MW01484053

Theorizing "Religion" in Antiquity

Studies in Ancient Religion and Culture

Series Editor:

Philip L. Tite, University of Washington

Studies in Ancient Religion and Culture (SARC) is concerned with religious and cultural aspects of the ancient world, with a special emphasis on studies that utilize social scientific methods of analysis. By "ancient world," the series is not limited to Greco-Roman and ancient Near Eastern cultures, though that is the primary regional focus. The underlying presupposition is that the study of religion in antiquity needs to be located within cultural and social analysis, situating religious traditions within the broader cultural and geopolitical dynamics within which those traditions are located.

This series also encourages cross-disciplinary research in the study of the ancient world. Due to the historical development of various academic disciplines, there has arisen a set of largely isolated and competing fields of study of the ancient world. Often this fragmentation in academia results in outdated or caricatured scholarly products when one discipline does use research from another discipline. A key goal of this series is to help facilitate greater cross- and inter-disciplinary work, bringing together those who study ancient history (especially social history), archaeology (of various methods and geographic focuses, as well as theorists in archaeology), ancient philosophy, biblical studies, early patristics/church history, Second Temple and formative Judaism, and Greek and Roman classics, as well as philologists.

Given the focus on the social and cultural context within which religion functions, the series also publishes studies which explore the various social locations in which real people in antiquity practiced or interacted with their religious traditions. Examples include the domestic cult, food production and consumption, temple worship, funerary practices/monuments, development of social networks, military cult, and ancient medicine.

Finally, the series encourages a broader application of theoretical and methodological tools to the study of the ancient world. While the main perspective is social-scientific (understood broadly), specific analyses from the reservoir of critical theory, narrative theories, economic theory, bio-archaeology, gender analysis, anthropology of religion, and cognitive theory are welcome.

Theorizing "Religion" in Antiquity

Edited by
Nickolas P. Roubekas

SHEFFIELD UK BRISTOL CT

Published by Equinox Publishing Ltd.

UK: Office 415, The Workstation, 15 Paternoster Row, Sheffield, South Yorkshire S1 2BX

USA: ISD, 70 Enterprise Drive, Bristol, CT 06010

www.equinoxpub.com

First published 2019

© Nickolas P. Roubekas and contributors 2019

All rights reserved. No part of this publication may be reproduced or transmitted in any form or by any means, electronic or mechanical, including photocopying, recording or any information storage or retrieval system, without prior permission in writing from the publishers.

British Library Cataloguing-in-Publication Data

A catalogue record for this book is available from the British Library.

ISBN-13   978 1 78179 356 5   (hardback)   978 1 78179 357 2   (paperback)
                    978 1 78179 674 0   (ePDF)

Library of Congress Cataloging-in-Publication Data

Names: Roubekas, Nickolas P. (Nickolas Panayiotis), 1979- editor.

Title: Theorizing 'religion' in antiquity / edited by Nickolas P. Roubekas.

Description: Bristol : Equinox Publishing Ltd., 2019. | Series: Studies in
    ancient religion and culture | Includes bibliographical references and
    index.

Identifiers: LCCN 2018000051 (print) | LCCN 2018030878 (ebook) | ISBN
    9781781796740 (ePDF) | ISBN 9781781793565 (hb) | ISBN 9781781793572 (pb)

Subjects: LCSH: Religion--Philosophy--History.

Classification: LCC BL51 (ebook) | LCC BL51 .T4245 2018 (print) | DDC
    210.1--dc23

LC record available at https://lccn.loc.gov/2018000051

Typeset by ISB Typesetting, Sheffield, UK

Contents

Editor's Preface

In November 2016, I received an anticipated email from one of the editors of a very well established journal in the field of Classics. A few months previously, I had volunteered to review an important multi-authored volume within the field of "Greek religion," which I had been expecting eagerly to appear in press. During the process of reading and taking notes in order to prepare my review, two notable issues drew my attention: the topic was treated almost exclusively by classicists and ancient historians (thus, excluding religious studies scholars), whereas throughout the volume all contributors had made sure to put the noun "religion" within quotation marks (at least at its first appearance within the individual chapters). My objection was to the absence of any explanation for the use of quotation marks. Neither the contributors nor the editors of that volume gave a reason for such an astounding consistency. These two issues became the focus of my review. However, to my surprise and dismay, in that November email the editor conveyed the "preoccupation" of two members of the editorial board, who gave a peer review of my review. To the first issue, the "review reviewers" maintained that (and I quote): (a) "Are these classifications [i.e., of classicists and ancient historians and the lack of religious studies scholars] made by the editors of the volume, and the reviewer is saying that the scholars should be classified according to the disciplines in which they were awarded their degrees? I find that strange: wouldn't a better metric be the disciplinary societies to which they belong, or the journals they tend to publish in?"; (b) "ancient Greek and Roman religion is usually studied in Classics departments, often at universities that do not have Religious Studies programs or departments. Also, in a traditional religious studies curriculum, at least in North America, most of the ancient scholarship is bible-adjacent: NT [New Testament], HB [Hebrew Bible], ancient Near East, etc."

I was struck by the contradictory comments I was given. On the one hand, the scholars who had contributed to the volume in question should not be classified according to their studies—although, they all held degrees in Classics and/or Ancient History and their academic positions were identified as "lecturer in classics," "professor of classics," "associate professor of ancient history," and so on—but the study of Greek religion "traditionally belongs" to departments of Classics—which, I presume, indicates that it is *classicists* who study ancient Greek religion within such departments (unless if it is now "tradition" to hire non-classicists within such departments, which is highly doubtful based on job advertisements—a quick online scanning of job listings will convince any skeptics). The second issue, that of the unjustified quotation marks, made one of the "review reviewers" even more hostile: "I wonder whether the reviewer might be able to figure out from context what those quotations are about ... I haven't read the book, but I suspect they are signaling the caution that multiple scholars of the ancient world are exercising with respect to the concept of religion, which varies from person to person. See, for example Nongbri 2013 and Boyarin/Barton 2016, just for starters."[1] Given that these were exactly the two books I was referring to in my own criticism as absent from the volume under review, the "review reviewers" simply repeated what I had long observed: the two disciplines, namely Classics/Ancient History and Religious Studies, almost never cooperate when studying the religions of the ancient world. Classicists and ancient historians tend to remain within the limits of their respective disciplines, whereas religious studies scholars simply utilize the findings of their colleagues from those departments. My review got rejected because of my refusal to make changes but was in turn accepted by another journal, itself also within Classics, without any required alterations.[2]

This incident is only one example of what I deem a "disciplinary chasm" apparent in the study of ancient religions.[3] In my view, this is not limited to Greek and Roman religions; it is also expanded into other cognate fields, such as Egyptology or Assyriology—let alone Christianity, for which classicists usually have nothing to say. Furthermore, classicists and religious studies scholars share an important difference: the former are or tend to be particularists; that is, they are interested in, say, Greek or Roman religion but not about religion as a category, which typically preoccupies the latter.

---

1.   Referring, of course, to Brent Nongbri, *Before Religion: A History of a Modern Concept* (New Haven, CT: Yale University Press, 2013) and Carlin A. Barton and Daniel Boyarin, *Imagine No Religion: How Ancient Abstractions Hide Ancient Realities* (New York: Fordham University Press, 2016). Note the protectionism in the phrase "I haven't read the book, but I suspect..."—if the "review reviewer" would have read the book, then the comment would have been a bit more convincing to me.

2.   See Nickolas P. Roubekas, "Review of E. Eidinow and J. Kindt (eds.): *The Oxford Handbook of Ancient Greek Religion*," *Revista Classica* 29.2 (2016): 221–4.

3.   There are, of course, some exceptions, although they employ different approaches than in the volume at hand. A good example is Sarah Iles Johnston, *Religions of the Ancient World: A Guide* (Cambridge, MA: The Belknap Press of Harvard University Press, 2004), and more recently Barbette Stanley Spaeth (ed.), *The Cambridge Companion to Ancient Mediterranean Religions* (Cambridge: Cambridge University Press, 2013). Both include classicists, ancient historians, and religious studies scholars (among others), but they are less interested in theoretical issues.

With that in mind, I approached Philip Tite back in the summer of 2014—as if I had anticipated the aforementioned incident—with an idea about bringing together classicists, ancient historians, and religious studies scholars to give their views on a topic that combined the moot point of the discipline of religious studies (i.e., theorizing about religion) and the field that is seen as an exclusivity to classicists and historians (i.e., the ancient world). Contrary to the book I reviewed, I decided to add the quotation marks in the very title of this volume, indicating from the beginning that this is a contested term within religious studies—and I did so in my initial invitation, two years before the publication of the volume I reviewed. But instead of remaining silent or failing to give an adequate explanation for my choice, allow me to elaborate very briefly given that the topic is discussed in greater length throughout this volume.

The issue of the applicability of the term "religion" outside the Christian or Christian-centric milieu was the focus of the influential *The Meaning and End of Religion* (1962) by Wilfred Cantwell Smith.[4] However, Smith's interest was not political, as it is for postmodernists, but rather theological. The term *religion* for Smith was an inadequate descriptor because it did not focus on the basic element of religiosity, that is, *faith*—Smith's alternative.[5] Since Smith, however, a number of scholars have taken his thesis to different venues, always adopting—often uncritically or, more than often, unpersuasively—the obvious postmodern and deconstructionist stance that such discourse essentially entails.[6] In the study of ancient religions the topic has lately received equal attention, primarily by the studies of Brent Nongbri—a contributor to this volume—and Carlin Barton and Daniel Boyarin (cf. n. 1 above). From the outset I must confess that the postmodernist approach is not one that I subscribe to. I have expressed my disagreement on different occasions, since I share Christopher Butler's constructive criticism of the "postmodernist culture" when he argues that "[i]t is worth asking, then, how far a postmodernist 'hermeneutics of suspicion' is justified. There is in any case a

---

4. See Wilfred Cantwell Smith, *The Meaning and End of Religion* (New York: Mentor Books, 1964).

5. For a discussion, cf. Robert A. Segal, "Diagnosis Rather Than Dialogue as the Best Way to Study Religion," in *The Legacy of Wilfred Cantwell Smith* (ed. Ellen Brandshaw Aitken and Arvind Sharma; New York: SUNY Press, 2017), 173–82.

6. To give just one example, see the extremely controversial—but also highly influential—article by Timothy Fitzgerald, "A Critique of 'Religion' as a Cross-Cultural Category," *Method & Theory in the Study of Religion* 9.2 (1997): 91–110, and the response given by one of the contributors to this volume, Kevin Schilbrack, "The Social Construction of 'Religion' and Its Limits: A Critical Reading of Timothy Fitzgerald," *Method & Theory in the Study of Religion* 24 (2012): 97–117, who offers a good bibliography for those further interested in this debate.

crippling contradiction at the heart of the analysis—if anyone says that every-thing is 'really' just constituted by a deceiving image, and not by reality, how does he or she *know*? They presuppose the very distinctions they attack."[7] In line with Butler's thesis, in a sense, my criticism lies at the problem of defi-nition. Arguing that the ancients did not have "religion" in the way mod-erns do begs for a definition of what "religion" is, to begin with. Because if the very criticism of ancient "religion" stems from identifying something as falsely termed "religion" in order for us to go ahead and deconstruct it—be it belief in gods, performing rituals and sacrifices, deifying potentates, embrac-ing myths, sharing a pantheon, and so on—we still need to explain why these elements are coined as "religion" or part of "a religion." Is this our definition? This question is a matter of theorizing rather than identifying.[8]

Theories of religion have received their share of criticism by the post-modernists exactly due to their nature of generalizing about religion. And, although postmodernism is kin to criticism and deconstructionism, it almost never offers answers or hypotheses. Butler puts it bluntly: "Books of a post-modernist persuasion are often advertised by their publishers, not for their challenging hypotheses or arguments, but for their '*use* of theory', their 'insights', their 'interventions', their 'addressing' (rather than answering) questions."[9] On the other hand, critical theory and postmodernism are seen as fruitful exercises if we wish to be intellectually and academically honest, as is maintained by exponents of such criticism towards how things "are done" in academia.[10]

It is within such an academic ambience that this volume appears, attempt-ing to include all the aforementioned issues but without favoring any camp.

7.   Christopher Butler, *Postmodernism: A Very Short Introduction* (Oxford: Oxford University Press, 2002), 118 (emphasis in the original). I have reviewed both Nongbri's and Barton and Boyarin's books expressing my concerns without this meaning, however, that their works are to be disregarded. See Nickolas P. Roubekas, "Review of B. Nong-bri: *Before Religion: A History of a Modern Concept*," *Relegere* 4.2 (2014): 261–4, and "Review of C. A. Barton and D. Boyarin: *Imagine No Religion: How Modern Abstrac-tions Hide Ancient Realities*," *Critical Research on Religion* 5.2 (2017): 217–21.

8.   For a more detailed discussion on this, see Nickolas P. Roubekas, "Should We Define Our Categories? On Jennifer Larson's *Understanding Greek Religion*," *Journal of Cognitive Historiography* 4.1 (2017): 42–6.

9.   Butler, *Postmodernism*, 11 (emphasis in the original). On a severe criticism of postmodernism from a "theories of religion" perspective, see Robert A. Segal, "All Gen-eralizations Are Bad: Postmodernism on Theories," *Journal of the American Academy of Religion* 74.1 (2006): 157–71.

10.   As Russell T. McCutcheon puts it (*Critics Not Caretakers: Redescribing the Public Study of Religion* [New York: SUNY Press, 2001], 120), traditionalists (or, in his parlance, caretakers) fail "to entertain the full implications of postmodernism in the study of religion."

This, however, is done due to the contributors' insights and erudition, to which I am indebted. In my initial invitation, I emphasized the first problem, that is, the disciplinary chasm, as well as the tendency by religious studies scholars to see theorizing about religion as a modern accomplishment. When the contributions started to arrive, I realized that the second issue, that is, the postmodern "culture" and the discussions and debates within academia it has generated, preoccupied many of the contributors. In many respects, these two elements that permeate the volume are interconnected. They portray a link between how the ancients theorized about their own religions and also how we, as moderns, discuss such discourses within our academic settings. Contrary to what most postmodernists maintain, the problem of language—that is, how nouns, verbs, adjectives, and so on are used—is not exclusively a postmodern concern; the ancients dealt with this as well. The debate between language and ideas is as "premodern" as it is "postmodern." For example, we only need to look at Seneca, who, in one of his many letters to Lucilius, laments the tendency of lovers of language to disregard the philosophical exercise that naturally emerges when reading a text:

> When Cicero's book *On the State* is opened by a philologist, a scholar, or a follower of philosophy, each man pursues his investigation in his own way. The philosopher wonders that so much could have been said therein against justice [*Philosophus admiratur contra iustitiam dici tam multa potuisse*]. The philologist takes up the same book and comments on the text as follows: There were two Roman kings—one without a father and one without a mother. For we cannot settle who was Servius's mother, and Ancus, the grandson of Numa, has no father on record. The philologist also notes that the officer whom we call dictator, and about whom we read in our histories under that title, was named in old times the *magister populi*; such is the name existing to-day in the augural records, proved by the fact that he whom the dictator chose as second in command was called *magister equitum*. He will remark, too, that Romulus met his end during an eclipse; that there was an appeal to the people even from the kings (this is so stated in the pontiffs' register and is the opinion of others, including Fenestella).[11]

In many respects, Seneca's observation is applicable to both issues I have raised in this short preface: classicists tend to preoccupy themselves with philology, often neglecting the theories and hypotheses one can formulate from a given text;[12] postmodernists, on the other hand, pay too much attention to

---

11.   Epistle 108.30, in Seneca, *Epistles 91–124* (trans. Richard M. Gummere; Cambridge, MA: Harvard University Press, 1925), 244. I borrow the excerpt and idea from the excellent review article by Andrew Hui, "The Many Returns of Philology: A State of the Field Report," *Journal of the History of Ideas* 78.1 (2017): 137–8.

12.   If my criticism seems too Religious-Studies-biased or anti-Classics, take the

the workings of language "à la Derrida" and how it is used, without allowing for scholars to offer theories—at least, not if they are not accompanied by the adjective *critical* (which, nowadays and within the cherished academic jargon, often implies postmodern/deconstructionist).[13]

In what follows, all voices are hopefully heard. My not siding with the postmodern approach did not mean that I would deny such approaches from being included in this volume; on the contrary, I sought to involve as many as possible in order, hopefully, to offer a fruitful debate that is also exemplified in Brent Nongbri's "Introduction" and Luther H. Martin's "Epilogue," two scholars representing rather opposite approaches to the study of ancient religions and "religion" in general.[14] Scholars should not fear criticism, and I believe that a complicated topic such as "theorizing 'religion'" needs pluralism and inclusion rather than marginalization and exclusion. Yet, the topic in question is vast and I am well aware that many important issues are not included or adequately addressed. This would have resulted in a huge volume. On the other hand, the structure of the volume could potentially raise some objections as well. Again, I will agree with such criticisms. However, the aim is not to exhaust the topic but rather to offer a tool to those interested in how "antiquity," "theory," and "religion" are conceived and could be studied, while anticipating other attempts that voice further concerns, insights, and alternative and/or opposite approaches, thus allowing our debates to unfold in a profitable manner for all scholarly "parties" involved.

* * *

I must thank a number of people who made this publication possible. First and foremost, I want to acknowledge the contributors for accepting

opinion of a well-respected contemporary classicist, who addressing the constant fear of this field known as "the decline of Classics" points out (among other reasons as they have been articulated by critics): "… maybe it is precisely because professors of Classics have refused to engage with modern theory and persisted in viewing the ancient world through rose-tinted spectacles (as if it was a culture to be admired) that the subject is in imminent danger of turning into an antiquarian backwater." See Mary Beard, *Confronting the Classics: Traditions, Adventures, and Innovation* (London: Profile Books, 2013), 6.

13. I have further discussed this in Nickolas P. Roubekas, "Theory in Distress? On Being 'Critical' with Everything," *Method & Theory in the Study of Religion* 30.4–5 (2018): 480–6.

14. It is rarely the case that editors of multi-authored works invite scholars to "criticize" or "review" the content of their volumes "from within." I decided to take another path. Both Brent's and (especially) Luther's contributions, in my view, act as exemplary cases of the richness and diversity encountered in the study of ancient religions, and should be seen as attempts to further elaborate on this complicated sub-field.

my invitation and for offering what I deem an excellent set of essays that address more issues that I had initially envisioned. Thanks are also due to the series editor, Phil Tite, for finding my idea appealing enough to include it in his series with Equinox. A number of people made suggestions and offered their help in different ways. I would like to thank Russell McCutcheon, Susan Deacy, Robert Segal, Brian Brock, Lukas Pokorny, and Aaron Hughes. Two of the contributions were published elsewhere in another form. I would like to extend my appreciation to the respective publishers for allowing the use of that material in a revised form to suit the needs of this volume: Equinox Publishing for permission to use segments of Panayotis Pachis's chapter "The Discourse of a Myth: Diodorus Siculus and the Egyptian *Theologoumena* During the Hellenistic Age," in *Chasing Down Religion: In the Sights of History and the Cognitive Sciences*, edited by Panayotis Pachis and Donald Wiebe (Sheffield, UK: Equinox, 2014), 303–36, and Oxford University Press for permission to use parts of Michael L. Satlow's article "Defining Judaism: Accounting for 'Religions' in the Study of Religion," *Journal of the American Academy of Religion* 74.4 (2006): 837–60.

Last but not least, I would like to thank Janet Joyce who, in a crucial moment, stepped in and offered a Solomonic solution to some issues that had occurred, actively showing her support to this project, as well as Audrey Mann, who worked so fast and efficiently on the manuscript when time was extremely limited, saving the book from numerous errors and inconsistencies. Eve Hooper and Valerie Hall, as always, have been a joy to work with.

Bibliography

Barton, Carlin A., and Daniel Boyarin. *Imagine No Religion: How Ancient Abstractions Hide Ancient Realities*. New York: Fordham University Press, 2016.

Beard, Mary. *Confronting the Classics: Traditions, Adventures, and Innovation*. London: Profile Books, 2013.

Butler, Christopher. *Postmodernism: A Very Short Introduction*. Oxford: Oxford University Press, 2002.

Fitzgerald, Timothy. "A Critique of 'Religion' as a Cross-Cultural Category." *Method & Theory in the Study of Religion* 9.2 (1997): 91–110. https://doi.org/10.1163/157006897X00070

Hui, Andrew. "The Many Returns of Philology: A State of the Field Report." *Journal of the History of Ideas* 78.1 (2017): 137–56. https://doi.org/10.1353/jhi.2017.0006

Johnston, Sarah Iles. *Religions of the Ancient World: A Guide*. Cambridge, MA: The Belknap Press of Harvard University Press, 2004.

McCutcheon, Russell T. *Critics Not Caretakers: Redescribing the Public Study of Religion*. New York: SUNY Press, 2001.

Nongbri, Brent. *Before Religion: A History of a Modern Concept*. New Haven, CT: Yale University Press, 2013. https://doi.org/10.12987/yale/9780300154160.001.0001

Roubekas, Nickolas P. "Review of B. Nongbri: *Before Religion: A History of a Modern Concept.*" *Relegere* 4.2 (2014): 261–4. https://doi.org/10.11157/rsrr4-2-655

—"Review of E. Eidinow and J. Kindt (eds.): *The Oxford Handbook of Ancient Greek Religion.*" *Revista Classica* 29.2 (2016): 221–4.

—"Review of C. A. Barton and D. Boyarin: *Imagine No Religion: How Modern Abstractions Hide Ancient Realities.*" *Critical Research on Religion* 5.2 (2017): 217–21. https://doi.org/10.1177/2050303217707248

—"Should We Define Our Categories? On Jennifer Larson's *Understanding Greek Religion.*" *Journal of Cognitive Historiography* 4.1 (2017): 42–6. https://doi.org/10.1558/jch.36261

—"Theory in Distress? On Being 'Critical' with Everything." *Method & Theory in the Study of Religion* 30.4–5 (2018): 480–6.

Schilbrack, Kevin. "The Social Construction of 'Religion' and Its Limits: A Critical Reading of Timothy Fitzgerald." *Method & Theory in the Study of Religion* 24 (2012): 97–117. https://doi.org/10.1163/157006812X634872

Segal, Robert A. "All Generalizations Are Bad: Postmodernism on Theories." *Journal of the American Academy of Religion* 74.1 (2006): 157–71. https://doi.org/10.1093/jaarel/lfj026

—"Diagnosis Rather Than Dialogue as the Best Way to Study Religion," 173–82 in *The Legacy of Wilfred Cantwell Smith.* Edited by Ellen Brandshaw Aitken and Arvind Sharma. New York: SUNY Press, 2017.

Seneca. *Epistles 91–124.* Translated by Richard M. Gummere. Cambridge, MA: Harvard University Press, 1925.

Smith, Wilfred Cantwell. *The Meaning and End of Religion.* New York: Mentor Books, 1964.

Spaeth, Barbette Stanley, ed. *The Cambridge Companion to Ancient Mediterranean Religions.* Cambridge: Cambridge University Press, 2013. https://doi.org/10.1017/CCO9781139047784

Chapter One

Introduction: The Present and Future of Ancient Religion

Brent Nongbri

When I was approached to contribute to this volume a few years ago, I was intrigued by the task of writing an introduction to a collection of essays that I had no hand in assembling. Having now read all the chapters, I am even more convinced than I already was that the study of "ancient religion" has come to a curious place. On the one hand, discomfort with the idea of ancient religion, the idea of seeing a discreet sphere of religion existing prior to the modern period, has become significantly more widespread in the past decade.[1] And in recent years, this kind of historicizing critique has been pushed to an extreme in two quite different directions. Carlin Barton and Daniel Boyarin, for example, have taken a hard line on the application of the concept of religion to ancient evidence, arguing that religion hopelessly distorts "ancient realities" and should simply be avoided completely by ancient historians.[2] From a rather different angle, Vaia Touna has argued that any proposed "ancient realities," religious or otherwise, as part of the past, are lost to us, and any writings we produce *about* the past are completely determined by our own interests here in the present.[3] Yet, even as these different types of critiques of the concept of religion continue to appear, so also do studies that advance the long-standing project of seeking more accurate descriptions of religion as an ancient reality. The approaches of these latter studies consider ancient Greek or Roman or Egyptian religions are parts of the past to which we have access. The authors of such works are unconvinced (or, for the purposes of their interventions, just uninterested) by efforts to historicize the concept of religion.

The present book reflects these conflicting trends, and that is one reason that it marks an especially useful contribution at this particular moment

---

1.   The literature is on the topic is growing quickly. See the overview of Russell T. McCutcheon, "The Category 'Religion' in Recent Publications: Twenty Years Later," *Numen* 62 (2015): 119–41.

2.   Carlin Barton and Daniel Boyarin, *Imagine No Religion: How Modern Abstractions Hide Ancient Realities* (New York: Fordham University Press, 2016).

3.   Vaia Touna, *Fabrications of the Greek Past: Religion, Tradition, and the Making of Modern Identities* (Leiden: Brill, 2017).

in the study of religion. The volume's editor has arranged the book's central chapters into divisions that mix geographic and cultural designations (Part II: The Greek World, Part III: From Mesopotamia to Rome, and Part IV: From Judaism to Christianity). Perhaps in response to the increasing preoccupation with meta-concerns throughout the field, these studies are bracketed by more theoretically themed sections—Part I: From Language to Method and Part V: Topics in the Study of (Ancient) Religion. The book can therefore profitably be read according to this organizational scheme. Yet, since all readers bring different sets of interests to the table, it is not surprising that some might perceive noteworthy continuities and discontinuities that cut across the editor's organization of the chapters. In fact, the most fundamental divide among these essays could be seen as reflecting the very division that I outlined above: several contributors concentrate on data taken to be relatively stable; that is to say, they seem to be reasonably confident that they know what religion is, what belief is, what science is, and consequently what objects and activities are religious and sacred in their ancient sources. They therefore proceed with the study of these manifestly religious data with greater and greater sophistication. The second group of contributors, however, subjects concepts like "religion" (or "belief" or "community" or "text") to various kinds of criticism. This second group of studies seems united by a commitment to the claim that classification (say, classification of some things as "religious" and other things as "not religious") is not simply a natural account of stuff in the world. It is rather, as James Crossley reminds us in his chapter, "a political act." This discontinuity among the writers, echoing what I see as important contemporary trends in our field, makes this volume a valuable snapshot of where the field currently sits—and it is this curious discontinuity that provides the lens through which some readers (especially those not necessarily trained in the study of ancient sources) might approach the volume.

Within the first group of chapters, one cluster focuses on textual exegesis of Greek sources. Donald Wiebe ("Philosophical Reflections on the Pre-Socratics: A Contribution to the Scientific Study of Religion") expands a dialogue with the work of Paul Veyne and makes the case that the presocratic philosophers, especially the Milesians and Ionians, can be seen as a "critical episode" in the development of "a scientific study of religion that, at times, has flourished in some of our research universities" (82).[4] Through a close reading of the fragments of Protagoras, Prodicus, and the lost play known as

---

4.   For Wiebe's earlier interaction with Veyne, see Donald Wiebe, *The Irony of Theology and the Nature of Religious Thought* (Montreal: McGill-Queen's University Press, 1991), 129 n. 175.

the *Sisyphus*, Emese Mogyoródi ("Impiety and Versions of Rationalization of Religion in Classical Greece") explores how certain theories about the gods and their origins posed "a challenge for traditional religious sensibility in the classical era" (104). In one of his two chapters, "Theorizing About (Which?) Origins: Herodotus on the Gods," the volume's editor, Nickolas P. Roubekas, examines the writings of Herodotus, arguing that the historian's "theory of the origins of the Greek gods (and, thus, Greek religion) constitutes one of the oldest attempts to theorize about religion" (132).[5] In "Manipulating 'Religion': The Egyptian *Theologoumena* in Diodorus Siculus," Panayotis Pachis concentrates on the ideology of Diodorus Siculus, who, he argues, manipulates his sources in his treatment of Egyptian gods by adjusting the ideas of Euhemerus of Messene in order "to justify the religio-political *status quo* of his time" (198).

Moving away from a primarily exegetical focus, the remaining four chapters in this first grouping provide more thematic treatments of metaphor, gender, space, and geography in the study of ancient religion. Spencer E. Cole ("Metaphor and Religion in Ancient Rome") brings contemporary developments in metaphor theory to bear on Roman evidence, proposing that metaphors, especially metaphors of death and the divine, "introduced new perspectives and shaped religious thought and practice" (240) in Republican-era Rome. Justin K. H. Tse ("Cultural Geography") highlights the place of Mircea Eliade in the disciplinary history of cultural geography and contends that "far from being hip and trendy, geography is foundational to the study of ancient religion" (377). In his second contribution, "Whither Shall We Go? Tertullian and Christian Identity Formation," Roubekas offers a reading of Tertullian's *De spectaculis* that emphasizes the ways in which actors imbue spaces with meaning. In his words, Tertullian's work is a good example of how "theorizing about the relationship between space and religion creates, enforces, and maintains new religious identities and how classification, as a set of human relations and ideas, transforms places from ordinary and neutral into ideologically and 'religiously' charged spaces" (290). Finally, in her chapter on "Gender," Irene Salvo explores "whether and in what ways issues of gender were relevant to the ancient religious reality," (398) with a focus on ancient Greek evidence.

In placing these eight chapters into a group, I do not mean to imply that they present a uniform point of view on the issues they address. On the contrary, and again reflecting discontinuities in the field, there is rather strong disagreement on a number of points. To take just one example, consider

---

5.   See further his related monograph, Nickolas P. Roubekas, *An Ancient Theory of Religion: Euhemerism from Antiquity to the Present* (London: Routledge, 2017).

4 Theorizing "Religion" in Antiquity

debates on the place of (or, perhaps better put, the lack of) belief in our understanding of religion: "Belief in gods constituted the crux of ancient Greek religion for many ancient thinkers, no matter how eagerly some scholars still prefer and promote the dichotomy between religious belief and religious practice within ancient Greek culture by prioritizing the latter and depreciating or even rejecting the former" (Roubekas, 131) versus "Greek religion was predominantly a matter of orthopraxy, compliance with cult and rituals prescribed by custom rather than orthodoxy, beliefs, or convictions about matters divine" (Mogyoródi, 103). Such contrasting interpretations abound in these chapters.

The chapters I would put in my second group are equally diverse in terms of individual approach. Some of these studies adopt a sharply articulated, self-consciously redescriptive standpoint. For example, after noting that the cultural specificity of the concept of religion "need not shut down our exploration of intellectual history to find earlier attempts to deal with matters and materials that we now deem religious," Alan Lenzi ("Ancient Mesopotamian Scholars, Ritual Speech, and Theorizing Religion Without 'Theory' or 'Religion'," 153) investigates what he calls "ritual speech" in ancient Mesopotamian evidence and draws what I find to be quite interesting parallels between the activities of ancient scribes and modern scholars of religious studies. Rita Lucarelli ("Magic and Religion in Ancient Egypt") proposes an avowedly functionalist approach to Egyptian magic, arranging the ancient evidence, "only from our etic perspective" (181), into four categories: defensive, funerary, curative, and transformative magic. Also in line with redescriptive work in the field, two contributions complicate our view of Judaism as an ancient phenomenon. Michael L. Satlow ("Defining Judaism: The Case of Philo") takes up Jonathan Z. Smith's challenge of giving a polythetic classification of Judaism by offering a bird's-eye view of the corpus of the Alexandrian philosopher. In a broader scope that includes discussions of modern Judaism, Sarah Imhoff ("Religion, Geography, and the Impossibility of Jewish Identity") advises that just as we are comfortable with the idea that modern Jewish identity is a "messy" affair (265), so also should we get used to the idea that ancient Jewish identity was also messy, albeit in different ways. Taken together, these two chapters probe the degree to which any kind of "Judaism" ("Hellenistic" or otherwise) is a viable object of study in antiquity.[6]

---

6.   For a viewpoint that sees more coherence in such a project, see John J. Collins, *The Invention of Judaism: Torah and Jewish Identity from Deuteronomy to Paul* (Berkley, CA: University of California Press, 2017).

Two contributions focus on the promises and perils of the cognitive science of religion. In "The Value(s) of Belief: Ancient Religion, Cognitive Science, and Interdisciplinarity," Jason P. Davies challenges us to work carefully through recent philosophical and historical debates about "belief" and uses selected scholarship on the ancient world to try to craft a responsible form of interdisciplinary encounter between the humanities and the sciences. Showing considerably greater assurance in the possibilities that cognitive science can transform religious studies, Leonardo Ambasciano ("Cognitive Study of [Ancient] Religions") provides reasons for including the study of cognition and evolution in the study of antiquity, using Roman cults as a case in point. Reading these two chapters in conversation with each other may raise a series of questions: Can scientific discourses ever explain something called "religious belief"? Or is the turn toward cognitive science simply a way to "medicalize," biologize, and thus authorize and naturalize one historically situated, culturally specific taxon, namely religion?[7] Might we do better to direct the lens of the cognitive sciences to the broader human phenomena of which religion is simply one local variant?[8] No clear answers are forthcoming, but the questions are worth pondering.

Three of the chapters reflect upon the usefulness of a series of concepts that frequently appear in studies of ancient religion (not least in the chapters in this volume): text, community, and, of course, religion. In a contribution simply entitled "Texts," James Crossley, undercuts the idea, still pervasive in biblical studies, religious studies, and classics, that texts are stable entities that unproblematically transfer an intended meaning from an author to an audience. Through an analysis of recent New Testament scholarship, Crossley draws our attention to the ways that "politicized mythmaking" inevitably accompanies the act of interpretation. Sarah E. Rollens ("The Anachronism of 'Early Christian Communities'") argues that the ubiquity of early Christian "communities" in New Testament scholarship is part of the legacy of early Protestant theology, German nationalism, and Romanticism. She further suggests that rather than finding a well-defined Christian community behind each surviving Christian author or text, "it is better to view a text as a discursive space dealing with identity and authority, in which a variety of authors engaged, some perhaps entirely disconnected from any coherent community" (307). Relying on a temporally and geographically broad range of ancient authors, Steve Mason ("Our Language

7.   Russell T. McCutcheon, "Will Your Cognitive Anchor Hold in the Storms of Culture?" *Journal of the American Academy of Religion* 78 (2010): 1185.
8.   Maurice Bloch, "Why Religion Is Nothing Special But Is Central," *Philosophical Transactions of the Royal Society B: Biological Sciences* 363 (2008): 2055–61.

and Theirs: 'Religious' Categories and Identities") tests the usefulness of insider and outsider modes of analysis of ancient cultures and concludes that "in terms of both social location and internal content, ancient Mediterranean societies had nothing that corresponded very closely [to religion]. The categories to which Graeco-Roman and Judaean writers resort on every page (*ethnos*, nature or character, ancestral custom, and law; *polis*, citizenship, and constitution [*politeia*]; and sacrifice-centered rituals for attending to the Gods of the *ethnos* and *polis*) suited a differently constructed world" (29).

A final chapter seems to me (and perhaps to its author as well) to straddle the two groups into which I have divided these contributions. Kevin Schilbrack ("Imagining Religion in Antiquity: A How To") argues that his preferred approach, critical realism, offers us a way to appreciate the historicizing studies of religion while maintaining the "reality" of ancient religion.[9] Schilbrack begins by making a distinction between "reflexive" and "debunking" approaches to the historicizing of religion. The former "examines where one's concepts come from, who invented them, and what purposes they were intended to serve" (60), but the latter "seeks not only to raise questions about the concept, but also to argue that to use the concept is to project its own referent, that—lacking the concept—there is no such entity operating 'out there' in the world" (61). Schilbrack endorses the "reflexive" approach, but argues forcefully against the debunking project on the grounds that it mistakes human conceptions for "reality outside how human beings experience the world," elsewhere phrased as "the actual character of the world," "real structure in the natural or social world," and "the social world distinct from our concepts about it" (70, 76, 65, 68). The adherent of critical realism, as he describes this position, can make reference to these "real structures" to show that historians "discover" rather than "invent" ancient religions. On most points, Schilbrack's chapter is admirably clear, but I must admit that it remains unclear how exactly the critical realist gains this privileged access to the "real structure" or "actual character of the world," and how these "real structures" can somehow adjudicate between competing, secondary conceptions of these structures by something other than the (socially determined, linguistically based, and thoroughly human) rules of the historical or interpretive enterprise.[10] I suspect readers will be divided on this point, but Schilbrack's chapter does cut to

---

9.   The chapter is part of Schilbrack's larger program to engage constructively with the historicizing critique of religion. See, for example, Kevin Schilbrack, "Religions: Are There Any?" *Journal of the American Academy of Religion* 78 (2010): 1112–38.

10.   For further reflections along these lines, see my contribution to a recent series of queries into the relationship between "Words and Things": Brent Nongbri, "On

the heart of an important problem not just in the study of religion but in historiography more broadly.

Similarly, the present collection of chapters helps us to see a number of debates that are currently animating the discipline as a whole. The volume also, I think, evinces a fairly clear divide between those studying ancient religion and those studying "religion" by means of ancient evidence. This diversity of approaches will no doubt persist, and the chapters collected here offer a stimulating opportunity to continue to think through these problems.

Biographical Note

Brent Nongbri is an Honorary Research Fellow at Macquarie University in Sydney, Australia. Previously he was Visiting Associate Professor of New Testament Studies at Aarhus University, Denmark, and held an Australian Research Council Discovery Early Career Research Fellowship in the Department of Ancient History at Macquarie University, Australia, as well as teaching positions at Oberlin College and Yale University. He is the author of *God's Library: The Archaeology of the Earliest Christian Manuscripts* (Yale University Press, 2018) and *Before Religion: A History of a Modern Concept* (Yale University Press, 2013). His research interests center on methodological problems in the study of religion and the material culture of the ancient Mediterranean world.

Bibliography

Barton, Carlin, and Daniel Boyarin. *Imagine No Religion: How Modern Abstractions Hide Ancient Realities*. New York: Fordham University Press, 2016.

Bloch, Maurice. "Why Religion Is Nothing Special But Is Central." *Philosophical Transactions of the Royal Society B: Biological Sciences* 363 (2008): 2055–61. https://doi.org/10.1098/rstb.2008.0007

Collins, John J. *The Invention of Judaism: Torah and Jewish Identity from Deuteronomy to Paul*. Berkley, CA: University of California Press, 2017. https://doi.org/10.1525/california/9780520294110.001.0001

McCutcheon, Russell T. "The Category 'Religion' in Recent Publications: Twenty Years Later." *Numen* 62 (2015): 119–41. https://doi.org/10.1163/15685276-12341358

——"Will Your Cognitive Anchor Hold in the Storms of Culture?" *Journal of the American Academy of Religion* 78 (2010): 1182–93. https://doi.org/10.1093/jaarel/lfq085

Nongbri, Brent. "On Religion, Words, and Things: A Reply." *Studying Religion in Culture*. Online: https://religion.ua.edu/blog/2017/03/01/on-religion-words-and-things/ (accessed 1 May 2017).

Religion, Words, and Things: A Reply," *Studying Religion in Culture*, online: https://religion.ua.edu/blog/2017/03/01/on-religion-words-and-things/ (accessed 1 May 2017).

Roubekas, Nickolas P. *An Ancient Theory of Religion: Euhemerism from Antiquity to the Present*. London: Routledge, 2017.

Schilbrack, Kevin. "Religions: Are There Any?" *Journal of the American Academy of Religion* 78 (2010): 1112–38. https://doi.org/10.1093/jaarel/lfq086

Touna, Vaia. *Fabrications of the Greek Past: Religion, Tradition, and the Making of Modern Identities*. Leiden: Brill, 2017.

Wiebe, Donald. *The Irony of Theology and the Nature of Religious Thought*. Montreal: McGill-Queen's University Press, 1991.

PART I

FROM LANGUAGE TO METHOD

Chapter Two

Our Language and Theirs:
"Religious" Categories and Identities

Steve Mason

Most of our surviving evidence for the Graeco-Roman world—literary, inscriptional, or numismatic—involves language. In order to understand it, we need to know something of how educated persons viewed their world and what categories they invoked in talking with each other. We use generic terms today—school, supermarket, "the office," police, income tax, justice system—in the confidence that others will know what we mean by them. But even moving from one English-speaking country to another requires us to make adjustments: Americans do not know verandas, Britons do not have sidewalks, and Australians have a whole treasury of terms incomprehensible to outsiders. Once we admit that the Roman world is alien to us, we must reckon with the need to understand not only its languages in the grammatical sense, but at least some of the categories most relevant to social structures, relations, and inter-communal conflict.

Beginning students of ancient history typically find themselves off balance in this area of categories. They quickly realize that even basic terms with fairly obvious meanings in English—history, democracy, state, country, city, empire/emperor, province, myth, religion, priest, philosophy, professional, law, police, army, military rank, economy, markets, social class, genre, geography, maps—bring with them a cartload of connotations that should not be imposed on any Greek and Latin (or Hebrew and Aramaic) terms, no matter how similar those may look at first glance. One-for-one translation from ancient agrarian cultures to post-industrial and post-modern worlds, conceptual and concrete, is bound to be hazardous. If we cannot relive the past, we can at least make an imaginative effort to enter a world that existed long before developments that have decisively shaped our language, values, and assumptions, to encounter it as alien. Our modern language concerning countries, religions, conversion, and so on is part of what we need to reconcile with the concepts and categories current among the ancients.

Before we explore such terms, we must deal with a thorny issue that sparks debate and can create misunderstandings even among specialists, namely: the legitimacy and status of "insider-language" research. An example concerning antiquity but not our present issues might clarify the problem. Every student of the ancient world learns that Roman society was held together by bonds of "patronage." That is, the few hundred men of senatorial standing in the Republic became socio-economic focal points and weight-bearing pillars for everyone else. Each was surrounded by a ring of "clients" dependent on the great man for material support. The relationship was one of disparity but also reciprocal exchange: the wealthy conferred tangible benefits on those who needed their support, who in return offered intangible support. For example, the client would visit the rich man's house in the morning to honor him, and would be on call to support him whenever he needed an entourage. Clients inside that first ring in turn became patrons for those further removed from the centers of power and wealth. Under the Empire, in the first century CE, an increasingly large class of equestrians and even freedmen (former slaves) became favored clients of the emperor, now the super-patron alongside the traditional senatorial class. This allowed such men to amass great wealth and power, and add their own patronage to the mix. All this is familiar to students.

In a 1978 study, however, Peter White argued that our investment in the language of patronage, which he admitted using himself as a convenience, and which sprang from a commendable effort to understand this alien culture, actually impeded our understanding of the way that *Romans themselves* thought and spoke about their social relationships. Focusing on Roman literature, he pointed out that the very term "patronage" suggests conditions present in the early modern world but not in first-century Rome, especially the financial support of otherwise resourceless writers by the wealthy. In Rome, by contrast, the one we call the "client" of a senator or emperor was a *relatively* wealthy person—likely to have equestrian status—and not dependent on his patron for day-to-day survival. What the greater man did for him was along the lines of lending his authority if the writer found himself in political trouble (for example if forgeries were circulating under his name), providing a venue and rounding up audiences for the writer's public recitations, and furnishing the author with accommodation and occasional gifts.

White's crucial point was that the Romans did not conceive of the two parties as "patrons" and "clients," or call them such, because this language would have highlighted their disparity in a crass and counterproductive way. They preferred the pleasant language of friendship (*amicitia*). It was blazingly obvious which was the more powerful friend, but the relationship would be cheapened if labeled so ostentatiously. *Amicitia* language was usefully vague, accommodating also relationships among virtual equals (say, a young senator and a wealthier and well-connected equestrian), without inviting close inspection of each person's net worth or status. White's interest, we might say, was in the *inside* of the Roman social world: the categories that people actually used and not those that may be most convenient for our analysis. To label the ancient structure patronage, he thought, was to obscure the Romans' own values and assumptions, even if in broad terms it facilitated our communication with each other.

But there is more. Richard Saller, a renowned expert in the Roman economy and its patronage patterns, responded to White in a 1983 article. Focusing there on one illustrative case, he argued that the Flavian poet Martial really was a *client* in the full and usual sense of the term. Having equestrian status, a country farm with slaves, and a small townhouse in Rome did not provide Martial with the financial stability he needed. He still felt desperately in need of money. Patrons of the time might give such poets direct cash payments from time to time, and many of the expensive gifts that Martial mentions were also convertible to cash. So, he really was a client of his patrons. Saller noted further that the Latin term *patronus* happens to turn up in a few inscriptions, if not in literature, a fact that casts doubt on White's claims about Roman resistance to such language in real life.

We need not declare White or Saller right, it seems to me. The two scholars differed primarily because of their different questions and methodological frameworks. Saller, experienced in social-scientific modes of historical analysis, considered the question about the ancients' own use of language a "red herring" to be "eliminated from the discussion."[1] Granting that they favored friendship (*amicitia*) language, he said:

> [i]t would be wrong to conclude that the modern scholar must therefore restrict himself to the vocabulary of friendship in his analysis and avoid the word "patronage". The historian never confines himself to the language and categories of the subjects of his study, though they must be taken into account. He always organizes and analyses his material in terms of his own questions, interests, and categories.[2]

For Saller, if the relationships found in ancient Rome qualify as "patronage, as we define it today" (viz., as "a continuing reciprocal but asymmetrical exchange relationship"), we should use the term without guilt or hesitation, also for ancient Rome. To justify this view philosophically, Saller cites a prominent study of "cause and meaning in the social sciences," which elaborates his points about investigator-driven analysis.[3]

1.   Richard P. Saller, "Martial on Patronage and Literature," *The Classical Quarterly* 33 (1983): 255.

2.   Saller, "Martial on Patronage," 256.

3.   See Ernest Gellner, *Cause and Meaning in the Social Sciences* (London: Routledge & Kegan Paul, 1973).

In my view, Saller is quite right that historians generally can only reconstruct the past in a methodical way (i.e., we can only *do history*) by posing and investigating our research problems. But this shared starting position leaves open the question of how we interpret the surviving evidence. Here, given Saller's interests in aggregates (in societies, groups, and types), he naturally appeals to social-scientific categories with external and analytical warrants: "patronage, as we define it today." Like a physician investigating my joint complaint according to her knowledge of types, whether I know her analytical terminology or not, Saller does not need the ancients to have recognized the labels or types that he defines and uses.

Both historians make good points, but they are evidently talking past each other, attempting different things by understandably different criteria. John Richardson's 2008 study of Rome's "language of empire" helps further to isolate the issue. Whereas many scholars before him tried to understand what *kind or type* of empire the late Republic represented, comparing Romans with other empire-builders, Richardson asks how *Romans conceived of* what they were doing—by examining the ways in which representative authors used empire-language in conversation with each other. He traces the evolving use of the Latin words *imperium* and *provincia* from the third century BCE to the second century CE.[4] Whereas we would evaluate a case that Republican Rome had a certain type of empire by scrutinizing the typology with its components, definitions, and analogies (much as Saller investigates patronage), we evaluate Richardson's proposals by quite different criteria: scrutinizing the texts that use *imperium*-language from inside Roman culture to decide whether we agree with the evolving senses he identifies.[5]

Such debates prompt me to clarify what I mean by exploring ancient categories of language and thought, and what I hope to achieve by doing so. Historical investigation begins with the historian's questions about the past (thus far, Saller). These questions may involve any event, institution, long-term situation, group, individual career, textual community, or much else. Some kinds of questions, involving material conditions or large social aggregates

---

4.   John Richardson, *The Language of Empire: Rome and the Idea of Empire from the Third Century BC to the Second Century AD* (Cambridge: Cambridge University Press, 2008). He defines his research problem as: "What did the Romans *think they were doing* as their power changed and expanded?" And continues: "relatively little has been written on what the Romans *thought their empire was* as opposed to what they did to create it" (p. 5, emphases added).

5.   See Israel Shatzman, "Review of J. Richardson: *The Language of Empire: Rome and the Idea of Empire from the Third Century BC to the Second Century AD*," *Scripta Classica Israelica* 29 (2010): 128–32.

(e.g., resource distribution for mines, food-production areas and capacities, shipping routes, military camp construction), may depend chiefly on uninterpreted material remains, inviting statistical or other social-scientific modelling. But all historical work involves locating, interpreting, and explaining the surviving evidence that bears on our question. And many questions, for example about specific events, conflicts, groups, and individuals, but also to some extent the large-scale issues above, involve written claims and expressions.

In such cases, understanding this ancient evidence will require us to enter into the mentality and discourse of those who wrote and understood it. We can only understand their thoughts and claims by reference to the written codes, assumptions, values, and categories of the script they shared and assumed in communicating with each other. For the reader who is willing to go this far, I must now offer three cautions. First, in using the word *category* I am not suggesting that the terms we are about to discuss provided a coherent *system* of classification like the biologist's phylum, class, order, family, genus, and species. On the contrary, all of the terms under discussion were impressively elastic. We seek to understand them not because they clearly defined some reality, but simply because they were the terms people used, and their semantic ranges were different from those of relevant modern terms. So, we try to understand them.

Second, we shall focus on *Greek and Latin* terminology. All the cultures of the Near and Far East had their own languages, dialects, and categories. By the first century CE, however, literate elites throughout the eastern Mediterranean basin and Near East, even in the Parthian world, had assimilated Greek ways of thinking and talking with each other. Today, by way of analogy, a desire for political self-determination, representative government, human rights, international law, and so forth may be universal, but European languages and especially English have provided the shared discourse for communication about these issues. Long use has generated a suitably refined vocabulary. In the eastern Mediterranean under Rome, Greek was the language in which Judaeans, their neighbors, and the Romans communicated with each other. That *shared discourse*, rather than the private thoughts of a Celt, Pict, Judaean, or Arab, or the in-house (and all but lost) conversations of North Africans or Phoenicians under Roman rule, is our concern.

Third, the discourse in question was not merely something overlaid on a reality that was qualitatively different, which might as easily have been described in other ways. To communicate in a language entails the ability to think and act in it. "Sales targets" and "manufacturing input" are modern buzzwords, but they provide a platform for action as well as discourse. Whether in the construction of *poleis* ("cities") or the Seleucid and later Roman administration of the subject territory through these recognized population centers, ancient realities on the ground were shaped by the discourse, and vice-versa. The imperial *legatus* (governor) of Syria made a circuit of the leading *poleis* in his province, knowing what a *polis* was. He knew that each one followed the distinctive laws, calendar, and customs of its populace, and had its own respected criteria of belonging (πολιτεία), which restricted the rights of foreigners. No matter how different the process that brought it into being, or the vernacular language used, he expected to find a body of leaders generically identifiable as "the first, the best, the elders" (οἱ πρῶτοι, ἄριστοι, πρεσβύτεροι) or similar, and normally a "council" (ἡ βουλή) with a leader serving for some term. Hebrew and Aramaic texts such as the Qumran Scrolls might offer insider, fascinating critique of such individuals. But such material is coded in ways that make understanding and dating difficult, and we do not know how widespread (spatially or chronologically) the views of any such text were. The most prolific Judaean authors, namely Philo writing in Alexandria and Josephus in Rome, are known to us only through their Greek compositions, and these use the language, assumptions, values, and categories shared (basically) by Greek elites from Herodotus, Thucydides, Plato, Aristotle, and Polybius through Dionysius of Halicarnassus, Diodorus of Sicily, Strabo of Amaseia (in Syria), and Cassius Dio (from Asia Minor). It is that common coin that interests us here.

To seek out the shared discourse does not imply that particular nations' outlooks or grievances were always adequately expressed in Greek. It may be that some Judaeans considered the shared Greek category "ancestral laws" (πάτριοι νόμοι, τὰ πάτρια) inadequate for *Torah* (divine "instruction"). Again, some Judaeans' conceptions of "freedom" may, depending on the Hebrew terms and given the context of a covenant with God, have meant something different from the valences of "freedom and independence" (ἐλευθερία καὶ αὐτονομία) in the larger culture. Each nation presumably considered its traditions unique. Nevertheless, the conflict that generated the Judaean war with Rome involved mutual perceptions of Judaeans, their neighbors, and Romans, who communicated in the shared discourse. Our main narrative source for the war, the Judaean aristocrat Josephus, felt confident in explaining the war in such language for "men who have partaken of the Greek wisdom" (*Apion* 1.51).

We turn, then, to the subset of the shared discourse bearing on what we call *religious* matters, with special reference to Roman Syria and Judaea. This prompts the further caveat that what follows is hardly meant to exhaust the subject or to compete with the rich monographs that continue to appear on Greek or Roman religion. My aims here are basic. Writing with an eye toward student readers, I want simply to emphasize those aspects of ancient discourse, and the life they reflect, that hinder our efforts to locate something like our *religion* in antiquity. There is much more to be said, of course, by way of complementing the *polis* norms on which I shall focus or even, as Tim Whitmarsh has recently emphasized, in making space for ancient doubters, agnostics, and atheists.[6] As far as I can see, however, such important qualifications and developments take nothing away from the basic picture of *polis*-centered life—as long as it is not thought to represent the whole picture or real life in all its complexity.

* * *

Whether we are thinking of the place of religion in western society today or the internal functions of what we call religions, the ancients had no conception of anything similar, and no language that closely corresponds to our *religion*. They could neither have asked nor have answered such standard modern questions as: "Are you religious? What is your religion? Has your religion changed from that of your parents?" The Latin word *religio*, from which we get English "religion," is indeed an ancient word, but its meaning has changed, much in the way that the Greek terms *ekklēsia* and *leitourgia*, which once had to do with basic features of *polis* life, came to mean "church" and "liturgy" in a Christian environment. Only in later Christian usage did *religio* come to mean "a system of religious belief, *a religion*." The etymology of the word was already disputed by the ancients, but in practical use its meanings ranged from sacrificial *ritual* in honor of a particular God to a *mentality of awe* or devoted scrupulousness. Carrying a basic sense of "solemn obligation or commitment," it might refer to *a superstition*, an oath in wartime, or a particular *sacred object* (or the sacredness of the object).[7] A person described as *religiosus* was someone deemed unusually scrupulous, whether in general life or in relation to sacrificial rituals, though some grammarians thought that the suffix *–osus* and not the root of the word implied the excess. Things described as *religiosus* were essentially *taboo*, or separate from ordinary life, whether in good or bad senses (Aulus Gellius 4.9).

In this world, accordingly, *priests* were not the official representatives of something called a religion, or a religious system such as Catholicism. They had little in common with modern clergy, who are professionally trained in

6.   See, respectively, Julia Kindt, *Rethinking Greek Religion* (Cambridge: Cambridge University Press, 2012) and Tim Whitmarsh, *Battling the Gods: Atheism in the Ancient World* (London: Faber & Faber, 2016).

7.   See the range of meanings even within Julius Caesar's literary corpus, e.g., *De Bello Alexandrino* 74.3; *Bellum Gallicum* 6.16.1, 37.8; *Bellum Civile* 1.11.2, 76.5; 2.32.10; 3.28.4 and the ten amply attested definitions offered by the *Oxford Latin Dictionary* (ed. P. G. W. Glare; Oxford: Clarendon Press, 1968), 1605–6.

the exposition of sacred texts, theology, religious history, foreign languages, pastoral counseling, and the orders of service for regular worship, as well as in assisting their congregants at birth, marriage, and death. An ancient priest, in addition to usually being a prominent civic leader, was a specialist in the sacrificial rituals customary for his *ethnos* and *polis*. He knew the ancient prescriptions for selecting, inspecting, preparing, slaughtering, sacrificing or immolating the animals, and separating their parts for consumption, as well as the appropriate offerings of wine, cakes, and incense. These last often accompanied animal sacrifice, or they might also be made on their own where an animal sacrifice was too elaborate. The priest was responsible for supervising all such activities, which might actually be executed by attendants and slaves, to ensure that they conformed to ancestral custom or law. He was also expert in the movements, gestures, music, and incantations that accompanied such sacrifices—the music serving partly to keep away evil spirits. The presence of priests was by no means necessary for every kind of Greek and Roman sacrifice, but they oversaw the major civic cults and preserved traditional knowledge of sacrificial etiquette.[8]

Paul Cartledge writes:

> [I]f there was one religious ritual that made a Greek conventionally and normatively "Greek", it was eligibility to participate in a bloody animal sacrifice, which constituted an act of communion in the strict sense. Thus for the full (adult male) citizen of a *polis* it was the very cornerstone of the city, defining precisely what it was to constitute and participate in that peculiar mode of political and social organization [i.e., the *polis*].[9]

As we read surviving ancient works and recognize their authors as fellow human beings, we tend to assimilate their values to ours and, in so doing, find it convenient to ignore the most alien and off-putting features of their world. One of these was the central place of animal sacrifice in *polis* life.[10] This problem is partly disguised or mitigated by the fact that many excellent studies of Greek and Roman *religion* use that familiar word in their titles. The reader soon discovers, however, that the books' contents have little to do with what we would recognize as religious activity today: what

---

8.   We do not have many literary accounts of sacrifice because it was such a common feature of daily life. But there are some, and John Scheid gives narrative examples of both public and private sacrifice (*An Introduction to Roman Religion* [trans. Janet Lloyd; Bloomington, IN: Indiana University Press, 2003], 86–9 and 92, respectively).

9.   Paul Cartledge, *The Greeks: A Portrait of Self and Others* (Oxford: Oxford University Press, 2002), 176.

10.   For comparative ancient perspectives, see Albert I. Baumgarten, ed., *Sacrifice in Religious Experience* (Leiden: Brill, 2002).

happens in our synagogues, temples, churches, and mosques.[11] Scholarly authors are quick to explain that they are writing about a rather different kind of "religious" expression, one centered in the ritualized offering of blood-soaked sacrifices—along with the bloodless offerings of grain, oil, wine, and incense—to a deity.[12]

Sacrificial ritual was integral to every facet of public life: politics, entertainment, sport, and military campaigning. In Athens, the whole civic center was a sacred space, barred to those facing disgrace and marked off by the same water basins for purification that were located outside temples. Meetings of the *polis* council or the political assembly would be preceded by the carrying of a sacrificed pig around the circumference. This sanctified the proceedings as well as the participants.[13] In Athens as elsewhere, dramatic festivals and athletic competitions were devoted to gods, particularly Asclepius and Dionysus, and marked by sacrifices and related rituals. Thus, the famous Athenian Dionsyia, from which some of Greece's tragedies were preserved to remain in our school curricula today, began with sacrifices to Asclepius (cf. Plato, *Ion* 530a) and especially to Dionysus, at his temple and in the Theatre of Dionysus, purified for the event by lavish sacrifices of a bull and other animals.[14] Actors were not members of modern-style professional

11.   E.g., Walter Burkert, *Greek Religion: Archaic and Classical* (trans. John Raffan; Oxford: Blackwell, 1985); Mary Beard, John North, and Simon Price, *Religions of Rome. Vol. II: A Sourcebook* (Cambridge: Cambridge University Press, 1998); Hans-Josef Klauck, *The Religious Context of Early Christianity: A Guide to Graeco-Roman Religions* (trans. Brian McNeil; Minneapolis, MN: Fortress Press, 2003); Scheid, *Introduction to Roman Religion*; Jörg Rüpke, *Religion of the Romans* (trans. Richard Gordon; Cambridge: Polity Press, 2007); James B. Rives, *Religion in the Roman Empire* (Oxford: Blackwell, 2007).

12.   So Burkert, *Greek Religion*, 8: "ritual and myth are the two forms in which Greek religion presents itself to the historian of religion." On pp. 55–60 he emphasizes the centrality of animal sacrifice in that ritual. Scheid (*Introduction to Roman Religion*, 18–29) carefully qualifies the meaning of religion in his study—focused on sacrificial ritual—to avoid anachronism. The central part of his book then explores ancient sacrifice with examples and insightful analysis (79–110). Rives (*Religion in the Roman Empire*, esp. 13–53) takes care to separate out many spheres of Roman life in which "religious" phenomena were to be found. Particularly clear, if less inviting for modern readers, are such books as Robert Turcan, *The Cults of the Roman Empire* (Oxford: Blackwell, 1996); Jennifer Larson, *Ancient Greek Cults: A Guide* (London: Routledge, 2007); and Beate Dignas and Kai Trampedach, eds., *Practitioners of the Divine: Greek Priests and Religious Officials from Homer to Heliodorus* (Washington, DC: Center for Hellenic Studies, 2008), which signal this interest in the title.

13.   See Robert Parker, *Miasma: Pollution and Purification in Early Greek Religion* (Oxford: Clarendon, 1983), 19.

14.   See Arthur Pickard-Cambridge, *The Dramatic Festivals of Athens* (ed. David Malcolm Lewis and John Gould; Oxford: Oxford University Press, 1988), 57–64.

guilds; through the Roman period their associations remained devoted to Dionysus. Elsewhere, drama festivals might be devoted to Asclepius or another deity.

Similarly, the Roman Senate could meet only in a consecrated building, and before each meeting its members ("Fathers") offered a sacrifice of incense. Rome and its colonies were defined by a sacred boundary (*pomerium*) marked out by the *augurs*, a threshold that had nothing directly to do with the city's defensive walls. From the area within this sacred boundary death and other forms of pollution were excluded, the dead being buried outside—before the inevitable growth of the city put some tombs inside. The powers granted to military commanders and provincial governors lapsed when they crossed this ritual boundary. In Republican times, armed soldiers were also banned, with few pragmatic exceptions, and the principle was respected as far as possible (e.g., excepting the imperial bodyguard) into the later Empire.[15] The entire city of Rome was thus a *templum*: at once a place marked out as ground for authoritative divination and a sacred space.

Roman military life, from camp routines to preparation for a military campaign or the solemn ceremonies marking the demobilization of long-service comrades, was shot through with rituals of divination and sacrifice— both the traditionally Roman rituals and those suited to the ethnic make-up of particular units.[16] In this the Romans were continuing a much older tradition among all armies. The Spartans, who were considered scrupulously observant of divine rites, would sacrifice a goat before engaging in battle.[17] The triumphal-memorial columns of Trajan (c. 113–117 CE) and Marcus Aurelius (c. 192 CE) conspicuously feature scenes of sacrifice in their frieze

---

15. Essentials are already Samuel B. Platner, *The Topography and Monuments of Ancient Rome* (2nd ed.; Boston, MA: Allyn and Bacon, 1911), 34–7, 43–8; James H. Oliver, "The Augustan Pomerium," *Memoirs of the American Academy in Rome* 10 (1932): 145–82. On purity and pollution, see the relevant essays in Valerie M. Hope and Eireann Marshall, eds., *Death and Disease in the Ancient City* (London: Routledge, 2000), especially therein the pithy summary by John R. Patterson, "On the Margins of the City of Rome," 88–97.

16. See Graham Webster, *The Roman Imperial Army of the First and Second Centuries A.D.* (3rd ed.; London: A. & C. Black, 1985), 275–81; Yann Le Bohec, *The Imperial Roman Army* (trans. Raphael Bate; London: Routledge, 1994), 236–54; Peter Herz, "Sacrifice and Sacrificial Ceremonies of the Roman Imperial Army," in Baumgarten, ed., *Sacrifice in Religious Experience*, 81–100 (with a valuable effort to recover concrete procedures); Oliver Stoll, "The Religions of the Armies," in *A Companion to the Roman Army* (ed. Paul Erdkamp; Oxford: Wiley-Blackwell, 2007), 451–76.

17. E.g., Burkert, *Greek Religion*, 59–60.

panels, as does the Arch of Trajan at Beneventum.[18] In some of these, the emperor in his priestly function supervises the traditional sacrifice of a pig (*sus*), sheep (*ovis*), and bull (*taurus*)—the so-called *suovetaurilia*—outside the fort, to purify the army before a campaign. In his work *On Agriculture* (142), Cato the Elder had prescribed the ritual (including prayers to Mars) for the *suovetaurilia* in the non-military context of purifying land. So, this fundamental ritual had several functions in addition to the army's purification for combat.

Pompey the Great, a candidate for the status of Rome's greatest general ever, illustrates well the integration of attendance on the gods with military life. When he had been granted unprecedented power over the entire Mediterranean and its contiguous lands, to deal with maritime threats, defeat King Mithridates VI of Pontus, and settle eastern lands for Rome, he reportedly first made a point of offering public sacrifice, as generals customarily did (Plutarch, *Pompeius* 26.1). Most telling are the coins issued following Pompey's three subsequent triumphs. Surprisingly to modern observers, perhaps, they feature the implements of Pompey's *priestly office* of augur: a jug and a crooked staff—a symbol preserved nowadays by Christian bishops. They show the close connection between Pompey and those priestly implements. This is seen too on the coins issued by his son and later by the Emperor Trajan in the second century CE, when the Pompey coins include the priest's jug and staff connected with image of the man they honor.[19]

If we imagine a modern general—Napoleon or Rommel, Montgomery or Patton, Schwarzkopf or Petraeus—choosing to be photographed for posterity in clerical garb, framing his battlefield maneuvers with elaborate modern-religious rituals, or thinking it important to dedicate a religious building after a successful conflict, we immediately see some important differences between the place of religion today and the ancient locations of cult, priest, and ritual.

Rome, the best-documented *polis* of our period, provides a good example of diversity within the standard categories of the Mediterranean world. By the first century BCE a complex collection of state priesthoods had developed. There were both colleges (*collegia*) of high officials and individual posts that were open only to the senatorial class or even the elite subset of patricians (families of ancient nobility). The latter included the "king and

18.   On the Beneventum arch, see Mary Beard, *The Roman Triumph* (Cambridge, MA: The Belknap Press of Harvard University Press, 2007), 126–8.

19.   Cf. the gold coin representing Pompey's first triumph (71 BCE), ref. 1867,0101.584 in the British Museum (http://www.britishmuseum.org/research.aspx), and the silver isues of 44–42 BCE and 112–114 CE, respectively (refs. 1860,0328.155, 1862,0415.8).

queen of sacrifices" (*rex* and *regina sacrorum*) as well as the *flamines* or individual priests of the leading gods: Jupiter, Mars, and Romulus (*Dialis*, *Martialis*, and *Quirinalis*). The great honor enjoyed by Jupiter's priest (the *flamen Dialis*) came with serious constraints. He was more or less confined to the city of Rome, was not permitted to touch a corpse or look on an arrayed army, and hence was disqualified from warfare. He could not touch bread made with yeast, and his clothing could contain no knots. He lived each and every day in the high state of holiness that was required of others only when they visited sacred sites.[20] These restrictions for the sake of purity will sound familiar to anyone studying the Judaean priesthood, temple access, and particularly the high priest's regimen.

Among the highest honors that the Emperor and military conqueror Augustus could claim for himself, in the autobiographical *Res gestae* that he published at the end of his life (14 CE), was membership in Rome's seven leading priestly colleges (*Res gestae* 7.2): "I have been *pontifex maximus*, *augur*, in the Commission of Fifteen Supervising the Sacred Activities, in the Commission of Seven Supervising Sacred Banquets, an Arval Brother, a *sodalis Titius*, and a *fetial* priest." These priestly bodies oversaw Rome's attention to the gods (*cura deorum*) and the interpretation of divine will through omens. The named colleges were the preserve of the senatorial class and, since they were life-long positions in contrast to year-long magistracies, avidly sought honors.[21] Augury was in its origins a form of divination by *auspicia* (from *aves* [birds] + *specto* [observe]): observing the flight patterns and noises of specified birds in a prescribed area and from a consecrated vantage point.

Auspicia had a long tradition in Rome. They were taken before various public undertakings, including the election of magistrates. But the great orator-statesman Cicero, a proud member of the senatorial College of Augurs, sounds rather like a modern liberal Protestant when—in a dialogue with his brother that ridicules the superstition involved in seeking the divine will through random animal movements—he writes (*De divinatione* 2.33):

> "It is hard for an augur to speak against auspices!" [you say]. For a Marsian,[22] no doubt; but for a Roman it is no problem. We are certainly not augurs who speak about the future by observing birds and the various other signs! I do believe that Romulus, who founded the city on the basis of auspices, held the view that knowledge of coming things lay in augury—for antiquity

20. So Aulus Gellius 10.15, summarizing in the mid-second century CE what he had read in Fabius Pictor, who wrote nearly four centuries earlier. For the priestly colleges see also the first-century BCE Dionysius of Halicarnassus, *Antiquitates Romanae* 2.64-76.

21. Beard, North, and Price, *Religions of Rome*, 55.

22. The Marsi were one of Rome's old neighboring tribes, northeast of Latium.

often went astray in these matters. But we can see that things have changed, whether you ascribe this to experience, to education, or to the great age [of the practice]. Still, with a view to both the imaginations of the rabble and expediency for the state, we maintain custom, superstition, discipline, the law of augury, and the authority of the [Augural] College.

Although this skepticism might remind British readers of stereotypical figures of the Church of England, as satirized in television comedy, who are not necessarily expected to believe cardinal Christian doctrines even as they represent the Church in high places (e.g., the House of Lords), the crucial difference is that the latter are professional religious figures whose eminence links them with politics, whereas Cicero and his colleagues were political-military-cultural leaders whose high status brought cultic responsibilities. Cicero's emphasis on the social utility of the ancient rites, including the perpetuation of superstition among the masses, was shared by many of this class.[23]

The College of Augurs was already by Cicero's time an elite body of great prestige. A century and a half later it was likewise political honor, and not the opportunity to exercise a spiritual or "religious" function, that delighted Pliny the Younger upon his appointment to the same College:[24]

You [Maturus Arrianus] may congratulate me on having been received among the Augurs, and you may congratulate me with justice: first because it's a fine thing to follow the judgments of such a great *princeps* as ours [i.e., Trajan as Augur] even in smaller matters; second, because this priesthood itself is old and sacred, and indeed has a clear and marked sanctity to it, *which is not taken away from a living incumbent*. Surely other positions of roughly comparable authority are granted, but they are also taken away. In this case the element of luck is limited to the giving of it.

That is, one had to wait on fortune for elevation to Augur status; once it was in hand, even a reversal of fortune could not take it away. Whereas a senator such as Pliny might aspire to one such college membership, the emperor dominated all possible rivals for prestige by holding *all* the important priesthoods at the same time. And he was in the unique position of securing memberships for others as new positions opened up.

23. Cf. Polybius 6.56.7-12, admiring the Romans' exploitation of superstition; similarly, Diodorus Siculus 1.2.2; 34-5.2.47. Josephus hints at the same principle when he allows that popular Greek beliefs about judgement after death (which he does not believe) are valuable in promoting virtuous behavior among the masses (*Bellum Judaicum* 2.158).

24. *Epistulae ad Familiares* 4.8 (emphasis mine); cf. 10.13, where Pliny requests the honor.

Like the other senatorial colleges, that of the Augurs preserved a body of secret ancient lore for advising the state. Each nation presumably had such elite experts in its own traditions. Josephus mentions a sub-group of "priests who were experts in the ancestral traditions," who were brought forward to convince their revolution-minded colleagues that excluding sacrifices from foreigners, as they were planning, would be both untraditional and dangerous (*Bellum Judaicum* 2.417). In Jerusalem, as elsewhere around the Mediterranean, priests were an integral part of *polis* leadership.

Augustus's self-representation provides ample evidence of the value he placed on public cult and its priesthoods. When describing his consulships in his autobiographical report (*Res Gestae* 8), which are offices that might sound to us purely secular and political, he mentions that he conducted the traditional expiatory sacrifices of a pig, a sheep, and a bull (the *lustrum*) upon completion of each population census. Imagine the Census Office of a modern government doing that! And he is frequently pictured on coins and reliefs offering sacrifice, his toga raised over his head in reverence to the divine. Beautiful gold coins portray his concern with proper sacrifice to the Roman gods.[25]

The importance that the emperor attached to his membership in the priestly colleges confirms the centrality of the gods to Roman life and his concern to control every avenue of upper-class influence and prestige. Particularly noteworthy is his title *pontifex maximus*. In its narrow sense, this term designated the leader of the sixteen or twenty men known as *pontifices*, who were charged with overseeing ritual correctness and advising the Senate as well as leading citizens. The *pontifices* constituted the most prestigious of Rome's priestly colleges.[26] But Julius Caesar's assumption of the position, which Augustus and his imperial successors followed, gave the title the *effective* sense of "high priest of the Roman state."[27] This sublime office was often mentioned first by emperors on their coins, inscriptions, and military diplomas (for auxiliary soldiers becoming citizens).[28]

25. See at http://www.britishmuseum.org/research.aspx the coins with reference numbers 1932,0408.2 (16 BC Rome), 1871,1203.6 (16 BC Spain), and 1864,1128.22 (13 BC Rome).

26. See Dionysius, *Antiquitates Romanae* 2.73.

27. See Beard, North, and Price, *Religions of Rome*, 191–2.

28. See in the British Museum collection (http://www.britishmuseum.org/research. aspx) reference numbers: 1843,0116.522 (coin of Caesar as *augur* and *pontifex*); R.3594, R.5033, R.6440, R.6441, R.6458, 1901,0601.150 (coins of Gaius Caligula, *pon. m.* or *p.m.*); 1912,0607.59, R.6583, 1874,0715.11 (coins of Galba *p.m.*); 1872,0709.465 (coin of Vitellius *p.m.*); 1894,1105.1 (inscription for new bridge built by Domitian, *pontf. maximus*); 1813,1211.1, 1813,1211.2 (diplomas from Trajan, *pontifex maximus*). Compare the examples from the reigns of Gaius Caligula (copper *as* of AD 37–38,

When Augustus' autobiographical record was published in the Greek-speaking provinces shortly after his death (19 August 14 CE), *pontifex maximus* was translated as Greek *archiereus* (*Res Gestae* 7.2). This is the same word that Greek used for the Judaean "high priest," the head of Jerusalem's cultic-sacrificial regime. The Judaean high priest also had important roles in general *polis* life, which had developed over time from simpler origins, in a somewhat similar way to the expanding profile of Rome's chief priest.[29] Likewise, the "high priest of Alexandria and all Egypt"—the man who supervised all of provincial Egypt's temples and its imperial cult—was the highest civic office to which a wealthy Alexandrian citizen could aspire.[30] Incidentally, *Pontifex Maximus* has survived to modern times as one of the Pope's unofficial titles.

Although the senatorial priestly colleges were the most visible and import-ant in Rome, at least half a dozen other colleges were for men of the lower-level equestrian rank, and a small few were open to ordinary Roman citizens or a subset of them. Of these last, the most famous was the college of *haurspices*, comprising sixty Etruscans of noble ancestry.[31] They are a good exam-ple of Rome's unique traditions because their functions arose from Rome's history of conquest and debts to the older civilization of Etruria to the north. At crucial points, Roman public ritual required these Etruscan specialists to read the internal organs, especially the liver, of a sacrificed animal. The organs were the parts of the sacrifice burned on the altar—for the god—whereas the rest of the roasted meat would be eaten. They were examined partly to deter-mine whether the sacrifice was accepted and partly, according to a tradition of divination, to read significance from the condition of various sections of the organ. The kind of secret knowledge required to undertake this divination could be viewed as a threat to the powerful.[32]

Just as the integration of cult with public and military life was a common feature of Mediterranean life, so also notions of pollution (*miasma*), taboo, and purification were widely shared, if differently addressed from place to place.[33] Pollution seems to have been understood essentially as

1853,0105.131) and Aulus Vitellius (denarius of April to December, AD 69, R.10252); both advertise their status as *pontifex maximus* and feature the Goddess Vesta with sac-rificial bowl (*patera*) on the reverse.

29. This development was of course different and driven by local conditions. Cf. Elias J. Bickerman, *Chronology of the Ancient World* (London: Thames & Hudson, 1980), 140–4.

30. Cf. Livia Capponi, *Augustan Egypt: The Creation of a Roman Province* (London: Routledge. 2005), 41–2.

31. See Rüpke, *Religion of the Romans*, 40 and 223–8.

32. See Rüpke, *Religion of the Romans*, 149–50 and 252–3.

33. For cross-cultural perspectives compare Parker, *Miasma*, e.g., 18–31, with Jacob

contamination: the mixing of things that ought to be kept separate, each in its proper place. Purification meant restoring things to their pure (that is, unmixed) state. In cultic contexts, proper separation meant above all keeping the immortal gods and the spaces consecrated to them free from exposure to the phenomena of mortality—the human processes associated with child-bearing and death, and sometimes including such bodily discharges as blood and semen. We see here an important difference from modern conceptions of *hygiene*, on the one hand, and from theological notions of *sin* on the other—though pollution certainly overlaps with both. Serious violations of the moral order such as murder were particular pollution-generators, but even naturally and unavoidably appearing bodily fluids associated with life and death, like death itself, had to be kept away from sacred areas.

Many kinds of pollution were considered communicable, contagious through contact, or inherently communal. For the last, consider the pollution of Thebes by Oedipus' unwitting outrages against the natural order, in *Oedipus Tyrannus*, or the growing atmosphere of doom that Josephus portrays as he describes wartime Jerusalem and the pollution of its sacred spaces.[34]

Purification, then, involved the restoration of a polluted person, group, or space to its proper place and whole condition. Those who wished to enter consecrated spaces needed to undergo a symbolic purification by washing with water. This was not for hygienic purposes in the modern sense, as bacteria were still unknown, though any obvious dirt or blood would certainly have needed to be removed on the simple ground that it was blemish. If they had contracted specific kinds of impurity, more elaborate rituals involving sacrifice and restitution might be needed to complete the process of restoration to proper order. Very serious cases, involving kin bloodshed or temple robbery, might place the perpetrators under a curse that only their suffering or death could resolve.

Such common notions were shared, at least in broad terms, from one *ethnos* and *polis* to another. Just as with the variety of phenomena classified as *ethnos* or *polis*, however, beneath the common language a wide range of local cultic practices was covered by such categories as *piety, sacred*

Milgrom, *Leviticus: A Book of Ritual and Ethics* (Minneapolis, MN: Fortress Press, 2004), and both of these with the seminal anthropological work of Mary Douglas, *Purity and Danger: An Analysis of Concepts of Pollution and Taboo* (London: Routledge & Kegan Paul, 1966); also, Baumgarten, *Sacrifice*. For an accessible summary with an emphasis on Israelite-Judaean conceptions, see Harold W. Attridge, "Pollution, Sin, Atonement, Salvation," in *Ancient Religions* (ed. Sarah Iles Johnston; Cambridge, MA: Harvard University Press, 2007), 71–83.

34. E.g., *Bellum Judaicum* 2.454-5, 562; 4.150, 159, 163, 201, 215, 242, 323; 5.10, 17-20, 377, 402; 6.95, 99, 110, 121-4, 127, 347; 7.267.

matters, cult, worship, and *rites.* Herodotus transmits stories about Persian and Scythian sacrifices, highlighting their differences from Greek practices. The Persians do not use temples, altars, or statues (as they do not think of gods in human form), he says. They take their sacrificial victims out to open spaces, cut them up, boil the meat, lay it out on the grass, receive the conse-crating chant of a priest (*magus*), and finally take away the whole lot to use as they wish (1.130-2). He contrasts Greek norms: a fixed altar for roasting the animal to accompanying music, ancillary offerings of wine and barley, and division of the victim so that part of it is burned up for the god, part goes to the priest(s), and part goes to the sacrificers (1.132.1).[35]

The Scythians, again, offer animals—mainly horses (not pigs, as the Greeks)—to various gods, with Greek-equivalent names, boiling the meat in a cauldron (again, no Greek-style roasting). They build a kind of altar, but only to honor their version of Ares (god of war), to whom they also barbari-cally sacrifice one *man* from every hundred they take prisoner (4.59-63). Still, in keeping with his ethnographic model Herodotus recognizes all these highly varied practices as the established customs (οἱ νόμοι, τὰ νόμαια) of those for-eign peoples, thus as generic counterparts to aspects of Greek culture.

The apparatus for worshipping and appeasing the deity thus varied with each *polis* and its local traditions. Although the same divine names turned up across the Hellenized world (Roman Jupiter, Syrian Baal-Shemim, and the Judaean Yahweh might all be identified with Zeus), their characteristics in each place varied considerably. Traditional cultic prescriptions and sys-tems for choosing priests and other officials were understood to be quite different even in Greek Athens, Sparta, and Corinth. A distinction was com-monly made, however, between the distinctive and central cults of each *polis* and those that functioned either below or above *polis* level. The latter were less definitive of distinct peoples and *poleis.*

Our focus must be on those public cults and festivals at the *polis* level, but we should at least acknowledge other related activities. First, throughout the Greek world (as also in Egypt, Judaea, and elsewhere) individuals and heads of households were free to bring sacrifices in fulfillment of vows, to accom-pany petitions (e.g., for a good harvest or health), and to express thanks to the deity.[36] Second, in the Hellenistic-Roman period male citizens and some-times even women and slaves could be initiated into a local group devoted to the worship of Demeter and Korē, Isis and Osiris, Sarapis, the Great Mother Cybelē, or Mithras. Or they might join a club or guild that, as part of its

35. See the discussion in Cartledge, *The Greeks*, 176.
36. See Robert Parker, *Polytheism and Society at Athens* (Oxford: Oxford Univer-sity Press, 2005), 9–49.

corporate life, worshiped a patron deity with regular sacrifices. Finally, there were various kinds of trans-local cultic activities: inter-*polis* festivals with athletic games every four years at Greece's pan-Hellenic sites (e.g., Delphi, Delos, and Olympia), which were deliberately sited at some distance from the powerful *poleis* and managed by committees; prestigious cults (such as that of Demeter and Korē at Eleusis in Attica) in which people from other *poleis* were welcome to celebrate; and Jerusalem's cult, which both served Judaeans everywhere and welcomed gifts and visits from non-Judaean visitors.

Judaeans throughout both the Roman and the Parthian Empires looked to their sole temple in the *mētropolis* of Jerusalem. They sent funds annually for its upkeep, and undertook pilgrimages to it if they had the means and inclination.[37] The exclusivity of Jerusalem as home of the Judaean cult is confirmed by these donations and pilgrimages, by the comments or complaints of outside observers about them (e.g., Tacitus, *Historiae* 5.4), and by biblical laws that developed out of earlier cultic variety and specified Jerusalem as the sole center of cultic activity (Deuteronomy 12.5-14). Nevertheless, there was a Judaean temple in Lower Egypt until the mid-70s CE, and some important sacrifices *may* have been offered elsewhere under some circumstances. We know very little about either of these complications.[38]

No matter what their personal beliefs may have been, then, citizens of either a Graeco-Roman or a Near-Eastern *polis*, including Jerusalem, would have had a constant awareness of the local god(s) and the traditional precautions for maintaining purity near spaces consecrated to that god. Ancient Hebrew, Aramaic, Greek, and Latin all had numerous words for laws, customs, observances, piety, ritual, sacrifice, pollution, purity, and so forth. They needed no word for a separate sphere of life comparable to *religion* in our world, and they had none.

---

37. On the relationship between pilgrims and Judaean locals, from several angles, see Reuben Lee, "Diaspora Judaeans and Proselytes in Early Roman Palestine: A Study of Ethnic, Social, and Cultural Boundaries" (PhD dissertation, University of Aberdeen, 2012).

38. The slight but intriguing literary and material evidence for sacrificial cult outside Jerusalem in the Graeco-Roman period is gathered in Anders Runesson, Donald D. Binder, and Birger Olsson, *The Ancient Synagogue from its Origins to 200 C.E.: A Source Book* (Leiden: Brill, 2008), 274–94. Cf. the suggestive remark of Josephus and *Antiquitates Judaicae* 2.313 with Federico M. Colautti, *Passover in the Works of Josephus* (Leiden: Brill, 2002), 7, 24–32, 231–5. On earlier temples in Egypt (at Elephantine), see Bickerman, *Chronology of the Ancient World*, 44–5, 239. On the temple in Leontopolis, Egypt, see Josephus, *Bellum Judaicum* 1.33; 7.421-36; *Antiquitates Judaicae* 12.388; 13.70, 285; 20.336, with critical analysis and reconstruction (exploiting relevant inscriptions) by Livia Capponi, *Il tempio di Leontopoli in Egitto: Identità Politica e Religiosa dei Giudei di Onia (c. 150 a.C–73 d.C.)* (Pisa: Edizioni ETS, 2007).

When I speak of religion today as (by contrast) separable from the rest of life, I recognize that for many this distinction may not be so obvious. They may feel that their religious outlook grounds and informs everything else they do: business and leisure activities, charity, diet, and dealings with others. But we are discussing societies, not personal outlooks, and the way in which *public life* is ordered. In modern western societies, religion is a voluntary sphere of activity, separate in principle from domestic and foreign politics, business and advertising, public education, sport, theatre, film, other kinds of entertainment, and military service—in other words, most of what we read about in the newspaper, outside of the small "religion section" or page, if there happens to be one. The internal content of this religion typically involves worship, prayer, the study and exposition of texts, moral exhortation, a certain life discipline, possibly including dietary implications, and rites of passage for birth, marriage, and death. Much of my point is that in terms of both social location and internal content, ancient Mediterranean societies had nothing that corresponded very closely to our modern sense of "religion." The categories to which Graeco-Roman and Judaean writers resort on every page (*ethnos*, nature or character, ancestral custom, and law; *polis*, citizenship, and constitution [*politeia*]; and sacrifice-centered rituals for attending to the gods of the *ethnos* and *polis*), suited a differently constructed world.

The sphere of life we recognize as *religion* would become recognizable first in the Christian reconstruction of the ancient-social lexicon, in which process elements of ethnic, political, ritual, and (mainly) philosophical life were fused to produce a category of chosen *systems of belief and practice*, called *religiones*. This new amalgam stripped and reconfigured what it needed from *ethnos*, *polis*, and cult, leaving the rest to wither on the carcass of classical civilization, in spite of the Emperor Julian's vigorous rearguard attempt to reestablish *polis* life, temples, altars, and sacrifice. After centuries of a new kind of faith-based integration of state and society during the medieval period, the transition to religious -isms was completed with a vengeance in the Enlightenment, with its placement of all religions on the same precarious level—of unfounded belief. In the American and French Revolutions, although religion was usually tolerated in principle, it was also clearly isolated as a voluntary pursuit of mind and spirit, distinct from governance, ideal education, and the essential operations of society.

Biographical Note

Steve Mason is Distinguished Professor of Ancient Mediterranean Religions and Culture at Groningen University, the Netherlands. Until 2011, he was at Toronto's York University, the last eight years holding the Canada Research

Chair in Greco-Roman Cultural Interaction. From 2012 until 2015 he held the Kirby Laing Chair in New Testament and Early Christianity at the University of Aberdeen, UK. A Fellow of the Royal Historical Society, he has held the Killam Research Fellowship and the Dirk Smilde Fellowship (Groningen), received a Humboldt Research Award (Berlin), and been Visiting Fellow in All Souls and Wolfson Colleges, Oxford. His books include *Flavius Josephus on the Pharisees* (Brill, 1991), *Josephus and the New Testament* (2nd ed., Hendrickson, 2003), *Josephus, Judea, and Christian Origins: Methods and Categories* (Hendrickson, 2009), and *The Jewish-Roman War, 66–74: A Historical Inquiry* (Cambridge University Press, 2016). He is the editor of the international multi-volume series *Flavius Josephus: Translation and Commentary*, published by Brill, to which he has so far contributed the volumes *Life of Josephus* (2011) and *Judean War 2* (2008).

Bibliography

Attridge, Harold W. "Pollution, Sin, Atonement, Salvation," 71–83 in *Ancient Religions*. Edited by Sarah Iles Johnston. Cambridge, MA: Harvard University Press, 2007.

Baumgarten, Albert I., ed. *Sacrifice in Religious Experience.* Leiden: Brill, 2002.

Beard, Mary. *The Roman Triumph.* Cambridge, MA: The Belknap Press of Harvard University Press, 2007. https://doi.org/10.4159/9780674020597

Beard, Mary, John North, and Simon Price. *Religions of Rome.* Vol. II: *A Sourcebook.* Cambridge: Cambridge University Press, 1998.

Bickerman, Elias J. *Chronology of the Ancient World.* London: Thames & Hudson, 1980 [1968].

Burkert, Walter. *Greek Religion: Archaic and Classical.* Translated by John Raffan. Oxford: Blackwell, 1985.

Capponi, Livia. *Augustan Egypt: The Creation of a Roman Province.* London: Routledge, 2005. https://doi.org/10.4324/9780203943946

—*Il tempio di Leontopoli in Egitto: Identità Politica e Religiosa dei Giudei di Onia (c. 150 a.C.–73 d.C.).* Pisa: Edizioni ETS, 2007.

Cartledge, Paul. *The Greeks: A Portrait of Self and Others.* Oxford: Oxford University Press, 2002.

Colautti, Federico M. *Passover in the Works of Josephus.* Leiden: Brill, 2002.

Dignas, Beate, and Kai Trampedach, eds. *Practitioners of the Divine: Greek Priests and Religious Officials from Homer to Heliodorus.* Washington, DC: Center for Hellenic Studies, 2008.

Douglas, Mary. *Purity and Danger: An Analysis of Concepts of Pollution and Taboo.* London: Routledge & Kegan Paul, 1966.

Gellner, Ernest. *Cause and Meaning in the Social Sciences.* London: Routledge & Kegan Paul, 1973.

Herz, Peter. "Sacrifice and Sacrificial Ceremonies of the Roman Imperial Army," 81–100 in Baumgarten, ed., *Sacrifice in Religious Experience*, 2002.

Hope, Valerie M., and Eireann Marshall, eds. *Death and Disease in the Ancient City.* London: Routledge, 2000.

Kindt, Julia. *Rethinking Greek Religion.* Cambridge: Cambridge University Press, 2012. https://doi.org/10.1017/CBO9780511978500

Klauck, Hans-Josef. *The Religious Context of Early Christianity: A Guide to Graeco-Roman Religions.* Translated by Brian McNeil. Minneapolis, MN: Fortress Press, 2003.

Larson, Jennifer. *Ancient Greek Cults: A Guide.* London: Routledge, 2007. https://doi.org/10.4324/9780203356982

Le Bohec, Yann. *The Imperial Roman Army.* Translated by Raphael Bate. London: Routledge, 1994.

Lee, Reuben. "Diaspora Judaeans and Proselytes in Early Roman Palestine: A Study of Ethnic, Social, and Cultural Boundaries." PhD dissertation, University of Aberdeen, 2012.

Milgrom, Jacob. *Leviticus: A Book of Ritual and Ethics.* Minneapolis, MN: Fortress Press, 2004.

Oliver, James H. "The Augustan Pomerium." *Memoirs of the American Academy in Rome* 10 (1932): 145–82. https://doi.org/10.2307/4238570

Oxford Latin Dictionary. Edited by P. G. W. Glare. Oxford: Clarendon Press, 1968.

Parker, Robert. *Miasma: Pollution and Purification in Early Greek Religion.* Oxford: Clarendon, 1983.

—*Polytheism and Society at Athens.* Oxford: Oxford University Press, 2005.

Patterson, John R. "On the Margins of the City of Rome," 85–103 in Hope and Marshall, eds., *Death and Disease in the Ancient City,* 2000.

Pickard-Cambridge, Arthur. *The Dramatic Festivals of Athens.* Edited by David Malcolm Lews and John Gould. Oxford: Oxford University Press, 1988.

Platner, Samuel B. *The Topography and Monuments of Ancient Rome.* 2nd ed. Boston, MA: Allyn and Bacon, 1911.

Richardson, John. *The Language of Empire: Rome and the Idea of Empire from the Third Century BC to the Second Century AD.* Cambridge: Cambridge University Press, 2008. https://doi.org/10.1017/CBO9780511575341

Rives, James B. *Religion in the Roman Empire.* Oxford: Blackwell, 2007.

Runesson, Anders, Donald D. Binder, and Birger Olsson. *The Ancient Synagogue from Its Origins to 200 C.E.: A Source Book.* Leiden: Brill, 2008.

Rüpke, Jörg. *Religion of the Romans.* Translated by Richard Gordon. Cambridge: Polity Press, 2007.

Saller, Richard P. "Martial on Patronage and Literature." *The Classical Quarterly* 33 (1983): 246–57. https://doi.org/10.1017/S0009838800034431

Scheid, John. *An Introduction to Roman Religion.* Translated by Janet Lloyd. Bloomington, IN: Indiana University Press, 2003.

Shatzman, Israel. "Review of J. Richardson: *The Language of Empire: Rome and the Idea of Empire from the Third Century BC to the Second Century AD.*" *Scripta Classica Israelica* 29 (2010): 128–32.

Stoll, Oliver. "The Religions of the Armies," 451–76 in *A Companion to the Roman Army.* Edited by Paul Erdkamp. Oxford: Wiley-Blackwell, 2007.

Turcan, Robert. *The Cults of the Roman Empire.* Oxford: Blackwell, 1996.

Webster, Graham. *The Roman Imperial Army of the First and Second Centuries A.D.* 3rd ed. London: A & C Black, 1985.

White, Peter. "*Amicitia* and the Profession of Poetry in Early Imperial Rome." *Journal of Roman Studies* 68 (1978): 74–92. https://doi.org/10.2307/299627

Whitmarsh, Tim. *Battling the Gods: Atheism in the Ancient World.* London: Faber & Faber, 2016.

Chapter Three

The Value(s) of Belief:
Ancient Religion, Cognitive Science, and Interdisciplinarity

Jason P. Davies

Anything ... which ... is usually hung on to the handy peg of "belief", will
be better said by recourse to some other word; and if we are clear about what
we want to say, we shall find that it can be said clearly only by another word.
— Rodney Needham[1]

In 2011, Henk Versnel published his *Coping with the Gods: Wayward Readings in Greek Theology*. It closes with an appendix "Did the Greeks Believe in Their Gods?" where he discusses a "vexing ... and sorely misguided recent campaign against the legitimacy of using the terms 'belief/believe' in the study of Greek religion."[2] In his argument, which particularly focuses on the case put by Manuela Giordano-Zecharya,[3] he identifies the anthropologist Rodney Needham as "the only regular guest" in the debate and concludes: "we are confronted here with a clash between cognitive and non-cognitive concepts of religion. And to date it seems that the former have prevailed: the notions belief/believe are thriving in current cognitive studies of religion."[4]

I shall use Versnel's account as a cue to consider what forces and customs lie behind the apparently endless disagreements on whether we should speak of ancient "belief." In so doing, I historicize his account, as it were, seeking insight into the dynamics of the debate and, if not some common ground, some understanding of why the topic has become so vexed. Normal

---

1. Rodney Needham, *Belief, Language and Experience* (Oxford: Oxford University Press, 1972), 229.
2. Henk S. Versnel, *Coping with the Gods: Wayward Readings in Greek Theology* (Leiden: Brill, 2011), 539.
3. Manuela Giordano-Zecharya, "As Socrates Shows, the Athenians Did Not Believe in Gods," *Numen* 52.3 (2005): 325–55.
4. Versnel, *Coping*, 539–40, citing Jensine Andresen, ed., *Religion in Mind: Cognitive Perspectives on Religious Belief, Ritual, and Experience* (Cambridge: Cambridge University Press, 2001), and Jesper Sørensen, "Religion in Mind: A Review Article of the Cognitive Science of Religion," *Numen* 52.4 (2005): 465–94.

historical argumentation seems not to have resolved what exponents of both sides think is a fairly straightforward matter.

The exasperation in Versnel's account is reminiscent of a project I was involved in some years ago, an interdisciplinary research program where strikingly similar expressions of frustration were indicative of disciplinary incommensurability beneath the surface of discussion.[5] Perhaps we are in a different kind of trouble than we thought.

I cannot think of a topic in ancient history that is so fraught with mutual misunderstanding, bafflement, and exasperation as the topic of "belief": a book could easily be filled about the conflation of "belief" as "any cognitive activity relating to religion" and "belief" as a term to *refer* to "cognitive activity relating to religion," but this book should not be written. It would be a labyrinth of attributing misunderstanding X of Professor Y to Doctor Z (irritating Doctor A in the process). In particular, two themes have struck me repeatedly: firstly, that the general argument ultimately rests on a particular scholar's innate and "natural" understanding of the term and, secondly, that it is not infrequent for scholars to attribute completely different implications to the same observation. I came to this conclusion from trying to frame clarifications (because it often seems to me that scholars have not quite understood each other) where I went full circle and it seemed to me far too often that I could no longer tell what people actually disagreed with.

To try to evoke this concept without getting distracted by specifics, if Professor B asserts that I must believe in trains or I would not set off to the station, I might wonder what it means to *believe in* trains. Does this describe my

5.   On that project, see Jason P. Davies, "The Messiness of Academics Speaking Across the Disciplines," in *Collaborative Working in Higher Education: The Social Academy* (ed. Lorraine Walsh and Peter Kahn; London: Routledge, 2010), 111–8, and "Disciplining the Disciplines," in *Evidence, Inference and Enquiry* (ed. Dimitra Vasilaki, William Twining, and Philip Dawid; Oxford: Oxford University Press, 2011), 37–72. Evelyn Brister ("Disciplinary Capture and Epistemological Obstacles to Interdisciplinary Research: Lessons from Central African Conservation Disputes," *Studies in History and Philosophy of Science Part C: Studies in History and Philosophy of Biological and Biomedical Sciences* 56 [2016]: 82–91) notes similar issues in conservation science and coins the phrase "disciplinary capture" for one discipline establishing hegemony. Des Fitzgerald and Felicity Callard (eds., *Rethinking Interdisciplinarity Across the Social Sciences and Neurosciences* [Basingstoke, UK: Palgrave Macmillan, 2015]) talk about entanglements of all kinds, especially emotional ones (pp. 11–128). I explore the concept of "disciplinary self-defence" in Jason P. Davies, "'Threshold Guardians': Threshold Concepts as Guardians of the Discipline," in *Threshold Concepts in Practice* (ed. Ray Land, Jan H. F. Meyer, and Michael Flanagan; Rotterdam: Sense Publishers, 2016), 121–34. On the "natural insularity" and incommensurability of disciplines, see also Jerry A. Jacobs, *In Defense of Disciplines: Interdisciplinarity and Specialization in the Research University* (Chicago, IL: University of Chicago Press, 2014).

mental state? "Believe" seems a little strong, it has overtones for me of being confident in the face of doubt: are there people who *don't*? A more plausible example would be whether I "believe in climate change" (not everyone does) but I find it distasteful to say I *believe* it: I would strenuously avoid using "believe" in this context as it would appear to be making it a matter of personal choice or opinion. Perhaps I should use a different word? But even if I *think* that the trains exist, which I concede I do at some level because Professor B seems to have impeccable logic on this matter, I am not particularly *aware* of it. Wondering whether the train will do what I expect is another matter entirely, of course—or is it? Is that implied in "believe in"? I am now wondering about "faith" but shall evade that term and return to "belief." Apparently, I believe in trains but I had no idea of this before it was pointed out, and I cannot help feeling something that was unimportant now occupies center-stage. At some stations in London rush hour, I would even be going *not* expecting a train (at least not for some time), but I dismiss that scenario as a red herring. Feeling a little uncomfortable, I cannot at this point deny that I believe in trains because that would not be true either. Now that we have put a spotlight on it, an anthropologist might helpfully point out that I have a *custom* of leaving at the same time in the morning, but Professor B quickly points out that I would not go if I was convinced there were no trains, so there *is* a cognitive aspect to this action. I might then assert that my cognition about trains is neither here nor there, but yes, since you ask, I think there will be a train there, but only because there usually is: I am not going to seek some kind of proof first. At which point Professor B says this is *exactly what he meant* and though I cannot deny either's claims, I am irritated with both of them, because what I was doing was *just going to work*.

Space does not permit a full history or rehearsal of the "belief" debate: rather, I follow Versnel in noting that Simon Price's book is an important landmark, that Needham's work on belief and experience is a critical part of it, and that cognitive science of religion has no qualms about using the term—indeed it is an essential part of their toolkit.[6] To brutally summarize the position against (use of the term) "belief" put by a range of scholars over the years, it is that if we are to understand ancient religion, we must effortfully discard the assumption that it is a primarily cognitive affair and that even passing invocation of "belief" runs the risk of implying dogmatism or intellectual contrariness. Rather, we should begin our enquiries with ritual and be particularly suspicious of diagnosing orthodoxy and authoritative exegesis.

---

6.   Cf. Simon R. F. Price, *Rituals and Power: The Roman Imperial Cult in Asia Minor* (Cambridge: Cambridge University Press, 1984); Needham, *Belief.*

This then opens the door to vacating issues of content ("what did they think?") and thinking rather about identity, particularly civic identity (thus *polis* or civic religion). The people of the ancient world did not turn up to festivals worrying whether they had got their ideas right about the god. "Belief," in short, was not where the action was: it was in *participation*.[7]

"Pro-belief" scholars tend to dispute Needham's argument that "belief" is a peculiarly western and secular term—or, more often, that its relevance and consequences are, and this is worth dwelling on: it is one example of opposite arguments made from the same observation. Needham concluded that belief was too imprecise to be of use but "if a word has no specific definition, then how could one know whether or not it could be rendered into the Nuer language?"[8] I confess to *aporia* at this point, in that it seems difficult to clarify Needham's original point that there is no word of equivalent *vagueness*. Charles King continues, perfectly logically, that we must prove that the word or concept does not exist in Rome to say it is anachronistic. Ignoring his sleight of hand in implying that Needham only studied Nuer,[9] I am still left feeling that I believe in trains again. Similarly, Needham argued that "belief" in its paradoxical sense of doubt *and* certainty was a distinctively western formulation, and warned against projecting it onto other cultures, but King, perfectly plausibly, points out that this does not prove it is not in that other culture.

Another related response is to say that the terms "religion" and "ritual" are also problematic, but we retain *them*. King notes Goody's demonstration of this move for ritual[10] and no-one disputes that "religion" is indeed deeply problematic: Benson Saler outlines the gulf between modern and anthropological understanding, before concluding that we have no choice

---

7.   The first chapter in Denis C. Feeney, *Literature and Religion at Rome: Cultures, Contexts, and Beliefs* (Cambridge: Cambridge University Press, 1998), 12–46, remains one of the best discussions; for a more polemical approach on the dangers of "belief," see Jason P. Davies, "Believing the Evidence," in *Evidence, Inference and Enquiry*, 395–449. On *polis* religion and its critics, see James B. Rives, "Graeco-Roman Religion in the Roman Empire: Old Assumptions and New Approaches," *Currents in Biblical Research* 8.2 (2009): 268–76; Julia Kindt, "Polis Religion: A Critical Appreciation," *Kernos* 22 (2009): 9–34; and John Scheid, *Les dieux, l'Etat et l'individu: Réflexions sur la religion civique à Rome* (Paris: Seuil, 2013) (to whom I shall return).

8.   Charles King, "The Organization of Roman Religious Beliefs," *Classical Antiquity* 22.2 (2003): 277.

9.   I count twenty-two languages, including Indo-European as a single item (Davies, "Believing the Evidence," 401).

10.   E.g., King, "Organization," 278. For a similar deconstruction of ancient "religion," see Brent Nongbri, *Before Religion: A History of a Modern Concept* (New Haven, CT: Yale University Press, 2013).

other than to begin with the anachronistic assumptions that students arrive with, and gradually dismantle them and progressively extend their model.[11] But once again, this point ultimately has no compelling force or persuasive traction: to mischievously borrow King's logic, why should these two examples, perfectly valid in themselves, mean we have a universal strategy on *not* abandoning words or concepts as hopelessly anachronistic? Though tempting, this would not resolve anything: by using his strategy against his objection, we are spiraling away from our material and will be unable to break the deadlock.

One strategy has been to reclaim "belief" by pruning it of its excesses to yield "low intensity" and "high-intensity" belief. The latter, Christianizing, credal and dogmatic, is unproblematically discarded for ancient history but for the former, Versnel quotes King: "Belief is a conviction that an individual (or group of individuals) hold independently of the need for empirical support."[12] King later rephrases slightly: "[T]he central element is not the conscious assertion of belief, but rather the existence of a conviction in the absence of the need for verification."[13] This then is the "new belief." The question is whether it does the job we want it to, particularly with regard to religious ideas.[14]

Sidestepping for now a concern that cognition has crept in to occupy center stage, there are problems with King's definition, in particular the juxtaposition of "conviction" and a "lack of empirical support or verification." Taken on their own, neither is unproblematic: we can all entertain a thought and we can all be convinced. When combined, however, it sums up beautifully the modern secular bafflement about religion and the sense of surprise that people made (and continue to make) apparently clear assertions about divine activity. As presented, it is a private interior (psychological) claim; however, to say someone believes something is a *social* judgment not an individualized one. There are *two* agents in this definition, the convinced and

11. See Benson Saler, *Conceptualizing Religion: Immanent Anthropologists, Transcendent Natives, and Unbounded Categories* (Leiden: Brill, 1993). Jonathan Z. Smith is a giant in this area; see, for instance, his collection *Relating Religion: Essays in the Study of Religion* (Chicago, IL: University of Chicago Press, 2004).

12. King, "Organization," 279.

13. King, "Organization," 280.

14. Though his definition is ostensibly not specifically limited to religion, King ("Organization," 279) says that "specifically religious beliefs tend to be unusually devoid of a mechanism for testing their validity, for any supporting evidence that could be cited would itself be filtered through additional belief"; he is therefore primarily talking about religious ideas. Rives also cites King approvingly ("Graeco-Roman Religion in the Roman Empire," 275).

the unconvinced.[15] "Belief" smuggles hegemony and counter-hegemony into the room—that's what makes the word so useful. In other words, the first difficulty is "lack of verification" *according to whom*? The answer when it is used of historical agents is inevitably according to *us*. *We* are the surprised hegemonic agents advertising our distance. But is it really worth emphasizing that we do not believe in Zeus?

Secondly, what happens when we talk of "conviction," even without any reference to "lack of verification"? There are two issues here; firstly, it is a strong word to use when we cannot always be sure of our reading: irony, rhetorical power, resignation, guesses, exaggeration for effect and deception—are all ruled out. If we want an example, we can use King's own: he translates "*quam nei esset credo nesci[o qui] inveidit deus*" as "I believe that some deity or another was jealous of her"[16] but we can equally translate *credo* as "I suppose": the example itself is not going to resolve the dispute.[17] Furthermore, my own sense of "conviction"[18] is that it is used not of someone "entertaining" a thought, or not thinking much at all, but rather of someone maintaining a position despite a strong and credible challenge: if we then compound that sense with an "absence of need for verification" we are implying cognitive activity stubbornly maintained by people with little credibility in the mainstream.[19] I am not convinced that the "pro-belief" scholars intend this but this definition does seem to me to point in that direction.

The question is: "is this the term we wish to use of ancient people?" Versnel is absolutely right to say that we are irredeemably etic but the responsibility that goes with being etic is that our terms must have relevant interpretative power: they should bring greater insight.[20] Here, we are

15. Observed decades ago by Jean Pouillon ("Remarques sur le verbe <croire>," in *La fonction symbolique: Essais d'anthropologie* [ed. Michel Izard, Pierre Smith, and Claude Lévi-Strauss; Paris: Editions Gallimard, 1979], 48): "[c]e n'est pas tellement le croyant ... qui affirme sa croyance comme telle, c'est plutôt l'incroyant qui *réduit à une simple croyance* ce qui pour le croyant est comme un savoir" (my emphasis). See also Needham's discussion of Wittgenstein's believers "being on another [epistemological] plane" (*Belief*, 73).

16. King, "Organization," 279.

17. More extensively, see Davies, "Believing the Evidence," 402.

18. As is done so often in these exchanges, I have hereby smuggled in my personal sense of the word as if it were a universal agreed meaning; see Versnel's exposition of this (*Coping*, 554) for Price, *Rituals and Power*.

19. We are, I note, talking about the supposedly mild "*low* intensity" version of "belief," as well as assuming that scholars have heeded Versnel's warning to clarify this, that the reader has read the book starting at the beginning *and* that their attention did not drift at that moment.

20. See Versnel, *Coping*, 548. In other word(s), we are engaged in "redescription" (cf. Smith, *Relating Religion*, 28–31; Nongbri, *Before Religion*, esp. 15–24).

reduced to invoking our personal sense of the word: though I agree entirely with Versnel that we live in "rapidly secularising times,"[21] we seem to use "belief" more specifically of religion. My sense is therefore that it only (and tautologically) implies that we no longer think the same way as they did, and adds an unnecessary layer of "alienness" to their thought. We would indeed be well-advised to use a different word here, and we certainly need to avoid claiming that no verification was felt necessary.

This is not a catastrophic error; it is essentially about a *missed opportunity* to highlight aspects of their religious practice that might be worth highlighting as part of the "necessary overhaul" of what is understood by religion. The repeated and habitual use of "belief" has a particularly numbing effect on any attempt to show subtlety in their thought: *all* judgments are equally untenable (to us), whether they debated for days or jumped to conclusions. "Belief" is a particularly barren backdrop, free of distinguishing features or landmarks. That is its drawback—but also its chief attraction.

Versnel puts his finger precisely on a key issue when he talks of *"resistance* to using the word 'belief/believe'" (my emphasis).[22] "Belief" is the incumbent and needs only fight off objections to remain the default term for religious cognition/thinking/reflection/assertion (and so on). He points out that even Price, champion of the anti-belief charge, has been repeatedly accused of unconscious Christianizing assumptions and we might add his apparently careless reference to "Roman beliefs" when citing Herodian IV 2 (he records ritual, not cognition).[23]

Easily done then—but I maintain that to use "belief" is often to evade the cognitive work of deciding more precisely what we are referring to, and why: are we talking about axiomatic assumptions that the gods involve themselves in human affairs? Particular deductions based on that axiom? An optimistic expectation that a ritual will have a particular "effect" (it did last time)? Reluctant acquiescence in wearing an amulet that someone does not really think will effect a cure, but it is what people do, so why not? Further, the question is not simply "how do we describe their state of mind?": this should only be asked after we have carefully considered *"why* would we describe their state of mind (and what would happen if we didn't)?"

That depends on our audience, of course, and we must hope that we are generally not speaking into a vacuum: our students arrive already thinking "they" were credulous except for those insightful skeptical philosophers who clearly saw through all the nonsense (*or* they overly romanticize a

21. Versnel, *Coping*, 547.
22. Versnel, *Coping*, 553–4.
23. See Versnel, *Coping*, 554 n. 31; Price, *Rituals and Power*, 116.

bygone age, which is equally problematic). The question in the room is usually "how could they *believe* this stuff?"[24] We do not need to cement this
sense of irrationality but rather to dismantle it and demonstrate how people
can indeed live their lives terrifyingly oblivious to our thinking that they
are utterly misguided: worse still, it might be a prompt to see how axiomatic our own thinking is, and the extent to which we simply accept what we
have been told. Very few of my readers have the faintest idea how electricity works and have as much verification (or interest in verification) as an
ancient Roman did about the support of the gods. Why and when would we
say we *believe in* electricity? This is where values start to show themselves
in our language which raises the question of just how serious are we about
casting the ancient world as "distinctive—different but not other"?

"Belief" is apparently too convenient, elastic, and entrenched to be
dethroned merely by pointing at its inconsistencies or failings but that does
not mean it furthers the middle course that Versnel (and most others, including myself) are committed to, of navigating between the two extremes of
depicting ancient cultures as "utterly alien" and "so similar as not to merit
discussion."[25]

I would therefore refashion Versnel's point: "Resistance to using the word
'belief/believe' can only be a pressing option for those who are still … under
the sway of their Christian heritage and assume that every other contemporary scholar submits to the same yoke."[26] This is not unreasonable and certainly not a categorically disputable position, but I would offer instead that:
resistance to using the word "belief/believe" is a pressing option for those
who expect to encounter students (and scholars) who are still deeply influenced by belief-centered perspectives on religion and wish to force on them,
and themselves, a careful and cautious inquiry into what cognitive and social
processes sustained apparently "alien" ways of thinking, and behaving.

* * *

Thus far, we have briefly considered the matter from within ancient history
though I promised an interdisciplinary perspective. Why should we take
any notice of what an anthropologist says—especially an anthropologist
who dabbled in philosophy? We shall return to belief after a survey of some
interdisciplinary considerations and interactions.

24. On ancient "atheism," see Nickolas P. Roubekas, "Ancient Greek Atheism?
A Note on Terminological Anachronisms in the Study of Ancient Greek 'Religion',"
Revista Ciências da Religião 12.2 (2014): 224–41, and Tim Whitmarsh, *Battling the
Gods: Atheism in the Ancient World* (London: Faber & Faber, 2016).
25. My paraphrase of Versnel, *Coping*, 15.
26. Versnel, *Coping*, 553–4.

The relationship of anthropology and ancient history is an interesting one: around a century ago, they were living next door to one another, as the likes of James Frazer and the "myth and ritual" school tackled the ancient material.[27] It was simpler in those days: anthropology worked horizontally (across the globe with contemporary subjects) and we worked vertically, delving into the lives of people long dead and idolizing the Greeks and (less frequently) the Romans.

Now, anthropology has a lot more past to deal with and the ancient world is a lot less special. The two disciplines have moved apart, perhaps to avoid the unintended absorption of one by the other, and meet only on relatively rare occasions. Anthropology politely ignores ancient material but ancient historians still borrow methods and approaches in an attempt to answer questions that we think they share. The criterion for success is how naturalized these borrowings can become, and that depends on how far they can answer local questions. Borrowing Needham, as an interdisciplinary act, is at the softer end of the spectrum—historians appropriating ideas and perspectives as starting points and support for intrinsically historical arguments. At the harder end of the spectrum is full-blown disciplinary imperialism, the appropriation of one discipline's material by another and its reconfiguration for new purposes. I shall return to this later.

What these all share is that they all experience greater resistance than is expected. Thus, for instance, attempts in 2010 in the *Journal of the History of the Neurosciences* to retrospectively diagnose Alexander the Great drew an acerbic response which threatened to turn the tables by historicizing past attempts at such diagnosis as indicative only of current medical fads at any given moment.[28] Neuroscience is particularly prone to this: there is a name for it ("neurocentrism")[29] but psychology also has a history of appropriating apparently easy targets.[30] Incommensurability runs deep, and authentically

27. On which, see Robert Ackerman, *The Myth and Ritual School: J. G. Frazer and the Cambridge Ritualists* (London: Routledge, 2013).

28. See Axel Karenberg and Ferdinand Peter Moog, "Next Emperor, Please! No End to Retrospective Diagnostics," *Journal of the History of the Neurosciences* 13.2 (2010): 143–9, on Hutan Ashrafian, "The Death of Alexander the Great: A Spinal Twist of Fate," *Journal of the History of the Neurosciences* 13.2 (2010): 138–42 (scoliosis), and Andrew N. Williams and Robert Arnott, "A Stone at the Siege of Cyropolis and the Death of Alexander the Great," *Journal of the History of the Neurosciences* 13.2 (2010): 130–7 (carotid artery dissection).

29. The title of Sally Satel and Scott O. Lilienfeld, *Brainwashed: The Seductive Appeal of Mindless Neuroscience* (New York: Basic Books, 2013) makes its trajectory clear from the start.

30. Cf., for example, James E. Dittes, "Continuities Between the Life and Thought of Augustine," *Journal for the Scientific Study of Religion* 5.1 (1965): 130–40.

borrowing from other disciplines often requires giving something up, or as Ray Land puts it "our disciplinary identity needs to be not abandoned—far from it—but loosened, perhaps weakened to an extent. Not surprisingly this can be experienced as a sense of loss and hence resisted."[31] I stress that I am not objecting to resistance: I am merely noting that it is surprisingly common for promising ideas to succeed only partially. For example, consider Anna Collar's *Religious Networks in the Roman Empire*, where we have the benefit of the author's response to criticism.[32]

Essentially, a promising idea (network theory) has been applied to the Roman Empire, and the author has been criticized for not fully anchoring the new perspective in the material (which she concedes) but nonetheless stands by her expectation that the model has yielded, and will continue to yield, useful results. I note the persistence of her enthusiasm for what the method promises and the acknowledgement that more could be done to embed it in the local (historical) data. In other words, she overestimated the persuasive power of the theory's *promises* and underestimated the extent to which it needed to be embedded to convince historians. They in turn wanted to see scrupulous, specifically historical, application of the new idea.

It is harder work than it first seems to transplant one discipline's established methods into another. However well proven a method or approach is in its home discipline, where it matured at its own pace chewing on local data and issues, it arrives only with promises in its new home: stripped of its established authority, it must prove itself again from scratch, and become amenable to local discussion, irrespective of whether this has repercussions for the theory in general. After all, it cannot easily be dismantled on its own terms (how many of us are in a position to dispute or tinker with the general workings of network theory?) so must be tested by traditional criteria.

31. Ray Land, "Interdisciplinarity as a Threshold Concept," in *Tribes and Territories in the 21st Century: Rethinking the Significance of Disciplines in Higher Education* (ed. Paul Trowler, Murray Saunders, and Veronica Bamber; Abingdon, UK: Routledge, 2012), 182. See also Stephen Rowland, *The Enquiring University: Compliance and Contestation in Higher Education* (Maidenhead, UK: Open University Press, 2006), 87–103; Davies, "Believing the Evidence" (more extensive general bibliography); Davies, "Threshold Guardians"; Jacobs, *In Defense of Disciplines*.

32. See Anna Collar, *Religious Networks in the Roman Empire: The Spread of New Ideas* (Cambridge: Cambridge University Press, 2013) and https://larryhurtado.wordpress.com/2015/12/08/collar-responds-to-reviews-of-her-book/ (accessed July 2016) for the author's response, and links to comments and a review. This was not network theory's first appearance in ancient history. Cf. Irad Malkin, Christy Constantakopoulou, and Katerina Panagopoulou, eds., *Greek and Roman Networks in the Mediterranean* (London: Routledge, 2009); Esther Eidinow, "Networks and Narratives: A Model for Ancient Greek Religion," *Kernos* 24 (2011): 9–38.

I stress I am deciphering some general contours of the debate rather than calling vaguely for more openness (the mantra of interdisciplinarians) or taking sides: I am inferring some telling similarities with "belief" where enthusiastic co-option led to partial adoption and then resistance (I am scrupulously evading judgments about whether it is justified or not). The explanatory promises still held though, and were restated, perhaps adopted by others: the debate continues. The process can only be completed by full localization.

I now intend to provide another example of this, not by citation but by enactment, by briefly considering cognitive science of religion.[33] A broad alliance drawn from linguistics, psychology, neuroscience, artificial intelligence studies, and anthropology, the field (or is it a discipline?) seeks to explain religion (we shall return to this phrase). To summarize, human minds are hard-wired to do certain things "naively": one is to detect agency via our "Agency Detection Device" (ADD, which is sometimes "Hypersensitive"—HADD). We are constantly generating these "unreflective" beliefs,

---

33.   In the last twenty years, hundreds of articles have been published with a connection to this field, too many to note here. Two useful snapshots, overviews, and responses are Léon P. Turner, "Neither Friends nor Enemies: The Complex Relationship Between Cognitive and Humanistic Accounts of Religious Belief," in *Evolution, Religion, and Cognitive Science: Critical and Constructive Essays* (ed. Fraser Watts and Léon P. Turner; Oxford: Oxford University Press, 2014), 152–70, and Harvey Whitehouse and James Laidlaw, eds., *Religion, Anthropology and Cognitive Science* (Durham, NC: Carolina Academic Press, 2007). In particular, I note that given rapid changes in emphasis, such as a recent increased emphasis on evolution and religion as complex adaptive systems (e.g., the collection by Fraser Watts and Léon P. Turner, eds., *Evolution, Religion, and Cognitive Science: Critical and Constructive Essays* [Oxford: Oxford University Press, 2014], and especially Richard Sosis and Jordan Kiper, "Religion Is More than Belief: What Evolutionary Theories of Religion Tell Us About Religious Commitment," in *Challenges to Religion and Morality: Disagreements and Evolution* [ed. Michael Bergmann and Patrick Kain; Oxford: Oxford University Press, 2014], 256–76) and challenges from a variety of quarters, swiftly make the claim of an "overview" treacherous. However, should a recommendation be required for the key ideas of CSR, an established and prominent member of the CSR community recently praised the "admirably clear summary" of the field by Aku Visala, *Naturalism, Theism and the Cognitive Study of Religion: Religion Explained?* (Surrey, UK: Ashgate, 2011), 3–84, in an otherwise hostile review (Luther H. Martin, "Review of A. Visala: *Naturalism, Theism and the Cognitive Study of Religion: Religion Explained?*" *The Journal of Religion* 94.4 [2014], 547). An also very lucid account is Justin L. Barrett, "Gods," in Whitehouse and Laidlaw, eds., *Religion, Anthropology and Cognitive Science*, 179–210, while a succinct history, especially with regard to the evolutionary perspective, is given by Turner, "Neither Friends nor Enemies." For an insider's recent overview and further references, see Ilkka Pyysiäinen, "The Cognitive Science of Religion," in Watts and Turner, eds., *Evolution, Religion, and Cognitive Science*, 21–37.

which sometimes develop into "reflective beliefs." It should be noted that we have not differentiated religion from other thinking at this point: the same mental processes underlie *all* understanding (e.g., physics).[34]

"Religion" starts when ideas about gods spread: "if only one person has a belief in a particular superhuman agent, that is not a religious belief but an … oddity. But when a group of people share the same beliefs in super-human agents, then we have religious belief."[35] This happens when "min-imally counter-intuitive" (MCI) ideas travel, which they do because they are especially memorable, more so than "intuitive" (obvious, common), "bizarre," or highly counterintuitive ideas. We shall explore MCI further in due course. Accounting for transmission is essential to get beyond a purely psychological remit: it is therefore "one (if not *the*) central idea of CSR writers."[36]

That deals with "horizontal transmission": for "vertical transmission" (inheritance by the next generation), there are "modes of religiosity," the *imagistic* and the *doctrinal*. The former centers on one-off unique and vivid transformative experiences (mystery cults come to mind) and the latter, the often boring repetition of ideas to drive them home. These have different qualities and consequences, such as the type of memory and understanding attached to them: my mother remembers what she was doing when news broke of JFK's assassination; I remember what I was doing when I was told Princess Diana was dead, and my elder son will never forget hearing about 9/11. None of us remember much about the circumstances of our learning multiplication tables.[37] Doctrinal memory would, as the name suggests, give rise to doctrinal religions of orthodoxy. Finally (for our purposes), Barrett

34. See Barrett, "Gods," 179 n. 2: "Note that religious beliefs are not alone in this regard." This parallelism is common in psychology and is described famously as "think-ing fast and slow" by Daniel Kahnemann, *Thinking, Fast and Slow* (London: Penguin, 2011). This "unreflective" cognition is, I assume, what King is alluding to.

35. Barrett, "Gods," 186–7. This is challenged frequently on the grounds that reli-gion is more than belief; most recently by Sosis and Kiper, "Religion Is More than Belief" but also in the same volume as Barrett by James Laidlaw, "A Well-Disposed Social Anthropologist's Problems with the 'Cognitive Science of Religion'," in White-house and Laidlaw, eds., *Religion, Anthropology and Cognitive Science*, 211–47.

36. Visala, *Naturalism*, 55.

37. Harvey Whitehouse, "Modes of Religiosity: Towards a Cognitive Explanation of the Sociopolitical Dynamics of Religion," *Method & Theory in the Study of Religion* 14.3–4 (2002): 293–315, is a useful summary of his earlier exposition of the theory in *Inside the Cult: Religious Innovation and Transmission in Papua New Guinea* (Oxford: Clarendon Press, 1995) and *Arguments and Icons: Divergent Modes of Religiosity* (Oxford: Oxford University Press, 2000). I have the impression that recent CSR schol-arship has focused less on this, although it is being applied to new areas; e.g., Risto Uro, *Ritual and Christian Beginnings* (Oxford: Oxford University Press, 2016) and Katrinka

has outlined a theory of "theological correctness": though subjects accurately understand doctrinal positions such as "God is boundless, eternal, and omnipotent," when they are instead asked questions embedded within everyday life or narrative, they assign anthropomorphic characteristics to God such as doing things in sequence or needing to answer one prayer at a time.[38] Thus epic poetry's depiction of the gods interacting (almost) like mortals, for instance, is absolutely typical.

It is my contention thus far that interdisciplinary engagement includes three broad kinds of interactions: opportunities (new starting points or perspectives), promises (optimistic claims that do not always pay off), and risks (unanticipated resistance to incursions). Of the last I dub the most extreme form "disciplinary imperialism." For instance, Luther H. Martin and Donald Wiebe define universities as (only) scientific institutions then lament the resistance of religious studies to that agenda: "[i]n no other department of the modern university do researchers systematically avoid critical studies and theoretically based explanations of their subject of study (except, of course, in the study of literature—at least in North America)" but award themselves the consolation prize that their theories predict this very outcome,[39] so they at least get to be right about "our species' anti-science proclivity."[40]

Speaking for the resistance, James Laidlaw, as a "well-disposed [to CSR] social anthropologist" notes, as I do, that its ideas and discoveries are of interest and consequence to other disciplines (anthropology, in his case) but shakes his head at the expectation in some quarters of "a complete revolution and ... the comprehensive superseding or encompassment of hermeneutic or interpretive by what they call scientific methods ... a 'complete

Reinhart, "Religion, Violence, and Emotion: Modes of Religiosity in the Neolithic and Bronze Age of Northern China," *Journal of World Prehistory* 28.2 (2015): 113–77.

38.   The idea was initially outlined in Justin L. Barrett, "Theological Correctness: Cognitive Constraint and the Study of Religion," *Method & Theory in the Study of Religion* 11.4 (1999): 325–39, and is usefully applied to theology by Nickolas P. Roubekas, "Whose Theology? The Promise of Cognitive Theories and the Future of a Disputed Field," *Religion & Theology* 20.3–4 (2013): 384–402 (but note the "promises").

39.   Luther H. Martin and Donald Wiebe, "Religious Studies as a Scientific Discipline: The Persistence of a Delusion," *Journal of the American Academy of Religion* 80.3 (2012): 594; cf. 589–94.

40.   Martin, "Review of A. Visala," 547, also has no truck with Visala's resistance and defense of deism: "[t]he fact remains, however: if scientific explanation can indeed explain away a phenomenon, no matter how widely held, then *a priori* ideological commitments, no matter how cleverly and coherently argued, simply do not constitute knowledge."

explanation of religion'."[41] Seven years later, in what is beginning to look just a little like "the token anthropologist in the collection of essays," Timothy Jenkins closes with the hope of reconciling "present oppositions. But the reconciliation will be through making nature historical, rather than making history natural, at the cost of the human."[42]

Moving away from the war-zones, there is no doubt that cognitive science of religion indeed presents us with opportunities:[43] it permits us, for instance, to be sure that some things are *less* problematic than they appear.[44] But like all good interdisciplinary ventures, their conclusions are our beginnings. I shall return to one particularly promising initiative after worrying about cognitive science of religion more generally.

There are also promises, ideas which remain unproven or less exciting than expected (perhaps being met with a shrug and "we knew that"). This will vary for individuals, but the news that people "naturally" ascribe agency to invisible entities did not particularly surprise me and is not earth-shattering news for anthropologists and historians of religion. Like other interdisciplinary ventures, it has those who see it as "the answer" because they mistake fitting material into *their* framework for explaining it in terms the *original* discipline understands or cares about: not only are we unconvinced that Alexander the Great, generally depicted as turning to face the sky, had scoliosis (curvature of the spine); I am unconvinced we are particularly *interested*, historically. Similarly, when encountering the theory of "theological correctness," we might respond by wordlessly handing over a tatty translation of Xenophanes.

Let us proceed to some "risks" and "resistance": firstly, with the zeal of a new discipline, there were ambitious calls for "explaining religion" and syntheses of perspectives (examples have already been noted). For cognitive

41.   Laidlaw, "Well-Disposed Social Anthropologist's Problems," 212.

42.   Timothy Jenkins, "The Cognitive Science of Religion from an Anthropological Perspective," in Watts and Turner, eds., *Evolution, Religion, and Cognitive Science*, 190.

43.   E.g., Roger Beck, "Four Men, Two Sticks, and a Whip: Image and Doctrine in a Mithraic Ritual," in *Theorizing Religions Past: Archaeology, History, and Cognition* (ed. Harvey Whitehouse and Luther H. Martin; Walnut Creek, CA: Altamira Press, 2004), 87–103, analyzes a Mithraic ritual by doctrinal and imagistic modes of representation.

44.   Roger Beck's sustained engagement with cognitive science and the study of Mithras cult is peppered with such moments: "the cognitive approach also lets us deproblematize what appear to be doctrinal contradictions" (*The Religion of the Mithras Cult in the Roman Empire: Mysteries of the Unconquered Sun* [Oxford: Oxford University Press, 2006], 95); see also p. 132 for cognitive and neuro-science "burying" psychic dualism. It also offers a rationale for apparently random facts, such as the two kinds of memory giving rise to particular forms of ritual and drawing our attention to features that we might not have focused on otherwise.

science of religion, all religious thought is faulty but explicable ("natural").
In terms of its values, this formulation is perfectly aligned with anthropology
and history's broad trajectory of avoiding (or at least regretting) any "other-
ing" of their subjects.[45] So far so good. But there is a price: "religion," now
(unproblematically defined)[46] can "be explained": we are all agency-detec-
tion machines (thus our invention of gods). However, as already mentioned
in the outline above, some of these "errors" prove more popular than others:
we therefore have to account for *transmission* (referring to *conversion* would
perhaps have highlighted some difficult issues earlier).

Thus Pascal Boyer rather ambitiously called his pivotal 1992 article
"Explaining Religious Ideas: Elements of a Cognitive Approach" and this
is arguably the moment that "optimal/minimal counterintuitiveness (MCI)"
began to emerge in earnest. MCI posits that the ideas which travel best vio-
late only a small number of "intuitive" assumptions of universal ontological
categories.[47] The idea was explored in various kinds of experiments (variations on asking people to read statements designed with various levels of
MCI). Early results were promising: "All that is needed to activate a religious interpretation is ontological violations. This finding in turn suggests
that there may be a common core to all religiosity."[48] This early optimism
has faded, both because of external resistance and 'internal' refinement.
Ilkka Pyysiäinen is, for instance, much more circumspect than he was in
2003 and calls for pluralism in explaining religion (not just MCI).[49] Indeed
Whitehouse's optimism that a combination of "cognitivist, ethnographic,
and historiographical perspectives on religion ... [will yield] a new synthesis of perspectives"[50] contrasts with the majority of the papers in Fraser

45. Efficiently encapsulated by Maurice Bloch's "anthropologists' 'exorcism
prayer'," to be recited before "essentialising a particular cultural position and then mer-
cilessly imposing it on defenceless people" ("Durkheimian Anthropology and Religion:
Going In and Out of Each Other's Bodies," in Whitehouse and Laidlaw, eds., *Religion,
Anthropology and Cognitive Science*, 64).

46. Laidlaw, "Well-Disposed Social Anthropologist's Problems" and Maurice
Bloch, "Are Religious Beliefs Counter-Intuitive?" in *Radical Interpretation in Religion*
(ed. Nancy Frankenberry; Cambridge: Cambridge University Press, 2002), 129–48, do
their best; see also Bloch, "Durkheimian Anthropology and Religion."

47. Pyysiäinen, "Cognitive Science," 27, has a short bibliography; cf. Barrett,
"Gods," 186–8, for a short summary. For those with serious interest, Benjamin Grant
Purzycki and Aiyana K. Willard, "MCI Theory: A Critical Discussion." *Religion, Brain
& Behavior* 6.3 (2016): 207–48 has eight and a half pages of bibliography and a thor-
ough critique from within cognitive science.

48. Ilkka Pyysiäinen, Marjaana Lindeman, and Timo Honkela, "Counterintuitiveness as the Hallmark of Religiosity," *Religion* 33.4 (2003): 353.

49. Pyysiäinen, "Cognitive Science of Religion."

50. Harvey Whitehouse, "Towards an Integration of Ethnography, History, and the

Watts and Léon Turner's work[51] which call for multiple (but not synthe-sized) perspectives and includes some which argue that the "naturalness of belief" is either a neutral onlooker on atheist/deist arguments or even sup-ports it: J. Wentzel Van Huyssteen argues directly that CSR supports reli-gious claims rather than undermining them[52] and elaborates an embodied sense of personhood—it will be interesting to see where this goes next.

We must note that MCI has come in for a battering recently[53] but our chief interest here is not whether it is valid within cognitive science but what happens when it is transplanted to history. Anders Lisdorf experi-ments with applying MCI to the Roman prodigy lists, and the results are interesting from an interdisciplinarity vantage point. His thesis one is con-firmed (counterintuitive concepts are more often transmitted than bizarre, and those more than common, 167) but thesis two (that certain "templates" will be more successful than others) is not. Throughout, he has had to work hard to stay within Boyer's scheme, interpreting culturally rather than ontologically, defining prodigies as "stories," giving wolves and owls spe-cial (Roman) treatment, and admitting a "cultural effect."[54] Both MCI and Roman history have been stretched a little out of shape in this process. The

Cognitive Science of Religion," in *Religion, Anthropology, and the Cognitive Science* (ed. Harvey Whitehouse and James Laidlaw; Durham, NC: Carolina Academic Press, 2007), 274.

51.   Watts and Turner, eds., *Evolution, Religion, and Cognitive Science*.

52.   See J. Wentzel Van Huyssteen, "From Empathy to Embodied Faith? Interdisci-plinary Perspectives on the Evolution of Religion," in Watts and Turner, eds., *Evolution, Religion, and Cognitive Science*, 149.

53.   Bloch, "Are Religious Beliefs Counter-Intuitive?" argues strongly against the theory for anthropology, whereas Justin L. Barrett, "Coding and Quantifying Counterin-tuitiveness in Religious Concepts: Theoretical and Methodological Reflections," *Method & Theory in the Study of Religion* 20.4 (2008): 308–38, sought an overhaul. Laidlaw, "Well-Disposed Social Anthropologist's Problems" breaks the circle of defining religion by beliefs in supernatural entities. Will M. Gervais and Joseph Henrich, "The Zeus Prob-lem: Why Representational Content Biases Cannot Explain Faith in Gods," *Journal of Cognition and Culture* 10.3 (2010): 383–9, highlight "the Zeus problem," namely that if MCI is a universal aspect and "explains" why particular religious ideas are so attrac-tive, why did we stop worshipping Zeus? Yvan I. Russell and Fernand Gobet, "What Is Counterintuitive? Religious Cognition and Natural Expectation," *Review of Philosophy and Psychology* 4.4 (2013): 715–49, argue that counterintuitiveness is subjective but are still optimistic about findings to date. Purzycki and Willard, "MCI Theory" is a damning critique from within the field: even though it ends with suggestions for improvement, it comes across more as an appeasement gesture for their argument than a blueprint for change. Given MCI's universalizing claims, making it cultural and subjective seem to me (as an outsider without authority) to deprive it of its distinctive explanatory power.

54.   Anders Lisdorf, "The Spread of Non-Natural Concepts," *Journal of Cognition and Culture* 4.1 (2004): 155, 154, and 157, 166, respectively.

historical findings in his summary are, by his own declaration, few and not especially new to us (e.g., that local cultural aspects affected transmission of prodigy reports): as he himself says, his chief interest is for cognitive science of religion, using historical material. While it is interesting for CSR to have some minor confirmation from historical material, given they have live subjects available who can answer predesigned questions, it is perhaps not surprising that Purzycki and Willard's impressive array of MCI experiments on subjects includes only one (Lisdorf's) with "dead ones."[55]

Lisdorf's foray illustrates what Maurice Bloch[56] argued for the Malagasy: that establishing counter-intuitiveness is not as simple as identifying universal categories and anonymizing violations. Perhaps the most interesting result is the relatively high proportion of supposedly hard-to-transmit "bizarre" items (frequently around forty percent): why did the reporting of Roman prodigies strain a universal trend? Put less promisingly, we have rediscovered their sensitivity to lightning striking temples.[57]

More broadly, though, I suspect we have little use for MCI in history. Any use of the theory to "explain" the spread of religion is going to be out of focus: we are not concerned with how minimally counter-intuitive ideas spread in the abstract, we are interested in why *this* particular cult spread (or died away) in this particular context, how it was differently adopted across different regions and so on (network theory makes more tangible promises in this regard).

One final example, of a very productive borrowing, will act as a stepping stone back to belief.[58] Stanley Stowers outlines four modes of religion, generated by positing two basic types and then expanding them. He focuses on Greece but suspects the patterns are broader.[59] Though the explicit debt to cognitive science is largely in the footnotes, he signals that it is an important scaffold.[60] To summarize, he calls the first mode "the religion of everyday social exchange." In this, gods are "interested parties" with local interests and sites of special significance to act as a focus for activities: divination, sacrifice, prayer and other "speaking practices." In this mode, valued knowledge was "how-to" knowledge, lore, and inferences about how gods behave

---

55. See Purzycki and Willard, "MCI Theory."
56. See Bloch, "Are Religious Beliefs Counter-Intuitive?"
57. See Lisdorf, "Non-Natural Concepts," 158.
58. The following is a compressed version of another piece, in preparation.
59. See Stanley Stowers, "The Religion of Plant and Animal Offerings Versus the Religion of Meanings, Essences, and Textual Mysteries," in *Ancient Mediterranean Sacrifice* (ed. Jennifer Wright Knust and Zsuzsanna Várhelyi; Oxford: Oxford University Press, 2011), 35.
60. See Stowers, "Plant and Animal Offerings," notes 5, 9, 13–5, 19, and 52.

(like people). As in many unequal relationships, "the dominant epistemological mood ... was uncertainty—not uncertainty about the existence of the gods ... but ... about how and when the gods act and about their moods and desires."[61] One item that he suggests is fairly reliable is that "the gods regularly give the fruit of the land ... [T]hese ... come from somewhere. Why not from someone?" (i.e., ADD). This creates open-ended *reciprocity* rather than contractual and limited market exchange. In this light, sacrifice is not "dramatic ... but relatively mundane" as meals were shared with the gods. As he continues, reciprocity can be complicated, gifts can be rejected, and relations can break down.

Stowers's second mode is that of the "literate cultural producer" who ranged from the still largely "local"-minded (e.g., poets) to the "independent operators" who competed in shows of disinterest and novelty, such as certain sophists and practitioners of independent religious entrepreneurs like Orphism.[62] "Religion here is not about the everyday interests of family, clan, friends, and neighbors; good crops; the health of a child; the powers of revenge for a perceived injustice; and so on. Rather it concerns products of mind, right belief about the divine, the true nature of the self, and discernment of one's place in the drama of world history."[63]

The third mode is an extension of the first to the domain of political power and civic ideology (i.e., civic paganism/*polis* religion) where elites organized and participated on behalf of the populace but retained the "local" and "everydayness" of religious practice. The fourth mode is a further extension, whereby the "reformed" version of religion, with its orthodox meanings, is fed back to the still-existent local networks to be enforced (he suggests the early Church as an example).

At this point it becomes important to enforce the "right meaning" of rituals and as a result "the butchering, cooking, and eating of animals came to seem like a crude gesture that had failed to grasp some deeper proposition or symbols revealed in texts that had been the true essence of the practice all along."[64] Stowers argues that we moderns have stayed too close to the second and fourth, "meaning-centered" mode. "What is the meaning of lunch? ... [Perhaps] lunch on a certain day will be eaten so as to commemorate a certain story. The problem would come from claiming that the essential, basic, or important thing about the everyday practice of eating lunch was that story or its meaning."[65] Stowers's debt to, and relationship with, the

61. Stowers, "Plant and Animal Offerings," 39.
62. Stowers, "Plant and Animal Offerings," 42.
63. Stowers, "Plant and Animal Offerings," 46.
64. Stowers, "Plant and Animal Offerings," 51.
65. Stowers, "Plant and Animal Offerings," 49.

"very young but highly promising field of the cognitive psychology (*sic*) of religion" is summed up by his comment that "history, ethnography, and perhaps cognitive science has shown that the everyday religion is the default mode."[66] His argument does not *require* cognitive science, but it offers suggestions, metaphors, and points at promising avenues of enquiry: it has, as he says, influenced his argument at several points.[67] It also shows the extent to which a successful argument must "go native" before it can provide any local insight and the right level of tentative engagement that is the hallmark of interdisciplinary work ("perhaps"). It also complicates "belief," serving as a reformulation and enrichment of the arguments against the use of "belief," to refocus on ritual, and to dethrone cognition, but simultaneously allowing us to acknowledge that "less everyday" questions *could* also be asked in the ancient world in particular contexts. It meshes with Versnel's citation of Wilhelm Fahr's *Theous Nomizein* (1969) to show that *nomizein* moved, over centuries, between meanings of "to practice or observe as a custom or institution" to "believe in the *existence* of the gods."[68] In Plato the "cognitive" notion is dominant (Stowers's second mode). Plato, of course, prescribed "mode four" in his writings.

This gives us a bigger canvas to work on, one that permits us to accommodate previously overcrowded views. Versnel mentions in passing Scheid's *Quand croire, c'est faire* as an example of going too far on eschewing "belief."[69] Scheid's recent foray is a strong restatement of his position, though his frustration is with critics of *polis* religion more generally.[70] Scheid here (and as ever) argues that *polis* religion is the persistent organizing principle for public religion in the ancient world, and is important because the state was a pivotal point of reference for its inhabitants. This is firmly in opposition to the theory's detractors who assert individual choice or alternatives as if they *displace* the state's religious formulations. Rather, he argues, the domain of the personal is a logical consequence of that state framework, because of the complementary legal distinction of public and private: thus Varro could be buried Pythagorean-style, *within* the minor state restrictions on funerals, without undermining the pivotal role of public cult in the slightest.[71] Many

---

66. Stowers, "Plant and Animal Offerings," 50.
67. Stowers, "Plant and Animal Offerings," 53 n. 13.
68. Versnel, *Coping*, 542–3.
69. Versnel, *Coping*, 546.
70. Scheid, *Les dieux, l'Etat et l'individu*; now translated into English: *The Gods, the State, and the Individual: Reflections on Civic Religion in Rome* (trans. Clifford Ando; Philadelphia, PA: University of Pennsylvania Press, 2016).
71. Scheid, *Les dieux, l'Etat et l'individu*, 186 citing Pliny, *Naturalis historia* 35.160.

cults, he points out, that were supposedly implicated in "individual prefer-ence" or choice, were themselves established by the elite on behalf of the whole state.[72] Pushing Scheid's argument further, the implication is that far from representing a subversion or rejection of state religion, individual choices should be treated more in the spirit of de Certeau's "practice of every-day life": people choose this or that (route to work, way of cooking, public ceremonies to attend) as part of their identity-construction, and they might (or might not) tell stories about their choice.[73] We might also, if space allowed, experiment with the kinds of arguments put forward by Mary Douglas, which again puts us in a domain of choice and individual orientation within a larger framework that can be construed as options by individuals.[74] The framework is not necessarily made up of options *per se*—if I find a route to work that suits me (but *could* choose another), it does not mean the buildings and roads could be easily rearranged as "options," just as from a state point of view the whole ritual calendar or range of public deities might be considered neces-sary for coherence. Nonetheless, any member of that state might have differ-ent levels of involvement and participation, as well as wildly varying stories to tell about them.

But one does not "believe in" a particular (circuitous but tree-rich) walk to work, going for a meal every Sunday evening, always (or never) buying a coffee at the same place at the same time and so on. Even if I articulate rea-sons for these, "belief" is absolutely the wrong word. This, in a nutshell, is the "first level" of the argument against use of the term "belief": when used of "religion," it is all too often used to refer to cognition that is potentially flimsy or transient and certainly *not* orthodox conviction. If I were asked "why do you walk a long route to work?" and answered "they say exercise is good for you," I might think this is very important, or I might be trying to evade a boring or unanswerable question: I go on long walks because I do. I may not even understand why I do in any satisfactory way: why do people like dancing, or broccoli, or sunshine? Any exegesis I might provide about why I walk might yield a whole range of answers that changed from week to week. Thus the changing interpretation of the *Parilia* at Rome[75] tells us

72. See Scheid, *Les dieux, l'Etat et l'individu*, 200.
73. See Michel de Certeau, *The Practice of Everyday Life* (Berkeley, CA: University of California Press, 1984) and Michel de Certeau, Luce Giard, and Pierre Mayol, *The Practice of Everyday Life*. Vol. 2: *Living and Cooking* (trans. Timothy J. Tomasik; Min-neapolis, MN: University of Minnesota Press, 1998).
74. See Mary Douglas, "In Defence of Shopping," in *The Shopping Experience* (ed. Pais Falk and Colin Campbell; London: Sage, 1997), 15–30.
75. See Mary Beard, "A Complex of Times: No More Sheep on Romulus' Birthday,"

about the current understanding and issues of the time but does *not* exhaust (and certainly does not prescribe) the "meaning" of the rituals.

Scheid has nicely fleshed out Stowers's third mode, the civic version of everyday religion, and rarely have we had such a clear response to Talal Asad's repeated question "how does power create religion?"[76] For Scheid, the gods are (extra) powerful members of the community, and since for most of antiquity the civic state underpinned what a community was, they were members of a *polis* community. Like all its members they were expected to behave in certain ways and operate in a web of reciprocity and appropriate behavior.[77] No wonder the Athenians were annoyed with Socrates, with his (second) modish ideas and behavior. In one of Versnel's translated examples (Aristophanes's *Knights*), Nicias and Demosthenes have an exchange where the latter asks his companion "do you really believe in (*hēgei*) gods?" and the reply is that Nicias's evidence that they exist is that they hate him: by restoring the discourse of "everyday experience," Nicias thus rejects the second mode: there is a lot at stake here.[78]

We therefore have a full clash of "religious modes" here, and it is encapsulated in one word's history: *nomizein*, as Versnel argues, refers to the *existence of* rather than the *customary treatment of* gods by this point in time (though perhaps both were inferred by contemporaries). Should even a "non-believer" acknowledge that the richer aspects of the term are relevant (for a change)? Before we decide, we must consider the "second level" of the argument against belief, namely that the word's multiple and treacherous overtones cannot be securely contained, even by redefinition. Versnel, as already noted, has used it as part of a general argument that we have a clash of "cognitive versus non-cognitive" concepts of religion[79] but risks upstaging ritual as the central element by insisting that the idea of communication with divine beings "*without* believing (that is taking as true) that these beings exist" is a contradiction.[80] Here, I suspect, he has misunderstood the argument that *belief is not the point nor even necessary*: I am just heading for the station because I need to get to work, and any etic term one uses to describe what I am doing should not lose sight of that to this

Proceedings of the Cambridge Philological Society 33 (1987): 1–15 and highlighted by Scheid, *Les dieux, l'Etat et l'individu.*

76. Talal Asad, *Genealogies of Religion: Discipline and Reasons of Power in Christianity and Islam* (Baltimore, MD: The Johns Hopkins University Press, 1993), 45.

77. Scheid, *Les dieux, l'Etat et l'individu*, 177–9.

78. See Versnel, *Coping*, 553.

79. See Versnel, *Coping*, 540.

80. Versnel, *Coping*, 552 (original emphasis).

extent. "Belief" just complicates matters, *especially* if we are interested in the nuances of my cognitive state regarding trains.

My point is that most of the time we are only enquiring into my cognitive state in the first place because we have an anachronistic assumption that it is important or even present. If this seems overstated, let us return to Charles King: "Roman religion consisted of worshippers holding disunified polythetic sets of beliefs."[81] This is as historically relevant as saying everyone wore slightly different clothes at a festival—that is, some preparatory work needs to be done to explain why this aspect is important, that goes beyond a mere insistence that "beliefs" are in any way a significant item in Roman religion. Roman religion did not *consist of* beliefs, whether overlapping or not—though we might be interested in plural interpretations whose mutability is their only common factor. But why would we want to call them "beliefs" in the first place apart from our fascination with religion as a cognitive affair? Why can they not be "ideas," "interpretations," "thoughts," "guesses," and, just occasionally, when it is merited by circumstance—"convictions"?

Thus the "second level" objection of the resistance emerges: the (possibly inexperienced) reader has their work cut out tracking these different and sometimes competing sub-meanings of "belief." If we are to talk of cognition, are we talking about freely shifting and often spontaneous or playful meanings, or convictions that require no evidence or verification? Is the cognition we are referring to even particularly noteworthy, whatever it was? Is it central or peripheral (beliefs like to be center-stage, after all)? Are we talking about axiomatic assumptions or fine-tuning ritual performance?

Versnel is attentive to this more than once, offering clarifications ("taking as true"; "the double meaning of the term [*nomizein*] is perhaps best rendered by English 'acknowledge'")[82] but has thereby acted on the same problem that led Needham and others to call for the use of more specific terms: that aspect, at least, has perhaps gone native.

The third and final argument I wish to make here is that in an inevitably interdisciplinary environment, we owe it to ourselves to use the word "belief" as a last resort, so that it becomes immediately visible when it appears as an interloper, with all its baggage and promises that must be carefully scrutinized. The more rarely the word is used, the more we must confront what we mean by it and why we mean it: for instance, Versnel has chosen his battle shrewdly and found an example where we might well grant something resembling "believing in" (the existence of the gods) but

81. King, "Organization," 191.
82. Versnel, *Coping*, 552 and 554, respectively.

he has found an exception rather than an everyday example. It does not prove that the general "anti-belief campaign" is misguided or absurd.

Biographical Note

Jason P. Davies is Senior Teaching Fellow at the UCL Arena Centre for Research-based Education at University College London, UK. He is the author of *Rome's Religious History: Livy, Tacitus and Ammianus on Their Gods* (Cambridge University Press, 2004) and has published articles on ancient religion, interdisciplinarity, and the notion of "belief." He is co-founder of the Teaching and Learning Ancient Religion Network (TLARNetwork.org).

Bibliography

Ackerman, Robert. *The Myth and Ritual School: J. G. Frazer and the Cambridge Ritualists*. London: Routledge, 2013.

Andresen, Jensine, ed. *Religion in Mind: Cognitive Perspectives on Religious Belief, Ritual, and Experience*. Cambridge: Cambridge University Press, 2001. https://doi.org/10.1017/CBO9780511586330

Asad, Talal. *Genealogies of Religion: Discipline and Reasons of Power in Christianity and Islam*. Baltimore, MD: The Johns Hopkins University Press, 1993.

Ashrafian, Hutan. "The Death of Alexander the Great: A Spinal Twist of Fate," *Journal of the History of the Neurosciences* 13.2 (2010): 138–42. https://doi.org/10.1080/0964704049052157

Barrett, Justin L. "Theological Correctness: Cognitive Constraint and the Study of Religion," *Method & Theory in the Study of Religion* 11.4 (1999): 325–39. https://doi.org/10.1163/157006899X00078

—"Gods," 179–210 in Whitehouse and Laidlaw, eds., *Religion, Anthropology and Cognitive Science*, 2007.

—"Coding and Quantifying Counterintuitiveness in Religious Concepts: Theoretical and Methodological Reflections," *Method & Theory in the Study of Religion* 20.4 (2008): 308–38. https://doi.org/10.1163/157006808X371806

Beard, Mary. "A Complex of Times: No More Sheep on Romulus' Birthday," *Proceedings of the Cambridge Philological Society* 33 (1987): 1–15. https://doi.org/10.1017/S0068673500004892

Beck, Roger. "Four Men, Two Sticks, and a Whip: Image and Doctrine in a Mithraic Ritual," 87–103 in Whitehouse and Martin, eds., *Theorizing Religions Past: Archaeology, History, and Cognition*, 2004.

—*The Religion of the Mithras Cult in the Roman Empire: Mysteries of the Unconquered Sun*. Oxford: Oxford University Press, 2006.

Bloch, Maurice. "Are Religious Beliefs Counter-Intuitive?" 129–48 in Frankenberry, ed., *Radical Interpretation in Religion*, 2002. https://doi.org/10.1017/CBO9780511613906.010

—"Durkheimian Anthropology and Religion: Going In and Out of Each Other's Bodies," 63–80 in Whitehouse and Laidlaw, eds., *Religion, Anthropology and Cognitive Science*, 2007.

Boyer, Pascal. "Explaining Religious Ideas: Elements of a Cognitive Approach," *Numen* 39.1 (1992): 27–57. https://doi.org/10.1163/156852792X00159

Brister, Evelyn. "Disciplinary Capture and Epistemological Obstacles to Interdisciplinary Research: Lessons from Central African Conservation Disputes," *Studies in History and Philosophy of Science Part C: Studies in History and Philosophy of Biological and Biomedical Sciences* 56 (2016): 82–91. https://doi.org/10.1016/j.shpsc.2015.11.001

de Certeau, Michel. *The Practice of Everyday Life*. Berkeley, CA: University of California Press, 1984.

de Certeau, Michel, Luce Giard, and Pierre Mayol. *The Practice of Everyday Life*. Vol. 2: *Living and Cooking*. Translated by Timothy J. Tomasik. Minneapolis, MN: University of Minnesota Press, 1998.

Collar, Anna. *Religious Networks in the Roman Empire: The Spread of New Ideas*. Cambridge: Cambridge University Press, 2013. https://doi.org/10.1017/CBO9781107338364

Davies, Jason P. "The Messiness of Academics Speaking Across the Disciplines," 111–8 in *Collaborative Working in Higher Education: The Social Academy*. Edited by Lorraine Walsh and Peter Kahn. London: Routledge, 2010.

—"Disciplining the Disciplines," 37–72 in Vasilaki et al., eds. *Evidence, Inference and Enquiry*, 2011. https://doi.org/10.5871/bacad/9780197264843.003.0003

—"Believing the Evidence," 395–449 in Vasilaki et al., eds. *Evidence, Inference and Enquiry*, 2011. https://doi.org/10.5871/bacad/9780197264843.003.0015

—"'Threshold Guardians': Threshold Concepts as Guardians of the Discipline," 121–34 in *Threshold Concepts in Practice*. Edited by Ray Land, Jan H. F. Meyer, and Michael Flanagan. Rotterdam: Sense Publishers, 2016. https://doi.org/10.1007/978-94-6300-512-8_10

Dittes, James E. "Continuities Between the Life and Thought of Augustine," *Journal for the Scientific Study of Religion* 5.1 (1965): 130–40. https://doi.org/10.2307/1384261

Douglas, Mary. "In Defence of Shopping," 15–30 in *The Shopping Experience*. Edited by Pais Falk and Colin Campbell. London: Sage, 1997. https://doi.org/10.4135/9781446216972.n2

Eidinow, Esther. "Networks and Narratives: A Model for Ancient Greek Religion," *Kernos* 24 (2011): 9–38. https://doi.org/10.4000/kernos.1925

Fahr, Wilhelm. *Theous Nomizein: Zum Problem der Anfänge des Atheismus bei den Griechen*. Hildesheim: G. Olms, 1969.

Feeney, Denis C. *Literature and Religion at Rome: Cultures, Contexts, and Beliefs*. Cambridge: Cambridge University Press, 1998.

Fitzgerald, Des, and Felicity Callard, eds. *Rethinking Interdisciplinarity Across the Social Sciences and Neurosciences*. Basingstoke, UK: Palgrave Macmillan, 2015.

Frankenberry, Nancy, ed. *Radical Interpretation in Religion*. Cambridge: Cambridge University Press, 2002. https://doi.org/10.1017/CBO9780511613906

Gervais, Will M., and Joseph Henrich. "The Zeus Problem: Why Representational Content Biases Cannot Explain Faith in Gods," *Journal of Cognition and Culture* 10.3 (2010): 383–9. https://doi.org/10.1163/156853710X531249

Giordano-Zecharya, Manuela. "As Socrates Shows, the Athenians Did Not Believe in Gods," *Numen* 52.3 (2005): 325–55. https://doi.org/10.1163/156852705774342824

Jacobs, Jerry A. *In Defense of Disciplines: Interdisciplinarity and Specialization in the Research University*. Chicago, IL: University of Chicago Press, 2014. https://doi.org/10.7208/chicago/9780226069463.001.0001

Jenkins, Timothy. "The Cognitive Science of Religion from an Anthropological Perspective," 173–91 in Watts and Turner, eds., *Evolution, Religion, and Cognitive Science*, 2014.

Kahneman, Daniel. *Thinking, Fast and Slow*. London: Penguin, 2011.

Karenberg, Axel, and Ferdinand Peter Moog. "Next Emperor, Please! No End to Retrospective Diagnostics," *Journal of the History of the Neurosciences* 13.2 (2010): 143–9. https://doi.org/10.1080/0964704049052158

Kindt, Julia. "Polis Religion: A Critical Appreciation," *Kernos* 22 (2009): 9–34. https://doi.org/10.4000/kernos.1765

King, Charles. "The Organization of Roman Religious Beliefs," *Classical Antiquity* 22.2 (2003): 275–312. https://doi.org/10.1525/ca.2003.22.2.275

Laidlaw, James. "A Well-Disposed Social Anthropologist's Problems with the 'Cognitive Science of Religion'," 211–47 in Whitehouse and Laidlaw, eds., *Religion, Anthropology and Cognitive Science*, 2007.

Land, Ray. "Interdisciplinarity as a Threshold Concept," 175–85 in *Tribes and Territories in the 21st Century: Rethinking the Significance of Disciplines in Higher Education*. Edited by Paul Trowler, Murray Saunders, and Veronica Bamber. Abingdon, UK: Routledge, 2012.

Lisdorf, Anders. "The Spread of Non-Natural Concepts," *Journal of Cognition and Culture* 4.1 (2004): 151–73. https://doi.org/10.1163/156853704323074796

Malkin, Irad, Christy Constantakopoulou, and Katerina Panagopoulou, eds. *Greek and Roman Networks in the Mediterranean*. London: Routledge, 2009.

Martin, Luther H. "Review of A. Visala: *Naturalism, Theism and the Cognitive Study of Religion*. Religion Explained?" *The Journal of Religion* 94.4 (2014): 547–8. https://doi.org/10.1086/679204

Martin, Luther H., and Donald Wiebe. "Religious Studies as a Scientific Discipline: The Persistence of a Delusion," *Journal of the American Academy of Religion* 80.3 (2012): 587–97. https://doi.org/10.1093/jaarel/lfs030

Needham, Rodney. *Belief, Language and Experience*. Oxford: Oxford University Press, 1972.

Nongbri, Brent. *Before Religion: A History of a Modern Concept*. New Haven, CT: Yale University Press, 2013. https://doi.org/10.12987/yale/9780300154160.001.0001

Pouillon, Jean. "Remarques sur le verbe <croire>," 43–51 in *La fonction symbolique: Essais d'anthropologie*. Edited by Michel Izard, Pierre Smith, and Claude Lévi-Strauss. Paris: Editions Gallimard, 1979.

Price, Simon R. F. *Rituals and Power: The Roman Imperial Cult in Asia Minor*. Cambridge: Cambridge University Press, 1984.

Purzycki, Benjamin Grant, and Aiyana K. Willard. "MCI Theory: A Critical Discussion," *Religion, Brain & Behavior* 6.3 (2016): 207–48. https://doi.org/10.1080/2153599X.2015.1024915

Pyysiäinen, Ilkka. "The Cognitive Science of Religion," 21–37 in Turner and Watts, eds., *Evolution, Religion, and Cognitive Science*, 2014. https://doi.org/10.1093/acprof:oso/9780199688081.003.0002

Pyysiäinen, Ilkka, Marjaana Lindeman, and Timo Honkela. "Counterintuitiveness as the Hallmark of Religiosity," *Religion* 33.4 (2003): 341–55. https://doi.org/10.1016/j.religion.2003.09.001

Reinhart, Katrinka. "Religion, Violence, and Emotion: Modes of Religiosity in the Neolithic and Bronze Age of Northern China," *Journal of World Prehistory* 28.2 (2015): 113–77. https://doi.org/10.1007/s10963-015-9086-4

Rives, James B. "Graeco-Roman Religion in the Roman Empire: Old Assumptions and New Approaches," *Currents in Biblical Research* 8.2 (2009): 240–99. https://doi.org/10.1177/1476993X09347454

Roubekas, Nickolas P. "Whose Theology? The Promise of Cognitive Theories and the Future of a Disputed Field," *Religion & Theology* 20.3–4 (2013): 384–402.

—"Ancient Greek Atheism? A Note on Terminological Anachronisms in the Study of Ancient Greek 'Religion'," *Revista Ciências da Religião* 12.2 (2014): 224–41.

Rowland, Stephen. *The Enquiring University: Compliance and Contestation in Higher Education*. Maidenhead, UK: Open University Press, 2006.

Russell, Yvan I., and Fernand Gobet. "What Is Counterintuitive? Religious Cognition and Natural Expectation," *Review of Philosophy and Psychology* 4.4 (2013): 715–49. https://doi.org/10.1007/s13164-013-0160-5

Saler, Benson. *Conceptualizing Religion: Immanent Anthropologists, Transcendent Natives, and Unbounded Categories*. Leiden: Brill, 1993. https://doi.org/10.1163/9789004378797

Satel, Sally, and Scott O. Lilienfeld. *Brainwashed: The Seductive Appeal of Mindless Neuroscience*. New York: Basic Books, 2013.

Scheid, John. *Les dieux, l'Etat et l'individu: Réflexions sur la religion civique à Rome*. Paris: Seuil, 2013. [English edition: *The Gods, the State, and the Individual: Reflections on Civic Religion in Rome*. Translated by Clifford Ando. Philadelphia, PA: University of Pennsylvania Press, 2016.] https://doi.org/10.9783/9780812291988

Smith, Jonathan Z. *Relating Religion: Essays in the Study of Religion*. Chicago, IL: University of Chicago Press, 2004.

Sørensen, Jesper. "Religion in Mind: A Review Article of the Cognitive Science of Religion," *Numen* 52.4 (2005): 465–94. https://doi.org/10.1163/156852705775219974

Sosis, Richard, and Jordan Kiper. "Religion Is More than Belief: What Evolutionary Theories of Religion Tell Us About Religious Commitment," 256–76 in *Challenges to Religion and Morality: Disagreements and Evolution*. Edited by Michael Bergmann and Patrick Kain. Oxford: Oxford University Press, 2014.

Stowers, Stanley. "The Religion of Plant and Animal Offerings Versus the Religion of Meanings, Essences, and Textual Mysteries," 35–56 in *Ancient Mediterranean Sacrifice*. Edited by Jennifer Wright Knust and Zsuzsanna Várhelyi. Oxford: Oxford University Press, 2011. https://doi.org/10.1093/acprof:oso/9780199738960.003.0001

Turner, Léon P. "Neither Friends nor Enemies: The Complex Relationship Between Cognitive and Humanistic Accounts of Religious Belief," 152–70 in Watts and Turner, eds., *Evolution, Religion, and Cognitive Science*, 2014.

Uro, Risto. *Ritual and Christian Beginnings*. Oxford: Oxford University Press, 2016.

Van Huyssteen, J. Wentzel. "From Empathy to Embodied Faith? Interdisciplinary Perspectives on the Evolution of Religion," 132–49 in Watts and Turner, eds., *Evolution, Religion, and Cognitive Science*, 2014. https://doi.org/10.1093/acprof:oso/9780199661176.001.0001

Vasilaki, Dimitra, William Twining, and Philip Dawid, eds. *Evidence, Inference and Enquiry*. Oxford: Oxford University Press, 2011 (for the British Academy).

Versnel, Henk S. *Coping with the Gods: Wayward Readings in Greek Theology*. Leiden: Brill, 2011. https://doi.org/10.1163/ej.9789004204904.i-594

Visala, Aku. *Naturalism, Theism and the Cognitive Study of Religion: Religion Explained?* Surrey, UK: Ashgate, 2011.

Watts, Fraser, and Léon P. Turner, eds. *Evolution, Religion, and Cognitive Science: Critical and Constructive Essays*. Oxford: Oxford University Press, 2014. https://doi.org/10.1093/acprof:oso/9780199688081.001.0001

Whitehouse, Harvey. *Inside the Cult: Religious Innovation and Transmission in Papua New Guinea*. Oxford: Clarendon Press, 1995.

—*Arguments and Icons: Divergent Modes of Religiosity*. Oxford: Oxford University Press, 2000.

—"Modes of Religiosity: Towards a Cognitive Explanation of the Sociopolitical Dynamics of Religion," *Method & Theory in the Study of Religion* 14.3–4 (2002): 293–315.

—"Towards an Integration of Ethnography, History, and the Cognitive Science of Religion," 247–80 in Whitehouse and Laidlaw, eds., *Religion, Anthropology, and the Cognitive Science*, 2007.

Whitehouse, Harvey, and James Laidlaw, eds. *Religion, Anthropology and Cognitive Science*. Durham, NC: Carolina Academic Press, 2007.

Whitehouse, Harvey, and Luther H. Martin, eds. *Theorizing Religions Past: Archaeology, History, and Cognition*. Walnut Creek, CA: Altamira Press, 2004.

Whitmarsh, Tim. *Battling the Gods: Atheism in the Ancient World*. London: Faber & Faber, 2016.

Williams, Andrew N., and Robert Arnott. "A Stone at the Siege of Cyropolis and the Death of Alexander the Great," *Journal of the History of the Neurosciences* 13.2 (2010): 130–7. https://doi.org/10.1080/0964704049052156

Chapter Four

Imagining Religion in Antiquity:
A How To

Kevin Schilbrack

Introduction

It is common today to speak of religion as a phenomenon that can be found around the world and throughout history. But the word "religion" is a relatively modern invention. How can the connotation of this modern term accurately capture a social reality that operated long before the concept emerged? Is it not anachronistic to say that what we now call "religion" existed in antiquity? That is the question of this chapter.

Jonathan Z. Smith raised the idea that religion is solely the creation of the modern imagination in his widely-read book *Imagining Religion: From Jonestown to Babylon*.[1] Since the publication of that book, many scholars have answered Smith's call for more attention to the ways that the word "religion" was developed and deployed to serve modern European interests.[2] These genealogical and deconstructive studies of "religion" trouble the central concept in the academic study of religion, and they also raise interesting philosophical questions about the difference between the ontology of the natural world and the social world, about the influence of present theorizing on how we understand the past, and about the relationship between words and objects. What then are the implications of the fact that contemporary scholars and laypeople are imagining or, as Russell McCutcheon says, "retrojecting" the category of religion onto cultures that lack the term?[3]

---

1. Jonathan Z. Smith, *Imagining Religion: From Babylon to Jonestown* (Chicago, IL: University of Chicago Press, 1982).
2. For a list of social constructionists writing about the concept of religion, see Kevin Schilbrack, "Religions: Are There Any?" *Journal of the American Academy of Religion* 78.4 (2010): 1112–38. To that list, one can add Brent Nongbri, *Before Religion: A History of a Modern Concept* (New Haven, CT: Yale University Press, 2013); Carlin A. Barton and Daniel Boyarin, *Imagine No Religion: How Modern Abstractions Hide Ancient Realities* (New York: Fordham University Press, 2016). I would also like to thank Stephen Young for comments that improved this chapter's argument.
3. See William E. Arnal and Russell T. McCutcheon, *The Sacred Is the Profane: The Political Nature of "Religion"* (Oxford: Oxford University Press, 2013).

To say that religion is "imagined" outside modern Europe suggests that the existence of religion outside modern Europe is merely imaginary. To say that religion is "retrojected" into the past suggests that claims about the existence of religion in the past are merely projections. The thesis of this chapter, however, is that when historians recognize that "religion" is a modern invention, they are not forced to treat the use of the term for premodern history as illegitimately anachronistic. Rather, one can choose between two critical approaches: a critical nonrealism that argues that nothing like what modern people call religion existed in antiquity, and a critical realism that says that something like what modern people call religion did. I make a philosophical case for critical realism, that is, a case for how one can imagine religion in antiquity without embarrassment.

An Ambiguity in the Critique of "Religion"

We should start by considering the arguments that religion is "imagined" or "invented" or "manufactured" at some point in the modern West.[4] Many of these social constructionist arguments straddle an ambiguity: are the scholars saying that what was invented in the modern West was the modern *concept* of "religion" or are they also claiming that what was invented, presumably simultaneously, was the *reality* of religion, that is, the alleged referent of that concept? That is, one can ask whether a given social constructionist argument is "idea-constructionist" or "object-constructionist."[5] If these scholars seek only to bring the concept into question, then we might call theirs a reflexive project. Their aim is to "pull the camera back," so to speak, in order to investigate the conceptual tools that scholars of religion use but typically take for granted. In a reflexive project, one examines where one's concepts come from, who invented them, and what purposes they were intended to serve. However, if these scholars seek to bring the reality of religion into question, then we might call theirs a debunking project.[6] In a debunking project, one seeks not only to raise questions about the

---

4.   Guy G. Stroumsa argues persuasively that the modern term emerges in the sixteenth century and the "science" of religion in the seventeenth. See Stroumsa, *A New Science: The Discovery of Religion in the Age of Reason* (Oxford: Oxford University Press, 2010).

5.   This distinction was introduced and developed in Ian Hacking, *The Social Construction of What?* (Cambridge, MA: Harvard University Press, 1999) and in Sally Haslanger, "Social Construction: The 'Debunking' Project," in *Socializing Metaphysics: The Nature of Social Reality* (ed. Frederick F. Schmitt; Lanham, MD: Rowman & Littlefield, 2003), 301–26.

6.   Cf. Haslanger, "Social Construction."

concept, but also to argue that to use the concept is to project its own referent, that—lacking the concept—there is no such entity operating "out there"
in the world. A debunker thus seeks to disabuse people of the assumption
that something they have taken as real actually is so. In this latter case, one
would be what Ian Hacking calls an "unmasking" or "rebellious" social
constructionist who not only wants to historicize the term "religion" but
also wants to argue that it is analytically useless and has no referent.[7] In this
latter camp I would put, among several others, Timothy Fitzgerald, Russell
McCutcheon, and Brent Nongbri.[8]

It is sometimes unclear whether the critics of "religion" are arguing for
the reflexive project or the debunking one, but it is important to identify
which position they are taking. For a first example, take Smith's *Imagining
Religion.* That book does not include an essay that shares the book's title,
but its short "Introduction" suggests an explanation of the title when Smith
writes: "There is no data for religion. Religion is solely the creation of the
scholar's study. It is created for the scholar's analytic purposes by his imaginative acts of comparison and generalization. Religion has no independent
existence apart from the academy."[9] These sentences claim that religion
is the product of the imagination of scholars of religion.[10] But is Smith

7.   Ian Hacking, "The Looping Effects of Human Kinds," in *Causal Cognition: A
Multi-Disciplinary Debate* (ed. Dan Sperber, David Premack, and Ann James Premack;
Oxford: Oxford University Press, 1999), 19–20.

8.   For example, Timothy Fitzgerald says: "the word ['religion'] has no genuine
analytic work to do and its continued use merely contributes to the general illusion that
it has a genuine referent." See Timothy Fitzgerald, *The Ideology of Religious Studies*
(Oxford: Oxford University Press, 2000), 14. Russell McCutcheon argues that "religion" lacks a referent in many places. I seek to show the weaknesses in Fitzgerald's
arguments in Kevin Schilbrack, "The Social Construction of 'Religion' and Its Limits:
A Critical Reading of Timothy Fitzgerald," *Method & Theory in the Study of Religion*
24.2 (2012): 97–117; the weaknesses in McCutcheon's in "A Realist Social Ontology of
Religion," *Religion* 47.2 (2017): 161–78; and the weaknesses in Nongbri's in the present
chapter.

9.   Smith, *Imagining Religion*, xi.

10.   Derek Peterson and Darren Walhof are clearer as they focus reflexively on the
ways in which the modern concept of religion has been constructed. But they object to
the idea (which they associate with Jonathan Z. Smith and Russell McCutcheon) that
"it is the study of religion that invented 'religion'." As they point out, rightly, since the
characterization of religion as something archaic, personal, and nonpolitical was part of
a post-Reformation strategy of marginalizing religion from the public sphere, both in
Europe and in colonized countries, this strategy was the work of legislators, clerics, and
colonial administrators long before the academic study of religion emerged: "inventing
religion was never purely an academic project" (1). Derek Peterson and Darren Walhof,
eds., *The Invention of Religion: Rethinking Belief in Politics and History* (New Brunswick, NJ: Rutgers University Press, 2002).

referring here to the word or the alleged referent of the word? The former argument would be that the word "religion" is relatively new, that its connotation in the modern word is not the same as that of *religio* from which it evolved, but is instead a novel conceptual category that treats a European social phenomenon as if it were a genus of which there are types to be found all around the world and throughout history. Smith argues exactly this point elsewhere.[11] If Smith's goal is to draw attention to the emergence of the central conceptual tool in the academic study of religion, then his project is the important reflexive one.

On the other hand, some have interpreted Smith as seeking not only to historicize the word, but also to undermine the assumption of the existence of the social reality to which the word ostensibly refers. If Smith's goal were this debunking one—and the final sentence in the quote above can certainly be read this way—then he would be arguing that the aspects of cultures that those in the West call "religion" do not exist outside the studies of scholars and that whatever social structures operated outside the modern West, they were not religion.[12] It is true that some entities that exist today simply did not exist in the past and to speak of them in the past is a sign of an error. "The Buddha was born in Nepal" provides an example. There are philosophically-informed ways in which one might make such a nonrealist argument: for instance, one might hold that human beings have no access to what is real apart from language, and so if the members of a given society lack the word "religion" then there is nothing but distortion and conceptual violence in claiming that without knowing it, they "really" practiced religion. If Smith's goal is to call into question the reality of what is called religion in such a way, then he would be debunking.

My own position is that on the subject of religion, scholars should accept the reflexive project but not the debunking one. That is, on the one hand, scholars should recognize that the central concept in our field has a history and that it was developed to address problems at a certain historical time and place, and therefore how one defines "religion" as a genus is crucial. Nevertheless, on the other hand, we can and should still be realistic about the referent of that concept. In fact, although Smith is not explicit about this, I would

11. See Jonathan Z. Smith, "Religion, Religions, Religious," in *Critical Terms for Religious Studies* (ed. Mark C. Taylor; Chicago, IL: University of Chicago Press, 1998), 269–84.

12. McCutcheon states this view: "Whether pre-seventeenth century Europeans, or people from contemporary cultures other than our own, believe(d) in gods or life after death, or whatever we today happen to define religion to be, I would argue that they were not religious" (*The Discipline of Religion: Structure, Meaning, Rhetoric* [London: Routledge, 2003], 271; cf. 253–4).

argue that this is precisely the position that Smith's essays embody. Smith's essays argue that there is a poor fit between what some have assumed religion is and what it actually is—a poor fit for which he provides evidence in the writings about religion by Mircea Eliade and by the British Polynesian Society, for example.[13] But Smith does not deny that the word "religion" has a referent in history. On the contrary, the claim that modern concepts fit the past reality poorly makes no sense unless one grants that the word "religion" refers to real social practices. Smith claims that those early modern Europeans who claimed that non-Europeans had no religion were "factually incorrect."[14] Smith's overarching project is therefore not to debunk the claim that religion existed before the word was invented. His project, rather, is the reflexive one or, as he calls it, a "double archaeology" that includes both the investigation of a social reality operating in history and the history of the concept by which people have sought to grasp that reality.[15] Smith is certainly not proposing that scholars of religion should stop imagining or stop retrojecting religion. Despite those who cite the "Introduction" to *Imagining Religion* to support a nonrealist conclusion, therefore, Smith treats what we now call religion as something that exists across cultures, including in antiquity—as he puts it, "from Babylon to Jonestown."

A different answer can be found in Brent Nongbri's *Before Religion: A History of a Modern Concept*. Nongbri's subtitle might make one think that his focus is just on the concept and not also on its referent. If, like Jonathan Z. Smith, Nongbri recognizes that the past has an ontological reality that is independent of the concepts we use to redescribe it, then his book would be, like Smith's, a reflexive project but not a debunking one. However, under the heading "Do You Need the Word to Have the Thing?," Nongbri argues that if a culture lacks the concept of religion, as all cultures outside the modern West did, then it is not plausible to posit that it includes the reality of religion as some sort of "extralinguistic thing."[16] For Nongbri, then, a society must know a concept if they are to have that reality. When scholars use a term not known in a given society, they are not describing something that already exists in history but rather *creating* it there.[17]

13.   See Jonathan Z. Smith, *Map Is Not Territory: Studies in the History of Religions* (Chicago, IL: University of Chicago Press, 1978), ch. 4; Smith, *Imagining Religion*, ch. 5.

14.   Smith, "Religion, Religions, Religious," 269.

15.   E.g., Jonathan Z. Smith, *Relating Religion: Essays in the Study of Religion* (Chicago, IL: University of Chicago Press, 2004), 10, 29.

16.   Nongbri, *Before Religion*, 23.

17.   See Brent Nongbri, "Dislodging 'Embedded' Religion: A Brief Note on a Scholarly Trope," *Numen* 55.4 (2008): 440.

A realist about religion might try to counter this debunking argument by arguing that society is not exhausted by the concepts of its participants, and so it may be accurate to label forms of life with terms not known by their participants. But, citing Russell McCutcheon, Nongbri rejects the idea that an outsider can be "sighted" when the participants are all "blind," and so he argues that where concepts roughly equivalent to "religion" are absent, one should not impose that label.[18] A realist might also argue that although the *modern* form of religion did not exist in antiquity, other forms could exist without being named by its participants. For example, in modern contexts where church and state are separated, religion is relegated to a limited role in public life, but in premodern or non-western contexts participants might not distinguish religion from the politics or the art or the other aspects of their culture.[19] It is understandable that people might not develop a concept for an aspect of their society that they have not distinguished from the society as a whole. But Nongbri also rejects this claim that "before 'religion'" what we now call religion was "embedded in" or "diffused in" a culture.[20] In short, then, Nongbri does not accept the realist distinction between concepts and their referents that we saw in Smith and therefore, with Russell McCutcheon,[21] instead rejects the existence of religion as a reality that operated in the world before the concept emerged. As one reviewer summarized Nongbri's thesis: "Religion does not exist, but people today think it does."[22]

However, Nongbri is not simply a nonrealist about religion in antiquity but instead introduces a third possibility that we have not yet considered. In addition to (1) those nonrealists who deny that religions existed in history without the concept and who therefore propose that scholars should drop the term,[23] and (2) those realists who hold that religions did exist without

18. Nongbri, *Before Religion*, 24; Russell T. McCutcheon, *The Discourse on Sui Generis Religion and the Politics of Nostalgia* (Oxford: Oxford University Press, 1997).

19. Bruce Lincoln marks these two forms of religion in society by distinguishing between a modern western "minimalist" mode and a "maximalist" mode in which religious commitments pervaded the society (*Holy Terrors: Thinking About Religion After September 11* [Chicago, IL: University of Chicago Press, 2003], ch. 4).

20. Nongbri, "'Embedded' Religion"; also Nongbri, *Before Religion*, 157–8; cf. 151–2. McCutcheon has also objected to the claim that religion pervaded pre-modern or non-western cultures (*Discipline of Religion*, 259).

21. See Russell T. McCutcheon, "Religion Before 'Religion'?" in *Chasing Down Religion: In the Sights of History and the Cognitive Sciences* (ed. Panayotis Pachis and Donald Wiebe; Sheffield, UK: Equinox, 2010), 285–301.

22. Nathan J. Ristuccia, "Review of B. Nongbri: *Before Religion: A History of a Modern Concept*," *Fides et Historia* 46.1 (2014): 84.

23. Both the review of Nongbri by Ristuccia cited above and that by Naomi Goldenberg put Nongbri in this category and chide him for holding that, after one historicizes

the concept and who therefore wish to retain the term, there is (3) a mixed position, namely: those who deny that religion existed without the concept but who hold that scholars may still use the word, as long as they treat the term as a heuristic, taxonomic, or analytic tool that does not correspond to real structures in the social world.[24] In this third position, one debunks the idea that what we now call religion really existed in the past but one retains the word for the scholar's own sorting purposes. Call this the heuristic view of "religion."[25]

The heuristic view includes the salutary reminder that the conceptual categories people invent are rarely neutral. The categories people invent follow what they find problematic. As instrumentalists and pragmatists in the philosophy of science have argued, concepts are tools and people conceptualize not simply to mirror the world but to help them do what they want to do to the world. The invention of concepts reflects our interests, and the diffusion of those concepts reflects how widespread those interests grow (or can be pushed). There are questions of power involved in theorizing. But it does not follow from the fact that a concept is invented by interested parties that it does not grasp a real structure in the natural or social world. Nor does it follow from the fact that people develop concepts in response to their own worried questions ("what causes this?") that their answers do not identify the actual causes. From the interested character of theory, one need not draw a nonrealist conclusion.

the term "religion," scholars can continue to use the term. Those reviewers champion the abolitionist position and recommend instead that scholars "cut the whole thing off," "simply jettison [it]." See Naomi Goldenberg, "Some (Mainly) Very Appreciative Comments on Brent Nongbri's 'Before Religion'," *Critical Religion*, online: https://criticalreligion.org/2013/05/06/some-mainly-very-appreciative-comments-on-brent-nongbris-before-religion/ (accessed February 2019).

24.   It is true that the term "heuristic" is sometimes used in a way that does not deny that it is meant to identify real aspects of the world. (I owe this reminder to Stephen Bush.) Some describe their theoretical terms as "heuristic devices" to mean that their purported reference to real things is tentative or not yet confirmed. But in such cases, the intention is nevertheless to grasp real structures in the world. In such cases, "heuristic" is there being used like the term "hypothesis"—that is, it is treated as an attempt to refer to real social structures in the world—and this is precisely the realist position about the relation of "religion" outside the modern West that the nonrealists are rejecting.

25.   Nongbri also calls this a "redescriptive account," a name that reflects the important distinction between a descriptive account of social phenomena that seeks to reproduce the classification of the participants and a redescriptive account that uses a foreign classification. I do not use that term for the heuristic position, however, since I would argue that redescriptive accounts typically seek to grasp real features of the world. That is, most historians and anthropologists who offer redescriptive, etic accounts of a society are realists and not merely heuristic about those accounts (*Before Religion*, 21–2, 24).

Nongbri does draw the nonrealist conclusion, however, and so he holds that scholars can use the term "religion" to redescribe aspects of antiquity only if they do not claim that the term corresponds to something that is really there.[26] A heuristic view like this is a problematic one for historians. It implies that one's redescriptions of the past reflect one's own interests but do not grasp any real patterns or causes in the societies studied. Given this heuristic view, one can argue that one's categories are useful for one's own purposes. But unless one commits to speaking of real structures in the society, that is, structures that operate independent of one's labels, one cannot argue that one's redescription of it is illuminating, explanatory, accurate, or true. All those terms require that one's inquiry does not create the reality it names. I therefore judge that a critical realist approach that sees theories as attempts to capture the real causes of events is more persuasive. I turn to a defense of that position now.

A Defense of Realism

The realist view is that one can accurately speak of religion as a form of life in antiquity that is real in the sense that the structures, roles, and institutions that make up that form of life explain aspects of that society. I accept the evidence put forward by genealogical and deconstructionist-minded historians that the word "religion" was invented in modern Europe to provide a conceptual tool to help manage the fragmentation of Christianity, the discovery by Europeans of cultures around the world of which they had been unaware, and the need to categorize the people in those cultures conceptually as part of colonial and imperialistic designs. But the invention of a new concept or word does not imply that the reality to which it allegedly refers is also an invention. What position must one hold to make this view coherent?

Realists must hold that the epistemic order of human concepts and the ontological order of what exists are distinct. This means that—with the exception of some odd cases, like one's ideas about one's ideas—changing one's ideas about the world does not change the things in the world. The existence of things does not depend on their being known. Such assertions strike most people as commonsense, especially when the alleged referent of some concept is in the natural world. The concept of "DNA," for example, has a history. The concept of a long molecular string that carried the blueprint of an organism's genetic information was hammered out over the twentieth century by contending biochemists. But the fact that the molecule to which the term "DNA" allegedly referred was first imagined as a

---

26. Nongbri, *Before Religion*, 151–2, 158.

single string, then modeled as a triple helix by Linus Pauling before it was re-imagined as a double helix by James Watson and Francis Crick does not imply that the molecule itself changed from a single helix to a triple helix to a double helix, much less that the referent of the concept was invented by Watson and Crick. Almost no one would argue that the natural world depends in this way on human imagination.

The philosopher/anthropologist of science Bruno Latour famously did defend the idea that facts about the natural world were social constructions, dependent for their existence on the laboratory work that produced them as facts. Latour proposed that human discourse and natural objects be treated "symmetrically" so that if a given concept only emerged at a certain place and time, then the reality to which that concept referred would only exist after that place and time. For this reason, Latour rejected as anachronistic the claim made by French doctors that the pharaoh Ramses II had died of tuberculosis, arguing that the tubercle bacillus was not discovered until the nineteenth century and so it could not properly be said to have existed before then. As Latour quipped, to claim that the pharaoh died of TB was as absurd as claiming that he died of machine-gun fire.[27] Latour had thought that denying that the world has a structure independent of human discourse would emancipate the public from ideologies that masqueraded as facts. But he came to judge that nonrealism actually undermines one's ability to critique ideologies. He now apologizes for his earlier debunking project that denied that the world is independent of and resists our conceptualization of it. He bemoans the fact that

> entire Ph.D. programs are still running to make sure that good American kids are learning the hard way that facts are made up, that there is no such thing as natural, unmediated, unbiased access to truth, that we are always prisoners of language, that we always speak from a particular standpoint, and so on.[28]

Not unlike the present chapter, Latour argues against confusing the ontological question "What is there?" with the epistemic question "How do we know it?"[29] He says that by collapsing these questions, social constructionists suffer from an excessive distrust of "good matters of fact ... real objective and incontrovertible facts," and he recommends the "cultivation of a stubbornly realist attitude," since, despite their claims, debunkers are

27. See Bruno Latour, "On the Partial Existence of Existing and Nonexisting Objects," in *Biographies of Scientific Objects* (ed. Lorraine Daston; Chicago, IL: University of Chicago Press, 2000), 248.

28. Bruno Latour, "Why Has Critique Run Out of Steam? From Matters of Fact to Matters of Concern," *Critical Inquiry* 30 (2004): 227.

29. Latour, "Why Has Critique Run Out of Steam?" 244.

always realists for the things that they care about in their own lives.[30] I read Latour's change of heart as part of a larger retrieval of realism that signals the tail end of what is usually considered poststructuralist thought.[31]

This independence of the natural world from human concepts also holds when one is speaking of the social world. What people do is not invented by how others describe those actions. Of course, social realities are not independent of the concepts of the agents. Intentional actions are the actions they are because of the concepts held by those who do them. This is why understanding the intentional activities of people differs from understanding the nonintentional behavior of, say, minerals. This is also why scholars who study history should distinguish between the description of human activities according to the self-understanding of the participants and the scholars' own redescription of those activities. But although actions are dependent on the self-understanding of the agents, they are not dependent on the understanding of the scholars. If one speaks of the kinship pattern in a given people as a phratry, this does not "manufacture" that kinship pattern. If one changes one's redescription of their kinship relations, those relations are not thereby changed. The social world has a structure that is distinct from our concepts about it.

There is an important exception to this world/word independence for some social realities, namely, those cases of feedback that Ian Hacking calls "looping effects."[32] Looping effects occur when people, described in a certain way, learn of and respond to how they are described, by either accepting it or rejecting it. As Hacking says, illustrating his point with example of human "kinds" like *authors*, *homosexuals*, *refugees*, and *Zulu*: "People of these kinds can become aware that they are classified as such. They can make tacit or even explicit choices, adapt or adopt ways of living so as to fit or get away from the very classification that may be applied to them."[33] It follows that when one employs the modern western concept of religion and uses it to redescribe an aspect of some culture in which the concept is not known, the use of this concept can have an effect on the social reality as those participating in it come to accept or reject it.[34] But although some social realities can be influenced by how they are described, this difference is eliminated when the social realities being described are in the past. The way that those in the present describe the past cannot change the past but

---

30. Latour, "Why Has Critique Run Out of Steam?" 227, 233.

31. Cf. Hubert L. Dreyfus and Charles Taylor, *Retrieving Realism* (Cambridge, MA: Harvard University Press, 2015).

32. Hacking, "Looping Effects."

33. Hacking, *Social Construction of What?*, 34.

34. E.g., Fitzgerald, *Ideology*, ch. 8.

only one's understanding of it. To claim otherwise is to confuse the wide and stable realm of what is real with the narrower and shakier realm of what has been named. The argument that what is real is coextensive with what has been named—sometimes under the slogan that "there is nothing outside the text"—was popular in poststructuralist thought. But the rejection of this slogan (or at least this use of the slogan) and a realist commitment to the autonomy of both the social and the natural worlds from human concepts about them are two features that unite those nascent intellectual movements called "new realism" and "new materialism," movements of which this essay is at least an ally.[35]

When those involved in the reflexive projects historicize the concept of "religion" without rejecting realism, they provide a tremendous service. These deconstructive and genealogical approaches can shift readers from an uncritical, naïve realism towards religion to a reflective stance that makes possible the critique of inadequate and distorting versions of the concept. Latour calls this benefit of critique "anti-fetishism." The critique of "religion" makes it possible to see how some accounts of religion distort the social reality in antiquity they are intended to describe and explain. I argued that this is precisely the tack taken by Jonathan Z. Smith. But one can critique a given concept—or even reject it entirely as misconceived, as with "phlogiston"—without denying that there is a real world, both human and extra-human, independent of our concepts. Taking seriously the historical and contentious aspect of our concepts need not lead to the conclusion of the "world well lost."

Russell McCutcheon argues against this view. He writes that saying that religion existed before the invention of the word "religion" is like saying that before the invention of cooking people ate "raw food"—"as if, prior to the invention of cooking … early humans simply had a natural sense that their food was raw."[36] He compares speaking of religion before "religion" to saying that before people invented sheltered dwellings, they lived "outdoors."[37] McCutcheon is right that without the distinction between raw and cooked, people would conceive of what they ate simply as "food," not as "raw food." Until they had experienced shelters, no one would have the category of "outdoors." The retrojection of these concepts to redescribe the past reflects distinctions only made later. But McCutcheon's argument

---

35. For representative examples of these two movements, see Maurizio Ferraris, *Introduction to New Realism* (London: Bloomsbury, 2015) and Diana Coole and Samantha Frost, eds., *New Materialisms: Ontology, Agency, and Politics* (Durham, NC: Duke University Press, 2010).
36. McCutcheon, "Religion Before 'Religion'?" 6.
37. McCutcheon, "Religion Before 'Religion'?" 13.

involves an unacknowledged shift. When a historian says that early people ate raw food, s/he means that the food they ate had certain properties: it had not been heated to the extent that bacteria had been killed and that proteins had been broken down, and so the effect of the food on digestive systems and its absorption by bodies was different. When McCutcheon points to the anachronism of the concept, however, he ignores the reference to the properties of the food and focuses on how insiders would have conceptualized their own experiences. That is, he shifts from the historian's ontic reference (which is completely accurate) to an epistemic one (which would not be accurate had this been what the historian was describing).[38] As an argument against the accuracy of retrojected terms, this argument only succeeds if there is no reality outside how human beings experience the world. In other words, McCutcheon's argument for critical nonrealism trades on the concept/reference ambiguity with which this chapter began.

The weakness of the "raw food" analogy applies as well to McCutcheon's treatment of "religion." A historian might speak of religion operating in antiquity to mean that that there were certain distinctive practices being performed—for instance, making offerings at an altar to some superempirical being. Such practices often assign certain roles to those who do them and they often require certain institutions to maintain them. But McCutcheon's argument shifts attention from these questions about social practices, roles, and institutions to a different question: whether those doing the practices understood themselves in a certain way. McCutcheon treats religion not as the properties of a society but as something possessed by individuals that is purely mental and private. He speaks of religion as "this inner thing," "something ... buried deep in my heart," something "deeply felt ... [that is] variously called experience, faith, authenticity, spirituality, meaning, the religious, and religiosity."[39] But from the fact that the practitioners did not use this concept or did not feel a mysterious something, it does not follow that religious practices, roles, and institutions were not operating in their society. When redescribing the properties of a given society in antiquity, therefore, it is no more inappropriate for historians to use the label "religion" than it is to say that before the invention of cooking people ate "raw food."

As scholars agree with the critics that the concept of "religion" is constructed and has a history, that it was produced in a particular social context

---

38. There is an irony in this unacknowledged shift of reference from the world to how the world was experienced by insiders, given McCutcheon's career-long antipathy to phenomenology. Fitzgerald similarly supports his nonrealism by relying on the phenomenological claims he castigates in his opponents. See Schilbrack, "Social Construction of 'Religion' and Its Limits," 107–8.

39. McCutcheon, "Religion Before 'Religion'?" 8, 9, 6, respectively.

to solve a particular conceptual problem, then they can see that having such a concept is not a necessary or natural aspect of human social life. On the contrary, the development and deployment of the concept of religion was part of a revolution in western thinking about social life. Those in antiquity did not see the world as the moderns did. They did not see what they were doing as religious. Appreciating this point lets us formulate the question of this chapter whether the term "religion" fits antiquity. But if we reject the nonrealist argument that "unless those in the past had the concept, religion could not exist then"—that is, if we do not collapse the epistemic and the ontological—then we reject the idea that the reality of social structures now called "religion" was simultaneously manufactured by the creation of the word. Realists who distinguish the epistemic and the ontological can then speak of the invention of the term "religion" as what made possible the modern discovery of religion in the past.[40]

Religion as a Discovery

What does it mean for critical realists to speak of religion as a modern discovery? Does it mean that religions were, so to speak, just lying there, like rocks, waiting to be discovered once Europeans created the magical word that revealed them? Even if this way of thinking were not anachronistic, a realist approach might suggest arrogance.

Religions are not like rocks, to be sure, since the emergence and continued existence of a religion depends on the joint commitments of a group of people. The ontology of things whose existence requires social agreement (like marriages or governments) is not like the ontology of those that do not (like amino acids or birds). In this sense, religions do not "just lie there" but instead grow and evolve and die depending on the shifting commitments of their practitioners. But it certainly is true that real aspects of the social world, no less than those of the natural world, come into focus only when one has a concept that identifies them.

The process of creating new words for social realities that occur in one's own time and place and then discovering that those terms also refer more generally to social realities that existed before those concepts were invented is commonplace. Take the concept of a "recession."[41] This term

40. E.g., Hans G. Kippenberg, *Discovering Religious History in the Modern Age* (trans. Barbara Harshav; Princeton, NJ: Princeton University Press, 2001); Stroumsa, *New Science: The Discovery of Religion in the Age of Reason.*
41. The example of recessions comes from John Searle, who notes a recession would be an example of "fallout" from deliberate social activities, and not a "ground-floor" social fact intended by the practitioners themselves. Elsewhere, I have used "patriarchy"

was invented only recently to get a handle on a certain pattern of reduced economic activity, but it is now retrojected into the past to redescribe financial downturns that share that pattern. The financial activity so described, obviously, is not a natural phenomenon; recessions depend for their existence on historically contingent human activities. Despite the fact that the term is a contemporary invention, however, there is nothing illegitimate about the claim that, once equipped with the term, historians can now discover recessions in the past.

I would argue that to speak of "discovering" religion outside the modern West provides a better explanation of the genealogy of the term than does the nonrealist view that the modern world simply invented religion. From the realist perspective, it is not the case that Europeans simply imposed the concept onto non-western cultures regardless of the structure of those cultures. Instead, there was a dialectical give and take between non-European practices (which, as data, were taken as difficult, challenging, and incongruous) and western theorizing about them. One can see the emergence of the modern sense of the world "religion" not as the imposition of a tool that Europe already had, but rather as the product of conflict between inherited categories and the facts about the new world. As Guy Stroumsa notes, "the concept of natural religion came to Hobbes and Locke from [missionary José de] Acosta, whom they read. The insertion of Christianity within the comparative history of religions, the loss of its absolute character ... stemmed from the missionaries' reflection on Amerindian religions."[42] It is only this confrontation with recalcitrant social facts that permits one to speak of the *study* of religion.

The critics of "religion" are right that to retroject this category on a culture in which the concept is not known inevitably carries assumptions that are distorting. If one assumes that when a people practice a religion they must have a building dedicated to those practices or else their religion is somehow incomplete, then one's use of the concept may distort one's understanding of the particularities of how that religion was actually practiced. The same is true if one assumes that their participation in those practices must be chosen, that it must mark a bounded community, or that that must preclude participation in other practices one would call religious. If one is to retroject "religion" as a genus (as I am recommending), then one should

as an example of a retrojected concept analogous to religion (see Schilbrack, "Social Ontology of Religion"), but as an example of discovering historical facts with contemporary concepts, the concept of recessions works just as well. See John Searle, *Making the Social World: The Structure of Human Civilization* (Oxford: Oxford University Press, 2010), 21–2.

42. Stroumsa, *New Science*, 23.

stipulate a generic definition that involves the least "conceptual violence." The push for that generic definition constitutes the history of "religion."

The realist notion that one might discover religion in antiquity requires that one treats "religion existed there" as a hypothesis, that is, as a claim confirmable or disconfirmable by the historian's tools. To treat the presence of religion as a hypothesis in turn requires one to be transparent about what one is seeking to discover and to develop a definition of religion that may not be identical to the colloquial sense of the term but serves the scholar's purposes.[43] There are two common ways of defining "religion" that undermine the notion that religion can be discovered in history. In the first place, if one defines religion with Paul Tillich as one's "ultimate concern," then the answer to the question of discovery is already settled. All human beings, both individually and collectively, have concerns; one of those concerns will be the highest or ultimate concern and so all societies will have had a religion. The answer would be true *a priori*, by definition, and would be the result not of a historical investigation but rather of a certain view of the nature of human being. In the second place, if one defines religion as "some inner thing, deeply felt," then the question again cannot be answered by a historian. Unless one defines religion in terms of publicly available discourse and behavior, the historian will not be able to find any evidence of it and the presence in antiquity of religion will have to remain purely speculative. As McCutcheon complained above, to claim that "religious feelings existed in antiquity" is to retroject on the past something that cannot be confirmed. This is no longer a historian's project.

However, if one defines religion as "forms of life predicated on the existence of superempirical realities"[44] (or another definition that includes a substantive element), then it is possible that some societies do, and other societies do not, include religion. A definition like this one makes the discovery of religion in antiquity an open question. It is possible that some Neolithic societies had not developed any idea of superempirical realities

43.   James Broucek also makes this case, noting that critical nonrealists often select a narrow definition of religion (for example, as an inner state or a set of beliefs about salvation), and ignore the history of Durkheimian and Weberian and other scholarly definitions of religion as a public reality ("Thinking About Religion Before 'Religion'," *Soundings* 98.1 [2015]: 98–125).

44.   This is the definition I recommend. Seeking to avoid the term "supernatural," I use the term "superempirical" in a specific way to refer to *non-empirical realities that are also not the product of empirical realities*. "Superempirical" as a category, then, would include, say, both person-like realities such as Allah or Shiva and non-person-like realities such as the Dao or the Logos, but not products of human creativity like one's nation or wealth. See Kevin Schilbrack, *Philosophy and the Study of Religions* (Oxford: Wiley-Blackwell, 2014), ch. 5.

and so they did not have any forms of life predicated on the belief in such things. If this is the case, then those early human societies lacked religion.[45] It is also possible that some contemporary societies are skeptical towards forms of life predicated on the existence of superempirical realities and deliberately eschew them. In such cases, they too would lack religion.[46] To retroject religion understood in this way, therefore, is to make a fallible proposal. One can imagine religion in antiquity and then look to see whether one is right.

My working assumption is that most cultures in history did include practices predicated on the existence of superempirical realities. But if one has settled the question of *whether* some ancient societies were religious, the question of *how* they were religious remains. For example, one might conclude that a given society's uses of oracles or home altars do constitute religious practices, but that these were not practices in the sense of worship but rather as gift exchanges. Historians doing this kind of detailed comparative work seek to remove anachronistic or inapt meanings and improve their redescriptive accounts. This work is asymptotic, never finished, always in a hermeneutic circle from one's initial descriptions and then back to critical reflection on one's conceptual tools. One cannot improve one's account of the past if one does not move into the reflexive mode. One must examine and re-examine one's conceptual vocabulary in the light of the recalcitrant reality of things. Despite this reflexive moment, one imagines religion in antiquity and does so legitimately. Critical realism is precisely this: namely, the recognition that our concepts are the tools we have invented and so they are in need of constant improvement in the light of what we learn about how people actually live.[47]

One can find critical realism informing scholarship that does not label itself in this way. For example, Jennifer Eyl argues that the word *ekklēsia*, when translated as "church," distorts our understanding of early Christianity.[48] Translating Paul's letters with the term "church" suggests that he

---

45. Cf. Ian Hodder, ed., *Religion at Work in a Neolithic Society* (Cambridge: Cambridge University Press, 2014).

46. Cf. Phil Zuckerman, *Society Without God: What the Least Religious Nations Can Tell Us About Contentment* (New York: New York University Press, 2008).

47. The best account of a critical realism of religion is Christian Smith, *Religion: What It Is, How It Works, Why It Is Still Important* (Princeton, NJ: Princeton University Press, 2017).

48. Jennifer Eyl notes that other examples of theologically-influenced distortions include translating *ta ethnē* as pagan, *hamartia* as sin, and *pneuma* as a kind of hypostatized spirit. See Jennifer Eyl, "Semantic Voids, New Testament Translation, and Anachronism: The Case of Paul's Use of *Ekklēsia*," *Method & Theory in the Study of Religion* 26 (2014): 315–39.

was speaking of and to a distinctly Christian community of people, but that social form had not yet emerged. This translation thus retrojects a term that reassures present-day Christian readers that their own contemporary institutions can be traced back to the origins of their tradition. She recommends that this anachronism be dropped. In this way, her work is critical. Moreover, Eyl argues that Paul was seeking not to convert pagans to Christianity but rather to incorporate gentiles into the people of the God of Israel, and so Paul's use of *ekklēsia* is better captured less anachronistically as "a gathering of a people" or "an assembly." Although no translation is perfect, these less theologically laden terms are closer to the social structures of the Jewish community in that time. In this way, her work is realist. In an analogous way, David Frankfurter argues that the use of the label "sacrifice" distorts our understanding of religious practices in antiquity.[49] Ancient Mediterranean "pagan" religions have often been described as centrally focused on sacrifice, a bloody ritual that is then overcome in Christianity. But Frankfurter argues that although animals are killed as part of some religious practices in antiquity, the goal of the killing may not be to offer the animal's life or flesh to a god, but to create a mummy as a votive sign, to ward off evil with pleasant aromas, to use its entrails as part of an extispicy divination technique, to prepare the animal for an incineration that symbolizes the destruction of enemies, or simply to eat it in a feast. In such cases, the killing of the animal is not a significant religious act—strictly speaking, it is not a sacrifice—but rather a means to some other end. The use of the term "sacrifice" obscures this diversity and also distorts one's understanding of each of these kinds of rituals, and so Frankfurter argues that the label should be decentered or even dropped. In this way, he is critical. But the critique of "sacrifice" leads to its replacement with labels like divination, mummification, apotropaic spells, and feasts that seek to better grasp the actual religious practices in antiquity. In this way, his work is realist.

Some have argued that religion in the past must be invented and not discovered since the reference of the concept shifts as one's definition shifts. This much is true: those who define religion as one's "ultimate concern" identify as a referent a different set of practices than those who define religion as "a form of life predicated on superempirical realities." It may seem that as one shifts from one definition to another, religion morphs in and out of existence. But in neither example is the referent invented or manufactured by the term. Rather, to both definitions there correspond real patterns

49. David Frankfurter, "Egyptian Religion and the Problem of the Category 'Sacrifice'," in *Ancient Mediterranean Sacrifice* (ed. Jennifer Wright Knust and Zsuzsanna Várhelyi; Oxford: Oxford University Press, 2011), 75–93.

in the world—human concerns in the one and human practices in the other. One invents "religion" but not religion. Thus, just as one person might use the term "politics" to refer only to what governments do and another might use it to refer to any interpersonal operations involving power, it would not follow that "there is no such thing as politics" or that with their discourse the speakers manufacture politics. One invents "politics" but not politics.

Critical realism means that the concepts one imagines as realities in the past may fit the world more or less accurately. When one's accounts of the past fit the actual character of the world poorly, it does not follow that the world has no structure, that reality is like cookie dough, a blooming buzzing confusion, waiting to be structured by human categorization. It only means that we should improve our accounts to better accord with the events of the past and the mechanisms that caused them. Imagining religion in antiquity requires one to resist the collapse of concept and world and instead to distinguish between the social structures of the past and how we describe them, in the name of continually improving our descriptions so that they grasp the past better.

Biographical Note

Kevin Schilbrack is Professor and Chair of Religious Studies at the Appalachian State University, USA. He previously taught at Florida International University, Wesleyan College, and Western Carolina University. He is the author of *Philosophy and the Study of Religions: A Manifesto* (Wiley-Blackwell, 2014) and of various articles on philosophy and the study of religion. He is the editor of *Thinking Through Rituals: Philosophical Perspectives* (Routledge, 2004), *Thinking Through Myths: Philosophical Perspectives* (Routledge, 2002), and *The Wiley-Blackwell Companion to Religious Diversity* (Wiley-Blackwell, 2019).

Bibliography

Arnal, William E., and Russell T. McCutcheon. *The Sacred Is the Profane: The Political Nature of "Religion"*. Oxford: Oxford University Press, 2013.

Barton, Carlin A., and Daniel Boyarin. *Imagine No Religion: How Modern Abstractions Hide Ancient Realities*. New York: Fordham University Press, 2016.

Broucek, James. "Thinking About Religion Before 'Religion'," *Soundings* 98.1 (2015): 98–125. https://doi.org/10.5325/soundings.98.1.0098

Coole, Diana, and Samantha Frost, eds. *New Materialisms: Ontology, Agency, and Politics*. Durham, NC: Duke University Press, 2010. https://doi.org/10.1215/9780822392996

Dreyfus, Hubert L., and Charles Taylor. *Retrieving Realism*. Cambridge, MA: Harvard University Press, 2015. https://doi.org/10.4159/9780674287136

Eyl, Jennifer. "Semantic Voids, New Testament Translation, and Anachronism: The Case of Paul's Use of *Ekklēsia*," *Method & Theory in the Study of Religion* 26 (2014): 315–39. https://doi.org/10.1163/15700682-12341289

Ferraris, Maurizio. *Introduction to New Realism*. London: Bloomsbury, 2015.

Fitzgerald, Timothy. *The Ideology of Religious Studies*. Oxford: Oxford University Press, 2000.

Frankfurter, David. "Egyptian Religion and the Problem of the Category 'Sacrifice'," 75–93 in *Ancient Mediterranean Sacrifice*. Edited by Jennifer Wright Knust and Zsuzsanna Várhelyi. Oxford: Oxford University Press, 2011. https://doi.org/10.1093/acprof:oso/9780199738960.003.0003

Goldenberg, Naomi. "Some (Mainly) Very Appreciative Comments on Brent Nongbri's 'Before Religion'," *Critical Religion* (2013). Online: https://criticalreligion.org/2013/05/06/some-mainly-very-appreciative-comments-on-brent-nongbris-before-religion/ (accessed November 2016).

Hacking, Ian. "The Looping Effects of Human Kinds," 351–83 in *Causal Cognition: A Multi-disciplinary Debate*. Edited by Dan Sperber, David Premack, and Ann James Premack. Oxford: Oxford University Press, 1995.

—*The Social Construction of What?* Cambridge, MA: Harvard University Press, 1999.

Haslanger, Sally. "Social Construction: The 'Debunking' Project," 301–26 in *Socializing Metaphysics: The Nature of Social Reality*. Edited by Frederick F. Schmitt. Lanham, MD: Rowman & Littlefield, 2003.

Hodder, Ian, ed. *Religion at Work in a Neolithic Society*. Cambridge: Cambridge University Press, 2014.

Kippenberg, Hans G. *Discovering Religious History in the Modern Age*. Translated by Barbara Harshav. Princeton, NJ: Princeton University Press, 2002.

Latour, Bruno. "On the Partial Existence of Existing and Nonexisting Objects," 247–69 in *Biographies of Scientific Objects*. Edited by Lorraine Daston. Chicago, IL: University of Chicago Press, 2000.

—"Why Has Critique Run Out of Steam? From Matters of Fact to Matters of Concern," *Critical Inquiry* 30 (2004): 225–48. https://doi.org/10.1086/421123

Lincoln, Bruce. *Holy Terrors: Thinking About Religion After September 11*. Chicago, IL: University of Chicago Press, 2003.

McCutcheon, Russell T. *Manufacturing Religion: The Discourse on Sui Generis Religion and the Politics of Nostalgia*. Oxford: Oxford University Press, 1997.

—*Critics Not Caretakers: Redescribing the Public Study of Religion*. Albany, NY: State University of New York Press, 2001.

—*The Discipline of Religion: Structure, Meaning, Rhetoric*. London: Routledge, 2003. https://doi.org/10.4324/9780203451793

—"Religion Before 'Religion'?" 285–301 in *Chasing Down Religion: In the Sights of History and the Cognitive Sciences*. Edited by Panayotis Pachis and Donald Wiebe. Sheffield, UK: Equinox, 2010.

Nongbri, Brent. "Dislodging 'Embedded' Religion: A Brief Note on a Scholarly Trope," *Numen* 55.4 (2008): 440–60. https://doi.org/10.1163/156852708X310527

—*Before Religion: A History of a Modern Concept*. New Haven, CT: Yale University Press, 2013. https://doi.org/10.12987/yale/9780300154160.001.0001

Peterson, Derek, and Darren Walhof, eds. *The Invention of Religion: Rethinking Belief in Politics and History*. New Brunswick, NJ: Rutgers University Press, 2002.

Ristuccia, Nathan J. "Review of B. Nongbri: *Before Religion: A History of a Modern Concept*." *Fides et Historia* 46.1 (2014): 84–5.

Schilbrack, Kevin. "Religions: Are There Any?" *Journal of the American Academy of Religion* 78.4 (2010): 1112–38. https://doi.org/10.1093/jaarel/lfq086

—"The Social Construction of 'Religion' and Its Limits: A Critical Reading of Timothy Fitzgerald," *Method & Theory in the Study of Religion* 24.2 (2012): 97–117. https://doi.org/10.1163/157006812X634872

—*Philosophy and the Study of Religions.* Oxford: Wiley-Blackwell, 2014.

—"A Realist Social Ontology of Religion," *Religion* 47.2 (2017): 161–78. https://doi.org/10.1080/0048721X.2016.1203834

Searle, John. *Making the Social World: The Structure of Human Civilization.* Oxford: Oxford University Press, 2010. https://doi.org/10.1093/acprof:osobl/9780195396171.001.0001

Smith, Christian. *Religion: What It Is, How It Works, Why It Is Still Important.* Princeton, NJ: Princeton University Press, 2017.

Smith, Jonathan Z. *Map Is Not Territory: Studies in the History of Religions.* Chicago, IL: University of Chicago Press, 1978.

—*Imagining Religion: From Babylon to Jonestown.* Chicago, IL: University of Chicago Press, 1982.

—"Religion, Religions, Religious," 269–84 in *Critical Terms for Religious Studies.* Edited by Mark C. Taylor. Chicago, IL: University of Chicago Press, 1998.

—*Relating Religion: Essays in the Study of Religion.* Chicago, IL: University of Chicago Press, 2004.

Stroumsa, Guy G. *A New Science: The Discovery of Religion in the Age of Reason.* Oxford: Oxford University Press, 2010.

Zuckerman, Phil. *Society Without God: What the Least Religious Nations Can Tell Us About Contentment.* New York: New York University Press, 2008.

PART II
THE GREEK WORLD

Chapter Five

Philosophical Reflections on the Presocratics:
A Contribution to the Scientific Study of Religion

Donald Wiebe

Ancient Greek Philosophy as a Critical Episode in the History of Human Thought

Implicit in the thought of the presocratic cosmologists from the Milesians to the Atomists lies a new understanding of "knowledge" in which beliefs are open to rational criticism and assessment. This kind of knowledge about the world and states of affairs in the world simply amounts to the espousal of beliefs about an objectively existing reality that have found rational and evidential support. This "knowledge as rationally justifiable beliefs" stands in radical contrast to knowledge as metaphysical "Truths" regarding indisputable realities such as the gods and the meaning of life vouchsafed to people either by way of revelation, intuition, or imagination. Such "Truths" are, in effect, local worldviews—that is, products of the human mind—rather than accounts of a rationally established reality. The transition from knowledge as "Truth" to knowledge as comprising beliefs that under rational criticism are potentially either true or false amounts to the creation of a new cultural value of "knowledge as rationally justified belief for the sake of that knowledge alone." And it is the emergence of this new conception of knowledge as entirely reliant on autonomous reason that constitutes a "critical episode" in the development of human thought essential to the eventual emergence of science (and of the scientific study of religion) as we understand it today.

Half a century ago, Jan de Vries gave serious attention to the importance of intellectual developments in ancient Greece for the field of religious studies as an academic discipline. Most important for de Vries, was the work of the Ionian (Milesian) natural philosophers which, he maintains, "wiped out the whole system of solid and simple belief in the Olympic gods" among the intellectuals of Athens, many of whom ultimately produced reductionist theoretical explanations of religion and the gods.[1] "In company with the

---

1.   Jan de Vries, *The Study of Religion: A Historical Approach* (New York: Harcourt, Brace & World, 1967), 5–6.

speculations of the philosophers," de Vries noted in his comments on Herodotus, "mention should be made of the germ of a science of religion, which one is almost inclined to call 'ethnological'."[2]

I am not persuaded by de Vries's suggestion that we can see the germ of a science of religion in the thought of the Ionian natural philosophers and other presocratic intellectuals. Nor am I persuaded by others who see the Ionians as having created science or a "truly scientific outlook." I am convinced, however, that this period in the history of human thought constitutes a "critical episode" in the ultimate emergence and development of a scientific study of religion that, at times, has flourished in some of our research universities. Ionian cosmological thought seems, in fact, not only to have undermined naive belief in the Olympian gods, but nurtured various forms of atheism, and fostered reductionist explanations for belief in gods and "the divine." Presocratic thought, however, is not uniform in this regard. Other presocratics provided alternative accounts of the gods, including the construction of what we would today refer to as natural theologies, as well as sophisticated conceptions of "the divine" that seem indistinguishable from the elemental substance or substances of their explanatory accounts of the cosmos. Although the emergence and development of atheism in this period—as a more radical form of criticism of religion than that contained in the sophisticated forms of religious thought just mentioned—was a significant factor in making a scientific study of religion possible, the very possibility of such criticism is itself the result of a more general revolutionary development in human thought. The attempt to explain the world without reference to myth and religion, that is, involves a "transitional mode of thought" that unconsciously amounted to a disenchantment of the world in favor of knowledge of the world that ultimately provided the foundation for a genuinely scientific study not only of the natural world but of the social world as well. That is, knowledge for the sake of knowledge alone, as well as the emergence of a form of critical reason (reasoning) as a non-moral instrument of inquiry necessary for obtaining such knowledge, emerged unintentionally as new cultural values from the "religiously disinterested this-worldliness" of presocratic thought.[3]

In this chapter I set out the import of the two hundred or so years of presocratic thought for the emergence and development of a scientific study of religion and religions in our modern research universities. My objective here is not that of trying to make a new and original contribution to "presocratic studies," or to interpretive studies of the fragments of any or several

2.   De Vries, *Study of Religion*, 11.
3.   See W. K. C. Guthrie, *The Greeks and Their Gods* (Boston, MA: Beacon Press, 1950), 92.

of the major presocratic philosophers. There is more than one mountain of critical analyses and philosophical interpretations by experts in this field and I hope here to take the measure of those studies insofar as they relate to their relevance for scientific study of religion and religions. I will focus attention, for the most part, on the Milesian/Ionian cosmologists, who were the first thinkers who attempted to provide a wholly rational account of the nature of the world in terms of a primary material substrate and natural processes of its transformation, and their successors, who found its culmination in the atomism of Leucippus of Miletus and Democritus of Abdera. As Geoffrey Kirk, John Raven, and Malcolm Schofield put it: "Atomism is in many ways the crown of Greek philosophical achievement before Plato. It fulfilled the Ultimate aim of Ionian material monism [...]."[4] I agree here with Kirk et al. that it is important "not to exaggerate the sheer irrationality" of the pre-Milesian thinkers and to recognize that Hesiod, for example, exercised "a useful kind of reasonableness in grading and synthesizing tales from different regions and with different emphases."[5] However, Kirk et al. also recognize that while many early Greek philosophers were slow in rejecting a mythic mode of thought, the Milesian revolution ultimately resulted in the substitution of logical and critical rational thought for myth in accounting for the world. The Milesians must in hindsight, then, be seen as having crossed a threshold in human modes of thought made possible not in terms of new cognitive capacities of the human brain but by significant changes in Greek society and culture.

It must be acknowledged that there are significant difficulties for scholars to have total confidence in understanding and in justifying their claims regarding the presocratics. Some may think, therefore, that this uncertainty will cast doubt on my claims about the import of presocratic thought for the study of religion. I recognize that judgments reached on the basis of this scholarship will be less than conclusive, but I believe it will provide a reasonable—non-arbitrary and plausible—basis for my claims about the revolutionary character of early presocratic thought.

Recognizing Ambiguity of the Evidence

Daniel Graham—editor of *The Texts of Early Greek Philosophy* (2010)[6]— rightly points out that what we know of presocratic thought is only available

4.   Geoffrey S. Kirk, John E. Raven, and Malcolm Schofield. *The Presocratic Philosophers: A Critical History with a Selection of Texts* (Cambridge: Cambridge University Press, 1983), 433.

5.   Kirk, Raven, and Schofield, *Presocratic Philosophers*, 72 and 73, respectively.

6.   Daniel Graham, ed., *The Texts of Early Greek Philosophy: The Complete*

in fragments and from reports on their thought by other philosophers, doxographers, and biographers who have made use of their work to support their own interests. This, clearly, is a serious handicap. As Geoffrey Lloyd warns: "We should never underestimate how difficult it is to recover ancient aims, goals, preoccupations, and expectations."[7] Even though Graham insists that no one is in a position "to offer any final readings" of the presocratic fragments, he acknowledges that contemporary philosophers have been able to "offer increasingly sophisticated interpretations" of them.[8] And it is on the basis of such modern and contemporary interpretations of presocratic thought that I will rely in arguing that the Milesians created a new, transitional, mode of thought that was not wholly under the constraints of myth and religion. I agree, for example, with Jean-Pierre Vernant's assessment that this Milesian mode of thought grew *out* of the past as well as *away* from it, and it is this growth away from the mythic past that crosses the threshold separating mythopetic and religious modes of thought from a new critically rational mode of thought.[9] Nevertheless, I remain aware that this assessment may be tagged as the product of "retrospective history," as historian of philosophy Michael Frede puts it. He writes: "it is very much in hindsight that we can see that Thales [of Miletus] started a tradition that contributed to the formation of the discipline that came to be known as philosophy."[10] Frede further claims that there "is no reason to suppose that Thales conceived of the wisdom he aspired to as entirely a matter of theoretical insight."[11] However, this does not constitute evidence in support of Frede's claim that Thales's cosmological speculation was wholly constrained by his pursuit of a "broader wisdom." Indeed, Frede admits that "we have to acknowledge that the Presocratics from Thales to Democritus, as part of the general concern for wisdom, tried to provide an account of reality as a theory of nature."[12] And it is precisely that interest in *a theory of nature* that constitutes a revolutionary development in the

---

Fragments and Selected Testimonies of the Major Presocratics (Vol. 1; Cambridge: Cambridge University Press, 2010).

7.   Geoffrey E. R. Lloyd, *Ancient Worlds, Modern Reflections: Philosophical Perspective on Greek and Chinese Science and Culture* (Oxford: Oxford University Press, 2004), 188.

8.   Graham, *Texts of Early Greek Philosophy*, 13.

9.   See Jean-Pierre Vernant, *Myth and Thought Among the Greeks* (trans. Janet Lloyd and Jeff Frost; London: Routledge & Kegan Paul, 1983), 365.

10.   Michael Frede, "The Philosopher," in *Greek Thought: A Guide to Classical Knowledge* (ed. Jacques Brunschwig and Geoffrey E. R. Lloyd; Cambridge, MA: Harvard University Press, 1996), 6.

11.   Frede, "Philosopher," 6.

12.   Frede, "Philosopher," 6.

long history of human thought, whether or not Thales intended to create that new tradition.

I am somewhat uncomfortable in trying to make a case that presocratic philosophy as a whole constituted a significant "episode" in ultimately making possible the scientific study of religion and religions. My anxiety is of a similar nature to that of Francis M. Cornford who wrote that any student in any branch of knowledge knows

> the expert will frown upon some of his statements as questionable in content and dogmatic in tone, and will mark the omission of many things for which no room could be found. But it will do him good to sit back in his chair and look for the main outline, so often obscured by detail.[13]

Like Cornford, I think it is possible for us to discern ways in which the early Greek philosophers contributed to the emergence and development of what we today recognize as science.

The Centrality of Socrates to Clarifying the Evidence

I shall begin my examination of the contribution of presocratic philosophy to modern life by drawing on Cornford's claim that Socrates must be seen as a central figure in assessing that influence because of Socrates's "conversion of philosophy from the study of Nature to the study of human life."[14] Cornford's account of that conversion of philosophy brilliantly, but inadvertently, captures the significance of the Milesians' transitional mode of thought that breaks free of what Gilbert Murray (1946) called the "inherited conglomerate" of ancient Greek culture even though Conford overstates its accomplishment as science.

Cornford's aim in his *Before and After Socrates* is "so to describe the early Ionian science as to show why it failed to satisfy Socrates," and to present Socrates's thought as "revolutionary."[15] I will show, however, that a critical analysis of Cornford's argument will reveal the thought of the Milesian/Ionian cosmologists to be a genuinely revolutionary development in the history of human thought and Socrates's "philosophy" to be counter-revolutionary. That Ionian transitional thought, however, is best understood as an "extended patchy revolution,"[16] starting with the Milesians

---

13. Francis MacDonald Cornford, *Before and After Socrates* (Cambridge: Cambridge University Press, 1965), ix.

14. Cornford, *Before and After Socrates*, ix.

15. Cornford, *Before and After Socrates*, ix n. 1.

16. See David Wooton, *The Invention of Science: A New History of the Scientific Revolution* (New York: Harper, 2015).

and culminating in the thought of the Atomists roughly two hundred years later. The new, non-mythic, mode of thought of the atomists, described by Benjamin Farrington as "an admirable introduction to scientific culture [and] an admirable training in rational thought," was achieved in a step-wise fashion, as he put it, "marked by the names of Thales, Anaximander, Anaximenes, Pythagoras, Parmenides, Zeno, Melissus, Empedocles, Anax-agoras, Leucippus and Democritus ... These names mark an epoch in the history of humanity."[17] Thales, as Farrington puts it in his *Science in Antiquity*, is the first person "known to history to have offered a general explanation of nature without invoking the aid of any power outside history."[18] In his later *Greek Science*, Farrington points to the significant difference in the Babylonian account of the appearance of the world as involving the god Marduk fashioning a rush mat piled high with dirt that rests upon the sea from that of Thales's account of the world as also resting on water by pointing out that "[w]hat Thales did was to leave Marduk out."[19] Even though this development did not create science as we understand it today, with the Milesian cosmologists, as I have intimated above, an "incipient new mode of thought" appeared, not wholly distinct from what preceded it, yet a new, religiously and mythically disinterested, way of thinking about the world that played a significant role in the eventual emergence of modern Western science and, therefore, the possibility of a scientific study of religions.

Socrates turned his back on this "science-like" tradition of thought which sought to provide a theoretical account of the world, and nearly brought that tradition of rational cosmological thinking to an end. As Kirk et al. put it:

> [U]nder the mature Socrates and the Sophists, the old cosmological approach—by which the primary aim was to explain the outside world as a whole, man being considered only incidentally—was gradually replaced by a *humanistic* approach to philosophy, by which the study of man became no longer subsidiary but the starting-point of all inquiry.[20]

Although one must also agree with Kirk et al. that this "reorientation" of philosophy was in some sense a natural product of the presocratic movement itself, (even though also determined in part by social factors), this does not undermine the counter-revolutionary character of Socratic thought; Socrates's "humanistic" approach to understanding "man," that is, amounted to

17. Benjamin Farrington, *Science and Politics in the Ancient World* (London: George Allen & Unwin, 1946), 60.

18. Benjamin Farrington, *Science in Antiquity* (London: Thornton Butterworth, 1936), 40.

19. Benjamin Farrington, *Greek Science (Thales to Aristotle): Its Meaning for Us* (Harmondsworth, UK: Penguin, 1944), 30.

20. Kirk, Raven, and Schofield, *Presocratic Philosophers*, 452 (emphasis added).

a return to a modified form of mythopoetic thought. Cornford, I think, captured that difference perfectly in the following passage:

> The Socratic philosophy is a reaction against this [Ionian] materialistic drift of physical science. In order to rediscover the spiritual world, philosophy had to give up, for the moment, the search after material substance in external Nature, and turn its eyes inwards to the nature of the human soul. This was the *revolution* accomplished by Socrates, with his Delphic injunction "Know thyself".[21]

It is clear, then, that Socrates represents not a revolutionary development in human thought but a reactionary and counter-revolutionary development because Socrates saw religiously disinterested Ionian cosmological thinking as a crisis for society that can only be resolved by a return to a religiously interested, self-involving mode of thought.

Even though the Ionian development is not the birth of what we understand as modern science, it does amount to a new mode of thought both continuous and discontinuous with that which precedes it, and Cornford is fully aware of this. "All the histories of Greek philosophy from Aristotle's time to this day," he writes,

> begin with Thales of Miletus. It is generally agreed, [he continues], that with him something new, that we call Western science, appeared in the world— science as commonly defined: the pursuit of *knowledge for its own sake*, not for any practical use it can be made to serve.[22]

Although I disagree with Cornford's definition of science here, he rightly recognizes that what has emerged with the Milesians is the new cultural value of seeking knowledge for the sake of knowledge alone that is so characteristic of modern science. As Cornford puts it, Milesian thought

> is marked by the tacit denial of this distinction between two orders of knowledge, experience and revelation, and between the two corresponding orders of existence, the natural and the supernatural. The Ionian cosmogonists assume (without even feeling the need to make the assertion) that the whole universe is natural, and potentially within the reach of knowledge as ordinary and rational as our knowledge that fire burns and water drowns.[23]

As I have intimated above, I am in agreement with Lloyd that the Ionian mode of thought is not a simple and "sudden breakthrough" to "truly modern science."[24] There was no quantum leap here, no absolute discontinuity from all that preceded it. The presocratics as a whole only slowly

21. Cornford, *Before and After Socrates*, 27–8 (emphasis added).
22. Cornford, *Before and After Socrates*, 5 (emphasis added).
23. Cornford, *Before and After Socrates*, 14–5.
24. See Lloyd, *Ancient Worlds, Modern Reflections*, 13.

rejected—overcame—what Gilbert Murray described as "the thick atmosphere of tradition and convention"[25] that defined their society. In *Demystifying Mentalities*, Lloyd points out that science emerges, at least in part, due
to "a rhetoric of legitimation," but he also insists that Greek science is not
either just a myth or magic.[26] I find his earlier discussion of Greek science in
his *Magic, Reason, and Experience* to the effect that there is general agreement that between the sixth and fourth centuries BCE a new mode of thought
emerged that has some appearance of being scientific even though it is also
continuous with myth and magic, reasonable in light of his insistence that the
new mode of thought has "some features of a paradigm switch."[27] Without
having to assume that there was a uniform set of beliefs among presocratic
thinkers as to the ideas (concepts) of cause and effect, and without drawing conclusions about the nature of ancient Greek speculative thought as a
whole,[28] Lloyd comes to a conclusion that I find reasonably encapsulates the
achievements of the Milesian cosmologists and many of their successors. As
he puts it:

> The development of philosophy and science in ancient Greece is a unique
> turning-point in the history of thought. So far as the Western world goes, our
> science is continuous with, and may be said to originate in, that of ancient
> Greece.[29]

In the following section I will lay out briefly what that unique turning-point
amounts to.

Transcending Myth: Not a Miracle, Just an Extended Patchy Revolution

In his "Prolegomena to the Study of Ancient Philosophy," Gilbert Murray
talks about "inherited conglomerates" that he describes as "the thick atmosphere of tradition and convention" found in almost all thought in ancient
human societies within which thought is "stifled and imprisoned." "One
of the great lessons which anthropology has taught us," he continues, "is
the overpowering influence on mankind of tradition and tribal custom, of

25. Gilbert Murray, "Prolegomena to the Study of Ancient Philosophy," in *Greek Studies* (Oxford: Clarendon Press, 1946), 66.
26. Geoffrey E. R. Lloyd, *Demystifying Mentalities* (Cambridge: Cambridge University Press, 1990), 43; cf. 70.
27. Geoffrey E. R. Lloyd, *Magic, Reason, and Experience: Studies in the Origins and Development of Greek Science* (Cambridge: Cambridge University Press, 1979), 26–7.
28. See Lloyd, *Magic, Reason, and Experience*, 233.
29. Lloyd, *Magic, Reason, and Experience*, 264.

inherited taboos and superstitions."[30] Murray rightly notes that even though "these inherited conglomerates have practically no chance of being true or even sensible," it seems that "no society can exist without them or even submit to any drastic correction of them without social danger."[31] Despite these claims, however, Murray also points out that the early Greek philosophers paid little or no regard to the Olympian gods and that "as soon as philosophy began [they] rose above their traditions and conventions."[32]

Karl Popper's essay "Back to the Presocratics" provides a brilliant analysis of the Milesian cosmologists that supports Murray's claim about philosophy transcending the "inherited conglomerate" as well as Lloyd's claim about philosophical thought in ancient Greece constituting a unique turning-point in the development of human thought. Like Murray, Popper is aware of how early Greek thought had been stifled and imprisoned in tradition. According to Popper, the Milesian cosmologists freed themselves from the "inherited conglomerate" by limiting their interests to seeking knowledge of how the world came to be what it is, and by creating a new way of achieving such knowledge by substituting critical debate and rational discussion for myth and religious revelation as legitimate sources of knowledge. Thales, Popper maintains, actively encouraged criticism of his views rather than encasing them in unchallengeable narratives (myths). This, Popper argues, was a "momentous innovation" because it led

> to the realization that our attempts to see and to find the truth are not final, but open to improvement; that our knowledge, our doctrine, is conjectural; that it consists of guesses, of hypotheses, rather than final and certain truths; and that criticism and critical discussion are our only means of getting nearer to the truth.[33]

Popper arrived at this conclusion by way of a close examination of the structure of Anaximander's theory of the architecture of the cosmos which, he argues, could only have been derived by way of criticizing Thales's theory. Thales, according to Popper, was the first thinker to try to understand the structure of the cosmos and to determine the material of which it is made. Anaximander, likely a student of Thales, sought the same kind of knowledge but was not persuaded by Thales's account of the cosmos. For Thales, the stable position of the earth was predicated on the assumption that it was supported by water. Anaximander, it appears, was clearly aware that

---

30. Murray, "Prolegomena," 66.
31. Murray, "Prolegomena," 67.
32. Murray, "Prolegomena," 69; cf. 71.
33. Karl R. Popper, *Conjectures and Refutations: The Growth of Scientific Knowledge* (New York: Harper & Row, 1965), 151.

if such a theory were developed consistently it would lead to an infinite regress, requiring a similar hypothesis to account for the stability of the ocean upon which the earth floats. Anaximander's theory avoids this problem by hypothesizing that the earth is a globe situated at the center of the universe and encircled by spheres on which the planets and stars were fixed. Anaximander, that is, attempts to account for the stability of the earth by appealing to its structural symmetry and the equality of its distance from all other bodies in the universe.

Popper sees Anaximenes as the least productive of the Milesian cosmologists but recognizes that, although he misunderstood Anaximander's theory, he did not shrink from criticizing it. Heraclitus and Parmenides, among other presocratic philosophers, Popper argues, also adopted this mode of thought in trying to understand the nature of the cosmos, leading ultimately to Leucippus and Democritus. Following these debates and discussions, he writes, amounts to a "splendid story" that is "almost too good to be true."[34] "In every generation" of the presocratics, he continues, "we find at least one new philosophy, one new cosmology of staggering originality and depth" made possible by the development of a tradition of critical thought that contributed not only to an escape from the "inherited conglomerate" of ancient Greece, but it also laid the groundwork for the ultimate emergence of modern science. As Popper put it:

> I assert that there is the most perfect possible continuity of thought between ... [the theories of the prescoratics] and the later development of physics. Whether they are called philosophers, pre-scientists, or scientists matters very little, I think. But I do assert that Anaximander's theory cleared the way for the theories of Aristarchus, Copernicus, Kepler, and Galileo.[35]

According to Popper, then, the hypotheses/theories of the Milesians clearly indicate that they were not interested either in reforming religion or in attempting to replace it. With respect to the objective of explaining the cosmos, they simply ignored it. This does not mean, however, that there is absolutely no continuity of thought from the pre-Milesians to the early Milesian and other presocratic philosophers. W. K. C. Guthrie, for example, has rightly reminded those interested in the earliest Greek philosophers to remember "how close were the Greeks in early times, and many of the common people throughout the classical period, to the magical stage of thought."[36] And E. R. Dodds was entirely right to criticize as "naive and

---

34. Popper, *Conjectures*, 148.
35. Popper, *Conjectures*, 141.
36. W. K. C. Guthrie, *The Greek Philosophers: From Thales to Aristotle* (London: Methuen, 1950), 12.

historically inaccurate" those who see "rationality bursting miraculously and full-blown onto the scene of human history at the time of the Milesians, totally distinct from the form of thought that precedes it ..."[37] More recently, Richard McKirahan has also pointed out that the Milesians took over much from Homer and Hesiod including "a belief in the divine governance of the world."[38]

Despite these reminders of continuity between ancient Greek myth and Milesian/Ionian philosophy, however, it is neither naive nor historically inaccurate to investigate the question as to whether there exists a significant difference between the mythic and Milesian modes of thought that follows on the heels of leaving the gods out of consideration in the search for an understanding of the cosmos. The question of continuity and discontinuity between the old and the new in the historical development of societies and cultures, that is, is not much different from the same issue in biology which recognizes that continuity in the evolution of species does not exclude development; that is, discontinuity. One need not, therefore, ignore the effect of the "inherited conglomerate" in the thought of the early Greek philosophers in order to recognize the genuinely new contributions made by them. This is clearly demonstrated by Robert Hahn in his account of how Anaximander's work builds on that of Hesiod. Anaximander's work, as he puts it, is a "rationalized version of Hesiod's *Theogony* [and] an Hellenized version of the Babylonian creation story, the *Enuma elish*" and not a mythological account.[39] Anaximander's account of the cosmos, that is, makes no reference to divine beings in order to determine the substance of which the world is made or to explain its structure.

I am not suggesting here that the "shelving of the Olympian gods" by the early Ionian thinkers amounted to an espousal of atheism *tout court*. However, their attempt to understand the world independent of religious thought and public cult amounts to a form of methodological atheism. Whether they were religious or not, that is, it is clear that their intellectual interests were simply to gain knowledge about the world—its primary substance, the principles of transformation of that substance, and the architecture of the universe and all that is in it—supported by reason and rational speculation and therefore open to criticism. And such a rational approach to understanding the world is, so to speak, methodologically incommensurable with mythic

37.   E. R. Dodds, *The Greeks and the Irrational* (Berkeley, CA: University of California Press, 1951), 108.

38.   Richard D. McKirahan Jr., *Philosophy Before Socrates: An Introduction with Texts and Commentary* (Indianapolis, IN: Hackett, 1994), 71.

39.   Robert Hahn, *Archaeology and the Origins of Philosophy* (Albany, NY: State University of New York Press, 2010), 11.

or religious accounts that invoke divine agents who capriciously intervene not only in human social events in the world but also in its natural processes. Their thinking, therefore, amounts to the crossing of an epistemic threshold that ultimately made possible a disenchantment of the world (by displacing agentic explanations in favor of natural/mechanical explanations) and the production of criticizable knowledge claims. They displaced narrative with argument in their accounts of the world. It is in this sense that one can speak of a Milesian/Ionian/presocratic *revolution* in human thought—referring to the development from the Milesians to the Atomists—despite the fact there is a degree of continuity between it and the mythic and quasi-rational modes of thought from which it emerged.

In making this argument, however, it should nevertheless be borne in mind that it is not the case that archaic societies ante-dating these philosophical developments did not investigate natural phenomena. It is obvious that our brains evolved for understanding and dealing with the immediate, everyday-ordinary world around us. Had our archaic forebears not been able to grasp/understand the external world for what it is, they would not have survived. However, as historian of science H. Floris Cohen, among other historians and paleoanthropologists, has argued, such knowledge was not carried out in a systematic and socially and culturally disinterested fashion. It was, rather, generally pursued within the framework of what he calls "a larger conception of how things in the universe cohere"—that is, within a narrative (mythic and metaphysical) framework of meaning. Moreover, I think Cohen is entirely right to argue that even if it had been "pursued as an activity in its own right [as with the Milesians], it is most unlikely to have survived at all."[40] Anthropologist and philosopher Ernest Gellner, in his account of the radical difference between "The Savage and the Modern Mind,"[41] also captures the essence of this development from traditional pragmatic societal interests in the natural world to a more focused and neutral interest in knowledge of the natural world for its own sake. In his analysis of the "gap" between archaic (mythopoetic) and modern modes of thought, he points out, for example, that the mythopoetic mode of thought in traditional societies provides a general vision of what is normal for society—its social and moral order—which grounds a framework of meaning within which its members function, and also constitutes its cognitive base lines for understanding the world. In such traditional societies, that is, there is a systematic conflation

40. H. Floris Cohen, *The Scientific Revolution: A Historiographical Inquiry* (Chicago, IL: University of Chicago Press, 1994), 506.

41. See Ernest Gellner, "The Savage and the Modern Mind," in *Modes of Thought: Essays on Thinking in Western and Non-Western Societies* (ed. Robin Horton and Ruth Finnegan; London: Faber & Faber, 1973), 162–81.

of the descriptive, evaluative, and status-conferring role of language that produces an enchanted framework of existence. What the early Greek philosophers achieved, to use Gellner's language, was to provide autonomy to knowledge from "the social, moral and political obligations and decencies of society." The presocratic philosophers therefore, even if not with conscious intent, in effect created a new cultural value of "knowledge for the sake of knowledge alone" that gave it what Gellner calls "diplomatic immunity" from all other cultural values and catapulted the Greeks beyond their "inherited (mythic) conglomerate." This intellectual achievement, as I note above, amounted to the crossing of a threshold in human modes of thought which can only be attributed to significant changes in the structure of Greek society, a matter that does not need elaboration here.

Religion, Criticism, and the Disenchantment of the World

A summary of the intellectual achievements of the "Milesian revolution" that have contributed to making a scientific study of religion possible include both those developments that have, in the long run, contributed to the emergence of modern western science two millennia later, and those that opened contemporary religion and religious thought to criticism. It is somewhat artificial to see these developments as independent from each other, but it will be helpful to look at them separately.

What is clear from the history of scholarship on the presocratic achievement—viewed as a cumulative development from the Milesians to the Atomists—is that even though this revolution cannot be accredited with the creation of a fully scientific mode of thought, it provided the foundation for its future development. It did so, one might say, in its inadvertent disenchantment of the world by way of its focused interest in explaining the physical/natural world. In seeking an explanation for the world in terms of a primal substance and transformations of that substance via physical/mechanical causes rather than by way of divine agency, the Milesians "discovered nature," which, in a sense, involved displacing the gods. The Milesians, that is, depended upon the creation of criticizable conjectures as to the "nature" of the physical/natural world and, with respect to their primary intellectual objectives, they ignored the mythic narratives about the inscrutable (uncriticizable) will of the gods. They depended instead on the unaided use of reason—autonomous reason as a kind of non-moral instrument of reasoning—in an intellectual atmosphere of critical discussion of one another's hypotheses. In proceeding as they did, therefore, the presocratics created several elements essential to the eventual development of scientific thought, namely, the liberation of reason from the constraints of a narrative (mythic-intuitive or revelational) mode of thinking and the creation of a new cultural value of "knowledge for the sake of knowledge alone." Furthermore, by not paying attention to the stories of the gods in Homer and Hesiod in their accounts of the cosmos, the Milesians not only undermined the myths as sources of knowledge—rather than as mere beliefs—about the world; they opened up the possibility of making the gods themselves objects of religiously disinterested (that is, a Popperian conjectural-refutational type of) explanation. Beliefs in the gods were subjected to reforming criticism and even given up entirely. The gods were often seen as mere human contrivances and, therefore, metaphysically non-existent. Consequently, we see in the presocratics, and in the atheism and atheist theories of religion they spawned, "the germ of a science of religion."[42]

The disbelief in the old mythological conceptions of the gods (and other forms of atheism) does not comprise the whole of the presocratic tradition. Xenophanes's reforming criticism of Olympian religion is a well-known example of this. Although Xenophanes had acquired an Ionian scientific outlook he did not reject belief in, or simply ignore, the gods. He was clearly aware of how the conception and descriptions of the gods varied from one culture to another. His interest appears to have been spurred by the potential for the harmful influence of beliefs in the gods on human behavior. He rejected the widespread belief that Homer and Hesiod possessed superhuman or special mental abilities that permitted them to see the gods, and denounced the way they depicted the gods. Nevertheless, he still held a belief in the gods. Although his conception of the gods was still anthropomorphic in character it was a moral improvement on the Olympian theology of Homer and Hesiod that held sway among the general populace in ancient Greece. Moreover, his argument for a morally more acceptable belief about the gods was presented not on the basis of a revelation but as rationally justifiable.

Xenophanes's explicit concern with transforming the widespread Homeric perception of the gods disseminated through the general populace is but one type of argument in support of belief in the existence of the divine in ancient Greek society. Belief in the divine, even if only implicit, persisted even among the intelligentsia despite the fact that although the "philosophers threw off the artificial creations of 'Homer and Hesiod,' [they] could not get rid of the more primitive and instinctive religion"—what Gilbert Murray called the "inherited conglomerate."[43] Jan Bremmer similarly points out that

---

42. See de Vries, *Study of Religion*, 11. Cf. the recent Tim Whitmarsh, *Battling the Gods: Atheism in the Ancient World* (New York: Alfred A. Knopf, 2015).

43. Murray, "Prolegomena," 71.

the atheism of the ancient Greeks was not a genuine rejection of belief in the gods but was rather a "soft atheism" involving the mere rejection of the gods as expressed in popular belief.[44] Philosopher James Thrower put forward a similar view writing: "What is certainly true [about the presocratics] is that they laid the foundations for the decline of the old mythological conception of the gods and of traditional religion—though this, of course, only at the intellectual level."[45] Thrower further maintains that one can discern in the presocratic period "the beginnings of a more sophisticated conception of the divine which will in Plato and Aristotle to a large extent displace the traditional religion and in its later developments became a genuine alternative to it."[46] Richard McKirahan, in summarizing the results of his examination of the presocratics, also maintains that although they did "away with gods governed by human passions, emotions, and caprices" in accounting for the world purely in terms of natural processes, he nevertheless insists that the Milesians were "unanimous in recognizing the divine nature of their primary substances [...]"[47]—a theme already presented by Werner Jaeger in his *The Theology of the Early Greek Philosophers*.[48] David Sedley in his *Creationism and Its Critics in Antiquity*, moreover, maintains that in presocratics like Anaxagoras and Empedocles we find the assumption that the world is governed by a divine power and that it is therefore not possible to assume that the naturalistic thinking of the presocratics and religion are "mutually exclusive modes of thought"[49]—a somewhat odd conclusion given that the *Phaedo* presents Socrates as questioning the coherence of Anaxagoras's philosophy which ultimately was the reason for Socrates's rejection of the entire tradition of cosmological speculation in the philosophical thought that preceded him.

There should be no surprise that belief in the Olympian gods was widespread among the general population of ancient Greece. Nor should we be surprised to find that some presocratic thinkers rejected the notion that any and every belief in a "divine" reality of some kind amounted to the espousal of an irrational belief. And it is clear that some attempted to "purify" traditional

---

44. See Jan N. Bremmer, "Atheism in Antiquity," in *The Cambridge Companion to Atheism* (ed. Michael Martin; Cambridge: Cambridge University Press, 2007), 11–26.

45. James Thrower, *Western Atheism: A Short History* (Amherst, NY: Prometheus Books, 2000), 17.

46. Thrower, *Western Atheism*, 33.

47. McKirahan, *Philosophy Before Socrates*, 70–1 and 60, respectively.

48. See Werner Jaeger, *The Theology of the Early Greek Philosophers* (Oxford: Clarendon Press, 1946).

49. David Sedley, *Creationism and Its Critics in Antiquity* (Los Angeles, CA: University of California Press, 2007), 31.

anthropomorphic religious beliefs by supplanting them with belief in a kind of non-anthropomorphic religionism that they considered to be complementary to the kind of knowledge of the natural world that interested the ancient Greek cosmologists. Such beliefs persist even today in a world that most scholars and intellectuals think of as scientific. As physicist Richard Feynman has put it, scientists have perpetually made discoveries about our world for the past few hundred years but not in the sense that science has played a large part in art, literature, or in the general population's attitudes to and understandings of the world.[50] The epistemic value of such religious belief, however, is ambiguous at best when compared with the kind of belief claims about the nature of the world and its contents that were open to critical discussion and possible rejection (an early form of falsification) that characterized the "epistemic results" of the new Milesian-to-Atomist methodology. The problem is particularly obvious with the application of this "new methodology" to the gods and religion as part of the "contents" of the world. It is unclear, that is, whether such religious belief—belief in the reality of divinity—actually transcends the boundaries of myth. It does not appear that it can. Paul Veyne, in his *Did the Greeks Believe in Their Myths?*, maintains, that myth and reason are not opposites since "[n]o positivist criticism can adequately deal with mythology and the supernatural"[51] and that historians of religion, therefore, will have much to gain in recognizing the reality of a discourse of "truth" in the plural rather than the singular. In effect, therefore, Veyne is denying that the Milesian-to-Atomist development of presocratic thought constitutes a revolutionary achievement in which reason, so to speak, gained its independence from myth and can therefore subject myth to critical reflection. His argument, however, is flawed and it is the revolution in thought created by the presocratics that will stand as the real contribution of ancient Greek philosophy to the historical and scientific study of religion.

Can Believing Re-Enchant the Universe?

Veyne is aware that there may have been many in ancient Greece who believed in the gods in a superstitious manner but he points out that there was also an educated public who understood that they could no longer believe in the "supernatural" (his term) "in the old way." Consequently, he claims, they created a "new type" of supernaturalism that would not conflict

50. See Richard P. Feynman, *The Meaning of It All* (New York: Basic Books, 1998), 62–3.

51. Paul Veyne, *Did the Greeks Believe in Their Myths? An Essay on the Constitutive Imagination* (trans. Paula Wissing; Chicago, IL: University of Chicago Press, 1988), 2.

with the rational thought that had emerged with the Milesians. Veyne sees such intellectuals as being in a "complicated state of mind" in that they rejected "the marvelous" and at the same time were convinced "that legends had a true basis."[52] According to Veyne, "[a]mong the learned, critical credulity, as it were, alternated with a global skepticism and rubbed shoulders with the unreflecting credulity of the less educated"; and he maintains that in ancient Greece these

> attitudes tolerated one another, and popular credulity was not culturally devalued. This peaceful coexistence of contradictory beliefs had a sociologically peculiar result. Each individual internalized the contradiction and thought things about myth that, in the eyes of the logician at least, were irreconcilable. The individual himself did not suffer from these contradictions; quite the contrary. Each one served a different end.[53]

"The truth,"—that is, the truth of the mythic tradition—is the world of values (the worldview) forged by a people (group, state, nation) in response to the plurality of forces it faced, and reflected the "marvelous" world of its myths. What the truth is for any particular group or person, then, is simply the value system within which each functions, which implies the existence of a plurality of truths and worldviews. As Veyne puts it:

> This [kind of] truth is the child of the imagination. The authenticity of our belief is not measured according to the truth of their object. Again we must understand the reason, which is a simple one: it is we who fabricate our truths, and it is not "reality" that makes us believe. For "reality" is the child of the constitutive imagination of our tribe.[54]

I agree with much of Veyne's analysis here: the plurality of truths in effect amount to comprehensive worldviews that embody the aims, objectives, goals, values of society/tribe/culture, and as such are subjective, imaginative constructs rather than discoveries of worlds of value existing independent of human thought. From the perspective of Ionian-type thinkers, of course, these truths do not amount to knowledge, although they are believed by the unsophisticated members of these societies, and in their framework such beliefs constitute knowledge—*for them*. But those beliefs do not amount to knowledge for the sophisticated members of society for, as Veyne notes, "[t]ruth is the name we give to choices to which we cling";[55] these are commitments to live by—*as if* these affirmations (beliefs) reflected the world as it is in itself. The notions of "true" or "false" do not apply to them.

---

52. Veyne, *Did the Greeks Believe*, 56–7.
53. Veyne, *Did the Greeks Believe*, 54.
54. Veyne, *Did the Greeks Believe*, 113.
55. Veyne, *Did the Greeks Believe*, 127.

Where I disagree with Veyne over this matter is that he talks of "scientific truth" as indistinguishable from the "imaginative" truths of myth and religion, maintaining that science itself is a myth (a truth). As he puts it:

> Science finds no truths, either mathematicized or formalized; it discovers unknown facts that can be interpreted in a thousand ways … Sciences are no more serious than the humanities, and since, in history, facts are not separable from interpretation and one can imagine all the interpretations one wishes, the same must be true in the exact sciences.[56]

Veyne, therefore, is unaware that science-like thinking—and the proto-scientific thinking of the Milesians—is not concerned with moral value and meaning. He fails to see that such thinking *values* only knowledge for the sake of knowledge alone, which engages one only in making justified empirical or theoretic propositional claims about the world or states of affairs in the natural and social worlds—that is, epistemic claims open to debate and criticism—and not with value or meaning (though knowledge for its own sake is a value). There is, moreover, a clear distinction between "scientific knowing" and "mythic belief" in that only the former is committed to the discovery of, and ongoing accumulation of, intersubjective knowledge about the world and events in it, while the latter is a (subjective) product of the collective imagination of the community that "discovers" (that is, creates) values that make possible a cooperative and meaningful existence for its members and ensures society's continued existence.

Contra Veyne, then, what is new in the "Milesian revolution" or the "Ionian Enlightenment" as many have referred to the philosophy of the presocratics, is the implicit distinction between belief and knowledge which is ultimately responsible for the (likely unintended) creation of the new cultural value of knowledge for the sake of knowledge alone. Veyne's account of the existence of an intellectual elite in ancient Greece, too sophisticated to take the stories of the gods in Homer and Hesiod at face value yet convinced of the existence of a divine, supernatural reality and of its value to society, is beyond question. However, that sophisticated belief in the supernatural is no more open to critical discussion and debate characteristic of the work of the Milesian and other Ionian cosmologists than are the mythic beliefs of the ordinary ancient Greek citizen because, as Veyne argues, those beliefs were not mere propositional claims (knowledge) about the world or states of affairs in the world that could be either true or false. They were instead moral truths about the meaning of human existence intuited (created) by the human imagination that reason cannot adequately explain or understand. But in being beyond critical rational examination and analysis

56. Veyne, *Did the Greeks Believe*, 115.

these truths, like the mythic accounts of the gods in Homer and Hesiod, would eventually be ignored by those thinkers seeking a naturalistic explanation of the world.

The transition in understanding of "knowledge" as beliefs that are open to rational criticism and assessment—and therefore potentially either true or false—that lay implicit in the thought of the presocratic cosmologists, therefore, amounts to possession of what classicist Henk Versnel refers to as "low intensity" beliefs (*assensus, fides*), that is, belief simply as holding a thing to be true even if it has not been fully demonstrated and is not therefore beyond falsification at some point in the future. Versnel contrasts that sort of belief with what he calls "high intensity" belief (*fiducia*), that is, belief that involves not only a cognitive conviction (certitude without certainty) but also commitment or trust.[57] The rationally supported low-intensity beliefs of the presocratic cosmologists, therefore, stand in radical contrast with the indisputably high-intensity beliefs ("truths") about the gods and the meaning of life vouchsafed to people either by way of revelation or intuition. It is the emergence of this new conception of knowledge as justified belief, obtained by way of reliance on unaided (autonomous) reason, that constitutes a "critical episode" in the development of human thought essential to the eventual emergence of science as we understand it today.

Ancient Greek Philosophy and the Historians

Just as the cosmologists were interested in the subject of change in the natural world, the early Greek historians were interested in accounting for changes that occur in the activities of human communities. Torrey Luce, Professor of Classics at Princeton, points to the influence of the work of the Ionian cosmologists—although not in any immediate or direct way—as a particularly important influence on the rise of history as a new genre of literature capable of "standing on its own and with a character and premises special to it."[58] He writes:

> Another important influence on the birth of history, in addition to Homer, was philosophy. The first philosophers, known as Pre-Socratics ... most of whom are preserved in fragments quoted in later writers, began to look at the world in a new spirit, rejecting simple acceptance of traditional beliefs (the "inherited conglomerate") in favor of critical inquiry and creative explanations.[59]

57. See Henk S. Versnel, *Coping with the Gods: Wayward Readings in Greek Theology* (Leiden: Brill, 2011), 539–59.

58. Torrey J. Luce, *The Greek Historians* (London: Routledge, 1997), 2.

59. Luce, *Greek Historians*, 7.

A number of histories of the origin and development of the study of religion suggest that we might find its origin in Herodotus (480–430 BCE). In some sense that is true—Herodotus took interest in a wide range of habits, customs, and religions of a number of the dozens of nations he visited in his travels, including, for example, those of the Assyrians, Babylonians, Egyptians, and various Greek city-states. In looking at the Babylonians, for example, he describes their religious practice of requiring every woman in the country having "once in her lifetime [to] go to the temple of Aphrodite and sit there and be lain with by a strange man" as one of the ugliest and most shameful among nations (*Histories* 1.199). In discussing the customs of the Egyptians, he claims that they are the exact opposite of that of other nations noting, for example, their reverence for the gods is excessive but that women are not dedicated to any god, male or female, while men are dedicated to all gods and goddesses. And of particular interest for Herodotus is the Egyptian acknowledgement of Heracles "as one of the twelve gods," as well as their lack of knowledge of the Heracles that the Greeks knew. These few instances, of course, do not make Herodotus a comparative religionist or historian of religion, but they do show that he is not so deeply entrenched in Greek life that he is simply taking the stories at face value. His *Histories*, therefore, constitute a radically different genre of literature that, as historian Moses Finley puts it, systematically questioned "the supposedly known facts … in rational, human form."[60] He, like the Ionian cosmologists before him, had an open mindedness about the gods and was willing to examine and debate their nature and history. In a sense, therefore, it is not inappropriate to suggest that just as the cosmologists engaged in a kind of proto-scientific work—as did the authors of the Hippocratic Corpus—Herodotus is also a kind of proto-historian of religions.[61]

Biographical Note

Donald Wiebe is Professor of Philosophy of Religion at Trinity College in the University of Toronto, Canada. His primary areas of research interest are philosophy of the social sciences, epistemology, philosophy of religion, the history of the academic and scientific study of religion, and method and theory in the study of religion. He is the author of *Religion and Truth: Towards an Alternative Paradigm for the Study of Religion* (Walter de Gruyter, 1981), *The Irony of Theology and the Nature of Religious Thought* (McGill-Queen's

---

60. Moses I. Finley, *The Portable Greek Historians* (New York: Viking Penguin, 1959), 2.

61. Cf. the discussion on Herodotus in Chapter 7, this volume.

University Press, 1991), *Beyond Legitimation: Essays on the Problem of Religious Knowledge* (Palgrave Macmillan, 1994), *The Politics of Religious Studies: The Continuing Conflict with Theology in the Academy* (Palgrave Macmillan, 1999), *Conversations and Controversies in the Scientific Study of Religion* (with L. H. Martin; Brill, 2016) and *The Science of Religion: A Defence* (Brill, 2019). He is a founding member of the North American Association for the Study of Religion, and served as President of that Association twice (1986–1987; 1991–1992).

Bibliography

Bremmer, Jan N. "Atheism in Antiquity," 11–26 in *The Cambridge Companion to Atheism*. Edited by Michael Martin. Cambridge: Cambridge University Press, 2007.

Cohen, H. Floris. *The Scientific Revolution: A Historiographical Inquiry*. Chicago, IL: University of Chicago Press, 1994.

Cornford, Francis MacDonald. *Before and After Socrates*. Cambridge: Cambridge University Press, 1965 [1932].

de Vries, Jan. *The Study of Religion: A Historical Approach*. New York: Harcourt, Brace & World, 1967.

Dodds, E. R. *The Greeks and the Irrational*. Berkeley, CA: University of California Press, 1951.

Feynman, Richard P. *The Meaning of It All*. New York: Basic Books, 1998.

Farrington, Benjamin. *Science in Antiquity*. London: Thornton Butterworth, 1936.

—*Greek Science (Thales to Aristotle): Its Meaning for Us*. Harmondsworth, UK: Penguin, 1944.

—*Science and Politics in the Ancient World*. London: George Allen & Unwin, 1946.

Finley, Moses I. *The Portable Greek Historians*. New York: Viking Penguin, 1959.

Frede, Michael. "The Philosopher," 3–19 in *Greek Thought: A Guide to Classical Knowledge*. Edited by Jacques Brunschwig and Geoffrey E. R. Lloyd. Cambridge, MA: Harvard University Press, 1996.

Gellner, Ernest. "The Savage and the Modern Mind," 162–81 in *Modes of Thought: Essays on Thinking in Western and Non-Western Societies*. Edited by Robin Horton and Ruth Finnegan. London: Faber & Faber, 1973.

Graham, Daniel. *The Texts of Early Greek Philosophy: The Complete Fragments and Selected Testimonies of the Major Presocratics*. Vol. 1. Cambridge: Cambridge University Press, 2010.

Guthrie, W. K. C. *The Greek Philosophers: From Thales to Aristotle*. London: Methuen, 1950.

—*The Greeks and Their Gods*. Boston, MA: Beacon Press, 1950.

Hahn, Robert. *Archaeology and the Origins of Philosophy*. Albany, NY: State University of New York Press, 2010.

Jaeger, Werner. *The Theology of the Early Greek Philosophers*. Oxford: Clarendon Press, 1947.

Kirk, Geoffrey S., John E. Raven, and Malcolm Schofield. *The Presocratic Philosophers: A Critical History with a Selection of Texts*. Cambridge: Cambridge University Press, 1983.

Lloyd, Geoffrey E. R. *Magic, Reason, and Experience: Studies in the Origins and Development of Greek Science*. Cambridge: Cambridge University Press, 1979.

—*Demystifying Mentalities*. Cambridge: Cambridge University Press, 1990. https://doi.org/10.1017/CBO9780511607691

—*Ancient Worlds, Modern Reflections: Philosophical Perspective on Greek and Chinese Science and Culture*. Oxford: Oxford University Press, 2004. https://doi.org/10.1093/0199270163.001.0001

Luce, Torrey J. *The Greek Historians*. London: Routledge, 1997. https://doi.org/10.4324/9780203299043

McKirahan, Richard D., Jr. *Philosophy Before Socrates: An Introduction with Texts and Commentary*. Indianapolis, IN: Hackett, 1994.

Murray, Gilbert. "Prolegomena to the Study of Ancient Philosophy," 65–86 in *Greek Studies*. Oxford: Clarendon Press, 1946.

Popper, Karl R. *Conjectures and Refutations: The Growth of Scientific Knowledge*. New York: Harper & Row, 1965.

Sedley, David. *Creationism and Its Critics in Antiquity*. Los Angeles, CA: University of California Press, 2007.

Thrower, James. *Western Atheism: A Short History*. Amherst, NY: Prometheus Books, 2000.

Vernant, Jean-Pierre. *Myth and Thought Among the Greeks*. Translated by Janet Lloyd and Jeff Fort. London: Routledge & Kegan Paul, 1983.

Versnel, Henk S. *Coping with the Gods: Wayward Readings in Greek Theology*. Leiden: Brill, 2011. https://doi.org/10.1163/ej.9789004204904.i-594

Veyne, Paul. *Did the Greeks Believe in Their Myths? An Essay on the Constitutive Imagination*. Translated by Paula Wissing. Chicago, IL: University of Chicago Press, 1988.

Whitmarsh, Tim. *Battling the Gods: Atheism in the Ancient World*. New York: Alfred A. Knopf, 2015.

Wooton, David. *The Invention of Science: A New History of the Scientific Revolution*. New York: Harper, 2015.

Chapter Six

Impiety and Versions of Rationalization of Religion in Classical Greece

Emese Mogyoródi

Greek religion was predominantly a matter of orthopraxy, compliance with cult and rituals prescribed by custom rather than orthodoxy, beliefs, or convictions about matters divine.[1] Hence, as long as they observed customs (*ta patria, ta nomizomena*), there was a relatively broad field of "freedom of thought" for intellectuals to voice what might be called today "heretic" or "unorthodox" ideas about or a critique of the gods in ancient Greece.[2] A straightforward assertion of atheism,[3] however, was definitely "a risky thesis to embrace"[4] and other unorthodox views were also suspect, especially around the last third of the fifth century, when due to some traumatic political and social events in Athens, religious sensitivity tended to be delicate.[5] *Asebeia* ("impiety") trials relevant to sacrilege or of presumable political motivations set aside,[6] three significant theories have come down to us

---

1.   As will be made clear below, I do not share Fontenelle's perspective, who characterized the Greeks' religious attitude as follows: "Faites comme les autres, et croyez ce qu' il vous plaira"; quoted in and discussed critically by Robert Parker, *On Greek Religion* (Ithaca, NY: Cornell University Press, 2011), 64ff.

2.   "Heretic" and "unorthodox" must be taken *cum grano salis*, since, as it is well known, in Greek polis religion there were no sacred scriptures or church authorities to prescribe religious creed. On this, see Parker, *Greek Religion*, 19–133.

3.   The adjective ἄθεος had a broader scope of meaning for the Greeks than its modern equivalent, "atheism." Apart from the explicit denial of the existence of gods, it also included acts of sacrilege (any kind of violation or repudiation of cult practice, the mysteries, sanctuaries, etc.) or repudiation of popular conceptions of gods. To avoid anachronism, "atheism" throughout this chapter refers to the denial of the existence of gods, whereas "impiety/impious" or "unorthodox" refer to unconventional views about the gods or the divine.

4.   David Sedley, *Creationism and Its Critics in Antiquity* (Berkeley, CA: University of California Press, 2013), 150.

5.   On this see, e.g., Martin Ostwald, *From Popular Sovereignty to the Sovereignty of Law: Law, Society and Politics in Fifth-Century Athens* (Berkeley, CA: University of California Press, 1987), esp. 528–36; Robert Parker, *Athenian Religion: A History* (Oxford: Clarendon Press, 1996), 199–217.

6.   Although he was notoriously labeled ἄθεος in his lifetime, Diagoras of Melos

from fifth-century Greece that provoked religious sentiment to the extent of being labelled "atheist": Protagoras's profession of ignorance with regard to the existence (and the nature) of gods; Prodicus's theory about the rise of belief in gods; and a different explanation to the same effect by the author (Critias or Euripides) of the *Sisyphus*.[7] These theories and their contrasts with earlier philosophical accounts of the divine are the subject of this essay.[8]

Why did these theories pose a challenge for traditional religious sensibility in the classical era? There have been numerous divergent answers to this apparently simple question, but none have gained unanimous currency. A general interpretative framework, however, remains largely prevalent to date: the novel way of thinking about the world—gods and humans included—initiated by some *sophoi* (later to be called *philosophoi*) in sixth-century Ionia inevitably led to an anti-religious outlook in the fifth century, an outlook that was countered by Plato's conservative reform in the fourth century. Thus, in the fifth century *mythos* eventually gave in to *logos* as a result of the collective effort, as it were, of the presocratic

was outlawed for mocking the mysteries; see Kenneth Dover, "Freedom of the Intellectual in Greek Society," *Talanta* 7 (1976): esp. 26–7; David Sedley, "The Atheist Underground," in *Politeia in Greek and Roman Philosophy* (ed. Verity Harte and Melissa Lane; Cambridge: Cambridge University Press, 2015), 331. The evidence for a trial against Anaxagoras is highly debated—compare the contrasting views of Dover, "Freedom," 31–2, and Ostwald, *Popular Sovereignty*, 196 and n. 73—but interpreters largely agree that, if there was a trial, it was motivated by political maneuvering against Pericles (see, e.g., Ostwald, *Popular Sovereignty*, 196, 257). Because of the complexity of Anaxagoras's tenets, save for a few references, his discussion is beyond the limitations of this chapter.

7.   On the Epicurean list of atheists (Prodicus, Diagoras, Critias), see Sedley, "Atheist Underground," 329–32, who notes the probability that Protagoras was also on the list. Cf. Ostwald, *Popular Sovereignty*, 274–5.

8.   In principle, Democritus should also be included, because he similarly proposed theories about the rise of belief in gods (DK 68 B 30, A 75). However, since it is not even clear whether or not he was considered an atheist by his contemporaries—see, S. Y. Luria, *Democritus: Texts, Translation, Investigations* (trans. C. C. W. Taylor, online: http://oxford.academia.edu/ChristopherTaylor), 395, *contra* Christopher C. W. Taylor, *The Atomists: Leucippus and Democritus. Fragments. A Text and Translation with a Commentary* (Toronto: University of Toronto Press, 1999), 211–5—and because his conception of gods as "images" (DK 68 B 166, A 74, A 77) is highly debated, his discussion is beyond the scope of the current chapter. The conclusions proposed might nonetheless be relevant to a clarification of the issue of Democritus's unorthodoxy. Unless otherwise noted, texts by the presocratics and the Sophists are quoted or referred to from Hermann Diels and Walther Kranz, *Die Fragmente der Vorsokratiker* (6th ed.; Zürich: Weidmann, 1951), Vols. 1–3 (DK) by the standard notation.

philosophers,[9] while Plato made a novel attempt to reinstate the religious outlook, much to the detriment of science.[10]

For the past couple of decades this somewhat gross and one-sided general framework has undergone considerable modification. It has been argued that although the explanations and theories of the early Greek philosophers about the world certainly contributed to the advancement of the mathematical and physical sciences, it is misleading to project onto their oeuvre a modern, "hard-line scientism"[11] with its strong emphasis on empiricism, naturalism, or materialism. Following this proviso is the suggestion that it is similarly misleading to attribute to them the modern notion of a stark contrast—let alone animosity—between reason and religion.[12] From this perspective, the story of the rise of theories that compromised traditional Greek piety in the classical era needs adjustment. It can no longer be taken for granted that the philosophical efforts of the early Greek philosophers from Thales through Parmenides to Anaxagoras were all aiming at a single *telos* culminating in atomism, a system of thought that finally got rid of all supernatural agency or causation at work in nature.[13]

9.   Although more nuanced than earlier studies that assumed a stark contrast of *mythos* and *logos*, the recent study by Tim Whitmarsh, *Battling the Gods: Atheism in the Ancient World* (New York: Alfred A. Knopf, 2016) is a good example for the prevalence of projecting onto presocratic philosophy patterns of thought characteristic of eighteenth-century Enlightenment with its materialistic and atheistic tendencies (see, esp. 100–14).

10.   See the summary of an account along these lines in Sedley, *Creationism*, 2.

11.   Robin Waterfield, "Introduction," in *The First Philosophers: The Presocratics and the Sophists* (Oxford: Oxford University Press, 2000), 24.

12.   See the pioneering work by Werner Jaeger, *The Theology of the Early Greek Philosophers* (Oxford: Oxford University Press, 1967), which found relatively slow followers, such as: P. A. Meijer, "Philosophers, Intellectuals and Religion in Hellas," in *Faith, Hope, and Worship: Aspects of Religious Mentality* (ed. Henk S. Versnel; Leiden: E. J. Brill, 1981), 227; Charles H. Kahn, "Greek Religion and Philosophy in the *Sisyphus* Fragment," *Phronesis* 42.3 (1997): 250–1; Glenn W. Most, "Philosophy and Religion," in *The Cambridge Companion to Greek and Roman Philosophy* (ed. David Sedley; Cambridge: Cambridge University Press, 2003), 307; George Boys-Stones, "Ancient Philosophy of Religion: An Introduction," in *The History of Western Philosophy of Religion.* Vol. 1: *Ancient Philosophy of Religion* (ed. Graham Oppy and Nick Trakakis; Durham, UK: Acumen, 2009), 1–6; David Sedley, "From the Pre-Socratics to the Hellenistic Age," in *The Oxford Handbook of Atheism* (ed. Stephen Bullivant and Michael Ruse; Oxford: Oxford University Press, 2013), 140. For a delicately balanced view of the relation of myth and science in early Greek thought, see Edward Hussey, "Ionian Inquiries: On Understanding the Presocratic Beginnings of Science," in *The Greek World* (ed. Anton Powell; London: Routledge, 1995), 530–49.

13.   See John Burnet, *Early Greek Philosophy* (London: Adam & Charles Black, 1892), 334, whose conception of a radical break between myth and science (cf. p. 3)

It is clear, however, that what came to be called the "Greek Enlighten-ment" was initiated by the presocratic philosophers, and that their novel way of speculating about the gods or the divine as well as their critique of religious conceptions did contribute to what might be broadly conceived of as a *rationalization* of religion. However, if it might be conceded that the presocratics were not unanimously working toward rationalizing religious conceptions *away*, but sought to make them compatible with the chang-ing social realities of the time and with the new framework of explanations provided by *historiê*, then it is expedient to address the issue of the differ-ences between theories that provided a rationalization within a fundamen-tally religious paradigm—as well as those that went along with it too far for Greek piety to tolerate. The main objective of this chapter is to discuss these differences through contrasting theorizing about the gods and religion around the last third of the fifth century with earlier attempts on the rational-ization of the divine that, despite their novel perspective of scientific con-cerns, did not compromise the religious paradigm. My argument is that the explanation for stronger religious sentiments against philosophical theories in the last third of the fifth century is not that the Greeks were the ancient forerunners of "freedom of thought" who, around the last third of the fifth century, lost their tolerant attitude, but that there were significant differ-ences between earlier presocratic speculations about the divine and later theories that rationalized them away.

Interpreters in favor of the view that assumes continuity rather than opposition between the mythical and the philosophical worldviews seek an explanation for the rise of unorthodox ideas in a development that was determined by historical, political, and social-psychological rather than purely philosophical-historical or intellectual factors. The latter might be summed up as culminating in what has been called the sophistic "antino-mian individualism," which typically promoted *phusis* in the *nomos* ("law, convention") versus *phusis* ("nature") debate.[14] If atheism is not a congenial development within philosophy, then this suggestion is historically plausi-ble and theoretically cogent. However, the link between scientific theories and sophistic antinomianism has not become entirely clear. Indeed, Robert

has been highly influential in the English-speaking world. For a similar recent account of the history of early Greek thought (with atomism as its denouement), see Daniel W. Graham, *Explaining the Cosmos: The Ionian Tradition of Scientific Philosophy* (Prince-ton, NJ: Princeton University Press, 2006), esp. 276.

14. See, e.g., Charles H. Kahn, "The Origins of Social Contract Theory," in *The Sophists and Their Legacy* (ed. George B. Kerferd; Wiesbaden: Franz Steiner Verlag, 1981), 92–108, and Kahn, "Greek Religion and Philosophy"; Parker, *Athenian Religion*, 212–3; Sedley, "Pre-Socratics to the Hellenistic Age."

Parker skeptically concludes that "it is impossible ... to fill in the details of the alliance between a scientific determinism that was pushed to an atheistic extreme and sophistic antinomianism."[15] I believe there is no reason for a skeptical conclusion if we consider that while certain cosmological or cultural historical views proposed by the presocratics were adopted by theoreticians under sophistic influence, they underwent considerable alterations. The contrast must be better clarified because, while identifying reasons for the rise of atheism without directly deriving them from presocratic thought, interpreters of early Greek philosophy nonetheless assume too much congruity with regard to religious matters between earlier presocratics and thinkers of the fifth century whose speculations proved intolerable from a pious perspective. It has been suggested, for example, that it was the relatively low status of gods (notably, that they were not creators and, as part of nature or causal forces, were compatible with materiality) in early Greek thought that precluded atheism to develop directly from philosophy.[16] In terms of its theoretical implications, this approach might ultimately yield what I think is a misleading conclusion; namely, that in so far as there was a theological strain underlying the history of presocratic thought, its objective was to "naturalize the divine" and make it entirely subject to "lawlike behavior."[17] In polar contrast, it has been argued that it was the highly sublime or detached nature of the gods of the presocratic philosophers (Anaximander's *Apeiron*; Heraclitus's *Logos*; Xenophanes's *Theos*; Anaxagoras's *Nous*) that contributed to the rise of atheism, since by dividing the natural and the supernatural, they made it easy to ignore the latter.[18] So, what was the status of gods or the divine in presocratic cosmologies that remained compatible with the religious paradigm? Another general issue that has not become sufficiently clear is how much the criticism of some early Greek

15. Parker, *Athenian Religion*, 213.
16. See Meijer, "Philosophers, Intellectuals," 224–8; cf. Simon Trépanier, "Early Greek Theology: God as Nature and Natural Gods," in *The Gods of Ancient Greece: Identities and Transformations* (ed. Jan N. Bremmer and Andrew Erskine; Edinburgh, UK: Edinburgh University Press, 2010), 276; Sedley, "Pre-Socratics to the Hellenistic Age," 140.
17. Daniel W. Graham, "The Theology of Nature in the Ionian Tradition," *Rhizomata* 1.2 (2013): 215. Hence, Graham suggests that Ionian philosophy must be understood as "theology of nature" (rather than natural theology). Similarly, Gregory Vlastos, "Theology and Philosophy in Early Greek Thought," *Philosophical Quarterly* 2 (1952): 97–123; cf. also Kahn, "Greek Religion and Philosophy," 253, where the theology of the early Greek philosophers is characterized as "a flexible polytheistic version of Spinoza's *deus sive natura*." See also Parker, *Athenian Religion*, 211–2.
18. See Adam Drozdek, *Greek Philosophers as Theologians: The Divine Arche* (Aldershot, UK: Ashgate, 2007), 119.

philosophers of the gods of traditional myth, or their skeptical tone with regard to their knowability, differs from a *critique of religion* or religious agnosticism.[19] So, how far do theories of sophistic provenance reaffirm or subvert traditional piety?

It might be tempting to conclude that the ultimate explanation for the provocative nature of these theories is that they belong to the sort of disillusioning explanations of religion, the ultimate rationale of which is the elimination of religious conceptions, such as those offered much later by Karl Marx or Sigmund Freud. If the rise of religious beliefs was felt by some to be in need of explanation (by Prodicus, Democritus, and the author of the *Sisyphus*), or the existence of gods as non-evident (by Protagoras), that suggests that the belief in gods was no longer considered natural of primordial, after all.[20] This restrained approach itself might well have provided some reason for concern to contemporary believers; but I do not think it would have sufficed to raise disapproval unless they exhibited other features believers found objectionable. In what follows I suggest that these other features partly concern the ontological status or nature of the gods, which in theories of religion is naturalistic and reductionist, and that this conception might fundamentally be contrasted with some earlier presocratic speculations about the divine or divinity. The second aspect of these theories, I propose, that played a part in considering them unorthodox has to do with their views about the human-divine relationship, a vital but rarely discussed aspect of Greek piety. For it is not by chance that, in considering other forms of impiety beyond the denial of the gods' existence, Plato enlists two beliefs, both of which concern the divine-human relationship: the first is that the gods do not care for us; the second that they can be bought off by sacrifice and prayer (*Laws* 885b). The belief about what the gods are like qualifies people's piety through determining their attitude towards the gods as well as their behavior towards their fellow humans. In the *polis* religious impiety was a social concern because it affected the community, after all.

---

19. See Jan N. Bremmer, "Atheism in Antiquity," in *The Cambridge Companion to Atheism* (ed. Michael Martin; Cambridge: Cambridge University Press, 2007), 19: "The increasing criticism of the gods by philosophers and poets had eroded the traditional beliefs in gods, and some intellectuals drew the inevitable consequence." For warnings against identifying constructive and destructive critiques of religion, see Boys-Stones, "Ancient Philosophy of Religion," 3; Nickolas P. Roubekas, "Ancient Greek Atheism? A Note on Terminological Anachronism in the Study of Ancient Greek 'Religion'," *Revista Ciências da Religião* 12.2 (2014): esp. 230. This fundamental distinction is blurred by the central conception of Whitmarsh, *Battling the Gods*.

20. See Parker, *Athenian Religion*, 213 n. 56 (on Prodicus's theory of the origins of religious beliefs).

Protagoras

Ancient sources report that Protagoras asserted ignorance regarding the existence of gods in a work entitled *About the Gods*:

> DK 80 B 4: Eusebius, *Praeparatio Evangelica* xiv.3.7.3-4
> Περὶ μὲν θεῶν οὐκ οἶδα οὔθ᾽ ὡς εἰσὶν οὔθ᾽ ὡς οὐκ εἰσὶν οὔθ᾽ ὁποῖοί τινες ἰδέαν.
> As to the gods I do not know whether they exist or not, nor what sort of form they might have.

> Diogenes Laertius IX.51.8-52.1
> περὶ μὲν θεῶν οὐκ ἔχω εἰδέναι οὔθ᾽ ὡς εἰσίν, οὔθ᾽ ὡς οὐκ εἰσίν· πολλὰ γὰρ τὰ κωλύοντα εἰδέναι, ἥ τ᾽ ἀδηλότης καὶ βραχὺς ὢν ὁ βίος τοῦ ἀνθρώπου.
> As to the gods, I am unable to know whether they exist or not; for the obstacles are many, such as the obscurity of the matter (*or* of the gods) and the brevity of human life.[21]

Although Diogenes of Oenoanda (DK 80 A 23) concludes that "this comes down to asserting that he knows that they do not exist" (τοῦτο δ᾽ ἐστὶν τὸ αὐτὸ τῶι λέγειν εἰδέναι ὅτι μὴ εἰσίν), he is obviously mistaken. As many have noted, this is not an atheist but an agnostic or skeptical thesis, the first one of its kind that has come down to us from antiquity.[22] It is puzzling for two main reasons. First, given that it does not assert nor even imply the non-existence of the gods, does it gives us any hint that it would give rise to concern in the context of traditional Greek religion at all? Second, how could or should its justification be interpreted? As to the first question, it might be noted that the assertion is made in the first person singular and hence it does not claim universal scope. This attenuates its poignancy and makes it even more puzzling with regard to its purported atheism. In order to realize the acuteness of the problem, consider the following: Protagoras's agnosticism might be interpreted as an assertion of a widely-held belief of pious implications, notably, of human ignorance vis-à-vis the nature of the gods or compared with divine knowledge. Xenophanes, for example, was similarly wary of epistemic certainty about the gods (and nature) while emphasizing the dissimilarity of God and humans, which explains his skepticism and suggests that he may well have believed that God is beyond representation or comparison:

---

21.   For various other paraphrases, see DK 80 A 2 (Philostratus); A 3 (Hesychius); A 12 (Sextus); A 23 (Plato, Cicero, Philodemus, Diogenes of Oenoanda). Unless otherwise noted, all translations are my own.

22.   E.g., Drozdek, *Greek Philosophers as Theologians*, 109; Boys-Stones, "Ancient Philosophy of Religion," 7.

B 34 Sextus, *Adversus mathematicos* 7.49.110
... and of course the clear and certain truth (τὸ ... σαφὲς) no man has seen nor will there be anyone who knows about the gods (ἀμφὶ θεῶν) and what I say about all things.
For even if, in the best case, one happened to speak just of what has been brought to pass (τετελεσμένον), still he himself would not know. But opinion is allotted to all (δόκος δ᾽ ἐπὶ πᾶσι τέτυκται).[23]

B 23 Clement, *Miscellanies* 5.109
One god (is) (εἷς θεὸς) greatest (μέγιστος) among gods and men,
not at all like mortals in body (δέμας) or in thought (νόημα) [...].[24]

So, what is the difference from Protagoras, if any? This is where a clarification of Protagoras's odd justification for his proclamation might be helpful. Discussing Protagoras in the larger context of the sophistic turn vis-à-vis presocratic thought—and especially Parmenides, "the philosopher as a new existential type"[25]—Eric Voegelin puts his finger on a vital change in perspective that he calls "the radical immanentism" of "sophistic thinking in the technical sense."[26] He suggests that this new attitude is fully developed in Protagoras in conjunction to his notorious "man is the measure" principle (DK 80 B 1):

Of his work *On Truth* the famous opening sentence is preserved:
Of all things the measure is man, of being that they are, of the not being that they are not (B 1).
The Parmenidean correlation between Nous-Logos and Being becomes the correlation between man and immanent things; the autonomy of the Logos in exploring the Truth about transcendent Being has become the autonomy of man in exploring his surrounding world. The consequences of this radical immanentism, as far as problems of transcendence are concerned, become tangible in the opening sentence of Protagoras' work *On the Gods* [B 4 ...]. The sentence does not express dogmatic atheism but rather a suspense of judgement concerning the existence of gods. This is the form in which the problem of transcendence will present itself to an immanentist who has no experience of transcendence, provided that his intellectual discipline will

23. Translation drawn from James H. Lesher, *Xenophanes of Colophon: Fragments. A Text and Translation with a Commentary* (Toronto: University of Toronto Press, 1992), 39.
24. Translation drawn from Lesher, *Xenophanes*, 31. Brackets have been added to indicate an ambiguity in the first verse of the fragment, notably, that it might be read as asserting that "one god" is "the greatest, etc." (as Lesher translates it), or as asserting something about "one greatest (etc.) god" in a missing third verse (following other enlisted qualifications of god contained in the fragment). On further possible readings of this debated fragment, see Lesher, *Xenophanes*, 96.
25. Eric Voegelin, *Order and History.* Vol. 2: *The World of the Polis* (Baton Rouge, LA: Louisiana State University Press, 1957), 292.
26. Voegelin, *Order and History*, 294.

prevent him from falling into dogmatic negation of divine existence. Nevertheless, the line of dogmatic derailment is indicated by the odd conclusion of the sentence which seems to assume that certainty in this obscure matter could be reached, presumably by immanent means, if life were longer. More impetuous sophists will find sooner or later that their life is long enough to arrive at a judgement, and it will be negative.[27]

Whether one approves or disapproves of the humanistic turn Voegelin himself censures as a "derailment," he is certainly correct in pointing out the inadequacy of seeking to give an account of the divine by immanent (anthropocentric) measures or means (i.e., in terms of human lifespan). Voegelin underlines the contrast between Protagoras's intellectual honesty and the "impetuousness" of the negative judgment of other sophists; nonetheless, his point is that the immanentist approach that first occurs in Protagoras is programmatic and in fundamental contrast with earlier presocratic thought. It would be injudicious to discuss Parmenides's views in the context of piety in such a brief chapter,[28] but we can opportunely contrast Protagoras on this score with Xenophanes and Heraclitus.

First, although by doing so, Xenophanes plainly contradicts his own skeptical assertion about the knowability of the gods, he nonetheless boldly proclaims theses about God that must have struck his contemporaries as radically new. After reflecting on the cultural differences of representations of gods, rather than promoting a suspension of judgment about them as Protagoras does, or the denial of the existence of any god as the *sophos* in the *Sisyphus*, Xenophanes emphatically asserts that God (the only God worthy of genuine worship) is beyond human likeness or comprehension—which, in turn, obviously implies his existence. This is certainly not a mere concession to religious tradition, but an attempt to reform or purify it, on pain of self-contradiction. Xenophanes is likely to have underlined divine sublimity or superiority in response to the erosion of civic morality that incited some to adduce the behavior of anthropomorphic gods for legitimizing human licentiousness,[29] or to cynically exploit the piety of others to one's own advantage.[30] By insisting on the utter dissimilarity of (the truly divine) God, Xenophanes sought to ward off any attempt to measure the Divinity

27. Voegelin, *Order and History*, 294–5.
28. Parmenides presents his metaphysical and natural philosophical views as revealed by a goddess (DK 28 B 1). Whether or not we should take the revelation motif seriously or metaphorically is one of the most debated issues of his oeuvre.
29. See Lesher, *Xenophanes*, 52–3 (with reference to *Republic* 378b and *Euthyphro* 6a).
30. James Warren, "Gods and Men in Xenophanes," in Harte and Lane, eds., *Politeia in Greek and Roman Philosophy*, 305–7 (on DK 22 A 14).

by precisely the sort of immanentist-anthropocentric perspective that Protagoras introduced into philosophical discourse. Hence, he set up a sharp division between the divine and the human and warned against the *impiety* of blurring the boundary between them.[31]

Heraclitus, on the other hand, does allow for a comparison between gods and humans; however, the comparison similarly serves to underscore divine superiority both in terms of knowledge (DK 22 B 78, B 79) and power (DK 22 B 41, B 64). And while Heraclitus uses language about gods and humans that would have outraged Xenophanes ("immortals are mortal, mortals immortal, living the others' death, dead in the others' life";[32] DK 22 B 62), it would be difficult to saddle him with the mistake that Xenophanes criticizes, notably, of impiously blurring the difference between them. Thus, however much Heraclitus and Xenophanes might differ in other respects in terms of their conceptions of the divinity, they both underline divine superiority vis-à-vis human knowledge, power, and dignity through stressing his/ its transcendence.[33]

Although Protagoras's agnostic stance seems at first sight to fit into the pious Greek tradition of stressing the contrast between gods and humans (especially in terms of knowledge), his "man is the measure" principle, which is curiously echoed both in the very formulation and the subjective implications of B 4 pointed out above, runs against traditional pious *eulabeia* ("caution").[34] Although the agnostic statement does not in itself express atheism, it suggests that such ideas were around, for it seems to have been formulated in response to them.[35] However, it does have its own implication of a denial of a general—one might even claim cosmological—import; notably, "a denial that religious language *adds* anything at all, that it *has*

31. See Warren, "Gods and Men," 300–5 (on DK 21 A 13).

32. Translation drawn from Charles H. Kahn, *The Art and Thought of Heraclitus* (Cambridge: Cambridge University Press, 1979), 71—similarly for all translations of all other fragments of Heraclitus quoted below.

33. On this see further below. It is important to note, however, that Heraclitus and Xenophanes differ significantly from poets of the Archaic age with their fear of divine *phthonos* ("jealousy") and profound sense of human *amêchaniê* ("helplessness")—on the latter, see E. R. Dodds, *The Greeks and the Irrational* (Berkeley, CA: University of California Press, 1951), 28–63. The cosmic theologies of the former are compatible both with traditional piety and the rising new humanism that eased the fears characteristic of the dismal theology of the Archaic age, which I consider as a hallmark of rationalization *within* religion.

34. On *eulabeia* as going closely with *eusebeia* in Greek religion, see Walter Burkert, *Greek Religion: Archaic and Classical* (trans. John Raffan; Oxford: Blackwell, 1985), 273.

35. See Sedley, "Pre-Socratics to the Hellenistic Age," 141.

meaningful content of its own. The universe will end up looking the same whether one calls its originative matter or structuring forces 'divine'."[36] In terms of the human-divine relationship, this stance implies an indifference of religious import: it is not that Protagoras would positively deny that the gods care for us (as one of the Platonic instances of impiety), but that he proclaims that he does not care whether they care for us or not. What is programmatic and significantly different from the stance of a Xenophanes or Heraclitus with regard to the nature or status of the divine in the world is the individual's *indifference* to the whole issue. Other sophists were not so indifferent, but for reasons other than piety.

Prodicus

From Prodicus we have one of the first fully-fledged "genealogies of religion" that has come down to us from antiquity. Apart from issues of language (mainly, synonymy) and religion, Prodicus was also preoccupied with cosmology and is hence one of those who refute the widely held view that the sophists radically broke with the presocratic tradition of natural philosophy. His most influential contribution to cultural history is his theory about the rise of beliefs in gods, in which he distinguished two stages: first, humans worshiped natural elements (such as the sun, moon, rivers) that were of use to them, that is, on which their existence depended; and then they divinized human benefactors whose inventions contributed to their sustenance:

> *PHerc* 1428 cols. ii 28-iii 13[37]
> It is clear that Persaeus indeed eliminates and does away with the divine or reveals his utter ignorance thereof when in his book, *About the gods*, he finds Prodicus's idea plausible, who wrote that the things that nourish and benefit us (τὰ τρέφοντα καὶ ὠφελοῦντα) were first considered and honored (νενομίσθαι καὶ τετειμῆσθαι) as gods, and then the discoverers or inventors of food, shelter and the other crafts, such as Demeter, Dionysus, and the Dioscuri.[38]

> DK 84 B 5: Sextus, *Adversus mathematicos* 9.18
> Prodicus of Ceos says, "The ancients considered (ἐνόμισαν) as gods the sun and moon, rivers, springs, and in general all the things that assist our life (τὰ ὠφελοῦντα τὸν βίον), on account of the help they give, just as the Egyptians (deify) the Nile." He adds that for this reason bread was called Demeter, wine

36. Boys-Stones, "Ancient Philosophy of Religion," 7 (emphasis in the original).

37. See Albert Henrichs, "Two Doxographical Notes: Democritus and Prodicus on Religion," *Harvard Studies in Classical Philology* 79 (1975): 116.

38. Cf. DK 84 B 5, where a shorter version of this text is included in an earlier edition by Gomperz. My translation is based on the edition by Henrichs, "Two Doxographical Notes."

Dionysus, water Poseidon, fire Hephaestus, and so on with everything that was of service.[39]

The language and the conception itself suggest that this theory was formulated in the purview of cultural, anthropological, and developmental theories about the transition from a natural human state to civilized society, a development which might also have included an interest in "first inventors." Religion itself is not an invention of some *sophos*, nor are the gods mere fictive artifacts as they are in the *Sisyphus*. Hence, it has been suggested that Prodicus did not mean to debunk religious conceptions, and that his theory did not imply the non-existence of gods; rather, he merely provided an explanation to the effect that "our early ancestors, in identifying crops with Demeter, were recognizing the manifestation of a genuinely divine power."[40] Although, in light of a papyrus found at Herculaneum (*PHerc* 1429 fr. 19) and attributed to Philodemus, the evidence that Prodicus openly declared himself an atheist can hardly be considered to be "poor,"[41] such a stance is indeed difficult to reconcile with the fact that both Plato and Xenophon treat him with respect. For the sake of the argument, then, let us put aside the late evidence for his impiety in the stronger sense of outright atheism and examine his theories in terms of unorthodoxy.

It is notable that the first stage of the development has strong affinities with Xenophanes's naturalistic explanations. Xenophanes reasoned that what was believed to be the goddess Iris was in reality just a colorful cloud in the sky (DK 21 B 32), and that the Dioscuri—the phenomenon called today St Elmo's fire—were an ignited cloud (DK 21 A 39). According to Prodicus, because their existence depended on them, people believed that the sun, the moon, and the rivers were gods—presumably out of gratitude; for *him*, however, these are obviously sheer natural phenomena, devoid of divine (supernatural) aspects.[42] This explanation not only implies a clear theoretical distinction of the natural and the supernatural by the author,

39. Translated by W. K. C. Guthrie, *The Sophists* (Cambridge: Cambridge University Press, 1971), 238. On the authenticity of the two-stage theory (*contra* Sextus's evidence at the end of the quoted passage), see Henrichs, "Two Doxographical Notes," 112 and 116–8.

40. Sedley, "Atheist Underground," 330.

41. Sedley, "Atheist Underground," 330. The papyrus runs: "[Prodicus] maintains that the gods of popular belief do not exist and that he does not recognize them (ὑπὸ τῶν ἀνθρώπων νομιζομένους θεοὺς οὔτ' εἶναι οὔτ εἰδέναι), but that primitive man, [out of admiration deified] the fruits of the earth and virtually everything that contributed to his subsistence" (*PHerc* 1429 fr. 19; text and translation by Henrichs, "Two Doxographical Notes," 107–8). For a detailed analysis of this text and arguments for Prodicus's atheism, see Henrichs, "Two Doxographical Notes," 108ff.

42. Cf. Guthrie, *Sophists*, 242; Christopher C. W. Taylor and Mi-Kyoung Lee, "The

but also strongly suggests that he himself did *not* share the beliefs of the ancients. This is supported especially by the second stage of the development of religious beliefs: whereas it makes some sense to assume that Prodicus meant that early people "recognized" what *he* also believed to be the manifestations of the divine in the sun, moon, and rivers, it is difficult to attribute to him the same belief about human benefactors or inventors.[43] If there ever was an *asebeia* trial against Anaxagoras, then it was because he similarly naturalized the sun—the god Helios—when he taught that it was a red-hot stone (λίθος) or ingot (μύδρος).[44] This theory is likely to have been taken as unorthodox and threatened religious sensibility, although Anaxagoras never explicitly denied the existence of gods.[45]

Prodicus's contrast with Xenophanes on this score is informative. It is true that Xenophanes naturalized (some of) the gods of popular religion, but his aim was to radically contrast a higher (more powerful, sublime, or venerable) God to the gods of traditional Greek myth.[46] And although this notion of God (with its monotheistic penchant) represented a considerable novelty in relation to traditional piety, Xenophanes believed that such a God might be worshiped by at least *some* form of ritual and—what may seem perhaps unexpected—even within the setting of a traditional cultic occasion, the symposium.[47]

While Heraclitus's notion of the divine is far more complex than—and in many respects different from—that of Xenophanes, nonetheless his way of rationalizing the religious tradition through his reflections on the divine can similarly be contrasted to the naturalism underlying Prodicus's theory. From some of his fragments it might occur that Heraclitus believed that the divine (or the deity)—especially if it is identified with fire as one of the

---

Sophists," *The Stanford Encyclopedia of Philosophy* (Fall 2015 Edition) (ed. Edward N. Zalta, online: http://plato.stanford.edu/archives/fall2015/entries/sophists/).

43. The two-stage theory is convincingly defended by Henrichs, "Two Doxographical Notes."

44. E.g., DK 46 A3, A12, A20a (λίθος); A1, A2, A19 (μύδρος).

45. Cf. Ostwald, *Popular Sovereignty*, 197; Parker, *Athenian Religion*, 209.

46. In his commentary to B5, Daniel Graham suggests that Prodicus "could have rejected traditional cults in favor of a more defensible religion, such as presented by Xenophanes" (ed., *The Texts of Early Greek Philosophy: The Complete Fragments and Selected Testimonies of the Major Presocratics* [Vol. 1; Cambridge: Cambridge University Press, 2010], 861). Such a "religion," however, could have been worthy of the name only if it assumed the existence of a more sublime god than those of traditional myth, as in Xenophanes. Had Prodicus proposed such a god, however, we would certainly have had some doxographical evidence for it.

47. See Emese Mogyoródi, "Xenophanes and the Rise of Theology in Early Greek Thought," *Philosophical Inquiry* 43.1–2 (2019): 11–6.

natural elements and/or with the *kosmos* (as cosmic Fire) as a whole—is
immanent in nature (intramundane):

> DK 22 B 67: Hippolytus, *Refutatio omnium haeresium* IX.10.8
> ὁ θεὸς ἡμέρη εὐφρόνη, χειμὼν θέρος, πόλεμος εἰρήνη, κόρος λιμός. ἀλλοιοῦται
> δὲ ὅκωσπερ ὁπόταν συμμιγῆι θυώμασιν, ὀνομάζεται καθ᾽ ἡδονὴν ἑκάστου.
> The god: day and night, winter and summer, war and peace, satiety and hun-
> ger. It alters, as when mingled with perfumes it gets named according to the
> pleasure of each one.[48]

> DK 22 B 30: Clement, *Stromata* V.103.6
> κόσμον τὸν αὐτὸν ἁπάντων, οὔτε τις θεῶν οὔτε ἀνθρώπων ἐποίησεν, ἀλλ᾽ ἦν
> ἀεὶ καὶ ἔστιν καὶ ἔσται πῦρ ἀείζωον, ἁπτόμενον μέτρα καὶ ἀποσβεννύμενον
> μέτρα.
> The ordering, the same for all, no god or man has made, but it ever was and is
> and will be: fire everliving, kindled in measures and in measures going out.[49]

Other fragments suggest, however, that this interpretation does not stand up
to scrutiny and that his conception of the divine is more refined:

> DK 22 B 32: Clement, *Stromata* V.115.1
> ἓν τὸ σοφὸν μοῦνον λέγεσθαι οὐκ ἐθέλει καὶ ἐθέλει Ζηνὸς ὄνομα.
> The wise is one alone, unwilling and willing to be spoken of by the name of
> Zeus.

> DK 22 B 108: Stobaeus III.1.174
> ὁκόσων λόγους ἤκουσα, οὐδεὶς ἀφικνεῖται ἐς τοῦτο, ὥστε γινώσκειν ὅ τι
> σοφόν ἐστι πάντων κεχωρισμένον.
> Of all those whose accounts I have heard, none has gone so far as this: to rec-
> ognize what is wise, set apart from all.[50]

Clearly, Fire as an aspect (manifestation? symbol?) of the divinity (among
other aspects, such as *to sophon*, *to xynon*, War, and *Logos*) is *not* identical
(consubstantial) with—and yet is obviously intrinsically related to—elemental (intracosmic) fire,[51] just as "the wise one" (B 41, B 32) is both willing and not willing to be called by the name of Zeus (B 108). Fire, then,
is and is not Zeus, and "the wise one," in turn, *is and is not* identical with
the *kosmos*. On a more general level, the divinity is both a principle of (or
manifested as) polar oppositions (B 67, B 80) and unity (B 41, B 114, B
106).[52] But the divine as "the one" (apparently, its most general conceptual expression or symbol) is both a *unity* of opposites (B 67, B 80) and

---

48. Texts, translations, and references are by Kahn, *Art and Thought of Heraclitus*
but fragment numbering is from DK.
49. Cf. DK 22 B 76, B 90.
50. Cf. DK 22 B 41, B 64, B 66, B 114.
51. On this, see Kahn, *Art and Thought of Heraclitus*, 23, 273.
52. Cf. Kahn, *Art and Thought of Heraclitus*, 277–8.

hence "common" to all (B 80, B 114), and "one" in the sense of *unique* on account of its being "alone" (B 32) and "set apart from all" (B 108). This adjective (κεχωρισμένον), unique in a presocratic text, may well be taken as the earliest expression for what is "transcendent," firstly in the literal spatial sense,[53] and secondly as signifying the metaphysical distinctness of what is other than (different from[54]) the physical. The divine in Heraclitus at the most abstract level is *coincidentia oppositorum*,[55] not merely in the sense of the unity of (intramundane) opposites, but also as the unity—but at the same time, conceptual *incompatibility*—of the immanent (constituted by opposites) and the transcendent (represented by "the one" as "set apart from all"). This paradoxical conception of the divinity in Heraclitus seems to be more traditional than that of Xenophanes with its monotheistic (or rather, henotheistic) theology.[56] For, if one might speak of traditional mythical theology in any meaningful sense, then what characterizes the Homeric conception of the divine is a paradoxical intertwining of what later came to be differentiated as the "natural" and the "supernatural." As Mircea Eliade suggested in his seminal study on the premodern (or what he generally calls "religious") worldview, although it is characterized by a fundamental distinction of the sacred and the profane, "a reality of a wholly different order from natural realities,"[57] nonetheless "for religious man nature is never only natural," and "the supernatural is indissolubly connected with the natural … nature always expresses something that transcends it."[58] This belief is characteristic of Greek religion, too, and was expressed by one of the first poets in Greece who speculated about the divine on a more abstract level by remarkable succinctness:

> Ζεύς ἐστιν αἰθήρ, Ζεὺς δὲ γῆ, Ζεὺς δ' οὐρανός,
> Ζεύς τοι τὰ πάντα χὤ τι τῶνδ' ὑπέρτερον.
> Zeus is *aithêr*, Zeus is earth, Zeus is *ouranos*,
> Zeus is indeed all, and whatever is beyond it all.

(Aeschylus fr. 70 Radt)[59]

53. As the perfect (passive) participle of χωρίζω ("separate, divide"), connected with χώρα ("space, room, place").

54. The sense of the passive (with genitive). For an interpretation along these lines, cf. Kahn, *Art and Thought of Heraclitus*, 115.

55. Cf. Meijer, "Philosophers, Intellectuals," 223.

56. See Mantas Adomenas, "Heraclitus on Religion," *Phronesis* 44.2 (1999): 87–113; Most, "Philosophy and Religion," 300–22.

57. Mircea Eliade, *The Sacred and the Profane: The Nature of Religion* (trans. Williard R. Trask; New York: Harcourt, Brace & World, 1959), 10.

58. Eliade, *Sacred and the Profane*, 151 and 117–8, respectively.

59. It is a riddle for me how Ulrich von Wilamowitz-Moellendorff, *Der Glaube der Hellenen* (Vol. 2; Berlin: Weidmannsche Buchhandlung, 1932), 133 n. 1, could have

Although it comes from a poet, this characterization of the highest divinity represents the sort of speculation that contributed to the process of rationalization *within* the traditional confines of Greek religion, whereby essential but theoretically latent or incoherent elements of religious beliefs are made articulate and compatible with the intellectual developments and language of *historiē* and/or the novel moral-religious (cooperative) values promoted within the changing social and historical circumstances. Albeit in their own different ways, Xenophanes and Heraclitus are both engaged in this enterprise in a more focused—and, in theoretical terms obviously more coherent—way than poets or most other presocratic thinkers. For his own practical purposes, Xenophanes underlines divine sublimity and transcendence; Heraclitus, as a more metaphysically inclined cosmologist, presents it as *coincidentia oppositorum* at two distinct levels, both in terms of opposites *within* the natural world and in terms of the polar contrast of the physical and the metaphysical. But neither Xenophanes nor Heraclitus conceive of the deity as reducible to the purely physical or immanent, and both highlight its/his inscrutability and superiority while warning against the hubris of thinking too highly about ourselves vis-à-vis the divine.

In contrast, the theoretical (and presumably emotional) personal detachment implied by Prodicus's genealogy of religion is expressed not merely in his theorizing about religious beliefs, but also in his conception of deities as (in reality) *merely* natural. As Christopher Taylor and Mi-Kyoung Lee succinctly put it, whereas the theologies of Xenophanes and Heraclitus are "naturalistic, but non-reductive," "in the fifth century the naturalistic approach to religion exhibits a more reductive aspect with a consequent move towards a world-view which is not merely naturalistic, but in the modern sense secular."[60] In Prodicus's theory the world is disenchanted and the gods are deprived of a mind-independent reality,[61] a conception that comes dangerously close to the theory voiced in the *Sisyphus*, where the belief in the gods is an illusion, albeit a "useful" one.

Another aspect of Prodicus's theory throws further light on "secularization." It was presumably due to his belief in progress and pride about

---

interpreted these lines as expressing "materialization of the divinity." The belief formulated ever so clearly by Aeschylus is fundamental to the Greeks' relation to their statues of gods that were believed to be "both matter and god" (Parker, *Greek Religion*, 15 n. 11).

60. Taylor and Lee, "Sophists"; similarly, Guthrie, *Sophists*, 242 (on Prodicus).

61. If for Prodicus bread and wine were mere physical substances, then the message is not that people "recognized" in them something that is "out there" (manifested in but not identical with them), but that they projected something onto them that only existed in their minds.

autonomous civilizational achievements—such as agriculture[62] and the crafts, that is, his "anthropocentric attitude"[63]—that played a central role in attributing to the ancients a deification of human benefactors. This is a special application of the immanentist-anthropocentric perspective of the Protagorean "man is the measure" principle. The second stage in the development of religious beliefs in Prodicus's theory reflects a way of thinking about humans that subjects them to an *apotheôsis*[64]—ironically a secular one. It was not the ancients who deified human inventors, but the secular interpreter of their beliefs, for whom humans were "divine" merely in a metaphorical sense since gods did not exist. The theory assumes a disenchanted mind seeking an explanation of a mentality that is alien to itself, by means of its own understanding, much like nineteenth-century secular-minded anthropologists.[65]

Finally, a further hallmark of the sophistic Enlightenment lying behind Prodicus's theory must be noted, namely, its spirit of "pragmatic utilitarianism."[66] It is not that Prodicus could be assumed to have held, as the *sophos* of the *Sisyphus* did, that, whatever its veracity, religion is socially beneficial and hence to be promoted. We do not know what Prodicus thought about the social utility of religious beliefs; nonetheless, his conception attests to the predominance of "the useful" (τὰ ὠφελοῦντα) as a "more potent norm than *nomos*"[67] in sophistic (and political) thought in the last decades of the fifth century. His projection of this norm as the social-psychological drive triggering the belief in the gods into the ancients' mind reflects the value preference of his own era.

The Sisyphus

Significantly, Sisyphus is one of the few gross transgressors to receive punishment in Hades for his hubris of defying the gods in Homer.[68] He is famously condemned eternally to roll a huge rock up on a hill, albeit with no success. He is called "the most cunning of men" (κέρδιστος ... ἀνδρῶν;

---

62. Cf. the testimony by Themistius in DK 84 B 5, on which see Henrichs, "Two Doxographical Notes," 118–9.

63. Henrichs, "Two Doxographical Notes," 112.

64. Cf. Meijer, "Philosophers, Intellectuals," 229.

65. On what he calls the "if I were a horse" fallacy in nineteenth-century theories of primitive religion, see E. E. Evans-Pritchard, *Theories of Primitive Religion* (Oxford: Clarendon Press, 1965), 24.

66. Henrichs, "Two Doxographical Notes," 112.

67. Ostwald, *Popular Sovereignty*, 255.

68. He is referred to, along with other similar transgressors (Orion, Tityus, Tantalus), at *Odyssey* 11.576-600.

Iliad VI.153) for chaining Thanatos (Death), hence liberating humans from death, at least for a while, and for outwitting Hades (or persuading Persephone) to escape his own death as punishment for this outrage till old age.[69] While the symbolism of his punishment has been variously interpreted, according to Kerényi it represents the vanity of all human efforts to subvert their apportioned lot, that is, death.[70] This is an attractive interpretation, given that Sisyphus challenged the gods with regard to their most crucial prerogative: immortality. Hence, Sisyphus is a fitting character to voice the theory of the origins of the belief in gods in the drama, given that it is presented as the invention of "some shrewd and wise man" (πυκνός τις καὶ σοφὸς γνώμην ἀνήρ, 12) for the benefit of humankind, comparable (if not, of course, equivalent) in significance to the abolition of death.

The narrative of the drama named after him goes in rough outlines as follows:[71] "Once upon a time" (ἦν χρόνος ὅτ') the life of humankind was without order (ἄτακτος) and beastly (θηριώδης), subservient to brute force (1-2); there was no reward for good, nor punishment for evil (3-4). Then people established retributive laws (νόμους θέσθαι κολαστάς), so that justice might prevail and there would be punishment for evil (5-8). The laws could prevent them from openly doing evil, but could not impede covert wrongdoing (9-11). Then, some shrewd and wise man (πυκνός τις καὶ σοφὸς γνώμην ἀνήρ) invented the fear of the gods for mortals so that they may not even ponder wrongdoing (11-5). He explained to them that there is an everlasting, omniscient supernatural creature (δαίμων) who pays attention and can hear and see everything they say or do, whether openly or in secret (16-24): "By telling such lies as these, he introduced [to humankind] the most pleasant of instructions (διδαγμάτων ἥδιστον εἰσηγήσατο), concealing the truth with his false story (ψευδεῖ καλύψας τὴν ἀλήθειαν λόγῳ)" (24-6). And to perpetuate his story, he placed the gods in the sky, which he realized was the source of their fear as well as gratitude for its benefits for their wretched life, such as lightning, thunder, and rain (27-36): "Such were the fears wherewith he encircled humankind, and by their means" he managed to extinguish "lawlessness by the imposition of law. So it was, I

69. The fullest version of the myth is in Pherecydes (fr. 119 Jacoby); the persuasion of Persephone is referred to by Theognis 703-5.

70. See Karl Kerényi, *Die Heroen der Griechen* (Zürich: Rhein-Verlag, 1958), 91.

71. The authorship and the title of the drama (and even its genre) is highly debated (attributed by some to Critias, by others to Euripides), but nothing hangs on these issues in my argument. On the debate, see, e.g., Kahn, *Art and Thought of Heraclitus* and Malcolm Davies, "Sisyphus and the Invention of Religion: 'Critias' *TrGF* 1 (43) F19 = B 25 DK," *Bulletin of the Institute of Classical Studies* 36 (1989): 16–32.

think, that some man first persuaded mortals to believe in the race of gods (νομίζειν δαιμόνων εἶναι γένος)" (37-42).[72]

This story exhibits several remarkable novelties or contrasts with other similar early accounts of human prehistory.[73] The traditional introductory formula, "once upon a time" (ἦν χρόνος ὅτ'), immediately suggests an informative contrast to a similar myth of cultural history told by Protagoras in Plato.[74] In the Protagorean version, the gods not only are primary in existence (and hence the creators of humankind; 320d1-3), but (unwritten) laws (*aidôs*, "shame" and *dikê*, "justice") to preclude wrongdoing are also devised by the chief of the gods for them (322c1-3). Remarkably, in this idiosyncratic myth religion precedes even the divine introduction of the moral code, together with the basics of technical know-how (along with fire), stolen from the gods and given to humankind by Prometheus (321c7-d3). In contrast, the story of the *Sisyphus* starts with a disorderly and beastly life; *nomoi* are somewhat casually established by humans, and, because of their imperfection (and human proclivity to wrongdoing), religion is sagaciously invented by a single individual thereafter. Traditionally, eulogies of the *prôtos heuretês* ("first inventor") of commodities specify gods.[75] Rather than praising gods (or even humans) for establishing laws in the first place, acclaim is reserved for the cunning individual who saved humankind by introducing the fear of the gods.[76] Hence, the normal priorities between gods and mortals are entirely reversed.[77] Rather than assuming the divine as the ultimate source and guarantor of civilizational order, the story assigns this role to a single individual, making it dependent on human contingency. This is another application of the Protagorean "man is the measure" principle, this time with grave political consequences, to which I shall return below. But before doing so, it is expedient to discuss atheistic aspects in the *Sisyphus*.

72. Direct quotes are translated by Davies, "Sisyphus"; the rest is my paraphrase with some Greek terms added in brackets from the text edited by Davies.

73. See Davies, "Sisyphus"; Kahn, "Greek Religion and Philosophy," 258ff.

74. "Once upon a time the gods already existed, but there was no human race yet" (Ἦν γάρ ποτε χρόνος ὅτε θεοὶ μὲν ἦσαν, θνητὰ δὲ γένη οὐκ ἦν) (*Protagoras* 320c8-d1). It is difficult to assess how much of the myth Plato puts into his mouth might be attributed to the historical Protagoras (see, e.g., the cautious position of Kahn, "Social Contract Theory," 98). In so far as its theory of the origins of religion is concerned, however, I do not think it is compatible with Protagoras's agnosticism. The categorical assertion of the gods' primordial existence itself contradicts it.

75. Davies, "Sisyphus," 21.

76. Davies, "Sisyphus," 20.

77. See Emily Kearns, "Order, Interaction, Authority," in Powell, ed., *Greek World*, 524. Cf. Guthrie, *Sophists*, 244; Davies, "Sisyphus," 21.

Atheism is most obvious in the characterization of the story told by the *sophos* as false or deceptive (ψευδεῖ … λόγῳ) by which he "concealed the truth" (καλύψας τὴν ἀλήθειαν). This clearly suggests that not only certain illicit myths about them,[78] but the very existence of the gods is a fiction, a mere human fabrication. But is this the whole concealed truth? No less important is the message that there is no divinity *as a source and guarantor of moral order* in the world. Humans are left to their own resources in determining right and wrong.[79] There is no guarantee or even hope, therefore, that justice will prevail, as it did not in the primordial "state of hubris," despite the introduction of punitive laws (1-11).

The story has its own theoretical or scientific underpinning in a relatively lengthy cosmological section, which describes the heavens by technical vocabulary borrowed from contemporary science (31-6). That this is also a disenchanted universe is most clearly indicated by the characterization of "the star-like flash of heaven" as "the beautiful ornament of the smart craftsman Time" (Χρόνου καλὸν ποίκιλμα, τέκτονος σοφοῦ, 34). The parallel with the *sophos* who devised religion for early humans is evident. Just as "the smart craftsman Time" fixed the stars on the vault of heaven and made them both delightful and frightening, "the shrewd and wise man" placed an omniscient god in heaven to assume the function of a cosmic police officer threatening humans with punishment for their transgressions.

"The smart craftsman Time" recalls Anaximander, but with significant contrasts, which suggest crucial differences between a disenchanted conception of the cosmos and one that retains essential aspects of the divine characteristic of a religious conception. In Anaximander the opposing elements constituting the cosmos "pay penalty and retribution to each other for their injustice according to the assessment of Time" (DK 12 B1).[80] "Time" here might seem to symbolize what we call "'natural necessity'"[81] in following a "law-like behavior." However, the personification of time as a judge in a law court suggests that justice will prevail not automatically or mechanically, but as a result of some discretion: it will inevitably be restored between the contending parties sooner or later (indicated by the phrase "according to necessity"), but its periods are assessed "appropriately

78. As in Xenophanes B 1.23, where he castigates myths about divine warfares as πλάσματα τῶν προτέρων ("fictions of old").
79. See Voegelin, *Order and History*, 322–3.
80. Translation drawn from Geoffrey S. Kirk, John E. Raven, and Malcolm Schofield, *The Presocratic Philosophers: A Critical History with a Selection of Texts* (2nd ed.; Cambridge: Cambridge University Press, 1983), 118.
81. Cf. the introductory phrase of the fragment, κατὰ τὸ χρεών ("according to necessity").

to each case."[82] This, I propose, is also a fine example of the sort of rational-ization of religious notions that retains the traditional pious paradigm with regard to its conception of the divine, while extracting its essence and trans-posing it into a cosmological setting. For among historians of philosophy it is not often realized that in Greek religion—from Homer through Hesiod, to Sophocles, Herodotus and beyond—"the idea of justice, order and the divine go very closely together," and not merely prescriptively, but also descriptively, "like a scientific law."[83] The divine would not, of course, be divine were it not at the same time capable of disrupting order; yet, "events none the less follow an overall pattern whereby undue prosperity and espe-cially the arrogance which results from this leads eventually to downfall."[84] Seen from this perspective and formulated at such a level of generaliza-tion, the essence of the Greeks' belief about the relation of the divine to order (and justice) is precisely mapped out onto Anaximander's cosmology. The elements are punished for their hubris of encroaching on one another as a rule. And the equivalent of something like a disruption of order in this system might be seen in the autonomy of Time in determining the periods of retribution. In both the religious and the "scientific" accounts, therefore, "the world as we perceive it is ultimately governed by something only par-tially accessible to normal perception: the universe is in some sense or other a religious universe."[85] This is very different from the universe of the *Sisy-phus*, and not merely because there is no divine guarantee for order and justice in the *kosmos* of the *sophos*, but because justice is merely a matter of human discretion and arbitration, hence never perfect or impartial. This brings us to the political dimensions of the text.

Before the notion of justice as a matter of human arbitration is perceived as an insight driven by democratic values, it might be noted that the *sophos* has a privileged position compared to the ordinary, deluded masses,[86] not merely because he knows the truth, but because by his imposition of a cru-cial belief he is (at least potentially) in a position of control.[87] Indeed, this is the first text in the West to present religion as an ideological construct, as false belief perpetuated in order to manipulate the masses. This might seem to be a far-fetched conclusion, since the *sophos* does not intend to invali-date legal order; on the contrary, confronted with the political disorder, he devises a means of promoting righteousness and group solidarity, thereby

82. Kirk, Raven, Schofield, *Presocratic Philosophers*, 121.
83. Kearns, "Order," 516.
84. Kearns, "Order," 517.
85. Kearns, "Order," 518.
86. Kearns, "Order," 524.
87. See Voegelin, *Order and History*, 322.

serving the interest of the community. Nonetheless, a theory that reduces religion to a function of morality[88] and considers pragmatic "usefulness" as "a more potent norm of political action than *nomos*"[89]—understood not as an overarching norm that transcends the power of individuals but something created and hence controlled by them—might easily be conceived of as a weapon by which the naive masses are kept within their ideological confines for the benefit of a ruling class.[90] The odd adjective ἥδιστον ("the most pleasant") qualifying the teachings of the *sophos* in 1.25—which, for this reason, some emend for κέρδιστον, "the most useful"[91]— might be explained from the perspective of "the natural aristocrat" who enjoys the benefits of the folly of those who naively believe his story. This is the sort of cynical misuse of others' piety that Xenophanes sought to come to terms with by propounding a most sublime Deity who, he believed, would respond to one's prayer for the ability of doing *ta dikaia* ("righteous deeds"; B 1.16).[92] In this conception, social expediency is subjected to a superhuman power that is the source of social order, and values human behavior that contributes to this order. In contrast, in the "sophistic myth"[93] of the *Sisyphus*, social expediency stands in the service of the superior power of (some) humans, while nature, disenchanted as it is, remains at best indifferent towards human behavior—or at worst provides an impersonal norm that runs counter to cooperative values.[94]

88. See Burkert, *Greek Religion*, 247 (on what he calls "the quasi-amoral justice of Zeus"); cf. Kearns, "Order," 515–9.

89. Ostwald, *Popular Sovereignty*, 255.

90. As in the conception of Thrasymachus in Plato's *Republic*, whose theory is that what people call "justice" is none other than behavior serving the interest of the stronger (343c-d), since they create laws for their own benefit (338c-9a). Complying with laws and justice is thus "noble simplicity" or "foolishness" (γενναία εὐήθεια; 348c12; cf. 343c6, 343d2).

91. Cf. Davies, "Sisyphus," 22, who complains of destroying the "pungent paradox" of the phrase, διδαγμάτων ἥδιστον, but provides no other reason for preferring the manuscript reading.

92. It is true that the major deity of the *Sisyphus* exhibits crucial resemblances to Xenophanes's God and that he criticizes the Homeric/Hesiodic depiction of gods for their licentiousness on pragmatic grounds (B 1.24: οὐδὲν χρηστὸν ἔνεστι; "there is nothing useful in them"), but it is difficult to assume that he would have been driven to his grander conception of the Deity by some such secular-minded social expediency as the *sophos*. He believed that this God could be worshiped and supplicated within the traditional confines of Greek cult (a *symposium*). On this, see Mogyoródi, "Xenophanes and the Rise of Theology."

93. Voegelin, *Order and History*, 322.

94. The latter is observable in the "genealogy of morality" proposed by Callicles in Plato's *Gorgias* (483a7-4c3).

Conclusion

Our investigations suggest that no presocratic natural philosophical or theological (skeptical or critical) development directly resulted in the elimination of gods without the presumable influence of a general political and
social development that brought with it an erosion of the authority of *nomoi*
and of social solidarity. For Anaximander and Heraclitus nature was not
devoid of supernatural aspects nor, consequently, was the divine merely a
part of nature. The sublime character of their cosmological divinities (and
especially that of the God of Xenophanes) certainly contributed to a clearer
differentiation of the natural and the supernatural. However, getting rid of
the latter altogether required the overall questioning of the validity and
authority of *nomoi*, a development that occurred only around the last third
of the fifth century for historical, political, and social-psychological reasons. Speculations that challenged the traditional status of *nomoi* adopted
elements of natural philosophy for theoretical support in such a way as to
facilitate the abolition of all underpinning of convention in nature. Since
nomoi were traditionally believed to have divine origins,[95] nature was to
be divested of all supernatural aspects. This left no room for theology, for
it makes no sense to speak of natural theology—let alone of a "theology of
nature," or even of supernatural theology—if nature is a self-contained and
self-regulating system, with nothing beyond its immanent order.

The disenchanted conception of the *kosmos* was conjoined with a developmental account of humanity, according to which humans developed as any
other animal (from mud) and civilizational achievements (including *nomoi*)
were artificial impositions on them.[96] Concomitant to this development was
a rising immanentist-anthropocentric attitude that boasted of civilizational
achievements to the extent of usurping divine status. If the existence of
gods was not indifferent to theorists of religion, it was because they conceived of it as arising from or serving social expediency. The dominance of
pragmatic concerns over *nomoi* (including the very belief in gods) affected
the conception of the divine-human relationship in similar ways to that of
the human-human relationship. The essentially "charismatic" nature[97] of all
personal (human or divine) relations eroded, and both "the original state of

95. See, e.g., Guthrie, *Sophists*, 76–8, 135–6.
96. Cf. Archelaus DK 60 A1, on which see Kahn, "Social Contract Theory," 102–3;
Ostwald, *Popular Sovereignty*, 260; Sedley, "Pre-Socratics to the Hellenistic Age,"
346–7.
97. See Burkert, *Greek Religion*, 273–4; Kearns, "Order," 519; and Parker, *Greek
Religion*, 9 who contrasts a simple *do ut des* relationship with "generalized reciprocity,"
characteristic of traditional religion.

humans" and the human-divine relationship were conceived of in terms of "masters" and "servants" engaged in a power struggle.[98]

If we consider that pragmatic utilitarianism is also characteristic of some of the religious attitudes current, then the issue of atheism or unorthodoxy becomes more complex than it might seem otherwise. Transposed into the sphere of the relationship of gods and humans, pragmatic utilitarianism might lead to the *do ut des* conception of religion that Plato subjected to severe criticism in his portrayal of Euthyphro (*Euthyphro* 14e1-8) and of Cephalus in the *Republic* (330d4-331b7). Of the three versions of impiety that Plato enlists, this is the one the Athenian finds the most impious (*Laws* 907b) and destructive in social terms, to be refuted above all (*Laws* 905d). The other one is that gods do not concern themselves with us. If they are part of nature, hence objects rather than persons, they obviously cannot— just like if they do not exist. No straightforward denial of the existence of the gods was needed for the Greeks to find such theories impious.

Biographical Note

Emese Mogyoródi is Associate Professor of Ancient Philosophy at the University of Szeged, Hungary. Her fields of interest include presocratic philosophy, Socrates, Plato's ethics and political philosophy, and moral psychological and theological issues in archaic and classical Greek thought. She has been granted the fellowship of the Center for Hellenic Studies (2003–2004) and the National Humanities Center (2012–2013). Her most recent book is a collection of essays entitled *Achilles and Socrates: Moral Psychology and Political Philosophy in the Archaic and Classical Age of the Greeks* (in Hungarian).

Bibliography

Adomenas, Mantas. "Heraclitus on Religion," *Phronesis* 44.2 (1999): 87–113. https://doi.org/10.1163/156852899321331752

Boys-Stones, George. "Ancient Philosophy of Religion: An Introduction," 1–22 in *The History of Western Philosophy of Religion*. Vol. 1: *Ancient Philosophy of Religion*. Edited by Graham Oppy and Nick Trakakis. Durham, UK: Acumen, 2009.

Bremmer, Jan N. "Atheism in Antiquity," 11–26 in *The Cambridge Companion to Atheism*. Edited by Michael Martin. Cambridge: Cambridge University Press, 2007.

Burkert, Walter. *Greek Religion: Archaic and Classical*. Translated by John Raffan. Oxford: Blackwell, 1985.

Burnet, John. *Early Greek Philosophy*. London: Adam and Charles Black, 1892.

98. As Kahn, "Social Contract Theory," 107 notes, the antinomians accepted the behavior of animals as a model for humans, as Callicles does at *Gorgias* 483d.

Davies, Malcolm. "Sisyphus and the Invention of Religion: 'Critias' *TrGF* 1 (43) F19 = B 25 DK," *Bulletin of the Institute of Classical Studies* 36 (1989): 16–32. https://doi.org/10.1111/j.2041-5370.1989.tb00560.x

Diels, Hermann, and Walther Kranz. *Die Fragmente der Vorsokratiker.* Vols. 1–3. 6th ed. Zürich: Weidmann, 1951.

Dodds, E. R. *The Greeks and the Irrational.* Berkeley, CA: University of California Press, 1951.

Dover, Kenneth. "Freedom of the Intellectual in Greek Society," *Talanta* 7 (1976): 24–54.

Drozdek, Adam. *Greek Philosophers as Theologians: The Divine Arche.* Aldershot, UK: Ashgate, 2007.

Eliade, Mircea. *The Sacred and the Profane: The Nature of Religion.* Translated by Williard R. Trask. New York: Harcourt, Brace & World, 1959.

Evans-Pritchard, E. E. *Theories of Primitive Religion.* Oxford: Clarendon Press, 1965.

Graham, Daniel W. *Explaining the Cosmos: The Ionian Tradition of Scientific Philosophy.* Princeton, NJ: Princeton University Press, 2006.

—ed. *The Texts of Early Greek Philosophy: The Complete Fragments and Selected Testimonies of the Major Presocratics,* Vol. 1. Cambridge: Cambridge University Press, 2010.

—"The Theology of Nature in the Ionian Tradition," *Rhizomata* 1.2 (2013): 194–216. https://doi.org/10.1515/rhiz-2013-0009

Guthrie, W. K. C. *The Sophists.* Cambridge: Cambridge University Press, 1971. https://doi.org/10.1017/CBO9780511627385

Harte, Verity, and Melissa Lane, eds. *Politeia in Greek and Roman Philosophy.* Cambridge: Cambridge University Press, 2015.

Henrichs, Albert. "Two Doxographical Notes: Democritus and Prodicus on Religion," *Harvard Studies in Classical Philology* 79 (1975): 93–123. https://doi.org/10.2307/311131

Hussey, Edward. "Ionian Inquiries: On Understanding the Presocratic Beginnings of Science," 530–49 in Powell, ed., *Greek World*, 1995.

Jaeger, Werner. *The Theology of the Early Greek Philosophers.* Oxford: Oxford University Press, 1967.

Kahn, Charles H. *The Art and Thought of Heraclitus.* Cambridge: Cambridge University Press, 1979. https://doi.org/10.1163/15685289760518153

—"The Origins of Social Contract Theory," 92–108 in *The Sophists and Their Legacy.* Edited by George B. Kerferd. Wiesbaden: Franz Steiner Verlag, 1981.

—"Greek Religion and Philosophy in the *Sisyphus* Fragment," *Phronesis* 42.3 (1997): 247–62.

Kearns, Emily. "Order, Interaction, Authority," 511–29 in Powell, ed., *Greek World*, 1995.

Kerényi, Karl. *Die Heroen der Griechen.* Zürich: Rhein-Verlag, 1958.

Kirk, Geoffrey S., John E. Raven, and Malcolm Schofield. *The Presocratic Philosophers: A Critical History with a Selection of Texts.* 2nd ed. Cambridge: Cambridge University Press, 1983.

Lesher, James H. *Xenophanes of Colophon: Fragments. A Text and Translation with a Commentary.* Toronto: University of Toronto Press, 1992.

Luria, S. Y. *Democritus: Texts, Translation, Investigations.* Translated by C. C. W. Taylor. Online: https://oxford.academia.edu/ChristopherTaylor, 2016. [Originally: *Democritea.* Leningrad: Nauka Publishing, 1970.]

Meijer, P. A. "Philosophers, Intellectuals and Religion in Hellas," 216–65 in *Faith, Hope, and Worship: Aspects of Religious Mentality*. Edited by Henk S. Versnel. Leiden: Brill, 1981.

Mogyoródi, Emese. "Xenophanes and the Rise of Theology in Early Greek Thought," *Philosophical Inquiry* 43.1–2 (2019): 4–30.

Most, Glenn W. "Philosophy and Religion," 300–22 in *The Cambridge Companion to Greek and Roman Philosophy*. Edited by David Sedley. Cambridge: Cambridge University Press, 2003. https://doi.org/10.1017/CCOL0521772850.012

—"Heraclitus on Religion." *Rhizomata* 1.2 (300–322): 153–67.

Ostwald, Martin. *From Popular Sovereignty to the Sovereignty of Law: Law, Society and Politics in Fifth-Century Athens*. Berkeley, CA: University of California Press, 1987.

Parker, Robert. *Athenian Religion: A History*. Oxford: Clarendon Press, 1996.

—*On Greek Religion*. Ithaca, NY: Cornell University Press, 2011.

Powell, Anton, ed. *The Greek World*. London: Routledge, 1995. https://doi.org/10.4324/9780203269206

Roubekas, Nickolas P. "Ancient Greek Atheism? A Note on Terminological Anachronism in the Study of Ancient Greek 'Religion'," *Revista Ciências da Religião* 12.2 (2014): 224–41.

Sedley, David. *Creationism and Its Critics in Antiquity*. Berkeley, CA: University of California Press, 2007.

—"From the Pre-Socratics to the Hellenistic Age," 139–51 in *The Oxford Handbook of Atheism*. Edited by Stephen Bullivant and Michael Ruse. Oxford: Oxford University Press, 2013.

—"The Atheist Underground," 329–48 in Harte and Lane, eds., *Politeia in Greek and Roman Philosophy*, 2015.

Taylor, Christopher C. W. *The Atomists: Leucippus and Democritus. Fragments. A Text and Translation with a Commentary*. Toronto: University of Toronto Press, 1999. https://doi.org/10.1017/CCOL0521441226.009

Taylor, Christopher C. W., and Mi-Kyoung Lee. "The Sophists," in *The Stanford Encyclopedia of Philosophy* (Fall 2015 Edition). Edited by Edward N. Zalta. Standford: Standford University, 2015. Online: http://plato.stanford.edu/archives/fall2015/entries/sophists/ (accessed August 2016).

Trépanier, Simon. "Early Greek Theology: God as Nature and Natural Gods," 273–317 in *The Gods of Ancient Greece: Identities and Transformations*. Edited by Jan N. Bremmer and Andrew Erskine. Edinburgh, UK: Edinburgh University Press, 2010.

Vlastos, Gregory. "Theology and Philosophy in Early Greek Thought," *Philosophical Quarterly* 2 (1952): 97–123. https://doi.org/10.2307/2216899

Voegelin, Eric. *Order and History*. Vol. 2: *The World of the Polis*. Baton Rouge, LA: Louisiana State University Press, 1957.

Warren, James. "Gods and Men in Xenophanes," 294–312 in Harte and Lane, eds., *Politeia in Greek and Roman Philosophy*, 2015.

Waterfield, Robin. "Introduction," in *The First Philosophers: The Presocratics and the Sophists*, xi–xxxiii. Oxford: Oxford University Press, 2000.

Whitmarsh, Tim. *Battling the Gods: Atheism in the Ancient World*. New York: Alfred A. Knopf, 2016.

Wilamowitz-Moellendorff, Ulrich von. *Der Glaube der Hellenen*, Vol. 2. Berlin: Weidmannsche Buchhandlung, 1932.

Chapter Seven

Theorizing About (Which?) Origins: Herodotus on the Gods

Nickolas P. Roubekas

Introduction

In his now classic *Totem and Taboo* (1913), Sigmund Freud, drawing on Darwinian evolutionism and totemism, maintained that deep in prehistory the earliest human groups—what he called primal hordes—were run by "a violent and jealous father who keeps all the females for himself and drives away his sons as they grow up." What followed, in Freud's discussion, gave rise to the phenomenon of religion:

> One day the brothers who had been driven out came together, killed and devoured their father and so made an end of the patriarchal horde. United, they had the courage to do and succeeded in doing what would have been impossible for them individually.[1]

The feelings of remorse that emerged from such an act gave rise to the idea of the totemic meal and the development of the notion of taboo. For Freud, the notion of god is nothing more than a substitute of the murdered father by the sons-culprits: "Totemic religion arose from the filial sense of guilt, in an attempt to allay that feeling and to appease the father by deferred obedience to him."[2]

A year earlier, however, Émile Durkheim argued for the abandonment of the pursuit of the historical origins of religion in his celebrated *The Elementary Forms of Religious Life* (1912):

> Granted, if by origin one means an absolute first beginning, there is nothing scientific about the question, and it must be resolutely set aside. There is no radical instant when religion began to exist, and the point is not to find a

---

1. Sigmund Freud, *Totem and Taboo* (trans. James Strachey; London: Routledge, 2004), 164.
2. Freud, *Totem and Taboo*, 168. For a more detailed discussion, see Nickolas P. Roubekas, "Sigmund Freud's Theory of Religion and the Sacrament of the Eucharist in the Orthodox Church," *Ekklesiastikos Pharos* 95 (2013): 266–82.

roundabout way of conveying ourselves there in thought. Like every other human institution, religion begins nowhere.[3]

Both Freud and Durkheim shared a genuine interest in origins within the context of a scientific study of religion, although both had significantly different perspectives. For Freud, origins of religion referred to the historical origin, that is, a specific moment in human history, albeit virtually undetermined, that religion appeared. Durkheim, conversely, shifted his attention to what is known as the recurrent origin of religion, that is, not "an absolute beginning but the simplest social state known at present—the state beyond which it is at present impossible for us to go."[4]

These two approaches from the early twentieth century are representatives of a continuing debate among religious studies scholars. The issue of origins, although having now somewhat lost its value while being dismissed within the postmodern academic ambient, remains a central issue in theorizing about religion. Already from the eighteenth century onward, theorists of religion addressed either the issue of origin or function (or both) of religion based on a certain need that can vary, including but not limited to a need for: shelter, clothing, and well-being (Karl Marx); coming into contact with the unconscious (Carl G. Jung); understanding the complexities of the functions of the universe (E. B. Tylor); or maintaining social cohesion (Émile Durkheim).[5] Although eventually origins became a problematic category due to an apparent inability to delve so deep into prehistory, it still preoccupies scholars of religion, most recently on a more "scientific" level represented by the field known as the cognitive science of religion.[6]

---

3.   Émile Durkheim, *The Elementary Forms of Religious Life* (trans. Karen E. Fields; New York: Free Press, 1995), 7.

4.   Durkheim, *Elementary Forms*, 7 n. 3.

5.   For an overview, see Robert A. Segal, "Theories of Religion," in *The Routledge Companion to the Study of Religion* (ed. John Hinnells; London: Routledge, 2005), 49–60, and "Origins of Religion," in *Vocabulary for the Study of Religion* (ed. Robert A. Segal and Kocku von Stuckrad; Leiden: Brill, 2016), Vol. 3, 579–85.

6.   For example, see the introduction as well as the individual papers in Dimitris Xygalatas and William McCorkle, eds., *Mental Culture: Classical Social Theory and the Cognitive Science of Religion* (London: Routledge, 2014); cf. the discussion in Ingvild S. Gilhus, "Founding Fathers, Turtles and the Elephant in the Room: The Quest for Origins in the Scientific Study of Religion," *Temenos* 50.2 (2014): 202–10. For a critique, see William Arnal and Russell T. McCutcheon, *The Sacred Is the Profane: The Political Nature of "Religion"* (Oxford: Oxford University Press, 2013), 91–101. A more detailed discussion on the cognitive science of religion (CSR) in general and in connection to ancient religions in particular can be found in Chapters 3 and 16, this volume (along with the overall discussion by Luther H. Martin in the Epilogue).

However, the pursuit of the origins of religion is not restricted to the modern era nor, even more so, is it an accomplishment of modern thought. In this chapter I address an attempt to account for the origins of religion as it was exemplified by one of the most influential figures from antiquity, namely Herodotus of Halicarnassus. However, as one might readily argue, Herodotus famously provides us with information pertaining to the origins of the Greek gods and not of religion as a phenomenon. Additionally, he does not deal with the issue of a need—be it a religious or social one—for which the idea of gods emerges, nor does he offer any tangible answer to the issue of function. In this regard, Herodotus can hardly be seen or regarded as a full-fledged theorist of religion in the same way as Freud, Durkheim, or other modern thinkers. The problem here, naturally, lies with what "religion" means and what kind of a definition one employs in order to consequently subsume, in our case, Herodotus under the rubric of "theorists of religion." I have no interest here to address the issue of the applicability of the term "religion" in antiquity, which is a problem that some scholars seem to consider an unsurpassable barrier when focusing on ancient cultures in general or Greek culture in particular.[7] As Robert Fowler recently pointed out, however,

> [w]ith respect to religion, I agree that it is not a Greek category, but do not think it matters; they had no categories "economy", "society", or "psychology" either, but we can study them nonetheless. Realising that some of the assumptions we bring about these terms to their analysis in an ancient context can get in the way of understanding does not negate the existence of the object of study, or prove that it is fantasy.[8]

What I wish to add, at this point, is that we can hardly talk about religion in ancient Greece without invoking the gods and the myths accompanying them. As I have argued elsewhere, belief in the gods constituted the crux of ancient Greek religion for many ancient thinkers, no matter how eagerly some scholars still prefer and promote the dichotomy between religious belief and religious practice within ancient Greek culture by prioritizing the latter and depreciating or even rejecting the former.[9] In this light, Herodotus's

7. There are numerous studies on the issue; a great starting point however is Brent Nongbri, *Before Religion: A History of a Modern Concept* (New Haven, CT: Yale University Press, 2013) and, more recently, Carlin A. Barton and Daniel Boyarin, *Imagine No Religion: How Modern Abstractions Hide Ancient Realities* (New York: Fordham University Press, 2016).

8. Robert L. Fowler, "Thoughts on Myth and Religion in Early Greek Historiography," *Minerva* 22 (2009): 22–3.

9. See Nickolas P. Roubekas, *An Ancient Theory of Religion: Euhemerism from Antiquity to the Present* (London: Routledge, 2017), 5–8. Also see the excellent argumentation by Henk S. Versnel, *Coping with the Gods: Wayward Readings in Greek*

second book of the *Histories*, where he presents his theory of the origins of the Greek gods (and, thus, the origins of Greek religion) constitutes one of the oldest attempts to theorize about religion, by focusing not on the function of religion nor the underlying need for which religion arises in general, but on the origins of a particular religion by employing a diffusionist approach—albeit a problematic one as I will argue—worth examining in relation to how he perceived origins and why he chose to incorporate such a discussion into a historical treatise that primarily dealt with the Graeco-Persian wars.

On the Origin of the (Greek) Gods

Since the nineteenth century Herodotus has been dealt with as an author lacking scientific methodology, prone to generalizations, not elaborate or critical enough, lacking credibility, and in general not of the stature of a Thucydides. However, as Neville Morley has pointed out, any criticism of Herodotus and his placement as less significant and "historical" than Thucydides "is not an eternal situation but the product of internal disciplinary disputes at specific historical moments."[10] Recently, however, Herodotus seems to have been revisited. One of the most central elements of the *Histories* is, of course, the place and role of divinity. However, and contrary to the traditional view that saw Herodotus as having the gods determining the development of history, scholars have lately argued that Herodotus is extremely skeptical when it comes to allowing for the divinity to interfere and control the outcome of historical events. As Robert Fowler has shown, although Herodotus expresses in many occasions his reservations for either the interference of the gods or the veracity of the testimonies about such interventions (e.g., 1.60.3; 1.182; 2.143; 3.123.1; 4.5.1; 4.11.1; 6.53.2; 7.61.3; 7.189.3), he nevertheless does not negate nor repudiates the existence of those gods. On the contrary, he allows for divinity to function outside the direct empirical realm and only via mediums and intermediary vehicles (e.g., oracles). As such, although Herodotus is "profoundly skeptical ... when the gods are supposed

---

Theology (Leiden: Brill, 2011), 552; cf. Mark Humphries, "Religion," in *A Companion to Ancient History* (ed. Andrew Erskine; Oxford: Wiley-Blackwell, 2009), 308–9, and Thomas Harrison, *Divinity and History: The Religion of Herodotus* (Oxford: Clarendon Press, 2002), 19. On the contrary, John Gould is an exponent of the traditional view and applies it to Herodotus's *Histories* ("Herodotus and Religion," in *Greek Historiography* [ed. Simon Hornblower; Oxford: Clarendon Press, 1994], 91–106). For a discussion on the problem of belief in ancient religions, see Chapter 3, this volume.

10. Neville Morley, "The Anti-Thucydides: Herodotus and the Development of Modern Historiography," in *Brill's Companion to the Reception of Herodotus* (ed. Jessica Priestley and Vasiliki Zali; Leiden: Brill, 2016), 149.

to have walked on to the stage of history, and spoken directly to humans or directly determined the course of events in the Biblical manner," he allows for the gods to "interact with the events of history indirectly on the micro-level and directly—in the sense that they take care of the course of events—on the remote macro-level."[11] Thus, any claims about Herodotus's disbelief, atheism, or refusal of the existence of gods are simply the result of misreading or misinterpreting the *Histories*.[12]

Herodotus's theory of the origin of the gods (and/or the gods' names) is encountered in the second book of his *Histories* (2.50-3). There we read:[13]

> Almost all the names of the gods have come to Greece from Egypt. For I am assured by inquiry that they come from foreigners, and I think that they have come chiefly from Egypt. Except for Poseidon, the Dioscuri ... and Hera, Hestia, Themis, the Graces and the Nereids, the names of all the gods have always existed in Egypt ... The gods whose names they say they do not know were, I think, named by the Pelasgians, save only Poseidon, of whom the Greeks learnt about from the Libyans ... And the Egyptians do not believe in heroes at all ... In previous times the Pelasgians used to make all their prayers and sacrifices to the gods, as I know from what I heard from Dodona, but they created no epithet or name for any of them. That is because they had not yet heard them. They called them gods because they had put in order and controlled all things and all distributions. And after a long time the Pelasgians learnt the names of the other gods that had come from Egypt, and, much later, the name of Dionysus; And after a time they consulted the oracle at Dodona about the names [... and] the oracle bid them to use them ... And the Greeks later received the names from the Pelasgians. From where each of the gods came to be, or if all always were existing, and how they look, the Greeks did not know until recently, just yesterday so to speak. For I think that Hesiod and Homer ... are the ones who created a divine genealogy for Greeks, gave their epithets to the gods, distributed their offices and their crafts, and marked out their outward appearances.

---

11.   Robert L. Fowler, "Gods in Early Greek Historiography," in *The Gods of Ancient Greece: Identities and Transformations* (ed. Jan N. Bremmer and Andrew Erskine; Edinburgh, UK: Edinburgh University Press, 2010), 324 and 331, respectively.

12.   See Fowler, "Gods," 319 (and n. 5 with further bibliography on this issue). Cf. Harrison, *Divinity and History*, 14, 156–7; Thomas Harrison, "'Prophecy in Reverse'? Herodotus and the Origins of History," in *Herodotus and His World* (ed. Peter Derow and Robert Parker; Oxford: Oxford University Press, 2003), 239.

13.   I am primarily drawing here from Jon D. Mikalson, *Herodotus and Religion in the Persian Wars* (Chapel Hill, NC: North Carolina University Press, 2012), 167–78, and Alan B. Lloyd, *Herodotus. Book II: Introduction* (Leiden: Brill, 1994), 148–9, although I will be taking a different approach. The translations of all excerpts from the *Histories* are based on Mikalson, *Herodotus and Religion*, 168, and Godley's LOEB edition, with some interventions of my own.

As it turns out, Herodotus does not here talk about the origins of the idea of the existence of the gods. Although the names are indeed what the Pelasgians import from Egypt, the gods preexist both in Egypt and in the Hellenic peninsula and, of course, so is the *idea* of gods that gives rise to religion. As Jon Mikalson has rightly noted, and contrary to the positions of the vast majority of other scholars, "[n]o one, in this account, imports or creates a *new* god. The gods seem to be there throughout: first they receive prayer and sacrifice, then the generic name θεοί, then Egyptian names, and, finally, from Hesiod and Homer their distinguishing attributes."[14] In this regard, Herodotus is not dealing with or speculating upon the origins of religion as a phenomenon. If we wish to necessarily assign an interest on origins, then we must concentrate on the origins of Greek religion in particular rather than religion *per se*. This is the context in which the idea of diffusionism in Herodotus makes its appearance. Before turning toward this thorny issue, however, I need to take a step back and attempt to determine why Herodotus is generally preoccupied with how the names of the gods came about. The problems in his discussion are many, but the most persistent is the most evident one; that is, if the names come from Egypt, then how can one linguistically or semantically reconcile names as dissimilar as, for example, Zeus/Amun, Demeter/Isis, Dionysus/Osiris, or Apollo/Horus? Unfortunately, there is no satisfactory solution to this problem, although scholars have promoted different explanations, from being a contradiction that Herodotus—either deliberately or inadvertently—chose not to address taking the term "names" as common designations that are nevertheless not linguistically identical.[15] Do names matter that much? Hardly. By demonstrating some kind of a common ancestry, on the other hand, Herodotus is attempting to persuade his readership of the existence of a unifying thread that connects the cultural dots of the various peoples he is discussing in his *Histories* (including the Scythians, Persians, Phoenicians, and others), without however neglecting or diminishing their striking differences.[16] With this in mind, perhaps we could identify in this endeavor not so much a

14. Mikalson, *Herodotus and Religion*, 171 (emphasis in the original).
15. For example, see Mikalson, *Herodotus and Religion*, 171–2; cf. the discussion in Scott Scullion, "Herodotus and Greek Religion," in *The Cambridge Companion to Herodotus* (ed. Carolyn Dewald and John Marincola; Cambridge: Cambridge University Press, 2007), 198–9. Carolina López-Ruiz, "Gods–Origins," in *The Oxford Handbook of Ancient Greek Religion* (ed. Esther Eidinow and Julia Kindt; Oxford: Oxford University Press, 2015), 372, on the other hand, takes the names as simply common denominators, even if their writing is so different.
16. Even when discussing the Egyptian origins of the Greek gods, he is reporting traditions alien to the Greeks, such as the lack of heroes (2.50), the depiction of the Egyptian gods as animals (2.65-7), the importance of dogs and cats (2.66), or even

conviction as an agenda, which is linked to a broader pattern that seeks to bring together and, then, ingeniously separate anew the protagonists of his work: the different peoples and their cultures.

Before I address this issue, however, I would like to return to the problem of diffusion, which has been identified by most scholars as the principal theory Herodotus employs to account for Greek religion.[17] I take this to be a problem since many scholars have failed to explain what they mean here by diffusionism. An example of the vague usage of this theory is found in Scott Scullion's article on Herodotus and religion, where he mentions: "It is in any case clear that Herodotus is a diffusionist … [He] concluded that the Greeks had taken theirs [i.e. their gods] over from the Pelasgians, who had in turn taken most of theirs over from the Egyptians."[18] Yet, a closer reading of the relevant excerpt, as I see it, does not do justice to such a seemingly straightforward conclusion.

First, one needs to establish what is here meant by the characterization of Herodotus as a diffusionist. A known theory in the field of anthropology for over a century, diffusionism has different expressions. Commonly seen as the opposite of classical evolutionism, diffusionism theory "presumes that humans are inherently conservative and uninventive and the major route of progress in culture history has been through the spread of civilisation from a very few culture centers."[19] Yet, there are certain qualifications that must be taken into consideration. First-level diffusionism, for example, mainly expressed by the anatomist G. Elliot Smith (1871–1937) and his disciple, geographer William James Perry (1887–1949), maintains that there is only one center or matrix of civilization through which progress spread to the globe. For Smith and Perry that center was Egypt. Second-level diffusionism, on the other hand, is more moderate, mainly promoted by the German-Austrian geographers and anthropologists of the nineteenth century—Friedrich Rätzel (1844–1904) being the most prominent one. This type of diffusionism is more of a hybrid between first-level diffusionism and classical evolutionism. The latter maintains that humankind is indeed inventive and that similar cultural achievements will appear in different

---

goats (2.46). Cf. the discussion in Donald Lateiner, *The Historical Method of Herodotus* (Toronto: University of Toronto Press, 1989), 149.

17.   For example, see Scullion, "Herodotus," 198–200; Harrison, *Divinity and History*, 209; Jennifer T. Roberts, *Herodotus: A Very Short Introduction* (Oxford: Oxford University Press, 2011), 28; Zachary S. Schiffman, *The Birth of the Past* (Baltimore, MD: Johns Hopkins University Press, 2011), 42.

18.   Scullion, "Herodotus," 198–9.

19.   Robert H. Winthrop, *Dictionary of Concepts in Cultural Anthropology* (New York: Greenwood Press, 1991), 83.

milieus and locations, albeit by employing different processes and having different timing. However, for these second-level diffusionists, this does not dismiss the transference of cultural units or even clusters among distinct cultures. As such, Rätzel maintained that "single items of culture tended to diffuse, whereas whole 'culture complexes' (clusters of related cultural features) were spread by migration."[20]

Herodotus's theory must be measured against these two primary types of diffusionism. First-level diffusionism does not allow for independent invention, the latter being, by definition, the opposite of diffusionism *per se*. By employing either the more radical Smith-Perry version or the multi-center alternative, we encounter a barrier. For Herodotus does not maintain that the idea of gods came from Egypt and Libya to the Greek world but only their respective names—although he does not account for all of them (for example, he says nothing about "the Dioscuri … and Hera, Hestia, Themis, the Graces and the Nereids"). The issue of the preexistence of the gods draws a line that cannot be overlooked merely due to the transference of a secondary element, such as the names of the gods. On the other hand, second-level diffusionism seems to better fit Herodotus. Yet again, in order to acknowledge Herodotus as a diffusionist in this respect, one needs to decide whether the idea of gods or their naming should be considered *the* actual cultural discovery. By definition, and Herodotus does not fall outside this norm, the idea of gods precedes their naming, description, offices, and so on. In this respect, Herodotus does nothing more than accounting historically—although the historicity of his theory is contestable—for the evolution of the idea of gods in the world rather than the emergence of the idea of gods *per se*. If, as Herodotus correctly maintains, the Egyptians are an older civilization, it was natural for them to have also developed further the idea of gods and the accompanying elements that constitute their religion, including their names. Similarly, the Pelasgians who are older than the Greeks, already had in place a group of deities, although unnamed. Given the connection between the Pelasgians and the Egyptians, both more ancient civilizations than the Greeks, it is not surprising to read in Herodotus the Greek debt to them for the more elaborated and sophisticated elements of their religion.

In this respect, then, Herodotus seems to belong more to an evolutionist camp rather than to a diffusionist one. An obvious objection, however, is that Herodotus maintains that the Greeks themselves had no concept of

---

20. Alan Barnard, *History and Theory in Anthropology* (Cambridge: Cambridge University Press, 2004), 50. Cf. his discussion in pp. 47–53. For more on diffusionism theory, see Jack D. Eller, *Introducing Anthropology of Religion* (London: Routledge, 2007), 14; Thomas H. Eriksen and Finn S. Nielsen, *A History of Anthropology* (London: Pluto Press, 2001), 27–9.

gods—or so it seems—and that they took theirs from the Pelasgians, who, in turn, had taken the names of their gods from the Egyptians. In his words: "[w]hen [the Pelasgians] consulted the oracle in Dodona if they should take up the names that had come from the foreigners, the oracle bid them to use them. And from this time on the Pelasgians were sacrificing using the names of the gods. And the Greeks later received the names from the Pelasgians." Although ostensibly straightforward, Herodotus does not explain whether the Greeks—among whom he chronologically prioritizes the Athenians[21]— already had the concept of gods and, just like the Pelasgians before, simply lacked names for their gods. If, as Herodotus argues, the Pelasgians shared the same land with the Athenians, then naming the Athenian gods was obviously due to the Pelasgian influence, without however verifying that the former took the very idea of the gods from the latter.

A second problem is the origins of the names of the gods for which Herodotus does not offer an explanation or a genealogy: the Dioscuri, Hera, Hestia, Themis, the Graces, and the Nereids. Although in the case of Poseidon the solution is easy as he informs the reader ("of whom the Greeks learnt about from the Libyans"), the same does not apply for the aforementioned group of deities. If, as Alan Lloyd argued some years ago, "[t]he only thing the remaining gods could be was Pelasgian,"[22] then Herodotus's origins scheme seems to rely on unsound foundations. The most apparent problem is a stunning contradiction in Herodotus's theory. If, as he argues and based on the testimony from Dodona, the Pelasgians "created no epithet or name for any of them [their gods]," then Lloyd's conclusion indicates that the Pelasgians did indeed have names for *some* of their gods but lacked names for some others. In this case, Herodotus is only interested in how the names of the Olympians came about—leaving out Hera however—rather than the names of all Greek deities.[23] Yet again, such an assertion implies that the Pelasgians had names for the secondary deities but not

21. "But they have not learned from the Egyptians to make the statues of Hermes have erect genitals. The Athenians first of all the Greeks took this from the Pelasgians, and then the others took it from the Athenians. The Pelasgians were dwelling in their land with the Athenians who already at that time were counted among the Greeks, and as a result the Pelasgians began also to be considered Greeks" (2.51).

22. Lloyd, *Herodotus. Book II*, 149.

23. Indeed, in 2.4 Herodotus argues that "the Egyptians (said they) first used the appellations of twelve gods (which the Greeks afterwards borrowed from them); and it was they who first assigned to the several gods their altars and images and temples, and first carved figures on stone." Although the identity of the twelve gods here remains problematic (e.g., the exclusion of Hera), Herodotus seems to be adding in the list Poseidon as well, although in 2.50ff. he argues that the Greeks received him from the Libyans. Cf. his discussion in 2.145 of the three different stages of the Egyptian pantheon—the

for their most powerful ones—which, typically, goes against any reasonable approach to a hierarchical pantheon. On the other hand, if what Herodotus maintains (and, perhaps, implied by Lloyd) is that the Pelasgians named those secondary gods after they received the names of their primary deities from Egypt and Libya, then, potentially, Herodotus could historically account for this since it follows what he learned at Dodona. His certainty that the Athenians took the names of their gods from the Pelasgians would allow him to further investigate the origins of those names. However, it seems that he actually did investigate and failed to encounter a satisfactory, historically sound answer. For this reason, he argues—with a degree of uncertainty nevertheless—that "[t]hose (Greek) gods whose names the Egyptians say they do not know were, I think, named by the Pelasgians, except for Poseidon." One could surmise that the impossibility of tracing the origins of those names could only indicate that they were indeed ancient Pelasgian names for which Herodotus could not possibly offer a historically acceptable and adequate explanation. Herodotus's failure to chronologically place the naming of those gods is certainly problematic to his whole discussion on the origins of the names of the gods.

Last, but not least, it seems to have been the norm to somehow neglect or overlook Herodotus's statement pertaining to the role of heroes: "And the Egyptians do not believe in heroes at all." The centrality of the heroes in Greek religion need not be repeated here.[24] Herodotus himself refers to heroic figures that assisted the Greeks in the battlefields or that play some role—sometimes central, in others secondary—in his narrative (e.g., 4.147; 6.53; 7.61; 7.170; 8.38-9; 8.44), although he is prepared to simply refer to his informants rather than express some kind of personal belief.[25] However, Herodotus does not explain how the Greeks came about honoring their heroes. No narrative of origins is offered, nor does he seem to be interested in dealing with the heroes as divine or semi-divine agents. As Robert Fowler has argued,

> Herodotus draws the conclusion that the gods did not walk with the heroes either. The reason must be that he regards them as much like us, if superior in attainments ... The gods did not intervene in the lives of heroes any more than they do in ours. We need to understand just how astonishing this

first consisting of eight gods including Pan; the second of twelve, including Herakles; and the third of most likely thirteen, since he adds here Dionysus.

24. See, for example, Gunnel Ekroth, "Heroes and Hero-Cults," in *A Companion to Greek Religion* (ed. Daniel Ogden; Oxford: Wiley-Blackwell, 2007), 100–14.

25. Cf. Mikalson, *Herodotus and Religion*, 188–9; Alan Griffiths, "Myth in History," in *Blackwell Companion to Greek Mythology* (ed. Ken Dowden and Niall Livingstone; Oxford: Wiley-Blackwell, 2011), 196–9.

conclusion is. It is completely at odds with every known predecessor, and requires a complete revision of traditional "mythology."[26]

Whatever the case might be regarding the origins of the idea of heroes, it is not insignificant to point out here that the principle of "everything came from Egypt" did not simultaneously mean for Herodotus the lack of independent invention; in this case, the notion and cult of the heroes seems to be a Greek-only characteristic, which, in turn, jeopardizes his alleged diffusionism stance.

The theory of diffusionism, in any of its expressions, is hardly a theory of the origins of a phenomenon. Adding to that its failure "to explain why some traits diffuse and others don't,"[27] I suggest that we should reevaluate Herodotus's view based not so much on the premise that he was a diffusionist but, rather, on an agenda he had that also permeated his take on religion. However, and following Russell McCutcheon's train of thought, "[i]t's not an easy shift to make—to see history and origins tales as being all about the tale-teller's present situation …"[28] Yet, if we wish to account for Herodotus's insertion of the origins tale in the second book of his *Histories*, we need to consider what was the underlying principle that prompted him to offer a seemingly diffusionism-like explanation.

Similarities, Yes; Diffusion, No: The Principles of "Antiqueness" and "Universalism"

It is well known that Herodotus incurred Plutarch's wrath for both his historical method and his take on religion. His criticisms appear in *On the Malice of Herodotus*, a polemical treatise against the historian from Halicarnassus. As Jon Marincola has shown, Plutarch's view of the divine was utterly different from that of Herodotus, especially in regard to the nature of the divine: for Herodotus (in his known Solon and Croesus story in 1.29-33) the divine is jealous, whereas for Plutarch the divine is a source of goodness. Additionally, Plutarch attacks Herodotus for ignoring many clear signs, as he maintains, of the involvement of the divine during the Persian Wars. By involvement,

---

26. Fowler, "Gods," 327.

27. Mark Moberg, *Engaging Anthropological Theory: A Social and Political History* (New York: Routledge, 2013), 151; on the problems with diffusionism, cf. pp. 149–51. Also see Luther H. Martin, "Comparison," in *Deep History, Secular Theory: Historical and Scientific Studies of Religion* (Berlin: Walter de Gruyter, 2014), 72, from a religious studies perspective, including his discussion on the *interpretatio Graeca* and syncretism (for more on this, see below).

28. Russell T. McCutcheon, "Introduction: Midnight in the Study of Origins," in *Fabricating Origins* (ed. Russell T. McCutcheon; Sheffield, UK: Equinox, 2015), 8.

of course, Plutarch concentrates on the divine interventions in favor of the Greeks. In other words, the Persian Wars were seen by Plutarch as straight-forward proof of a Greek glory that should not be in any way diminished or taken lightly.[29] On the contrary, as Emily Baragwanath has argued in her monograph *Motivation and Narrative in Herodotus*, Herodotus's primary concern in his *Histories* is to unveil "the reasons behind actions," which does not mean divine interventions—as Plutarch would prefer—but primarily an "explanation on the human level," that is, "the representation of human moti-vation."[30] Without, however, avoiding or utterly extracting from his narrative the divine element, Herodotus is remarkable in bringing both the human and the divine to the forefront, although he is obviously more interested in the former in composing his *Histories*. The significance of destiny/fate—along with the power of the oracles—is, for example, one of the most central divine elements in his work, which includes both the culmination of the Persian Wars and the control even of the divine world itself.[31] In regard to the oracles, Herodotus returns to his favorite hypothesis of an interconnection between Greece and Egypt, when he argues (cf. 2.54-8) that the oracles at Dodona and at the Siwah oasis came from Egypt.[32] This, as he claims, derives from tes-timonies he heard from priests while at Thebes as well as the prophetesses of Dodona. The reason he took those testimonies at face value, although he does try to strip away the mythical narrative he collects from his sources, is his firm conviction that the antiquity of Egypt suffices to justify the intercon-nections: "I hold this proved, because the Egyptian ceremonies are manifestly very ancient, and the Greek are of late origin" (2.58).[33] In the same fashion, as we have already seen, he accepts the transference of the Egyptian names to

29. On the attacks of Plutarch to Herodotus regarding the divine, see John Marin-cola, "Defending the Divine: Plutarch on the Gods of Herodotus," in *God in History: Reading and Rewriting Herodotean Theology from Plutarch to the Renaissance* (ed. Anthony Ellis; Newcastle upon Tyne: Newcastle University, 2015), 41–83. On the broader attack against Herodotus's historical method and Plutarch's understanding of the Persian Wars as an indication of Greek grandeur, see John Marincola, "History With-out Malice: Plutarch Rewrites the Battle of Plataea," in Priestley and Zali, eds., *Brill's Companion to the Reception of Herodotus*, 101–19; cf. Emily Baragwanath, *Motivation and Narrative in Herodotus* (Oxford: Oxford University Press, 2008), 10–1.

30. Baragwanath, *Motivation and Narrative*, 3.

31. "None may escape his destined lot, not even a god" (1.91). Cf. François Hartog, "'Myth into Logos': The Case of Croesus, or the Historian at Work," in *From Myth to Reason? Studies in the Development of Greek Thought* (ed. Richard Buxton; Oxford: Oxford University Press, 1999), 188–9. On the role of fate in the *Histories*, see Esther Eidinow, *Luck, Fate, and Fortune* (London: I. B. Tauris, 2011), 96–118.

32. Cf. the discussion in Erich Gruen, *Rethinking the Other in Antiquity* (Princeton, NJ: Princeton University Press, 2011), 82–3.

33. For a discussion on the value and credibility of the Egyptian priests' testimonies

Greece. What does this mean, however, within the context of theorizing about origins linked to an alleged diffusion theory?

Virtually, nothing. If diffusion—either in the stricter or its more moderate versions—was the case, then it is hard for the reader of the *Histories* to fit into the theory the numerous differences Herodotus traces between the various peoples,[34] including of course the Egyptians and the Greeks. For example, in 2.37 we read:

> [The Egyptians] are beyond measure religious (Θεοσεβέες δὲ περισσῶς ἐόντες), more than any other nation; and these are among their customs: They drink from cups of bronze, which they cleanse out daily; this is done not by some but by all. They are especially careful ever to wear newly-washed linen raiment. They practice circumcision for cleanliness' sake; for they set cleanness above seemliness. Their priests shave the whole body every other day, that no lice or aught else that is foul may infest them in their service of the gods. The priests wear a single linen garment and sandals of papyrus: they may take no other kind of clothing or footwear. Twice a day and twice every night they wash in cold water. Their religious observances are, one may say, innumerable (ἄλλας τε θρησκηίας ἐπιτελέουσι μυρίας ὡς εἰπεῖν λόγῳ).

If we add to this description the Egyptian depiction of gods not in an anthropomorphic but in animal-like fashion (2.65-7), their mourning in the household for the death of a cat or a dog (2.66), the community's grief for the loss of a Mendesian goat (2.46), or considering cremation of the dead as unholy (3.16), one wonders how exactly an alleged diffusionism functions in such a context. Herodotus is apparently contradicting himself when, although offering the various differences, he also argues that almost (if not) all Greek rituals and practices came from Egypt; from the Orphic and Bacchic rituals (2.81) to the Thesmophoria, which arrived from Egypt by Danaus's daughters (2.171).

However, as Elena Muñiz Grijalvo recently argued, religion is not an end in itself in the *Histories*. Rather, it is an instrument that sought to construct "different limits for the concept of Greekness."[35] In this way, Herodotus's contradictions have a common denominator that explains the apparent problem in the *Histories*. In Muñiz Grijalvo's view, Greek religion for Herodotus was a fluid system comprised of indigenous (Pelasgian), late-comer (Greek), and

---

in Herodotus's work, see Ian S. Moyer, *Egypt and the Limits of Hellenism* (Cambridge: Cambridge University Press, 2011), 42–63.

34. See 1.131-2 on the Persian beliefs and practices; 1.216 on the Massagetai; 2.29 on the Ethiopians; 4.26 on the Issidones; 5.7 on the Thracians. Cf. Mikalson, *Herodotus and Religion*, 197.

35. Elena Muñiz Grijalvo, "The Frontiers of Graeco-Roman Religions: Greeks and Non-Greeks from a Religious Point of View," in *Frontiers in the Roman World* (ed. Ted Kaizer and Olivia Hekster; Leiden: Brill, 2011), 134.

foreign wisdom (Egyptian), in a sense consistent with his position that "no man knows about the gods more than another (νομίζων πάντας ἀνθρώπους ἴσον περὶ αὐτῶν ἐπίστασθαι)" (2.3).[36] For Scott Scullion, this phrase indicates not knowing equally enough but equally little, thus aligning Herodotus with previous thinkers, like Xenophanes and—primarily—Protagoras and his known statement "[c]oncerning the gods I am unable to know that they exist, or that they do not exist, or what they are like in appearance."[37] The link between Protagoras (and Xenophanes) and Herodotus can be found in the last segment, the one pertaining to the gods' appearance. According to Scullion, Herodotus portrays the Protagorean influence in 2.53:

> From where each of the gods came to be, or if all always were existing, and how they look, the Greeks did not know until recently, just yesterday so to speak. For I think that Hesiod and Homer … are the ones who created a divine genealogy for Greeks, gave their epithets to the gods, distributed their offices and their crafts, and marked out their outward appearances.

The same idea is repeated, as Scullion maintains, in 1.131, where Herodotus discusses the lack of anthropomorphism in the Persian understanding of the gods.[38] However, I find Tim Whitmarsh's approach to be a more compelling argument for a connection between Herodotus and Protagoras. If such a connection is indeed desired, then Protagoras's philosophical determinism—which is to be found throughout his (admittedly, extremely fragmented) work—needs to be taken into consideration. As Whitmarsh has shown, existence for Protagoras is predicated on appearance; things cannot exist if they do not manifest: "the being of things that are consists in being manifest."[39] In this sense, to claim that Herodotus belongs to the Protagorean tradition means that he also maintained such a relativism that leaned more towards atheism rather than mere religious skepticism as, for example, Scullion and Walter Burkert maintain.[40]

Jon Mikalson's approach to the issue, however, seems to be getting closer to my own reading of Herodotus's views on the gods. Homer and Hesiod

---

36. Muñiz Grijalvo, "Frontiers," 136–7. A different interpretation is offered by Fowler, "Thoughts on Myth," 27.

37. See Scullion, "Herodotus," 200–1.

38. Scullion, "Herodotus," 202, following Walter Burkert's discussion ("Herodot als Historiker fremder Religionen," in *Hérodote et les peuples non grecs* [ed. Giuseppe Nenci; Geneva: Fondation Hardt, 1990], 1–39).

39. Fragment 12 in Daniel D. Graham, ed., *The Texts of Early Greek Philosophy: The Complete Fragments and Selected Testimonies of the Major Presocratics* (Cambridge: Cambridge University Press, 2010). Cf. Tim Whitmarsh, *Battling the Gods: Atheism in the Ancient World* (New York: Alfred A. Knopf, 2015), 87–91.

40. See Burkert, "Herodot als Historiker."

created the Greek version of a "divine sphere" that is, although in different forms, fundamentally the same throughout the world. They "essentially
made Greek these Pelasgian gods with Egyptian names. In giving them
their genealogies, offices, crafts, and outward appearances they did not discover a hitherto unknown truth but rather invented a poetic truth about the
nature of the gods."[41] This, in turn, means that the Greek pantheon should
not be deemed superior or inferior to the Egyptian or to any other ethnic god
or pantheon. On the contrary, the Greek gods for Herodotus constitute "just
one system among many other systems of conceiving of and dealing with
the universal 'divine,'" which is why Herodotus is extremely cautious in
criticizing either the Greek or any other religious worldview.[42] That universal "divine" is undoubtedly the silent actor behind Herodotus's discussion
on the origins of the gods,[43] but its existence does not simultaneously point
toward a diffusion theory employed by Herodotus as I have already argued.

It is in this context where the notion of the *interpretatio Graeca* enters
the scene anew. Rather than talking about diffusion, one will be better off
by returning to this old but still valid concept, which of course is derived
from perhaps the earliest recorded attempt of an ethnographical comparative exercise, as Jonathan Z. Smith argued more than forty years ago. This
class of comparison, in which Smith identified Herodotus as the first exponent, is "basically a set of traveler's impressions. Something other has been
encountered, and it is surprising either in its similarity or dissimilarity to
what is familiar 'back home'. In such a context, comparison becomes primarily a means of overcoming strangeness."[44] The problems of this type of
comparativism notwithstanding,[45] it becomes evident that Herodotus was
more interested in reconciling the religious differences in favor of a powerful religious universalism. The methodological tool of what was later called
interpretatio Graeca served his needs by allowing him to invoke and note
the analogies between the Greek and Egyptian deities and practices. This
has been neatly summarized by Robert Parker:

41. Mikalson, *Herodotus and Religion*, 173.
42. Mikalson, *Herodotus and Religion*, 174. Cf. *Histories* 3.38: "Each people thinks
that its own traditions are by far the best. Therefore no one but a madman ought to laugh
at such things."
43. This is a point on which I strongly agree with Scullion, "Herodotus," 196–7.
44. Jonathan Z. Smith, "Adde Parvum Parvo Magnus Acervus Erit," *History of Religions* 11.1 (1971): 73.
45. Smith has discussed extensively the problems with all four categories of comparison that he identifies—that is, ethnographic, encyclopaedic, morphological, and
evolutionary—throughout his diverse work. The best starting point would be Jonathan
Z. Smith, "In Comparison a Magic Dwells," in *Imagining Religion: From Babylon to
Jonestown* (Chicago, IL: University of Chicago Press, 1982), 19–35.

> Herodotus (and other Greeks too) worked on the assumption that the difference between, say, "Zeus" and "Amoun" was no different from that between the Greek and Egyptian words for "bread"; the god, like the bread, is the same everywhere, and Amoun is not a different god from Zeus but simply the Egyptian word for him.[46]

If one accepts the existence of a universal "divine" in Herodotus's thought which manifests itself or, better, is conceived by the various historical peoples in different manners, then Herodotus could be deemed, *mutatis mutandis*, a very early predecessor of Mircea Eliade's notion of the "sacred" or John Hick's "the Real" in the sense that there exists "a common 'essence' or basis of all religions."[47] Although the representation of the divine varies in different cultures and peoples, this does not at the same time mean that one representation is superior or more advanced than the other. As a matter of fact, as Jon Mikalson has put it,

> [t]he Hesiodic/Homeric scheme of the pantheon is millennia younger than the Egyptian, but to Herodotus it is apparently no better or worse, no more or less valid. It is simply different, with two cultures coming to different characterizations and representations of what is in origin the *same divine world*. The deities of Herodotus' world are culturally determined, but the "divine," in essence, is not.[48]

If Herodotus was indeed arguing in favor of such a religious universalism, he did so only in a subtle way,[49] albeit one that was as radical as Plutarch's attack indicates.[50] But Herodotus's take on the culturally determined deities throughout the world perhaps served yet another aim.[50]

---

46. Robert Parker, *On Greek Religion* (Ithaca, NY: Cornell University Press, 2011), 68–9.

47. Malory Nye, *Religion: The Basics* (2nd ed.; London: Routledge, 2008), 111 and 111–5 for a discussion of Eliade and Hick.

48. Mikalson, *Herodotus and Religion*, 173 (emphasis added).

49. Universalism's variants are numerous as William E. Paden, "Comparative Religion," in Hinnells, ed., *The Routledge Companion to the Study of Religion*, 211–2 has shown.

50. It is interesting to think that Plutarch could have agreed with Herodotus on such a universalism, considering how he approached the issue in another context. However, his Platonic religious worldview perhaps is the key of their fundamental difference here:

> Nor do we think of the gods as different gods among different peoples, nor as barbarian gods and Greek gods, nor as southern and northern gods ; but, just as the sun and the moon and the heavens and the earth and the sea are common to all, but are called by different names by different peoples, so for that one rationality which keeps all these things in order and the one Providence which watches over them and the ancillary powers that are set over all, there have arisen among different peoples, in accordance with their customs, different honours and appellations (*On Isis and Osiris* 67; translation drawn from F. C. Babbitt's LOEB edition).

Talking About Gods, Talking About Peoples

Considering that according to Herodotus the Greeks only needed from the gods to make the war against the Persians simply a "fair fight" (θεῶν τὰ ἴσα νεμόντων) and not intervene in order to help either camp,[51] I suggest that although he dedicated considerable space on the origins of the gods in a historical treatise about the Persian Wars, his aim was primarily to show that it was indeed the peoples who determined the outcome of the wars. Yet, in order to understand the different peoples, in Herodotus's view, one needs to understand their culture—and, for Herodotus, religious beliefs[52] and practices were at the core of each culture. If the Greeks won the war, this victory happened due to the common identity the Greeks shared and which allowed them to unite against the common enemy; nevertheless, it was an identity "that was consolidated in the Persian Wars," as Thomas Harrison has correctly pointed out. And as he goes on to argue,

> [t]his sense of common identity, together with the easy narrative framework
> of Persian invasion, defeat and flight, made it possible and meaningful (for
> example) to record the background history of different cities in the context of
> their response to Persian demands for submission, or to frame the traditions
> and marvels of the cities of Thrace and Thessaly within a narrative of Persian
> invasion ... Herodotus' religious beliefs had a similarly enabling effect.[53]

In this respect, and in accordance to Mikalson's focus on the culturally determined gods as the indicative factor of the different peoples' self-identification, one could argue that Herodotus sought to (a) bring together the alleged different gods in order to show the existence of a common religiosity throughout the ancient world—but primarily among Greeks and Egyptians—while at the same time (b) indicated that it constituted such a strong self-identification mechanism that functioned as the determinative factor of a kind of ethnic/national self-consciousness. In an interesting passage, Herodotus clearly demonstrates how religion indeed functioned as the quintessential element of certain peoples' self-identification:

---

51. See, 6.11; 6.109; 8.13. Cf. the discussion in Jon D. Mikalson, "Religion in Herodotus," in *Brill's Companion to Herodotus* (ed. Egbert J. Bakker, Irene J. F. De Jong, and Hans Van Wees; Leiden: Brill, 2002), 192.

52.   Although, as I mentioned in the introduction, the issue of belief in ancient Greek religion is contested by many ancient historians, Thomas Harrison has correctly demonstrated how the verb νομίζω in the *Histories*—when, e.g., referring to the Persians or the Getae—indicates Herodotus's interest in both beliefs and practices (*Divinity and History*, 221).

53. Harrison, "Prophecy," 255.

> The men of the cities of Marea and Apis, in the part of Egypt bordering on
> Libya, believing themselves to be Libyans and not Egyptians, and disliking
> the injunction of the religious law that forbade them to eat cows' meat, sent to
> Ammon saying that they had no part of or lot with Egypt: for they lived (they
> said) outside the Delta and did not consent to the ways of its people, and they
> wished to be allowed to eat all foods. (2.18)

Although the god decided that they were indeed Egyptians, thus rejecting
their request, one gets a clear view of how important the religious ideas and
practices were in Herodotus's view pertaining to national or ethnic classification. The same of course applies—perhaps even more clearly—when one
brings into mind the known passage (8.144) of what defines "Greekness":
common blood (kinship), common language, and the common gods along
with their dedicated sanctuaries and sacrifices. In this respect, although
Herodotus's agenda in the second book of his *Histories* seems like an
attempt to eliminate such borders of the mechanisms of self-identification,
he nevertheless constantly returns to those borders only to reinforce them,
although he seemingly attempts to diminish them.

One can hardly claim that Herodotus manages to leave out from his *Histories* his personal religious beliefs as Harrison has shown.[54] But his theory of
the origins of the gods' names can hardly be qualified as an accurate scientific
theory. The motives behind Herodotus's choice of talking about those origins
must be sought in his own need to promote a complicated and hitherto quite
unusual religious universalism, while at the same time indicating how loans
and influences through cultural exchanges—rather than a straightforward diffusionism—managed not to lead into a better understanding of that religious
universalism, but rather strengthened and established on more concrete foundations the borders that made the Greeks who they were or thought they were.
After all, the perceived origin vis-à-vis the "true" origin of a cultural item
"usually plays a greater role in its reception and history" as Carolina López-
Ruiz has argued,[55] which brings us back to McCutcheon's view that "origins
are therefore not about the past" but rather about the "one who is making the
claim."[56] By promoting his theory of the origins of the Greek gods, Herodotus was making a claim that was touching upon issues of self-identification,
ethnic/national classification, and religious universalism.

---

54. Harrison, *Divinity and History.*
55. López-Ruiz, "Gods–Origins," 369.
56. Russell T. McCutcheon, "Afterward: Origins Today," in McCutcheon, ed., *Fabricating Origins*, 77.

Biographical Note

Nickolas P. Roubekas is Assistant Professor of Religious Studies at the University of Vienna, Austria. Previously he held a postdoctoral research fellowship at the University of South Africa, a teaching fellowship at the University of Aberdeen, UK, and a research fellowship at the North-West University, South Africa. He has published articles and book reviews in various journals and is the author of *Αναζητώντας τους Θεούς: Θρησκεία, Μύθος, Ουτοπία στον Ευήμερο τον Μεσσήνιο* (Vanias, 2011) and *An Ancient Theory of Religion: Euhemerism from Antiquity to the Present* (Routledge, 2017). His research focuses on the Graeco-Roman world, method and theory in the study of religion, and the disciplinary intersection of Religious Studies, Classics, and Ancient History.

Bibliography

Arnal, William, and Russell T. McCutcheon. *The Sacred Is the Profane: The Political Nature of "Religion."* Oxford: Oxford University Press, 2013.

Baragwanath, Emily. *Motivation and Narrative in Herodotus*. Oxford: Oxford University Press, 2008. https://doi.org/10.1093/acprof:oso/9780199231294.001.0001

Barnard, Alan. *History and Theory in Anthropology*. Cambridge: Cambridge University Press, 2004.

Barton, Carlin A., and Daniel Boyarin. *Imagine No Religion: How Modern Abstractions Hide Ancient Realities*. New York: Fordham University Press, 2016.

Burkert, Walter. "Herodot als Historiker fremder Religionen," 1–39 in *Hérodote et les peuples non grecs*. Edited by Giuseppe Nenci. Geneva: Fondation Hardt, 1990.

Durkheim, Émile. *The Elementary Forms of Religious Life*. Translated by Karen E. Fields. New York: Free Press, 1995 [1912].

Eidinow, Esther. *Luck, Fate, and Fortune*. London: I. B. Tauris, 2011.

Ekroth, Gunnel. "Heroes and Hero-Cults," 100–14 in *A Companion to Greek Religion*. Edited by Daniel Ogden. Oxford: Wiley-Blackwell, 2007.

Eller, Jack D. *Introducing Anthropology of Religion*. London: Routledge, 2007. https://doi.org/10.4324/9780203946244

Eriksen, Thomas H., and Finn S. Nielsen. *A History of Anthropology*. London: Pluto Press, 2001.

Fowler, Robert L. "Thoughts on Myth and Religion in Early Greek Historiography," *Minerva* 22 (2009): 21–39.

—"Gods in Early Greek Historiography," 318–34 in *The Gods of Ancient Greece: Identities and Transformations*. Edited by Jan N. Bremmer and Andrew Erskine. Edinburgh, UK: Edinburgh University Press, 2010.

Freud, Sigmund. *Totem and Taboo*. Translated by James Strachey. London: Routledge, 2004 [1913].

Gilhus, Ingvild S. "Founding Fathers, Turtles and the Elephant in the Room: The Quest for Origins in the Scientific Study of Religion," *Temenos* 50.2 (2014): 193–214.

Gould, John. "Herodotus and Religion," 91–106 in *Greek Historiography*. Edited by Simon Hornblower. Oxford: Clarendon Press, 1994.

Graham, Daniel D., ed. *The Texts of Early Greek Philosophy: The Complete Fragments and Selected Testimonies of the Major Presocratics.* Cambridge: Cambridge University Press, 2010.

Griffiths, Alan. "Myth in History," 195–207 in *Blackwell Companion to Greek Mythology.* Edited by Ken Dowden and Niall Livingstone. Oxford: Wiley-Blackwell, 2011. https://doi.org/10.1002/9781444396942.ch10

Gruen, Erich. *Rethinking the Other in Antiquity.* Princeton, NJ: Princeton University Press, 2011.

Harrison, Thomas. *Divinity and History: The Religion of Herodotus.* Oxford: Clarendon Press, 2002. https://doi.org/10.1093/acprof:oso/9780199253555.001.0001

——"'Prophecy in Reverse'? Herodotus and the Origins of History," 237–55 in *Herodotus and His World.* Edited by Peter Derow and Robert Parker. Oxford: Oxford University Press, 2003.

Hartog, François. "'Myth into Logos': The Case of Croesus, or the Historian at Work," 183–95 in *From Myth to Reason? Studies in the Development of Greek Thought.* Edited by Richard Buxton. Oxford: Oxford University Press, 1999.

Hinnells, John, ed. *The Routledge Companion to the Study of Religion.* London: Routledge, 2005. https://doi.org/10.4324/9780203412695

Humphries, Mark. "Religion," 301–11 in *A Companion to Ancient History.* Edited by Andrew Erskine. Oxford: Wiley-Blackwell, 2009.

Lateiner, Donald. *The Historical Method of Herodotus.* Toronto: University of Toronto Press, 1989. https://doi.org/10.3138/9781442675773

Lloyd, Alan B. *Herodotus. Book II: Introduction.* Leiden: Brill, 1994. https://doi.org/10.1163/9789004295094

López-Ruiz, Carolina. "Gods–Origins," 369–82 in *The Oxford Handbook of Ancient Greek Religion.* Edited by Esther Eidinow and Julia Kindt. Oxford: Oxford University Press, 2015.

Marincola, John. "Defending the Divine: Plutarch on the Gods of Herodotus," 41–83 in *God in History: Reading and Rewriting Herodotean Theology from Plutarch to the Renaissance.* Edited by Anthony Ellis. Newcastle upon Tyne: Newcastle University, 2015. https://doi.org/10.1163/9789004299849_007

——"History Without Malice: Plutarch Rewrites the Battle of Plataea," 101–19 in Priestley and Zali, eds., *Brill's Companion to the Reception of Herodotus*, 2016.

Martin, Luther H. "Comparison," 66–79 in *Deep History, Secular Theory: Historical and Scientific Studies of Religion.* Berlin: Walter de Gruyter, 2014. https://doi.org/10.1515/9781614515005

McCutcheon, Russell T. "Introduction: Midnight in the Study of Origins," 1–8 in McCutcheon, ed., *Fabricating Origins*, 2015.

——"Afterward: Origins Today," 77–92 in McCutcheon, ed., *Fabricating Origins*, 2015.

——ed. *Fabricating Origins.* Sheffield, UK: Equinox, 2015.

Mikalson, Jon D. "Religion in Herodotus," 187–98 in *Brill's Companion to Herodotus.* Edited by Egbert J. Bakker, Irene J. F. De Jong, and Hans Van Wees. Leiden: Brill, 2002.

——*Herodotus and Religion in the Persian Wars.* Chapel Hill, NC: North Carolina University Press, 2012.

Moberg, Mark. *Engaging Anthropological Theory: A Social and Political History.* New York: Routledge, 2013.

Morley, Neville. "The Anti-Thucydides: Herodotus and the Development of Modern

Historiography," 143–66 in Priestley and Zali, eds., *Brill's Companion to the Reception of Herodotus*, 2016.

Moyer, Ian S. *Egypt and the Limits of Hellenism*. Cambridge: Cambridge University Press, 2011. https://doi.org/10.1017/CBO9780511894992

Muñiz Grijalvo, Elena. "The Frontiers of Graeco-Roman Religions: Greeks and Non-Greeks from a Religious Point of View," 133–48 in *Frontiers in the Roman World*. Edited by Ted Kaizer and Olivia Hekster. Leiden: Brill, 2011.

Nongbri, Brent. *Before Religion: A History of a Modern Concept*. New Haven, CT: Yale University Press, 2013. https://doi.org/10.12987/yale/9780300154160.001.0001

Nye, Malory. *Religion: The Basics*. 2nd ed. London: Routledge, 2008. https://doi.org/10.4324/9780203927977

Paden, William E. "Comparative Religion," 208–25 in Hinnells, ed., *Routledge Companion to the Study of Religion*, 2005.

Parker, Robert. *On Greek Religion*. Ithaca, NY: Cornell University Press, 2011.

Priestley, Jessica, and Vasiliki Zali, eds. *Brill's Companion to the Reception of Herodotus*. Leiden: Brill, 2016.

Roberts, Jennifer T. *Herodotus: A Very Short Introduction*. Oxford: Oxford University Press, 2011. https://doi.org/10.1093/actrade/9780199575992.001.0001

Roubekas, Nickolas P. "Sigmund Freud's Theory of Religion and the Sacrament of the Eucharist in the Orthodox Church," *Ekklesiastikos Pharos* 95 (2013): 266–82.

—*An Ancient Theory of Religion: Euhemerism from Antiquity to the Present*. London: Routledge, 2017.

Schiffman, Zachary S. *The Birth of the Past*. Baltimore, MD: Johns Hopkins University Press, 2011.

Scullion, Scott. "Herodotus and Greek Religion," 192–208 in *The Cambridge Companion to Herodotus*. Edited by Carolyn Dewald and John Marincola. Cambridge: Cambridge University Press, 2007.

Segal, Robert A. "Theories of Religion," 49–60 in Hinnells, ed., *Routledge Companion to the Study of Religion*, 2005.

—"Origins of Religion," 579–85 in *Vocabulary for the Study of Religion*, Vol. 3. Edited by Robert A. Segal and Kocku von Stuckrad. Leiden: Brill, 2016.

Smith, Jonathan Z. "Adde Parvum Parvo Magnus Acervus Erit," *History of Religions* 11.1 (1971): 67–90. https://doi.org/10.1086/462642

—"In Comparison a Magic Dwells," 19–35 in *Imagining Religion: From Babylon to Jonestown* Chicago, IL: University of Chicago Press, 1982.

Versnel, Henk S. *Coping with the Gods: Wayward Readings in Greek Theology*. Leiden: Brill, 2011. https://doi.org/10.1163/ej.9789004204904.i-594

Whitmarsh, Tim. *Battling the Gods: Atheism in the Ancient World*. New York: Alfred A. Knopf, 2015.

Winthrop, Robert H. *Dictionary of Concepts in Cultural Anthropology*. New York: Greenwood Press, 1991.

Xygalatas, Dimitris, and William McCorkle, eds. *Mental Culture: Classical Social Theory and the Cognitive Science of Religion*. London: Routledge, 2014.

PART III
FROM MESOPOTAMIA TO ROME

Chapter Eight

Ancient Mesopotamian Scholars, Ritual Speech, and Theorizing Religion Without "Theory" or "Religion"

Alan Lenzi

Europeans in the centuries following the Reformation were the first to theorize "religion" and in so doing invented our modern notion of the term. So goes a growing consensus among contemporary scholars of religion.[1] Although this historical assessment is accurate, it need not shut down our exploration of intellectual history to find earlier attempts to deal with matters and materials that we now deem religious.[2] In this brief contribution, I explore some of the ways ancient Mesopotamian scholars of the first millennium BCE designated and organized ritual speech and in so doing I will identify some of their unarticulated ideas surrounding divine-human relations. These ideas, I suggest, contribute to what may be profitably considered an implicit theory of religion. Although the presentation is only illustrative and the results partial, providing a view on one narrow swath of a much larger conceptual field, this chapter, drawing on parallel discussions in the history of science, finds an intellectual kinship between ancient and modern scholars and thus suggests that there is value in framing our modern discipline of Religious Studies in an intellectual history broader than western civilization since 1500.

Setting the Scene

There is no word in Akkadian for "religion" or "theory."[3] This absence is not surprising since the scribes never name let alone discuss explicitly many

---

1.   Brent Nongbri, *Before Religion: A History of a Modern Concept* (New Haven, CT: Yale University Press, 2013) provides a recent summation.

2.   See Nongbri, *Before Religion*, 156–9.

3.   Akkadian is the most important language for understanding first millennium ancient Mesopotamian sources. For a description of this ancient Semitic language, see John Huehnergard and Christopher Woods, "Akkadian and Eblaite," in *The Cambridge Encyclopedia of the World's Ancient Languages* (ed. Roger D. Woodard; Cambridge: Cambridge University Press, 2004), 218–87. Abbreviations used: CAD = *Chicago Assyrian Dictionary* (see A. Leo Oppenheim, Erica Reiner, and Martha Roth, *The Assyrian*

of the abstract concepts that we find useful for organizing the artifacts—
material, social, and symbolic—of our own social formations.[4] For example, there is no general word for "ethics," "law," "music," "art," "science,"
"economy," "technology," "government," "media," or "culture."[5] There
are, however, many words in Akkadian for various kinds of "ritual speech."
And there is very good evidence for how the ancient scribes identified some
texts as ritual speech, classified them by function and/or genre, and organized them into series and within ritual complexes. This sort of scholarly
activity extended to many other kinds of texts (e.g., literary, lexical, divinatory, etc.) and offers the contemporary historian a path into understanding
ancient Mesopotamian notions of textuality and, as has been argued recently,
epistemology and science.[6] In the first millennium BCE, the men responsible for these intellectual pursuits—they were all men—were called *ummânū*
("scholars"). They worked for the great institutions of society, temples and

Dictionary of the Oriental Institute of the University of Chicago [Chicago, IL: Oriental
Institute, 1956–2010]); *AHw* = *Akkadisches Handwörterbuch* (see Wolfram von Soden,
Akkadisches Handwörterbuch [Vols. 1–3; Wiesbaden: Harrassowitz, 1972–1985]).
   4.   This is not due to an inability to express abstract concepts, as is readily shown,
for example, by the widespread use of the Akkadian morpheme *–ut*, which when
attached to a substantive creates an abstract noun (e.g., *abu*, "father" + *–ut* > *abbūtu*,
"fatherhood"; *āšipu*, "exorcist" + *–ut* > *āšipūtu*, "exorcism"; *gitmālu*, "perfect," + *–ūt*
> *gitmālūtu*, "perfection"). A quick survey of Jeremy Black, Andrew R. George, and
Nicholas Postgate, eds., *A Concise Dictionary of Akkadian* (Wiesbaden: Harrassowitz,
1999) shows about 450 examples of such nouns. For this morpheme in Akkadian nomi-
nal formation, see Wolfram von Soden, *Grundriss der akkadischen Grammatik* (3rd ed.;
Rome: Pontifical Biblical Institute), §56s.
   5.   It is important to note that I have mentioned only the absence of *words* and not
the absence of *concepts*. There is no word for "genre" in Akkadian, for example. But it
is quite clear that the scribes understood the concept, if only tacitly, because they could
make lists of similar works and create texts that parody specific genres. To conclude the
absence of a concept in a Babylonian's head on the basis of the absence of a word in his
language for that concept would be to agree with the unproven "strong version" of the
Sapir-Whorf Hypothesis, for which see Barbara C. Scholz, Francis Jeffry Pelletier, and
Geoffrey K. Pullum, "Philosophy of Linguistics," *The Stanford Encyclopedia of Philosophy* (Fall 2015 Edition), online: http://plato.stanford.edu/archives/fall2015/entries/
linguistics/, §4 generally and Michael Streck, "Sprache und Denken im altem Mesopotamien: Am Beispiel des Zeitausdrucks," in *Studia Semitica* (ed. Leonid Kogan; Moscow:
Russian State University for the Humanities, 2003), 431 n. 21 in the context of a discussion about the Akkadian language in particular. Contrast Nongbri, *Before Religion*, 23.
   6.   See, e.g., Marc Van de Mieroop, *Philosophy Before the Greeks: The Pursuit
of Truth in Ancient Babylonia* (Princeton, NJ: Princeton University Press, 2015); Niek
Veldhuis, *History of the Cuneiform Lexical Tradition* (Münster: Ugarit-Verlag, 2014);
Alan Lenzi, "Mesopotamian Scholarship: Kassite to Late Babylonian Periods," *Journal
of Ancient Near Eastern History* 2.2 (2015): 145–201.

palaces, to insure proper relations with the gods—and their most important client was the king, whose ability to rule was dependent on their counsel and expertise. The scholars' corpus was called *ṭupšarrūtu* ("scribal art, scholarship").[7] Like scholars today, each specialized in one or more disciplines (extispicy, celestial divination, exorcism, medicine, and ritual lamentation/ appeasement) and curated a corpus of associated texts, which they used to insure proper relations with the gods, as well as other learned materials—literary, lexical, and mathematical. A focus on ritual speech, a specific aspect of Mesopotamian culture that intersects significantly with—although is not comprehended by—this ancient scholarship, provides one way to get at a context and locus for understanding, if only partially, the scholars' implicit theory of divine-human relations of interest here.

For the present purpose, I define "ritual speech" as any human linguistic communication that was not used to communicate between humans but sought by performative means to elicit or effect change in some situation for which the communication was invoked. Ritual speech was often, although not always, directed at a superhuman entity and often, although not always, accompanied by symbolic actions. The evidence for ritual speech from ancient Mesopotamia is much too extensive to present comprehensively; thus, I limit myself to representative examples from the Akkadian materials of the first millennium BCE, presented under two separate though inter-related categories: lexical and scribal classificatory. The latter material provides invaluable indigenous evidence for second-order thinking about the matter at hand.

Methodological Prelude: Ancient Science or Ancient Religion?

The scholars of the first millennium BCE traced the origins of their disciplines and the texts that they curated back via seven ancient sages to Ea, god of water, wisdom, and magic.[8] This lineage gave the scholars prestige at court and their corpora of texts an unmatched authority in maintaining divine-human relations for both palace and temple. Considered as a whole, these scholars were responsible for a wide variety of intellectual activities, from celestial observation and calculation to the maintenance and execution

---

7.   Some even translate the term as "Scripture" since the corpora were authoritative to the scholars. See Frances Reynolds, *The Babylonian Correspondence of Esarhaddon and Letters to Assurbanipal and Sin-šarru-iškun from Northern and Central Babylonia* (Helsinki: University of Helsinki Press, 2003), no. 204 (cited below). For an overview of scholarship in first millennium BCE Mesopotamia, see Lenzi, "Mesopotamian Scholarship."

8.   See Alan Lenzi, *Secrecy and the Gods: Secret Knowledge in Ancient Mesopotamia and Biblical Israel* (Helsinki: The Neo-Assyrian Text Corpus Project, 2008), 67–134.

of various rituals. Most modern readers of this book will associate the former tasks within the gambit of science (i.e., astronomy and mathematics) and thus related to the natural realm, whereas they will likely connect the latter tasks to the domain of religion (i.e., liturgy and theology) and thus related to the supernatural realm. These tasks, however, as apparently disparate as they are to us, were conceptually related to one another, indeed, inextricably so in some cases[9] for the ancient Mesopotamian scholars, for whom there was no concept of nature and super-nature and thus no absolute division between the human and divine spheres.[10] Indeed, the scholars—all too human, if their correspondence is any evidence[11]—thought themselves to be the professional descendants of semi-divine sages, the emissaries of a god.

It would seem then that looking for something akin to a theory of religion among these ancient scholars would distort the evidence. Yet confronting the absence of distinctions in the ancient scholars that are so crucial to our own thinking offers several openings. The first among these are opportunities to develop a critical self-awareness of our own analytical categories and to question our compartmentalization of the history of science and the history of religions. After considering briefly some broad currents within the two fields, I note that they share a common concern and a common methodological point of departure when it comes to analyzing ancient historical data. Reflecting on the ancient data in terms of the history of science versus the history of religions leads also to the recognition that our research interests steer the circumscription and inform the interpretation of the data. Brief discussions of these matters provide a methodological prelude to the presentation of evidence.

The fields of the history of religions and the history of science in the last century have by and large moved in opposite directions in terms of their willingness to include within their purview the intellectual activities encoded in texts from ancient societies. As the twentieth century unfolded and positivism died off, contemporary historians of science grew more willing to talk about pre-modern (and non-western) people's observations and

9.   For example, the observation (or prediction) of a lunar eclipse announced impending evil and therefore required an elaborate apotropaic ritual.

10.   See Francesca Rochberg, *Before Nature: Cuneiform Knowledge and the History of Science* (Chicago, IL: University of Chicago Press, 2016). Mesopotamian mythology exemplifies this point repeatedly. For example, Gilgamesh follows the sun god's (probably) subterranean path; Etana ascends to the heavens on the back of an eagle; and Enkidu descends into the netherworld to fetch Gilgamesh's ball and mallet. For a detailed presentation of ancient Mesopotamian cosmography, see Wayne Horowitz, *Mesopotamian Cosmic Geography* (Winona Lake, IN: Eisenbrauns, 1998).

11.   See Simo Parpola, *Letters from Assyrian and Babylonian Scholars* (Helsinki: Helsinki University Press, 1993).

understandings of the phenomenal world as science, and to do so in the peo-ple's own cultural terms rather than in the standards of modern science. In broad strokes, the early reticence to include the ancients in history of sci-ence gave way to a socio-culturally contextualized understanding of their activities as scientific.[12] It is acceptable now, for example, to talk about sci-ence in ancient Mesopotamia.[13]

   Philologists and historians of religion, on the other hand, with ancient texts chocked full of gods, rituals, and prayers—all intuitive denizens in modern notions of religion—have been quite willing (often without much self-aware-ness) to describe their materials in terms of religion. For ancient Mesopo-tamia, scholars have readily used "religion" as a descriptive term since the nineteenth century, when thousands of cuneiform texts poured into European museums.[14] In recent decades, however, scholars in religious studies have lain bare the genealogy of religion—one intimately related to the historical contingencies of western civilization—and called into question the field's common assumptions and definitions as Eurocentric and crypto-Protestant.[15] Whereas once scholars of ancient societies took for granted the applicability

   12.   Clearly, this un-nuanced generality does not do justice to the complexities of the matter, which has not been without controversy and continues to be debated. For a useful and succinct presentation of these historiographical changes (and the implications for the historiography of the Chemical Revolution), see John G. McEvoy, "Modernism, Postmodernism and the Historiography of Science," *Historical Studies in the Physi-cal and Biological Sciences* 37.2 (2007): 383–408. Peter Dear, "What is the History of Science the History *Of*?: Early Modern Roots of the Ideology of Modern Science," *Isis* 96.3 (2005): 390–406 provides a broad view on how these new developments have raised anxieties about the field's identity and content. Interestingly, Dear draws a parallel between the problems in defining science for the history of science to the problems of defining religion in what he calls the field of comparative religion (392).

   13.   See Francesca Rochberg, *The Heavenly Writing: Divination, Horoscopy, and Astronomy in Mesopotamian Culture* (Cambridge: Cambridge University Press, 2004), especially ch. 1, for a thorough presentation of the changing reception of Babylonian celestial observations, moving from exclusion to acceptance, within the field of the his-tory of science. Rochberg applies the term "scientific" to Mesopotamian materials in a qualified sense (see below and 244–6). See also Rochberg, *Before Nature*, in which she argues for including Mesopotamia in the history of science despite the fact that the Mes-opotamians did not have a concept of "nature." (I thank Professor Rochberg for allowing me to read her book before its publication.) Van de Mieroop, *Before the Greeks* uses a much more relativistic definition of science in his treatment of Babylonian epistemology as manifested in lexicography, divination, and jurisprudence.

   14.   A mammoth book on ancient Mesopotamian religion, Morris Jastrow's *The Reli-gion of Babylonia and Assyria* (Boston, MA: Ginn, 1898), was published just over forty years after the confirmed decipherment of Akkadian in 1857.

   15.   See, e.g., Talal Asad, *Genealogies of Religion: Discipline and Reasons of Power in Christianity and Islam* (Baltimore, MD: Johns Hopkins University Press, 1993), 27–54.

of religion as a descriptive category for understanding the ancient texts from Greece, Rome, Egypt, and the Near East, they are now increasingly calling its utility into question.[16]

Both history of science and history of religions, despite their differences, are responding, broadly speaking, to the same intellectual issues raised by postmodernism. Having grown aware of the situatedness of their own categories of cultural analysis, scholars in both fields have (rightly) reassessed how they deploy these categories and have developed methodological stances to remedy or at least ameliorate their hegemonic use. Among these various strategies is one utilized recently by both ancient historians of science and religion. Brent Nongbri has recently summarized the case against using "religion" as a descriptive category with ancient texts because it is anachronistic. Rather than giving up "religion" entirely, however, he suggests we use the term as a second-order, *re*-descriptive concept; that is, "religion" may prove useful as a heuristic or analytical concept that helps the present-day scholar mediate the interpreted content of ancient texts to a contemporary world for whom religion is a significant cultural category.[17] Nongbri's basic definition of religion, "things involving gods or other superhuman beings and the technologies for interacting with such beings,"[18]

16. See Nongbri, *Before Religion* generally and 143–53 for Mesopotamia specifically. See, likewise, Niek Veldhuis, *Religion, Literature, and Scholarship: The Sumerian Composition Nanše and the Birds, with a Catalogue of Sumerian Bird Names* (Leiden: Styx/Brill, 2004), 11–3 for ancient Mesopotamia (also cited by Nongbri). The message is still working its way through the field. For example, the most recent book about Mesopotamian religion written by an Assyriologist (Ivan Hrůša, *Ancient Mesopotamian Religion: A Descriptive Introduction* [Münster: Ugarit-Verlag, 2015]) does not even offer a working definition of religion but simply presumes his readership knows what it is.

17. See Nongbri, *Before Religion*, 156–8. For a brief description of religion as a descriptive vs. redescriptive category, see 21–2. Advocating for the second-order use of religion is not new in Religious Studies; see, e.g., Jonathan Z. Smith, *Imagining Religion: From Babylon to Jonestown* (Chicago, IL: University of Chicago Press, 1982) and Russell T. McCutcheon, *Critics Not Caretakers: Redescribing the Public Study of Religion* (Albany, NY: State University of New York Press, 2001). Nongbri cites Stanley Stowers, "The Ontology of Religion," in *Introducing Religion: Essays in Honor of Jonathan Z. Smith* (ed. Willi Braun and Russell T. McCutcheon; London: Equinox, 2008), 434–49, who advocates religion's usefulness specifically as a second-order analytical concept in the study of *ancient* societies; likewise, Alan Lenzi, ed., *Reading Akkadian Prayers and Hymns: An Introduction* (Atlanta, GA: Society of Biblical Literature Press, 2011), 2–8. The philosophical difficulty that this distinction runs into—a problem literally introduced in a standard "Ethnography 101" textbook (see, e.g., Martyn Hammersley and Paul Atkinson, *Ethnography* [3rd ed.; London: Routledge, 2007], 230–3)—is that the tidy distinction between description and analysis (redescription) is a theoretical ideal that in practice is not so tidy.

18. Nongbri, *Before Religion*, 157.

seems appropriate for investigating ritual speech as religious data and its treatment by ancient scholarship as a means for identifying and understanding elements of an ancient theory of religion.

Something like Nongbri's approach is likewise advocated by Assyriologist and historian of science Francesca Rochberg, who states at the beginning of her book on Babylonian celestial science that

> an investigation of [Babylonian] "science" is, strictly speaking, an exercise in anachronism … But we come to historical material from a distant vantage point, and with analytical categories that may or may not apply to the subject of interest. As long as the goal is, in this case, to make the cuneiform texts concerning celestial inquiry intelligible, the use of non-Mesopotamian categories to analyze these texts can be productive … [R]ather than condemn the very question of "how is cuneiform celestial inquiry classifiable as science" as unintelligible within the context of ancient Mesopotamian cultural values, I maintain its continuing interest and value for the history of science, because finally, the question is not how "they" thought about science, but how we do. Indeed, cuneiform texts of divinatory, astrological, and astronomical content belong to the history of science not because the Babylonians thought of these intellectual inquiries as "science," but because, in assessing the nature and practice of their activities, we can reasonably place Mesopotamian divination, astrology, and astronomy in a larger context that is meaningful within and for the history of science.[19]

If one replaces "science" with "religion" and reads Rochberg's statement as applying to cuneiform texts generally, one sees a statement very much in keeping with Nongbri's methodology and this study's suggestion with regard to the ancient Mesopotamian scholars. In light of these statements, why, one might ask, should the present study use "religion" rather than "science" as its analytical category of choice?

In fact, other contemporary scholars have presented the intellectual activity of the ancient Mesopotamian scholars, viewed at a more general and thus more inclusive level than is done here,[20] as an aspect of Mesopotamian science.[21] I am interested in a subset of their intellectual activity, namely, their treatment of ritual speech and especially incantations. And this evidence, I suggest, when viewed in terms of religion, defined again as "things involving gods or other superhuman beings and the technologies for interacting with such beings,"[22] offers a perspective useful to those of us who study religion. Indeed, the Mesopotamian evidence provides a corrective in

---

19. Rochberg, *Heavenly Writing*, xv–xvi.

20. For example, a more inclusive approach to scribal textual classificatory practices might include data from, e.g., divinatory, literary, legal, and lexical text forms.

21. See, e.g., Van de Mieroop, *Before the Greeks*.

22. Nongbri, *Before Religion*, 157.

some ways to recent trends since it views the ancient scholars as our fore-bears in the study of religion. It is a truism in historical investigation that the questions, methods, emphases, and perspectives we bring to bear upon our data influence the results of our investigation. Looking at the data through the lens of religion rather than science highlights different facets of the data. The results are complementary perspectives that yield insights on a culture that recognized neither science nor religion in our sense of those words.

I am not claiming that the ancient Mesopotamian evidence reviewed here proves the scholars had a "theory of religion" in the same sense that we expect those words to have today.[23] Rather, I claim that the activity of ancient scholars points to a kinship—not so much genetic as analogical—to elements of modern theoretical work on religion undertaken by contem-porary scholars,[24] for whom circumscription of data and its taxonomy are the results of (in the best cases, explicit) theoretical commitments or judg-ments. The ancients are usually not explicit about their theoretical com-mitments. But their circumscription of data and their taxonomic practices suggest the presence of a tacit theory in operation. This I deem worthy of explication and exploration.

Ritual Speech: Lexical and Scribal Classificatory Evidence

Ritual speech, considered broadly, could have been formal or informal, written and/or oral. We know ancient Mesopotamian ritual speech today, however, only to the extent that it is preserved in written form in, for exam-ple, prayers, laments, hymns, queries, and incantations, or mentioned in other documents such as letters and royal propaganda. These documents, like most other texts we have from ancient Mesopotamia, were usually inscribed on clay tablets and unearthed during archaeological excavations of the last one hundred and seventy years. Although contemporary muse-ums hold about a million tablets of all genres, the tablets range over three millennia and are thus uneven in geographical and chronological cover-age. The period I have chosen to focus on, the first millennium BCE, offers some of the richest tablet finds, including the famed library of Ashurbani-pal at Nineveh,[25] and represents the most self-conscious stage of Babylo-nian intellectual activity available to us. It thus serves the present purpose quite well.

23. That is, the origins of religion or the reason for its perpetuation.
24. I have borrowed the kinship metaphor from Rochberg, *Before Nature*.
25. For a brief overview of the main sites and libraries, see Lenzi, "Mesopotamian Scholarship."

As noted earlier, I approach this material from two perspectives: the lexical and the scribal classificatory,[26] that is, the ways scholars designated and organized ritual speech. The evidence shows ambiguities and overlaps in ritual speech and non-ritual speech. It also shows distinctive treatment of incantations. All of this provides evidence that contributes to an implicit theory of divine-human relations.

Lexical Evidence: Designations

Among first millennium sources there are many Akkadian words that designate ritual speech, both in terms of content and the act of producing it. Many of these terms were used by people who were not scholars, although the latter certainly used them, too. Thus, this first domain of evidence provides a general backdrop against which to understand the second dealing with classification. To illustrate the variety of words for ritual speech, I offer the following inventory,[27] identified by searching *A Concise Dictionary of Akkadian*[28] for lexemes glossed with "beseech," "entreat," "entreaty," "hymn," "incantation," "lament," "praise," "pray," "prayer," "supplicate," and "supplication." The resulting list is arranged in three categories.[29]

(1) Words used to describe ritual speech in some general manner: *angillu*, "lament";[30] *atnu*, "prayer"; *dalīlu*, "praise"; *gerrānu*, "wailing, lament"; *ikribu*, "prayer, dedication"; *karābu* I, "prayer, blessing"; *minûtu*, "recitation (of an incantation)"; *naqbītu*, "utterance, wording (of a prayer)"; *nīru* III, "prayer";[31] *nissatu*, "wailing, lament"; *qibītu*, "command, prayer"; *sīpu*, "prayer"; *sul(l)û*, "prayer"; *sup(p)û*, "supplication"; *surāru*, "prayer"; *ṣerḫu* I, "dirge, lamentation"; *ṣul(l)û*, "supplication"; *šigû*, "a cry of lamentation"; *šiptu*, "incantation"; *tanattu*, "praise, glory"; *tanīdu*, "(hymn of) praise"; *tanittu*, "(hymn of) praise, renown"; *tarsītu*, "prayer";[32] *tēmīqu*, "(deep) prayer, presentation of

---

26. I make no claim to this approach being the only one for gathering evidence for the present concerns.

27. Although I have cast the net broadly and thus acquired a good representative cross-section, the resulting list is not comprehensive. As far as I know, there is no complete treatment of "ritual speech" as a semantic domain.

28. Black, George, and Postgate, eds., *Concise Dictionary of Akkadian.*

29. The usage of each word was checked in the CAD or *AHw*, both standard dictionaries in the field, to ensure that it was in fact related to ritual speech. A few words that did not meet that criteria or were the product of a scribal corruption were omitted.

30. See CAD I/J, 57–9, s.v. *ikkillu*.

31. Only in lexical lists, CAD N/2, 265.

32. Only in lexical lists, CAD T, 241.

case"; *tēnintu*, "lamentation, prayer"; *tēnīnu*, "lamentation, prayer"; *teslītu*, "appeal, prayer"; *tespītu*, "prayer"; *tû*, "incantation"; *unnīnu*, "prayer"; *urubātu*, "wailing"; and *utnēnu* I, "supplication."

(2) Verbs that implied the production of some form of ritual speech: *bâlu*, "to supplicate"; *dalālu* II, "to praise"; *elû* (D-stem), "to extol"; *emēqu* (Št-stem), "to pray devoutly";[33] *enēnu* IV, "to pray";[34] *karābu* II, "to pray, bless"; *ma'û* (D-stem), "to praise(?)"; *nâdu*, "to celebrate, praise"; *qerēbu* (Štn-stem), "constantly present request, pray"; *rabû* (Š-stem), "to magnify"; *sarruru*, "to pray"; *sullû* (D-stem), "to appeal, pray";[35] *suppû* II (D-stem), "to pray"; *šamāru* (Gt-and Gtn-stems), "to praise"; *šaqû* (Š-stem), "to exalt"; *šarāḫu* (D-stem), "to glorify"; and *(w)ašāpu*, "to exorcise, to chant a spell."

(3) Words used to identify or label *a particular kind of* ritual speech:[36] *eršaḫungû*, "a kind of Emesal prayer"; *ikribu*, "(diviner's) prayer"; *ki'utukku*, "a kind of incantation"; *muḫru*, "a special kind of prayer"; *pāru*, "a kind of hymn"; *šerdingirgallakku*, "a divine hymn"*; *šigû*, "a kind of prayer"; *šu'illakku*, "a hand-raising prayer"; *šutanīdû*, "antiphonal hymn,"*;[37] *urubātu*, "ceremonial wailing"; and *zipadû*, "an incantation formula."

A full treatment of these words is beyond the purview of this short chapter and unnecessary for its purpose. A perusal of their attested contexts in the CAD indicates that most of the terms in the first two groups were not exclusively used to describe what we have defined as ritual speech.[38] For example, *unnīnu*, a common word for prayer, describes supplication to a

---

33. This verb is not recognized in the CAD. See *AHw*, 214.

34. Including *utnēnu* II, "to pray."

35. Including *ṣullû*.

36. A number of these designated a kind of lament only attested in lexical lists: *aḫulabakku*; *ergididû*; *erkitušû*; *ersaḫarḫubbû*; *ersiskurrû*; *eršabadarû*; *eršannešakku*; *ertabadarû*; and *irarazakku*.

37. * indicates these words are only attested in the hymnic catalog KAR 158 (cf. Brigitte Groneberg, "Searching for Akkadian Lyrics: From Old Babylonian to the 'Liederkatalog' KAR 158," *Journal of Cuneiform Studies* 55 [2003]: 55–74).

38. Some words in the first two lists are only used (on present evidence) to describe human intercession with superhuman beings and thus may hint that these are distinctive lexical designations for ritual speech. Examples include *atnu*, *sīpu*, *tēnīnu*, and *sarruru*. It seems imprudent to draw conclusions from this since the words are attested so rarely—two to four contexts outside of lexical lists (see CAD A/2, 499; S, 304; T, 343; and S, 414, respectively). The word *šigû* is also only used for ritual speech and in fact seems to have become a designation for a kind of lamentation, as noted in the third list (see Margaret Jaques, *Mon dieu qu'ai-je fait? Les* diĝir-šà-dab$_{(5)}$-ba *et la piété privée en Mésopotamie* [Fribourg: Academic Press / Göttingen: Vandenhoeck & Ruprecht, 2015], 9, 12–3).

deity or to a human;[39] *gerrānu,* "wailing, lament," describes ritual wailings directed at the gods or simply an emotional outburst due to social alienation and loss of status;[40] and *šarāḫu* (D-stem), "to glorify," can describe praise directed to a god or a king.[41] Such usage is not at all surprising and reveals the first of several implicit theoretical principles our investigation reveals about divine-human relations.

As with many cultures around the world, Mesopotamian conceptions of the divine realm were patterned on human society. Just as there is a human king, there is a king of the gods; just as there is a royal council, there is a divine council; just as one writes a letter to one's family, one may write a letter to one's god; just as one greets a social superior with a specific hand-raising gesture, one may do the same when approaching a deity (in prayer);[42] and thus it is not surprising that just as one may entreat or direct a lament to a social superior, one may entreat or lament to a deity—the ultimate social superior. And to do so, one would draw on the same words (and often genres)[43] used in that kind of communication between humans. Cognitive studies of religious activity provide an additional reason for this phenomenon: people in unreflective moments tend to treat a deity as a human person (with limitations, etc.), despite official theological statements to the contrary, because the human brain is cognitively predisposed to do so. As Todd Tremlin writes, "*Person* is the only natural ontological category that the mind possesses for comprehending the type of entities that gods are said to be."[44] Although this is not distinctively Mesopotamian or an exclusive characteristic of the ancient scholars, this point provides important background information for conceptualizing the scholars' understanding of divine-human relations.

39. See CAD U/W, 162–4. Although most of the contexts in which the word describes speech directed to a human are from second millennium letters, there is one use in a royal inscription from the mid-first millennium.

40. CAD G, 89. For the latter use, see *Ludlul* I 105 cited there.

41. CAD Š/2, 37–8.

42. For the hand-raising (Sum. šu-íl-lá) gesture and its use in a prayer of the same name, see Christopher G. Frechette, *Mesopotamian Ritual-Prayers of "Hand-lifting" (Akkadian Šuillas): An Investigation of Function in Light of the Idiomatic Meaning of the Rubric* (Münster: Ugarit-Verlag, 2012).

43. Thus, we have "letter-prayers," which look just like letters between humans (Lenzi, *Reading Akkadian Prayers*, 53–5), and "incantation-prayers," which are very clearly modeled on the interaction of a social inferior gaining an audience with and entreating a social superior; see Annette Zgoll, "Audienz — Ein Modell zum Verständnis mesopotamischer Handerhebungsrituale. Mit einer Deutung der Novelle vom *Armen Mann von Nippur*," *Baghdader Mitteilungen* 34 (2003): 173–95; Frechette, *Mesopotamian Ritual-Prayers*, 11–106.

44. Todd Tremlin, *Minds and Gods: The Cognitive Foundations of Religion* (Oxford: Oxford University Press, 2006), 96; cf. 93–106 for the fuller context.

The words *šiptu* and *tû* in the first list are interesting exceptions to the rule. They are *never* used of non-ritual human speech. Both terms are traditionally translated "incantation" in Assyriology, although they are better rendered with "ritual wording" or "divine adjuration," and designate the most populous general category of Mesopotamian ritual speech—there are many hundred incantations.[45] *Šiptu* and *tû* are terms for a potent form of speech typically directed at gods, demons, monsters, ghosts, personified illnesses, witches, cultic substances, animals, and sometimes other people (although not interpersonally), often accompanied by symbolic actions, to effect change in the speaker's situation via its utterance.[46] Although these two words obviously designate ritual speech and distinctively so, there is an issue: the semantic coverage of both words goes beyond the human realm since gods also spoke incantations.[47] In fact, it is precisely *because* the gods spoke incantations that these texts had power when humans used them.[48] This finds support in incantations that assert near their conclusions that the words do not belong to the speaker, rather, a god spoke them and the human speaker has repeated them. For example:

> *Ea u Asalluḫi šipat mašmaš ilī Marduk šunu iddū-ma*
> *anāku ušanni*
> Ea and Asalluḫi cast the incantation of Marduk, the exorcist of the gods, and I repeated it.

> *ina qibīt Ištar Šamaš Ea Asalluḫi*
> *šiptu ul yuttun šipat Ea u Asalluḫi šipat Ištar bēlet rami*
> By order of Ishtar, Shamash, Ea, and Asalluḫi. The incantation is not mine;

---

45.   Unfortunately, no comprehensive catalog exists. For an overview, see Benjamin Foster, *Akkadian Literature of the Late Period* (Münster: Ugarit-Verlag, 2007), 91–5, 74–7 (the so-called incantation-prayers; a differentiation not followed here).

46.   Compare Wilfred G. Lambert, "The Classification of Incantations," in *Proceedings of the 51st Rencontre Assyriologique Internationale Held at The Oriental Institute of the University of Chicago July 18-22, 2005* (ed. Robert D. Biggs, Jennie Myers, and Martha T. Roth; Chicago, IL: The Oriental Institute of the University of Chicago, 2008), 95.

47.   Akkadian mythology makes this point clear. Ea uses an incantation to subdue his enemy Apsu in the creation account *Enuma Elish* (Tablet I, lines 59-70), and both Marduk and his foe Tiamat use incantations in their battle to the death in the same poem (IV 61-94); see Wilfred G. Lambert, *Babylonian Creation Myths* (Winona Lake, IN: Eisenbrauns, 2013), 52–5 and 88–91.

48.   There is no comprehensive study of first millennium incantations. For divine legitimation, see Alan Lenzi, "*Šiptu ul Yuttun*: Some Reflections on a Closing Formula in Akkadian Incantations," in *Gazing on the Deep: Ancient Near Eastern, Biblical, and Jewish Studies in Honor of Tzvi Abusch* (ed. Jeffrey Stackert, Barbara Neveling Porter, and David P. Wright; Bethesda, MD: CDL Press, 2010), 131–66.

it is the incantation of Ea and Asalluḫi; *it is* the incantation of Ishtar, goddess of love.[49]

In light of this, we ought better to understand *šiptu* and *tû* as designating divine speech that humans have appropriated into their own ritual speech. By "people" I mean scholars, since our evidence limits incantations in the first millennium context to scholars who expended countless hours reciting, copying, editing, and organizing incantations within the context of the *ṭupšarrūtu*, specifically, within exorcism and to some extent ritual lamentation.[50] In appearances there is still a blurring of the separation between divine and human, albeit in the opposite direction: people take up what is divine. But in linguistic designation this form of divine ritual speech is labeled distinctively, suggesting a second implicit theoretical principle that our examination of ritual speech contributes to understanding divine-human relations—one related more closely to the ancient scholars. That is, when humans designate ritual speech understood as having a divine origin, such is labeled distinctly with terms not used of other forms of speech, ritual or non-ritual in kind. Although significant in its own right, this point will also be important in our examination of scribal classificatory practices.

The third group of words is of an entirely different order since they designate specific kinds of ritual speech, defined in terms of form, content, and/or function. Whatever their origin,[51] these terms—joined by many other Akkadian and Sumerian terms not captured in my survey—operate essentially as technical terms and occur within the scribal classificatory system, to which we turn presently. Their existence supports the idea that the scholars carefully sorted and labeled ritual speech.

Scribal Classificatory Evidence: Organization

A wealth of what we may call scribal meta-data exists in the various means scribes used to label, organize, and classify the texts they curated on clay tablets in the first millennium BCE.[52] For our purposes, the most important of these are colophons, incipits, rubrics, and superscriptions, all of which are

49. Both texts are cited in Lenzi, "*Šiptu ul Yuttun*," 144 and 146, respectively, with full references there.

50. Non-scholars probably used incantations, too, but we lack documentation.

51. Note that the generic word *ikribu* also designates a kind of prayer, even though it was not always used to designate ritual speech but could be used for interpersonal speech, too. See CAD I/J, 62–6. A similar dual use may hold true for *urubātu*, "ceremonial wailing, wailing" (see CAD U/W, 267), and *tamītu*, "oath, speech," which became a name for a specific kind of oracle query; see Wilfred G. Lambert, *Babylonian Oracle Questions* (Winona Lake, IN: Eisenbrauns, 2007), 5–7.

52. For an introduction to this material, see Lenzi, "Mesopotamian Scholarship."

defined below. Thousands of cuneiform tablets offer evidence of these classifiers, representing a wide array of genres: from astronomical texts to literary catalogs; from the *Epic of Gilgamesh* to a lexical list of occupations; and
from liver omens to incantations against illnesses and demons. These traditional texts comprised *ṭupšarrūtu* and defined the scholars' canon (if not
knowledge or interests), as implied in this letter from a scholar to his king:

> Rites that are written in *ṭupšarrūtu are* our rites. Our fathers performed these.
> And they were established for the needs of kingship. *There are* a hundred, a
> thousand *rites* that may serve for purification of the kings, my lords, as far
> as I am concerned. But because they *are* not our rites, they are not written in
> *ṭupšarrūtu.*[53]

Our review of the scribal classificatory means to organize this traditional
material suggests an evidentiary parallel to the lexical inventory surveyed
earlier. Generally, the classificatory means are not exclusively used with
ritual speech; but one practice used to demarcate the beginning of an incantation is distinctive. Before this review, however, a caveat is in order.

Not all ritual speech was fitted with scribal meta-data. For example,
the Neo-Assyrian diviners' inquiries to Shamash, spoken before the performance of an extispicy, were preserved on tablets but never subjected
to organizational techniques as were the related *tamītu*-texts.[54] Unlike the
latter, the former were specific to one situation and thus were not organized
for a future use, although they were preserved in the royal archive. The
same single-use intent likely explains why Old Babylonian letter-prayers
lack scribal meta-data.[55] Thus, although ritual speech intersects significantly
with the scholars' intellectual interests and therefore their scribal classificatory activities under discussion, not all ritual speech was classified. The
needs and principles of *ṭupšarrūtu* define what the scholars curated, which
again suggests that an implicit theory is actively shaping the process.

At the end of a clay tablet bearing a copy of a traditional text there is
often a colophon, a space set apart on the tablet from the main text with
a dividing line, where scribes stated that the tablet was a copy and then
recorded various other bits of information, including the contents of the text
designated by its first line (its incipit), its position in a series, and the name

53. Reynolds, *Babylonian Correspondence of Esarhaddon*, no. 204, rev. 5-10; my
translation (emphases in the original).

54. For the NA queries, see Ivan Starr, *Queries to the Sungod: Divination and Politics in Sargonid Assyria* (Helsinki: Helsinki University Press, 1990); for the *tamītu*
texts, see Lambert, *Babylonian Oracle Questions*; and for a brief description of both,
see Lenzi, *Reading Akkadian Prayers*, 49–53.

55. For an introduction to the OB letter-prayers, see Lenzi, *Reading Akkadian
Prayers*, 53–5.

of the composition, series, or ritual type to which it belongs (its rubric).[56] A tablet colophon is comparable to a book's copyright page. The following example, taken from the end of a tablet bearing the seventh chapter of the anti-witchcraft ritual *Maqlû* ("Burning"), is typical:

> ÉN *adi tappuḫa uqâka bēlī Šamaš*
> [D]UB.7.KAM* *Maqlû*
> Incantation. Until you appear, I wait for you, my lord, Shamash.
> It is the seventh tablet. Burning.[57]

The first line in the citation above identifies the opening line of the next chapter of the ceremony (Tablet VIII). The second line marks the end of the present chapter ("tablet") and identifies the composition by means of its rubric, which is also the name of the ritual ceremony. The very same devices were used to link and identify chapters in other genres, such as lexical lists, omen collections, and literary texts. We need not multiply references, although many, many more examples could easily be cited.[58] Like the many general words used for ritual speech, the scribal meta-data in colophons do not show any distinguishing characteristics that would suggest texts or tablets mainly comprised of ritual speech were treated differently from texts or tablets of non-ritual speech.

Rubrics were sometimes placed in the middle of a tablet to identify the text that comes before it and separate that material from the text that follows the rubric. Rubrics were usually only a line or two long and distinguished from the body text with dividing lines incised in the tablet before and after the rubric. Sometimes the rubric's identification names the composition or larger ritual series to which the textual unit belongs. For example, at the conclusion of most incantations in the series *Utukkū Lemnūtu*, "Evil Demon," we find a rubric that states in Sumerian:

---

56.   Colophons may also state the number of lines a tablet contains, its place of origin, the copyist's name, for whom it was copied, the date it was copied, the reason the tablet was copied, the care with which it was copied, and/or whether it was a complete copy. What is included varies widely. See Hermann Hunger, *Babylonische und assyrische Kolophone* (Neukirchen-Vluyn: Neukirchener / Kevelaer: Butzon & Bercker, 1968), 1–15, which offers more than five hundred and sixty examples.

57.   Tzvi Abusch, *The Magical Ceremony* Maqlû: *A Critical Edition* (Leiden: Brill, 2016), 191, 360.

58.   To compare the variable content of colophons of manuscripts of the same chapter in an omen series and lexical text, see Sally Freedman, *If a City Is Set on a Height: The Akkadian Omen Series* Shumma Alu ina mele Shakin. Vol. 1: *Tablets 1-21* (Philadelphia, PA: University Museum, 1998), 260–3 (and passim for other examples) and Ivan Hrůša, *Die akkadische Synonymenliste* malku = šarru: *Eine Textedition mit Übersetzung und Kommentar* (Münster: Ugarit-Verlag, 2010), 376, respectively.

ka-inim-ma udug-ḫul-a-kam
It is the ritual wording of an "evil demon" ritual.[59]

This rubric simply specifies that the preceding incantation was part of the larger ritual series. If more than one incantation was inscribed on a single tablet, then this rubric would occur several times on that tablet.

In other cases, the rubric's identification names a specific function such as a ritual use. For example:

ka-inim-ma šu-íl-lá ᵈDN
It is the ritual wording of a *shuila*-ritual (Akk. *šu'illakku*) to {insert divine name}.

This rubric, written in Sumerian, as is often the case, is quite common. For example, it occurs five times on a tablet that belongs to a royal purificatory ritual and contains five incantation-prayers directed to as many gods.[60] A similar use of rubrics occurs in the *tamītu*-queries (posed to the gods before an extispicy), where multiple *tamītu*s are compiled on a single tablet and separated from one another by an Akkadian rubric that identifies each text as a query and gives its topic of reference.[61] Many other examples could be provided.[62]

If we define a rubric as an intermittent insertion between blocks of text for purposes of identification and classification, then rubrics are not limited to texts containing ritual speech. In fact, they are a rather common scribal technique. For example, a literary catalog lists several compositions followed by a rubric that identifies their putative author before moving on to the next group of texts and their author.[63] Tablets bearing the text of several prophetic oracles arranged serially separate each oracle with a rubric

---

59. Stephen Geller, *Evil Demons: Canonical* Utukkū Lemnūtu *Incantations* (Helsinki: The Neo-Assyrian Text Corpus Project, 2007), passim.

60. See, e.g., Claus Ambos, *Der König im Gefängnis und das Neujahrsfest im Herbst: Mechanismen der Legitimation des babylonischen Herrschers im 1. Jahrtausend v. Chr. und ihre Geschichte* (Dresden: ISLET, 2013), 204–9.

61. For example, a *tamītu* "concerning the safety of the city," "for the safety of those who go out of the city," etc. See Lambert, *Babylonian Oracle Questions*, no. 1, lines 95, 160 (and 183, 231, 345).

62. See Lenzi, *Reading Akkadian Prayers*, 47–8 for a series of *ikribu*-prayers, that is, prayers spoken during each step of an extispicy ritual, marked off from one another by rubric.

63. See Wilfred G. Lambert, "A Catalogue of Texts and Authors," *Journal of Cuneiform Studies* 16 (1962): 64–7. This catalog illustrates well the idea that important works of scholarship came from Ea, god of wisdom and magic, and his sages (the *apkallū*), while human scholars (*ummânū*) of a later age are their professional successors. See Lenzi, *Secrecy and the Gods*, 119–20.

identifying the human speaker.[64] And Assyrian records related to the acquisition of scholarly and literary works for Ashurbanipal's famed library follow a similar list-rubric structure.[65] These are but a small sample of a rather widespread practice.

Again, we must conclude that this classificatory method was merely part of the curation of tablets comprising traditional scholarship. As with colophons, rubrics therefore do not tell us anything distinctive about the treatment of ritual speech. But this should not be that surprising. As mentioned above, the various branches of ancient Mesopotamian scholarship (*ṭupšarrūtu*) included a great many disciplines and genres of texts. As a curated corpus of intellectual activity, we would expect some level of consistency in organizational mechanisms across genres, which implies that curated ritual speech generally did not enjoy a higher status than, say, divination or medicine. Is there, then, anything in the scribal classificatory repertoire that would mark some ritual speech in a distinctive manner? I suggest there is: the én superscription.

Scribes used various superscriptions, a sign or short series of signs placed at the head of a block of text, for a very practical purpose: to mark the beginning of a distinct subunit within the larger document. For example, the "item sign," a single vertical wedge, often marks the beginning of a new entry in a sign list and three signs, DÙ.DÙ.BI (Sum. dù.dù.bi, "its ritual"), often signal the beginning of ritual instructions, usually placed after the accompanying ritual recitation. In a similar fashion, the ÉN sign (Sum. én and Akk. *šiptu*, both meaning "incantation") functions as a superscription in first millennium texts to indicate the beginning of an incantation.[66] It is rarely absent.[67]

Unlike the other superscriptions, however, ÉN is distinctive in that it is written even when only the incipit of the incantation appears in a list,[68] is

64. See Simo Parpola, *Assyrian Prophecies* (Helsinki: Helsinki University Press, 1997), nos. 1 and 2.

65. See Simo Parpola, "Assyrian Library Records," *Journal of Near Eastern Studies* 42 (1983): 1.

66. This sign seems to have largely replaced the longer formula, én é-nu-ru, used in earlier times (Lambert, "Classification," 93).

67. Due to space constraints, I leave aside a discussion of the subscription TU$_6$ ÉN, which sometimes appears at the end of the last line of an incantation. Unlike ÉN, the appearance of TU$_6$ ÉN is unpredictable and its precise meaning unclear. It may form an envelope structure with the superscription ÉN, encasing, as it were, the ritual speech with a divine origin within. I thank my colleague Laura Bathhurst for discussing this phenomenon with me from a broader anthropological perspective.

68. E.g., Stephen Geller, "Incipits and Rubrics," in *Wisdom, Gods and Literature: Studies in Assyriology in Honour of W. G. Lambert* (ed. Andrew R. George and Irving L. Finkel; Winona Lake, IN: Eisenbrauns, 2000), 225–58.

cited in ritual instructions,[69] or is mentioned in a letter from a scholar to the king.[70] As Wilfred Lambert notes, ÉN was "a marker in the script to communicate something to the reader, but not to be pronounced. It was then a real classifier."[71] I suggest that its function was to mark incantations as a kind of ritual speech that derives from the gods themselves. This is similar to what we saw in the lexical survey: Akkadian reserves *šiptu* and *tû* for ritual speech of divine origin and never uses these terms for human interpersonal speech.

This interpretation of ÉN's function may find support in the form of the cuneiform sign itself (𒂗), which the scribes recognized as comprising the signs ŠÚ (𒋙) and AN (𒀭).[72] The latter sign may be read as both "heaven" (Sum. an; Akk. *šamû*) and "god" (Sum. dingir; Akk. *ilu*), expressing in either case the idea of divinity.[73] As for the former sign, one is tempted to read the ŠÚ as the Sumerian word šú, which typically means *kiššatu*, "totality, world" in Akkadian or, following ancient scholarly lexical speculations, as Akkadian *erēbu*, "to enter."[74] Thus, the scribes may have applied their traditional hermeneutics to the ÉN sign and read it as "the totality of heaven / divinity" or "entering heaven / divinity." Although these attempts to specify the precise meaning of the ÉN sign are speculative, it does seem to be the case that the sign somehow encodes in its actual shape the mythology of the divine origination of incantatory speech—a special form of speech restricted to the gods and to humans in specific circumstances speaking the words given by the gods themselves to effect circumstances performatively. So closely are incantations associated with the gods and Ea specifically that a major god list actually apotheosizes "incantation," thus writing ᵈÉN, that

69. E.g., Ambos, *König im Gefängnis*, 158–71.

70. E.g., Parpola, *Letters from Assyrian*, nos. 194, 201, 238, 240, and 295.

71. Lambert, "Classification," 93.

72. See the sign list Ea I 345 in Miguel Civil, *Ea A = nâqu, Aa A = nâqu, with Their Forerunners and Related Texts* (with Collaboration of Margaret W. Green and Wilfred G. Lambert; Rome: Pontifical Biblical Institute, 1979), 194, where the sign name for ÉN (𒂗), understood as ŠÚ-AN (𒋙 - 𒀭), is named BAR(𒀭)-*tenanaku*. BAR-*ten* stands for BAR-*tenû*, which means "the slanting or oblique BAR sign" (𒁇). See Yushu Gong, *Die Namen der Keilschriftzeichen* (Münster: Ugarit-Verlag, 2000), 32–4. And *anaku* seems to be an Akkadianized form of the Sumerian word an, "heaven," followed by the Sumerian genitive element -ak. Thus, "the slanting BAR-sign of heaven."

73. See already Jean Bottéro, "Magie. A.," *Reallexikon der Assyriologie* 7 (1987–1990): 213.

74. For the latter speculation, see Ea II 151 in Civil, "*Ea A = nâqu, Aa A = nâqu*," 253. One might even suggest that we read the two signs as Akkadian: *šū ilu* / *šamû*, "it *is* divinity / heaven."

is, the god "incantation," and lists it as one of the names of Ea, the god to whom the scholars attributed the origins of their learned corpora.[75]

The implicit principle at work in using the ÉN sign as a superscription before the text of an incantation is: the part of the scholarly corpus that is explicitly conceived as divine words is to be marked as such.[76]

Conclusions

This investigation of the intersection of ritual speech and scribal scholarship has revealed several unarticulated principles about divine-human relations. Although these do not represent the entirety of the scholars' implicit theory of religion,[77] they certainly contribute towards its understanding. First, the ancient Mesopotamians designated ritual speech in general with the same words they used to address social superiors. At the broadest level, the scholars' notion of divine-human relations conforms to the common idea that the divine realm reflects human society. They also developed a group of technical terms that they applied to specific kinds of ritual speech. When ritual speech, however, was believed to have a divine point of origination (as with incantations), it was designated by distinctive terms that are never used for non-ritual, human speech. This distinction holds despite an ontology that generally does not draw a sharp line between the divine and human or natural and supernatural domains. Some ritual speech was selected for incorporation into the scholarly corpora (*ṭupšarrūtu*) and was organized in similar ways as were other materials (e.g., divinatory, literary, etc.). Thus again, at a broad level, the scribal classification of ritual speech was indistinguishable from other kinds of curated materials because it was but one subsection within the scholar's intellectual repertoire. However, the scholars used the lexicographical distinction of words for "incantation" taxonomically: the ÉN sign became a superscription to mark the beginning of an incantation within the curated *ṭupšarrūtu*, a corpus transmitted to the

75. See Richard L. Litke, *A Reconstruction of the Assyro-Babylonian God-Lists*, AN : ᵈa-nu-um *and* AN : anu ša amēli (New Haven, CT: Yale Babylonian Collection, 1998), 85 at line 154.

76. It may seem to us that marking the incantations used in ritual activities with a special determinative to indicate divine origins was superfluous or redundant. But an analogy may put this objection in a different perspective. Many contemporary Christians believe the entire Bible to be inspired by God and yet they value a text that marks the words of Christ in red. They are somehow doubly marked divine.

77. For example, I have completely ignored the major issue of divination in all of its varied forms in my discussion here. For a survey, see Ulla Susanne Koch, *Mesopotamian Divination Texts: Conversing with the Gods. Sources from the First Millennium BCE* (Münster: Ugarit-Verlag, 2015).

scholars ultimately from the god Ea. The incantations preserving divine words, therefore, were doubly marked divine.

We might be tempted to interpret these principles as mere theology rather than theory-driven scholarship. But the two need not be mutually exclusive.[78] The ancient scholars were certainly writing in a normative mode. But, they were also utilizing terminology and classifiers rooted in specific principles to circumscribe and organize materials related to divine and superhuman entities within their intellectual purview. Since we now identify much of their material as religious in nature, is it not valuable in an effort to broaden the context in which we understand the on-going human attempts to think about "religion" to consider this activity as akin to what we religious studies scholars do?[79]

Biographical Note

Alan Lenzi is Professor and Chair of Religious Studies at University of the Pacific, Stockton CA, USA. He specializes in the study of ancient Assyrian and Babylonian scholarship, literature, and religion during the first millennium BCE. His books include a monograph entitled *Secrecy and the Gods: Secret Knowledge in Ancient Mesopotamia and Biblical Israel* (Helsinki, 2008), a text edition of *Ludlul Bēl Nēmeqi: The Standard Babylonian Poem of the Righteous Sufferer* (with Amar Annus; Helsinki, 2010), and two edited volumes: *Reading Akkadian Prayers and Hymns: An Introduction* (SBL Press, 2011) and *Divination, Politics, and Ancient Near Eastern Empire* (with Jonathan Stökl; SBL Press, 2014).

Bibliography

Abusch, Tzvi. *The Magical Ceremony* Maqlû: *A Critical Edition*. Leiden: Brill, 2016.
Ambos, Claus. *Der König im Gefängnis und das Neujahrsfest im Herbst: Mechanismen der Legitimation des babylonischen Herrschers im 1. Jahrtausend v. Chr. und ihre Geschichte*. Dresden: ISLET, 2013.
Asad, Talal. *Genealogies of Religion: Discipline and Reasons of Power in Christianity and Islam*. Baltimore, MD: Johns Hopkins University Press, 1993.
Black, Jeremy, Andrew R. George, and Nicholas Postgate, eds. *A Concise Dictionary of Akkadian*. Wiesbaden: Harrassowitz, 1999.
Bottéro, Jean. "Magie. A." *Reallexikon der Assyriologie* 7 (1987–1990): 200–34.
Civil, Miguel. *Ea A = nâqu, Aa A = nâqu, with Their Forerunners and Related Texts*.

---

78. Rochberg, *Heavenly Writing*, 244–5 supports a similar claim about science and theology.

79. I thank Jeffrey Cooley and Kevin McGinnis for comments on an earlier draft of this study.

With Collaboration of Margaret W. Green and Wilfred G. Lambert. Rome: Pontifical Biblical Institute, 1979.

Dear, Peter. "What is the History of Science the History *Of*? Early Modern Roots of the Ideology of Modern Science," *Isis* 96.3 (2005): 390–406. https://doi.org/10.1086/447747

Foster, Benjamin. *Akkadian Literature of the Late Period*. Münster: Ugarit-Verlag, 2007.

Frechette, Christopher G. *Mesopotamian Ritual-Prayers of "Hand-lifting" (Akkadian Šuillas): An Investigation of Function in Light of the Idiomatic Meaning of the Rubric*. Münster: Ugarit-Verlag, 2012.

Freedman, Sally. *If a City Is Set on a Height: The Akkadian Omen Series* Shumma Alu ina mele Shakin. Vol. 1: *Tablets 1-21*. Philadelphia, PA: University Museum, 1998.

Geller, Stephen. "Incipits and Rubrics," 225–58 in *Wisdom, Gods and Literature: Studies in Assyriology in Honour of W. G. Lambert*. Edited by Andrew R. George and Irving L. Finkel. Winona Lake, IN: Eisenbrauns, 2000.

—*Evil Demons: Canonical* Utukkū Lemnūtu *Incantations*. Helsinki: The Neo-Assyrian Text Corpus Project, 2007.

Gong, Yushu. *Die Namen der Keilschriftzeichen*. Münster: Ugarit-Verlag, 2000.

Groneberg, Brigitte. "Searching for Akkadian Lyrics: From Old Babylonian to the 'Liederkatalog' KAR 158," *Journal of Cuneiform Studies* 55 (2003): 55–74. https://doi.org/10.2307/3515954

Hammersley, Martyn, and Paul Atkinson. *Ethnography*. 3rd ed. London: Routledge, 2007. https://doi.org/10.4324/9780203944769

Horowitz, Wayne. *Mesopotamian Cosmic Geography*. Winona Lake, IN: Eisenbrauns, 1998.

Hrůša, Ivan. *Die akkadische Synonymenliste* malku = šarru: *Eine Textedition mit Übersetzung und Kommentar*. Münster: Ugarit-Verlag, 2010.

—*Ancient Mesopotamian Religion: A Descriptive Introduction*. Münster: Ugarit-Verlag, 2015.

Huehnergard, John, and Christopher Woods. "Akkadian and Eblaite," 218–87 in *The Cambridge Encyclopedia of the World's Ancient Languages*. Edited by Roger D. Woodard. Cambridge: Cambridge University Press, 2004.

Hunger, Hermann. *Babylonische und assyrische Kolophone*. Neukirchen-Vluyn: Neukirchener / Kevelaer: Butzon & Bercker, 1968.

Jaques, Margaret. *Mon dieu qu'ai-je fait?* Les diĝir-šà-dab(5)-ba *et la piété privée en Mésopotamie*. Fribourg: Academic Press / Göttingen: Vandenhoeck & Ruprecht, 2015.

Jastrow, Morris. *The Religion of Babylonia and Assyria*. Boston, MA: Ginn, 1898.

Koch, Ulla Susanne. *Mesopotamian Divination Texts: Conversing with the Gods. Sources from the First Millennium BCE*. Münster: Ugarit-Verlag, 2015.

Lambert, Wilfred G. "A Catalogue of Texts and Authors," *Journal of Cuneiform Studies* 16 (1962): 59–77. https://doi.org/10.2307/1359154

—*Babylonian Oracle Questions*. Winona Lake, IN: Eisenbrauns, 2007.

—"The Classification of Incantations," 93–7 in *Proceedings of the 51st Rencontre Assyriologique Internationale Held at the Oriental Institute of the University of Chicago July 18-22, 2005*. Edited by Robert D. Biggs, Jennie Myers, and Martha T. Roth. Chicago, IL: The Oriental Institute of the University of Chicago, 2008.

—*Babylonian Creation Myths*. Winona Lake, IN: Eisenbrauns, 2013.

Lenzi, Alan. *Secrecy and the Gods: Secret Knowledge in Ancient Mesopotamia and Biblical Israel*. Helsinki: The Neo-Assyrian Text Corpus Project, 2008.

—"*Šiptu ul Yuttun*: Some Reflections on a Closing Formula in Akkadian Incantations," 131–66 in *Gazing on the Deep: Ancient Near Eastern, Biblical, and Jewish Studies in Honor of Tzvi Abusch*. Edited by Jeffrey Stackert, Barbara Neveling Porter, and David P. Wright. Bethesda, MD: CDL Press, 2010.

—ed. *Reading Akkadian Prayers and Hymns: An Introduction*. Atlanta, GA: Society of Biblical Literature Press, 2011.

—"Mesopotamian Scholarship: Kassite to Late Babylonian Periods," *Journal of Ancient Near Eastern History* 2.2 (2015): 145–201.

Litke, Richard L. *A Reconstruction of the Assyro-Babylonian God-Lists*, AN : ᵈa-nu-um *and* AN : anu ša amēli. New Haven, CT: Yale Babylonian Collection, 1998.

McCutcheon, Russell T. *Critics Not Caretakers: Redescribing the Public Study of Religion*. Albany, NY: State University of New York Press, 2001.

McEvoy, John G. "Modernism, Postmodernism and the Historiography of Science," *Historical Studies in the Physical and Biological Sciences* 37.2 (2007): 383–408. https://doi.org/10.1525/hsps.2007.37.2.383

Nongbri, Brent. *Before Religion: A History of a Modern Concept*. New Haven, CT: Yale University Press, 2013. https://doi.org/10.12987/yale/9780300154160.001.0001

Oppenheim, A. Leo, Erica Reiner, and Martha Roth. *The Assyrian Dictionary of the Oriental Institute of the University of Chicago*. Chicago, IL: Oriental Institute, 1956–2010.

Parpola, Simo. "Assyrian Library Records," *Journal of Near Eastern Studies* 42 (1983): 1–29. https://doi.org/10.1086/372983

—*Letters from Assyrian and Babylonian Scholars*. Helsinki: Helsinki University Press, 1993.

—*Assyrian Prophecies*. Helsinki: Helsinki University Press, 1997.

Reynolds, Frances. *The Babylonian Correspondence of Esarhaddon and Letters to Assurbanipal and Sin-šarru-iškun from Northern and Central Babylonia*. Helsinki: University of Helsinki Press, 2003.

Rochberg, Francesca. *The Heavenly Writing: Divination, Horoscopy, and Astronomy in Mesopotamian Culture*. Cambridge: Cambridge University Press, 2004. https://doi.org/10.1017/CBO9780511617409

—*Before Nature: Cuneiform Knowledge and the History of Science*. Chicago, IL: University of Chicago Press, 2016. https://doi.org/10.7208/chicago/9780226406275.001.0001

Scholz, Barbara C., Francis Jeffry Pelletier, and Geoffrey K. Pullum. "Philosophy of Linguistics," *The Stanford Encyclopedia of Philosophy* (Fall 2015 Edition). Online: http://plato.stanford.edu/archives/fall2015/entries/linguistics/ (accessed 16 March 2015).

Smith, Jonathan Z. *Imagining Religion: From Babylon to Jonestown*. Chicago, IL: University of Chicago Press, 1982.

Starr, Ivan. *Queries to the Sungod: Divination and Politics in Sargonid Assyria*. Helsinki: Helsinki University Press, 1990.

Stowers, Stanley. "The Ontology of Religion," 434–49 in *Introducing Religion: Essays in Honor of Jonathan Z. Smith*. Edited by Willi Braun and Russell T. McCutcheon. London: Equinox, 2008.

Streck, Michael. "Sprache und Denken im altem Mesopotamien: Am Beispiel des Zeitausdrucks," 424–31 in *Studia Semitica*. Edited by Leonid Kogan. Moscow: Russian State University for the Humanities, 2003.

Tremlin, Todd. *Minds and Gods: The Cognitive Foundations of Religion*. Oxford: Oxford University Press, 2006. https://doi.org/10.1093/0195305345.001.0001

Van de Mieroop, Marc. *Philosophy Before the Greeks: The Pursuit of Truth in Ancient Babylonia*. Princeton, NJ: Princeton University Press, 2016. https://doi.org/10.1515/9781400874118

Veldhuis, Niek. *Religion, Literature, and Scholarship: The Sumerian Composition Nanše and the Birds, with a Catalogue of Sumerian Bird Names*. Leiden: Styx/Brill, 2004.

—*History of the Cuneiform Lexical Tradition*. Münster: Ugarit-Verlag, 2014.

von Soden, Wolfram. *Akkadisches Handwörterbuch*. Vols. 1–3. Wiesbaden: Harrassowitz, 1972–1985.

—*Grundriss der akkadischen Grammatik*. 3rd ed. Rome: Pontifical Biblical Institute, 1995.

Zgoll, Annette. "Audienz — Ein Modell zum Verständnis mesopotamischer Handerhebungsrituale. Mit einer Deutung der Novelle vom *Armen Mann von Nippur*," *Baghdader Mitteilungen* 34 (2003): 173–95.

Chapter Nine

Magic and Religion in Ancient Egypt

Rita Lucarelli

The last decade has seen a very strong interest from the scholarly community for magic in antiquity and in particular in ancient Egypt.[1] In a world— that of Pharaonic and Graeco-Roman Egypt—where religion was at the base of the political and social structure of society and the care for the dead and the funerary cults were a daily practice, magic was a necessary element of any kind of ritual and cultic performance. However, Egyptologists are still debating on how to define magic according to an emic perspective and on the basis of the vast and very variegated evidence coming from the material and written sources of ancient Egypt. The main issue, similar to what has been debated in the study of other magical traditions in antiquity and in disciplines other than Egyptology, is whether to consider magic as part of religion or to attempt to isolate specific magical techniques and performances to compare and confront with other religious phenomena such as rituals, cults, and divination.[2] The latter is also at the center of a scholarly debate focusing on definition and interpretation of different categories of religious practices; divination can be seen both as magical performance or a

---

1. A few new publications on ancient Egyptian magic have recently appeared, such as Andrea Jördens, ed., *Ägyptische Magie und ihre Umwelt* (Wiesbaden: Harrassowitz, 2015) and Christoffer Theis, *Magie und Raum: Der magische Schutz ausgewählter Räume im alten Ägypten nebst einem Vergleich zu angrenzenden Kulturbereichen* (Tübingen: Mohr Siebeck, 2014). On the ancient Egyptian magic in comparison to other magical traditions in antiquity, see Grażyna Bąkowska-Czerner, Alessandro Roccati, and Agata Świerzowska, eds., *The Wisdom of Thoth: Magical Texts in Ancient Mediterranean Civilizations* (Oxford: Archaeopress Archaeology, 2015); Gideon Bohak, "The Diffusion of the Greco-Egyptian Magical Tradition in Late Antiquity," in *Greco-Egyptian Interactions: Literature, Translation, and Culture, 500 BCE-300 CE* (ed. Ian Rutherford; Oxford: Oxford University Press, 2016), 357–81.

2. "Ritual" and "divination" are also at the center of a scholarly debate focusing on the definition and interpretation of religious practices. On ritual, magic, and religion in ancient Egypt, see Jan Assmann, "Magie und Ritual im alten Ägypten," in *Magie und Religion* (ed. Jan Assmann and Harald Strohm; München: Wilhelm Fink, 2010), 23–43; on ancient Egyptian rituals in the Graeco-Roman period, see Joachim Friedrich Quack, ed., *Ägyptische Rituale der griechisch-römischen Zeit* (Tübingen: Mohr Siebeck, 2014).

phenomenon on its own, with more of a focus on questioning the gods and waiting for answers than on creating or provoking something to happen, as in general magical practices.[3]

Another issue is related to the use of the singular and general term "magic" to indicate a series of indigenous words differently related to the sphere of magic in ancient Egypt and in antiquity in general. Attempts to avoid the use of the term in order not to generalize the ancient sources did not really succeed; even speaking of "ritual power"[4] or "ritual expertise"[5] in order to highlight the main role that ritual practices play in what we call "magic" cannot cover the vast semantic sphere of the ancient Egyptian magical lexicon. Curiously enough, in the earlier German studies on ancient Egyptian magic, two separate terms were employed, namely "Magie" and "Zauber," the latter indicating a sort of ancient Egyptian witchcraft whereas the former referred to official religious practices and beliefs. Such a distinction cannot be made at all if looking at the ancient Egyptian sources, in which witchcraft does not enter into the picture.[6]

Aside from the ritual component of ancient Egyptian magic, one has to consider the importance that magic had, within ancient Egyptian theology, as a sort of impersonal and abstract force of creation provided by the gods for humankind.[7] In the *Instructions for King Merikara* of the Tenth Dynasty, which belongs to the genre of ancient Egyptian wisdom literature, we read:

3.   On divination in ancient Egypt, see Alexandra von Lieven, "Divination in Ägypten," *Altorientalische Forschungen* 26.1 (1999): 77–126; Laslo Kákosy, "Divination and Prophecy: Egypt," in *Religions of the Ancient World: A Guide* (ed. Sarah Iles Johnston; Cambridge, MA: Belknap Press of Harvard University Press, 2004), 371–3. For divination in the Graeco-Roman period, see Franziska Naether, *Die Sortes Astrampsychi: Problemlösungsstrategien durch Orakel im römischen Ägypten* (Tübingen: Mohr Siebeck, 2010). See also my remarks at the end of this chapter.

4.   See Marvin Meyer and Paul Mirecki, "Introduction," in *Ancient Magic and Ritual Power* (ed. Marvin Meyer and Paul Mirecki; Leiden: Brill, 1995), 1–10. See also Robert K. Ritner, "The Religious, Social, and Legal Parameters of Traditional Egyptian Magic," in Meyer and Mirecki, eds., *Ancient Magic and Ritual Power*, 43–60.

5.   Cf. David Frankfurter, "Dynamics of Ritual Expertise in Antiquity and Beyond: Towards a New Taxonomy of 'Magicians'," in *Magic and Ritual in the Ancient World* (ed. Paul Mirecki and Marvin Meyer; Leiden: Brill, 2002), 159–78.

6.   Hans Bonnet, "Hike," in *Lexikon der ägyptischen Religionsgeschichte* (Hamburg: Nikol, 2005), 301–2, has three different entries: "Hike" (personified magic), "Magie," and "Zauber." The *Lexikon der Ägyptologie* includes also two different entries for "Magie" and "Zauber."

7.   Joris F. Borghouts, "Magie," in *Lexikon der Ägyptologie* (ed. Wolfgang Helk and Eberhardt Otto; Wiesbaden: Harrassowitz, 1980), Vol. 3, 1137–51 defines magic as an "impersonal, morally neutral mystical force."

> It was in order to be weapons to ward off the blow of events that he made
> magic for them (scil. "men").[8]

We may therefore distinguish two main understandings of magic: theory
(magic as an abstract force of creation) and practice (magic as ritual expertise). These two aspects come together in the understanding of *Heka*
("magic") as a god who is participating in creation.

It is especially in the textual sources that we understand the ancient Egyptian specifications of "magic." Already in the earlier stages of the ancient
Egyptian language, we can find different terms in order to distinguish
between a divine, personified entity or a more abstract but highly effective
supernatural power, which we could translate with "magic" rather than with
"religion." On the other hand, there is not a specific term, in ancient Egypt,
which could correspond to the Latin *religio* / our modern English *religion*;
the expression *ir.t ḥ(w).t* ("doing [sacred] things") is probably the most close
verbal construction employed to indicate ritual performances in religion.[9]
Therefore, from an emic perspective and on an abstract level, there was no
distinction between magic and religion.[10] On the other hand, when coming to
the personification of the concept, we have abundant evidence on a "minor"
god, called *ḥkꜣ(w)* (*Heka*), who personifies the concept of magic as a divine
manifestation. Heka plays a role in maintaining the order of creation together
with *Maat*, the principle of cosmic and social justice. The representation of
this god occurs very often in the mythic imagery of the gods of creation,
beside the sun god and other deities involved in the maintenance of creation.[11] In particular, Heka is depicted in the vignettes decorating the funerary papyri as a complement to the written incantations and he is depicted as
a male anthropomorphic god holding one or two snake-like rods, being part

8.   Translation by Robert K. Ritner, *The Mechanics of Ancient Egyptian Magical
Practice* (Chicago, IL: Oriental Institute of University of Chicago, 1993), 20. Although
this passage can be translated in many ways, its main message does not change: *Heka*
originates from the gods. See also n. 79 and the translation in French by Joris F. Borghouts, "Les Textes magiques de l'Egypte ancienne: Théorie, mythes et themes," in *La
magie en Egypte: Actes du colloque organisé par le Musée du Louvre les 29 et 30 septembre 2000* (ed. Yan Koenig; Paris: Documentation française, 2002), 23: "La magie
[*hekau*] est une arme que le dieu supreme a donnée à l'humanité ..."

9.   See Carolyn Routledge, "Ancient Egyptian Ritual Practice: *Ir-xt* and *nt-a*" (PhD
dissertation, University of Toronto, 2001).

10.   For an updated discussion and bibliography on the definition of magic in antiquity and its relationship with religion, see Dietrich Boschung and Jan N. Bremmer, eds.,
The Materiality of Magic (München: Fink, 2015), 10–2.

11.   For the role of Heka in the ancient Egyptian cosmology and as a power of creation, see Susanne Bickel, *La cosmogonie égyptienne: Avant le Nouvel Empire* (Göttingen: Universitätsverlag and Vandenhoeck & Ruprecht, 1994), 152–7.

of the solar boat's crew during the daily journey of Ra, the sun god, in the netherworld.[12] The fact that Heka is a god[13] also means the whole concept of magic was accepted within the official religion of the temple and in the rituals officially performed by the king; on the contrary, the very meaning of the ancient Greek word μαγεία, in use from the fifth century BCE, was negative. It referred to a practice basically forbidden by and performed against the deities.[14] In incantations composed already in the second millennium BCE, such as Spell 261 of the *Coffin Texts*, the deceased wishes to be identified with the god ("to become the god Heka" is the title of the spell itself) or to make sure that Heka does not leave his/her belly.[15] "Great of magic" (*wr ḥkꜣw*) is one of the most common epithets used for gods, as well as being used as a name for the sacred uraeus, an important royal emblem and solar symbol through the whole Pharaonic period. "Great of magic" was also the name given to a ritual tool, namely a serpent-shaped rod employed in one of the most important funerary rituals of ancient Egypt, the so-called "Opening of the Mouth" ritual, which aimed at restoring the physical abilities of the deceased in the netherworld.[16]

Aside from the personification of magic as a god, the ancient Egyptians were also envisioning different kinds of magical acts and performances, which they expressed through specific terminology in the magical texts. Written and spoken magic was indicated by the term *r/rꜣ* (*ra*; "spell"), namely by the "mouth" ideogram ⟨⟩, and employed to open the title of the incantations copied in magical handbooks. When magical invocations are mixed with medical prescriptions against illnesses and medical treatment, *pḫr.t* (*pekheret*; literally "remedy") is employed, still with reference to the

12. For a complete list of occurrences of Heka in texts and iconography, see Christian Leitz, ed., *Lexikon der ägyptischen Götter und Götterbezeichnungen* (Leuven: Peeters, 2002), 552–4.

13. Although Heka was not venerated in any major temple in Egypt, there is evidence of cult places devoted to this god in Memphis (see Bonnet, "Hike"). In the Late, Graeco, and Roman periods, similar to other male anthropomorphic gods, Heka was also venerated as a primeval child-god, son of Ptah and Sekhmet (ibid.); its mythological role was especially stressed in temple contexts.

14. See Alan Lloyd, "Egyptian Magic in Greek Literature," in *Ancient Egyptian Demonology: Studies on the Boundaries Between the Demonic and the Divine in Egyptian Magic* (ed. Panagiotis Kousoulis; Leuven: Peeters, 2012), 99–120.

15. See also Laslo Kakosy, "Heka," in *Lexikon der Ägyptologie* (ed. Wolfgang Helk and Eberhardt Otto; Wiesbaden: Harrassowitz, 1977), Vol. 2, 1108–10; for Heka in the funerary texts (*Coffin Texts*), see Brigitte Altenmüller, *Synkretismus in den Sargtexten* (Wiesbaden: Harrassowitz, 1975), 160–2.

16. See Eberhard Otto, *Das ägyptische Mundöffnungsritual* (Wiesbaden: Harrassowitz, 1960).

magical efficacy of these medico-magical texts.[17] The efficacy of magic is especially expressed by the term *ȝḥw* (*akhw*), which is used to indicate the creative function of magical spells and words.[18] There would actually be many more terms to include in a lexicographical list connected to the sphere of magic in ancient Egypt, many of which survived in Coptic.[19] As a matter of fact, the need to compile a magical lexicon for ancient Egypt has been noted for decades and unfortunately not yet fulfilled.[20] The main difficulty for a comprehensive lexicographical analysis and a consequent uniform definition of magic in ancient Egypt lies in the heterogeneity of the written sources produced during a very long span of time (from the third millennium BCE to the Graeco-Roman period). These texts are written in different languages and scripts (from Classic Egyptian to Demotic and Coptic), and undergo an evolution in meaning and use following the religious and theological principles of each period. Because some terms only occur in certain textual contexts, we also need a specific lexicographical study for each period.

On the other hand, when looking at the *materia magica* and in general at the iconic, non-written sources, we almost always have to face a lack of archaeological contexts, which could help the reconstruction of the social and cultural sphere of magical practices and their relationship to specific sacred spaces such as temples, tombs, sleeping places, and other areas which were felt to be particularly at risk of demonic attack and in need of protection.[21] Moreover, even when found *in situ*, very often we are facing objects that have been moved already in antiquity or ended up in deposits of debris and, therefore,

17. On the close relationship between magic and medicine in ancient Egypt, see Wolfhart Westendorf, *Erwachen der Heilkunst: Die Medizin im Alten Ägypten* (Zürich: Artemis & Winkler, 1992), 19–39; Geraldine Pinch, *Magic in Ancient Egypt* (London: British Museum Publications, 1994), 133–46.

18. See Ritner, *Mechanics of Ancient Egyptian Magical*, 30ff. Ritner's chapter comments and reviews the earlier essay on the terminology used for "magic" by Borghouts, "Magie"; cf. Joris F. Borghouts, "*ȝḥ.w* (*akhu*) and *ḥkȝ.w* (*hekau*): Two Basic Notions of Ancient Egyptian Magic, and the Concept of the Divine Creative Word," in *La magia in Egitto ai tempi dei faraoni: atti, convegno internazionale di studi, Milano, 29-31 ottobre 1985* (ed. Alessandro Roccati and Alberto Siliotti; Verona: Rassegna internazionale di cinematografia archeologica arte e natura libri, 1987), 29–46. On the different nuances among the words *ḥkȝ* and *ȝḥ.w*, see Theis, *Magie und Raum*, 35–40.

19. For a list of other related terms on magic, especially referring to the recitation of charms, see Table 1 in Ritner, *Mechanics of Ancient Egyptian Magical*, 50.

20. See Joris F. Borghouts, "Lexicographical Aspects of Magical Texts," in *Textcorpus und Wörterbuch: Aspekte zur ägyptischen Lexikographie* (ed. Stefan Grunert and Ingelore Hafemann; Leiden: Brill, 1999), 149–77.

21. The recent study of Theis, *Magie und Raum*, is focused on the way magic works as protection of sacred or dangerous places. The need for protection is related in particular to defensive magic (see below).

their original context of use and the identity of their owner (the magical prac-
titioner) are still problematic to understand. Apart from a few isolated cases
where tools employed in magical rituals have been found together during
excavations of cemeteries and villages,[22] most of the magical objects from
ancient Egypt—and currently spread out through the museums around the
world—are not of a secure provenance. It is thanks to the ritual papyri and the
instructions added to the magical spells on *how* to use them and on what kind
of images to recite them, that we can basically understand the use of many
magical objects such as bowls, figurines, and other apotropaic tools. The figurines and broken pottery found in military fortresses, such as at Mirgissa,
are representative examples of this kind of *materia magica*, found *in situ* (the
so-called "execration deposit"), whose use and purpose can be understood
thanks to the ritual texts. The one hundred and ninety-seven inscribed red
vases and ostraca and the four hundred and thirty-seven non-inscribed vases
found broken in pieces at Mirgissa are clearly connected to rituals described
in texts such as the "breaking of the red vases."[23]

The execration texts and figurines mentioned above are only one among
many examples of magic contexts and performance. We can discern,
although only from our etic perspective, four categories of magic, based
mainly on the function and aim of the spells and tools employed during
the ritual performances: defensive, funerary, curative, and transformative
magic. The basic concept applying to all these categories is that of *s3w*
("protection"). Expressed by the hieroglyphic variants ▦ 𓀀, the derivative
s3w.w an be translated as "protector" and was used to indicate benevolent
demons protecting sacred places in the netherworld or on earth.[24] Moreover,

---

22.   Especially interesting is the case of the village of Karanis in Roman Fayyum,
whose remains of magical practices have been thoroughly studied by Andrew T. Wilburn, *Materia Magica: The Archaeology of Magic in Roman Egypt, Cyprus and Spain*
(Ann Arbor, MI: University of Michigan Press, 2012). For Pharaonic Egypt, see the case
of the so-called "tomb of the magician" found near the Ramesseum in West Thebes and
dated to the Middle Kingdom, where both magical papyri and uninscribed artifacts have
been found: Ritner, *Mechanics of Ancient Egyptian Magical Practice*, 223ff. and Theis,
Magie und Raum, 107ff.

23.   Ritner, *Mechanics of Ancient Egyptian Magical Practice*, 153–5. The color red
had a recognized apotropaic character in ancient Egypt until the Graeco-Roman period,
when rituals on red vessels are attested also in the Greek Magical Papyri. In total, two
thirds of the Mirgissa deposit is constituted by red vessels (see Theis, *Magie und Raum*,
74–5).

24.   See Rita Lucarelli, "The So-called Vignette of Spell 182 of the Book of the Dead,"
in *Herausgehen am Tage: Gesammelte Schriften zum altägyptischen Totenbuch* (ed. Rita
Lucarelli, Marcus Müller-Roth, and Annik Wüthrich; Wiesbaden: Harrassowitz, 2012),
79–91.

sꜣw.w occurs in titles of magicians who are also experts in medical practices and together with the title of *swnw* ("doctor"), therefore testifying to the close relationship of magic and medicine in ancient Egypt.[25]

The need for protection, which is closely connected to that of prevention from harm, applies to any sort of dangerous or menacing situation, which could occur everywhere at home, in the village, in the street, and even in the temple or in the tomb. Protection was also needed in the netherworld during the journey through the Realm of the Dead, where the deceased had to face menacing supernatural guardians while passing gates, lakes of fire, and demons-inhabited mounds, as described in the funerary texts of the *Pyramid Texts*, *Coffin Texts*, *Book of the Dead*, and *Books of the Netherworld*.[26]

Defensive magic, also known as "apotropaic" or "protective" magic, therefore covers all kind of protective magical acts in daily life on earth and in the afterlife, while funerary magic can be considered a subcategory, which only concerns the protection of the tomb and in the netherworld. Some of the dangers and malevolent agents from which protection was sought vary and we can distinguish between defensive magic used on earth and in the netherworld; while the former could be directed against personal and public (of the state/king) human enemies, the latter was used mainly against or in order to appease and deal with liminal beings populating the Realm of the Dead. On the other hand, disease-carrier or nightmare demons and evil ghosts were affecting humankind on earth. Spells for warding off poisonous snakes were used in both contexts of daily and netherworldly life. Therefore, the spells of defensive magic for daily life on earth can be very similar in structure and content to the incantations for protection in the tomb and in the netherworld. Their basic layout of a title and of a central invocation, very often including a mythical allusion, is employed both for short and very extensive texts. The need of magic protection goes together with that of the use of amulets, which are among the most popular and spread-out artifacts from ancient Egypt. What differentiates an amulet from other kinds of magical objects is its small size, which allows its owner to carry it on his/her body. They can be associated with those objects that in other civilizations, both ancient and modern, are called talismans. However, while a talisman is believed to be empowered by forces that bring good luck to its owner and provide successful endeavors in life, an amulet has as its

---

25. See Theis, *Magie und Raum*, 49ff.
26. For an overview on the funerary literature of ancient Egypt and its relationship with other religious texts, see Ronald J. Leprohon, "Egyptian Religious Texts," in *Egyptology Today* (ed. Richard H. Wilkinson; Cambridge: Cambridge University Press, 2008), 230–47.

main aim the protection of its owner.[27] Moreover, we can distinguish two main temporal contexts in which amulets were used: they were worn for protection during particular moments or periods (pregnancy and childbirth; while traveling or being ill) or, their use was prolonged in order to grant protection at any moment. Amulets of this latter type, which can be in the form of jewelry items or as short strips of inscribed papyrus to be worn as a pendant, are generally those that have survived in the largest number.[28]

Among the vast array of inscribed and non-inscribed amulets produced in ancient Egypt, textual amulets are especially interesting for the way they combine magic designs, materials (papyrus, linen and in the later period also metal), and texts in one powerful apotropaic object, which could be inserted in a leather or linen pouch or in a metal tube (especially in the Graeco-Roman period) to wear round the neck.[29] Some of the most interesting textual amulets have been found in the workmen's village of Deir el Medina in Thebes (modern Luxor) and are strong evidence for personal piety and defensive magic for everyday use. They generally contain a recipe for recovering or "saving" someone from a demonic illness or attack, followed by instructions on how to use the amulet and, occasionally, a few protective images of deities and divine symbols.[30] These kinds of documents are also a useful source for the study of the scribal practices of magic and the modality of transmission of magical formularies through the centuries, since the textual amulets were still in use in Roman Egypt. There is evidence of some types of textual amulets only in certain periods, such as the so-called *Oracular Amuletic Decrees*, attested in the early Third Intermediate Period (1986–712 BCE, corresponding to Dynasties Twenty-one to Twenty-four of the Egyptian

27. On the difference between amulets and talismans in medieval and modern Europe, see Pinch, *Magic in Ancient Egypt*, 105.

28. See Pinch, *Magic in Ancient Egypt*, 104–19. For an overview on amulets in ancient Egypt, see Carol Andrews, *Amulets of Ancient Egypt* (London: British Museum Press, 1994).

29. A new recent study of ancient Egyptian textual amulets is Jacco Dieleman, "The Materiality of Textual Amulets in Ancient Egypt," in Boschung and Bremmer, eds., *Materiality of Magic*, 23–58.

30. A few amuletic papyri from Deir el Medina have been published by Yvan Koenig in a series of publications: "Un revenant inconvenant? (Papyrus Deir el-Medineh 37)," *Bulletin de l'Institut Français d'Archéologie Orientale* 79 (1979): 103–19; "Deux amulettes de Deir el-Médineh," *Bulletin de l'Institut Français d'Archéologie Orientale* 82 (1982): 283–93; "Le contre-envoûtement de Ta-i.di-Imen: pap. Deir el-Médineh 44," *Bulletin de l'Institut Français d'Archéologie Orientale* 99 (1999): 259–81; and "Le papyrus de Moutemheb," *Bulletin de l'Institut Français d'Archéologie Orientale* 104.1 (2004): 291–326.

history).[31] These were actually "divine deliberations" (*sḥr.w*), which a god would pass to a priest through oracular practices in a temple. They were meant to provide protection for newborns and were apparently also used for individuals of the non-elite. The text of the *Oracular Amuletic Decrees* includes, after a fixed opening formula ("I shall protect him/her/NN from …"), a lengthy list of dangers one could encounter in life. Most of these were represented by encounters with evil demons such as the *wrt*-demons, the evil *ꜣḫ.w*-spirits, female and male dead and evil gods.[32] These "apotropaic lists"[33] are also found in earlier and later magical texts and refer to belief in a world where protection against the supernatural was strictly necessary and where dangers of any type could be demonized. It is especially from the Ramesside Period (Dynasties Nineteen and Twenty, about 1350–1090 BCE) that we have a conspicuous number of magical papyri,[34] including medical prescriptions for curing demonic diseases and assaults. The linguistic register used in these documents is the colloquial one, the popular speech of Late Egyptian; this use of the colloquial speech shows how demons were felt to be part of daily life and distinguished from the higher, greater gods of the temple, who are generally addressed in the classic literary linguistic register of Middle Egyptian in religious and ritual texts.[35]

Protection was felt to be especially necessary in certain periods of the year, such as during the Nile's flood at the end of the year. The five epagomenal days, which were added to the Egyptian lunar calendar in order to compensate for the difference with the astronomical year, were thought to be particularly ominous since they were not provided by the divine

31. The main edition of the *Oracular Amuletic Decrees* is I. E. S. Edwards, *Hieratic Papyri in the British Museum. Fourth Series: Oracular Amuletic Decrees of the Late New Kingdom Edited, Together with Supplementary Texts in Other Collections* (Vols. 1–2; London: Published by the Trustees of the British Museum, 1960). See also Briant Bohleke, "An Oracular Amuletic Decree of Khonsu in the Cleveland Museum of Art," *Journal of Egyptian Archaeology* 83 (1997): 155–67; Terry G. Wilfong, "The Oracular Amuletic Decrees: A Question of Length," *Journal of Egyptian Archaeology* 99 (2013): 295–300.

32. See Rita Lucarelli, "Popular Beliefs in Demons in the Libyan Period: The Evidence of the Oracular Amuletic Decrees," in *The Libyan Period in Egypt: Historical and Cultural Studies into the 21st-24th Dynasties. Proceedings of a Conference at Leiden University, 25-27 October 2007* (ed. G. P. F. Broekman, R. J. Demarée, and O. E. Kaper; Leiden: Nederlands Instituut voor het Nabije Oosten and Peeters, 2009), 231–9.

33. See David Frankfurter, *Evil Incarnate: Rumors of Demonic Conspiracy and Satanic Abuse in History* (Princeton, NJ: Princeton University Press, 2007).

34. See, e.g., those published by Christian Leitz, *Magical and Medical Papyri of the New Kingdom* (London: British Museum Press, 1999).

35. See Alessandro Roccati, "Demons as Reflection of Human Society," in Kousoulis, ed., *Ancient Egyptian Demonology*, 89–96.

cosmological order. Defensive, protective magic was therefore essential and specific magical texts and calendars of lucky and unlucky days were composed in order to face this period of the year.[36] A very peculiar composition, in which beliefs in magic and demons mingle with the daily temple rituals, is the so-called "Calendars of the Lucky and Unlucky Days" (the ancient Egyptian title being: *ḥ3t-ꜥ m ḥ3t nḥḥ pḥ.wy ḏt*, the Book of "the beginning is *neheh*, the end is *djet*" [*neheh* and *djet* are both words used for eternity]), which was composed in the Ramesside Period and include directions for activities and rituals during the epagomenal days too.[37]

Besides the abundant textual evidence, defensive magic was also available through the use of apotropaic objects such as the ivory magic wands, also known as knives or *apotropaia* as Altenmüller named them in the first and main publication of these peculiar objects. These seem to have been in use from 2000 to 1600 BCE, namely from the end of the Eleventh to the Seventeenth Dynasty, for protection during birth-giving.[38] The row of protective creatures (named indeed *s3w.w*, "protectors," or *nṯr.w*, "gods") represented on the wands are anonymous, but their iconography allows us to recognize some of them—like the apotropaic dwarf god Bes/Aha and its female counterpart Beset, or the composite hippo goddesses Taueret or Ipet. Other hybrids and animal figures (lions, donkeys, frogs, vultures, and snakes among other) are less easily identifiable, but they appear to be very similar to those liminal beings depicted in rows on other apotropaic objects also used in private spheres of magic, such as headrests,[39] which also included more composite figures of Bes-like demons with snakes in their hands, spitting from their mouth, and with daggers on the feet.[40]

36. See Martin Bommas, *Die Mythisierung der Zeit: Die beiden Bücher über die altägyptischen Schalttage des magischen pLeiden I 346* (Wiesbaden: Harrassowitz, 1999), which is a thorough study of one papyrus filled with incantations to use during the epagomenal days. Cf. Maarten J. Raven, "Charms for Protection During the Epagomenal Days," in *Essays on Ancient Egypt in Honour of Herman te Velde* (ed. Jacobus van Dijk; Groningen: Styx, 1997), 275–91.

37. The main edition of the Calendars, based on Pap. Cairo JE 86637 and on Pap. Sallier IV (recto), is that of Christian Leitz, *Tagewählerei: Das Buch ḥ3t nḥḥ pḥ.wy ḏt und verwandte Texte* (Wiesbaden: Harrassowitz, 1994).

38. See Hartwig Altenmüller, "Die Apotropaia und die Götter Mittelägyptens: Eine typologische Untersuchung der sog. "Zaubermesser" des Mittleren Reichs. Vols. 1–2" (PhD dissertation, University of München, 1965), and Stephen Quirke, *Birth Tusks: The Armoury of Health in Context – Egypt 1800 BC*. Middle Kingdom Studies 3. London: Golden House Publications, 2016.

39. See Milena Perraud, "Appuis-tête à inscription magique et *apotropaïa*," *Bulletin de l'Institut Français d'Archéologie Orientale* 102 (2002): 309–26.

40. See, e.g., the specimen published in Siegfried Schott, "Eine Kopfstütze des Neuen Reiches," *Zeitschrift für ägyptische Sprache und Altertumskunde* 83 (1958):

Finally, in everyday life, protection was needed against the bite of poisonous and aggressive animals as well as in order to expel or keep away demonic diseases. Among the reptiles and insects mentioned in the spells, such as crocodiles and scorpions, snakes played a main role as incarnations of danger to be repelled, especially in the netherworld. The *Pyramid Texts* of the Old Kingdom contain many such "snake spells" which covered the walls of the pyramid's sarcophagus chamber.[41]

Spells against demonic illnesses are known from what Egyptologists call "medico-magical papyri," where incantations were complementary to medical recipes and prescriptions.[42] The close relationship between magic and medicine in the ancient world has been widely recognized by scholars. For Egyptologists, it is a central aspect of the study of religion and science in the Pharaonic period.[43] Health was a main concern for the ancient Egyptians as it is now in the Western world; the *swnw.w* ("doctors") were also priests and magicians who possessed the knowledge of the human physiology and possible symptoms and diseases aside from being able to write and recite incantations. In these documents, defensive magic mingles with curative magic: papyrus Ebers (dated to 1534 BCE in the New Kingdom), one of the main and longest documents of this corpus, includes spells for curing both known and unknown diseases together with treatises and treatment descriptions for migraines, skin, gastric, and anal diseases, heart-related issues, and even tumors.[44] The spells copied in this kind of papyri are based most often on mythological allusions to the myth of Horus-son-of-Isis (Horus Harsiese), the child hidden in the marshes and protected by his mother (and great magician) Isis against his uncle Seth. The mythic reference here plays the role of

141–4. On the iconography of the magic wands and its relationship also with the imagery found in the so-called *Books of the Netherworld*, see Joshua Roberson, "The Early History of 'New Kingdom' Netherworld Iconography: A Late Middle Kingdom Apotropaic Wand Reconsidered," in *Archaism and Innovation: Studies in the Culture of Middle Kingdom Egypt* (ed. David Silverman, William Kelly Simpson, and Josef Wegner; New Haven, CT: Department of Near Eastern Languages and Civilizations, Yale University, 2009), 427–45.

41.   See Christian Leitz, "Die Schlangensprüche in den Pyramidentexten," *Orientalia* 65 (1996): 381–427.

42.   A comprehensive translation (in French) of the most important medical papyri is that of Thierry Bardinet, *Les papyrus médicaux de l'Egypte pharaonique: Traduction intégrale et commentaire* (Paris: Fayard, 1995).

43.   For an overview on the subject of magic and medicine, see Pinch, *Magic in Ancient Egypt*, 133–46.

44.   On Papyrus Ebers, see Hans-Werner Fischer-Elfert, ed., *Papyrus Ebers und die antike Heilkunde: Akten der Tagung vom 15.-16.3.2002 in der Albertina/UB der Universität Leipzig* (Wiesbaden: Harrassowitz, 2005).

enhancing the power of the spell and of the cure by assimilating the patient and the magician to the deities. Religion, medicine, and magic are all in one. It is interesting that currently the texts copied on these papyri still attract the interest of doctors and scientists, who have provided some of the most important studies of them and on medicine in ancient Egypt in general.[45]

The texts and knowledge found in the magico-medical papyri were however not the only source of curative magic. Healing statues and objects were widely used in private and temple contexts, testifying to the central role of magic rituals and the preoccupation with survival in often adverse climate and living conditions. Plagues, poor hygiene customs, droughts, and different kinds of pathologies affected people no matter their social conditions. The so-called Horus *cippi* (or "Horus on the crocodiles") were particularly important objects in this regard; these stelae start to be attested from the thirteenth century BCE and become especially popular in the Graeco-Roman period. The main figure and focus of these stelae is Horus the Child, who is trampling on crocodiles and holding snakes, scorpions, lions, and oryxes; the mythic episode recalled here is again the one mentioned above, when the god had to hide in the marshes in order to avoid Seth's wrath. However, the earlier iconography of a god called Shed the Savior and attested also on stelae and other amuletic objects, closely recalls that of the *cippi* and seems to be its predecessor as well.[46] The so-called *Metternich Stela*, which comes from a temple in Heliopolis and dates to the Thirtieth Dynasty, is one of the most popular and rich specimens of this typology of curative and amuletic objects. The figure of the main deity (Horus the Child) is surrounded by a series of other apotropaic deities and by magical and mythical texts meant to cure snake bites and scorpion stings. The *Metternich Stela* and the other smaller and less richly decorated *cippi*, constitute a unique source for the study of ancient Egyptian theology and mythology as well as magic, since their decoration must have been copied from theological treatises and mythic accounts kept in temple archives.[47]

Healing statues of particular deities were also widely used in temples. More than seven hundred sitting statues of the lion-headed goddess

45. See, e.g., the publication by John F. Nunn, *Ancient Egyptian Medicine* (London: British Museum Press, 1996).

46. On the development of the Shed-the-Savior and Horus-the-Child iconographies, see Heike Sternberg-El Hotabi, *Untersuchungen zur Überlieferungsgeschichte der Horusstelen: Ein Beitrag zur Religionsgeschichte Ägyptens im 1. Jahrtausend v. Chr* (Wiesbaden: Harrassowitz, 1999).

47. See Laslo Kákosy, "A New Source of Egyptian Mythology and Iconography," in *Proceedings of the Seventh International Congress of Egyptologists, Cambridge, 3-9 September 1995* (ed. C. J. Eyre; Leuven: Peeters, 1998), 619–24.

Sekhmet have been found in New Kingdom Thebes and were originally placed in temples with a healing function. Sekhmet and her plague-carrying demons, the fearful *ḫ3yty.w* ("the slayers"), the *wpwty.w* ("the messengers"), and the *šm3y.w* ("the wanderers") were much feared, and rituals to appease the angry goddess in order to ward off the pestilences and plagues of the country were widely attested. The priests of Sekhmet were especially popular in their function as doctors, and the already mentioned magico-medical papyri—such as papyrus Edwin Smith—include spells against the demonic messengers of Sekhmet. The demons' breath is the plague and they were especially active during the epagomenal days.

The role of divine statues in healing is also mentioned in literature. The tale of the so-called *Bentresh Stela* is about a Persian princess from Bactria (modern Afghanistan), who was healed by a statue of the god Khonsu sent over by Ramses II.[48] These healing statues, together with the many statues of deceased persons populating tombs and funerary monuments, were thought to be a double of the represented person or deity and a sort of repository of its spirit. Their magic power was intrinsic to the belief that any image could be empowered through magic performances if placed in the right ritual context and taken care of by ritual specialists.[49]

Although an integral part of defensive magic, funerary magic needs further explanation in its aims and function since it covers a vast array of sources and rituals. At the basis of funerary magic is the belief in life after death, which begins with a journey of the deceased (body and soul) through a celestial and subterranean netherworld/underworld, during which a high level of protection and sacred, magic knowledge is needed. The deceased had to face a series of encounters with gods and demons guarding mounds, gates, and doors of the Realm of the Dead, and therefore needed lists of divine and demonic names, as well as maps of those regions. The final aim and fulfillment for the dead was his/her transfiguration into an *3ḫ (Akh)*: a glorified, effective spirit.

The mortuary literature of ancient Egypt is an essential source for the understanding of religious thought and ideas on death and the afterlife. The main collections of funerary texts—namely the *Pyramid Texts* of the Old

---

48. See the recent study of Orell Witthuhn et al., *Die Bentresch-Stele: Ein Quellen- und Lesebuch: Forschungsgeschichte und Perspektiven eines ptolemäerzeitlichen Denkmals aus Theben (Ägypten)* (Göttingen: Seminar für Ägyptologie und Koptologie der Georg-August-Universität Göttingen, 2015).

49. On healing statues, see Laslo Kákosy, "A propos des statues guérisseuses et d'une statue de Bès au musée du Louvre," in *La magie en Egypte: A la recherche d'une définition. Actes du colloque organisé par le Musée du Louvre les 29 et 30 septembre 2000* (ed. Yvan Koenig; Paris: Documentation Française, 2002), 273–84.

Kingdom; the *Coffin Texts* of the Middle Kingdom; and the *Book of the Dead* (in use from the beginning of the New Kingdom to the Roman Period)—are attested on tomb walls, coffins, magical objects, and especially on papyri, of which thousands have survived and were placed beside the mummy as a sort of *vademecum* during the journey in the other world. It has to be mentioned that scholars of funerary literature are now conscious that the distinction between these three main textual collections is only a conventional one, deriving from the different periods of production for each of these corpora and from their media (pyramid walls for the earliest of them, coffins and papyri for the other two collections). However, their scope and character is basically the same and gets perpetuated and even reinforced and expanded (from the king to the private/elite person) through the millennia.

With the exception of the *Pyramid Texts*, these textual collections had in their illustrations (the so-called "vignettes" in the *Book of the Dead*) a powerful complement, which testifies to the importance of figurative magic in ancient Egypt (the German *Bildzauber*).[50] Some funerary papyri, composed during the Third Intermediate Period (1070–712 BCE) at Thebes and belonging to the powerful priests of Amun, were even exclusively made of images only, showing how funerary symbols and scenes were a powerful amuletic medium on their own and did not necessarily need a textual counterpart.[51] Moreover, these figural papyri seem to represent a sort of catalogue of funerary and mythical motifs, which were also used in similar selections and sequences on the longer scrolls, which were then personalized by adding the name of the buyer at the moment of sale. It is mostly through these scrolls, authentic masterpieces of the ancient Egyptian scribal culture, that writing techniques and the "book" culture from ancient Egypt can be studied and understood.

Among the many religious themes illustrated in the funerary papyri, spells for warding off dangerous beings and happenings were among the most popular ones, and these tend to be very similar to those spells of defensive magic used in daily life on earth. The borders between funerary and defensive magic are therefore superficial: based only on the context of use—either the tomb or the house. We may mention, however, a few specific themes occurring in the funerary texts, such as the occurrence of Apopis, the arch-enemy

---

50. See Peter Eschweiler, *Bildzauber im alten Ägypten: Die Verwendung von Bildern und Gegenständen in magischen Handlungen nach den Texten des Mittleren und Neuen Reiches* (Göttingen: Universitätsverlag and Vandenhoeck & Ruprecht, 1994).

51. On the funerary papyri of the Third Intermediate Period, the main reference publication is that of Andrzej Niwiński, *Studies on the Illustrated Theban Funerary Papyri of the 11th and 10th Centuries B.C.* (Göttingen: Universitätsverlag and Vandenhoeck & Ruprecht, 1989).

of the sun god and daily attacker of the solar boat during its journey in the netherworld. Spell 39 of the *Book of the Dead* is one explicative example of how rituals and incantations against Apopis were necessary—not only for the individual deceased, but in order to ensure the perfect functioning of the cosmos and the daily renewal of creation through mythic allusions.[52] Funerary magic cannot be understood without the knowledge of the myths of creation and ideas on cosmology in ancient Egypt. Once again, like other types of magic literature from ancient Egypt, funerary texts were composed and handled mainly within a temple context by literate priests and scribes.

* * *

Another popular group of spells and illustrations included in the funerary literature, in particular in the *Coffin Texts* and in the *Book of the Dead*, belong to what we have previously named as transformative magic; in these texts, the purpose is to "become/transform" (*ḫpr* in ancient Egyptian, which is also the root of the name *Khepry*, the sun god in its scarab manifestation) into a different divine state, either that of a divine animal, plant, or anthropomorphic god.[53]

A different and definitely more aggressive type of what we could also call transformative magic was more popular in documents used in daily contexts and based on personal wishes to manipulate the desire of a loved one. In reference books on ancient Egyptian magic this is also called "love magic" and "binding magic,"[54] and it is still popular among modern pagan and esoteric groups that use ancient Egyptian magic as their main secret lore. However, until the Graeco-Roman period and the production of what has been called the "Theban magic library," namely the collection of the Greek Magical Papyri (PGM), we do not have any textual source speaking of rites of love magic which could imply the use and manipulation of figurines in order to bind the victim to its perpetuator through inducted sexual desire.[55] The few "love spells" attested in the Pharaonic period have a different flavor and mostly use mythological allusions to the stories of the gods in order to

52. See Joris F. Borghouts, *Book of the Dead [39]: From Shouting to Structure* (Wiesbaden: Harrassowitz, 2007).

53. See Frédéric Servajean, "Les formules des transformations du Livre des Morts," *Égypte, Afrique & Orient* 43 (2006): 47–56.

54. See Ritner, *Mechanics of Ancient Egyptian Magical Practice*, 142–4, 176–8.

55. This manipulation of images recalls curse rituals employed within the ancient Mediterranean societies which have been erroneously compared to the practices used in modern voodoo, although we cannot speak of "voodoo dolls" in ancient Egypt (see Chris Faraone, "Binding and Burying the Forces of Evil: The Defensive Use of 'Voodoo Dolls' in Ancient Greece," *Classical Antiquity* 10.2 [1991]: 165–205).

fulfill their intent. One spell from an *ostracon* found in the village of Deir el Medina writes: "Hail to you, gods, lords of heaven and earth—let (the woman) NN born of NN come after me like a cow after grass, like a maid-servant after her children, like a herdsman after his cattle. If they fail to make her come after me, I will set <fire to> Busiris and burn up <Osiris>!"[56]

Finally, one open issue within Egyptology, is whether to consider divina-tion as part of magic or as a purely religious practice connected to the tem-ple-controlled rituals of the Pharaonic and Graeco-Roman period. Also in this case, the borders between magic and religious aspects of the phenome-non are hard to define; however, most of the practices connected to ancient divination (oneiromancy, lecanomancy, and necromancy) are based on the somewhat passive interpretation of divine signs and on the prediction (orac-ular practices) of the future already established by the gods, where magic, in all its forms, is mainly characterized by performances aimed at *changing* a current state of being or *preventing* something from happening on earth or in the Realm of the Dead. We may therefore speak of "divinatory magic" only when the use of magic is employed in order to communicate with the gods. Magic and divination belong to the same sphere of religious thinking and action in other Near Eastern societies, such as Mesopotamia, as well as being very prominent in the Jewish world of Late Antiquity. Therefore, it would be illogical to advocate for a different approach for ancient Egypt, although the sources at our disposal are not really clear on this matter and are especially scanty for the earliest periods. In Ptolemaic Egypt divination was still part of the official religion of the temple, and it was only during the Roman Christian condemnation of the pagan religion that it was banned and seen as a sort of witchcraft. One of the few early sources from Phara-onic Egypt where magic and divinatory texts occur together is the Rames-side papyrus Chester Beatty 3, a book of dream interpretation, which also includes a spell to ward off bad dreams.[57] Dream books, as well as most divinatory magic practices, become more frequently attested in the Grae-co-Roman period and in the Demotic literature, showing the high popular-ity of this genre not only within the temple but also in the private sphere of everyday magical practices.[58]

56.   Joris F. Borghouts, *Ancient Egyptian Magical Texts: Translated* (Leiden: Brill, 1978), 1 (text n. 1).

57.   This papyrus has been published by Alan Henderson Gardiner, *Hieratic Papyri in the British Museum. Third series: Chester Beatty Gift* (London: British Museum Press, 1935), I 9–27; II Pls. 5-12.

58.   See Luigi Prada, "Classifying Dreams, Classifying the World: Ancient Egyptian Oneiromancy and Demotic Dream Books," in *Current Research in Egyptology 2011: Proceedings of the Twelfth Annual Symposium Which Took Place at Durham University,*

The abundance of textual and material sources on magic in ancient Egypt and the variety of the sources and languages employed for the texts requires a common effort by the egyptological community, in order to get a comprehensive understanding of magic in ancient Egypt. Unlike other ancient cultures, such as the ancient Jewish world, we lack an organized discourse on the part of the ancient Egyptian theologians and literates as to how magic and magic practices were conceptualized within the wider frame of religion. In other words, we lack an "ancient Egyptian" theoretical approach to magic. In order to reconstruct it, however, we have access to a series of evidence, which can be fully studied also in comparison with similar sources from other magic traditions in the Mediterranean and in the ancient world at large. A comparative approach to magic in ancient Egypt would indeed be very fruitful and could lead scholars to think at a broader level and to propose new, more fluid, and less limited definitions of phenomena such as demons and demonology, which are an integral part of magic as well.[59]

Biographical Note

Rita Lucarelli is Associate Professor of Egyptology at the University of California, Berkley, USA. She specializes in the religions of ancient Egypt, demonology, and magic in the Near East, and the funerary culture and literature of ancient Egypt. She has held positions at the University of Verona, Bonn University, University of Bari, and she was a visiting research scholar at the Italian Academy of Advanced Studies of Columbia University (2009) and at the Institute for the Study of the Ancient World of New York University (2012). She is the author of *The Book of the Dead of Gatseshen: Ancient Egyptian Funerary Religion in the 10th Century BC* (Brill, 2006), *Agents of Punishment and Protection: Assessing the Demonic in First Millennium BCE Egypt* (Brill, forthcoming), and co-editor of *Handbook of the Ancient Egyptian Book of the Dead* (with Martin Stadler; Oxford University Press, forthcoming) and *Herausgehen am Tage: Gesammelte Schriften zum altägyptischen Totenbuch* (with Marcus Müller-Roth and Annik Wüthrich; Harrassowitz Verlag, 2012).

United Kingdom, March 2011 (ed. Heba Abd El Gawad et al.; Oxford: Oxbow Books, 2012), 167–77.

59. See Rita Lucarelli, "Towards a Comparative Approach to Demonology in Antiquity: The Case of Ancient Egypt and Mesopotamia," *Archiv für Religionsgeschichte* 14 (2013): 11–25. See also, in the same volume, David Frankfurter, "Amente Demons and Christian Syncretism," *Archiv für Religionsgeschichte* 14 (2013): 83–101.

Bibliography

Altenmüller, Brigitte. *Synkretismus in den Sargtexten*. Wiesbaden: Harrassowitz, 1975.

Altenmüller, Hartwig. "Die Apotropaia und die Götter Mittelägyptens: Eine typologische Untersuchung der sog. 'Zaubermesser' des Mittleren Reichs. Vols. 1–2," PhD dissertation, University of München, 1965.

Andrews, Carol. *Amulets of Ancient Egypt*. London: British Museum Press, 1994.

Assmann, Jan. "Magie und Ritual im alten Ägypten," 23–43 in *Magie und Religion*. Edited by Jan Assmann and Harald Strohm. München: Wilhelm Fink, 2010.

Bąkowska-Czerner, Grażyna, Alessandro Roccati, and Agata Świerzowska, eds. *The Wisdom of Thoth: Magical Texts in Ancient Mediterranean Civilizations*. Oxford: Archaeopress Archaeology, 2015.

Bardinet, Thierry. *Les papyrus médicaux de l'Egypte pharaonique: Traduction intégrale et commentaire*. Paris: Fayard, 1995.

Bickel, Susanne. *La cosmogonie égyptienne: Avant le Nouvel Empire*. Göttingen: Universitätsverlag and Vandenhoeck & Ruprecht, 1994.

Bohak, Gideon. "The Diffusion of the Greco-Egyptian Magical Tradition in Late Antiquity," 357–81 in *Greco-Egyptian Interactions: Literature, Translation, and Culture, 500 BCE-300 CE*. Edited by Ian Rutherford. Oxford: Oxford University Press, 2016.

Bohleke, Briant. "An Oracular Amuletic Decree of Khonsu in the Cleveland Museum of Art," *Journal of Egyptian Archaeology* 83 (1997): 155–67. https://doi.org/10.1177/030751339708300109

Bommas, Martin. *Die Mythisierung der Zeit: Die beiden Bücher über die altägyptischen Schalttage des magischen pLeiden I 346*. Wiesbaden: Harrassowitz, 1999.

Bonnet, Hans. "Hike," 301–2 in *Lexikon der ägyptischen Religionsgeschichte*. Hamburg: Nikol, 2005.

Borghouts, Joris F. *Ancient Egyptian Magical Texts: Translated*. Leiden: Brill, 1978.

—"Magie," 1137–51 in *Lexikon der Ägyptologie*. Edited by Wolfgang Helk and Eberhardt Otto. Vol. 3. Wiesbaden: Harrassowitz, 1980.

—"ꜣḫ.w (*akhu*) and ḥkꜣ.w (*hekau*): Two Basic Notions of Ancient Egyptian Magic, and the Concept of the Divine Creative Word," 29–46 in *La magia in Egitto ai tempi dei faraoni: atti, convegno internazionale di studi, Milano, 29-31 ottobre 1985*. Edited by Alessandro Roccati and Alberto Siliotti. Verona: Rassegna internazionale di cinematografia archeologica arte e natura libri, 1987.

—"Lexicographical Aspects of Magical Texts," 149–77 in *Textcorpus und Wörterbuch: Aspekte zur ägyptischen Lexikographie*. Edited by Stefan Grunert and Ingelore Hafemann. Leiden: Brill, 1999.

—"Les Textes magiques de l'Egypte ancienne: Théorie, mythes et themes," 17–39 in *La magie en Egypte. Actes du colloque organisé par le Musée du Louvre les 29 et 30 septembre 2000*. Edited by Yan Koenig. Paris: Documentation française, 2002.

—*Book of the Dead [39]: From Shouting to Structure*. Wiesbaden: Harrassowitz, 2007.

Boschung, Dietrich, and Jan N. Bremmer, eds. *The Materiality of Magic*. München: Fink, 2015.

Dieleman, Jacco. "The Materiality of Textual Amulets in Ancient Egypt," 23–58 in Boschung and Bremmer, eds., *The Materiality of Magic*, 2015.

Edwards, I. E. S. *Hieratic Papyri in the British Museum. Fourth Series: Oracular Amuletic Decrees of the Late New Kingdom Edited, Together with Supplementary Texts in Other Collections*. Vols. 1–2. London: Published by the Trustees of the British Museum, 1960.

Eschweiler, Peter. *Bildzauber im alten Ägypten: Die Verwendung von Bildern und Gegenständen in magischen Handlungen nach den Texten des Mittleren und Neuen Reiches*. Göttingen: Universitätsverlag and Vandenhoeck & Ruprecht, 1994.

Faraone, Chris. "Binding and Burying the Forces of Evil: The Defensive Use of 'Voodoo Dolls' in Ancient Greece," *Classical Antiquity* 10.2 (1991): 165–205. https://doi.org/10.2307/25010949

Fischer-Elfert, Hans-Werner, ed. *Papyrus Ebers und die antike Heilkunde: Akten der Tagung vom 15.-16.3.2002 in der Albertina/UB der Universität Leipzig*. Wiesbaden: Harrassowitz, 2005.

Frankfurter, David. "Dynamics of Ritual Expertise in Antiquity and Beyond: Towards a New Taxonomy of 'Magicians'," 159–78 in *Magic and Ritual in the Ancient World*. Edited by Paul Mirecki and Marvin Meyer. Leiden: Brill, 2002.

—*Evil Incarnate: Rumors of Demonic Conspiracy and Satanic Abuse in History*. Princeton, NJ: Princeton University Press, 2007.

—"Amente Demons and Christian Syncretism," *Archiv für Religionsgeschichte* 14 (2013): 83–101. https://doi.org/10.1515/arege-2012-0006

Gardiner, Alan Henderson. *Hieratic Papyri in the British Museum. Third series: Chester Beatty Gift*. London: British Museum Press, 1935.

Jördens, Andrea, ed. *Ägyptische Magie und ihre Umwelt*. Wiesbaden: Harrassowitz, 2015. https://doi.org/10.2307/j.ctvc2rjv4

Kákosy, Laslo. "Heka," 1108–10 in *Lexikon der Ägyptologie*. Edited by Wolfgang Helk and Eberhardt Otto. Vol. 2. Wiesbaden: Harrassowitz, 1977.

—"A New Source of Egyptian Mythology and Iconography," 619–24 in *Proceedings of the Seventh International Congress of Egyptologists, Cambridge, 3-9 September 1995*. Edited by C. J. Eyre. Leuven: Peeters, 1998.

—"A propos des statues guérisseuses et d'une statue de Bès au musée du Louvre," 273–84 in *La magie en Egypte: A la recherche d'une définition. Actes du colloque organisé par le Musée du Louvre les 29 et 30 septembre 2000*. Edited by Yvan Koenig. Paris: Documentation Française, 2002.

—"Divination and Prophecy: Egypt," 371–73 in *Religions of the Ancient World: A Guide*. Edited by Sarah Iles Johnston. Cambridge, MA: Belknap Press of Harvard University Press, 2004.

Koenig, Yvan. "Un revenant inconvenant? (Papyrus Deir el-Medineh 37)," *Bulletin de l'Institut Français d'Archéologie Orientale* 79 (1979): 103–19.

—"Deux amulettes de Deir el-Médineh," *Bulletin de l'Institut Français d'Archéologie Orientale* 82 (1982): 283–93.

—"Le contre-envoûtement de Ta-i.di-Imen: pap. Deir el-Médineh 44," *Bulletin de l'Institut Français d'Archéologie Orientale* 99 (1999): 259–81.

—"Le papyrus de Moutemheb," *Bulletin de l'Institut Français d'Archéologie Orientale* 104.1 (2004): 291–326.

Kousoulis, Panagiotis, ed. *Ancient Egyptian Demonology: Studies on the Boundaries Between the Demonic and the Divine in Egyptian Magic*. Leuven: Peeters, 2011.

Leitz, Christian. *Tagewählerei: Das Buch ḥзt nḥḥ pḥ.wy ḏt und verwandte Texte*. Wiesbaden: Harrassowitz, 1994.

—"Die Schlangensprüche in den Pyramidentexten," *Orientalia* 65 (1996): 381–427.

—*Magical and Medical Papyri of the New Kingdom*. London: British Museum Press, 1999.

—ed. *Lexikon der ägyptischen Götter und Götterbezeichnungen*. Leuven: Peeters, 2002.

Leprohon, Ronald J. "Egyptian Religious Texts," 230–47 in *Egyptology Today*. Edited by Richard H. Wilkinson. Cambridge: Cambridge University Press, 2008.

Lloyd, Alan. "Egyptian Magic in Greek Literature," 99–120 in Kousoulis, ed., *Ancient Egyptian Demonology*, 2012.

Lucarelli, Rita. "Popular Beliefs in Demons in the Libyan Period: The Evidence of the Oracular Amuletic Decrees," 231–9 in *The Libyan Period in Egypt: Historical and Cultural Studies into the 21st-24th Dynasties. Proceedings of a Conference at Leiden University, 25-27 October 2007*. Edited by G. P. F. Broekman, R. J. Demarée, and O. E. Kaper. Leiden: Nederlands Instituut voor het Nabije Oosten and Peeters, 2009.

—"The So-called Vignette of Spell 182 of the Book of the Dead," 79–91 in *Herausgehen am Tage: Gesammelte Schriften zum altägyptischen Totenbuch*. Edited by Rita Lucarelli, Marcus Müller-Roth, and Annik Wüthrich. Wiesbaden: Harrassowitz, 2012.

—"Towards a Comparative Approach to Demonology in Antiquity: The Case of Ancient Egypt and Mesopotamia," *Archiv für Religionsgeschichte* 14 (2013): 11–25.

Meyer, Marvin, and Paul Mirecki. "Introduction," 1–10 in Meyer and Mirecki, eds., *Ancient Magic and Ritual Power*, 1995.

—eds. *Ancient Magic and Ritual Power*. Leiden: Brill, 1995.

Naether, Franziska. *Die Sortes Astrampsychi. Problemlösungsstrategien durch Orakel im römischen Ägypten*. Tübingen: Mohr Siebeck, 2010.

Niwiński, Andrzej. *Studies on the Illustrated Theban Funerary Papyri of the 11th and 10th Centuries B.C.* Göttingen: Universitätsverlag and Vandenhoeck & Ruprecht, 1989.

Nunn, John F. *Ancient Egyptian Medicine*. London: British Museum Press, 1996.

Otto, Eberhard. *Das ägyptische Mundöffnungsritual*. Wiesbaden: Harrassowitz, 1960.

Perraud, Milena. "Appuis-tête à inscription magique et *apotropaïa*," *Bulletin de l'Institut Français d'Archéologie Orientale* 102 (2002): 309–26.

Pinch, Geraldine. *Magic in Ancient Egypt*. London: British Museum Publications, 1994.

Prada, Luigi. "Classifying Dreams, Classifying the World: Ancient Egyptian Oneiromancy and Demotic Dream Books," 167–77 in *Current Research in Egyptology 2011: Proceedings of the Twelfth Annual Symposium which took place at Durham University, United Kingdom, March 2011*. Edited by H. Abd El Gawad, N. Andrews, M. Correas-Amador, V. Tamorri, and J. Taylor. Oxford: Oxbow Books, 2012.

Quack, Joachim Friedrich, ed. *Ägyptische Rituale der griechisch-römischen Zeit*. Tübingen: Mohr Siebeck, 2014.

Quirke, Stephen, *Birth Tusks: The Armoury of Health in Context – Egypt 1800 BC*. Middle Kingdom Studies 3. London: Golden House Publications, 2016

Raven, Maarten J. "Charms for Protection During the Epagomenal Days," 275–91 in *Essays on Ancient Egypt in Honour of Herman te Velde*. Edited by Jacobus van Dijk. Groningen: Styx, 1997.

Ritner, Robert K. *The Mechanics of Ancient Egyptian Magical Practice*. Chicago, IL: Oriental Institute of University of Chicago, 1993.

—"The Religious, Social, and Legal Parameters of Traditional Egyptian Magic," 43–60 in Meyer and Mirecki, eds., *Ancient Magic and Ritual Power*, 1995. https://doi.org/10.1163/9789004283817_005

Roberson, Joshua. "The Early History of 'New Kingdom' Netherworld Iconography: A Late Middle Kingdom Apotropaic Wand Reconsidered," 427–45 in *Archaism and Innovation: Studies in the Culture of Middle Kingdom Egypt*. Edited by David

Silverman, William Kelly Simpson, and Josef Wegner. New Haven, CT: Department of Near Eastern Languages and Civilizations, Yale University, 2009.

Roccati, Alessandro. "Demons as Reflection of Human Society," 89–96 in Kousoulis, ed., *Ancient Egyptian Demonology*, 2011.

Routledge, Carolyn. "Ancient Egyptian Ritual Practice: *Ir-xt* and *nt-a.*," PhD dissertation, University of Toronto, 2001.

Schott, Siegfried. "Eine Kopfstütze des Neuen Reiches," *Zeitschrift für ägyptische Sprache und Altertumskunde* 83 (1958): 141–4. https://doi.org/10.1515/zaes-1958-0118

Servajean, Frédéric. "Les formules des transformations du Livre des Morts," *Égypte, Afrique & Orient* 43 (2006): 47–56.

Sternberg-El Hotabi, Heike. *Untersuchungen zur Überlieferungsgeschichte der Horusstelen: Ein Beitrag zur Religionsgeschichte Ägyptens im 1. Jahrtausend v. Chr.* Wiesbaden: Harrassowitz, 1999.

Theis, Christoffer. *Magie und Raum: Der magische Schutz ausgewählter Räume im alten Ägypten nebst einem Vergleich zu angrenzenden Kulturbereichen.* Tübingen: Mohr Siebeck, 2014.

von Lieven, Alexandra. "Divination in Ägypten," *Altorientalische Forschungen* 26.1 (1999): 77–126. https://doi.org/10.1524/aofo.1999.26.1.77

Westendorf, Wolfhart. *Erwachen der Heilkunst: Die Medizin im Alten Ägypten.* Zürich: Artemis & Winkler, 1992.

Wilburn, Andrew T. *Materia Magica: The Archaeology of Magic in Roman Egypt, Cyprus and Spain.* Ann Arbor, MI: University of Michigan Press, 2012.

Wilfong, Terry G. "The Oracular Amuletic Decrees: A Question of Length," *Journal of Egyptian Archaeology* 99 (2013): 295–300. https://doi.org/10.1177/030751331309900119

Witthuhn, Orell, Heike Sternberg-el Hotabi, Moritz Klimek, Melanie Glöckner, and Gernot Demuth. *Die Bentresch-Stele: Ein Quellen- und Lesebuch: Forschungsgeschichte und Perspektiven eines ptolemäerzeitlichen Denkmals aus Theben (Ägypten).* Göttingen: Seminar für Ägyptologie und Koptologie der Georg-August-Universität Göttingen, 2015.

Chapter Ten

Manipulating "Religion":
The Egyptian *Theologoumena* in Diodorus Siculus

Panayotis Pachis

In the study of the cultures and societies that developed around the Medi-terranean basin, the sources play the most important role, being the safest means for our understanding the way the historical context was shaped in each period. The unreflective and uncritical usage of the sources and tes-timonies not only complicates one's work, but often leads to exaggerated historical generalizations. Thus, the student of history is obliged to try to understand the available sources and, primarily, to untangle the reasons for their production. Historical studies have demonstrated that, in all historical periods, each element is intertwined with others, constituting a unity that must be studied as such. Similarly, if we wish to approach the "religions" of antiquity and the various ideas that accompanied them, we need to do so by employing methodologies that will allow us to see but also comprehend what lay "behind the familiar metaphors, typologies, or sets of concepts proposed on the modern historical assumptions."[1] This can be achieved if we deal with our research similar to the investigations of a detective, who patiently and insightfully tries to find solutions to unresolved problems. It is in this fashion that we are able to achieve "a theoretical filling-in of the evidential gaps ... that is based upon testable hypotheses."[2]

In many respects, the same applies to scholars dealing with the religions of the ancient world. The treatment of "religion" as a *sui generis* phenom-enon constitutes a one-sided utilization of history. Contemporary scholars of religion need to be alerted to the fact that the different testimonies that shape the framework of their study are parts of a system, which cannot be overlooked when addressing those testimonies. Addressing "religion" as a social system that is "regularized" by resorting to a divine power constitutes the *sine qua non* for the contemporary study of religion, which struggles to

1. Luther H. Martin, "The Promise of Cognitive Science for the Historical Study of Religions with Reference to the Study of Early Christianity," unpublished lecture held in Helsinki (1 September 2005), 5.
2. Martin, "Promise of Cognitive Science," 5.

be "purged" from the generalizations of the past. Therefore, failing to take into consideration all those elements that shape the era in which a given religious phenomenon appears, leads us to simplified and superficial conclusions.[3] Such a problematic approach, however, is not restricted solely to the study of religion, but is often encountered in other fields. For example, traditional classicists often read and use the available sources coming from antiquity in a way that makes it actually impossible to allow for a way to understand the motives behind the composition of those works. Moreover, such a selective and often isolated utilization of the ancient sources also promotes ideologies that can rarely be seen as illustrative of the historical period under examination.

In this chapter, I am approaching these issues through the work of Diodorus Siculus in regards to the Egyptian *theologoumena*. Diodorus employs a strategy of manipulation of his sources in the first book of his *Library of History*. As I will argue, he indirectly adopts and adjusts Euhemerus's ideas with the aim of justifying the religio-political *status quo* of his time. Surprisingly, his strategy shifts in the fifth and sixth book of his *Library*, where he names Euhemerus of Messene and offers a long summary of the *Sacred Record*, the work in which Euhemerus promoted his ideas. As Ivan Strenski recently put it, what do we "see" when we "look" at the various data we use in our studies? How do we understand the various testimonies and events that are both directly and indirectly related to our data? Or, most importantly, how are they presented to our eyes, when we read, interpret, and utilize them?[4] These questions are indeed crucial when we address the more general and important question of "[w]hat are we trying to bring out when we say that we 'see' something 'religious' amid the 'political'?"[5]

* * *

In the first book of his *Library of History*, Diodorus presents a panorama of ideas and practices that dominated Egyptian life during his own time (first century BCE). Diodorus lived in an unstable and constantly changing world in which everything was contested. After the death of Alexander the Great, new social, political, economic, and religious ideas and worldviews came to the surface—ideas that complete the image of the Classical world. The traditional principles and values of the city-state were gradually replaced by

3.   See Gary Lease, "The History of 'Religious' Consciousness and the Diffusion of Culture: Strategies for Surviving Dissolution," *Historical Reflections/Reflections Historiques* 20.3 (1994): 454–5, 466–7.
4.   See Ivan Strenski, *Why Politics Can't Be Freed from Religion* (Oxford: Wiley-Blackwell, 2011), 1.
5.   Strenski, *Why Politics*, 6.

an ecumenical ideal. Cosmopolitanism was creating new conditions with regards to the coexistence of different people within the borders of the vast *oecumene*. The expansion of the limits of the traditional world led to the questioning of the conventional cosmological way of thinking. This phenomenon is later amplified with the emergence, during the second century CE, of a new cosmology created by Claudius Ptolemy.[6]

The information that Diodorus provides about the religious practices of Egypt is of particular significance. "Egyptomania" is the new trend of this period and, thus, everything that comes from this country is of great importance and begs for examination and description.[7] There are constant innuendos in his work to the oppositions between the local and ecumenical character of the cults of the Egyptian deities. The first tendency is represented by the priests of Egypt, who remain loyal to their religious traditions. The second one is represented by the ecumenical and syncretistic character, which is evident in the worshiping of these deities already from the beginning of the Hellenistic era. The tendency towards ecumenism is directly related to the Ptolemaic attempts for a renewal of the traditional character of the Egyptian religion.

In order to understand the way Diodorus describes the land of the Nile, we should observe the choices he makes. Every writer makes descriptions based on the ideas and views of his or her own time. This constitutes an essential factor for understanding a writer's thoughts and intentions. Diodorus is influenced by both the mindset and the intellectual tendencies that dominated the period in which he lived. His description of Egypt is based on reports of earlier writers, mainly Hecataeus of Abdera, whose travel descriptions of Egypt are the main source on which most of the subsequent writers rely for their own accounts. Hecataeus, who lived in the last quarter of the fourth century BCE, concentrated on matters relating to the origin of religion and kingship.[8] He considers both phenomena to be divine benefactions towards humanity. His reasoning influences the so-called (ancient) "euhemerism," which is one of the dominant religio-philosophical ideas of the Hellenistic world.[9]

6.   See Luther H. Martin, *Hellenistic Religions: An Introduction* (Oxford: Oxford University Press, 1987); Panayotis Pachis, *Ἶσις Καρποτόκος*. Vol. I: *Οἰκουμένη. Προλεγόμενα στόν συγκρητισμό τῶν ἑλληνιστικῶν χρόνων* (Thessaloniki: Vanias, 2003).

7.   Concerning the so-called phenomenon of "Egyptomania" during the Graeco-Roman age, see Mariette de Vos, *L'egittomania in pittura a mosaici Romano-Campani nella prima età imperiale* (Leiden: Brill, 1980); Robert Wild, *Water in the Cultic Worship of Isis and Sarapis* (Leiden: Brill, 1981), 87, 230; Sally-Ann Ashton, *Roman Egyptomania* (London: Golden House Publications, 2004).

8.   See *FGrH* 264 F25 = Diodorus Siculus 1.13.1. Cf. Peter M. Fraser, *Ptolemaic Alexandria* (Oxford: Clarendon Press, 1972), Vol. IIa, 450–1 and n. 815.

9.   *FGrH* 264 cited in Felix Jacoby, "Euemeros," *Realencyclopädie der classischen*

Euhemerism is ostensibly portrayed in Diodorus's descriptions in the first book of his *Library* and constitutes the main feature of his approach.[10] This specific tactic, which decisively shapes Diodorus's mythical narration, deals with the presentation and description of the Egyptian divine world. It is indeed an audacious hermeneutical method, since it challenges the peculiarity of the divine world. This new theory is critical because, while it is being shaped, it simultaneously provides information about the religious ideas and worshiping practices that prevail in the capital city of the Ptolemies during the third century BCE. Euhemerism remains in fashion during the second century BCE, when it deals with the teachings about the gods. The uncertainty of the religious and political scene during the last decades of the first century BCE is an additional factor for the dominance of euhemerism, which justifies its influence on Diodorus's work.

Euhemerus of Messene, the introducer of this theory, lived during the late fourth and early third century BCE.[11] He most likely spent a period of his life in the diplomatic service of King Cassander of Macedonia, but, for the longest part of his life, he is found in Alexandria. During this period, he wrote a book called *Sacred Record* ('Ιερὰ Ἀναγραφή), in which he developed his ideas. According to Diodorus's interpretation of the theory in book one, the gods or, to be more specific, the "terrestrial gods," were charismatic people (kings) who contributed to the dissemination of the "gentle and useful fruits" to mankind and were generally responsible for many benefactions.[12]

Many scholars believe that Euhemerus's theory coincides with the ideas of the sophist Prodicus.[13] Both ancient writers maintained a common line of

Altertumswissenschaft 6 (1907): 969; cf. Fraser, *Ptolemaic Alexandria*, Vol. I, 293, 497; Vol. IIa, 453–4 and n. 827–8; Vol. IIb, 720 and n. 15–6.

10. Diodorus Siculus 1.13.1. Diodorus discusses Euhemerus by name in books five and six. In the first book, as I argue, the theory is implied. This implied utilization is closely related to the way Diodorus used his sources throughout the *Library*. Rather than a mere compiler or copyist, he has recently been seen as a very capable and cautious author who uses his sources to serve his own agenda. For example, see Nickolas P. Roubekas, *An Ancient Theory of Religion: Euhemerism from Antiquity to the Present* (London: Routledge, 2017), 51–71, 179–83.

11. See Martin P. Nilsson, *Geschichte der Greichischen Religion* (3rd ed.; München: C. H. Beck, 1974), Vol. II, 283–9; Marek Winiarczyk, *Euhemerus Reliquiae* (Stuttgart and Leipzig: De Gruyter, 1991) and *Euhemeros von Messene: Leben, Werk, und Nachwirkung* (München and Leipzig: De Gruyter, 2002); Fraser, *Ptolemaic Alexandria*, Vol. I, 289–96, 298, 301; Vol. IIa, 453–7 and n. 800–43; Pachis, *'Ισις Καρποτόκος*, 61, 199, 339; Franco De Angelis and Benjamin Garstad, "Euhemerus in Context," *Classical Antiquity* 25.2 (2006): 211–42.

12. See Diodorus Siculus 1.2.2, 12.10-3.1.

13. See Albert Henrichs, "The Sophists and Hellenistic Religion: Prodicus as the

argumentation, and used the same terminology; for example, the view pertaining to the "ferocious living" of mankind and the decisive influence of the spread of cultivated fruits in people's life. These ideas affected a group of writers and shaped in a conclusive way their thought.[14] Hecataeus of Abdera, for example, also influenced Euhemerus.[15] Moreover, both writers lived during the first years of the Ptolemaic dynasty and were affected by Prodicus's ideas as well as those of another writer, Leon of Pella, who lived during the same period. Leon was an Egyptian priest who was considered to be an authority on the divine world of Egypt.[16]

Such ideas, however, would be considered insolence (ὕβρις) in previous periods, especially during the Classical era; in the Hellenistic period, on the contrary, such ideas formed the people's worldviews. We should not disregard the fact that the people who wandered in the vast *oecumene*, and in particular within the newly established cities (Alexandria, Pergamos, Antiochia, Efessos, etc.), were feeling more and more detached from their homes; this is a tendency that led to the emergence and dominance of similar innovative ideas, such as the theory of "euhemerism.'[17] According to the "spirit of this time," monarchs were deified and euhemerism constituted one of the

Spiritual Father of the ISIS Aretalogies," *Harvard Studies in Classical Philology* 88 (1984): 139–58.

14. Henrichs, "Sophists and Hellenistic Religion," 141 n. 10, 142 n. 14–5, 143–7.

15. Henrichs, "Sophists and Hellenistic Religion," 147–52.

16. About Leon of Pella, see Hyginus, *De astronomica* 2.20.4; Augustine, *De civitate dei* 5.12.11; Minucius Felix, *Octavius* XXI 3. Cf. Lily R. Taylor, *The Divinity of Roman Emperor* (Middletown, CT: American Philological Association, 1975), 26–7; W. Spuerri, "Leon von Pella," *Kleine Pauly* 3 (1979): 565; Fraser, *Ptolemaic Alexandria*, Vol. II, 447–8 and n. 847; 800–36; Nilsson, *Geschichte*, 283–9; Marianne Zumschlinge, "Euhemeros: Staatstheoretische und Staatsutopische Motive" (PhD dissertation, University of Bonn, 1976); Henrichs, "Sophists and Hellenistic Religion," 147–52; Jürgen Ebach, "Euhemerismus," in *Handbuch religionswissenschaftlichen Grundbegriffe* (ed. Hubert Cancik, Burkhard Gladigow, and Matthias Laubscher; Stuttgart and Berlin: Kohlhammer, 1990), Vol. 2, 365–8; Frank W. Walbank, *Ο Ελληνιστικός Κόσμος* (trans. Tasos Varveris; Thessaloniki: Vanias, 1993), 307–8; Reinhold Richter, "Politische Ordnung und fremde Kultur im Bild der hellenistischen Utopie," in *Hellenismus, Beiträge zur Erforschung von Akkulturation und politischen Ordnung in den Staaten des hellenistischen Zeitalter* (ed. Bernd Funk; Tübingen: J. C. B. Mohr, 1996), 638–40.

17. See Martin, *Hellenistic Religions*, 23–5; Luther H. Martin, "The Anti-Individualistic Ideology of Hellenistic Culture," *Numen* 41 (1994): 125–31; Panayotis Pachis, "Η Έννοια της Περιπλάνησης κατά τη Διάρκεια των Ελληνιστικών Χρόνων," *Επιστημονική Επετηρίδα Θεολογικής Σχολής* (n.s.) 12 (2002): 273–323 and "'*Hominibus vagis vitam*': The Wandering of *Homo Hellenisticus* in an Age of Transformation," in *Introducing Religion: Essays in Honor of Jonathan Z. Smith* (ed. Willi Braun and Russell T. McCutcheon; London: Equinox, 2008), 388–405.

most important means of advocating their absolute power, resulting in the establishment of ideas such as their divine descent.[18]

Euhemerus's approach offers the best possible explanation about the dominance of this particular political system. The limits that always separated the divine from the human world are now being minimized. It is possible that these ideas come from Protagoras (fifth century BCE), who claimed that "man is the measure of all things."[19] On the contrary, the old Delphic motto "know thyself" invited individuals to realize that they are mortals and have nothing in common with the immortal gods, an idea that we also encounter in Pindar's work and in the great tragic writers of the fifth century BCE.[20] All these result in the novel ideas that are being shaped by the people of the Hellenistic world, who were thus placing *Tychē* at the top ranks of the pantheon[21] and deified their monarchs.

This new tendency starts with Alexander the Great and continues with the Ptolemies and the Seleucids. The emergence of kingship is one of the best recorded and characteristic phenomena of the Hellenistic period.[22] There is a transition from the local worshiping practices—that are connected with

18. See Luther H. Martin, "Kingship and the Hellenistic Consolidation of Religio-Political Power," in *Theoretical Frameworks for the Study of Graeco-Roman Religions* (ed. Luther H. Martin and Panayotis Pachis; Thessaloniki: University Studio Press, 2003), 89–96.

19. See Plato, *Cratylus* 385E6-A1; Menander, *fragm.* E 240; K 203. Sextus Empiricus, *Outlines of Pyrrhonism* 1.216.1-2. Cf. Carl Schneider, *Kulturgeschichte des Hellenismus* (München: Beck, 1967–1969), Vol. I, 72.

20. See Plutarch, *De E apud Delphos* 392A6. Cf. Nilsson, *Geschichte*, Vol. I, 561; 736; Frederick M. Schroeder, "The Self in Ancient Religious Experience," in *Classical Mediterranean Spirituality: Egyptian, Greek, Roman* (ed. Arthur H. Armstrong; London: Routledge, 1989), 346–7; Martin, "Anti-Individualistic," 122–3.

21. About *Tychē*, see Iiro Kajanto, "Fortuna," *Aufstieg und Niedergang der römischen Welt* II.17 (1972): 502–58; Nilsson, *Geschichte*, Vol. II, 200–10; Martin, *Hellenistic Religions*, 21–3; Giulia Sfameni Gasparro, "Daimon and Tychē in the Hellenistic Experience," in *Conventional Values of the Hellenistic Greeks* (ed. P. Bilde, T. Engberg-Pedersen, L. Hannestad, and J. Zahle; Aarhus: Aarhus University Press, 1997), 67–109 and "Iside-Fortuna: Fatalismo e divinità sovrane del destino nel mondo ellenistico-romano," in *Le Fortune dell'età arcaica nel Lazio ed in Italia e la loro posterità* (Palestrina: Comune di Palestrina, Assessorato alla Cultura, 1998), 301–23; Pachis, Ἶσις Καρποτόκος, 22, 56–7, 317–24, 336, 348.

22. See Christian Habicht, *Gottmenschentum und griechische Städte* (2nd ed.; München: C. H. Beck, 1970); Ludwig Koenen, "The Ptolemaic King as a Religious Figure," in *Images and Ideologies: Self-Definition in the Hellenistic World* (ed. Anthony Bulloch et al.; Berkeley, CA: University of California Press, 1993), 25–115; Pachis, Ἶσις Καρποτόκος, 247–89; Angelos Chaniotis, "The Divinity of Hellenistic Rulers," in *A Companion to the Hellenistic World* (ed. Andrew Erskine; Oxford: Blackwell, 2005), 431–45.

the family—to the broad kinship groups of the public cults of the city-state, and then to kingship and the legitimation of their power. Whereas in the former two cases we find a collective distribution of power in the frame of social organization, in the latter power is restricted only to the king.[23]

The citizens of the *oecumene* suffered from the authoritarian expression of royal power in every aspect of their lives, and that is why they were trying to find a way to justify its existence. They no longer participated in the public life of the city they lived in. The writers, as well as the representatives of the philosophical schools of this period, acted as supporters, through their works, of the newly established order, as well as the quintessential *voice* of the idea of the monarchs' deification. It is the monarchs who covered the living expenses of all those who resided in their courts, who, in turn, declared that only the monarchs could resolve the problems that people faced.[24] At the same time, the representatives of the royal courts were considered to be responsible, with their actions and way of government, towards the gods. Through the works and ideas of this period, the "principle of the divine command" is established, which constitutes the best way for justifying their absolute power.

This demonstrates the religio-political *status quo* of Euhemerus's age. It is a manifestation of the views of this period, according to which the monarchs were protectors and constant carriers of civilization throughout the *oecumene*. They were the representatives of harmony, order, and stability—in other words, the divine saviors and benefactors.[25] The monarchs were recipients of divine honors due to their political tactics since, according to Diodorus,[26] they did many things of service to the social life

---

23. See Martin, "Kingship."

24. Cf. Peter Green, *Alexander to Actium: The Historical Evolution of the Hellenistic Age* (Berkeley, CA: University of California Press, 1990), 84–91, 173–82; Pachis, Ἶσις Καρποτόκος, 48–9; R. A. Hazzard, *Imagination of a Monarchy: Studies in Ptolemaic Propaganda* (Toronto: University of Toronto Press, 2000).

25. See Arthur D. Nock, "Notes on Ruler Cult I-IV," in *Arthur Darby Nock: Essays on Religion and the Ancient World* (ed. Zeph Stewart; Cambridge, MA: Harvard University Press, 1972), Vol. I, 134–59 and "Soter and Euergetes," in *Arthur Darby Nock: Essays on Religion and the Ancient World* (ed. Zeph Stewart; Cambridge, MA: Harvard University Press, 1972), Vol. II, 720–9; Vera F. Vanderlip, *The Four Greek Hymns of Isidorus and the Cult of Isis* (Toronto: Scholars Press, 1972), 15; Françoise Dunand, "Culte royal et culte imperial en Egypte: Continuités et ruptures," in *Das Römisch-Byzantinische Ägypten* (ed. Grimm Günter, Heinz Heinen, and Erich Winter; Mainz am Rhein: Philipp von Zabern, 1983), 49; Ludwig Koenen, "Die Adaptation ägyptischer Königsideologie am Ptolemäerhof," in *Egypt and the Hellenistic World* (ed. Edmond van 't Dack, Peter van Dessel, and Wilfried van Gucht; Louvain: Orientaliste, 1983), 152–70; Green, *Alexander to Actium*, 402; Pachis, Ἶσις Καρποτόκος, 269–70.

26. Diodorus Siculus 1.13.5: καὶ τὸν μὲν Ὄσιριν μεθερμηνευόμενον εἶναι Διόνυσον,

of their subjects (πολλὰ πρᾶξαι πρὸς εὐεργεσίαν τοῦ κοινοῦ βίου). This is directly related to the ideology of this period, according to which the king is deemed the constant representative of harmony and law in the whole country.[27] People knew that the wealth and prosperity depended mainly on the abundant crops of the land. The monarchs' "philanthropy" was directly related to their overall policies and constituted the indication *par excellence* of their influence on their subjects, especially when the latter were in danger.[28] Testimonies for all these can be found in various governmental decrees issued during this period, where the simultaneity of religion and politics becomes even clearer.[29]

This is especially important if we take into consideration that the dissemination of a mythical narration in a specific historical period, according to Bruce Lincoln,

> will depend on a great many factors, many of which are contingent to the specific situation ... First, there is the question of whether a disruptive discourse can gain a hearing, that is, how widely and effectively can it be propagated ... Second, there is the question of whether the discourse is persuasive or not, which is partially a function of its logical and ideological coherence. Although such factors, which are by nature internal to the discourse, have their importance, it must be stressed that persuasion does not reside within any discourse *per se* but is, rather, a measure of audiences' reaction to, and interaction with the discourse.

Furthermore, Lincoln maintains that

> there is the question of whether—and the extent to which—a discourse succeeds in calling forth a following; this ultimately depends on whether a discourse elicits those sentiments out of which new social formation, operating along rational (or pseudorational) and moral (or pseudomoral) lines, but it is also an instrument of sentiment evocation.[30]

The innovation of the Hellenistic period regarding the beneficial influence of the gods on people's lives lies in the transition from the mythical to the historical time; as Lincoln mentions, "a dialectic interaction of past and present

τὴν δὲ Ἶσιν ἔγγιστά πως Δήμητραν. ταύτην δὲ γήμαντα τὸν Ὄσιριν καὶ τὴν βασιλείαν διαδεξάμενον πολλὰ πρᾶξαι πρὸς εὐεργεσίαν τοῦ κοινοῦ βίου.

27. See *OGIS* 56, 68. Cf. Fraser, *Ptolemaic Alexandria*, Vol. I, 193–210; Green, *Alexander to Actium*, 402; Simon R. F. Price, *Rituals and Power: The Roman Imperial Cult in Asia Minor* (Cambridge: Cambridge University Press, 1984), 31; Pachis, Ἶσις Καρποτόκος, 192–3.

28. See Pachis, Ἶσις Καρποτόκος, 186–206.

29. See *OGIS* I 90; *SEG* 8, 463, 33; 1357. Cf. Pachis, Ἶσις Καρποτόκος, 204–5.

30. Bruce Lincoln, *Discourse and the Construction of Society: Comparative Studies of Myth, Ritual, and Classification* (Oxford: Oxford University Press, 1989), 8–9.

is evident in the myths."³¹ This is further reinforced if we take into account Russell McCutcheon's view who points out that "we should not forget that despite the attempts to construct a past or future long removed from the present, mythmaking takes place in a specific socio-political moment and supports a specific judgement about the here and now."³² Diodorus's narrations about the mythical world of Egyptian religion can be considered as retrojective applications of such views. Among the cultural goods that are offered to people by Osiris and Isis, the most important are: the creation of laws; the foundation of new cities; the learning of how to make new tools that will be useful in people's everyday life (such as in agriculture, hunting, etc.). In this cultural enterprise, the divine couple was helped by another god, Hermes-Thoth.³³ Diodorus's strategy aimed at ascribing to the monarchs of Egypt the benefactory attributes of the divine couple Isis and Osiris, who spread agriculture to the world and thus created more prosperous conditions for the development of civilization.³⁴ This actually determines the monarchs' political behavior: as new gods, they travelled around the *oecumene* and disseminated cultural goods to all people, who in turn recognized them as providers of culture and benefactors of humanity.

The main feature of their civilizing project was the offering of laws. The meaning of laws, as prerequisites of civilization, can be linked to the overall ideology of the Hellenistic and Roman periods. In this regard, the adjective "law-giver" (*Thesmophoros*)³⁵ that is attributed to Isis by Diodorus, demonstrates the important role that laws played in the creation of the appropriate conditions that would contribute to the people's harmonious coexistence. This also applies to the divine characterizations "Just" (*Dikaia*) and "Justice" (*Dikaiosynê*) that are attributed to Isis.³⁶

31. Lincoln, *Discourse*, 28.
32. Russell T. McCutcheon, "Myth," in *Guide to the Study of Religion* (ed. Willi Braun and Russell T. McCutcheon; London and New York: Cassell, 2000), 204.
33. See Diodorus Siculus 1.16.1; 1.20.6; 1.45.6; 1.94.1; 1.96.6. Cf. Iris Sulimani, *Diodorus' Mythistory and the Pagan Mission: Historiography and Culture-Heroes in the First Pentad and the Bibliotheke* (Leiden: Brill, 2011), 265–80.
34. Diodorus Siculus 1.13.5-20.6.
35. Diodorus Siculus 1.14.4: διὸ καὶ τοὺς παλαιοὺς Ἕλληνας τὴν Δήμητραν θεσμοφόρον ὀνομάζειν, ὡς τῶν νόμων πρῶτον ὑπὸ ταύτης πειθομένων. 1.25.1: καθόλου δὲ πολλὴ τίς ἐστι διαφωνία περὶ τούτων τῶν θεῶν. τὴν αὐτὴν γὰρ οἱ μὲν Ἶσιν, οἱ δὲ Δήμητραν, οἱ δὲ θεσμοφόρον, οἱ δὲ Σελήνην, οἱ δὲ Ἥραν, οἱ δὲ πάσαις ταῖς προσηγορίαις ὀνομάζουσι. Cf. *Aretalogy of Kyme* 16; *Aretalogy of Andros* 20; *Aretalogy of Thessaloniki* 4; *Aretalogy of Cassandrea* [*Potidea*] 4 = *RICIS*, 113/1201.
36. See ID 2079; *CIG* II, 2295 = *ID* 2079 = *RICIS*, 202/0282; *ID* 2103; *RICIS*, 202/288. Cf. Fraser, *Ptolemaic Alexandria*, Vol. I, 221, 241; Vol. IIa, 335–6 and n. 76, 392, 413; Jon D. Mikalson, *Religion in Hellenistic Athens* (Berkeley, CA: University of

The foundation of cities by Osiris, with altars for the veneration of gods, indirectly implies the monarchs and their tactics.[37] Another characteristic feature of this era is the establishment of cities in the successors' kingdoms. The civilizing activity of the monarchs was clearly established by specific actions: the monarchs had monuments and temples built, with inscribed texts commemorating their benefactions to the citizens of the *oecumene*. Furthermore, we should not forget that temples of Isis were built throughout the Graeco-Roman world.[38]

The spread of civilization by these specific deities can be connected to relevant theories about the origin of civilization in which emphasis is given to the cultural role of grains as well as to the direct relationship between religion and politics. The latter holds an important place in Diodorus's work and is linked to the hermeneutical approaches offered by Euhemerus. Both Osiris and his wife Isis are responsible for the civilizing activity that benefits humanity as a whole. Isis is considered to be the one who discovers the grains, whereas Osiris discovers the methods of agriculture.[39] For this reason Diodorus characterizes Osiris as "the one who was interested in agriculture" (φιλογεωργός),[40] thereby placing special emphasis on Osiris as the most important agent of this development. In this way, Osiris, as Diodorus maintains, is the one who spreads (διαδούς) all the goods of civilization to people.[41] The correspondence between grain and civilization was also dominant in previous periods, especially in fifth century BCE Athens. This phenomenon is connected to the "cultural heroes" (ἥρωες εὑρετές), who spread agriculture. What is really important among the accomplishments of the cultural heroes is the end of cannibalism, which, according to Diodorus, was a usual phenomenon prior to the spread of agriculture.[42] It is through this development that the transition from the environment of the wild to the civilized

California Press, 1998), 276–7. All these adjectives are related to the diffusion of grains and they display the identification of Demeter with Isis. See Diodorus Siculus 1.14. Cf. Panayotis Pachis, "'Manufacturing Religion' in the Hellenistic Age: The Case of Isis-Demeter Cult," in *Hellenisation, Empire and Globalisation: Lessons from Antiquity* (ed. Luther H. Martin and Panayotis Pachis; Thessaloniki: Vanias, 2004), 163–207.

37.   See Diodorus 1.5.1-5.

38.   See *RICIS*, 204/0346?; 202/0350; 101/0210; 202/0282; 202/0288; Sulimani, *Diodorus' Mythistory*, 280–304.

39.   See Diodorus Siculus 1.14. Cf. Henri Frankfort, *Kingship and the Gods: A Study of Ancient Near Eastern Religion as the Integration of Society and Nature* (Chicago, IL: University of Chicago Press, 1978), 187–9; Sulimani, *Diodorus' Mythistory*, 230–65.

40.   Diodorus Siculus 1.15.6.

41.   Diodorus Siculus, 1.14-20.

42.   Diodorus Siculus 1.14.1; 1.27. Cf. *Aretalogie of Kyme*. About culture heroes, see Sulimani, *Diodorus' Mythistory*, 13–5, 156–61; Panayotis Pachis, *Δήμητρα Καρποφόρος:*

way of life takes place. Diodorus reckons that each god plays a different role in this process. Isis spreads wheat and barley, which are already known to other peoples, whereas Osiris teaches them how to cook them.[43] In this way, it is made clear that any "savage" habits of the previous periods (such as scavenging) are done away with; at this point we encounter a barrier between the people's "thorny (uncivilized)" (ἀκανθώδης) and the "cultivated (civilized) way of life" (ἀληλεμένος βίος).[44] The next step is the establishment of laws. It is necessary to point out that all the above-mentioned reports attribute to Osiris and Isis the discovering of agriculture, that is, the exploitation of the vegetal world in favor of the human world, paying attention only to the use of plants and not to the reason for which they exist. This omission is justified by the adoption of the peripatetic teachings by Hecateus. This philosophical school teaches the eternity of the world, in which the elements of the cosmos (the astral and planetary world) and all species of the animal and vegetal world participate. Thereby, when Hecataeus of Abdera and Diodorus Siculus present Isis and Osiris as founders of agriculture and civilization, they continue an already formed tradition. This adjusted concept was further emphasized in the thought of other writers of this era (between the fifth and the first century BCE), and clearly reflects the Greek ideas of the fifth century BCE.[45]

The collaborating activity of Osiris and Isis can be further explained by yet another interpretation. The eccentric activity of the two deities seems to correspond to the analogous task of Demeter and Triptolemus.[46] We should keep in mind that Demeter's cult acquired great importance during the reign of Ptolemus I the Soter,[47] mainly due to the influence of Eumolpides's priest

---

Θρησκεία και Αγροτική Οικονομία του Αρχαιοελληνικού Κόσμου (Athens: Ellinika Grammata, 1998).

43. Diodorus Siculus 1.14. Cf. Henrichs, "Sophists and Hellenistic Religion," 142; Pachis, *Δήμητρα Καρποφόρος*, 144.

44. See Suda, s.v. "βίος ἀκανθώδης" and "βίος ἀληλεμένος." Cf. Henrichs, "Sophists and Hellenistic Religion," 142 and n. 15; 145–50; Marcel Detienne, *The Gardens of Adonis: Spices in Greek Mythology* (trans. Janet Lloyd; Princeton, NJ: Princeton University Press, 1994), 117; Pachis, *Δήμητρα Καρποφόρος*, 132–6, 157.

45. See Henrichs, "Sophists and Hellenistic Religion," 140–52; Pachis, *Δήμητρα Καρποφόρος*, 125–40.

46. Cf. Pachis, *Δήμητρα Καρποφόρος*, 160–76.

47. See Schneider, *Kulturgeschichte*, Vol. I, 552–3; Fraser, *Ptolemaic Alexandria*, Vol. I, 198–201; Vol. IIa, 333–42 and n. 64–95; Nilsson, *Geschichte*, Vol. II, 94–5; Dorothy J. Thompson, "Demeter in Graeco-Roman Egypt," in *Egyptian Religion: The Last Thousand Years. Studies Dedicated to the Memory of Jan Quaegebeur* (ed. Willy Clarysse, Antoon Schoors, and Harco Willems; Leuven: Peeters, 1998), 699–707; J. J. Herrmann, "Demeter-Isis or the Egyptian Demeter? A Graeco Roman Sculpture from an Egyptian Workshop in Boston," *Jahrbuch des Deutschen Archäologischen Instituts* 114 (1999): 74–5.

Timotheus, whose participation was decisive for the Ptolemies' religious reformative project.[48] The special meaning that they attributed to the cult of the Greek goddess becomes obvious by the fact that the name "Eleusis" is given, according to Polybius,[49] to a suburb of the new capital,[50] as well as to a village in the area of Fayum,[51] where the *Thesmophorion* was possibly established in honor of Demeter. The worship of the goddess was also portrayed in the feasts of Kalathos[52] and Demetria,[53] the two important festivals of this period, as mentioned in Zeno's Papyrus.[54] At the same time, during the reign of the Ptolemies, Triptolemus received great honors in Egypt. His cultural activity set a permanent example for the activity of the Egyptian rulers.[55]

48. See J. Gwen Griffiths, *Plutarch's De Iside et Osiride* (Cardiff: University of Wales Press, 1970), 76, 78, 84, 92–3, 394–5, 403; Francois Chamoux, *Hellenistic Civilization* (trans. Michel Roussel; Oxford: Wiley-Blackwell, 2003), 330, 345; Susan A. Stephens, *Seeing Double: Intercultural Poetics in Ptolemaic Alexandria* (Berkeley, CA: University of California Press, 2003), 142; Robert Parker, "Timotheos," *Neue Pauly* 12.1 (2002): 598–9. Cf. *FGrHist* 273 F74; Arnobius, *Adversus Nationes* 5.5–7.

49. See Polybius 15.27.2; 15.29.8; 15.33.8.

50. See Strabo 17.1.16; Livy, *Ab urbe condita* 45.12.2. Cf. Fraser, *Ptolemaic Alexandria*, Vol. I, 35, 200; Vol. IIa, 110 and n. 276–7, 338 and n. 81–2.

51. See Françoise Dunand, *Le culte d'Isis dans le bassin oriental de la Méditerranée* (Leiden: Brill, 1973), Vol. I, 73. See also *OGIS* 83; *SB* 2674; *PPetr.* III. 41.1-7; 66B 1.5-8; 5 *P.Cair.Zen.* III 59350, 1-8 [Thesmophoria, Nesteia]; Polybius 15.29.8.33 [Thesmophoria].

52. Fraser, *Ptolemaic Alexandria*, Vol. IIa, 339 and n. 87: "In any case it seems clear that the procession described is part of the Thesmophoria, and not of the Eleusinian mysteries as the scholiast (on line 1 of Callimchus, *Hymn* VI) suggests: ὁ Φιλάδελφος Πτολεμαῖος κατὰ μίμησιν τῶν Ἀθηνῶν ἔθη ἵδρυσε ἐν Ἀλεξάνδριαι, ἐν οἷς καὶ τὴν καλάθου πρόοδον. ἔθος ἦν ἐν Ἀθήναις ἐν ὡρισμένηι ἡμέραι ἐπὶ ὀχήματος φέρεσθαι κάλαθον εἰς τιμὴν Δήμητρος. Cf. Vol. IIa, 334–5 and n. 71: "I do not believe that the background of Callimachus' *Hymn to Demeter* VI, which contains a description of the 'Procession of the Basket' in the goddess's honour, if it is of any particular city, is Alexandria. A very strong case can be made out for Cos […]."

53. See *P.CairZen* I 59028 [Demetreia] [258 BCE]; III 59350,1-8 [Thesmophoria, Nesteia] [244 BCE]; *P.Tebt.* III 21079, 1, 1-4 [Demetreia] [third–second c. BCE]; III, 2826, 1, 3-5 [Verenice's Thesmophorion]. Cf. Giulia Sfameni Gasparro, *Misteri e culti di Demetra* (Roma: L'Erma Di Bretschneider, 1986), 249.

54. About the so-called Zenon Papyrus, see Pieter W. Pestman, *A Guide to the Zenon Archive* (Leiden: Brill, 1981); Tony Reekmans, "Archives de Zénon: Situation et comportment des entrepreneurs indigènes," in Van 't Dack et al., eds., *Egypt and the Hellenistic World*, 325–50; Joseph G. Manning, *Land and Power in Ptolemaic Egypt: The Structure of Land Tenure* (Cambridge: Cambridge University Press, 2003), 16, 102, 110–8, 140–1. Cf. *P.Col.Zen* 1.8.9; *P.CairZen* 1.59056; 2.59177; 2.59202; 2.59203; 2.59204; 2.59209.

55. Pachis, *Δήμητρα Καρποφόρος*, 171–4.

Diodorus gives us, in this context, some information concerning Triptolemus.[56] This report is directly related to the fact that, during the reign of the
Ptolemies in Egypt, the cult of Triptolemus was also spread and gained great
popularity. The idea of the civilizing activity of the hero became particularly
popular in the environment of Alexandria. The rulers of Egypt were identified
with Triptolemus, which led to the connection of the latter with Osiris,[57] both
of whom, according to Diodorus, were connected with the discovery of agriculture. However, Diodorus goes in this case one step further, by identifying
Triptolemus with Osiris, without separating the Greek from the Egyptian tradition. The formation of such an idea, which defined Egypt as the birthplace
of civilization, corresponded to the tendency of many cities to impropriate
this primacy.

In the fifth book of his *Library*, Diodorus mentions the mythical traditions of Sicily, his birthplace, in relation to the cults of Demeter and Korē.
He focuses on the divine donation of the goddess to humanity, thus con-
firming the special bonds of Sicily with her cult.[58] This cult is connected
with the religio-political life of the island, from its emergence (between
the seventh and the sixth century BCE) until the Roman domination (211
BCE), when it became the symbol of the state power.[59] In his description of
the divine donation, Diodorus combines the two dominant mythical traditions (the Attic and the Sicilian). The Alexandrian writers use the same tactic.[60] In the Classical period, the accepted birthplace of civilization was the
city of Athens, due to its cultural effulgence and political power. But when,
during the Hellenistic era, Alexandria is gradually getting acknowledged as
a political and cultural center, it is natural for the geographical position of
the "birthplace" to adjust to the new conditions, with the Ptolemaic capital
being considered as the birthplace of civilization.[61] This was amplified by
the prevalence of the syncretistic spirit, evident in Alexandria, due to the
favorable geographical and historical conditions that allowed the conflation
of heterogeneous cultural elements. The Egyptian descent of Triptolemus
and the assignment of his project by Isis reflected these two tendencies: the

56. Diodorus Siculus 1.14.1; 1.18.2; 1.20.3; 1.29.1.
57. Diodorus Siculus 1.18-9; 1.20.3-4.
58. Diodorus Siculus 5.2.3; 6.4.1-6.
59. See Luther H. Martin, "Greek Goddesses and Grain: The Sicilian Connection,"
Helios 17.2 (1990): 251–61; Pachis, *Δήμητρα Καρποφόρος*, 123–4.
60. Diodorus Siculus 5.2.1; Nicander, *Theriaca* 483-7. Cf. Sfameni Gasparro,
Misteri e culti, 151, 157; Pachis, *Δήμητρα Καρποφόρος*, 122.
61. Diodorus Siculus 5.69.1-3; Strabo 17.1.7; 17.1.13. Cf. Pachis, *Δήμητρα
Καρποφόρος*, 176–96; Green, *Alexander to Actium*, 80–91, 157–8, 313–5; Pachis, *Ἶσις
Καρποτόκος*, 46.

appropriation of the beginning of civilization and syncretism. These beliefs resulted in the hero's identification with the monarchs. The relevant tradition affected the house of the Ptolemies—after all, this was a period in which the deification of humans, and mainly monarchs, is a practice that received great attention. The new reality will be maintained during the Hellenistic era and will reach its climax during the imperial age.

It is worth mentioning an innovation that we find in Diodorus's text regarding the common beneficial activity of Osiris and Isis. This practice seems to fade in Diodorus's narration as we can see in the so-called "Aretalogy of Isis," which is found among his descriptions about the Egyptian mythical world. This text is the most ancient testimony regarding the hymns in honor of the goddess, which accompany the spread of her cult in the Graeco-Roman world, and in which the goddess herself declares her benefactions towards humanity. The "I am" (ἐγὼ εἰμί), that characterizes the personal style of these hymns, is for the first time presented by Diodorus and is related to the gods, the kings, and the priests of the East. The same notion is a common locus in all subsequent Aretalogies, according to which the goddess, and not Osiris, takes over the obligation to perform all the civilizing actions in the Greaco-Roman *oecumene*.[62] Diodorus, in the beginning of this particular hymn, characteristically mentions: "[T]he tombs of these gods [that is, Osiris and Isis] lie in Nysa in Arabia, and for this reason Dionysus is also called Nysaeus. And in that place there stands also a stele of each of the gods bearing an inscription in hieroglyphs,"[63] in which are written, according to what Isis mentions, all her divine benefactions towards humankind. This report constitutes one more piece of evidence regarding the explicit influence of Euhemerus on Diodorus's *theologoumena*, since this passage comprises a clear analogy to Euhemerus's text.

This idea is directly connected to the religious reality of Diodorus's time, according to which Isis began to attract—during the second half of the second century BCE—greater attention than her husband Osiris.[64] This wider acceptance of the goddess is generally attributed to the increased role that the queens of Egypt held in religio-political affairs. This affected the overall way in which the goddess was presented in subsequent periods.[65]

62. Cf. Panayotis Pachis, "The Hellenistic Era as an Age of Propaganda: The Case of Isis' Cult," in Martin and Pachis, eds., *Theoretical Frameworks*, 97–125.

63. Diodorus Siculus 1.27.

64. See Frankfort, *Kingship and the Gods*, 181–212; Panayotis Pachis, "Το Νερό και το Αίμα στις Μυστηριακές Λατρείες της Ελληνορωμαϊκής Εποχής" (PhD dissertation, Aristotle University, Greece, 1988), 7, 79–80.

65. Diodorus Siculus 1.22. Cf. Dunand, *Le culte d'Isis*, Vol. I, 34–5, 41; Françoise Dunand, *Religion populaire en Egypte romaine* (Leiden: Brill, 1979), 112–3; Hazzard,

Additionally, we should mention another determinative factor, that is, the coexistence of tradition and renewal.[66] The latter contributes to the gradual retreat of the local spirit of traditional society. Diodorus was aware of this, as mentioned above, and therefore it was natural to insert innuendos in his relevant narrations. By adjusting the Egyptian mythical world to this particular historical reality, we can argue that Osiris was, in this case, the quintessential model of the centripetal society of Egypt, whereas Isis, on the contrary, was entirely identified with the ideals of the centrifugal ecumenical world.[67] The henotheistic character of Isis was an example of this new reality—it expressed the religio-political ideals of the imperial age.[68]

Diodorus differentiates himself from contemporary terminology, which constitutes another innovation pertaining to the adjustment of his narration to the demands of his era. He uses the term "benefactress" (εὐεργέτρια) as one of Isis's attributes in order to underscore her connection with the ideology of the monarchs' benefactions that dominated the broader ideology of the Ptolemaic period. This particular trait, found initially in texts from Memphis, was replaced in the Greek territory during the first century BCE by the terms πρώτη εὑρίσκειν and εὑρέτρια.[69] But Diodorus uses the traditional term. Isis's benefactory character is displayed in the context of these hymns and in the usage of terms such as "κατέδειξε – ἔδειξε."[70] Seeking (ζήτησις) and finding (εὕρεσις) constituted the basic features of the Eleusinian ideology, which greatly influenced the cult of Isis.[71] The same stands for the presentation of the myth by Plutarch during the second century CE,

Imagination of a Monarchy, 111, 129, 135–7, 158. According to Hazzard (136 n. 173) we find the first relevant evidence in an inscription that is dated back to 136 BCE. Cf. *BGU* 6.1249.

66. Nilsson, *Geschichte*, Vol. II, 1–10; Mikalson, *Hellenistic Athens*, 307 as well as "Greek Religion: Continuity and Change in the Hellenistic Period," in *The Cambridge Companion to the Hellenistic World* (ed. Glenn R. Bugh; Cambridge: Cambridge University Press, 2006), 208–22; Pachis, *Ἰσις Καρποτόκος*, 35 and n. 26.

67. See Jonathan Z. Smith, *Map Is Not Territory: Studies in the History of Religions* (Chicago,: University of Chicago Press, 1993), 10, 131–2.

68. See Henk S. Versnel, *Ter Unus: Isis, Dionysus, Hermes. Three Studies in Henotheism* (Leiden: Brill, 1990), 39–95.

69. *UPZ* 81, 9-10. Cf. Vanderlip, *Four Greek Hymns*, 4–6; *Aretology of Kyme* 7; *Aretalogy of Thessaloniki* 7; *Aretalogy of Cassandrea* (*Potidea*) 7 = *RICIS* 113/1201; Sulimani, *Diodorus' Mythistory*, 65–6.

70. Diodorus Siculus 5.68.1-3 and 5 [Demeter]. See also *Orphic Hymn* 76 [Muses]; 78.3 [Themis].

71. Plutarch, *Isis and Osiris* 371B–372C. Cf. Griffiths, *Plutarch's De Iside et Osiride*, 469–9; Vanderlip, *Four Greek Hymns*, 22–3; Pachis, *"Hominibus vagis vitam,"* 389.

while, in the same spirit, Apuleius uses the terms *quaestionis* (*petionis*) and *repertus* (*inventio*).[72]

The climax of the goddess' beneficial donations to humanity was the spread and establishment of the mystery rituals of her own cult. Isis is considered to have established the mystery rituals in honor of her husband, as suggested by the use of the terms "mystery" (μυστήριο)[73] and "mystery rituals"[74] found in Diodorus's text. The Sicilian writer, in contrast to Herodotus's analogous usage, relates the term to the new form that it received during his lifetime in the environment of the goddess' cult.[75] The development of mutual relationships between gods and humans—and the support that the divine world offers to mortals—constituted one of the basic features of her cult, a communication that resulted in their salvation. But at the same time the notion of salvation was connected—both in this and in subsequent periods—to ideas about the believers' posthumous bliss;[76] this expectation becomes "real" through their initiation rites that lead to their complete transformation. The influence of the Eleusinian mysteries, which are the alternative form of religiosity *par excellence*, continued undisturbed and unchanged during this period.

A prevalent element in the descriptions of the Egyptian divine world by Diodorus is the connections of Isis with Demeter and Osiris with Dionysus.[77] However, the identification of those gods and goddesses by Diodorus is different to that made by Herodotus,[78] despite the fact that they both depended on the *interpretatio Graeca*.[79] Herodotus dealt with the Egyptian tradition as a Greek of the Classical period, while Diodorus was an exponent of the cosmopolitan spirit of the Hellenistic era. In Herodotus,

72. Apuleius, *Metamorphoses* 11.2.

73. Diodorus Siculus 1.29.2-3.

74. Diodorus Siculus 1.96.4: Ὀρφέα μὲν γάρ τῶν μυστικῶν τελετῶν τὰ πλεῖστα καὶ τὰ περὶ τὴν ἑαυτοῦ πλάνην ὀργιαζόμενα καὶ τὴν τῶν ἐν ᾅδου μυθοποιίαν ἀπενέγκασθαι.

75. Herodotus 2.170-1.6.

76. Diodorus Siculus 1.25.6.

77. Diodorus Siculus 1.11.

78. Herodotus 2.41-2; 2.47-8; 2.56-9; 2.121-2; 2.143; 2.155-6; 2.158. Cf. Dunand, *Le culte d'Isis*, Vol. I, 9–71, 85–6; Herrmann, "Demeter-Isis or the Egyptian Demeter," 71 and n. 7.

79. About the *interpetatio Graeca* and *interpretatio Romana*, see Wolfgang Schwenk, "Interpretatio Graeca–Interpretatio Romana: Die hellenistische Syncretismus als semiotisches Problem," in *Innovationen in Zeichen Theorien* (ed. Peter Schmitter and H. Walter Schmiz; Münster: Nodus, 1989), 83–121; Luther H. Martin, "Comparison," in Braun and McCutcheon, eds., *Guide to the Study of Religion*, 51; Clifford Ando, *The Matter of the Gods: Religion and the Roman Empire* (Berkeley, CA: University of California Press, 2008), 43–58.

the contrast between Greeks and barbarians was the one that defined the
ideological orientation, shaped the criteria of the cultural evaluation, and
eventually designated the points of agreement or disagreement with other
peoples. The citizens' position within the Greek city-states and their democratic institutions ensured an *a priori* acceptance of the conditions and
principles according to which the city-states were operating. One observes,
however, that Diodorus criticizes the way in which Herodotus provides his
information about Egypt, as the former does not try to simply describe the
Egyptian world but to understand it;[80] moreover, he places emphasis on the
ethical and political principles that are related to law. This leads to a more
intense worshiping of Isis—more than that of all the other deities—because
she was the one who gave the goods of civilization to mankind. On the contrary, Herodotus primarily bases his inquiry on what he has heard, or on
popular beliefs.[81]

We should not overlook, however, Diodorus's narration about the connection of Osiris with Dionysus and their actions pertaining to the founding
and dissemination of civilization.[82] This identification of the Egyptian with
the Greek god constitutes, as in the case of Isis and Demeter, a continua-
tion of the idea first found in Herodotus; but, in this case, Diodorus's goals
are very different. He aims to demonstrate—or, better, praise—the policies
of the Egyptian monarchs, whom he presents as gods, since he considers
them to be the legal successors of the Pharaohs and Alexander the Great.
After all, it is Dionysus that constitutes the god-protector of this dynasty. In
Diodorus's descriptions, Osiris is identified with Dionysus and both gods
undertake the task of civilizing humanity. Thus, the local character of the
Egyptian myth acquires a clearly ecumenical character that is connected
to Diodorus's overall view. The dissemination of this kind of ideas was
expected during the Ptolemaic period, because the humanitarian ecumenical activity of Osiris—which is a Greek influence—reflects the policies of
the Egyptian monarchs. The culture-giver Osiris, according to Diodorus, is
Dionysus's *alter ego*.[83] Osiris is presented not only as the master of grains
but also of grapevines. These are the goods the god spreads in the world,
and the reason for being identified by the Greeks with Dionysus. At the
point where Diodorus mentions that the god is spreading the cultivation of

80. Diodorus Siculus 1.37.11; 1.39; 1.69.
81. See Herodotus 2.42.2; 2.47; 2.91. Cf. Thompson, "Demeter," 705.
82. Diodorus Siculus 1.25; 1.27; 2.38. Cf. Pachis, *Δήμητρα Καρποφόρος*, 171–2;
Sulimani, *Diodorus' Mythistory*, 165–8.
83. Diodorus Siculus 1.13.

grapevine, he does not imply Osiris but rather Dionysus.[84] In this way, he refers to the spread of the cultivation of grapevine and the use of wine in Egypt by the Ptolemies. This approach is part of the general enterprise of the new monarchs to renew the economic conditions of the country. Their strategy is part of a successful coexistence of the cultural ideas of the two peoples, leading to decisive results in the outlook of this period. There is no doubt that the Egyptians were not aware, during the reign of the Pharaohs, of wine but only beer, which they produced from barley, something that is confirmed by Herodotus.[85]

Osiris continues his civilizing task in many countries, including Arabia and India;[86] then, he assigns the task to Triptolemus.[87] These narrations imply the civilizing activity of Alexander the Great. In any way, this theme receives great attention in the narratives of the fourth and third centuries BCE (for example, in Nonnos's *Dionysiaka*). We can discern in Diodorus's description an innuendo about the expansionary pretensions of the Ptolemies. India was always considered to be the quintessential source of wealth and that is why everyone aimed, already from the beginning of the Hellenistic era, to control this region. The development of commercial transactions between Alexandria and India, through the Arabic peninsula, is mentioned in many sources of the Ptolemaic period.[88]

Undoubtedly, Dionysus is an amalgam of the Hellenistic era. The "hellenization" of Osiris's cult takes place in Ptolemaic Alexandria according to the teachings of Dionysus's cult. Proof for the hellenization of the Egyptian myth is found in Diodorus's narration regarding the dismemberment of the god's body, a choice that shows the direct influence from Hecataeus's narration who was interested in this kind of syncretism. According to the mythical description, Isis looks for Osiris's dismembered body. She manages to collect all of the pieces with the exception of his genitals, which the Greeks and the Egyptians[89] used to worship during the Osiris's rituals. The origins of these rituals can be traced, according to Diodorus, to the "feasts" that Isis establishes in memory of her husband.[90] It is possible that our writer implies at this point the actualization of the *phallophoria*, which held a central position in Dionysus' cult.

---

84. Diodorus Siculus 1.15.8.
85. Herodotus 2.77.4; Diodorus Siculus 1.34.10-1.
86. Diodorus Siculus 1.19.5-8.
87. Diodorus Siculus 1.19.
88. Fraser, *Ptolemaic Alexandria*, Vol. I, 180–4; Vol. IIa, 310–7 and n. 380–415; Green, *Alexander to Actium*, 329–30, 365, 370.
89. Diodorus Siculus 1.21.5.
90. Diodorus Siculus 1.27.6.

Diodorus seems to follow both the Greek and the Egyptian traditions regarding the identification of the two deities. In the former, Dionysus is the leading figure, whereas in the latter Osiris is the most important Egyptian god. The common denominator is the direct and indirect influences stemming from the environment of Orphism. Osiris's culture-giving and humanitarian activity is connected to the relevant feature of Dionysus (Orpheus), which constitutes a hint regarding the special position of Orphism within the Egyptian environment—especially during the reign of the Ptolemies, when Orphism became one of the main instruments of the dynasty's political propaganda.[91] Diodorus seems to follow the same scheme when it comes to the identification of Isis and Demeter. Thus, Osiris's rituals are identified with Dionysus's (Orpheus's), while those dedicated to Isis with Demeter's. There is only one differentiation, and this is the deities' names, with the essence remaining the same.[92]

* * *

Diodorus's approach in his Egyptian *theologoumena* may comprise further confirmation that we should always "pay attention to the man behind the curtain."[93] This is even more apparent when we take into account that the particular mythical narration could be considered "as an ideological activity,"[94] which is an "ongoing process of constructing, authorizing and reconstructing social identities or social formations."[95] As Bruce Lincoln has put it:

> [I]deology ... is not just an ideal against which social reality is measured or an end toward the fulfillment of which groups and individuals aspire. It is also, and more importantly, a screen that strategically veils, mystifies, or distorts important aspects of real social processes ... [A]ll human doing is contextualized within historical (social, political, economic, gendered etc.) pressures and

---

91. Diodorus Siculus 1.11; 1.23. Cf. Walter Burkert, *Ancient Mystery Cults* (Cambridge, MA: Harvard University Press, 1987); J. Bottéro, "L'anthropogonie mésopotamienne et l'élément divin en l'homme," in *Orphisme et Orphée: en l'honneur de Jean Rudhardt* (ed. Philippe Borgeaud; Genève: Librairie Droz, 1991), 221–5; Reinhold Merkelbach, "Die goldenen Totenpässe: Agyptisch, orphisch, bakchisch," *Zeitschrift für Papyrologie und Epigraphik* 128 (1999): 1–13; and Fritz Graf and Sarah Iles Johnston, *Ritual Texts for the Afterlife: Orpheus and the Bacchic Gold Tablets* (London: Routledge, 2007), 50–1, 150–5, 177–8, 188–90.

92. Diodorus Siculus 1.96.4-9.

93. I am adopting here the subtitle found in McCutcheon, "Myth," 205; cf. 206–7.

94. McCutcheon, "Myth," 203.

95. McCutcheon, "Myth," 202.

influences, we must therefore understand all such doings, partial and linked to specific temporally and culturally located words.[96]

This is further emphasized if we approach them under the spectrum of a panorama of beliefs and practices that are a characteristic of the "system" of the Hellenistic age. As Theodosis Nikolaides writes in the preface of the Greek translation of Peter Brown's *The Making of Late Antiquity*:

> [A]ll functions cohere; one cannot possibly isolate an event and understand it without viewing it, first of all, as part of the whole, of a system. The use of this common—at first sight—suggestion is explicit in the study of religious forms ... The people around the Mediterranean Sea had a *Koinē* (common language) that they used to describe their social experiences, their relations to one another, as well as their relations to the holders of power. Aspects of the *Koinē*, however, were also used to describe their relations to the numinous power—as P. Veyne would say: tout se tient.[97]

Biographical Note

Panayotis Pachis is Professor of Religious Studies at the Aristotle University of Thessaloniki, Greece. His publications include *Religion and Politics in the Graeco-Roman World: Redescribing the Isis-Sarapis Cult* (Barbounakis, 2010) and many articles on the Graeco-Roman religions and the cognitive study of religion. He is also the author of five books in Greek and co-editor of four volumes, including *Chasing Down Religion: In the Sights of History and the Cognitive Sciences* (with Donald Wiebe; Equinox, 2014) and a collection of papers written by Luther H. Martin entitled *Studies in Hellenistic Religions* (Cascade, 2018).

Bibliography

Ando, Clifford. *The Matter of the Gods: Religion and the Roman Empire*. Berkeley, CA: University of California Press, 2008.
Ashton, Sally-Ann. *Roman Egyptomania*. London: Golden House Publications, 2004.
Bottéro, J. "L'anthropogonie mésopotamienne et l'élément divin en l'homme," 221–5 in *Orphisme et Orphée: En l'honneur de Jean Rudhardt*. Edited by Philippe Borgeaud. Genève: Librairie Droz, 1991.
Braun, Willi, and Russell T. McCutcheon, eds. *Guide to the Study of Religion*, 2000.
Burkert, Walter. *Ancient Mystery Cults*. Cambridge, MA: Harvard University Press, 1987.

96. Cited in McCutcheon, "Myth," 204–5.
97. Theodosis Nikolaides, "Ιστορία και Ανθρωπολογία. Η Δημιουργία της Ύστερης Αρχαιότητας. Εισαγωγή του Μεταφραστή," in Peter Brown, *Η Δημιουργία της Ύστερης Αρχαιότητας* (trans. Theodosis Nikolaides; Athens: Estia, 2001), 18–9.

Chamoux, Francois. *Hellenistic Civilization.* Translated by Michel Roussel. Oxford: Wiley-Blackwell, 2003.

Chaniotis, Angelos. "The Divinity of Hellenistic Rulers," 431–45 in *A Companion to the Hellenistic World.* Edited by Andrew Erskine. Oxford: Blackwell, 2005.

De Angelis, Franco, and Benjamin Garstad. "Euhemerus in Context," *Classical Antiquity* 25.2 (2006): 211–42. https://doi.org/10.1525/ca.2006.25.2.211

De Vos, Mariette. *L'egittomania in pitture a mosaici Romano-Campani nella prima età imperiale.* Leiden: Brill, 1980.

Detienne, Marcel. *The Gardens of Adonis: Spices in Greek Mythology.* Translated by Janet Lloyd. Princeton, NJ: Princeton University Press, 1994.

Dunand, Françoise. *Le culte d'Isis dans le bassin oriental de la Méditerranée.* Vols. 1–3. Leiden: Brill, 1973.

—*Religion populaire en Egypte romaine.* Leiden: Brill, 1979.

—"Culte royal et culte imperial en Egypte: Continuités et ruptures," 47–58 in *Das Römisch-Byzantinische Ägypten.* Edited by Grimm Günter, Heinz Heinen, and Erich Winter. Mainz am Rhein: Philipp von Zabern, 1983.

Ebach, Jürgen. "Euhemerismus," 365–8 in *Handbuch religionswissenschaftlichen Grundbegriffe.* Edited by Hubert Cancik, Burkhard Gladigow, and Matthias Laubscher. Vol. 2. Stuttgart and Berlin: Kohlhammer, 1990.

Frankfort, Henri. *Kingship and the Gods: A Study of Ancient Near Eastern Religion as the Integration of Society and Nature.* Chicago, IL: University of Chicago Press, 1978.

Fraser, Peter M. *Ptolemaic Alexandria.* Vols. 1–3. Oxford: Clarendon Press, 1972.

Graf, Fritz, and Sarah Iles Johnston. *Ritual Texts for the Afterlife: Orpheus and the Bacchic Gold Tablets.* London: Routledge, 2007.

Green, Peter. *Alexander to Actium: The Historical Evolution of the Hellenistic Age.* Berkeley, CA: University of California Press, 1990.

Griffiths, J. Gwen. *Plutarch's De Iside et Osiride.* Cardiff: University of Wales Press, 1970.

Habicht, Christian. *Gottmenschentum und griechische Städte.* 2nd ed. München: C. H. Beck, 1970.

Hazzard, R. A. *Imagination of a Monarchy: Studies in Ptolemaic Propaganda.* Toronto: University of Toronto Press, 2000. https://doi.org/10.3138/9781442676008

Henrichs, Albert. "The Sophists and Hellenistic Religion: Prodicus as the Spiritual Father of the ISIS Aretalogies," *Harvard Studies in Classical Philology* 88 (1984): 139–58. https://doi.org/10.2307/311449

Herrmann, J. J. "Demeter-Isis or the Egyptian Demeter? A Graeco Roman Sculpture from an Egyptian Workshop in Boston," *Jahrbuch des Deutschen Archäologischen Instituts* 114 (1999): 65–124.

Jacoby, Felix. "Euemeros," *Realencyclopädie der classischen Altertumswissenschaft* 6 (1907): 952–72.

Kajanto, Iiro. "Fortuna," *Aufstieg und Niedergang der römischen Welt* II.17 (1972): 502–58.

Koenen, Ludwig. "Die Adaptation ägyptischer Königsideologie am Ptolemäerhof," 143–90 in Van 't Dack et al., eds., *Egypt and the Hellenistic World,* 1983.

—"The Ptolemaic King as a Religious Figure," 25–115 in *Images and Ideologies: Self-Definition in the Hellenistic World.* Edited by A. Bulloch, E. Gruen, A. A. Long, and A. Stewart. Berkeley, CA: University of California Press, 1993.

Lease, Gary. "The History of 'Religious' Consciousness and the Diffusion of Culture:

Strategies for Surviving Dissolution," *Historical Reflections/Reflections Histo-riques* 20.3 (1994): 452–79.

Lincoln, Bruce. *Discourse and the Construction of Society: Comparative Studies of Myth, Ritual, and Classification.* Oxford: Oxford University Press, 1989.

Manning, Joseph G. *Land and Power in Ptolemaic Egypt: The Structure of Land Tenure.* Cambridge: Cambridge University Press, 2003. https://doi.org/10.1017/CBO9780511482847

Martin, Luther H. *Hellenistic Religions: An Introduction.* Oxford: Oxford University Press, 1987.

—"Greek Goddesses and Grain: The Sicilian Connection," *Helios* 17.2 (1990): 251–61.

—"The Anti-Individualistic Ideology of Hellenistic Culture," *Numen* 41 (1994): 117–40. https://doi.org/10.2307/3270256

—"Comparison," 45–56 in Braun and McCutcheon, eds., *Guide to the Study of Religion,* 2000.

—"Kingship and the Hellenistic Consolidation of Religio-Political Power," 89–96 in Martin and Pachis, eds., *Theoretical Frameworks,* 2003.

—"The Promise of Cognitive Science for the Historical Study of Religions with Reference to the Study of Early Christianity," 1–35. Unpublished lecture delivered in Helsinki, 1 September 2005.

Martin, Luther H., and Panayotis Pachis, eds. *Theoretical Frameworks for the Study of Graeco-Roman Religions.* Thessaloniki: University Studio Press, 2003.

McCutcheon, Russell T. "Myth," 190–208 in Braun and McCutcheon, eds., *Guide to the Study of Religion,* 2000.

Merkelbach, Reinhold. "Die goldenen Totenpässe: Agyptisch, orphisch, bakchisch," *Zeitschrift für Papyrologie und Epigraphik* 128 (1999): 1–13.

Mikalson, Jon D. *Religion in Hellenistic Athens.* Berkeley, CA: University of California Press, 1998.

—"Greek Religion: Continuity and Change in the Hellenistic Period," 208–22 in *The Cambridge Companion to the Hellenistic World.* Edited by Glenn R. Bugh. Cambridge: Cambridge University Press, 2006.

Nikolaides, Theodosis. "Ιστορία και Ανθρωπολογία. Η Δημιουργία της Ύστερης Αρχαιότητας. Εισαγωγή του Μεταφραστή," 13–19 in Peter Brown, *Η Δημιουργία της Ύστερης Αρχαιότητας.* Translated by Theodosis Nikolaides. Athens: Estia, 2001.

Nilsson, Martin P. *Geschichte der Greichischen Religion.* Vols. 1–2. 3rd ed. München: C. H. Beck, 1974.

Nock, Arthur D. "Notes on Ruler Cult I-IV," 134–59 in *Arthur Darby Nock: Essays on Religion and the Ancient World.* Edited by Zeph Stewart. Vol. 1. Cambridge, MA: Harvard University Press, 1972.

—"Soter and Euergetes," 720–35 in *Arthur Darby Nock: Essays on Religion and the Ancient World.* Edited by Zeph Stewart. Vol. 2. Cambridge, MA: Harvard University Press, 1972.

Pachis, Panayotis. "Το Νερό και το Αίμα στις Μυστηριακές Λατρείες της Ελληνορωμαϊκής Εποχής," PhD dissertation, Aristotle University, Greece, 1988.

—*Δήμητρα Καρποφόρος: Θρησκεία και Αγροτική Οικονομία του Αρχαιοελληνικού Κόσμου.* Athens: Ellinika Grammata, 1998.

—"Η Έννοια της Περιπλάνησης κατά τη Διάρκεια των Ελληνιστικών Χρόνων," *Επιστημονική Επετηρίδα Θεολογικής Σχολής* (n.s.) 12 (2002): 273–323.

—*Ίσις Καρποτόκος.* Vol. I: *Οικουμένη. Προλεγόμενα στόν συγκρητισμό τῶν ἑλληνιστικῶν χρόνων.* Thessaloniki: Vanias, 2003.

—"The Hellenistic Era as an Age of Propaganda: The Case of Isis' Cult," 97–125 in Martin and Pachis, eds., *Theoretical Frameworks*, 2003.

—"'Manufacturing Religion' in the Hellenistic Age: The Case of Isis-Demeter Cult," 163–207 in *Hellenisation, Empire and Globalisation: Lessons from Antiquity.* Edited by Luther H. Martin and Panayotis Pachis. Thessaloniki: Vanias, 2004.

—"'*Hominibus vagis vitam*': The Wandering of *Homo Hellenisticus* in an Age of Transformation," 388–405 in *Introducing Religion: Essays in Honor of Jonathan Z. Smith.* Edited by Willi Braun and Russell T. McCutcheon. London: Equinox, 2008.

Parker, Robert. s.v. "Timotheos." *Neue Pauly* 12.1 (2002): 598–9.

Pestman, Pieter W. *A Guide to the Zenon Archive.* Leiden: Brill, 1981.

Price, Simon R. F. *Rituals and Power: The Roman Imperial Cult in Asia Minor.* Cambridge: Cambridge University Press, 1984.

Reekmans, Tony. "Archives de Zénon: Situation et comportment des entrepreneurs indigènes," 325–50 in Van 't Dack et al., eds., *Egypt and the Hellenistic World*, 1983.

Richter, Reinhold. "Politische Ordnung und fremde Kultur im Bild der hellenistischen Utopie," 629–52 in *Hellenismus, Beiträge zur Erforschung von Akkulturation und politischen Ordnung in den Staaten des hellenistischen Zeitalter.* Edited by Bernd Funk. Tübingen: J. C. B. Mohr, 1996.

Roubekas, Nickolas P. *An Ancient Theory of Religion: Euhemerism from Antiquity to the Present.* London: Routledge, 2017.

Schneider, Carl. *Kulturgeschichte des Hellenismus.* Vols. 1–2. München: Beck, 1967–1969.

Schroeder, Frederick M. "The Self in Ancient Religious Experience," 336–59 in *Classical Mediterranean Spirituality: Egyptian, Greek, Roman.* Edited by Arthur H. Armstrong. London: Routledge, 1989.

Schwenk, Wolfgang. "Interpretatio Graeca–Interpretatio Romana: Die hellenistische Syncretismus als semiotisches Problem," 83–121 in *Innovationen in Zeichen Theorien.* Edited by Peter Schmitter and H. Walter Schmiz. Münster: Nodus, 1989.

Sfameni Gasparro, Giulia. *Misteri e culti di Demetra.* Roma: L'Erma Di Bretschneider, 1986.

—"Daimon and Tychē in the Hellenistic Experience," 67–109 in *Conventional Values of the Hellenistic Greeks.* Edited by P. Bilde, T. Engberg-Pedersen, L. Hannestad, and J. Zahle. Aarhus: Aarhus University Press, 1997.

—"Iside-Fortuna: Fatalismo e divinità sovrane del destino nel mondo ellenistico-romano," 301–23 in *Le Fortune dell' età arcaica nel Lazio ed in Italia e la loro posterità.* Palestrina: Comune di Palestrina, Assessorato alla Cultura, 1998.

Smith, Jonathan Z. *Map Is Not Territory: Studies in the History of Religions.* Chicago, IL: University of Chicago Press, 1993.

Spuerri, W. "Leon von Pella." *Kleine Pauly* 3 (1979): 565.

Stephens, Susan A. *Seeing Double: Intercultural Poetics in Ptolemaic Alexandria.* Berkeley, CA: University of California Press, 2003.

Strenski, Ivan. *Why Politics Can't Be Freed from Religion.* Oxford: Wiley-Blackwell, 2011.

Sulimani, Iris. *Diodorus' Mythistory and the Pagan Mission: Historiography and Culture-Heroes in the First Pentad and the Bibliotheke.* Leiden: Brill, 2011. https://doi.org/10.1163/ej.9789004194069.i-409

Taylor, Lily R. *The Divinity of Roman Emperor.* Middletown, CT: American Philological Association, 1975.

Thompson, Dorothy J. "Demeter in Graeco-Roman Egypt," 699–707 in *Egyptian*

Religion: The Last Thousand Years. Studies Dedicated to the Memory of Jan Quaegebeur. Edited by Willy Clarysse, Antoon Schoors, and Harco Willems. Leuven: Peeters, 1995.

Van 't Dack, Edmond, Peter van Dessel, and Wilfried van Gucht, eds. *Egypt and the Hellenistic World.* Louvain: Orientaliste, 1983.

Vanderlip, Vera F. *The Four Greek Hymns of Isidorus and the Cult of Isis.* Toronto: Scholars Press, 1974.

Versnel, Henk S. *Ter Unus: Isis, Dionysus, Hermes. Three Studies in Henotheism.* Leiden: Brill, 1990.

Walbank, Frank W. *Ο Ελληνιστικός Κόσμος.* Translated by Tasos Varveris. Thessaloniki: Vanias, 1993.

Wild, Robert. *Water in the Cultic Worship of Isis and Sarapis.* Leiden: Brill, 1981. https://doi.org/10.1163/9789004295674

Winiarczyk, Marek. *Euhemerus Reliquiae.* Stuttgart and Leipzig: Walter de Gruyter, 1991.

—*Euhemeros von Messene: Leben, Werk, und Nachwirkung.* München and Leipzig: Walter de Gruyter, 2002. https://doi.org/10.1515/9783110965117

Zumschlinge, Marianne. "Euhemeros: Staatstheoretische und Staatsutopische Motive," PhD dissertation, University of Bonn, 1976.

Chapter Eleven

Metaphor and Religion in Ancient Rome

Spencer E. Cole

> For we all of us, grave or light, get our thoughts entangled in metaphors, and act fatally on the strength of them.
>
> — George Eliot, *Middlemarch*

> Metaphor is not simply an ornamental aspect of language, but a fundamental scheme by which people conceptualize the world and their own activities.
>
> — Raymond Gibbs[1]

Recent decades have seen fundamental transformations in the study of metaphor and also the study of ancient Roman religion. While these consequential scholarly revaluations have overlapped chronologically, the study of ancient Roman religion still has much to gain methodologically from conceptual metaphor theories that explore how metaphor shapes thought and action. The contemporary, cognitive approach to the study of metaphor pioneered by scholars like George Lakoff and Mark Johnson has had transformative influence in the study of politics, law, psychology, and neurosciences.[2] Even national intelligence agencies have started to analyze how metaphors shape perception and social practices.[3] This chapter will examine how contemporary metaphor theory can coalesce in productive ways with recent innovations in the study of ancient Roman religion. An introductory overview of conceptual metaphor theory is followed by a suggestive

---

1. Raymond W. Gibbs, "Metaphor and Thought: The State of the Art," in *The Cambridge Handbook of Metaphor and Thought* (ed. Raymond W. Gibbs; Cambridge: Cambridge University Press, 2008), 3.

2. See George Lakoff and Mark Johnson, *Metaphors We Live By* (Chicago, IL: University of Chicago Press, 2003), 267–72, for a succinct overview of applications of metaphor theory in the humanities, sciences, and social sciences. Robert Sapolsky, "This Is Your Brain on Metaphors," *The New York Times* (14 November 2011) offers a fascinating discussion of studies in the neurosciences exploring how metaphor influences understanding and actions.

3. Alexis C. Madrigal, "Why Are Spy Researchers Building a 'Metaphor Program'?" *The Atlantic* (27 May 2011) and John Naughton, "Metaphor Is the New Weapon in the 'War' on Terror," *The Guardian* (5 June 2011) discuss a US government program dedicated to analysis of cultural mindsets through the study of metaphors in English, Farsi, Russian, and Spanish.

case-study on metaphor and the cultural processing of new concepts of death and divinity in ancient Rome.

Conceptual Metaphor Theory and Roman Religious Discourse

Stretching back as far as Aristotle, there has been an entrenched tradition of conceiving metaphor as poetic flourish and rhetorical frills, simply an inert instance of language employed figuratively, in a sense markedly different from its normal usage. Classical scholars have traditionally explained away metaphor as *just* metaphor, expressions of language on an elevated register with perhaps provocative but ultimately superficial juxtapositions of different entities involving words and rhetoric, not thoughts and actions. Linguists and cognitive scientists, most notably George Lakoff, have productively challenged this traditional approach to metaphor. Lakoff argues that "the locus of metaphor is not in language at all, but in the way we conceptualize one mental domain in terms of another."[4] Much contemporary metaphor research focuses on the cognitive ordering and "cross-domain mapping" that metaphors perform in a culture's conceptual frameworks. Metaphor is seen as a pervasive phenomenon that often structures our understanding of everyday experience and influences our actions and decisions. And since we categorize and create meaning with metaphor, metaphor can

---

4.   George Lakoff, "The Contemporary Theory of Metaphor," in *Metaphor and Thought* (ed. Andrew Ortony; Cambridge: Cambridge University Press, 1993), 1–2, where he offers an important programmatic statement on the cultural, cognitive orientation in metaphor research:

> The generalizations governing poetic metaphorical expressions are not in language, but in thought: They are general mappings across conceptual domains. Moreover, these general principles which take the form of conceptual mappings, apply not just to novel poetic expressions, but to much of ordinary everyday language. In short, the locus of metaphor is not in language at all, but in the way we conceptualize one mental domain in terms of another. The general theory of metaphor is given by characterizing such cross-domain mappings. And in the process, everyday abstract concepts like time, states, change, causation, and purpose all turn out to be metaphorical. The result is that metaphor (that is, cross-domain mapping) is absolutely central to ordinary natural language semantics, and that the study of literary metaphor is an extension of the study of everyday metaphor. Everyday metaphor is characterized by a huge system of thousands of cross-domain mappings, and this system is made use of in novel metaphor. Because of these empirical results, the word *metaphor* has come to be used differently in contemporary metaphor research. The word *metaphor* has come to mean *a cross-domain mapping in the conceptual system.* The term *metaphorical expression* refers to a linguistic expression (a word, phrase, or sentence) that is the surface realization of such a cross-domain mapping (this is what the word *metaphor* referred to in the old theory).

introduce new conceptual possibilities into social knowledge systems.[5] To take a key illustration from Lakoff's seminal *Metaphors We Live By*: Time is Money. In American English, these three commonplace expressions show that time is conceived as a resource and commodity: Those years in Seattle were well *spent*. Slow traffic *cost* us three hours. She *invested* a lot of time in education.[6] Those using these expressions might not think of themselves in a metaphorical mode, but they are since they are using money, finite resources, and commodities to conceptualize time. There is no essential and intrinsic connection between time and money: in another culture, time could be construed using conceptual mapping drawn from everyday experience using, for example, familiar properties of plant life or an ocean.[7] But in each case, the realm of everyday experience that is used to conceptualize time is more than a culturally idiosyncratic "cross-domain" mapping manifesting itself simply as a turn of phrase: it can influence our thoughts and actions, which is why spies as well as scholars are now attuned to the cognitive dimensions of metaphor. An intriguing series of empirical studies discussed by Robert Sapolsky in an aptly titled article "This is Your Brain on Metaphors" (2011) show how metaphor shapes perceptions and influences decisions. He cites, for example, a study where "[s]ubjects either did or didn't read an article about the health risks of airborne bacteria. All then read a history article that used imagery of a nation as a living organism with statements like, 'Following the Civil War, the United States underwent a growth spurt.' Those who read about scary bacteria before thinking about the U.S. as an organism were then more likely to express negative views

---

5.   On how metaphors help normalize new cultural concepts, see Donald Schön, "Generative Metaphor: A Perspective on Problem-Setting in Social Policy," in Ortony, ed., *Metaphor and Thought*, 137:

> Much of the interest in metaphor on the part of linguists and philosophers of language has had to do with metaphor as a species of figurative language which needs explaining, or explaining away. Metaphor, in this tradition, is a kind of anomaly of language, one which must be dispelled in order to clear the path for a general theory of reference or meaning. There is a very different tradition associated with the notion of metaphor, however—one which treats metaphor as central to the task of accounting for our perspectives on the world: how we think about things, make sense of reality, and set the problems we later try to solve. In this second sense, "metaphor" refers both to a certain kind of product—a perspective or frame, a way of looking at things—and a certain kind of process—a process by which new perspectives on the world come into existence.

6.   Adapted from Lakoff and Johnson, *Metaphors We Live By*, 8.

7.   While time = money is certainly not a necessary, universal construction, an interesting parallel from ancient Rome is found in Seneca's *Moral Epistles*: in his first letter Seneca urges Lucilius to conceive of time as a precious, finite commodity.

about immigration.["8] Ancient Romans also conceived of a nation as a living organism (e.g., Cicero, *De republica* 2.3), a metaphor used by Aristotle and Polybius as well, even personifying the Republic (Cicero, *In Catilinam* 1.11) and framing its perceived enemies as disease-bringers (Cicero, *Orationes Philippicae* 5.43; *De domo sua* 2). We can entertain the possibility that Romans—like the subjects in the study discussed by Sapolsky—make conceptual distinctions that are affected by metaphorical expressions and "act fatally on" their understandings of the *life* or perceived *health* of the republic. Like Lakoff's "Time is Money" example, the Nation as a Living Organism could be deeply entrenched in a society's everyday thoughts with speakers, listeners, and readers unconsciously making such conceptual connections. Hearing Cicero label Antony with an explicit metaphorical expression like "disease-bringer" would activate conceptual mappings deeply embedded in Roman knowledge systems.

Recent work on Roman religion has yet to attract its share of a national defense budget, but it too has productively challenged traditional orthodoxies, and done so in ways that make new approaches to metaphor an especially valuable heuristic tool. Well into the twentieth century, the study of Roman religion proceeded from the premise that Roman religious practice in the historical period was aridly legalistic, detached from any "true" religious meaning and experience, and hence in a terminal state of decline that is only decisively reversed when Christianity finally fills a purported spiritual void. Since the days of the Christian apologists up through the hugely influential studies of Mommsen and Cumont, much of the apparatus of Roman religion had been seen as a set of tools cynically used by elites for social control and cohesion. This traditional dismissal of Roman religion as a formalistic political tool and contrived (if artful) charade as distinct from "real religion" has been productively challenged in a series of formative studies for being premised on anachronistic criteria:[9] unduly prioritizing Christian conceptual categories (e.g., "belief") over ritual practice and naively assuming a stark categorical division between politics and

---

8. Sapolsky, "Brain on Metaphors."
9. See H. D. Jocelyn, "The Roman Nobility and the Religion of the Republican State," *Journal of Religious History* 4 (1966): 89–104; Simon R. F. Price, *Rituals and Power: The Roman Imperial Cult in Asia Minor* (Cambridge: Cambridge University Press, 1984); Mary Beard, John North, and Simon Price, *Religions of Rome*. Vol. 1: *A History* (Cambridge: Cambridge University Press, 1998); Denis Feeney, *Literature and Religion at Rome: Cultures, Contexts, and Beliefs* (Cambridge: Cambridge University Press, 1998); John Scheid, *An Introduction to Roman Religion* (trans. Janet Lloyd; Bloomington, IN: Indiana University Press, 2003).

religion.[10] Newer scholarly paradigms no longer see Roman religion as stale and prosaic, but rather a dynamic, adaptive set of cultural practices that were performed, perpetuated, and interrogated in a range of media. And since H. D. Jocelyn (1966), the timeworn consensus that Roman elites had uniformly skeptical and even cynical attitudes about their own religious traditions has been steadily unraveling.[11]

A corollary development in the study of Roman religion has been a more inclusive approach to assessing our sources and sets of data for Roman religion. Reappraisals of the relationship between literature and religion at Rome underscore how literary discourses and other discourses that constitute Roman religion are implicated in each other. Since Denis Feeney's *Literature and Religion at Rome* (1998), the relationship between literature and religion is no longer seen as simply a case of literature autonomously reflecting on more essentially religious cultural forms (like ritual) that comprise the primary core of "real religion." While *orthopraxis* was central to Roman religious practices, critical analysis of religious traditions actively shaped religious culture. So a huge body of surviving texts once relegated far off from the real workings of Roman religious culture offers rich evidence for the study of metaphorical structures in Roman religious discourses. The largest, most diverse body of this written evidence comes from late-Republican Rome, the period once held to be especially representative of decline and neglect in religious culture at Rome that is increasingly being explored as a dynamic phase of accelerated change and cultural innovation.[12] The myriad channels for diffusion of new religious ideas and practices in late-Republican Rome have been influentially conceived as a "marketplace" by Andreas Bendlin. This model eschews a conventional public/private dualism and conceives of the religious landscape

10.   On "belief" in antiquity, see Chapter Three, this volume.

11.   See Jocelyn, "Roman Nobility." On the question of religious skepticism among Roman elites, see Mary Beard, "Cicero and Divination: The Formation of a Latin Discourse," *Journal of Roman Studies* 76 (1986): 33–46; Malcolm Schofield, "Cicero for and against Divination," *Journal of Roman Studies* 76 (1986): 47–65; Feeney, *Literature and Religion*, 3, 12–21; Spencer Cole, "Elite Skepticism in the Apocolocyntosis: Further Qualifications," in *Seeing Seneca Whole: Perspectives on Philosophy, Poetry and Politics* (ed. Katharina Volk and Gareth D. Williams; Leiden: Brill, 2006), 174–82, and *Cicero and the Rise of Deification at Rome* (Cambridge: Cambridge University Press, 2013), 149–63.

12.   Beard, North, and Price, *Religions of Rome*, 116–7, underscores the importance of late-Republican texts for our understanding of Roman religion: "It is in all this writing that we can glimpse for the first (and arguably the only) time in Roman history something of the complexity of religion and its representations, the different perspectives, interests, practices and discourses that constitute the religion of Rome."

of Republican Rome as a dynamic, decentralized space in which an array of religious practices vied for influence and power.[13] This marketplace would be awash in both written and spoken "communicative signs" with both conventional and original metaphors shaping Roman patterns of thought.[14]

One reason to think of late-Republican Rome as a hub of religious innovation and speculation—and a reason why this period is rich with sources for the study of Roman religion—is that this generation at Rome produced the first series of critical, analytical studies of Roman religious institutions and traditions. Cicero and his peer Varro (the antiquarian scholar) developed critical studies of cult, ritual, and divinities that categorized and systematized Roman religious knowledge to an unprecedented degree. This creative surge of analytical discourse and its dissemination of religious knowledge yielded some vivid images of cultural salvation that themselves, perhaps somewhat paradoxically, helped bolster scholarly arguments about religious neglect and narratives of decline. Cicero hailed Varro's books for showing Romans who had supposedly become strangers in their own city the way home, to understanding sacrifice, priesthoods, and "all things divine and human."[15] Varro himself presented his antiquarian work with a striking image as well; his books were rescuing the gods from oblivion much like Aeneas saved the penates from the sack of Troy.[16] Varro's intellectual mission was epic in its own way, but it did not preserve cultural artifacts in an act of selfless stewardship. Along with Cicero, his image of the past was configured by present cultural priorities. Much of Varro's work is now lost but the range of works surviving from Cicero—"the leading philosopher, theologian and theorist of his generation" according to Beard, North, and

---

13. See Andreas Bendlin, "Looking Beyond the Civic Compromise: Religious Pluralism in Late Republican Rome," in *Religion in Archaic and Republican Rome and Italy: Evidence and Experience* (ed. Edward Bispham and Christopher Smith; Edinburgh, UK: Edinburgh University Press, 2000), 134: "The market model allows us to conceptualise both the competition between different religious choices, cults and gods and the disappearance of some of these choices as natural processes in a self-regulating system. Elite laments about the demise of traditional gods and their cults in the late republic must be seen in this context of the religious system's constant optimisation in times of changing fashions."

14. Bendlin, "Beyond the Civic Compromise," 130: "As a matter of fact, from the late third century the city of Rome provided a backdrop to a plethora of different communicative signs, both religious and secular, whose over-abundance in the urban space, which lacked efficient control mechanisms for scrutinising the truthfulness of oral or literary propositions, precluded the emergence of unchangeable orthodoxies."

15. *Academica* 1.3.

16. Augustine, *De civitate dei* 6.2.248.

Price[17]—presents a rich array of evidence for the study of Roman religious discourses. From his ostensibly theological works like *De natura deorum* and *De divinatione* to his prominent public speeches, Cicero was a prolific producer of "communicative signs" and inventive metaphor in the religious marketplace of late-Republican Rome. His speeches, delivered to a range of elite and non-elite audiences and subsequently published, are therefore a rich vein to mine for the study of metaphor and religion at Rome. As Beard, North, and Price note on Cicero's speech *De domo sua*: "It does not reflect or record the discourse of religion; it *is* that discourse."[18] The connected case-studies presented below will consider the cultural work performed by metaphor to introduce and naturalize new ideas about the divinization of humans and the afterlife.

Gods' Gifts and Heaven's Gate

The quickening exchange of goods, people, and ideas between Rome and the eastern Mediterranean in the fourth through first centuries BCE was slow on one front: new ideas about the divinization of humans influenced religious practice in the east earlier and much more pervasively than they did in Italy. We can perhaps gauge distinct Roman attitudes about comparing humans to gods with a fragmentary detail from the *Odusia*, Livius Andronicus's (c. third century BCE) adaptation of the *Odyssey* into Latin. Livius, considered the originator of Latin literature by the late-Republicans Varro and Cicero, did not simply translate the poem but adapted and transformed it for a Roman audience. On a macro level, he recreates the poem in the Italic Saturnian meter; on the micro level, he alters a Homeric presentation of a hero as "equal to the gods" to *summus adprimus* ("greatest and most excellent") with a critical conceptual shift for a Roman audience. Gian Biagio Conte, in his discussion of "alteration of what is untranslatable" on Livius Andronicus observes that, with this Greek poet working in an Italian context, "translating means both preserving what can be assimilated and altering what proves to be untranslatable, either because of the limits of the linguistic medium or because of differences of culture and mind."[19] Here Conte aptly suggests that Livius's conceptual reconfiguration of the Homeric "equal to gods" to "greatest and most excellent" is due to the human/god collocation being "unacceptable to the Roman mind."[20]

---

17. Beard, North, and Price, *Religions of Rome*, 116.
18. Beard, North, and Price, *Religions of Rome*, 114 (emphasis in the original).
19. See Gian B. Conte, *A History of Latin Literature* (trans. Joseph B. Solodow; Baltimore, MD: Johns Hopkins University Press, 1994), 41.
20. Conte, *History of Latin Literature*, 41.

Romans of course had gods and humans in their conceptual inventory but were much less accustomed to making conceptual mappings between these particular domains than cultures in the eastern Mediterranean. From Livius's time through the first century BCE, this geographical and cultural distinction erodes as Romans progressively become more attuned to considering humans as "equal to gods" in language, thought, and action. A proliferation of related metaphorical expressions are both symptomatic of this change and instrumental in making such conceptual mappings more conventional and acceptable.

The language and logic of deification gained particular currency and theoretical elaboration in the age of Alexander the Great (d. 323 BCE) and its aftermath as divine honors and cult for Hellenistic dynasts—both male and female—appeared throughout the Mediterranean. The Egyptian Canopus decree of 238 BCE (*OGIS* 56, A), for example, shows that cultural benefaction provided a familiar ideological framework that increasingly became a basis for mortals making their way into the ranks of the gods. This trilingual inscription (Greek, Egyptian Demotic, Egyptian hieroglyphs) records a set of resolutions passed by Egyptian priests hailing Ptolemy III and Queen Berenice as "benefactor gods" descended from "savior gods" and also proclaiming the apotheosis of their deceased daughter Princess Berenice. Although a Roman seems to have first received such divine honors in Sicily—Marcus Marcellus was celebrated by the Syracusans in an annual festival after the city was taken from the Carthaginians—for centuries the divinization of humans was largely an eastern phenomenon. Prominent examples of Romans being divinized as saviors and benefactors in the east include: the general Flamininus by the Chalcidians in the second century BCE; Pompey in Athens in the first century BCE; and Caesar, declared the divine "universal savior of humanity" in Ephesus.[21] The concept of divinity achieved by human benefactors was elaborated in the *Sacred Record* of Euhemerus of Messene (fourth-third century BCE) which presents Zeus as a king elevated to divinity after a life of benefaction. Euhemerus's ideas had an impact at Rome via the *Euhemerus* of Ennius, a major cultural player who—unlike his poetic predecessor Livius—made innovative conceptual assimilations of mortals and gods for Roman audiences.[22] Ennius's *Annales* is our earliest source for the apotheosis of Romulus, Rome's legendary

21. Ephesus = *SIG* 760. On divinization of dynasts in the Hellenistic east, see Price, *Rituals and Power* and Duncan Fishwick, *The Imperial Cult in the Latin West* (Leiden: Brill, 1987), Vol. I, 3–45.

22. On the reception of Ennius's *Euhemerus* and its impact on imperial cult at Rome, see Brian Bosworth, "Augustus, the *Res Gestae* and Hellenistic Theories of Apotheosis," *Journal of Roman Studies* 89 (1999): 1–18.

founder—very plausibly an Ennian innovation inspired by Euhemerist the-ology.[23] With this new legitimizing prototype of the first Roman benefactor crossing the line to divinity along with Ennius's inventive use of diviniz-ing language for living Romans, the process of consolidating a conceptual nexus between humans and gods at Rome effectively launches.

While Ennius's *Euhemerus* survives, we are otherwise forced to feast on scraps. But his reception at Rome points to his formative role in Roman religious culture. Jörg Rüpke, for example, convincingly argues that texts like Ennius's *Annales*—with its representation of Romulus and Remus taking the auspices—could have a normative impact on a key Roman ritual like divination.[24] Cicero incorporates the Romulus auspices passage in his *de Divinatione* and likewise appeals to Ennius in his explorations of the divinization of humans. Unlike Ennius, Cicero has left one of the largest bodies of work from antiquity, presenting comparatively ample material for a "corpus study" analysis of conceptual metaphor and religion in Republican Rome.[25] Indeed, Cicero provides most of the first-century BCE public mani-festations of metaphorical expressions activating human/gods cross-domain mappings. In extant Latin, Cicero introduces the use of *divinus* ("divine") for humans and their qualities into public speech communication, and his recurrent late-Republican usages of this expression quantitatively surpass prior and subsequent usage in the classical Latin corpus. The scarcity of precedents for this use of *divinus* (hardly surprising if Conte is right about Livius's careful alteration of Homer) and the fact that divinizing metaphor-ical expression are not discussed in Republican Roman rhetorical treatises suggest that Cicero's metaphorical mappings were innovative in their orig-inal cultural contexts. While we cannot conduct the type of empirical stud-ies employed in the study of contemporary conceptual metaphor, we can attempt to reconstruct insofar as possible the webs of discourse and emer-gent religious practices in dialogue with Cicero's metaphorical expressions.

Cicero had helped establish the concept of the divinized human at Rome with his public presentation of Pompey. In his *Pro lege Manilia* of 66 BCE, Cicero took initial steps toward introducing divine honors that were bestowed

23. Otto Skutsch (*The Annals of Quintus Ennius* [Oxford: Oxford University Press, 1985], 205) argues that Ennius (under the influence of Euhemerus) introduced the apo-theosis into Roman tradition.

24. See Jörg Rüpke, "Acta aut agenda: Relations of Script and Performance," in *Rit-uals in Ink* (ed. Alessandro Barchiesi, Jörg Rüpke, and Susan Stephens; Stuttgart: Franz Steiner Verlag, 2004), 23–43.

25. As Gibbs ("Metaphor and Thought," 3) notes, contemporary metaphor research largely focuses on experimental studies and corpus studies.

on Pompey in the eastern Mediterranean onto Italian soil.[26] In the speeches of his consular year (63 BCE), Cicero set the possibility of divinity for deserving Romans on the agenda and initiated strategies that he pursued in the years to come: divinizing savior-figures who intervene in political crises (like himself) and using Romulus as a proxy-figure to explore the prospect of posthumous divinity for Roman benefactors.[27] Cicero again speculated publicly about the deification of Roman statesmen in an important post-exilic speech: the *Pro Sestio* of 56 BCE. In the following years, he treated his innovative proposal in depth in the *De re publica*.[28] Cicero formulated estimable Republican genealogies for his religious speculations in the *De re publica* by using Romulus's apotheosis to establish a Roman precedent for the divinization of statesmen. The prospect of posthumous rewards for Roman benefactors akin to those of Romulus is a central tenet of the *Somnium Scipionis* in book six of the *De re publica*. All of this myriad speculative activity for both elite and non-elite audiences was undertaken in the dynamic religious marketplace of Republican Rome where ritual practices like the triumph and the *supplicatio* as well as art and iconography (coins; statuary) were assimilating humans and gods and collectively effecting conceptual shifts.[29] And this constituting conversation of the first century BCE shapes both thought and

26. Beard, North, and Price, *Religions of Rome*, 147, gives a brief overview of Pompey's eastern honors which include cult and celebration as *soter* ("savior").

27. At *Pro Rabirio Perduellionis Reo* 29-30, Cicero speculates that the *mentes* of Marius and other departed *boni* are now divine. At *In Catilinam* 3.2, Cicero notes that Romans deified Romulus for founding the city and then wonders what honors he might earn as a latter-day *pater patriae*, since saving Rome (as he just did) is an equal or even greater accomplishment.

28. Cicero, at *Pro Sestio* 143, proposes that luminaries, like the Scipios, be ranked among the gods. The most radical statement in this passage—one that presents these religious ideas as present reality—is restricted to Cicero himself in the first person singular (*quos equidem in deorum immortalium coetu ac numero repono*). Cicero's *equidem* ("I at any rate") here flags the originality of Cicero's declaration. As Robert A. Kaster, (*Cicero: Speech on Behalf of Publius Sestius* [Oxford: Clarendon Press, 2006], 388) notes, Cicero's *equidem* "acknowledges that his view stands outside the mainstream." *Pro Sestio* 143 is echoed at *De republica* 6.13, when the elder Scipio reveals the heavenly rewards awaiting the devoted statesman.

29. On the ways that triumphal ritual in the later Republic became an active medium for testing ideas about human/divine identification and assimilation at Rome, see Mary Beard, *The Roman Triumph* (Cambridge, MA: Harvard University Press, 2007), 233–8. On how the *supplicatio*, the ritual thanksgiving traditionally offered to the gods, became increasingly focused on humans in the late Republic, see Frances Hickson-Hahn, "Pompey's *supplicatio duplicata*: A Novel Form of Thanksgiving," *Phoenix* 54 (2000): 244–54; Andrew Wallace-Hadrill, "Roman Arches and Greek Honours: The Language of Power at Rome," *Proceedings of the Cambridge Philological Society* 36 (1990): 143–81. A comprehensive overview of the art, coins, and architecture that blurred the

action: conceptual connections of humans and gods—transgressive or even taboo in earlier centuries—become more prevalent and a Roman leader, Caesar, is officially consecrated as a god and given cult.

Zooming in on the moment of cultural upheaval after the assassination of Caesar, we can see how novel conceptual mappings are activated with heightened frequency in a pivotal political crisis. We can also consider how ideas and practices common in the eastern Mediterranean but previously atypical at Rome became naturalized Roman modes of thought and action. The *Philippics* are a series of speeches composed by Cicero in 44 to 43 BCE in the wake of Caesar's assassination. The fourteen surviving speeches were mostly delivered to the senate and in *contiones*, the public gatherings that were a vital venue for public communication at Rome.[30] The language and ideas in these speeches also found further audiences as they were published and circulated after their initial performance. A central thrust of Cicero's public intervention with these speeches is to legitimize Caesar's heir Octavian while marginalizing the consul Antony. Cicero's representations of Octavian have potent conceptual possibilities for a Roman audience in 43 BCE (*Orationes Philippicae* 3.3):

> *C. Caesar adulescens, paene potius puer, incredibili ac divina quadam mente atque virtute, cum maxime furor arderet Antoni cumque eius a Brundisio crudelis et pestifer reditus timeretur, nec postulantibus nec cogitantibus, ne[c] optantibus quidem nobis, quia non posse fieri videbatur, firmissimum exercitum ex invicto genere veteranorum militum comparavit patrimonium-que suum effudit: quamquam non sum usus eo verbo quo debui; non enim effudit: in salute rei publicae collocavit.*

> Gaius Caesar the young man, rather almost a boy, with an incredible and a certain divine mind and virtue, when the fury of Antony was raging and we feared his cruel and disease-bearing return from Brundisium, with us neither asking nor thinking or even praying for such a thing because it seemed impossible, he gathered the strongest army of veteran, undefeated soldiers, and discharged his patrimony, though I use the wrong word, he did not discharge it but rather employed it for the salvation of the republic.

The representations of Octavian here and elsewhere in the *Philippics* are a conceptual "collage" of more conventional metaphorical mappings with

---

boundaries between the human and divine domains is offered by Stefan Weinstock, *Divus Julius* (Oxford: Clarendon Press, 1971).

30.   Bendlin ("Beyond the Civic Compromise," 127) stresses the centrality of the non-voting *contio* assemblies in Republican Rome's religious marketplace. Robert Morstein-Marx maintains that these public meetings at Rome were "perhaps the most important for the purposes of self-advertisement, communication, and ritualized communal action" (*Mass Oratory and Political Power in the Late Roman Republic* [Cambridge: Cambridge University Press, 2004], 9).

newer, erstwhile culturally incongruous expressions.[31] "The nation as a living organism" conceptual mapping is activated by representing Antony's as *pestifer* ("disease-bearing") for the republic while Octavian is the agent of the republic's salvation. The term used for salvation/safety, *salus*, has an expansive sematic range with powerful religious dimensions. *Salus* had been divinized at Rome since the fourth century BCE and in Roman comedy *salus* appears as a personal savior and also as a distinct divinity.[32] The concept embodied by this divine quality coheres well conceptually with the nation as a living organism metaphor and it also served to normalize conceptual correlations of humans with gods. Here the saving agent Octavian has his own divine qualities ("an incredible and a certain divine mind and valor") with the adjective *divinus* applied in an innovative fashion that is substantiated by conventional cultural thinking about *salus*. Presenting Octavian as the republic's savior connects to the Greek concept *soter* and the cult language used for Greek and Roman rulers in the eastern Mediterranean, but conceptual adjustments are made to support the development of new patterns of thought at Rome.[33]

Cicero also evokes familiar, fundamental cultural practice when he represents Octavian as a gift. The following three instances from the *Philippics* illustrate Cicero's provocative conceptual assemblies:

31. I borrow the "collage" image from Joe Grady's discussion of dynamic variations in metaphors for communication ("The 'Conduit' Metaphor Revisited: A Reassessment of Metaphors for Communication," in *Discourse and Cognition: Bridging the Gap* [ed. Jean-Pierre Koenig; Stanford, CA: CSLI Publications, 1988], 1–16).

32. A temple for *Salus* was built at the end of the fourth century BCE (Livy 9.43.25) and related coins with the head of *Salus* were minted; see Michael Crawford, *Roman Republican Coinage* (Cambridge: Cambridge University Press, 1974), 337–9. For *Salus* as a personal savior in Roman comedy, see Plautus *Bacchides* 879; for the god *Salus*, see *Mercator* 867.

33. *Salus* may have been incorporated into the cult for Julius Caesar: Dio claims that oaths based upon those sworn to extant gods were sworn by Caesar's *salus*. For further analysis, see David Wardle, "Caesar and Religion," in *A Companion to Julius Caesar* (ed. Miriam T. Griffin; Oxford: Oxford University Press, 2009), 106. On cross-cultural variation in common conceptual metaphors, see Zoltán Kövecses, *Metaphor in Culture: Universality and Variation* (Cambridge: Cambridge University Press, 2005); Ning Yu, "Metaphor from Body and Culture," in *The Cambridge Handbook of Metaphor and Thought* (ed. Raymond W. Gibbs; Cambridge: Cambridge University Press, 2008), 247–61. For culturally specific case studies on the nation as a living organism conceptual metaphor, see Kathryn Banks, "Interpretations of the Body Politic and of Natural Bodies in Late Sixteenth-Century France," in *Metaphor and Discourse* (ed. Andreas Musolff and Jörg Zinken; New York: Palgrave MacMillan, 2009), 205–18; Andreas Musolff, "Metaphor in the History of Ideas and Discourses: How Can We Interpret a Medieval Version of the *Body-State* Analogy?" in Musolff and Zinken, eds., *Metaphor and Discourse*, 233–47.

C. Caesar deorum immortalium beneficio, divina animi, ingeni, consili magnitudine.

Gaius Caesar, a gift of the immortal gods, with divine greatness of spirit, talent, and judgment. (5.23)

* * *

quis tum nobis, quis populo Romano obtulit hunc divinum adulescentem deus? qui, cum omnia ad perniciem nostram pestifero illi civi paterent, subito praeter spem omnium exortus prius confecit exercitum quem furori M. Antoni opponeret quam quisquam hoc eum cogitare suspicaretur.

What god then gave to us and the Roman people this divine young man? Who, when every means for our destruction lay open to that disease-bearing citizen, he suddenly to the surprise of all he arose and sooner than anyone could realize his plans, gathered an army to oppose Marcus Antonius's madness. (5.43)

* * *

quo maior adulescens Caesar, maioreque deorum immortalium beneficio rei publicae natus est, qui nulla specie paterni nominis nec pietate abductus umquam est et intellegit maximam pietatem conservatione patriae contineri

So much greater is the young man Caesar, born as a greater gift for the commonwealth from the immortal gods, who has never been carried away by a show of his father's name or by filial duty, and who understands that the highest filial duty is the preservation of the fatherland. (13.46)

Again, the provocative presentations of Octavian with his own divine powers are merged with a conceptual category deeply embedded in Roman culture. Gifts and reciprocal obligations were an everyday part of the networks of patronage and central to the major religious festival Saturnalia. And the logic of offerings and exchange informed sacrifice and much of cult practice. So, conceiving of Octavian as a benefaction provided by the gods would trigger powerful Roman cultural connotations to shape perceptions of this young new leader and affect political decision-making. The metaphorical expression evokes a traditional concept, but does so in an innovative way: prior Roman evocations of this conceptual blend come from the Ciceronian corpus in this phase of religious change.[34] The third passage ties the gift concept to *pietas* and familial duty to saving the "fatherland." Rome as family is

---

34. E.g., the *De haruspicum responsis* of 56 BCE, where Cicero presents Milo as a gift sent from the gods to cure Rome's ills (6): *sic T. Annius ad illam pestem comprimendam, exstinguendam, funditus delendam natus esse videtur et quasi divino munere donatus rei publicae* [so Titus Annius seems to have been born and given as if a divine gift for the commonwealth to stop, eradicate, and utterly destroy this pestilence].

an omnipresent governing conceptual metaphor of Roman society.[35] Social distinctions like patrician, patron, the "fathers" designation for senators all reflect this embedded concept as does late-Republican religio-political language. Octavian's "father" here is of course Caesar, who had *parens patriae* (parent of the fatherland) among his cult titles, which would evoke Romulus, the original parent of Rome.[36] As with the gift concept, a pre-established conceptual framework helps to normalize new religious thought and practice.

Zoltán Kövecses's application of "intratextuality" and "intertextuality" for metaphor analysis can provide a useful interpretive framework for these examples from the *Philippics*.[37] Processing Cicero's words intratextually, a listener or reader could make connections with related representations of Octavian in the *Philippics* as a gift and think of the divine attributes and designations he is given.[38] One might also retrieve thoughts of Caesar's assassins being conceived of as gifts as well.[39] Thinking intertextually, a Roman could recall Cicero framing Caesar's exceptional position to deliver salvation (*salus*) to the republic as divine in the *Pro Marcello* and *Pro Ligario*. Prior public, affective conceptual mappings with related underlying logic could come to mind: Pompey being presented to a Roman audience as a gift from gods or Lentulus being publicly hailed as a "parent, god, and savior."[40] An elite, literate Roman may have associations from Cicero's *De re publica* activated: the closing dream vision of astral immortality for Roman benefactors represents human life as a gift from the gods.[41] And such intertextual generation of meaning is diachronic as well as synchronic.

---

35. George Lakoff, *Moral Politics: How Liberals and Conservatives Think* (Chicago, IL: University of Chicago Press, 1996) analyzes American political culture through opposing conceptual family/parenting metaphors shaping progressive and conservative policy and patterns of thought. At *De domo sua* 94, Cicero represents himself as a lenient parent of the Roman people in a Roman cultural variant of Lakoff's analytical scheme.

36. The term *pater patriae* ("father of the fatherland"') first appears in extant Latin at Cicero, *Pro Rabirio Perduellionis Reo* 27, where Marius is also called the "parent (*parens*) of your liberty." Romulus is called *pater* in Ennius's *Annales* (106-8 Sk.) and *parens* at Cicero *De divinatione* 1.3 (*huius urbis parens Romulus* [Romulus parent of this city]). *Parens patriae* becomes Caesar's honorary cognomen (Weinstock, *Divus Julius*, 200). Suetonius *Divus Iulius* 85 mentions that a column inscribed with *Parenti Patriae* ("to/for the parent of the fatherland") was erected in the forum after Caesar's funeral and served as a cult site where sacrifice was offered and oaths and vows were taken.

37. See Zoltán Kövecses, *Metaphor: A Practical Introduction* (Oxford: Oxford University Press, 2010).

38. Elsewhere at *Orationes Philippicae* 7.9; 12.9; 13.19; 14.24.

39. At *Orationes Philippicae* 3.34; 4.7.

40. Pompey as a gift from the gods = *Pro Lege Manilia* 49. Lentulus as *parens, deus, salus* = *Post reditum ad populum* 11.

41. *De re publica* 6.15, 17.

The human savior and divine benefaction concepts trace genealogies to Greece and Egypt. This pervasive metaphoric activity shaped thought and influenced religious practice: Octavian (who will take the name Augustus) like Caesar will become a Roman state god.

A related set of concepts where metaphor is again enmeshed with emergent religious practice can also be tracked in our evidence from 44 and 43 BCE. In the fourth *Philippic* delivered at a public gathering of the Roman people for political deliberation (*contio*), Cicero hails Octavian's benefactions for the republic, which are divine in accord with his appearance itself being an act of divine beneficence that is awaiting fitting honors from the senate (4.4). These divine benefactions involve thwarting Antony, who is metaphorically reconfigured as the *parricida patriae* ("patricide of the fatherland")[42] in a conceptual blend of the powerful, culturally pervasive Roman nation as living organism and nation as family metaphors. For his efforts in saving the fatherland, Octavian is said to be "carried into heaven/ the skies" (*Caesar fertur in caelum*, 4.6), a charged expression gaining currency in the late Republic.[43] Caesar's assassin Brutus, in Cicero's recollection to his confidante Atticus, had similarly elevated Piso skyward (*Pisonem ferebat in caelum*) for giving an anti-Antony speech (*Epistulae ad Atticum* 16.7.5), and elsewhere Cicero tells Atticus that the "tyrannicides" (including Brutus) were *in caelo* ("in heaven/the sky") because of their brazen benefaction (14.6.2). What seems to be meant in these instances is "praised to the skies" and interpretation has held these metaphorical expressions to be rhetorical flourish and simply hyperbole—which treats metaphor as an a-contextual linguistic trope and overlooks the relative newness of the surviving original iterations of these expressions and their conceptual connections to religious developments in this phase of cultural reordering. These expressions are indeed hyperbolic praise, but that does not exhaust their significance when they are analyzed through their original contexts. When working as a provincial governor in the eastern Mediterranean in 50 BCE, Cicero tells Atticus that the grateful people of Salamis had extolled him *in caelum* with their public decrees (*Salamini nos in caelum decrstis suis*

---

42. For Antony as a *parricida*, see *Orationes Philippicae* 2.17; 12.13; 13.21; 13.42; 14.4; 14.35; for *parricida patriae*, see 2.17.

43. Cicero, for example, had recently used the expression for Julius Caesar in the *Pro Marcello* (29): *cum alii laudibus ad caelum res tuas gestas efferent, alii fortasse aliquid requirent, idque vel maximum, nisi belli civilis incendium salute patriae restinxeris* [Some will lift your achievements to heaven with praise, others perhaps will find something lacking—something most critical—if you do not quench the fire of civil war for the safety of the fatherland]. Cf. *ista, quae tu verbis ad caelum extulisti* (*De Oratore* 3.146); *sua quisque fortia facta ad caelum fert* (Sallust, *Bellum Iugurthinum* 53.8).

sustulerunt, 6.2.9), which presumably refers to the divinizing language customary for civic benefactors in the eastern Mediterranean. That same year, Cicero wrote from Laodicea telling Atticus he allowed verbal honors but refused other divinizing offerings like statues, shrines, and chariot statues (5.21.7). Cicero had presented Pompey—accorded with honors in the Greek east—as a man thought by the Greeks to be sent from heaven (*De caelo*; *Pro Lege Manilia* 40-2), and tells his eastbound brother Quintus that he will be treated as a heaven-sent (*de caelo*) divine man (*divinus homo*) (*Epistulae ad Quintum fratrem* 1.1.7).

Surviving evidence suggests that Romans were not simply predisposed to conceive of human achievement and exaltation as cosmic super-elevation. The proliferation of this metaphorical mapping coincides temporally with emergent concepts of death and afterlife, and such conceptual innovations work in mutually reinforcing ways to establish new categories and cognitive paths. These expressions are—to borrow Donald Schön's term—*generative* metaphors.[44] Cicero described the decrees at Salamis as hailing him *in caelum*, an image he had elaborated upon in detail to the college of pontiffs in representing the decrees for his recall from exile in Greece as divine and immortal and framing his return as a skyward ascent (*De domo sua* 75):

> *nam quid ego illa divina atque immortalia municipiorum et coloniarum et totius Italiae decreta commemorem, quibus tamquam gradibus mihi videor in caelum ascendisse, non solum in patriam revertisse?*

> Why should I recollect the divine and immortal decrees of the municipalities and colonies, and of the whole of Italy, the steps by which I seem to have not only returned to the fatherland, but ascended into the sky?[45]

---

44. Schön, "Generative Metaphor."

45. Cf. *Pro Milone* 97, where strikingly similar language of a skyward ascent by steps is integrated with the conventional aristocratic concept of *gloria*:

> *sed tamen ex omnibus praemiis virtutis, si esset habenda ratio praemiorum, amplissimum esse praemium gloriam; esse hanc unam quae brevitatem vitae posteritatis memoria consolaretur, quae efficeret ut absentes adessemus, mortui viveremus; hanc denique esse cuius gradibus etiam in caelum homines viderentur ascendere.*

> But nevertheless, out of all the rewards of virtue, if there must be a reckoning of rewards, the most ample reward is glory; which consoles the brevity of life with the remembrance of posterity, which makes us present in absence and alive in death; on the steps of which people seem even to ascend into heaven.

Slightly before this passage, Cicero argues that Milo would be duly celebrated with divine honors—not punished—for ridding the city of a tyrant if he had been in Greece (*Pro Milone* 80).

This figurative transmigration up into the sky has vital religious resonances, as is evident in the initial appearance of the Greek noun *apotheosis* in the Latin corpus. The relatively rare Greek word—used in the Ptolemaic Canopus decree (see above p. 228) by priests to describe a mortal's posthumous ascent to divinity—is first attested in Roman texts in Cicero's letters. The Greek word first appears very figuratively as Cicero relaying to Atticus that Curio had deemed the achievements of Cicero's consulship an *apotheosis* (*Epistulae ad Atticum* 1.16.13). Cicero then uses this word found in constitutive cultic decree to describe his public presentation of Caesar (4.5.2), the first Roman to be deified by official decree at Rome. The final iterations of the Greek word *apotheosis* in the Ciceronian corpus are used much like the word is used in the Canopus decree: they appear in letters to Atticus wherein the grief-stricken Cicero makes a radical, experimental departure from traditional Roman practices: he plans to deify his deceased daughter Tullia and searches for a high-profile site to build her a cult shrine, a *fanum*, the very type of divine cult shrine he himself had refused in the Greek east (12.12.1; 12.36.1; 12.37a).[46]

In the months when the assassins of Caesar were being praised to the heavens and deemed *di futuri* ("future gods," *Epistulae ad Atticum* 14.11.1) by Cicero, he observes that the bloody but brave civic benefaction on the Ides of March has earned them entrance to heaven (14.14.3, 28-9):

> *quem ad modum tu praecipis, contenti Idibus Martiis simus; quae quidem nostris amicis, divinis viris, aditum ad caelum dederunt.*

> As you recommend, let us be content with the Ides of March, which gave entrance to heaven to our friends, divine men.

Traditional Roman thinking about death and afterlife and related ritual practice conceived of the dead as a collective body (*manes*) under the earth.[47] Cicero's representation of death as passage through an entrance in the sky is an innovative formulation in 44 BCE, and cognate metaphorical expressions are also conceptually inventive. In the previous year, in his *Tusculan*

---

46. For Tullia's *apotheosis* Cicero wanted a shrine in the public eye distinct from a customary tomb. The specific Greek monument type he wanted was an *Aphidruma* (*Epistulae ad Atticum* 13.29) which was used to introduce cult; see, Michael Koortbojian, *The Divinization of Caesar and Augustus: Precedents, Consequences, Implications* (Cambridge: Cambridge University Press, 2013), 237.

47. On the traditional earthly orientation of the collective *Manes* spirit of the dead, see John Scheid, "Die Parentalien fur die verstorbenen Caesaren als Modell fur den romischen Totenkult," *Klio* 75 (1993): 188–201; Keith Hopkins, *Death and Renewal: Sociological Studies in Roman History* (Cambridge: Cambridge University Press, 1983), 227.

Disputations, Cicero legitimizes his speculative positions on a posthumous astral ascent by appealing to ancestral authority, pontifical law, and also the earlier Republican poet Ennius (27-28):

> *itaque unum illud erat insitum priscis illis, quos cascos appellat Ennius, esse in morte sensum neque excessu vitae sic deleri hominem, ut funditus interiret: idque cum multis aliis rebus, tum e pontificio iure et e caerimoniis sepulcrorum intellegi licet, quas maxumis ingeniis praediti nec tanta cura coluissent nec violatas tam inexpiabili religione sanxissent, nisi haereret in eorum mentibus mortem non interitum esse omnia tollentem atque delentem, sed quandam quasi migrationem commutationemque vitae, quae in claris viris et feminis dux in caelum soleret esse, in ceteris humi retineretur et permaneret tamen. ex hoc et nostrorum opinione 'Romulus in caelo cum diis agit aevum', ut famae adsentiens dixit Ennius.*

> And so it was ingrained in those of former times who Ennius called "the ancients" that there was sensation in death and in this departure from life a person is not entirely destroyed, this can be discerned from, among other things, pontifical law and burial ritual: these rituals would not have been so carefully observed by those endowed with such talents, and the violation of these rituals would not be punished without hope of atonement if it was not their deeply held belief that death was not an annihilation obliterating and destroying everything, but like a migration and transfer of life which was customarily a guide to heaven for exceptional men and women, while the rest of the people remained underground but still survived. Hence our notion "Romulus spends eternity in heaven with the gods" as Ennius said in accord with tradition.

Cicero's argument from ancestral authority is not antiquarian fidelity to Roman tradition: giving revolutionary concepts the sanction of ancestral tradition was a critical method of legitimization in the cultural revolutions of the late Republic. In this period, Andrew Wallace-Hadrill aptly observes, "to invoke the ancestors is to invoke a stable model of legitimacy: they are most invoked when legitimacy is most at issue."[48] Reference is made to ancestral practice with mention of the dead abiding underground, but with a consequential innovative development incorporated: exceptional men and women make a skyward posthumous ascent (*in caelum*). Ennius, the creative cultural force who propagated Euhemerus at Rome, corroborates this with his Romulus abiding in the sky post-apotheosis. In the cultural moment when Romans were becoming hard-wired to conceptualize high achievement as ascending skyward, corresponding religious ideas about an afterlife were gaining traction.

Roughly a decade earlier Cicero had mapped theoretical coordinates for this innovative shift in his dialogue *De re publica*, which closes with

48. Andrew Wallace-Hadrill, *Rome's Cultural Revolution* (Cambridge: Cambridge University Press, 2008), 217.

a vision of cosmic super-elevation *in caelum* for civic benefactors. Here too Ennius's texts are embedded to authorize and naturalize new theological outlooks. A passage on the death of Romulus from Ennius's *Annales* is read by Cicero's primary interlocutor Scipio as providing evidence that early Romans called him "father" and "god" (1.64), while an Ennian epigram raises the prospect of a rise to the sky for Scipio: (incer. 6): *si fas endo plagas caelestum ascendere cuiquam est, / mi soli caeli maxima porta patet* [If it is right for anyone to ascend to the heavenly precincts, for me alone the greatest gate of heaven remains open]. This "gate of heaven" conceptual metaphor originates in extant Latin with Ennius, and remains associated with him in classical Roman texts, the other instances are in the Latin vulgate Bible.[49] The consequential cognitive power of metaphor is evident here with such formative constructions of the topography of the afterlife: life after death awaits in the sky and this passage is made through a restricted entrance, a *porta*, a term familiar from everyday life at Rome, a gateway built into the city walls. Cicero does not use Ennius's exact wording for his astral topography in Scipio's dream, but there is a regulated entrance (*aditus*, 6.15) to an exclusive space in the sky (*in caelo*, 6.13) for Rome's benefactors. This conceptual formulation is echoed later in the posthumous journey won by Caesar's assassins (*Epistulae ad Atticum* 14.14.3): *contenti Idibus Martiis simus; quae quidem nostris amicis, divinis viris, aditum ad caelum dederunt* [let us be content with the Ides of March, which gave entrance to heaven to our friends, divine men].

The atmospheric changes in Roman religious culture in the late Republic involving death and divinization were facilitated in part by metaphor's capacity to effect cognitive realignments. These metaphorical expressions that developed transformative cognitive connections between humans and gods and conceived of death as a rise to the sky share underlying conceptual logic with a metaphorical reconfiguring of death. This is made quite explicit in the *De re publica*, where Romulus's apotheosis into the sky is reframed as a departure (*post obitum vel potius excessum Romuli* [after the death or rather departure of Romulus], 2.52). In the *Tusculan Disputations* passage cited above, novel ideas about an afterlife in the sky entail the same death metaphor (*excessu vitae*, "departure from life," 1.27), and early imperial Roman sources adopt this metaphor for the apotheosis of Augustus: *circa divi Augusti excessum* ("around the departure of the god Augustus").[50] And the nascent early imperial apotheosis rituals are in fact anxious to consecrate

49. See Bosworth, "Augustus," 5 n. 32.
50. Seneca, *Quaestiones naturales* 1.1.3; cf. Pliny, *Naturalis historia* 4.98.

a "departure" rather than commemorate a death.[51] This "departure" metaphor spreads beyond late-Republican theological theorizing and the imperial apotheosis ritual. Outside of Rome in the early imperial period at Bovillae, a magistrate and *rex sacrorum* was given permission to set up a portrait shield (*clipeus*)—an honor originally associated with the emperor—for his sister Manlia Severina, the chief Vestal priest.[52] The commemorative inscription represents her death as a departure (*excessum vitae*; *Corpus Inscriptionum Latinarum* 14.2410). As with the deification of Caesar and Augustus, Manlia's monument intimates major shifts in Roman ideas about death and afterlife. After the inventive ferment in late-Republican Rome, death was increasingly represented by Romans as a skyward journey for benefactors both public and private. A dynamic conceptual nexus of language and social practices facilitated this consequential change by introducing new religious ideas through embedded Roman cognitive frameworks like gift, reciprocity, and the family. The unparalleled proliferation of metaphorical mappings between humans and gods and human accomplishment and heaven in late-Republican Rome is no coincidence. Metaphor introduced new perspectives and shaped religious thought and practice in this phase of cultural revolutions at Rome.

Biographical Note

Spencer E. Cole is Associate Professor of Classics at the University of Minnesota, USA. His publications include *Cicero and the Rise of Deification at Rome* (Cambridge University Press, 2013) and articles on Roman religion in the republican and imperial periods, Augustan poetry, and Greek drama. He is also a contributor to *The Routledge Dictionary of Ancient Mediterranean Religions*.

Bibliography

Banks, Kathryn. "Interpretations of the Body Politic and of Natural Bodies in Late Sixteenth-Century France," 205–18 in Musolff and Zinken, eds., *Metaphor and Discourse*, 2009. https://doi.org/10.1057/9780230594647_13

Beard, Mary. "Cicero and Divination: The Formation of a Latin Discourse," *Journal of Roman Studies* 76 (1986): 33–46. https://doi.org/10.2307/300364

---

51. On how nascent imperial apotheosis ritual studiously avoided traditional funereal rituals to observe the skyward transmigration of apotheosis, see Elias J. Bickerman, "Consecratio," in *Le Culte des Souverains dans l'Empire Romain* (ed. Elias J. Bickerman and Willem den Boer; Geneva: Vandoeuvres, 1972), 1–25; Scheid, "Die Parentalien."

52. On Manlia Severina and monuments divinizing women in imperial Italy, see Emily A. Hemelrijk, *Hidden Lives, Public Personae: Women and Civic Life in the Roman West* (Oxford: Oxford University Press, 2015), 297–303.

—*The Roman Triumph*. Cambridge, MA: Harvard University Press, 2007. https://doi.org/10.4159/9780674020597

Beard, Mary, John North, and Simon Price. *Religions of Rome*. Vol. 1: *A History*. Cambridge: Cambridge University Press, 1998.

Bendlin, Andreas. "Looking Beyond the Civic Compromise: Religious Pluralism in Late Republican Rome," 115–35 in *Religion in Archaic and Republican Rome and Italy: Evidence and Experience*. Edited by Edward Bispham and Christopher Smith. Edinburgh, UK: Edinburgh University Press, 2000.

Bickerman, Elias J. "Consecratio," 1–25 in *Le Culte des Souverains dans l'Empire Romain*. Edited by Elias J. Bickerman and Willem den Boer. Geneva: Vandoeuvres, 1972.

Bosworth, Brian. "Augustus, the *Res Gestae* and Hellenistic Theories of Apotheosis," *Journal of Roman Studies* 89 (1999): 1–18. https://doi.org/10.2307/300731

Cole, Spencer. "Elite Skepticism in the *Apocolocyntosis*: Further Qualifications," 174–82 in *Seeing Seneca Whole: Perspectives on Philosophy, Poetry and Politics*. Edited by Katharina Volk and Gareth D. Williams. Leiden: Brill, 2006.

—*Cicero and the Rise of Deification at Rome*. Cambridge: Cambridge University Press, 2013. https://doi.org/10.1017/CBO9781139506373

Conte, Gian B. *A History of Latin Literature*. Translated by Joseph B. Solodow. Baltimore, MD: Johns Hopkins University Press, 1994.

Crawford, Michael. *Roman Republican Coinage*. Vols. 1–2. Cambridge: Cambridge University Press, 1974.

Feeney, Denis. *Literature and Religion at Rome: Cultures, Contexts, and Beliefs*. Cambridge: Cambridge University Press, 1998.

Fishwick, Duncan. *The Imperial Cult in the Latin West*. Vol. 1. Leiden: Brill, 1987.

Gibbs, Raymond W. "Metaphor and Thought: The State of the Art," 3–13 in *Cambridge Handbook of Metaphor and Thought*, 2008. https://doi.org/10.1017/CBO9780511816802

—ed. *The Cambridge Handbook of Metaphor and Thought*. Cambridge: Cambridge University Press, 2008. https://doi.org/10.1017/CBO9780511816802

Grady, Joe. "The 'Conduit' Metaphor Revisited: A Reassessment of Metaphors for Communication," 1–16 in *Discourse and Cognition: Bridging the Gap*. Edited by Jean-Pierre Koenig. Stanford, CA: CSLI Publications, 1998.

Hemelrijk, Emily A. *Hidden Lives, Public Personae: Women and Civic Life in the Roman West*. Oxford: Oxford University Press, 2015. https://doi.org/10.1093/acprof:oso/9780190251888.001.0001

Hickson-Hahn, Frances. "Pompey's *supplicatio duplicata*: A Novel Form of Thanksgiving," *Phoenix* 54 (2000): 244–54. https://doi.org/10.2307/1089058

Hopkins, Keith. *Death and Renewal: Sociological Studies in Roman History*. Cambridge: Cambridge University Press, 1983. https://doi.org/10.1017/CBO9780511552663

Jocelyn, H. D. "The Roman Nobility and the Religion of the Republican State," *Journal of Religious History* 4 (1966): 89–104. https://doi.org/10.1111/j.1467-9809.1966.tb00489.x

Kaster, Robert A. *Cicero: Speech on Behalf of Publius Sestius*. Oxford: Clarendon Press, 2006.

Koortbojian, Michael. *The Divinization of Caesar and Augustus: Precedents, Consequences, Implications*. Cambridge: Cambridge University Press, 2013.

Kövecses, Zoltán. *Metaphor in Culture: Universality and Variation*. Cambridge: Cambridge University Press, 2005. https://doi.org/10.1017/CBO9780511614408

—*Metaphor: A Practical Introduction*. Oxford: Oxford University Press, 2010.

Lakoff, George. "The Contemporary Theory of Metaphor," 202–51 in Ortony, ed., *Metaphor and Thought*, 1993. https://doi.org/10.1017/CBO9781139173865.013

—*Moral Politics: How Liberals and Conservatives Think*. Chicago, IL: University of Chicago Press, 1996.

Lakoff, George, and Mark Johnson. *Metaphors We Live By*. Chicago, IL: University of Chicago Press, 2003. https://doi.org/10.7208/chicago/9780226470993.001.0001

Madrigal, Alexis C. "Why Are Spy Researchers Building a 'Metaphor Program'?" *The Atlantic*, 27 May 2011.

Morstein-Marx, Robert. *Mass Oratory and Political Power in the Late Roman Republic*. Cambridge: Cambridge University Press, 2004. https://doi.org/10.1017/CBO9780511482878

Musolff, Andreas. "Metaphor in the History of Ideas and Discourses: How Can We Interpret a Medieval Version of the *Body-State* Analogy?" 233–47 in Musolff and Zinken, eds., *Metaphor and Discourse*, 2009. https://doi.org/10.1057/9780230594647_15

Musolff, Andreas, and Jörg Zinken, eds. *Metaphor and Discourse*. New York: Palgrave MacMillan, 2009. https://doi.org/10.1057/9780230594647

Naughton, John. "Metaphor Is the New Weapon in the 'War' on Terror," *The Guardian*, 5 June 2011.

Ortony, Andrew, ed. *Metaphor and Thought*. Cambridge: Cambridge University Press, 1993. https://doi.org/10.1017/CBO9781139173865

Price, Simon R. F. *Rituals and Power: The Roman Imperial Cult in Asia Minor*. Cambridge: Cambridge University Press, 1984.

Rüpke, Jörg. "Acta aut agenda: Relations of Script and Performance," 23–43 in *Rituals in Ink*. Edited by Alessandro Barchiesi, Jörg Rüpke, and Susan Stephens. Stuttgart: Franz Steiner Verlag, 2004.

Sapolsky, Robert. "This Is Your Brain on Metaphors," *The New York Times*, 14 November 2010.

Scheid, John. "Die Parentalien fur die verstorbenen Caesaren als Modell fur den romischen Totenkult," *Klio* 75 (1993): 188–201. https://doi.org/10.1524/klio.1993.75.75.188

—*An Introduction to Roman Religion*. Translated by Janet Lloyd. Bloomington, IN: Indiana University Press, 2003.

Schofield, Malcolm. "Cicero for and against Divination," *Journal of Roman Studies* 76 (1986): 47–65. https://doi.org/10.2307/300365

Schön, Donald. "Generative Metaphor: A Perspective on Problem-Setting in Social Policy," 137–63 in Ortony, ed., *Metaphor and Thought*, 1993. https://doi.org/10.1017/CBO9781139173865.011

Skutsch, Otto. *The Annals of Quintus Ennius*. Oxford: Oxford University Press, 1985.

Wallace-Hadrill, Andrew. "Roman Arches and Greek Honours: The Language of Power at Rome," *Proceedings of the Cambridge Philological Society* 36 (1990): 143–81. https://doi.org/10.1017/S0068673500005265

—*Rome's Cultural Revolution*. Cambridge: Cambridge University Press, 2008.

Wardle, David. "Caesar and Religion," 100–11 in *A Companion to Julius Caesar*. Edited by Miriam T. Griffin. Oxford: Oxford University Press, 2009.

Weinstock, Stefan. *Divus Julius*. Oxford: Clarendon Press, 1971.

Yu, Ning. "Metaphor from Body and Culture," 247–61 in *Cambridge Handbook of Metaphor and Thought*, 2008. https://doi.org/10.1017/CBO9780511816802.016

PART IV
FROM JUDAISM TO CHRISTIANITY

Chapter Twelve

Defining Judaism:
The Case of Philo

Michael L. Satlow

Religion, we have often been told, did not exist as such in antiquity. No word in any ancient language prior to Late Antiquity fully captures what modern scholars often mean (rightly or wrongly, thoughtfully or not) by "religion." A variety of terms denote specific dimensions of what we often mean by the term religion (e.g., *eusebeia* in Greek or *religio, pietas*, and *superstitio* in Latin) but there is no single, first-order term that separates "religion" from the complex web of ethnic and national identity (which are themselves unstable and weakly theorized concepts in antiquity).[1]

More than three decades ago, Jonathan Z. Smith recognized this issue and suggested a remedy. Smith advocated for a polythetic approach to ancient Judaism.[2] Using terminology derived from biological classificatory schemes, Smith understands a "monothetic" classificatory model for religion to be equivalent to the essentialism most frequently used by scholars to classify religion. Throughout his essay, Smith complains that scholars remain locked into the monothetic classificatory schemes bequeathed to them from the first-order definitions. That is, the scholar's understanding (of, for example, Judaism) is drawn from that definition formulated by a specific group that usually understands itself as the religion's authentic interpreters (for example, the Rabbis). Instead of locating essences, he

---

1.   This point is made strongly, perhaps too much so, by Carlin A. Barton and Daniel Boyarin, *Imagine No Religion: How Modern Abstractions Hide Ancient Realities* (New York: Fordham University Press, 2016) and Brent Nongbri, *Before Religion: A History of a Modern Concept* (New Haven, CT: Yale University Press, 2013). As it applies especially to Judaism, see Daniel Boyarin, *Judaism: The Genealogy of a Modern Notion* (New Brunswick, NJ: Rutgers University Press, 2019). For discussions of this issue, see Steve Mason, "Jews, Judaeans, Judaizing, Judaism: Problems of Categorization in Ancient History," *Journal for the Study of Judaism* 38.4–5 (2007): 457–512, and Michael L. Satlow, "Jew or Judaean?" in *The One Who Sows Bountifully: Essays in Honor of Stanley K. Stowers* (ed. Caroline Johnson Hodge, Saul M. Olyan, Daniel Ullucci; Providence, RI: Brown Judaic Studies, 2013), 165–76.

2.   See Jonathan Z. Smith, *Imagining Religion: From Babylon to Jonestown* (Chicago, IL: University of Chicago Press, 1982), 1–18.

argues, scholars should be developing maps of characteristics that may or may not be shared by the members of a group. Two specific members of a group might share several of these characteristics, some overlapping set, or even none at all. This "polythetic" model accounts for a wide diversity of actual religious manifestations while at the same time requiring the development of the basic map of characteristics that underlie a single "religion": "We need to map the variety of Judaisms, each of which appears as a shifting cluster of characteristics which vary over time."[3]

In the more than three decades since this essay appeared, there has been little serious attempt to follow through on Smith's suggestion. Perhaps this should not be surprising, for a polythetic classification of Judaism is easier said than done and while Smith provides some micro-examples of how he might start such a project, the project itself is daunting. How, in actuality, might a polythetic map of any particular Judaism appear, and how is it to be related to maps of other "Judaisms"?

This chapter will seek to develop Smith's polythetic model and to apply it to one ancient thinker, Philo. In the first part of the chapter I will briefly trace the genealogy of "Judaism" as a first-order category and attempt to show its limitations for modern analytical work. The second part, drawing especially on the work of Smith and Jacob Neusner, will develop a polythetic framework for analysis. In the third part of this chapter, in order to test the utility of this framework, I will apply this framework to the writings of Philo, a Jewish (or Judaean) philosopher who lived in Alexandria around the turn of the era.[4]

Judaism: A Short Genealogy

The first attestation of the word "Judaism" occurs in 2 Maccabees, a Greek abridgement of a history of the Maccabean revolt that was written circa 124 BCE. The Greek term *ioudaismos* appears first in the prefatory letter attached by the abridger: "[Jason of Cyrene, the author of the history] has also given an account of the wars with Antiochus Epiphanes and with his son Eupator, and he has described the apparitions from heaven that were made for those who were struggling with bravery and honor for *ioudaismos*" (2 Maccabees 2.21-2). Jason of Cyrene himself, though, appears to have coined the word. 2 Maccabees 8.1 describes how Judah Maccabee gathered those who, in the face of persecution, remained faithful to *ioudaismos*, and at 14.38 he describes a certain man Razis, known as "father of the Jews," as having been tried and having risked his life "for *ioudaismos*."

---

3.   Smith, *Imagining Religion*, 18.
4.   See Mason, "Jews, Judaeans, Judaizing"; Satlow, "Jew or Judaean?"

2 Maccabees understands *ioudaismos* as the antonym to another new word, *hellenismos*, often translated as "Hellenism."[5]

As scholars have noted, in all Jewish sources from antiquity *ioudaismos* means something akin to "Judaeanness," a complex distinctive identity that intermingled characteristics that we might call "religious" with those that we would call "ethnic."[6] It combined a kin identity, whether actual or fictive, as in the case of those non-Judaeans who "converted" or who otherwise entered the Judaean community, with adherence to a way of life that was authorized in some fashion by the Law of Moses.

In his book *Border Lines*, Daniel Boyarin has argued that it was the early Christians who brought "Judaism" as a more strictly religious category into existence: "[O]ne cannot speak of Judaism as existing before Christianity but only in part of the process of the invention of Christianity … Christianity, in its constitution as a religion, therefore needed religious difference, needed Judaism to be its other—the religion that is false."[7] Although this claim might be exaggerated, it does highlight the transformation that the term *ioudaismos* underwent in non-Jewish writings of Late Antiquity. The Church Fathers constructed "Judaism" as an antonym to "Christianity," as a definable entity that contained an identifiable essence and stood in relationship to "Christianity." When the Church Fathers wished to stress continuity with Christianity, they were more likely to locate this essence in God's covenant; when they wanted to sharpen Christian self-identity, they emphasized the Law as the essence of Judaism. In both cases, however, their construction of "Judaism" was clearly self-interested, deployed for their own needs of self-identification and divorced from the lives of real Jews. This understanding seeps into imperial legislation in Late Antiquity, which increasingly conceived of the "religion" of the Jews, most often denoted with the Latin terms *religio* and *superstitio*, as a voluntary religious system similar to that of the Christians.[8]

Whether Jews themselves accepted this "colonial" understanding of their own Judaism is not entirely clear. Boyarin claims that by the second century

5.   2 Macc. 4.11-3; cf. Daniel Schwartz, *Sefer Makabim 2: Mavo, Targum, Perush* (Jerusalem, Israel: Yad Yitshak Ben-Tsevi, 2004), 95.

6.   See Yehoshua Amir, "The Term *Ioudaismos*: A Study in Jewish-Hellenistic Self-Identification," *Immanuel* 14 (1972): 34–41; Shaye J. D. Cohen, *The Beginnings of Jewishness: Boundaries, Varieties, Uncertainties* (Berkeley, CA: University of California Press, 1999), 7–8, 105–6.

7.   Daniel Boyarin, *Border Lines: The Partition of Judaeo-Christianity* (Philadelphia, PA: University of Pennsylvania Press, 2004), 11. See most recently Boyarin, *Judaism*, 33–59.

8.   See Seth Schwartz, *Imperialism and Jewish Society, 200 B.C.E. to 640 C.E.* (Princeton, NJ: Princeton University Press, 2001), 179–202.

CE, the Rabbis had created "the rudiments of a full-fledged heresiology" that knows of "historical and genealogical Israelites who are not 'Israel'."[9] That is, the rabbinic project mirrored that of the Church Fathers, understanding membership in true Israel to be determined by rules of faith. Yet "[t]he Rabbis, in the end, reject and refuse the Christian definition of religion."[10] Moreover, at the same time the Rabbis were more rigidly drawing the lines of Jewish identity.[11] Jewish—or at least rabbinic—understandings of Judaism might flirt with an essence, but they seemed never to adopt it.

Only in the Middle Ages do we find the penetration of the concept of "Judaism" into Hebrew. One of the first, perhaps even the first, attestation of the Hebrew term for Judaism, *yahadut*, appears in Abraham Abulafia's *Book of the Testimony*. In it, Abulafia describes his attempts to meet with the pope in 1280 to speak "in the name of *yahadut*."[12] According to Moshe Idel, by *yahadut* Abulafia meant the different permutations of God's name, knowledge of which would help to hasten redemption.[13] Abulafia's eclectic use of the term mirrors other mediaeval Jewish writers, who never seemed to use the term to denote a complete religious system.

Jewish self-understandings changed in the modern period. Several factors played a role in this emerging Jewish self-definition. The Enlightenment category of "religion" drew heavily upon prior Christian understandings.[14] This definition of religion emphasized an intrinsic essence located in a system of rational belief. Western and Central European Jewish thinkers, seeking to understand their "religion" in Enlightenment terms, naturally adopted a similar notion.[15] This, however, was not a mere intellectual exercise of categorization. The Jewish need for religious self-definition in secular terms was exacerbated by the political situation in which they found themselves. Jews were fighting for civic rights, and at least in the public

9.   Boyarin, *Border Lines*, 61.

10.   Boyarin, *Border Lines*, 224.

11.   Cf. Cohen, *Beginnings of Jewishness*, 263–349.

12.   Moshe Idel, "Abraham Abulafia and the Pope: An Account of an Abortive Mission (Hebrew Section)," *AJS Review* 7–8 (1982–1983): 6.

13.   See Idel, "Abraham Abulafia," 13–4. See also, Boyarin, *Judaism*, 60–101.

14.   See Talal Asad, *Genealogies of Religion: Discipline and Reasons of Power in Christianity and Islam* (Baltimore, MD: Johns Hopkins University Press, 1993), 27–54; Wilfred Cantwell Smith, *The Meaning and End of Religion: A New Approach to the Religious Traditions of Mankind* (New York: Macmillan, 1963), 37–50.

15.   Cf. Arthur Hertzberg, *The French Enlightenment and the Jews* (New York: Columbia University Press, 1968), 268–313; Adam Sutcliffe, *Judaism and Enlightenment* (Cambridge: Cambridge University Press, 2003), 165–90, and "Can a Jew be a Philosopher? Isaac de Pinto, Voltaire, and Jewish Participation in the European Enlightenment," *Jewish Social Studies* 6.3 (2000): 31–51.

discourse the primary obstacle was "Judaism": Was it a "religion" that was compatible with civic society?[16] Perhaps this issue was nowhere as starkly presented as in the "Paris Sanhedrin" of 1806–1807, at which Napoleon put to a Jewish assembly twelve questions meant to elicit from it a commitment to French law and social intercourse.[17]

From the perspective of most European Jewish thinkers in the late eighteenth to mid-nineteenth centuries, the answer was clearly affirmative. Moses Mendelssohn asserted that Judaism's essence, its universal morality, was identical to the essence of Christianity—only Judaism, through its distinctive ceremonial laws, realized this essence more effectively.[18] Throughout the nineteenth and well into the twentieth century, this self-defining articulation of Judaism as having a distinctive moral essence became increasingly attractive for western Jews. Leo Baeck entitled his 1905 book *Das Wesen des Judentums*. Nineteenth-century neo-Orthodox thinkers such as Samson Raphael Hirsch and ultra-Orthodox thinkers such as Akiba Joseph Schlesinger both subscribed to essentialist notions of Judaism, even if the former located that essence in the covenant made at Sinai and the latter, increasingly, in peoplehood.[19]

The notion of "Judaism" as a distinctive religious system with an essence has been remarkably persistent, albeit not unchallenged. As some Jews in Europe joined the Zionist movement, they began to see "Judaism" as a national phenomenon; "Judaism" was the complex of distinctive customs and practices of the Jewish nation. As William Scott Green states, "[a]lthough all who practice and affirm Judaism are Jews, not all Jews affirm(ed) and practice(d) Judaism. This habit of mind subsumes Judaism under Jewish social identity and mistakes ethnicity for religion."[20] In the United States at the beginning and through the middle of the twentieth century, where despite their repeated attempts at presenting themselves as

16. See Michael A. Meyer, *Response to Modernity: A History of the Reform Movement in Judaism* (Oxford: Oxford University Press, 1988), 10–61.

17. Cf. *Transactions of the Parisian Sanhedrim; or, Acts of the Assembly of Israelitish Deputies of France and Italy* (trans. Diogène Tama; Landham, MD: University Press of America, 1985).

18. Cf. Allan Arkush, *Moses Mendelssohn and the Enlightenment* (Albany, NY: State University of New York Press, 1994); David Sorkin, *Moses Mendelssohn and the Religious Enlightenment* (Berkeley, CA: University of California Press, 1996).

19. See Michael K. Silber, "The Emergence of Ultra-Orthodoxy: The Invention of Tradition," in *The Uses of Tradition: Jewish Continuity in the Modern Era* (ed. Jack Wertheimer; New York: Jewish Theological Seminary of America, 1992), 23–84.

20. William Scott Green, "Old Habits Die Hard: Judaism in the *Encyclopaedia of Religion*," in *The Blackwell Reader in Judaism* (ed. Jacob Neusner and Alan Avery-Peck; Oxford: Blackwell, 1989), 9–10.

Americans of a different religion they were most often seen as a distinctive ethnic group, Jews began to reconceptualize "Judaism" as a matter of ethnicity and culture. As Mordechai Kaplan succinctly put it, Judaism was a "civilization."[21] For Kaplan, Jewish laws were "folkways," part of the culture of the Jews.

Kaplan's definition, of course, joins "religion" and "culture"; they are, for him, almost synonymous categories. On a theoretical level, as has been well observed, "the relation between 'culture' and 'religion' appears to be multiple, complex, and contradictory to some extent."[22] This is an apt characterization of Jewish life in contemporary America and Israel, where "Judaism" sometimes anchors and at other times stands in opposition to constructions of "Jewish culture."[23] As Cohn-Sherbok's definition of Judaism illustrates, this popular blurring of the categories "Judaism" and "Jewish culture"— which in turn is symptomatic of modern understandings of religion as individual and subjective (e.g., Judaism is whatever I consider it to be)—has also crept into the scholarly literature.

This survey is, of course, far too brief and schematic, but it nevertheless highlights the fact that all of the understandings of "Judaism" surveyed above are first-order definitions, created by communities for their own definitional purposes. When early Christians used the term "Judaism," they did so to help define themselves—"Judaism," as they understood it, was necessary for them to tell the story of Christianity. These Christian definitions of Judaism ultimately had an impact on Jewish self-understandings, and to the extent that Jews have understood themselves as practitioners of "Judaism," they have primarily adopted a model of a religious tradition that emerged from the Enlightenment's adaptation of a Christian notion. In this respect, Judaism is but one example of a more general phenomenon, in which the new scholars of "religion" defined religious communities in their own terms, only to see the members of those very communities come to see themselves in that way.[24]

---

21. See Mordecai M. Kaplan, *Judaism as a Civilization: Toward a Reconstruction of American Jewish Life* (New York: Macmillan, 1934).

22. See Tomoko Masuzawa, "Culture," in *Critical Terms for Religious Studies* (ed. Mark C. Taylor; Chicago, IL: University of Chicago Press, 1998), 70.

23. See Stephen J. Whitfield, "Declarations of Independence: American Jewish Culture in the Twentieth Century," in *Cultures of the Jews: A New History, 1099–1146* (ed. David Biale; New York: Schocken, 2002), 1099–145.

24. This phenomenon has been best documented for the nineteenth-century western creation of "Hinduism" out of the Indic religions. Cf. Peter van der Veer, *Imperial Encounters: Religion and Modernity in India and Britain* (Princeton, NJ: Princeton University Press, 2001); Gavin Flood, *An Introduction to Hinduism* (Cambridge: Cambridge University Press, 1996).

From First-Order to Second-Order

The preceding survey brings into focus the very blurriness of the relationship between the first-order definitions of religion and their use as second-order, academic, and value-neutral categories of organization. "Judaism," without critical reflection, brings with it the basic elements of its first-order formulation—either the notion of an objective essence and a normative set of belief and practices, or, following Kaplan's influential definition, a messier cultural complex that gives no place to religion, however defined, *per se*. Moreover, as has been amply documented, the implicit assumption that "Judaism" stands in opposition to Christianity, a legacy of first-order Christian definitions of Judaism, permeates modern scholarship. In an extensive review published in 1921, George Foot Moore argued that beginning in the nineteenth century scholars increasingly presented a Judaism that stood directly opposite Christianity, and E. P. Sanders has shown that the very understanding of Judaism that Moore sought to discredit was alive and well through the 1970s.[25]

First-order self-definitions are useful as data; they tell us about a group's self-perception. They are, however, far less useful as analytical or explanatory scholarly categories. First-order definitions of "Judaism" do not seek to describe a religious phenomenon but to create an "authentic" community by drawing lines between "orthodox" and "heterodox" manifestations.[26] They are inherently normative. Such definitions might be entirely appropriate for the community that wishes to define itself, but they are less appropriate for the academic student of Judaism who seeks to develop descriptive and analytical models. Any study of religion must begin, as Jonathan Z. Smith has frequently insisted, with the development of second-order concepts and definitions.

To my knowledge, Jacob Neusner has been one of the few scholars who has sought to offer a second-order definition of Judaism. For Neusner, *a Judaism* is a "religious system" that can best be described through attention to its ethnos, ethics, and ethos:

> [A Judaism] is composed of three elements: a world view, a way of life, and a social group that, in the here and now, embodies the whole. The world view explains the life of the group, ordinarily referring to God's creation, the revelation of the Torah, the goal and end of the group's life in the end of time. The way of life defines what is special about the life of the group. The social

---

25. See E. P. Sanders, *Paul and Palestinian Judaism: A Comparison of Patterns of Religion* (Philadelphia, PA: Fortress Press, 1977), 33–59.

26. Cf. Boyarin, *Border Lines*, 22–6.

> group, in a single place and time, then forms the living witness and testimony
> to the system as a whole and finds in the system ample explanation for its
> very being. That is *a Judaism*.[27]

At any given time, according to Neusner, there may be either competing
"Judaisms" or a single dominant one, but each requires investigation in its
own right. Despite this diversity of Judaism, Judaism, more so than even the
Jewish people, has a history: "[W]hile there may be no single, unitary 'Jewish
history,' there is a single (but hardly unitary) history of Judaism. The history
of Judaism itself is extraordinarily complex, involving, as it does, the construction of definitions of 'Judaism' capable of both defining and linking data
spread over a long continuum."[28] Indeed, in *The Way of the Torah* Neusner
attempts to describe the four "periods in the history of Judaisms and the paramount status of one Judaism."[29] That one Judaism, he goes on to explain, is
made into a coherent whole through the single "conception that the Jews are
in exile but have the hope of coming home to their own land, which is the
Land of Israel (also known as Palestine)."[30] This is the story of the Five Books
of Moses, the Torah, which each Judaism "retells in its own way and with its
distinctive emphases."[31]

There is much that is attractive about this definition of Judaism. It starts by
taking seriously a community's first-order definition: "The first requirement
is to find a group of Jews who see themselves as 'Israel' … That same group
must tell us that it uniquely constitutes 'Israel,' not *an* Israel […]."[32] Neusner's definition thus grapples with the critical problem of explaining how a
group of diverse religious communities can all see themselves as "Israel."
That any adequate description of a Jewish community ("a Judaism," in Neusner's terminology) must take into account its "worldview" (or ethos) and
"way of life" (or ethics) is also undoubtedly correct.

Yet there are also weaknesses with this definition. Neusner's definition of
Judaism posits (1) a religious system anchored (2) by a worldview that, in
its basic structure, (3) is essential to all "Judaisms" and therefore (4) can be
linked into a single (if complex) history. Ultimately, Neusner relies on the

---

27. Jacob Neusner, *The Way of Torah: An Introduction to Judaism* (5th ed.; Belmont, CA: Wadsworth, 1993), 8 (emphasis in the original).

28. Jacob Neusner, "Review of Ideas of Jewish History. Edited, with Introduction and Notes, by Michael A. Meyer," *History and Theory* 14.2 (1975): 218.

29. Neusner, *Way of Torah*, 9.

30. Neusner, *Way of Torah*, 14.

31. Neusner, *Way of Torah*, 15.

32. Neusner, *Way of Torah*, 7 (emphasis in the original).

kind of structuralist model set forth by Clifford Geertz, in which a religion can primarily be seen as a "system of meaning."[33]

This structuralist model has been heavily critiqued. Talal Asad has argued that by focusing on overarching cognitive meanings, Geertz's structuralist model ignores issues of power, practice, discourse, and discipline. Religions, Asad argues, are "products of historically distinctive disciplines and forces";[34] they cannot be conceived or understood outside of social and historical contexts. By conceiving religion as a "system of meaning," Geertz pigeonholes it into one specific and itself historically contingent understanding of "religion." Other scholars have preferred understanding religions as cultural repertoires that agents use "in complex, varying ways on various occasions, shifting the cultural framing of a problem in mid-discourse."[35] In all cases, however, the same critiques can be leveled at Neusner's emphasis of Judaism's "worldview."

Moreover, despite rejecting the essentialism inherent in almost all first-order definitions of Judaism, Neusner adopts his own essentialism (point 3 above). Essentialism is not an *a priori* reason to reject Neusner's definition. Indeed, as I will argue below, most communities that identify themselves as Jewish do share a discourse rather than an ethos, whose parameters can be traced back to the Torah.[36]

Finally, Neusner never quite works out to my satisfaction how either the diverse Judaisms or their "paramount status of one Judaism" can have a history. Contrary to Neusner's formulation, human communities have histories whereas abstract, second-order conceptions do not—except, at times, as histories of ideas. Although "Jewish history" remains a problematic category, the history of large communities of Jews can be told with more intellectual justification and integrity than can a history of "Judaism," however non-linear that history might be. More specifically, for Neusner the link between the four different stages of Judaism is the formation, definition, ascendancy, and weakening of the status of the rabbinic tradition. This privileging of the rabbinic tradition in this history sits uneasily with his fuller conceptual model; he is really attempting to tell the history of Rabbinic Judaism, without fully explaining what this is and how it relates to "Judaism." Here again

33. See Clifford Geertz, *The Interpretation of Cultures* (New York: Basic Books, 1973), 87–125.

34. Asad, *Genealogies of Religion*, 54.

35. Robert Ford Campany, "On the Very Idea of Religions (in the Modern West and in Early Medieval China)," *History of Religions* 42.4 (2003): 318; cf. Ann Swidler, *Talk of Love: How Culture Matters* (Chicago, IL: University of Chicago Press, 2001).

36. Cf. Bruce Lincoln, "Theses on Method," *Method & Theory in the Study of Religion* 17.1 (2005): 8–10.

I think that Neusner is correct to identify the rabbinic tradition as an important component for understanding Judaism, but he has not succeeded in fitting it into his broader model.

In order to move forward I suggest that we return to Jonathan Z. Smith's polythetic approach. If Smith usefully and convincingly advocates for a polythetic classification, it is Neusner who helps to lend specificity to which maps we might draw. The potential payoff for this new polythetic definition of "Judaism" is an analytical model that helps to account for a diverse group of religious communities that each sees itself as constituting a single Israel.

The three maps onto which Judaism can be plotted are Israel, textual tradition, and ritual. By Israel I refer to self-identity, the act of identifying as a member of *am yisrael* and the particular self-understanding of what that identification means. All groups that self-identify as Jews "count," and, however much other Jewish communities contest their identity, their own self-characterization puts them on the map. These communities identify themselves as Jews, locating themselves (or not) within a sacred narrative and a bloodline. The objective truth of this claim is less important in this case than the community's self-perception; being part of Israel begins with the claim to be, not with some outsider judging whether that claim is correct. At the same time, though, Jewish self-perception is hardly consistent or static. Different communities, and their individual members, use different strategies for identifying as Jews.

The second map charts the communities' canonical texts. Jewish communities throughout history have tended to ascribe authority of some type to a bounded and largely similar set of texts. Nearly every community from Late Antiquity to the present that identifies itself as Jewish has held in high regard the Hebrew Bible and the rabbinic textual tradition, although the precise nature of that regard and of the authority given to these texts is complex, contested, and varies from community to community. These texts constitute an ongoing dialogue that has been remarkably consistent, providing a set of resources upon which Jewish communities have drawn in order to authorize their understandings of Judaism.

Texts, however, are not the only vehicles of tradition. Jewish communities also transmit ritual practices, some of which coexist uneasily with the textual tradition. On the one hand, by absorbing traditional practices and even ritualizing them, rabbinic texts preserve them for later generations. Yet, on the other hand, these texts tend to structure the practices and ascribe meanings to them that do not always survive the test of time, and frequently a practice breaks from the texts that attempt to ritualize and interpret it.

It is important to emphasize that this is an explicitly non-normative framework. Judaism is an abstraction here, a second-order category created in the "scholar's study."[37] There is no attempt to judge *a priori* what counts as "authentic" or not. Indeed, it takes as its data all discourse and practices that some individual or group claims to be "Jewish." Once a large number of such groups are mapped, clusters and patterns will emerge; some definitions of Israel, for example, will stand on the margins, unshared by others. This might be interesting and significant, although it does not allow us any conclusions about its validity or authenticity. This distinction, I believe, is critical to the work of the scholar of religion.

The goal of any theoretical model is to help us to see and frame our evidence in a different and more useful way. That is, a theory should have utility. In what follows, in order to gauge the utility of the theoretical model developed above I will apply it to the writings of one particular ancient writer, Philo, who has often been held up as the exemplar of "Hellenistic Judaism."

Philo: A Case Study

Philo offers a more complex account of Jewish identity. His life provides an intriguing example of Jewish identity and its negotiation in a Greek city. Born in the first century BCE to what appears to be a wealthy and distinguished Jewish family, Philo spent his life (to the best of our knowledge) in Alexandria, Egypt. His brother had a position of political authority in Alexandria and his nephew, Tiberius Julius Alexander, achieved such prominence that the Romans appointed him procurator in Judaea in 46–48 CE. Otherwise we know little of Philo's life. He is barely mentioned by other contemporary authors (Josephus calls him "no mean philosopher") although later Christian writers (who preserved his works) ascribed to him a biography that appears to be largely fictional.[38]

From his own meagre self-referential words, Philo appears to have been devoted to the study and writing of philosophy. He laments the day that this life came to an end, when the Jewish community of Alexandria called on him to lead a delegation to Rome to protest their treatment. Before being called into public service, though, he was prolific. While most of his work was focused on interpreting the stories of the Torah (in its Greek translation) and presenting the lives of biblical figures as exemplars, he also wrote

37. Smith, *Imagining Religion*, xi.
38. Josephus, *Jewish Antiquities* 18.8.1. On the Christian reception of Philo, see David T. Runia, *Philo in Early Christian Literature: A Survey* (Assen: Van Gorcum; and Minneapolis, MN: Fortress Press, 1993).

about issues of Jewish law and composed some short historical and apologetic tracts.[39]

Philo is far from representative of his Jewish contemporaries, either in his personal history or his thought. Moreover, despite his best efforts to create a coherent set of ideas about the nature of Judaism, he frequently falls short; he often contradicts himself or simply does not follow through with the thread of his arguments. Nevertheless, it is possible to draw some conclusions about his "map" of Judaism, that is, his stance toward (1) identity; (2) traditional texts; and (3) practices. I will deal with each of these in turn.

Identity

Philo curiously distinguishes the communities "Israel" and the "Jews." He explicitly discusses what he means by "Israel." After critiquing those who follow present trends and their own "senses" rather than their rational and unerring intelligence, Philo continues:

> And yet the present time and the many important questions decided in it are strong enough to carry conviction even if some have come to disbelieve that the Deity takes thought for men, and particularly for the suppliants' race which the Father and King of the Universe and the Source of all things has taken for his portion. Now this race is called in the Hebrew tongue Israel, but expressed in our tongue, the word is "he that sees God" and to see Him seems to me of all possessions, public or private, the most precious. For if the sight of seniors or instructors or rulers or parents stirs the beholders to respect for them and decent behaviour and the desire to live a life of self-control, how firmly based is the virtue and nobility of conduct which we may expect to find in souls whose vision has soared above all created things and schooled itself to behold the uncreated and divine, the primal good, the excellent, the happy, the blessed, which may be called better than the good, more excellent than the excellent, more blessed than blessedness, more happy than happiness itself, and any perfection there may be greater than these.[40]

For Philo, "Israel" in general is not tied to a biological race or ethnicity. All who can achieve the perfection of their rational faculty can "see" the Deity. In this account, "Israel" becomes a notional and permeable category, open to all but whose members are very few.

Where, though, does this leave the *ioudaioi*, normally translated as "Jews" or "Judaeans"? *Ioudaioi* are distinct from the community of Israel. They are, for Philo, a social or ethnic group (*ethnos*). This cleavage between Israel and

---

39. For an overview of Philo's work, see Torrey Seland, ed., *Reading Philo: A Handbook to Philo of Alexandria* (Grand Rapids, MI: William B. Eerdmans, 2014).

40. Philo, *Embassy to Gaius* 3-5 (unless otherwise noted, all translations are drawn from LCL).

ioudaioi is not, however, clean. He posits an overlap between the two categories, in which the Jews are fundamentally identified with Israel.[41] A similar strategy appears later in Paul's Letter to the Romans.

The distinction between Israel and *ioudaioi* is particularly interesting in the case of "conversion." For Philo, the act of conversion (or maybe better, the state of becoming a proselyte) has to do with joining the *ioudaioi*. One can only attain status as a member of Israel through intellectual perfection. This formulation confuses what to us are distinct categories of religion, intellect, and the social.

Philo's model is ambiguous and leaves many unanswered questions: Is one's membership in Israel stable depending on one's continuing experience? Would he have considered Plato a member of Israel, and, if so, would Philo say that he remained a non-Jew, or does acquiring status as "Israel" in some way translate into Jewishness? At the same time, this understanding of Israel broadens its potential membership. How this was to work on the ground remains fuzzy, but Israel is here mostly separated from ethnicity.

Traditional Texts

Nearly every individual or social group in antiquity that identified itself as "Israel" or *ioudaioi* gave a place of some status to the Torah. The precise nature (and strength) of the authority given to this and related texts varied, but especially among the Judaean elite some engagement with them was common.[42] Philo's work, like the extant fragments of earlier Egyptian Jews in Greek, demonstrates a deep and serious engagement with these texts.

Philo set out to interpret the Torah as a rational and universalist text. Far from being the simple story of a particular *ethnos* and their cultic practices, the Torah for Philo is a sublime statement of the nature of the divine, the cosmos, and the human being. It is a document for Israel, not necessarily for the *ioudaioi*.

Philo's *a priori* assumption that the Torah is rational and targeted at strengthening and perfecting the individual's rational faculty leads him to immediate problems. Many statements in the Torah are, taken at face value, quite irrational. Since that, however, cannot be correct in Philo's reading, the seemingly irrational statements in the Torah must mean something other than what they seem to say. This leads him to rely heavily on allegorical interpretation. One example of this approach can be seen in Philo's

41. See Ellen Birnbaum, *The Place of Judaism in Philo's Thought: Israel, Jews, and Proselytes* (Brown Judaic Studies; Atlanta, GA: Scholars Press, 1996).
42. See Michael L. Satlow, *How the Bible Became Holy* (New Haven, CT: Yale University Press, 2014).

approach to the rampant anthropomorphism found in biblical texts. Philo relentlessly argues against anthropomorphic readings, which are at odds with (some) contemporary philosophical notions that the deity (or deities) is transcendent and perfect. Philo's God is not only not like a human being but in fact is barely conceivable by mere mortals:

> Just so anyone entering this world, as it were some vast house or city, and beholding the sky circling round and embracing within it all things, and planets and fixed stars without any variation moving in rhythmical harmony and with advantage to the whole, and the earth with the central space assigned to it ... and over and above these, living creatures, mortal and immortal beings, plants and fruits in great variety, he will surely argue that these have not been wrought without consummate art, but that the Maker of this whole universe was and is God. Those, who thus base their reasoning on what is before their eyes, apprehend God by means of a shadow cast, discerning the Artificer by means of His works.[43]

Except by the purest of minds (exemplified by, and perhaps limited to, Moses), God cannot be apprehended directly. Like other ancient philosophers, Philo saw the world and the cosmos as the best witness to God's existence.

Philo was certainly not the first writer to emphasize God's absolute otherness. Aristobulus, sometimes called the first Jewish philosopher, also has a palpable discomfort of biblical anthropomorphism. He exhorts his reader "to receive the interpretations [i.e., biblical anthropomorphisms] according to the laws of nature and to grasp the fitting conception of God and not to fall into the mythical and human way of thinking about God."[44] God's descent on Sinai could not be local, "for God is everywhere"—the Torah only portrays God's descent on Sinai in order to show "that the power of fire, which is marvelous beyond all things because it consumes all things, blazes without substance and consumes nothing, unless the power from God (to consume) is added to it."[45] When Aristobulus read the Hebrew Bible, he did so as a Greek-trained philosopher: He, like Philo, really believed that this was what the Hebrew Bible meant. The Torah may have been at the center of their self-understanding as Jews, but it was the Torah as read through the lens of their own Hellenistic culture.

This same tendency is clear in Philo's other writing. As in the Hebrew Bible, Philo attributes free choice to human beings; his anthropology, however, is entirely more pessimistic. The Hebrew Bible makes no real distinction

---

43. Philo, *Allegorical Works* 3.99.

44. Aristobulus, fragment from Eusebius, *Praeparatio Evangelica* 8.10.2 (translation by A. Yarbro Collins in James Charlesworth, ed., *The Old Testament Pseudepigrapha* [Garden City, NY: Doubleday, 1982–1985], II.838).

45. Aristobulus, fragment from Eusebius, *Praeparatio Evangelica* 8.10.15 (II.839).

between a material body and an eternal soul, a binary anthropology widely accepted by ancient Greek philosophers. Philo does. Although his anthropology is not consistent, several times he insists that humans are eternal souls trapped in imperfect bodies. The human's—ultimately unachievable—task is to strive like Moses to elevate, or even free, the soul from its earthly constraints. Pure piety is pure mind. If the ordinary person, or even philosopher, cannot achieve purity, he (for Philo, women were constitutionally unable to do this) can at least work to subdue the body and elevate the soul. One way to develop the mind is through the study of philosophy. Philo reads the Torah's value as containing philosophical truths, unlocked through allegorical interpretation. The Torah's account of creation, for example, is not really about the creation of the world and the drama of Adam and Eve: it is primarily an allegorical statement about the nature of human beings.

Practices

Philo discusses traditional Jewish practices primarily in two ways. First, and somewhat abstractly, he sees the legislation of the Torah as an embodiment of the law of nature. To behave according to the Torah's laws is to behave according to this universal law of nature and thus—in a Stoic sense—to be at one with the world. Simultaneously, Philo holds the laws of the Torah up as being the best and most moral of any nation. Philo ingeniously groups all the laws under the rubric of the Ten Commandments. Each precept, no matter how seemingly random, thus points toward a higher morality. Second, and more concretely, each of the Torah's laws is rational and is given for the good of the individual. Observance of the Torah's laws both inculcates morality and helps the individual to achieve self-perfection.[46]

It is worth pausing here momentarily to reflect on the theoretical ramifications of Philo's stance. Philo has here accepted as powerful and in some sense authoritative a set of practices. His project is in one sense to infuse these practices—stable in and of themselves—with new meaning. Philo's approach is thus reminiscent of the "Myth and Ritual" school which generally argued for the priority of ritual over myth; rather than the myth giving rise to the rituals, the rituals gave rise to a number of myths.[47] Philo similarly accepts the priority of the Torah's commandments but seeks to fit them into his rationalist understanding of the Torah. This is why Philo also insists that understanding how the Torah embodies the law of nature is not enough.

---

46. See Michael L. Satlow, "Philo on Human Perfection," *Journal of Theological Studies* 59.2 (2008): 500–19.

47. See Robert Ackerman, *The Myth and Ritual School: J. G. Frazer and the Cambridge Ritualists* (London: Routledge, 2002).

One must also actually perform the commandments. He thus draws a strong contrast with those (shadowy figures) in his community who come to the opposite conclusion:

> There are some who, regarding laws in their literal sense in the light of symbols of matters belonging to the intellect, are overpunctilious about the latter, while treating the former with easy-going neglect. Such men I for my part should blame for handling the matter in too easy and off-hand a manner: they ought to have given careful attention to both aims, to a more full and exact investigation of what is not seen and what is seen to be steward without reproach ... These men are taught by the sacred word to have thought for good repute, and to let go nothing that is part of the customs fixed by divinely empowered men greater than those of our time. It is quite true that the Seventh Day is meant to teach the power of the Unoriginate and the non-action of created beings. But let us not for this reason abrogate the laws laid down for its observance, and light fires or till the ground or carry loads or institute proceedings in court or act as jurors or demand the restoration of deposits or recover loans or do all else that we are permitted to do as well on days that are not festival seasons.[48]

Philo, unlike the (Jewish?) allegorizers against whom he argues, understands the physical practices, exemplified by those dealing with the Sabbath, to be essential.

This passage raises a more complicated issue about the actual practices performed by Philo's community. Much of Philo's discussion follows the laws as articulated in the Torah and as such it is often unclear if he is referring to practices common in his own community. The passage above serves as a window of sorts. Several of the practices that he mentions concerning the Sabbath do not in fact appear in the Torah (e.g., carrying loads or instituting lawsuits) and so most likely do reflect more common practices.

Yet understanding Judaism as a philosophy never, in the eyes of these Jewish writers, decreased the need for Jews to subscribe to the actual physical behaviors that they saw as commanded by the Torah. Philo insists that allegorical interpretation of the Torah's laws (as he understood them) supplements rather than replaces their literal applicability. Indeed, he rails against those Jewish "allegorizers" who were advocating a strictly allegorical reading of the Torah. If Philo was true to his word, in his own life he was a follower of the commandments. He prescribes a paschal sacrifice, but he suggests that it need not be made at the Temple in Jerusalem. He follows the biblical prohibitions against eating certain kinds of animals, but he seems unaware of any special way of slaughtering the permitted animals or of separating milk from meat products. He nowhere mentions regular prayer

---

48. Philo, *Migration of Abraham* 89-91.

(except on the Sabbath) or phylacteries. He interprets the "Festival of Trumpets" (Rosh Hashanah), as having a twofold significance, symbolizing both the trumpets that sounded at the giving of the Torah on Mount Sinai as well as the trumpets of war—he shows no awareness of this holiday as a New Year festival. He might be reflecting the practice of his own community when he states that Yom Kippur "is carefully observed not only by the zealous for piety and holiness but also by those who never act religiously in the rest of their life."[49] At times Philo can go beyond the letter of the law. He says that the law condemns a prostitute to death, which is nowhere stated in the Torah or the later rabbinic tradition. His treatments of paedophilia and child abandonment draw upon early Jewish extensions of biblical prohibitions. Philo's comments on such matters, and his prescription of draconian penalties, here most likely derive more from his "Judaism" than from what he saw practiced around him.

Conclusion

Through this chapter I have argued for the usefulness of understanding "Judaism" in antiquity not as a stable, self-evident category (systematic or not) but as a polythetic, second-order scholarly abstraction. Philo would not have understood what he was doing as defining "Judaism" but by charting his definition of the *ethnos* of the Jews; his interactions with texts that he thought were authoritative; and his conception and practice of acts that he regarded as "ancestral" and binding, we might arrive at a snapshot—however messy and incomplete—of Philo's approach to what we might call religion.

Philo has often been taken as an exemplar of a larger category labeled "Hellenistic Judaism." This chapter, I hope, can help us to rethink or refine this category. What do we mean here by both "Hellenistic" and "Judaism"? Do we mean the polythetic Judaism of all Jewish communities outside of the Land of Israel? What does "Judaism" without a modifying adjective look like—indeed, is one even possible?[50] Closer attention to these questions, as well as to mapping out the various characteristics of different ancient Jewish communities throughout the Mediterranean basin, could open new questions and lines of research.

Finally, there are broader applications of this argument beyond "Judaism." I do not believe that Judaism is a *sui generis* case. "Christianity," or Roman and Greek "religion," are themselves hardly stable categories and

49. Philo, *The Special Laws* 1.186.
50. See Aryeh Edrei and Doron Mendels, "A Split Jewish Diaspora: Its Dramatic Consequences," *Journal for the Study of the Pseudepigrapha* 16.2 (2007): 91–137.

the members of the latter two in particular do not self-reflect in any extensive way on their own first-order boundaries. An explicitly second-order polythetic approach to all "religions" of the ancient Mediterranean might help us not only to provide a new paradigm for the study of ancient religion but also to do a better and more rigorous job of comparison between different and among different "religions."[51]

Biographical Note

Michael L. Satlow is Professor of Religious Studies and Judaic Studies at Brown University, USA. His research focuses on the social and religious history of Jews and Judaism in antiquity, but he also has broader research interests on Jews and Judaism as well as on issues of method and theory in the study of religion. He is the author of *How the Bible Became Holy* (Yale University Press, 2014), *Creating Judaism: History, Tradition, Practice* (Columbia University Press, 2006), *Jewish Marriage in Antiquity* (Princeton University Press, 2001), *Tasting the Dish: Rabbinic Rhetorics of Sexuality* (Brown Judaic Studies, 1995), and he has edited and coedited *The Gift in Antiquity* (Wiley-Blackwell, 2013) and *Religion and the Self in Antiquity* (with David Brakke and Steven Weitzman; Indiana University Press, 2005).

Bibliography

Ackerman, Robert. *The Myth and Ritual School: J. G. Frazer and the Cambridge Ritualists*. London: Routledge, 2002.

Amir, Yehoshua. "The Term *Ioudaismos*: A Study in Jewish-Hellenistic Self-Identification," *Immanuel* 14 (1972): 34–41.

Arkush, Allan. *Moses Mendelssohn and the Enlightenment*. Albany, NY: State University of New York Press, 1994.

Asad, Talal. *Genealogies of Religion: Discipline and Reasons of Power in Christianity and Islam*. Baltimore, MD: Johns Hopkins University Press, 1993.

Barton, Carlin A., and Daniel Boyarin. *Imagine No Religion: How Modern Abstractions Hide Ancient Realities*. New York: Fordham University Press, 2016.

Birnbaum, Ellen. *The Place of Judaism in Philo's Thought: Israel, Jews, and Proselytes*. Brown Judaic Studies; Atlanta, GA: Scholars Press, 1996.

Boyarin, Daniel. *Border Lines: The Partition of Judaeo-Christianity*. Philadelphia, PA: University of Pennsylvania Press, 2004. https://doi.org/10.9783/9780812203844

—*Judaism: The Genealogy of a Modern Notion*. New Brunswick, NJ: Rutgers University Press, 2019.

---

51. See, e.g., Jonathan Z. Smith, "Prologue: In Comparison a Magic Dwells," in *A Magic Still Dwells: Comparative Religion in the Postmodern Age* (ed. Kimberley C. Patton and Benjamin C. Ray; Berkeley, CA: University of California Press, 2000), 23–46.

Campany, Robert Ford. "On the Very Idea of Religions (in the Modern West and in Early Medieval China)," *History of Religions* 42.4 (2003): 287–319. https://doi.org/10.1086/378757

Charlesworth, James, ed. *The Old Testament Pseudepigrapha*. Garden City, NY: Doubleday, 1983–1985.

Cohen, Shaye J. D. *The Beginnings of Jewishness: Boundaries, Varieties, Uncertainties*. Berkeley, CA: University of California Press, 1999.

Edrei, Aryeh, and Doron Mendels. "A Split Jewish Diaspora: Its Dramatic Consequences," *Journal for the Study of the Pseudepigrapha* 16.2 (2007): 91–137. https://doi.org/10.1177/0951820706074303

Flood, Gavin. *An Introduction to Hinduism*. Cambridge: Cambridge University Press, 1996.

Geertz, Clifford. *The Interpretation of Cultures*. New York: Basic Books, 1973.

Green, William Scott. "Old Habits Die Hard: Judaism in the *Encyclopaedia of Religion*," 8–18 in *The Blackwell Reader in Judaism*. Edited by Jacob Neusner and Alan Avery-Peck. Oxford: Blackwell, 1989.

Hertzberg, Arthur. *The French Enlightenment and the Jews*. New York: Columbia University Press, 1968.

Idel, Moshe. "Abraham Abulafia and the Pope: An Account of an Abortive Mission (Hebrew Section)," *AJS Review* 7–8 (1982–1983): 1–17.

Kaplan, Mordecai M. *Judaism as a Civilization: Toward a Reconstruction of American Jewish Life*. New York: Macmillan, 1934.

Lincoln, Bruce. "Theses on Method," *Method & Theory in the Study of Religion* 17.1 (2005): 8–10. https://doi.org/10.1163/1570068053429910

Mason, Steve. "Jews, Judaeans, Judaizing, Judaism: Problems of Categorization in Ancient History," *Journal for the Study of Judaism* 38.4–5 (2007): 457–512.

Masuzawa, Tomoko. "Culture," 70–93 in *Critical Terms for Religious Studies*. Edited by Mark C. Taylor. Chicago, IL: University of Chicago Press, 1998.

Meyer, Michael A. *Response to Modernity: A History of the Reform Movement in Judaism*. Oxford: Oxford University Press, 1988.

Neusner, Jacob. "Review of Ideas of Jewish History. Edited, with Introduction and Notes, by Michael A. Meyer," *History and Theory* 14.2 (1975): 212–26.

—*The Way of Torah: An Introduction to Judaism*. 5th ed. Belmont, CA: Wadsworth, 1993.

Nongbri, Brent. *Before Religion: A History of a Modern Concept*. New Haven, CT: Yale University Press, 2013. https://doi.org/10.12987/yale/9780300154160.001.0001

Runia, David T. *Philo in Early Christian Literature: A Survey*. Assen: Van Gorcum; and Minneapolis, MN: Fortress Press, 1993.

Sanders, E. P. *Paul and Palestinian Judaism: A Comparison of Patterns of Religion*. Philadelphia, PA: Fortress Press, 1977.

Satlow, Michael L. "Philo on Human Perfection," *Journal of Theological Studies* 59.2 (2008): 500–19. https://doi.org/10.1093/jts/fln089

—"Jew or Judaean?" 165–76 in *The One Who Sows Bountifully: Essays in Honor of Stanley K. Stowers*. Edited by C. J. Hodge, S. M. Olyan, D. Ullucci, and E. Wasserman. Providence, RI: Brown Judaic Studies, 2013.

—*How the Bible Became Holy*. New Haven, CT: Yale University Press, 2014.

Schwartz, Daniel. *Sefer Makabim 2: Mavo, Targum, Perush*. Jerusalem, Israel: Yad Yitshak Ben-Tsevi, 2004.

Schwartz, Seth. *Imperialism and Jewish Society, 200 B.C.E. to 640 C.E.* Princeton, NJ: Princeton University Press, 2001.

Seland, Torrey, ed. *Reading Philo: A Handbook to Philo of Alexandria.* Grand Rapids, MI: William B. Eerdmans, 2014.

Silber, Michael K. "The Emergence of Ultra-Orthodoxy: The Invention of Tradition," 23–84 in *The Uses of Tradition: Jewish Continuity in the Modern Era.* Edited by Jack Wertheimer. New York: Jewish Theological Seminary of America, 1992.

Smith, Jonathan Z. *Imagining Religion: From Babylon to Jonestown.* Chicago, IL: University of Chicago Press, 1982.

—"Prologue: In Comparison a Magic Dwells," 23–46 in *A Magic Still Dwells: Comparative Religion in the Postmodern Age.* Edited by Kimberley C. Patton and Benjamin C. Ray. Berkeley, CA: University of California Press, 2000.

Smith, Wilfred Cantwell. *The Meaning and End of Religion: A New Approach to the Religious Traditions of Mankind.* New York: Macmillan, 1963.

Sorkin, David. *Moses Mendelssohn and the Religious Enlightenment.* Berkeley, CA: University of California Press, 1996.

Sutcliffe, Adam. "Can a Jew be a Philosopher? Isaac de Pinto, Voltaire, and Jewish Participation in the European Enlightenment," *Jewish Social Studies* 6.3 (2000): 31–51. https://doi.org/10.2979/JSS.2000.6.3.31

—*Judaism and Enlightenment.* Cambridge: Cambridge University Press, 2003.

Swidler, Ann. *Talk of Love: How Culture Matters.* Chicago, IL: University of Chicago Press, 2001. https://doi.org/10.7208/chicago/9780226230665.001.0001

Transactions of the Paris Sanhedrim, or Acts of the Assembly of Israelitish Deputies of France and Italy. Translated by Diogène Tama. Lanham, MD: University Press of America, 1985.

Van der Veer, Peter. *Imperial Encounters: Religion and Modernity in India and Britain.* Princeton, NJ: Princeton University Press, 2001.

Whitfield, Stephen J. "Declarations of Independence: American Jewish Culture in the Twentieth Century," 1099–145 in *Cultures of the Jews: A New History, 1099–1146.* Edited by David Biale. New York: Schocken, 2002.

Chapter Thirteen

Religion, Geography, and the Impossibility of Jewish Identity

Sarah Imhoff

In Israel, secular Jews, religious Jews who are also nationalists, religious Jews who abhor nationalism, Ashkenazi Jews, Sephardi Jews, Mizrahi (Middle Eastern) Jews, Ethiopian Jews, and many others all make claims to Jewishness. In the United States, people identify as "half-Jewish" or "Franken-Jews" while others "discover" they are Jewish when a personal DNA testing company tells them part of their heritage is "Ashkenazi Jewish." Contemporary Jewishness, then, holds a number of categories in tension: there is religion, there is race or ethnicity, and there is descent. The question of who, precisely, belongs under the umbrella of Jewishness has also become foregrounded. Who is a Jew: those with two Jewish parents, a Jewish mother, one Jewish parent? Those who convert? Those who participate in religious ritual? And there are other complications. What about, for example, assisted reproductive technologies where descent seems less clear-cut? What constitutes Jewishness there?[1] Each one of these possibilities has many competing answers. Jewishness in today's world is complex, and its borders are shifting.

But while some of these particular forms of Jewishness are modern phenomena, the fuzziness of Jewish identity and Jewish community are not. In fact, the study of Jewish life in antiquity illuminates the contemporary study of Jews and Judaism for precisely this reason. Materials from Jewish life in the Graeco-Roman and Persian worlds show us that a problem that looks like a contemporary one is actually not new. The questions of what it means for a person or a thing to be "Jewish," and what, precisely, the contours of

---

1. For scholars who analyze some of these questions, see Susan M. Kahn, "The Multiple Meanings of Jewish Genes," *Culture, Medicine and Psychiatry* 29 (2005): 179–92, and "Are Genes Jewish?" in *Boundaries of Jewish Identity* (ed. Susan Glenn and Naomi Sokolov; Seattle, WA: University of Washington Press, 2010), 12–26; Nadia Abu El-Haj, *The Genealogical Science* (Chicago, IL: University of Chicago Press, 2012); Sarah Imhoff, "Half Jewish, Just Jewish, and the Oddities of Religious Identity," in *Religion and Identity* (ed. Ronald A. Simkins and Thomas M. Kelly; *Journal of Religion & Society* Supplement 13, 2016), 76–89; Julie Iny, "Ashkenazi Eyes," in *The Flying Camel: Essays on Identity by Women of North African and Middle Eastern Jewish Heritage* (ed. Loolwa Khazzoom; New York: Seal Press, 2003), 81–100.

Jewishness are turn out to be problems not only in the present, but also in antiquity.

Jewishness in antiquity is messy for two related reasons. First, it shifts among our ideas of "religion," "ethnicity," and "nationality," never a perfect fit for any one category. Second, the social borders of who participated in and could make claims to Jewishness are permeable. Jewishness, in this sense, never functioned as an utterly clear-cut binary of Jewish and non-Jewish.

Theory and Terminology

"Race," "ethnicity," and "religion" are all modern categories. They may, at times, be helpful in understanding the distant past, but none existed as an emic category in antiquity. In this way, to ask whether the ancient residents of Judea were a race, an ethnicity, or a religion is a profoundly modern question. One option for scholars, then, would be to refuse to use these categories when analyzing antiquity. Taking this option would imply that since "religion" in the way we understand it now did not exist, and the people living in antiquity would not have recognized it, scholars today would only be misrepresenting the past if they used "religion" to help explain antiquity. But equally, completely refusing to use analytical categories such as "religion" and "race" might mean missing out on cultural, theological, and even political insights into the past.

So, what is a scholar to do? One answer, and the one I have taken up here, is to own up to our own cultural context and embrace it. We are modern scholars with modern categories at our disposal, and we cannot completely abandon our own viewpoints and time-travel to the past. Instead, scholars can pursue both options: analyzing the past using etic modern categories, and also analyzing it as best as possible under the emic terms available from antiquity. To do this well, scholarly self-consciousness is essential. This idea of scholarship from multiple perspectives insists that we ask several kinds of questions. For instance, scholars should ask what we can see if we use religion to think about this group of people, their lives, their sense of belonging and community, and their practices. And then scholars should also ask what we can see when we sideline our ideas about religion and think about them as a national group, or, to use yet another modern category, an "ethnic" group. Then, to take the emic route, scholars must ask: what terms do they use to describe themselves, and how do these categories structure their world?

As part of this strategy to think about the past without an *a priori* commitment to the utility or accuracy of any of these categories, I will often use the term "Jewishness" here. "Jewishness," although neither a perfect nor somehow objective signifier of the past, has the advantage of possessing a modern connotation that can include ethnic and national identity as well as religious identity without forcing us to differentiate among them. If instead, this analysis used "Judaism" as the central idea throughout, it would have been structured on the assumption that religion is what made this people group distinctive. Using "Judeans" as the central term would assume a national or ethnic definition. "Jewishness" refers to the shared culture and sense of identity of the people group without already deciding what category (religious group, ethnic group, national group) they belong to.

Terminology is not merely incidental. In fact, in many ways it structures our knowledge. Many recent debates in ancient Jewish scholarly circles have been about terminology. For instance, scholars have an ongoing debate about whether the Greek *ioudaious* should be translated as "Jews" or "Judeans." Some argue that "Jews" is better because of its religious connotations; others argue that "Judeans" is more appropriate because of its geographic and descent-based connotations. The debate has such staying power—and is also quite muddled at times—because it rotates on several axes: the best or most accurate representation of the past; the creation of ethical representations for the religious present; and often the assumption that we can know the distinctions between ethnic and religious identity. As this debate suggests, terminology has become a major flashpoint that demonstrates the relevance of the study of antiquity for the present.

In this chapter, I will use "Jews" to describe the people who had religious ties to the temple and/or traced their lineage to Judea. But this choice of "Jews" needs an important clarification. I do not think, as some scholars of antiquity have suggested, that the English language term "Jew" necessarily connotes religious identity.[2] The significant cultural presence of today's secular Jews who celebrate their Jewishness suggests otherwise. And even in scholarly circles, the number of books and articles about Jews that never mention religion also shows that, in today's usage, "Jew" does not necessarily imply a connection to Judaism. It is also important to keep in mind that these Jews of antiquity were not like today's Jews. Their self-conceptions, their culture, their religious practices (Judaism, Graeco-Roman traditions, Christianity, or otherwise) were not the same as the self-conceptions, culture, and religious practices of the people we would call Jews today. With

---

2.   For one instance of a scholar who sees "Jew" as a religious term, see Adele Reinhartz, "The Vanishing Jews of Antiquity," in *Jew and Judean: A Marginalia Forum on Politics and Historiography in the Translation of Ancient Texts* (ed. Timothy Michael Law and Charles Halton; 2014, online: http://marginalia.lareviewofbooks.org/vanishing-jews-antiquity-adele-reinhartz/).

this terminological sketch, we can now begin to see the ways that the study of antiquity reflects much of the study of Jewish history—as well as some of the Jewish present.

Historical Narratives of Decline

When historians tell the long tale of Jewish history, they often tell it with an underlying narrative of decline. Heinrich Graetz, in many ways the father of modern Jewish history, presented a lachrymose view of that story, and many historians have followed in his tracks.[3] One component of this generalized decline narrative is what many people now call "Jewish identity." We see this from a variety of ideological camps: traditional and progressive Jews; Jews for and against intermarriage; and Jews optimistic and pessimistic about the future of Jewry. A succinct version from a progressive Jewish author reads:

> For most of Jewish history, peoplehood was straightforward. In most places and most times, Jews retained their separateness in every respect: Economically, linguistically, and socially, they were a distinct people in lands not their own. And this separateness was reinforced by a religion that instructed them that they possessed an exclusive covenant with a deity who favored them above all others. Their nationhood was both sacred and real. Today, all of this is gone.[4]

In short, the narrative arc about Jewishness goes like this: once upon a time, everyone knew who was Jewish and who was not. It assumes that before the modern period, and especially in antiquity, deciding on what it meant to be Jewish and deciding who was Jewish were uncomplicated tasks. These narratives recognize that some people converted, and some Jews occasionally passed as non-Jews, but they assume that the lines between Jew and non-Jew were visible, and everyone agreed on where those lines were.

With modernity, the story takes a turn; then came emancipation and its unfortunate companions, assimilation and intermarriage, and things became more complicated. Some people converted for reasons of social gain or for love. Some Jews married non-Jews, and then some people had one Jewish

---

3.   This is the Jewish historian Salo Baron's ("Ghetto and Emancipation: Shall We Revise the Traditional View?" *The Menorah Journal* 14 [1928]: 515–26) famous characterization of the tendencies of modern Jewish history writing. He referred not only to history-as-decline, but also the tendency to emphasize persecution over everyday life. "Surely it is time to break with the lachrymose theory," he wrote, and move toward more expansive understandings of Jewish life.

4.   Joey Kurtzman, "The End of the Jewish People," 2007, online: http://jewcy. com/jewish-religion-and-beliefs/joey1.

parent and one non-Jewish parent. These individual actions changed the face of Jewish communal identity. They made the borders of the Jewish community permeable and made deciding who is a Jew a thorny matter. Even the eastern European shtetl, characterized as "an impregnable citadel of Jewishness," disappeared.[5] Today's intermarriages, assimilation, and the thorniness of deciding who is a Jew bring this narrative of decline into the present. Thus, Jewish identity became diffuse, partial, mixed—in a word, messy. The stable center of Jewishness was lost.

These popular grand narratives of Jewish history, however, are too simple. During the Inquisition and following, Jews who converted to Christianity existed in a quasi-Jewish, quasi-Christian social and theological limbo. The Church constantly worried that they were "Judaizing," that is, converting and then continuing to practice Judaism in private. Jewish communities rarely required returners to "convert back," which also suggests that they thought that Jewishness was not erased by conversion to Christianity.

Even before the Middle Ages, defining Jewishness and demarcating Jewish life were no easy tasks. When we look at sources from antiquity, we see a complex mix of factors influencing individual and communal identities. And, as this chapter will show, these factors lead to pictures in which the meaning of Jewishness shifted and the lines between Jewish and non-Jewish were not hard and fast.[6] Perhaps most widely known are the complex borders between Judaism and early Christianity. Jewish-Christian synagogues in Palestine in the first two centuries of the common era served as the worship sites for Jews who believed Jesus was the messiah, and, as Annette Yoshiko Reed has explained, "the sources traditionally studied under the rubric of 'Jewish Christianity' shed doubt on any tidy narrative about an unavoidable, mutual, and final split between Christianity and Judaism in the first or second century CE."[7] Other examples abound.

---

5.   See Maurice Samuels, *Little Did I Know* (New York: Knopf, 1963), 137. For a more realistic version of the cultural and literary exchange of shtetl life, see the demonstration of the interconnections of Jewish and non-Jewish literatures by Amelia Glaser, *Jews and Ukrainians in Russia's Literary Borderlands: From the Shtetl Fair to the Petersburg Bookshop* (Evanston, IL: Northwestern University Press, 2016).

6.   The study of Jewish antiquity has also recently recognized that there was no single, homogenous, monolithic Judaism, but rather a diversity of Jewish lives. See, e.g., Sian Jones, "Identities in Practice: Towards an Archaeological Perspective on Jewish Identity in Antiquity," in *Jewish Local Patriotism and Self-Identification in the Graeco-Roman Period* (ed. Sian Jones and Sarah Pierce; Sheffield, UK: Sheffield Academic Press, 1998), 29–49.

7.   Annette Yoshiko Reed, "'Jewish Christianity' after 'The Parting of the Ways': Approaches to Historiography and Self-Definition in the Pseudo-Clementines," in *The Ways That Never Parted: Jews and Christians in Late Antiquity and the Early Middle*

Rabbinic sources, for instance, refer to the *yirei shamaim* (god-fearers) who were non-Jews who nevertheless worshipped the Jewish god and lived with Jewish communities.[8] Jewishness had elements of descent, of birthplace, and of ritual, but which of those was the central defining characteristic of Jewishness shifted continually and according to cultural context.

Despite these historical accounts, however, the decline story's general plot line from certainty about Jewishness to uncertainty and characters persists in both popular and academic accounts of Jewish history and sociology.[9] Why might scholars cling to this specious narrative? Jewish Studies scholars might valorize certainty and stability of Jewishness for a variety of reasons—the analytical appeal of certainty, a holdover from the centrality of objectivity to the nineteenth-century origins of Jewish Studies called *Wissenschaft des Judentums* ("the science of Judaism"), or even a theological desire for clarity about who is a Jew. Whatever the reasons, the narrative of decline persists.

However, abandoning the romantic notion that in antiquity Jewishness was clear, obvious, and apparent helps the broader picture of Jewish Studies scholarship. A close and careful look at antiquity demonstrates that the perception of modernity as a watershed with respect to the messiness of Jewish identity is a false one. If we abandon the decline narratives, we may see a richer Jewish past, as well as gain a better perspective on the complex Jewish present.

The Shape of Jewishness in Late Antiquity

Jewishness in antiquity developed in different times, places, and cultures, and so historical generalizing becomes a difficult task. Jews in first-century BCE Palestine did not live the same Jewishness as Jews in fifth-century BCE Babylonia or even first-century CE Alexandria. Rather than attempting to describe broadly, then, this chapter will offer several key examples from different historical locations—specifically, Greek, Roman, and

Ages (ed. Adam Becker and Annette Yoshiko Reed; Minneapolis, MN: Fortress Press, 2007), 191.

8.   See Joyce M. Reynolds and Robert Tanenbaum, *Jews and God-Fearers at Aphrodisias: Greek Inscriptions with Commentary* (Cambridge: Cambridge Philosophical Society, 1987); Emil Schurer, *The History of the Jewish People in the Age of Christ* (Edinburgh, UK: T&T Clark, 1987); L. Michael White, "The Delos Synagogue Revisited: Recent Fieldwork in the Graeco-Roman Diaspora," *Harvard Theological Review* 80 (1987): 133–60.

9.   See Steven M. Cohen and Jack Wertheimer, "Whatever Happened to the Jewish People?" *Commentary* 121 (2006): 33–7.

Persian cultures, the three major centers of late ancient Jewish life. These examples by no means create a comprehensive narrative of the development of ancient Jewish life. Yet together, the evidence disrupts the historical decline narrative by showing that Jewishness was a messy and porous category in each historical location.

Despite the difficulty of cross-cultural generalization, a few observations can be helpful to provide some historical grounding. First, ancient writings almost never used the word "Judaism." They used words to talk about Jewish people: the Hebrew *yehudim* and the Greek *ioudaioi*, most commonly. But as Brent Nongbri and others have argued, the ancient world did not quite have a thing called "Judaism."[10] The Greek word *Ioudaismos*, sometimes translated as "Judaism," might better be translated as "Jewishness" because of its broad connotations including both those traits we would consider religious as well as those we would consider ethnic. *Yahadut*, the Hebrew word for Judaism, does not appear in the Hebrew Bible at all, and only very seldom appears in other ancient texts.[11] The religion practiced by fourth- and fifth-century BCE Jews of Elephantine in Egypt included Passover, Sabbath observance, and temple sacrifice—but, seemingly unaware of deuteronomic prohibitions against other sites of sacrifice, they had their own temple![12] Communities like that of Elephantine suggest that even if there were a "Judaism" in antiquity, it would be vastly diverse and multiple.

Second, despite what reading rabbinic sources might imply, Jewish leadership was not concentrated solely in the religiously learned circles of the Rabbis. In fact, most scholars now agree that the Rabbis were relatively marginal figures, especially in Graeco-Roman societies. They never had the religious or cultural authority to dictate popular practices or institute sweeping change. And so, while these texts remain valuable resources, scholars cannot take rabbinic texts as objective reports of the history of the Jews, or as representative of all Jews of the time.

Third, and contrary to many older Jewish histories, Jews participated in a shared culture with their non-Jewish neighbors. Nor were Greek, Roman, or Sassanian rule characterized entirely by persecution, as some older histories imply. The story of Jewishness in antiquity, then, is largely a story of

10. See Brent Nongbri, *Before Religion: The History of a Modern Concept* (New Haven, CT: Yale University Press, 2013), 2.

11. See Daniel Schwartz, "Doing Like Jews or Becoming a Jew? Josephus on Women Converts to Judaism," in *Jewish Identity in the Greco-Roman World* (ed. Jörg Frey, Daniel Schwartz, and Stephanie Gripentrog; Leiden: Brill, 2007), 93.

12. See Bezalel Porten and Ada Yardeni, eds., *Textbook of Aramaic Documents from Ancient Egypt Newly Copied, Edited and Translated into Hebrew and English* (Vols. 1–4; Jerusalem: Hebrew University Press, 1986–1999).

interchange, contact, and cultural specificity rather than uniformity across time and space.

From archaeological and textual evidence, historians tend to think of Jewish life in historical periods as being demarcated by who ruled Jerusalem and the surrounding area. The Babylonian army conquered the city and destroyed the First Temple in 586 BCE, taking part of the population into exile. Some of the exiled population began to return around 538 BCE following the Edict of the Persian king Cyrus, and began the long period of reconstruction and rededication of a Second Temple. Then came a series of historical periods: the Post-Exilic (538–332 BCE); the Hellenistic (332–142 BCE); the Hasmonean (142 BCE–63 CE) which was punctuated by the Maccabaean revolt; and the Roman (63–476 CE).[13] During these times, Jews moved into and out of Judea, and settled in many other places. Many Jews went to Babylonia (modern day Iraq); others settled in a variety of Graeco-Roman cities in the region. Running parallel to this periodization is the periodization of rabbinic texts, including the religiously central Mishnah (c. 200 CE) and the Babylonian Talmud (sixth or seventh century CE). The corpus of rabbinic texts, authored and redacted from roughly the second to the seventh century CE, came from two main centers: Palestine and Babylonia. Thus, while a linear story marked by periodization is helpful for heuristic purposes, its focus on the changing rule over Jerusalem does not tell the whole story of ancient Jewish life.

Each of the cultural moments gathered here will give an all-too-brief snapshot of ancient Jewish life. But together these snapshots will also show a wider conclusion: Jewishness in antiquity was characterized by permeable borders, shifting identities, and cultural sharing. It was not, as many modern historians have liked to imagine, a time of certainty or bright, clear lines around the idea of Jewishness.

The Graeco-Roman Jewish world, sometimes also characterized as "Hellenistic Judaism," is relatively well documented. Philo of Alexandria (20 BCE–40 CE) wrote a series of biblical retellings and commentaries, philosophical treaties, and historical writings.[14] The vast writings of Flavius Josephus, (37–c.100 CE), have provided scholars with a significant source of Graeco-Roman Jewish data in particular, as well as a huge amount of data for antiquity more generally. The Roman-Jewish historian's multi-volume works *The Jewish War* and *Antiquities of the Jews* seem to have

---

13. These dates are heuristic rather than definitive. Some of these particular dates are a matter of debate in the historiography, but these conversations are beyond the scope of this essay.

14. For more on Philo, see Chapter Twelve, this volume.

been considered significant at the time, and later became essential for understanding both Jewish and early Christian histories.

Although Josephus's main concern was to present historical narratives, he also conveyed information about Jewish life and thought in his own moment. Around 100 CE, Josephus wrote a text to counter the critique of the grammarian Apion, who had accused Jewish culture and religious practice of newness, derivativeness, and inferiority to Greek culture, philosophy, and practices. In *Against Apion*, Josephus wrote:

> [T]o all who desire to come and live under the same laws with us, [Moses] gives a gracious welcome, holding that it is not family ties alone which constitute relationship, but agreement in the principles of conduct. On the other hand, it was not his pleasure that casual visitors should be admitted to the intimacies of our daily life.[15]

Later in the text, he explained succinctly: "while we have no desire to emulate the customs of others, yet gladly welcome any who wish to share our own."[16] While these statements did not play a critical role in Josephus's defense of "the antiquity of our nation,"[17] they did demonstrate something about Jewishness in his own cultural context. For instance, Josephus assumed the possibility of conversion—or at least the possibility of newcomers joining the community. And what is more, the text suggested the possibility of cohabitators who came and participated in Jewish communal customs and rituals perhaps without formal conversion. Josephus claimed that descent is not the only criterion for Jewishness, a statement he puts in the mouth of Moses, whose word carries great religious authority. Beyond descent, Josephus argued, it was "agreement in the principles of conduct"— or more specifically, practices and the principles that underlie those practices—that is the crucial defining characteristic of Jewishness.

Even in the texts of Josephus, who set out to explain and defend the history of the Jews, the concept of Jewishness shifts and the boundaries of the community are porous. To use modern categories, Josephus portrays Jewishness as both nation (where "nation" is defined by geography, descent, and peoplehood) and religion (where "religion" is defined by personal choice of community, practices, and philosophical principles). Not only does the definition of Jewishness shift among concepts of nation, ethnicity, and religion, but it is also clear that the borders of the community were porous, perhaps even with various shades of belonging.

This Jewish embeddedness in Graeco-Roman culture and ideas ranges

15. Josephus, *Against Apion* 2.210 (translation LCL).
16. Josephus, *Against Apion* 2.261.
17. Josephus, *Against Apion* 1.2.

far beyond Josephus. Well-known texts include the *Letter of Aristeas*, which predates Josephus and carves out a social and intellectual space for Jews *as* Greeks. It does so in the context of its larger narrative about the Septuagint—a Greek translation of the Hebrew Bible. The philosophical tracts of Philo of Alexandria also present Jewish traditions as part of the Greek philosophical tradition.

Surviving evidence of the shape of Jewishness in Hellenistic context also includes more enigmatic texts, such as the *Third Sibylline Oracle*. The oracle is a combination of Graeco-Roman and Jewish stories, includes Greek and Jewish modes of cultural authorization, and suggests a largely but not exclusively Jewish audience. There is a general scholarly consensus that it is one of the earliest such oracles, and that it was written by members of the Jewish community in Egypt.[18] But dating is still a matter of controversy, which is further complicated by the fact that various portions show evidence of having been composed at different times.

Even without a firm date, however, the *Third Sibylline Oracle* demonstrates the fluidity of Jewishness and its interconnection with Graeco-Roman cultures. Its very form combines elements of Jewish and Hellenistic cultures: the Sibyl is Jewish, but her speech appears in Homeric hexameters.[19] The Sibyl also uses both cultures to claim authority: she presents herself as a Hellenic prophetess as well as the daughter-in-law of the biblical Noah. Her content, too, combines both Jewish and Greek mythical events, without demarcating them apart from one another. For instance, the Sybil forecasts both the fall of Troy and the Exodus from Egypt. And perhaps most crucially, the Sybil asserts that Jewishness (or at least some aspects of it) is available to non-Jews. "Greeks who show themselves worthy are invited to partake of the values of the Jews," as Erich Gruen explains.[20]

Perhaps this seeming syncretism should make scholars question how Jewish the Jews of Alexandria were. If they spoke Greek, heard prophecy in a Greek form, and mixed Greek mythological and historical content with Jewish ("their own" content), then perhaps they were not very Jewish at all.

18. As Sylvie Honigman ("The Birth of a Diaspora: The Emergence of a Jewish Self-Definition in Ptolemaic Egypt in the Light of Onomastics," in *Diasporas in Antiquity* [ed. Shaye J. D. Cohen and Ernest S. Frerichs; Atlanta, GA: Scholars Press,1993], 93–127) demonstrates, Jews in Egypt had a long history of shared culture and political position as Greeks.

19. See Erich S. Gruen, "Jews, Greeks, and Romans in the Third Sibylline Oracle," in *Jews in a Graeco-Roman World* (ed. Martin Goodman; Oxford: Oxford University Press, 1998), 35.

20. Erich S. Gruen, *Heritage and Hellenism: The Reinvention of Jewish Tradition* (Berkeley, CA: University of California Press, 1998), 290.

This kind of critique was part of what fueled the well-known Maccabean revolt of many years earlier (167–160 BCE): Jews were being too Greek, and not Jewish enough. But, of course, for scholars to ask "how Jewish" the community around the Sibyl was entails having an *a priori* set of metrics for measuring Jewishness. And these metrics tend to be modern and dependent on modern categories such as religion and nationhood. In this sense, questioning how Jewish the Jews of Alexandria were amounts to a normative evaluation of ancient peoples using contemporary criteria, and is thus not a helpful scholarly path.

The *Third Sibylline Oracle* is, in some ways, an enigma. One scholar calls it "a mass of confused material."[21] But in other ways, it is not. Part of the reason it appears to us as an enigma, or confused material, is because of modern ideas about the separation of Judaism, Christianity, and Greek traditions as religions, and our assumptions about the separation of cultures. If we are no longer committed to thinking of Jewishness and Hellenism as representing two separate religions, and two distinct cultures, the Sybil becomes less an enigma and more an artifact of cultural and religious complexity. As Tessa Rajak notes, "Greek culture was deeply entwined with Jewish life from the early Hellenistic period to an extent where contemporaries were not themselves wholly aware of the strands."[22]

A third piece of evidence from the Graeco-Roman world has generated a robust scholarly discussion. This literature examines the *yirei shamayim* or "god-fearers"—people who did not halakhically convert to Judaism, but participated in Jewish community and performed Jewish rituals to varying degrees. These fellow-travelers most famously appear in the New Testament, but they also appear in rabbinic literature. There is also supporting textual evidence from Graeco-Roman writers, Philo, Josephus, and Christian Church Fathers, as well as inscriptions.[23] Yet scholars disagree about whether god-fearers existed, and how numerically significant they might have been.[24]

One of the strongest material examples is a third-century inscription from Aphrodisias that refers to Jews, converts, and "sympathizers." Such a

21.   Raymond Surburg, *Introduction to the Intertestamental Period* (St. Louis, MO: Concordia, 1975), 147.

22.   Tessa Rajak, *The Jewish Dialogue with Greece and Rome: Studies in Cultural and Social Interaction* (Leiden: Brill, 2002), 4.

23.   See Louis H. Feldman and Gōhei Hata, eds., *Josephus, the Bible, and History* (Leiden: Brill, 1989), 416.

24.   See Robert MacLennan and A. Thomas Kraabel, "The God-Fearers: A Literary and Theological Invention," *Biblical Archaeology Review* 12.5 (1986): 46–53; Louis H. Feldman, "The Omnipresence of the God-Fearers," *Biblical Archaeology Review* 12.5 (1986): 58–69.

three-fold typology strongly implies a version of Jewishness that has multiple layers and porous boundaries. It suggests communities that have people who identify with Jewishness from birth or because of descent, people who have chosen to adopt Jewishness officially, and those who engage in Jewishness voluntarily. And perhaps even these categories were not entirely differentiable. If "Jew" was a different category from "convert," then was descent (or a modern notion of ethnicity) an integral part of this Jewishness? What were the lines between the convert and the sympathizer?

And must conversion match up with modern notions of religious conversion? As historian Jason BeDuhn argues, "[t]here existed, even before the emergence of 'religions', something akin and antecedent to conversion in the voluntary act of joining another ethnicity." Like the tradition of the biblical Ruth, a person could move to another land and join their ethnicity. "But in the cosmopolitan conditions of the Hellenistic and Roman periods, different ethnicities found themselves juxtaposed in urban areas, and people could be attracted to a 'foreign' enclave right outside their door."[25] The inscription and presence of the *yirei shamayim* would demonstrate both the multi-focal meanings of Jewishness (in ways that both do and do not line up with the modern categories of the "ethnic," "religious," and "national") as well as the openness of the borders of the Jewish community. Here we connect back to the Jew/Judean debate: Daniel Schwartz suggests that scholars simply translate *ioudaios* as "Jew" when they are talking about religion and "Judean" when they are talking about birth or residence because "it should not be too difficult to decide which [Jew or Judean] to use in which context."[26] However, as these examples show, the difficulty is significant. The discussions of *yirei shamayim* demonstrate that it is not always easy or possible to decide between religion and descent, or religion and ethnicity.

Other scholars argue that there were really no such things as *yirei shamayim*, and that the category was a rhetorical invention of the writers of the gospels.[27] These scholars note that there is not much archaeological evidence for the presence of god-fearers in the synagogues of the Graeco-Roman world. This opens a far longer scholarly discussion, but here it is

---

25. Jason Beduhn, "Mani and the Crystallization of the Concept of 'Religion' in Third Century Iran," in *Mani at the Court of the Persian Kings: Studies on the Chester Beatty Kephalaia Codex* (ed. Iain Gardner, Jason BeDuhn, and Paul Dilley; Leiden: Brill, 2014), 252.

26. Daniel Schwartz, "The Different Tasks of Translators and Historians," *Marginalia Forum* 18 (2014), online: https://marginalia.lareviewofbooks.org/different-tasks-translators-historians-daniel-r-schwartz/.

27. E.g., see A. Thomas Kraabel, "The Disappearance of the 'God-Fearers'," *Numen* 28.2 (1981): 113–26; MacLennan and Kraaber, "The God-Fearers."

at least worth noting that a lack of archaeological evidence is not in itself proof that there were no god-fearers.

In the end, perhaps what is most important is that the writers of both the New Testament and rabbinic literature saw a world in which these god-fearing border figures—sort of Jewish and sort of not—occupied a plausible position. They did not think that the borders of Jewishness were clear and fixed, or that Jewishness was a binary category. Some, such as some early Christians, wanted the borders between people groups to be more fixed and better defined.[28] And yet most seemed to recognize that that was not the reality on the ground.

Jewish life in the Roman world shared many features with Hellenistic Jewish life, and the scholarly literature often groups these together as Jewish life in the Graeco-Roman world. While there were many historical and social differences, the evidence suggests that Jewishness in ancient Roman contexts was much like Jewishness in ancient Greek contexts: porous, interactive with other cultures, and never a precise or easy fit with modern categories of "religion," "ethnicity," or "nationhood."

A branch of Jews called the Essenes, the group most commonly associated with the Dead Sea Scrolls, left one document of particular interest for considering Jewishness in the Roman context. The Damascus Document (CD) lists the *ger* (usually translated as "convert") separately. It lists the people in the community: "the priests first, the Levites second, the sons of Israel third, the *gerim* fourth."[29] CD, like many Essene documents, has an interest in orderliness and division. It seems to offer little option for mobility among social categories; once a *ger*, always a *ger*, it implies. CD seems to offer a model of Jewishness that is strongly ethnic, in the sense that one can join the community but never quite become the same as a born member.

Scholars have often read it this way, but it also offers additional possibilities. Daniel Schwartz reads the line between the *ger* and the rest of the members as a hard and fast line: "However welcome it might be that non-Israelites undertake to worship the Jewish God, and therefore associate themselves with a Jewish community, that cannot make them into Israelites, any more than cats can become dogs, even if they learn to bark."[30] In

---

28. See Daniel Boyarin, *Borderlines: The Partition of Judeo-Christianity* (Philadelphia, PA: University of Pennsylvania Press, 2004); Isabella Sandwell, *Religious Identity in Late Antiquity: Greeks, Jews, and Christians in Antioch* (Cambridge: Cambridge University Press, 2011).

29. Damascus Document 14.3-6. On the CD (and its limitations), see Maxine L. Grossman, *Reading for History in the Damascus Document: A Methodological Study* (Leiden: Brill, 2009).

30. Schwartz, "Doing Like Jews," 24.

one sense, this is true. But in another sense, it opens up another reading: to continue with Schwartz's metaphor, it would change our conception of dog-ness if cats could bark. The boundaries of dog-ness would be less obvious, its characteristics less distinctive. And here the presence of *gerim* along-side different kinds of Jews similarly suggests that Jewishness cannot be reduced to the simple binary Jew/non-Jew.

Furthermore, CD demonstrates that even the sect that was considered the most religiously strict—the Essenes—had in practice a Jewishness with somewhat porous borders. They were the strictest, and they had the stron-gest sense of belonging as a matter of descent (in modern terms, we might say that they most closely associated "Jewish ethnicity" with "Jewish reli-gion"). But as CD makes clear, even the sectarians had varying levels of adjacent membership and belonging.[31]

And the sectarians at Qumran were an extreme case. What holds for them holds all the more so for Jewishness in other Roman cities. Scholars have shown this in a variety of ways. To take a range of examples from across the Graeco-Roman world, Benjamin Isaac uses Eusebius's *Onomasticon* to argue that most Roman and Byzantine cities had mixed populations—Jews, Christians, and pagans.[32] Legal language, from marriage to inheritance to business contracts, also shows a shared culture. Hannah Cotton remarks on the difficulty of defining what, exactly, makes a legal contract a Jewish legal contract: "What makes a contract Jewish is not its language, content, or par-ticular ingredients."[33] Ultimately, Cotton decides to call things Jewish only if this is later reflected in halakhic sources. Because there is no helpful criterion for deciding the Jewishness of a contract from its own historical time, Cotton relies on a retrospective metric, that is, whether or not later tradition would call it Jewish. Burial practices, inscriptions, and catacombs also show simi-lar integration.[34] Many Jewish cities in the Graeco-Roman world used coins with Graeco-Roman figures. Similarly, Jewish cities, such as Tiberias, Sep-phoris, lower Galilee, and even Beth Shearim show almost no discernable distinctive archaeological signs of Jewishness.[35] In addition to the permeable

---

31. See Alison Schofield, *From Qumran to the Yahad: A New Paradigm of Textual Development for The Community Rule* (Leiden: Brill, 2008).

32. See Benjamin Isaac, "Jews, Christians, and others in Palestine: The Evidence from Euseubius," in Goodman, ed., *Jews in a Graeco-Roman World*, 66.

33. Hannah M. Cotton, "The Rabbis and the Documents," in Goodman, ed., *Jews in a Graeco-Roman World*, 171.

34. Cotton, "Rabbis and the Documents," 171; cf. Leonard V. Rutgers, *The Jews in Late Ancient Rome: Evidence of Cultural Interaction in the Roman Diaspora* (Leiden: Brill, 1995).

35. See Jones, "Identities in Practice," 35.

social and legal boundaries of Jewish culture, Jewishness in Roman Palestine also confounds easy applications of modern identity categories. Studies that mix textual and archaeological evidence, such as Cynthia Baker's, also show that Jewishness is a shifting mix, wherein people "participated in negotiations of gender, class, ethnicity, and 'nation'."[36]

Even rabbinic texts (ranging roughly from the second to the seventh century CE), which frequently represent the world in binary Jewish-non-Jewish ways, contain evidence of the social mores and assumptions that Jews shared with their neighbors. For example, Jews in Roman Palestine shared a construction of sexuality with their Roman counterparts far more than their Jewish counterparts in Babylonia. In Michael Satlow's words, the Palestinian rabbis' "fundamental way of thinking at least about sexuality is virtually identical to those whom they label the 'other'."[37] In fact, as Daniel Boyarin and Virginia Burrus argue, it is often the places where people stress purity and religious difference that most reflect mixed and hybrid identities.[38] Rabbinic literature is one of these places.

The rabbis were not the dominant and far-reaching religious authorities one might assume from rabbinic texts. In legal and cultural matters, these rabbis were on the margins. Legal and political power rested with the Roman state and local officials, and as historian Seth Schwartz explains, "the cultural norms, even in the countryside, were overwhelmingly set by the elites of the Palestinian cities ... These norms were pervaded by pagan religiosity and were basically shared by imperial Greek cities generally."[39] Thus the common cultural norms of Jewishness shared much of their basis with Greek culture.

Unlike rabbinic texts, which largely offer views of a world divided between Jews and non-Jews, other evidence strongly suggests that the lines between Jews and non-Jews, as well as Jewish culture and Roman culture, were often indistinct and permeable. Seth Schwartz writes that Jews adopted "important elements of the common urban culture of the Roman east, suffused though this culture was with Greek, Roman, and Greco-Semitic religion."[40] The

36. Cynthia Baker, *Rebuilding the House of Israel: Architectures of Gender in Jewish Antiquity* (Stanford, CA: Stanford University Press, 2002), 4.

37. Michael L. Satlow, "Romans and Rabbis on Sex," in Goodman, ed., *Jews in a Graeco-Roman World*, 143.

38. See Daniel Boyarin and Virginia Burrus, "Hybridity as Subversion of Orthodoxy? Jews and Christians in Late Antiquity," *Social Compass* 52.4 (2005): 431–41.

39. Seth Schwartz, *Imperialism and Jewish Society, 200 B.C.E. to 640 C.E.* (Princeton, NJ: Princeton University Press, 2001), 104.

40. Schwartz, *Imperialism and Jewish Society*, 142.

archaeological evidence shows mixes of Graeco-Roman and Jewish elements in iconography in Palestinian synagogues.

In the fourth century, this picture changed. As the Roman Empire came under Christian rule, Jews were recognized as a group with a distinctive kind of otherness. Whereas before Jews were not specially singled out, as Christianity became the official creed and practice of the Empire, many Christians sought to emphasize the borders between Judaism and Christianity. This differentiation pushed the development of a more distinctive Jewish community.

And yet, even with Christian rule, Jewishness did not become utterly clear, distinct, and separate. For instance, John Chrysostom complained about Christians going to synagogues in general, and he was particularly appalled that Christians went to a synagogue in Daphne: "I have heard that many of the faithful go up to sleep beside the place."[41] Christians who should have rejected the synagogue continued to engage in Jewish rituals. Later, Roman Emperors would prohibit Jews converting their slaves to Judaism.[42] Here we see objection to what has probably long been going on. It creates weird boundaries, such as slaves who probably followed many of the customs of the household but were not officially converted. (And what it means for women converts is even fuzzier, and we know there were women converts.)[43] These brief Roman examples, like the Greek ones, demonstrate that Jewishness had elements of both what we might think of as "religion" and "ethnicity," as well as permeable borders for those who would identify with the Jewish community.

Persia, like the Graeco-Roman world, was the site of Jewish life across many centuries. The "Persian period," when Yehud was a colony of Aramaic-speaking Persian Empire, stretched from 538 BCE (with Cyrus's decree of return) to 323 BCE (Alexander's conquest of the Persian Empire). Many centuries later, the Sassanian Persian Empire was the context for the compilation of the Babylonian Talmud. These Jewish communities remained in contact with Jewish communities elsewhere, and so there were shared traditions, and even many instances of one community writing about another.

41. See A. D. Lee, *Christians and Pagans in Late Antiquity: A Sourcebook* (London: Routledge, 2016), 165–6.

42. See Peter Schaefer, *History of the Jews in Antiquity* (London: Routledge, 1995), 178.

43. See Margaret H. Williams, *The Jews Among the Greeks and Romans: A Diasporic Sourcebook* (Baltimore, MD: Johns Hopkins University Press, 1998), 172; Lee, *Christians and Pagans*, 166–7; Louis H. Feldman, "Proselytism by Jews in the Third, Fourth and Fifth Centuries," *Journal for the Study of Judaism in the Persian, Hellenistic, and Roman Period* 24 (1993): 1–58; Martin Goodman, "Jewish Proselytizing in the First Century," in *The Jews Among Pagans and Christians in the Roman Empire* (ed. Judith Lieu, John North, and Tessa Rajak; London: Routledge, 1992), 53–79.

A few texts written outside of Persia tell stories of Jewish life there, and these reflect a porous Jewishness. The story of the first-century Queen Helena of Adiabene suggests both the interaction of Jewish and non-Jewish cultures, but also the interpenetrating nature of our modern categories of ethnicity and religion in the Persian context. Helena and her family were likely Iranian, Zoroastrian, or Magian, but she embraced Jewishness as an adult. Stories about Queen Helena, her husband King Monobaz, and her son Izates appear in several places: in Josephus, in the Talmud and Tosefta, and in religious historians of later antiquity.

Josephus wrote that Queen Helena and Izates "changed their course of life, and embraced the Jewish customs."[44] They heard about the Jewish god, desired to worship him, learned about Jewish practices, and even monetarily supported the temple. If modern scholars approach this episode under the framework of "religion," then this seems fairly straightforward: Helena and Izates converted to Judaism.

However, it is also clear from the ancient texts that their own subjects thought that Helena and her family had abandoned their own culture and *ethnos*.[45] For these ancients, the idea of following Jewish law and worshiping the Jewish god was inseparable from the idea of *ethnos*—a concept encompassing, among other things, common ancestors and common customs.[46] When Josephus explained that Helena and Izates abandoned their own culture to embrace "foreign customs," he meant that their former subjects saw them as foreign both in the sense of *strange* and in the sense of *from a different place*. Helena and Izates traded not only their beliefs and practices (what we might call "religion"), but also their place and peoplehood (what we might call "ethnicity"). And yet neither modern category works perfectly. The ancient idea of *ethnos* is not identical with the modern ethnicity, which scholars argue has a strong component of elective affiliation.[47]

Josephus's telling of the episode—which admittedly may well tell us as much about Josephus's culture as about Persian culture—also suggests other complex Jewish identifications. At least two men, according to the text, convinced non-Jews to engage in worship of the Jewish god. A Jewish merchant named Ananias spread Jewish customs. According to Josephus, he

44. Josephus, *Antiquities of the Jews* 20.2.1. Queen Helena also appears in rabbinic literature, such as BT Baba Bathra 11a.

45. See Beduhn, "Concept of 'Religion'," 252.

46. For more on ancient conceptions of *ethnos*, see Jonathan Hall, *Ethnic Identity in Greek Antiquity* (Cambridge: Cambridge University Press, 1997).

47. For this contemporary sense of voluntary components of ethnicity, see, for instance, David Hollinger, *Post-Ethnic America: Beyond Multiculturalism* (New York: Basic Books, 1995).

got among the women that belonged to the king, and taught them to worship God according to the Jewish religion. He, moreover, by their means, became known to Izates, and persuaded him, in like manner, to embrace that religion; he also, at the earnest entreaty of Izates, accompanied him when he was sent for by his father to come to Adiabene; it also happened that Helena, about the same time, was instructed by a certain other Jew and went over to them.[48]

There is no indication of the formal conversion of the women. And Izates also did not convert according to law, at least at first: "[H]e said that he might worship God without being circumcised, even though he did resolve to follow the Jewish law entirely, which worship of God was of a superior nature to circumcision."[49] Here we have stories of the rulers Helena and Izates, as well as other women in the court, joining Jews in worshiping the Jewish god. Formal conversion happened in some cases, but Jewishness was not strictly confined to the terms of Jewish law. Jews invited, and even convinced, non-Jews to join in their religious practices. If Josephus's stories reflect something of Persian society, they strongly suggest the permeability of Jewish community.

Especially in the years following the destruction of the Second Temple (70 CE), Babylonia became an increasingly important center of Jewish life. The Babylonian Talmud, arguably the textual centerpiece of today's Judaism, was redacted there. Rabbinic leaders passed down what would become Talmudic traditions orally, compiled and redacted them over several centuries. Apart from rabbinic sources, other Jewish writings from Babylonia in the early common era are nearly nonexistent. And so, scholars have turned to these rabbinic texts in order to try to reconstruct history. And these rabbinic texts are (sort of) reconstructed conversations among rabbis, and seem to include few other voices. The picture they paint of Jewish life is one firmly structured by *halakhah* or "Jewish law" and clearly differentiated from non-Jewish life.

Traditionally, many scholars have argued that Jewish life was characterized by disengagement from surrounding communities.[50] Rabbinic literature can often give this impression. It was written by Jews for Jews. It addresses Jews in an environment that contains non-Jews, but it never addresses non-Jews. It seems to represent an insular Jewish world. More recently, however, these assumptions have been challenged.[51] As Naomi Janowitz writes, "[g]one are the days when Josephus' neat template of sects or the rabbis'

---

48. Josephus, *Antiquities* 20.2.3.

49. Josephus, *Antiquities* 20.2.4.

50. See Arnaldo Momigliano, "Review of *The Jews of Ancient Rome* by Harry J. Leon," *Gnomon* 34.2 (1962): 179–80.

51. For responses, see Leonard V. Rutgers, "Archaeological Evidence for the

narrow gaze supplied the rubric for conceptualizing late antique Judaism."[52] Much of the evidence giving the picture of an insular Jewish community in Babylonia comes from rabbinic texts. But the social location of these texts is quite specific, and scholars have come to agree that rabbinic materials do not directly reflect the everyday lives of most Jews.[53] There is a growing recognition that rabbinic literature was written by an upper crust of religious authorities who created a world through creation of a text, but the text was not necessarily a historically accurate version of their world. It was ideological, not purely descriptive. And these rabbis did not hold nearly as much social power as one might assume from reading their texts. They were, instead, rather marginal.

And yet, because of the paucity of non-rabbinic Jewish textual materials in the Persian context, many scholars have long allowed the rabbinic materials to speak for themselves, as if they presented accurate, rather than ideological, historical descriptions. However, there has recently been a move to consider the Babylonian Talmud in its Sassanian context.[54] As scholars begin to look at textual materials in Persian, material evidence such as the Aramaic bowls (which have Zoroastrian or other non-Jewish rituals or incantations written in Aramaic), and other evidence, it seems likely that they will also show that the borders of Jewishness in Sassanian Persia were porous.

Conclusion

This brief series of examples from Jewish antiquity demonstrate that the boundaries of Jewishness were fuzzy even in antiquity, and therefore

Interaction of Jews and Non-Jews in Late Antiquity," *American Journal of Archaeology* 96.1 (1992): 101–18.

52. Naomi Janowitz, "Rethinking Jewish Identity in Late Antiquity," in *Ethnicity and Culture in Late Antiquity* (ed. Stephen Mitchell and Geoffrey Greatrex; London: Duckworth, 2000), 205.

53. Jonathan Pomerantz, "Ordinary Jews in the Babylonian Talmud: Rabbinic Representations and Historical Interpretation" (PhD dissertation, Yale University, 2016) makes the case for using the Babylonian Talmud to find traces of the rabbis' connections to non-elite Jews.

54. See, e.g., Yaakov Elman, "Middle Persian Culture and Babylonian Sages: Accommodation and Resistance in the Shaping of Rabbinic Legal Traditions," in *The Cambridge Companion to the Talmud and Rabbinic Literature* (ed. Charlotte Fonrobert and Martin Jaffee; Cambridge: Cambridge University Press, 2006), 165–97; Shai Secunda, *The Iranian Talmud: Reading the Bavli in its Sassanian Context* (Philadelphia, PA: University of Pennsylvania Press, 2013); Jason Mokhtarian, *Rabbis, Sorcerers, Kings, and Priests: The Culture of the Talmud in Ancient Iran* (Berkeley, CA: University of California Press, 2015).

narratives of historical decline from clear and definite Jewish identity to modern muddled and disintegrating "Jewishness" cannot hold water. How, then, should scholars tell the story of Jewish history? In particular, how do we understand Jews in antiquity, especially in relation to our own cultural contexts? A close look at antiquity shows us that what we might call "Jewish identity" has long been diffuse, mixed, and even partial. What we now see as "ethnic identity" was malleable even in antiquity.[55] Nor was what we now see as "religious identity" fixed.

These remain live issues for scholars. Most often, disagreements are not, in fact, about anything that happened in antiquity. It is about how we should represent antiquity to people today. For instance, the intensity and recurrence of the Jew/Judean translation debate also suggests that scholars cannot decide whether the ancient *ioudaios* was "religious," "ethnic," or "national." And for good reason. These *ioudaioi* do not neatly fit into any one of these established modern categories. Like the second-century rabbinic discussions about the fictional animal called a *koi*,[56] they were sometimes one, sometimes the other, sometimes both, and sometimes neither. In the end, the ancient material suggests that "Jewishness" had—and has—no easy definition and no fixed set of borders.

Thus, the task of the scholar of Jewish studies, from antiquity to the present, is to remember that these established categories of "religion," "race," "nation" are *our* established categories. The question is not one of historical precision.[57] From where I sit as a scholar, it is also not one of ethics. It is rather, I suggest, a question of what each of these terms illuminates, what ways of thinking it opens up, and what it obscures. What does using "Jew" for *ioudaios* help scholars to see? What does using "Judean" show? Each, in fact, illuminates something useful for the scholar. "Jew" helps us think about a long trajectory of Jewish history. It can highlight reception history, the way that Josephus, for instance, functions when mediaeval and modern Jewish communities think about their own communities. "Religion" can help illuminate the intersections of ritual, material objects, and philosophies. "Judean" and its related categories of "ethnicity" and "nation" train the eye on geographic, military, and political aspects of Jewishness in antiquity. Religion,

55. See, e.g., Denise Kimber Buell, *Why This New Race: Ethnic Reasoning in Early Christianity* (New York: Columbia University Press, 2005).

56. Tosefta *Bikkurim* 2.2.

57. Steve Mason makes this point in "Ancient Jews or Judeans? Different Questions, Different Answers," in Law and Halton, eds., *Jew and Judean*. In an earlier article, however, he argues that *ioudaoi* were an ethnic group, despite ethnicity's status as a modern category; see Steve Mason, "Jews, Judaeans, Judaizing, Judaism: Problems of Categorization in Ancient History," *Journal for the Study of Judaism* 38 (2007): 457–512.

ethnicity, nation: these categories are not true or false in and of themselves. They are tools, and should be used when they are useful and put aside when they are not.

Studying Jewishness in antiquity suggests to us that Jewishness has always been multi-faceted and messy. The particulars of the messiness shift as cultural context shifts, so that the twenty-first century messiness of defining who is a Jew and what it means to be Jewish will be different from the second-century messiness. But a decline narrative is a romanticization, not a clear-eyed reflection, of the past.

Biographical Note

Sarah Imhoff is Associate Professor of Jewish Studies and Religious Studies at Indiana University, Bloomington, USA. She writes on gender and American Judaism, the role of the body and medical discourse in the construction of Jewishness, the history of the field of Jewish Studies, and the history of the field of Religious Studies, especially in its relation to US law. She is the author of *Masculinity and the Making of American Judaism* (Indiana University Press, 2017). Her work has appeared in the *Journal of Religion*, *Culture and Religion*, *Critical Research on Religion*, the *Bulletin of the Study of Religion*, and *American Jewish History*.

Bibliography

Abu El-Haj, Nadia. *The Genealogical Science*. Chicago, IL: University of Chicago Press, 2012. https://doi.org/10.7208/chicago/9780226201429.001.0001

Baker, Cynthia. *Rebuilding the House of Israel: Architectures of Gender in Jewish Antiquity*. Stanford, CA: Stanford University Press, 2002.

Baron, Salo. "Ghetto and Emancipation: Shall We Revise the Traditional View?" *The Menorah Journal* 14 (1928): 515–26.

Beduhn, Jason. "Mani and the Crystallization of the Concept of 'Religion' in Third Century Iran," 247–75 in *Mani at the Court of the Persian Kings: Studies on the Chester Beatty Kephalaia Codex*. Edited by Iain Gardner, Jason BeDuhn, and Paul Dilley. Leiden: Brill, 2014. https://doi.org/10.1163/9789004282629_010

Boyarin, Daniel. *Borderlines: The Partition of Judeo-Christianity*. Philadelphia, PA: University of Pennsylvania Press, 2004.

Boyarin, Daniel, and Virginia Burrus. "Hybridity as Subversion of Orthodoxy? Jews and Christians in Late Antiquity," *Social Compass* 52.4 (2005): 431–41. https://doi.org/10.1177/0037768605058148

Buell, Denise Kimber. *Why This New Race: Ethnic Reasoning in Early Christianity*. New York: Columbia University Press, 2005. https://doi.org/10.7312/buel13334

Cohen, Steven M., and Jack Wertheimer. "Whatever Happened to the Jewish People?" *Commentary* 121 (2006): 33–7.

Cotton, Hannah M. "The Rabbis and the Documents," 167–80 in Goodman, ed., *Jews in a Graeco-Roman World*, 1998.

Elman, Yaakov. "Middle Persian Culture and Babylonian Sages: Accommodation and Resistance in the Shaping of Rabbinic Legal Traditions," 165–97 in *The Cambridge Companion to the Talmud and Rabbinic Literature*. Edited by Charlotte Fonrobert and Martin Jaffee. Cambridge: Cambridge University Press, 2006.

Feldman, Louis H. "The Omnipresence of the God-Fearers," *Biblical Archaeology Review* 12.5 (1986): 58–69.

—"Proselytism by Jews in the Third, Fourth and Fifth Centuries," *Journal for the Study of Judaism in the Persian, Hellenistic, and Roman Period* 24 (1993): 1–58. https://doi.org/10.1163/157006393X00097

Feldman, Louis H., and Gōhei Hata, eds. *Josephus, the Bible, and History*. Leiden: Brill, 1989.

Glaser, Amelia. *Jews and Ukrainians in Russia's Literary Borderlands: From the Shtetl Fair to the Petersburg Bookshop*. Evanston, IL: Northwestern University Press, 2016.

Goodman, Martin. "Jewish Proselytizing in the First Century," 53–79 in *The Jews Among Pagans and Christians in the Roman Empire*. Edited by Judith Lieu, John North, and Tessa Rajak. London: Routledge, 1992.

—ed. *Jews in a Graeco-Roman World*. Oxford: Oxford University Press, 1998.

Grossman, Maxine L. *Reading for History in the Damascus Document: A Methodological Study*. Leiden: Brill, 2009.

Gruen, Erich S. *Heritage and Hellenism: The Reinvention of Jewish Tradition*. Berkeley, CA: University of California Press, 1998.

—"Jews, Greeks, and Romans in the Third Sibylline Oracle," 15–36 in Goodman, ed., *Jews in a Graeco-Roman World*, 1998.

Hall, Jonathan. *Ethnic Identity in Greek Antiquity*. Cambridge: Cambridge University Press, 1997. https://doi.org/10.1017/CBO9780511605642

Hollinger, David. *Post-Ethnic America: Beyond Multiculturalism*. New York: Basic Books, 1995.

Honigman, Sylvie. "The Birth of a Diaspora: The Emergence of a Jewish Self-Definition in Ptolemaic Egypt in the Light of Onomastics," 93–127 in *Diasporas in Antiquity*. Edited by Shaye J. D. Cohen and Ernest S. Frerichs. Atlanta, GA: Scholars Press, 1993.

Imhoff, Sarah. "Half Jewish, Just Jewish, and the Oddities of Religious Identity," 76–89 in *Religion and Identity*. Edited by Ronald A. Simkins and Thomas M. Kelly. *Journal of Religion & Society* Supplement 13; Creighton University, 2016. Online: http://moses.creighton.edu/JRs/toc/SS13.html

Iny, Julie. "Ashkenazi Eyes," 81–100 in *The Flying Camel: Essays on Identity by Women of North African and Middle Eastern Jewish Heritage*. Edited by Loolwa Khazzoom. New York: Seal Press, 2003.

Isaac, Benjamin. "Jews, Christians, and others in Palestine: The Evidence from Euseubius," 65–74 in Goodman, ed., *Jews in a Graeco-Roman World*, 1998.

Janowitz, Naomi. "Rethinking Jewish Identity in Late Antiquity," 205–19 in *Ethnicity and Culture in Late Antiquity*. Edited by Stephen Mitchell and Geoffrey Greatrex. London: Duckworth, 2000.

Jones, Sian. "Identities in Practice: Towards an Archaeological Perspective on Jewish Identity in Antiquity," 29–49 in *Jewish Local Patriotism and Self-Identification in the Graeco-Roman Period*. Edited by Sian Jones and Sarah Pierce. Sheffield, UK: Sheffield Academic Press, 1998.

Kahn, Susan M. "The Multiple Meanings of Jewish Genes," *Culture, Medicine and Psychiatry* 29 (2005): 179–92. https://doi.org/10.1007/s11013-005-7424-5

—"Are Genes Jewish?" 12–26 in *Boundaries of Jewish Identity*. Edited by Susan Glenn and Naomi Sokolov. Seattle, WA: University of Washington Press, 2010.

Kraabel, A. Thomas. "The Disappearance of the 'God-Fearers'," *Numen* 28.2 (1981): 113–26. https://doi.org/10.1163/156852781X00160

Kurtzman, Joey. "The End of the Jewish People," 2007. Online: http://jewcy.com/jewish-religion-and-beliefs/joey1 (accessed 19 May 2016).

Law, Timothy Michael, and Charles Halton, eds. *Jew and Judean: A Marginalia Forum on Politics and Historiography in the Translation of Ancient Texts*. 2014. Online: http://marginalia.lareviewofbooks.org/ancient-jews-judeans-different-questions-different-answers-steve-mason/ (accessed 22 June 2016).

Lee, A. D. *Christians and Pagans in Late Antiquity: A Sourcebook*. London: Routledge, 2016.

MacLennan, Robert, and A. Thomas Kraabel. "The God-Fearers: A Literary and Theological Invention," *Biblical Archaeology Review* 12.5 (1986): 46–53.

Mason, Steve. "Jews, Judaeans, Judaizing, Judaism: Problems of Categorization in Ancient History," *Journal for the Study of Judaism* 38 (2007): 457–512. https://doi.org/10.1163/156851507X193108

—"Ancient Jews or Judeans? Different Questions, Different Answers," in Law and Halton, eds., *Jew and Judean*, 2014.

Mokhtarian, Jason. *Rabbis, Sorcerers, Kings, and Priests: The Culture of the Talmud in Ancient Iran*. Berkeley, CA: University of California Press, 2015. https://doi.org/10.1525/california/9780520286207.001.0001

Momigliano, Arnaldo. "Review of *The Jews of Ancient Rome* by Harry J. Leon," *Gnomon* 34.2 (1962): 178–82.

Nongbri, Brent. *Before Religion: The History of a Modern Concept*. New Haven, CT: Yale University Press, 2013. https://doi.org/10.12987/yale/9780300154160.001.0001

Pomerantz, Jonathan. "Ordinary Jews in the Babylonian Talmud: Rabbinic Representations and Historical Interpretation," PhD dissertation, Yale University, 2016.

Porten, Bezalel, and Ada Yardeni, eds. *Textbook of Aramaic Documents from Ancient Egypt Newly Copied, Edited and Translated into Hebrew and English*. Vols. 1–4. Jerusalem: Hebrew University Press, 1986–1999.

Rajak, Tessa. *The Jewish Dialogue with Greece and Rome: Studies in Cultural and Social Interaction*. Leiden: Brill, 2002.

Reinhartz, Adele. "The Vanishing Jews of Antiquity," in Law and Halton, eds., *Jew and Judean*, 2014.

Reynolds, Joyce M., and Robert Tanenbaum. *Jews and God-Fearers at Aphrodisias: Greek Inscriptions with Commentary*. Cambridge: Cambridge Philosophical Society, 1987.

Rutgers, Leonard V. "Archaeological Evidence for the Interaction of Jews and Non-Jews in Late Antiquity," *American Journal of Archaeology* 96.1 (1992): 101–18. https://doi.org/10.2307/505760

—*The Jews in Late Ancient Rome: Evidence of Cultural Interaction in the Roman Diaspora*. Leiden: Brill, 1995. https://doi.org/10.1163/9789004283473

Samuels, Maurice. *Little Did I Know*. New York: Knopf, 1963.

Sandwell, Isabella. *Religious Identity in Late Antiquity: Greeks, Jews, and Christians in Antioch*. Cambridge: Cambridge University Press, 2011.

Satlow, Michael L. "Romans and Rabbis on Sex," 135–44 in Goodman, ed., *Jews in a Graeco-Roman World*, 1998.

Schaefer, Peter. *History of the Jews in Antiquity*. London: Routledge, 1995.

Schofield, Alison. *From Qumran to the Yahad: A New Paradigm of Textual Development for The Community Rule*. Leiden: Brill, 2008.

Schurer, Emil. *The History of the Jewish People in the Age of Christ*. Edinburgh, UK: T&T Clark, 1987.

Schwartz, Daniel. "Doing Like Jews or Becoming a Jew? Josephus on Women Converts to Judaism," 93–110 in *Jewish Identity in the Greco-Roman World*. Edited by Jörg Frey, Daniel Schwartz, and Stephanie Gripentrog. Leiden: Brill, 2007. https://doi.org/10.1163/ej.9789004158382.i-435.16

—"The Different Tasks of Translators and Historians," *Marginalia Forum* 18 (2014). Online: https://marginalia.lareviewofbooks.org/different-tasks-translators-historians-daniel-r-schwartz/ (accessed 30 June 2016).

Schwartz, Seth. *Imperialism and Jewish Society, 200 B.C.E. to 640 C.E.* Princeton, NJ: Princeton University Press, 2001.

Secunda, Shai. *The Iranian Talmud: Reading the Bavli in its Sassanian Context*. Philadelphia, PA: University of Pennsylvania Press, 2013.

Surburg, Raymond. *Introduction to the Intertestamental Period*. St. Louis, MO: Concordia, 1975.

White, L. Michael. "The Delos Synagogue Revisited: Recent Fieldwork in the Graeco-Roman Diaspora," *Harvard Theological Review* 80 (1987): 133–60. https://doi.org/10.1017/S0017816000023579

Williams, Margaret H. *The Jews Among the Greeks and Romans: A Diasporic Sourcebook*. Baltimore, MD: Johns Hopkins University Press, 1998.

Yoshiko Reed, Annette. "'Jewish Christianity' After 'The Parting of the Ways': Approaches to Historiography and Self-Definition in the Pseudo-Clementines," 189–231 in *The Ways That Never Parted: Jews and Christians in Late Antiquity and the Early Middle Ages*. Edited by Adam Becker and Annette Yoshiko Reed. Minneapolis, MN: Fortress Press, 2007.

Chapter Fourteen

Whither Shall We Go?
Tertullian and Christian Identity Formation

Nickolas P. Roubekas

"But what frightened you in this discussion of laughter? You cannot eliminate laughter by eliminating the book."

"No, to be sure. But laughter is weakness, corruption, the foolishness of our flesh. It is the peasant's entertainment, the drunkard's license."[1]

In Umberto Eco's famous mystery novel *The Name of the Rose* (1980), the blind librarian monk Jorge of Burgos, who felt revulsion at the emotions created by laughter, hid the only copy of the lost second book of Aristotle's *Poetics* in the library of a Benedictine remote monastery in northern Italy and, by poisoning the pages, murdered anyone who tried to handle it. In the dramatic last chapter of the book, the protagonist William of Baskerville, a Franciscan friar, and his student Adso of Melk, expose Jorge's secret so forcing him to admit to the murders. As Jorge asserts, laughter is the source of destruction, corruption, and mental as well as physical weakness. By hiding the book, and thus preventing everyone from reading it and consequently dying, Jorge argued that the eradication of laughter from life would prevent people from going astray and becoming heretics: "You saw yesterday how the simple can conceive and carry out the most lurid heresies, disavowing the laws of God and the laws of nature."[2] Jorge's delusion was that by coming into contact with Aristotle's works, the devout Christians were jeopardizing their (Roman-Catholic) Christian identity and were liable to join one of the prevailing heretical groups of the Middle Ages. It is the "Philosopher," as Jorge puts it, whose works have allowed Christians to doubt and re-evaluate the Christian scripture; thus, prohibiting people from reading Aristotle's works was a means of securing the Christian identity and the theological principles according to which that identity was shaped and maintained within the Roman-Catholic Christian world of the Middle Ages.

---

1. Umberto Eco, *The Name of the Rose* (trans. William Weaver; iPad edition, 1980).
2. Eco, *Name of the Rose*.

Although Eco's plot is unfolding in a completely different historical period, one may discern *mutatis mutandis* the similarities between Jorge's argumentation—pertaining to the necessity of maintaining and protecting the Christians from the pagan[3] teachings that can corrupt and alienate them from the Christian life and worldview—and Tertullian's project as is portrayed in the *De Spectaculis* regarding the pagan spectacles of the Roman Empire and the involvement of Christians as spectators. Writing for recently converted Christian and baptismal candidates, the North African apologist argues that Christians should avoid participating in the various shows organized by the Roman Empire. For Tertullian, those spectacles clash with the Christian way of life. However, Tertullian is writing in an era in which specific church laws or norms were not yet firmly established, and some newly converted Christians and catechumens were prone to attend the Roman spectacles. The African apologist, responding to the arguments put forward by both pagans and Christians in favor of the spectacles and the lack of any kind of threat to the faith of those who attended them, compiled the *De Spectaculis* in which a spatial approach to religion is at work that unfolds around two central pivots that are of interest to the study of religion in general, and the study of early Christianity in particular. First, the way theorizing about the relationship between space and religion creates, enforces, and maintains new religious identities; and second, how classification, as a set of human relations and ideas, transforms places from ordinary and neutral into ideologically and "religiously" charged spaces. By examining Tertullian's arguments, one can see an early classificatory system at work, one that was not yet established in the early Christian world and, especially, within the North African context. Tertullian's argumentation lacks strong theoretical coherence but it nevertheless remains an early attempt to classify places and actions by arguing against specific practices, such as the Roman spectacles. It is known that the christianization of North Africa has a complex history, while Christian practices in Africa were considerably different from the ones in Rome. The different Christian groups had experienced various conflicts both within their communities and against the arch-enemy, Rome.[4] Paul

---

3.   I use the term "pagan" by convention, although it is a problematic and biased term attributed by Christians to all non-Jew outsiders. See Christopher P. Jones, *Between Pagan and Christians* (Cambridge, MA: Harvard University Press, 2014), 1–8; Doug Lee, *Pagans and Christians in Late Antiquity: A Sourcebook* (London: Routledge, 2000), 10–1.

4.   See David E. Wilhite, *Tertullian the African* (Berlin: Walter de Gruyter, 2007), 31–5; Geoffrey D. Dunn, "Roman and North African Christianity," in *The Routledge Companion to Early Christian Thought* (ed. D. Jeffrey Bingham; London: Routledge, 2010), 154–71.

himself addressed issues pertaining to space in Rome, where early Christians were to be found within specific regions of the city—more particularly, in perimeter areas outside the walls.[5] Tertullian, however, is dealing with a more complicated issue, which is closely related to the way people classify their religious and cultural worlds.

As Craig Martin has put it, since Émile Durkheim, many scholars of religion have argued that "some things are what they are not because of their material properties but because of a set of human social relations. In these cases, the relation between the thing and the human practice makes it what it is."[6] Undeniably, Mary Douglas's seminal work *Purity and Danger* (1966) remains the classic study of how classification functions. In an oft-cited passage, Douglas argued that

> [d]irt is the by-product of a systematic ordering and classification of matter, in so far as ordering involves rejecting inappropriate elements ... In short, our pollution behaviour is the reaction which condemns any object or idea likely to confuse or contradict *cherished classifications.*[7]

The emphasis here holds a key role in discussing Tertullian's arguments in the *De Spectaculis*. Were there any *cherished classifications* among the Christians that functioned as the norm against which pagan spectacles were compared, examined, and rejected by Christians along with the actual loci wherein they took place? What I will argue is that, given the absence of such cherished classifications, Tertullian virtually acts as the introducer of such categorizations in light of the new faith within the North African context. By concentrating on space and spatializing practices, Tertullian becomes an early exponent—though not as systematic as later authors—of a basic principle that scholars of religion have discussed in the last hundred years or so and which is succinctly summarized by Craig Martin: "the way we classify or divide up the world is fundamental to understand how religious traditions function to reinforce social order."[8]

---

5.   See the detailed study by Peter Lampe, *From Paul to Valentinus: Christians at Rome in the First Two Centuries* (trans. Michael Steinhauser; Minneapolis, MN: Fortress Press, 2003), esp. 43–7.

6.   Craig Martin, *A Critical Introduction to the Study of Religion* (Sheffield, UK: Equinox, 2012), 19–20.

7.   Mary Douglas, *Purity and Danger: An Analysis of the Concepts of Pollution and Taboo* (London: Routledge, 1984 [1966]), 36–7 (emphasis added). For an analysis, see Richard Fardon, *Mary Douglas: An Intellectual Biography* (London: Routledge, 1999), 75–101.

8.   Martin, *Critical Introduction*, 20. Also see Jonathan Z. Smith, "Classification," in *Guide to the Study of Religion* (ed. Willi Braun and Russell T. McCutcheon; London: Cassell, 2000), 35–44.

The De Spectaculis, *Roman Imperial Identity, and Disaffiliation*

Tertullian was a converted Christian who lived in the later part of the second century and the first half of the third century CE in Carthage.[9] He wrote the *De Spectaculis* around the beginning of the third century to address a rising issue faced by the early Christian communities of Carthage, namely, the tendency of recently baptized and baptismal candidates to participate in the various spectacles organized by the Roman Empire. Tertullian offers to his readers an outline of his work that seeks to condemn the Roman spectacles and the spaces in which they take place (games, circus, theater, amphitheater):

> We shall, therefore, set forth the origins of the various spectacles, explaining in what nurseries they grew up; next in order, the titles of some of them, that is, the names by which they are called; then their equipment and the superstitions observed in them; thereafter the places and the presiding spirits to whom they are dedicated; and finally the arts employed in them and the authors to whom they are ascribed. (4.4)[10]

The work was meant for internal consumption; that is, even though it belongs to the so-called apologetic works, the audience and readership of the *De Spectaculis* were not outsiders but rather insiders.[11] This applies to many works of the same genre, contrary to the traditional opinion that those works were addressed to and read by outsiders, namely the pagans. Although it is clear that the apologetic works arose in response to the attacks coming from the outside, they were most likely primarily read by Christians, acting as handy references to be used by the members of the new religious communities. As Simon Price has shown, both the *De Spectaculis* and

---

9.   About Tertullian's life, see Timothy D. Barnes, *Tertullian: A Historical and Literary Study* (Oxford: Clarendon, 1971); Wilhite, *Tertullian the African*, 18–25; Geoffrey D. Dunn, *Tertullian* (London: Routledge, 2004), 2–8. Cf. the discussion in Éric Rebillard, "The West (2): North Africa," in *The Oxford Handbook of Early Christian Studies* (ed. Susan Ashbrook Harvey and David G. Hunter; Oxford: Oxford University Press, 2008), 303–7, where an estimation of the population of Christians in North Africa is given.

10.   Unless otherwise noted, all passages are quoted after Rudolph Arbesmann, Emily Joseph Daly, and Edwin A. Quain, eds., *Tertullian: Disciplinary, Moral and Ascetical Works* (Washington, DC: Catholic University of America Press, 1959).

11.   "Learn, o you servants of God who are just now entering upon His service, and you who have already solemnly sworn allegiance to Him recall what principle of faith, what reason inherent in truth, what rule in our way of life forbid, along with the other errors of the world, also the pleasures of the spectacles" (1.1). Also, see Robert D. Sider, "Tertullian on the Shows: An Analysis," *Journal of Theological Studies* 29.2 (1978): 339; Maijastina Kahlos, *Debate and Dialogue: Christian and Pagan Cultures c. 360–430* (Aldershot, UK: Ashgate, 2007), 63 n. 26.

the *De Idololatria* were "in fact esoteric, addressing existing Christians" and sought to "define a boundary between Christianity and paganism."[12] Similarly, Anders-Christian Jacobsen has argued that the use of irony as an apologetic strategy, especially in the works of Tertullian and primarily in his famous apologetic work *Apologeticum*, could not possibly act as an acceptable and efficient way to persuade the non-Christians. It is more likely that the general tone of those works addressed those Christians who needed solid arguments against the practices and beliefs of the pagans that demonstrated the overall superiority of Christianity.[13]

The decision to dedicate a whole treatise against the spectacles indicates that, at Tertullian's time, there was a considerable number of Christians who attended the spectacles without thinking that such practices could somehow harm their faith. On the contrary, those Christians seem to have presented convincing arguments in favor of their attendance, which had led to advanced discussions within the Christian communities and to which Tertullian wished to reply.[14] Thus, those Christians did not participate in the spectacles out of fear but by choice.[15] The entertainment industry set up by Rome served several aspects of imperial life. Already since the beginning of the first century BCE, professional athletes had formed synods, while gladiators and actors gained large amounts of money and glory.[16] Moreover, the various

12. Simon Price, "Latin Christian Apologetics: Minucius Felix, Tertullian, and Cyprian," in *Apologetics in the Roman Empire: Pagans, Jews, and Christians* (ed. M. Edwards, M. Goodman, S. Price, and C. Rowland; Oxford: Oxford University Press, 1999), 106.

13. See Anders-Christian Jacobsen, "Main Topics in Early Christian Apologetics," in *Critique and Apologetics: Jews, Christians and Pagans in Antiquity* (ed. Anders-Christian Jacobsen, Jörg Ulrich, and David Brakke; Frankfurt: Peter Lang, 2009), 108. One can here add that Christians could not, like pagans, make a career of oratory during that period and that writing for the attacks from the outsiders did not simultaneously mean that the responses came from the same direction. For a discussion, see Edwards et al., "Introduction: Apologetics in the Roman World," in Edwards et al., eds., *Apologetics in the Roman Empire*, 8–9.

14. For example, in 8.8 Tertullian says: "What will happen, you say, if I enter the circus at some other time? Shall I be then, too, in danger of contamination?" I will discuss his reply later; it is clear that for Tertullian such dialogues within the Christian communities of Carthage were obviously at least dangerous and threatening. The idea that there was a group of Christians who did not see any harm in attending the spectacles was already presented by Reginald M. Chase, "De Spectaculis," *The Classical Journal* 23.2 (1927): 108.

15. "What will you do when you are caught in that surging tide of wicked applause? Not that you are likely to suffer there at the hands of men (no one recognizes you as a Christian)" (27.2). Also, see Dunn, *Tertullian*, 29.

16. See David Potter, "Entertainment," in *A Companion to Ancient History* (ed. Andrew Erskine; Oxford: Blackwell, 2009), 389.

shows and games were not only an expression of pagan beliefs but, primarily, constituted the means through which imperial power was portrayed. Richard Beacham has demonstrated that, during the first three centuries CE, "[i]nside Rome's imperial theaters the audience often was presented with dazzling spectacles calculated to impress and to cast reflected glory upon the rulers and patrons (or their representatives) whose presence frequently added to the excitement and splendor of the occasion and ceremony."[17] It is well known that the emperors of Rome attended the games—a practice that continued when the capital moved to Constantinople—and were the central figures that received honors and acclamations or disapprobations from the crowds.[18] In his short introduction to the Roman Empire, Christopher Kelly has shown that the places where the games were taking place in Rome constituted a microcosm of the actual society, a structure that Emperor Augustus introduced: seats allocated according to social status, age, and occupation. Similarly, in the provincial cities, local authorities would have the best seats, with male citizens next, while professional associations and other social groups would follow.[19] Such practices were also vivid in Carthage, where Tertullian composed the *De Spectaculis*.

The various Roman spectacles served both the entertainment industry and the regime that sought to keep the masses happy, engaged, and "Roman." In the theater, the religious element in most cases "became a part of the spectators' experience of the performance,"[20] while for many Romans the circus was a representation of the actual cosmos that was reflected "in the links between religion and architecture."[21] Thus participation at the spectacles meant recognition by the spectators of their religious and cultural identity, that is, being pagans and Roman citizens. This religious element and the relationship between religion and architecture lie at the core of Tertullian's argumentation against Christians attending the spectacles: "Every ornament of the circus is a temple by itself" (8.3) he asserted, in demonstrating the all-pagan nature of virtually every single object that was found where the spectacles

17. Richard C. Beacham, *The Roman Theater and Its Audience* (Cambridge, MA: Harvard University Press, 1991), 167.

18. See Beacham, *Roman Theater*, 167; R. Malcolm Errington, *Roman Imperial Policy from Julian to Theodosius* (Chapel Hill, NC: University of North Carolina Press, 2006), 146–7; Christopher Kelly, *The Roman Empire: A Very Short Introduction* (Oxford: Oxford University Press, 2006), 81.

19. See Kelly, *Roman Empire*, 79. Also see Livy 34.54; Suetonius, *Augustus* 44. As Alison Futrell has pointed out, the local officials were the representatives of Rome and of the imperial power, seeking to assert control and the favor of Rome (*The Roman Games: A Sourcebook* [Oxford: Blackwell, 2006], 29).

20. Beacham, *Roman Theater*, 21.

21. Futrell, *Roman Games*, 76.

were taking place. Although Tertullian openly agrees with the counter-argument that all those objects were created by God and, thus, cannot be in themselves corrupted, he nevertheless makes clear that it is the way objects are used that determines whether they are defiled, sordid, and pagan—and thus must be rejected by the Christians:

> Obviously ... the very structures of the places—the squared stones, unhewn stones, marble slabs and columns—also are all the handiwork of God who gave them to furnish the earth; indeed, the performances themselves take place under God's heaven [...] (2.2). We must, then, consider not only by whom all things were created, but also by whom they were perverted [...] (2.6). The whole reason for condemnation is, rather, the *misuse* of God's creation by God's creatures. (2.11; emphasis added)

This implies that for Tertullian it is human actions and the ideologies at work behind the way physical objects are used that determine the nature of those things. In other words, by agreeing that certain objects have specific functions, a group of people will determine whether those objects are deemed sacred, profane, holy, pagan, Christian, Roman, North African, and so on. It is this social convention which for Tertullian establishes, regulates, and reinforces religious identity: by participating in the spectacles, one accepts the pagan—and, thus, corrupted—nature of the surroundings and of every object found in the circus, the amphitheater, the theater, and so on. As such, by attending the spectacles one cannot simultaneously be Christian, since the very physical presence indicates the acceptance of the pagan nature of the practices, the objects, and the space itself. Tertullian's core argument is encountered in 8.10, where he states:

> It is not the places in themselves that defile us, but the things done in them, by which the places themselves, as we have contended, are defiled; it is by the defiled that we are defiled.

In 15.1 Tertullian further elaborates on this, by arguing that

> we have already mentioned above that they do not contaminate us of themselves, but on account of what is done in them, that is, once these places have imbibed contamination by such actions, they spit it out again to the same degree on other.

Thus, it follows, that it is by their sheer presence that Christians are defiled by the sordid spaces and their Christian identity is endangered. For Tertullian, it is the disaffiliation from all pagan activities that will allow them to participate in the most splendid spectacle of all time, the second coming of Christ (30.1; 3-5), which will separate them from the defiled pagans and acknowledge them as a distinct group that worships the real God. This rhetoric obviously operated as a means for the establishment and reinforcement of the newly acquired identity that all converts were experiencing. Tertullian's spatial classification of the spaces where spectacles are presented as defiled invites further examination in regards to how space is here conceived by the North African apologist.

Avoiding Places: From Pagan to Christian Identity

In her book *The Location of Religion* (2005), Kim Knott argued that "like 'religion', 'space', 'place' and 'location' are concepts that have helped people to think about their social, cultural, and physical experience, their relationships to other people, things and the cosmos."[22] However, it is not the concepts themselves that make people think about their experiences, relationships, and the cosmos, but what those concepts *mean* and *do* when thought in specific contexts, which often changes according to different perspectives and developments. This socialization of space is the result of certain meanings and connections made by people pertaining to specific places, which are prone to changes depending on how cultures—either local or broader—evolve or radically transform.[23] In Tertullian's treatise, space plays a fundamental role regarding the spectacles. But such an approach implies that space is something more than the absolute space, that is, the given and non-changing space, such as the very places where the spectacles came about. The French philosopher and sociologist Henri Lefebvre identified three moments in spatial theorizing in his influential *The Production of Space* (1991): spatial practices; representations of space; and spaces of representation. The first refers to the various ways people experience space materially, including via their physical body and their senses; the second moment is related to how space is understood and grasped, what otherwise is known as "absolute space"; finally, spaces of representation are the lived spaces through the various symbols and images.[24] The latter is an important spatial moment that is central in Tertullian's work. As William Thalmann put it, it is

22. Kim Knott, *The Location of Religion: A Spatial Analysis* (London: Equinox, 2005), 11.

23. See Martyn Smith, *Religion, Culture, and Sacred Space* (New York: Palgrave, 2008), 7.

24. See Henri Lefebvre, *The Production of Space* (trans. Donald Nicholson-Smith; Oxford: Blackwell, 1991). For an excellent discussion, cf. Andy Merrifield, "Henri Lefebvre: A Socialist in Space," in *Thinking Space* (ed. Mike Crang and Nigel Thrift; London: Routledge, 2000), 167–82; Knott, *Location of Religion*, 35–58; Kim Knott, "Spatial Theory and Method for the Study of Religion," *Temenos* 41.2 (2005): 162–6. For a brilliant approach to Lefebvre's spatial theorizing in the ancient world that is also applicable to Tertullian's *De Spectaculis*, see William G. Thalmann, *Apollonius of Rhodes and the Spaces of Hellenism* (Oxford: Oxford University Press, 2011), 22–3.

the space constructed by and constructing social relations. It is often subject to appropriation and domination by structures of power with their representations of space but it can also be the site of alternative practices and understandings, of resistance and new possibilities.[25]

The circus, amphitheater, theater, and the arena were such places where both social relations and spaces of representation (pagan and Roman) were constructed. The disaffiliation and separation, which practically lie at the core of Tertullian's treatise,[26] are explicit cases of resistance and alternative (Christian) practices. Even though Tertullian seeks to make a case based on the emotional consequences participation could bring to the Christians, he is nevertheless preoccupied by his fear that such practices would eventually make the recent converts return to their old beliefs that were, of course, related to the Roman culture. As Geoffrey Dunn has shown, Tertullian was not interested in establishing theologically sound arguments but to simply win arguments put forward by both heathens and recently converted Christians.[27] In his *Apologeticum* 38.4-5, Tertullian is again dealing with the spectacles and the emotions they produce (madness, shamelessness, brutality, vanity) as being completely foreign to the Christian way of life. Just like in the *De Spectaculis*,[28] he argues that Christians should remain "separate from those institutions of pagan Rome that clash with Christian norms."[29] However, what is at work here is the rhetoric of an early Christian writer to establish and reinforce a new religious and cultural identity; the attention must shift from what Tertullian says to the context of what is being said.[30] When we add to this his ability to change positions based on his audience— for example, regarding the rejection or not of Christian military service as well as his exhortation to his fellow Carthaginians to abandon the toga in favor of their native dress, the pallium, which would indicate that they had become Christians (thus, not Romans/pagans anymore)—it becomes clear that the *De Spectaculis* has little to do with theological issues but a great deal to do with identity issues.[31] Tertullian's separative and disaffiliative

25. Thalmann, *Apollonius of Rhodes*, 23.

26. Disaffiliation is the first step in cases of religious conversion. For a discussion, see Henri Gooren, *Religious Conversion and Disaffiliation: Tracing Patters of Change in Faith Practices* (New York: Palgrave, 2010).

27. Dunn, "Roman and North African Christianity," 155.

28. "If we claim that cruelty, impiety, and brutality are permitted us, let us by all means go to the amphitheater" (19.1).

29. Futrell, *Roman Games*, 166.

30. I am borrowing this phrase, with the necessary alterations, from Smith, *Religion, Culture, and Sacred Space*, 5.

31. Regarding Tertullian's position on military service, see Dunn, "Roman and North African Christianity," 157; Maureen A. Tilley, "North Africa," in *The Cambridge*

strategy is even more explicit in the *De Idololatria*, where he urges the newly baptized Christians to avoid all pagan activities, including education that comes from pagans. He attacks the schoolmasters (*ludimagister*) themselves, since their classes are inevitably idolatrous. In addition, the works taught in those classes assume the reality of the pagan gods; as such, he poses a rhetorical question: "Consider whether the one who catechizes about idols isn't guilty of idolatry."[32] Although Tertullian tries to be moderate, he is essentially being radical. As such, on the one hand, he acknowledges the necessity of non-Christian literature for the proper education of the Christians but, on the other hand, Christians "should treat it as they would treat a poisoned drink: it may have benefits and attractions (of color and smell), and these may properly be relished and used. But if you drink it, it will kill you."[33]

The recently converted Christians and the baptismal candidates that were in favor of attending the spectacles were experiencing what Peter Burke and Jan Stets call "conflicting identities." This emerges when "a behavior is at odds with one identity but in accord with another ... [but] another reason may be that we don't fully see the consequences of a behavior or a decision."[34] Tertullian's argumentation points towards both aspects. However, this complex issue is not unique in Tertullian's treatises or in the apologetic works in general; rather, the North African apologist is among the many early Christian authors that dealt with similar issues. The new faith and its exponents promoted a new identity and advocated a separation from the existing religious and cultural groups. Paul was the first to touch upon spatiality when in 1 Corinthians 1.2 he stated that one can worship the Lord in every place. At the same time, the spatial element in Paul's teaching was closely related to the separation of the followers of Jesus from the old Jewish practices, such as circumcision and dietary restrictions (Galatians 2.16 and Romans 2.25-6).[35] In Paul's time, it was apart from the Jewish religion that Christians needed to be distinguished, whereas in Tertullian's

History of Christianity. Vol. 1: *Origins to Constantine* (ed. Margaret M. Mitchell and Frances M. Young; Cambridge: Cambridge University Press, 2008), 392. The encouragement to his fellow citizens to adopt the native dress can be found in *De Pallio* 6.2; also, see Dunn, *Tertullian*, 28.

32. Cited in Paul J. Griffiths, *Religious Reading: The Place of Reading in the Practice of Religion* (Oxford: Oxford University Press, 1999), 159.

33. Cited in Griffiths, *Religious Reading*, 159.

34. Peter J. Burke and Jan E. Stets, *Identity Theory* (Oxford: Oxford University Press, 2009), 185.

35. See the excellent discussion in Kimberly B. Stratton, "Identity," in *The Cambridge Companion to Ancient Mediterranean Religions* (ed. Barbette Stanley Spaeth; Cambridge: Cambridge University Press, 2013), 235, 241.

era it is the Roman culture and religion that threatens the Christian identity of the recent converts and the baptismal candidates. In both cases, the cultural "others," as Judith Lieu has argued, were the groups against which the Christians needed to define and distance themselves in establishing the new "race" that Tertullian speaks of in his *Apologeticum* (37.4-6).[36]

The lack of *cherished classifications*, to return to Douglas's terminology, during the early Christian era and the conflicting identities of the recent converts lies at the heart of Tertullian's agony for the future of the diverse Christian communities of North Africa at the beginning of the third century CE. Tertullian's exhortatory and advisory treatise denotes the existence of a sub-group of recently converted Christians and catechumens for whom the boundaries between novelty and tradition were not (or, most likely, should not be) that strict.[37] But at the same time, it also shows that there were others who subscribed to Tertullian's drawing of social (and spatial) borders that ought to be explicit and unique in distinguishing the new faith from the old traditions. By drawing on Bruce Lincoln's work, Chad Kile has demonstrated the various ways those individuals were approached in the works of the early Christian writers in order to be persuaded not to return to their old practices and beliefs. The members of a society, as Kile puts it, are "continually (and actively) contesting and negotiating the very terms by which society will be ordered ... between what is acceptable and what is not, between who may participate and who may not."[38] However, within a given society there is a plethora of individuals who have their own ideas, and consensus is rarely (if ever) accomplished. The means of persuasion of the various opposing voices of individual members is a wearisome task that is based on the "ability to evoke a sentimental response ... one of 'affinity' or of 'estrangement'."[39]

---

36. See Judith M. Lieu, *Christian Identity in the Jewish and Graeco-Roman World* (Oxford: Oxford University Press, 2004), 17–21. Regarding the view of Christians as a new distinct race in relation to Jews and pagans, see Denise Kimber Buell, *Why This New Race: Ethnic Reasoning in Early Christianity* (New York: Columbia University Press, 2005). Again, it is with Paul that the idea of a new *genos* (race) or *ethnos* (people) is introduced, with the members of the community belonging to a single body, that of Christ (e.g., 1 Corinthians 12.12). This was accomplished via baptism, as Tertullian also maintains in the *De Spectaculis*. See Stratton, "Identity," 241.

37. Maijastina Kahlos (*Debate and Dialogue*, 4) characterizes such newly converted as "luke-warm Christians," although I think that the underlying problem was not a matter of religious enthusiasm, but rather of hybrid identities.

38. Chad Kile, "Feeling Persuaded: Christianization as Social Formation," in *Rhetoric and Reality in Early Christianities* (ed. Willi Braun; Waterloo: Wilfrid Laurier University Press, 2005), 229.

39. Kile, "Feeling Persuaded," 230.

Tertullian is well aware that Christians cannot alienate nor completely separate themselves from the existing (predominantly Roman/pagan) world; but they can nevertheless remain distanced from that world: "For the world is God's, but the things of the world are the Devil's" (15.8). This detachment is related to the spectacles and is extended to the spatial aspect of those practices. It is the meanings related to the "worldly things" encountered in the spectacles that pose a threat to the Christians. In his *Cosmopolitanism and the Geographies of Freedom* (2009), the anthropologist and geographer David Harvey eloquently argued that

> [i]f, furthermore, I ask the question, of what the Basilica of Sacré-Coeur in Paris, Tiananmen Square in Beijing, or "Ground Zero" in Manhattan *means*, then I cannot come to a full answer without invoking relationalities. And that entails coming to terms with the things, events, processes, and socio-ecological relations that have produced those places in spacetime.[40]

It is those meanings—and the things done related to them—that "defile" the places rather than the actual places being defiled in and of themselves. Tertullian makes sure to distinguish between the two when he replies to the question of the recent converts regarding whether their entrance to the circus when spectacles are not taking place will have any negative effect on them:[41]

> There is no law laid down with regard to places as such. For not only these places where people gather for the spectacles but also the temples may be entered by the servant of God without peril to his rule of life, provided that he do [sic] so for an urgent and honest reason which has no connection with the business and function proper of the place. (8.8)

For Tertullian, the space of representation "overlays physical space, making symbolic use of its objects"[42] and, eventually, defiles it. Just like societies, places are not static but dynamic and relational; they are spaces where people interact "with their natural and social environment, invested with meaning and charged with feelings from the uses people make of them,"[43] and it is through such interactions that societies or communities/groups are "constantly constructing, deconstructing, reconstructing themselves."[44] The close ties between the social and the spatial in the construction, reinforcement, and establishment of both a social and religious identity is Tertullian's

40. David Harvey, *Cosmopolitanism and the Geographies of Freedom* (New York: Columbia University Press, 2009), 140 (emphasis in the original).

41. See above, n. 14.

42. Lefebvre, *Production of Space*, 39.

43. Thalmann, *Apollonius of Rhodes*, 19; also, Knott, *Location of Religion*, 29–30.

44. Kile, "Feeling Persuaded," 228.

ultimate concern. It is through the notion of "sordidness" that the North African apologist attempts to create certain cherished classifications that will allow Christians to distinguish themselves from their cultural others and bring about disaffiliation from their previous groups, while evoking the feeling of affinity among the members of the new faith.

However, one should not overlook two important elements that are either mute or implicit in Tertullian's argumentation. First and foremost, the core problem is not merely the places where the shows are presented simply because they are presented *there*, but the beliefs related to practices that construct what for Tertullian constitutes "defiled or sordid spaces." As William Arnal and Russell McCutcheon argued in another context, the boundaries of the category "religion" "are defined *not* in terms of material practices, events, or structures, but in terms of the nature and content of the *beliefs* associated with those practices, events, or structures."[45] Tertullian seems to be essentially promoting a similar approach, which could be extremely useful in understanding how "religion" was perceived in antiquity—which brings me to the second element worthy of our attention. Already from the opening lines of the *De Spectaculis*, Tertullian sets the agenda regarding what is "religion":

> Some may perhaps be allured by the opinions of pagans who commonly use the following arguments against us in this matter: such comforting and merely external pleasures of the eyes and ears are not opposed to religion, which is found in one's mind and conscience; nor is taking delight in such enjoyment in its proper time and place a sin as long as the fear of God and God's honor remain unimpaired. But this is precisely what we intend to prove: that these things are not compatible with *true religion* and true obedience to the true God [*quemadmodum ista non competant verae religioni et vero obsequio erga verum deum*]. (1.3-4)[46]

Tertullian's mission is to explicate to new Christians the proper way of understanding what religion—or, better, *true* religion—is, which in turn must be approached as a set of internal and external elements, albeit the latter are presented in the *De Spectaculis* primarily as things not to be done. Although the term *religio* in Tertullian functions quite differently than its derivative "religion,"[47] the North African apologist appears to be making

45. William Arnal and Russell T. McCutcheon, *The Sacred is the Profane: The Political Nature of "Religion"* (Oxford: Oxford University Press, 2013), 142 (emphasis in the original).
46. I am quoting here from Robert D. Sider, *Christian and Pagan in the Roman Empire: The Witness of Tertullian* (Washington, DC: Catholic University of America Press, 2001) (emphasis added).
47. See the discussion in Carlin A. Barton and Daniel Boyarin, *Imagine No Religion: How Modern Abstractions Hide Ancient Realities* (New York: Fordham University

the case here of "religion" being about both internal beliefs and external actions/practices—it seems that one cannot stand without the other. After all, throughout the treatise, he emphasizes how the shows are an extension of pagan beliefs, mainly by linking each and every element of the spectacles (the games, theater, amphitheater, etc.) with the respective deities to whom they were dedicated. In this respect, the *De Spectaculis* also functions as a treatise about what religion is, and how people can be deemed adherents of a given religion by combining beliefs and practices within a particular setting.

* * *

I opened this chapter with an excerpt from Umberto Eco's *The Name of the Rose* in order to show that, as William of Baskerville put it, one cannot eliminate something by simply eliminating its agent(s). In Eco's novel, Jorge of Burgos asserted that by hiding Aristotle's book he could eradicate something as natural as laughter. William's statement is rational and straightforward: laughter is inherent, a characteristic of the human existence, a medium of expression of feelings, a means of maintaining social life and group coherence. In Tertullian's *De Spectaculis* a similar though profoundly different strategy is at work. The North African apologist is trying to eliminate the need for certain recently converted Christians and catechumens to participate in the Roman spectacles, by presenting all the disastrous results such practices evoke; as he persuasively puts it in addressing his fellow Christians who were in favor of attending the spectacles: "how would you fare in heaven?" (27.2).

However, what makes Tertullian's approach noteworthy is both its spatial aspect and the absence of a clear ideology of what was meant to be Christian in North Africa at the turn of the third century CE. As Éric Rebillard has successfully shown, "Christianness was only one of the many affiliations that mattered in everyday life ... Christians, as the other inhabitants of the Roman Empire, did not belong to only one collectivity that determined their identity."[48] Rebillard's statement also applies to the *De Spectaculis* even though he concentrates more on other works written by Tertullian and does not deal with the spatial aspect discussed in this chapter. The close ties between place and identity are central to Tertullian's argumentation, indicating the need to not only make Christians refrain from their pagan traditions,

---

Press, 2016), 55–118; cf. Brent Nongbri, *Before Religion: A History of a Modern Concept* (New Haven, CT: Yale University Press, 2013), 26–34.

48. Éric Rebillard, *Christians and Their Many Identities in Late Antiquity, North Africa, 200-450 CE* (Ithaca, NY: Cornell University Press, 2012), 33.

but primarily to infuse a new understanding of what it meant to be Christian. Rejecting the spectacles was not only a subject for Christian authors but also concerned other sub-groups of Roman society. Kathryn Mammel has brilliantly presented this issue by identifying three such groups: the educated elitist Romans; the Romans that rejected the Greek athletics; and the Christians versus the corrupted pagans. All groups expressed their oppositions from different perspectives and with different motives lying behind their objections: "For elitist Roman literary figures, including the Stoics, the 'other' meant the uneducated, unphilosophical masses; for Romans opposed to Greek athletics, it meant effeminate and immoral Greeks or athletes and their trainers who jeopardized their own physical and spiritual well-being through athletic training; for Jews and Christian authors, it meant corrupt pagans who did not share their religious identities or their codes of morality."[49] Mammel successfully points out the connection between Tertullian's oppositions and the influence of the Stoic thought.[50] In all three cases and, as I have argued in this chapter, in Tertullian's *De Spectaculis*, what is at stake is not the participation in the spectacles *per se* and the presence of Christians at places deemed defiled and sordid, but what those practices and places *mean* and *do* regarding the more important and broader issue of establishing, reinforcing, or challenging practices that pertain to cultural, religious, and ethnic identification and identity formation. Just as in the case of sacralization and desacralization of places—a practice that became extremely popular in Late Antiquity with new shrines and religious centers replacing old ones or constructing new ones in different locations—so in Tertullian's treatise Beatrice Caseau's observation holds great importance: "defining sacredness in each religion required the setting of the boundaries of licit and illicit behavior … What was impure for one religion was not for another; what was considered impious by some was perceived as pious by others."[51]

The setting of boundaries constitutes the primary aim of Tertullian's argumentation in defining Christianness as a distinct identity that needed to be elevated above all previous existing affiliations that the recently converted Christians shared in the Roman world within the North African context of the second and third centuries CE. This was obviously a challenging endeavor, one that demonstrates how fluid the religious scene was in Tertullian's cultural

---

49. See Kathryn Mammel, "Ancient Critics of Roman Spectacle and Sport," in *The Blackwell Companion to Sport and Spectacle in Greek and Roman Antiquity* (ed. Paul Christesen; Oxford: Blackwell, 2014), 605.

50. See Mammel, "Ancient Critics," 610.

51. Beatrice Caseau, "Sacred Landscapes," in *Interpreting Late Antiquity: Essays on the Postclassical World* (ed. Glen W. Bowersock, Peter Brown, and Oleg Grabar; Cambridge, MA: Belknap Press of Harvard University Press, 2001), 23.

milieu. If, as John Gager argued some forty years ago in another context, (a) the degree to which individuals define themselves as members of a particular group, so that any threat to the group immediately becomes a threat to every individual, and (b) how intellectuals transform personal motivations into eternal truths,[52] constitutes any indication of how religious communities are conceived, formed, and established, then Tertullian's *De Spectaculis* represents an excellent case of a discourse on religious identity formation.

Biographical Note

Nickolas P. Roubekas is Assistant Professor of Religious Studies at the University of Vienna, Austria. Previously he held a postdoctoral research fellowship at the University of South Africa, a teaching fellowship at the University of Aberdeen, UK, and a research fellowship at the North-West University, South Africa. He has published articles and book reviews in various journals and is the author of *Αναζητώντας τους Θεούς: Θρησκεία, Μύθος, Ουτοπία στον Ευήμερο τον Μεσσήνιο* (Vanias, 2011) and *An Ancient Theory of Religion: Euhemerism from Antiquity to the Present* (Routledge, 2017). His research focuses on the Graeco-Roman world, method and theory in the study of religion, and the disciplinary intersection of Religious Studies, Classics, and Ancient History.

Bibliography

Arbesmann, Rudolph, Emily Joseph Daly, and Edwin A. Quain, eds. *Tertullian: Disciplinary, Moral and Ascetical Works*. Washington, DC: Catholic University of America Press, 1959.

Arnal, William, and Russell T. McCutcheon. *The Sacred Is the Profane: The Political Nature of "Religion."* Oxford: Oxford University Press, 2013.

Barnes, Timothy D. *Tertullian: A Historical and Literary Study*. Oxford: Clarendon, 1971.

Barton, Carlin A., and Daniel Boyarin. *Imagine No Religion: How Modern Abstractions Hide Ancient Realities*. New York: Fordham University Press, 2016.

Beacham, Richard C. *The Roman Theater and Its Audience*. Cambridge, MA: Harvard University Press, 1991.

Buell, Denise Kimber. *Why This New Race: Ethnic Reasoning in Early Christianity*. New York: Columbia University Press, 2005. https://doi.org/10.7312/buel13334

Burke, Peter J., and Jan E. Stets. *Identity Theory*. Oxford: Oxford University Press, 2009. https://doi.org/10.1093/acprof:oso/9780195388275.001.0001

---

52. See John G. Gager, *Kingdom and Community: The Social World of Early Christianity* (Englewood Cliffs, NJ: Prentice-Hall, 1975), 82; cf. Vernon K. Robbins, *The Tapestry of Early Christian Discourse: Rhetoric, Society, and Ideology* (London: Routledge, 1996), 192.

Caseau, Beatrice. "Sacred Landscapes," 21–59 in *Interpreting Late Antiquity: Essays on the Postclassical World*. Edited by Glen W. Bowersock, Peter Brown, and Oleg Grabar. Cambridge, MA: Belknap Press of Harvard University Press, 2001.

Chase, Reginald M. "De Spectaculis," *The Classical Journal* 23.2 (1927): 107–20.

Douglas, Mary. *Purity and Danger: An Analysis of the Concepts of Pollution and Taboo*. London: Routledge, 1984 [1966].

Dunn, Geoffrey D. *Tertullian*. London: Routledge, 2004. https://doi.org/10.4324/9780203642870

—"Roman and North African Christianity," 154–71 in *The Routledge Companion to Early Christian Thought*. Edited by D. Jeffrey Bingham. London: Routledge, 2010.

Eco, Umberto. *The Name of the Rose*. Translated by William Weaver. iPad edition, 1980.

Edwards, Mark, Martin Goodman, Simon Price, and Christopher Rowland. "Introduction: Apologetics in the Roman World," 1–13 in Edwards et al., eds., *Apologetics in the Roman Empire*, 1999.

—eds. *Apologetics in the Roman Empire: Pagans, Jews, and Christians*. Oxford: Oxford University Press, 1999.

Errington, R. Malcolm. *Roman Imperial Policy from Julian to Theodosius*. Chapel Hill, NC: University of North Carolina Press, 2006.

Fardon, Richard. *Mary Douglas: An Intellectual Biography*. London: Routledge, 1999.

Futrell, Alison. *The Roman Games: A Sourcebook*. Oxford: Blackwell, 2006.

Gager, John G. *Kingdom and Community: The Social World of Early Christianity*. Englewood Cliffs, NJ: Prentice-Hall, 1975.

Gooren, Henri. *Religious Conversion and Disaffiliation: Tracing Patters of Change in Faith Practices*. New York: Palgrave, 2010. https://doi.org/10.1057/9780230113039

Griffiths, Paul J. *Religious Reading: The Place of Reading in the Practice of Religion*. Oxford: Oxford University Press, 1999. https://doi.org/10.1093/acprof:oso/9780195125771.001.0001

Harvey, David. *Cosmopolitanism and the Geographies of Freedom*. New York: Columbia University Press, 2009.

Jacobsen, Anders-Christian. "Main Topics in Early Christian Apologetics," 85–110 in *Critique and Apologetics: Jews, Christians and Pagans in Antiquity*. Edited by Anders-Christian Jacobsen, Jörg Ulrich, and David Brakke. Frankfurt: Peter Lang, 2009.

Jones, Christopher P. *Between Pagan and Christians*. Cambridge, MA: Harvard University Press, 2014. https://doi.org/10.4159/9780674369511

Kahlos, Maijastina. *Debate and Dialogue: Christian and Pagan Cultures c. 360–430*. Aldershot, UK: Ashgate, 2007.

Kelly, Christopher. *The Roman Empire: A Very Short Introduction*. Oxford: Oxford University Press, 2006. https://doi.org/10.1093/actrade/9780192803917.001.0001

Kile, Chad. "Feeling Persuaded: Christianization as Social Formation," 219–48 in *Rhetoric and Reality in Early Christianities*. Edited by Willi Braun. Waterloo: Wilfrid Laurier University Press, 2005.

Knott, Kim. *The Location of Religion: A Spatial Analysis*. London: Equinox, 2005.

—"Spatial Theory and Method for the Study of Religion," *Temenos* 41.2 (2005): 153–84.

Lampe, Peter. *From Paul to Valentinus: Christians at Rome in the First Two Centuries*. Translated by Michael Steinhauser. Minneapolis, MN: Fortress Press, 2003.

Lee, Doug. *Pagans and Christians in Late Antiquity: A Sourcebook*. London: Routledge, 2000.

Lefebvre, Henri. *The Production of Space*. Translated by Donald Nicholson-Smith. Oxford: Blackwell, 1991.

Lieu, Judith M. *Christian Identity in the Jewish and Graeco-Roman World*. Oxford: Oxford University Press, 2004. https://doi.org/10.1093/0199262896.001.0001

Mammel, Kathryn. "Ancient Critics of Roman Spectacle and Sport," 603–16 in *The Blackwell Companion to Sport and Spectacle in Greek and Roman Antiquity*. Edited by Paul Christesen. Oxford: Blackwell, 2014.

Martin, Craig. *A Critical Introduction to the Study of Religion*. Sheffield, UK: Equinox, 2012.

Merrifield, Andy. "Henri Lefebvre: A Socialist in Space," 167–82 in *Thinking Space*. Edited by Mike Crang and Nigel Thrift. London: Routledge, 2000.

Nongbri, Brent. *Before Religion: A History of a Modern Concept*. New Haven, CT: Yale University Press, 2013. https://doi.org/10.12987/yale/9780300154160.001.0001

Potter, David. "Entertainment," 381–91 in *A Companion to Ancient History*. Edited by Andrew Erskine. Oxford: Blackwell, 2009.

Price, Simon. "Latin Christian Apologetics: Minucius Felix, Tertullian, and Cyprian," 105–29 in Edwards et al., eds., *Apologetics in the Roman Empire*.

Rebillard, Éric. "The West (2): North Africa," 303–22 in *The Oxford Handbook of Early Christian Studies*. Edited by Susan Ashbrook Harvey and David G. Hunter. Oxford: Oxford University Press, 2008.

—*Christians and Their Many Identities in Late Antiquity, North Africa, 200-450 CE*. Ithaca, NY: Cornell University Press, 2012.

Robbins, Vernon K. *The Tapestry of Early Christian Discourse: Rhetoric, Society, and Ideology*. London: Routledge, 1996.

Sider, Robert D. "Tertullian on the Shows: An Analysis," *Journal of Theological Studies* 29.2 (1978): 339–65. https://doi.org/10.1093/jts/XXIX.2.339

—*Christian and Pagan in the Roman Empire: The Witness of Tertullian*. Washington, DC: Catholic University of America Press, 2001.

Smith, Jonathan Z. "Classification," 35–44 in *Guide to the Study of Religion*. Edited by Willi Braun and Russell T. McCutcheon. London: Cassell, 2000.

Smith, Martyn. *Religion, Culture, and Sacred Space*. New York: Palgrave, 2008. https://doi.org/10.1057/9780230616172

Stratton, Kimberly B. "Identity," 220–51 in *The Cambridge Companion to Ancient Mediterranean Religions*. Edited by Barbette Stanley Spaeth. Cambridge: Cambridge University Press, 2013.

Thalmann, William G. *Apollonius of Rhodes and the Spaces of Hellenism*. Oxford: Oxford University Press, 2011. https://doi.org/10.1093/acprof:oso/9780199731572.001.0001

Tilley, Maureen A. "North Africa," 381–96 in *The Cambridge History of Christianity*. Vol. 1: *Origins to Constantine*. Edited by Margaret M. Mitchell and Frances M. Young. Cambridge: Cambridge University Press, 2008.

Wilhite, David E. *Tertullian the African*. Berlin: Walter de Gruyter, 2007. https://doi.org/10.1515/9783110926262

Chapter Fifteen

The Anachronism of "Early Christian Communities"

Sarah E. Rollens

Introduction

It has long been common to speak of "early Christian communities," and especially to assume that specific communities were associated with texts evincing ostensibly unique theologies. Several scholars have begun to question this connection, albeit for very different reasons. This chapter joins that conversation and argues that presumptions of "early Christian communities" are anachronistic, because they depend on and embody modern understandings of religious identity: in particular, that religion is a private, interior matter that is shared among a wider group of believers who all orient their collective identity around these beliefs. Furthermore, the idea that doctrinal differences evident in ancient texts should correspond to particular communities is a legacy of the Protestant Reformation, which saw the proliferation of new Christian "communities" when differences of doctrine, authority, or practice emerged. Other influences, such as German nationalism, German Romanticism, and modern western conceptions of the category of "religion," help enable this tendency as well. Rather than view each distinct text as corresponding to a particular community, it is better to view a text as a discursive space dealing with identity and authority, in which a variety of authors engaged, some perhaps entirely disconnected from any coherent community. To be clear, the goal in this chapter is not to disparage those who have tried to define the contours of groups of people who were interested in Jesus; I have shared that curiosity. My interest, rather, is in recognizing the logic of this strategy and thinking about the *intellectual legacy* that makes it possible.

Communities Everywhere, As Far As the Eye Can See

For many scholars, the conclusion that most texts correspond to a community has needed little justification; it has been a matter of fact. This assumption was evident in B. H. Streeter's seminal work on the four canonical gospels, wherein he matched each of the traditions behind the gospels to a particular geographical locale.[1] As Richard Bauckham observes, "Streeter would seem to be one of the first scholars to stress the local origins of all four Gospels in such a way as to fuse the two questions of the local context *in which* a Gospel was written and the audience *for which* it was written."[2] The habit of connecting texts to discrete communities probably found its best support in form criticism, which sought to identify how certain forms of tradition were passed down through communities and addressed their interests. Consider the following statement found at the opening of Rudolf Bultmann's classic study of the Synoptic Gospels: "[T]he literature in which the life of a given community, even the primitive Christian community, has taken shape," he explained, "springs out of quite definite conditions and wants of life from which grows up a quite definite style and quite specific forms and categories."[3] Elsewhere, he imagines the Q document— for many, one of the earliest sources for the Galilean Jesus movement—as "a primary source from which we can reconstruct a picture of the primitive community in which the Logia arose."[4] Thus, for Bultmann, it was a matter of fact that communities had "lives" and ideas which could be directly correlated first to oral tradition and later to literary forms. Indeed, communities are virtually required alongside the notion of *Sitz im Leben*, the social situation proposed by form critics that makes the most sense of a given unit of tradition.[5] Whereas form critics sometimes only vaguely defined the contours of the group settings they envisioned (such as an "eschatological community" or "Palestinian" and "Hellenistic" Christianity), we observe more specificity in redaction criticism, which sought to identify the local concerns to which an author was reacting when he edited a text.[6]

1.   See B. H. Streeter, *The Four Gospels, A Study of Origins, The Manuscript Tradition, Sources, Authorship, & Dates* (Oxford: MacMillan, 1924), 12. Cf. Edward W. Klink III, "The Gospel Community Debate: State of the Question," *Currents in Biblical Research* 3.1 (2004): 61.

2.   Richard Bauckham, "For Whom Were the Gospels Written?" in *The Gospels for All Christians: Rethinking the Gospel Audiences* (ed. Richard Bauckham; Grand Rapids, MI: Eerdmans, 1998), 15 (emphasis in the original).

3.   Rudolf Bultmann, *The History of the Synoptic Tradition* (trans. John Marsh; New York: Harper & Row, 1963), 4.

4.   Rudolf Bultmann, "The New Approach to the Synoptic Problem," *Journal of Religion* 6.4 (1926): 341.

5.   See Bultmann, *Synoptic Tradition*, 4. In fact, the existence of communities behind units of tradition emerges from cyclical reasoning for Bultmann: units of tradition require a community which produced them, while the community, in turn, is required to understand the meaning of said units (5).

6.   Bultmann, *Synoptic Tradition*, 17–8.

This history is clearly dated, and certainly many have moved away from this interest in communities behind texts. Moreover, not all who study form criticism have sought to outline the contours of specific communities, and not all who study the geographical spread of Christianity have connected it to known or hypothesized communities. But yet it is often *implicit* when scholars outline the supposed unique theology of a text or the distinctive practices that it endorses. We feel justified in imagining the people who *must have* adhered to such unique theologies or fostered them in a group. It seems clear, in the words of one scholar, that "[n]early all scholars writing about the Gospels now treat it as virtually self-evident that each evangelist addressed the specific context and concerns of his own community."[7]

More recently, the concept of community has been endorsed (again, implicitly) by discussions of oral tradition and its transmission. What has happened here is that scholars emphasize the social context of oral tradition, often based on studies of modern oral culture, and then conclude that a community is *required* to sustain the transmission of an ancient tradition. Consider James Dunn's study on Q, in which he distills an early, oral stratum of material. Oral tradition, he then stresses, "is essentially communal in nature," and so to identify an oral "core" in Q material puts us in touch with the community that sustained it. Elsewhere, he claims that these communities were likely not isolated from one another, so we ought not assume that a text functions *only* for one community.[8] His categories are even more precise (and anachronistic) than "community" though; he speaks, for instance, of the "first churches" and how they shared and knew of a variety of texts.[9] This is part of his wider thesis that "oral communities" nurtured the social memories of Jesus in the early years of the movement.[10] This seems to be an updated version of Bultmann and others' earlier form critical models. Others have similarly noticed the "communal" nature of text production, especially that an author would develop his ideas in conversation with an audience or even different audiences over time.[11] This is likely accurate, given that there are several famous instances of authors composing in this

7.   Richard Bauckham, "Introduction," in Bauckham, ed., *Gospels for All Christians*, 1.

8.   James Dunn, "Jesus in Oral Memory: The Initial Stages of the Jesus Tradition," in *SBL Seminar Papers* 39 (Atlanta, GA: Society of Biblical Literature, 2000), 324. This position is self-consciously in agreement with Bauckham's thesis in *Gospels for All Christians*.

9.   Dunn, "Jesus in Oral Memory," 325.

10.   See James Dunn, "Social Memory in the Oral Jesus Tradition," in *The Oral Gospel Tradition* (ed. James Dunn; Grand Rapids, MI: Eerdmans, 2013), 244.

11.   See Pieter J. J. Botha, "Authorship in Historical Perspective and Its Bearing on New Testament and Early Christian Texts and Contexts," *Scriptura* 102 (2009): 506.

manner,[12] but perhaps the term "communal" is not quite accurate. Particularly if a varied audience is in view, to use a term such as "social setting" or even just "group setting" may be more useful, otherwise we run the risk of imagining a fixed group who shared a certain level of familiarity and ideological similarity.

A major challenge to the notion that each gospel corresponds to a discrete community is found in Richard Bauckham's provocative essay "For Whom Were the Gospels Written?"[13] Bauckham had begun to notice the frequency with which scholars spoke of "John's community" or "Matthew's community," as if every text automatically arose from a coherent community and embodied its unique theological ideas; this connection, he argues, "has been entirely taken for granted in most Gospels scholarship for some decades now."[14] Instead, Bauckham imagines "a perfectly obvious alternative possibility,"[15] that the gospels were addressed to "any and every Christian community in [the author's] time in which Greek was understood."[16] The narratives of Jesus were not meant to be used only by one community. This, he claims, is in keeping with the ways that ancient literature circulated and with what we know about intra-group networks and communication.

His criticisms are well-taken and important starting points for my discussion, but two things must be noted. First, his solution is no more

12. Robyn Faith Walsh points to Athenaeus's episode of the "Sophists at Dinner" ("Q and the 'Big Bang' Theory of Christian Origins," Paper presented at the Annual Meeting of the Society of Biblical Literature. Baltimore, MD, 2014). Pliny the Younger also evinces this compositional model.

13. Bauckham edits the volume in which this essay is found—*Gospels for All Christians: Rethinking the Gospel Audiences*—and his essay acts as a programmatic introduction for other contributors.

14. Bauckham, "For Whom Were the Gospels Written?" 10.

15. Bauckman, "For Whom Were the Gospels Written?" 11.

16. Bauckham, "Introduction," 4. So also, Martin Hengel's study on the four canonical gospels claimed that the gospels reflect the activity of the apostles spreading a shared message among different churches: "[T]he missionaries of the early church traveled a great deal and could be authoritative teachers at different place" (*The Four Gospels and the One Gospel of Jesus Christ* [Harrisburg, PA: Trinity, 2000], 107). Thus, both Hengel and Bauckham presuppose a certain homogeneity among these groups and downplay local concerns. As someone who is carefully attentive to socio-economic experiences of different groups in the ancient world, I necessarily think that writings are products of their localized environment, whether than means a self-conscious community or not. Therefore, I cannot agree with them that the texts were directed toward any and all folks who followed Jesus. Any introduction to the New Testament will outline the most famous of these localized interests: John's polemic against his particular understanding of "Jews"; Matthew's on-going conflicts with Pharisees; Luke's frequent attention to gentile figures.

sociologically sophisticated than those with whom he takes issue. Whereas he had faulted others for proceeding under the unargued assumption that gospels correlated to specific Christian communities, he himself proceeds with the notion that a "community" is a self-evident social form that requires no argumentation. Second, his criticisms of the idea of isolated Christian communities are very confessionally motivated, as one of his major concerns is that "reading the Gospels as texts about their communities rather than as texts about the historically particular human Jesus implies a 'denial that the Word became flesh'."[17] It is thus clear how his understanding of what ancient Christianity *must be theologically* was the impetus for his challenges to more socio-historically interested scholarship.

Others who are ostensibly critical of some "community" models still implicitly endorse it as a viable sociological category. Bauckham, for instance, still assumed Christian communities existed, but just denied that any particular text was written to be a *direct reflection* of their interests. In Birger Pearson's assessment of how scholars have treated the Q community, he argues against the idea of a Q community in Galilee for a different reason, namely, that the ideas in Q do not show enough differentiation from the so-called Jerusalem community. Thus, though he is critical of a so-called "Q community," it is in service of giving priority to an unargued Jerusalem "community," which is evident in his conclusion: "we can legitimately conclude that the religion believed and practiced by the early Galilean Christians was essentially the same as that of the mother church in Jerusalem."[18] This conclusion, however, is guided by his understanding of what is "essential" to construct a coherent "Christian community"—in this case, a similar set of ideas about Jesus and the Pharisees. Moreover, it illustrates the evident anxiety that many feel in the possibility of finding *too many* communities, and consequently, of fracturing a particular portrait of Christian origins that depends on a certain homogeneity.

Whereas Bauckham, Dunn, and Pearson's apparent critiques are animated by interests homogenizing early Christian teachings and groups, Stanley Stowers's critique of the communities model is more sociologically nuanced. Stowers notes in his recent discussion of "communities" that we too often assume that there must be a "tight fit between a writer and a highly

17. Bauckham, "Introduction," 7.
18. Birger Pearson, "A Q Community in Galilee?" *New Testament Studies* 50 (2004): 494. Pearson understands his proposal to be "heretical" (p. 494) alongside the so-called hegemony in North American scholarship that argues for a distinct form of Galilean Jesus followers. His "heresy" is, in my opinion, one of the most traditional portraits of Christian origins in existence.

coherent social group with commonality in belief and practice."[19] In fact, as critical historians, our first impulse when we see this language should be to assume that the coherent community is *not* there and that the language is in fact trying to *create* it. Indeed, this is how Stowers proposes we should treat Paul's letters—not as a *reflection* of a community that is already in place, but as the very attempt to construct a not-in-place community out of a collection of individuals with diverse interests and commitments.[20] In addition, he argues that many of our ideas about what so-called communities looked like have resulted from portraits in the Book of Acts and Eusebius's writings, texts that have clear investments in depicting Christian origins as visible, coherent, and fairly homogenous. Yet there is even more to be said about the lack of sociological feasibility in this matter. In what follows, I explain why the term "community" is problematic from a sociological perspective, and then turn to exploring the intellectual heritage that makes the use of the term so common in the field of biblical studies.

Sociological Ambiguity and Theories of Identity

According to Anthony Cohen, "'Community' is one of those words—like 'culture', 'myth', 'ritual', 'symbol'—bandied around in ordinary, everyday speech, apparently readily intelligible to speaker and listener, which, when imported into the discourse of social science, however, causes immense difficulty."[21] The first question for biblical scholars, then, is: what kind of social formation do we even have in mind when we use the category "community"? And second, given what we know about identity and views of the self in the ancient world, is this social formation feasible? To be clear, this is not just a debate over a definition, but rather, the appropriateness and utility of a heuristic category in the ancient context.

Regina Schwartz lists a number of ways that the Bible tends to imagine collectives of people: "[A] group with a common deity and cultic practices, a population who hold a territory in common, a nation with a bureaucracy, a kinship group, an exiled community united by a common literature."[22] In general, scholars conflate many of these dimensions into bases for communities, vaguely understood as groups of individuals adhering to propositional

19. Stanley Stowers, "The Concept of 'Community' and the History of Early Christianity," *Method & Theory in the Study of Religion* 23 (2011): 248.

20. Stowers, "Concept of 'Community'," 242–4.

21. Anthony Cohen, *The Symbolic Construction of Community* (London: Routledge, 1985), 11.

22. Regina M. Schwartz, *The Curse of Cain: The Violent Legacy of Monotheism* (Chicago, IL: University of Chicago Press, 1997), 6.

beliefs and thus recognizing their identity on this basis as part of a larger collective. How would ancient peoples have understood these various affiliations? A common statement is that the Mediterranean world was a "collectivist" society, meaning that individuals understood their identity to be embedded in wider social forms such as family, village, or tribe.[23] This is opposed to our modern understanding of identity, which views an individual as emerging from these social forms but also as creating a unique, personal identity. On one hand, I think this distinction is somewhat overdrawn in much scholarship, and it often embodies some stereotypical assumptions about the differences between ancient and modern peoples. Collectivistic and individualistic identity traits should not be understood as *mutually exclusive*, but rather two common, cross-cultural identity strategies that people use in varying degrees in different settings.[24] We do, on the other hand, notice that people in the Roman Empire tended to understand their primary identity markers as those associated with family and heritage, ethnicity and homeland. These were not easily cast off. This does not mean, of course, that people did not understand themselves as singular entities, but rather that their identity was an *extension* of other groups in which they were embedded. This means that a person's understanding of his or her own identity should not be expected to automatically change when they participated in meals with a Christ group, gathered with them to sing hymns, or even opted to be baptized by a fellow Jesus follower—all things that we typically imagine as markers for so-called conversion to Christianity.

In fact, the notion of participating in various meetings, meals, or other activities with fellow Christ-believers may have had little to no impact on a person's sense of their own identity. For the purpose of the present discussion, this means that the notion of "joining a Christian community," could such a formation be positively identified, may have had little effect on an

23. See Harry C. Triandis, "Cross Cultural Studies in Individualism and Collectivism," in *Nebraska Symposium on Motivation* (ed. Richard A. Diensber and John J. Berman; Lincoln, NE: University of Nebraska Press, 1990), 56; so also, using Triandis's theory: Richard L. Rohrbaugh, *The New Testament in Cross-Cultural Perspective* (Eugene, OR: Cascade, 2007), 64–5; Wolfgang Stegemann, Bruce J. Malina, and Gerd Theissen, eds., *The Social Setting of Jesus and the Gospels* (Minneapolis, MN: Fortress Press, 2002), 30; Coleman A. Baker, *Identity, Memory, and Narrative in Early Christianity: Peter, Paul, and Recategorization in the Book of Acts* (Eugene, OR: Pickwick Publications, 2011), 44–9.

24. So also, stressing somewhat different nuances, Zeba A. Crook, *Reconceptualising Conversion: Patronage, Loyalty, and Conversion in the Religions of the Ancient Mediterranean* (Berlin: Walter de Gruyter, 2004), 33 and "Honor, Shame, and Social Status Revisited," *Journal of Biblical Literature* 128.3 (2009): 599.

individual's identity construction.[25] And, I would even argue that few texts witness the idea that converts "join" communities. Rather, what we read about in texts are situations in which people are still wrestling and coming to terms with other dimensions of their collective identity (e.g., kinship, occupational, regional, ethnic) since having accrued an interest in Jesus.

More to the point, the effort to pin ancient peoples into a particular religious group is based on a flawed notion of how identity construction occurs. In particular, this strategy focuses on a *singular* feature of a person's identity and treats it in an all-determining fashion; thus, one's interest in Jesus and occasional affiliation with similar folks becomes the basis for assuming that a community must result from this shared feature. This strategy is commonplace even when theorizing contemporary identity. Economist and political theorist Amartya Sen points to a similar tactic of dividing modern people into groups based on religio-cultural affiliation, what he calls the "civilizational model" of understanding humanity. As he explains,

> [t]he religious partitioning of the world produces a deeply misleading understanding of the people across the world and the diverse relations among them, and it also has the effect of magnifying one particular distinction between one person and another to the exclusion of all other important concerns.[26]

It is easy for scholars to put people into categories based on a particular feature that they have identified (a belief, a practice, a stated political or national loyalty), but that may bear no relation to how the individual in question understands their own identity. In addition, most are well aware of the variety of ways that people can participate in any given form of discourse, and so to fix a set of beliefs as unique to or definitive of a singular "community" privileges only those ideas that were heard. The "orthodox" beliefs of a particular social form may not be shared by all who participate in it. As Sen goes on to explain, "[t]he singular classification gives a commanding voice to the 'establishment' figures in the respective religious hierarchy while other perspectives are relatively downgraded and eclipsed."[27]

It seems to be a related assumption that modern, globalized identities are more complex than ancient ones (as Amartya Sen's concerns take for granted), which provides ostensible comfort to historians seeking nascent Christian communities. For instance, Jean-Luc Nancy, an identity theorist, imagines an ideal age when identities were easily constructed from minimal social dimensions. He muses:

25. As in Dunn, "Social Memory," 244.

26. Amartya Sen, *Identity and Violence: The Illusion of Destiny* (New York: W. W. Norton, 2006), 76

27. Sen, *Identity and Violence*, 77.

> We are floating on an ocean of identity-forming materials that nothing seems
> any longer to be able to crystallize into "identities" … In the past, one was a
> Kanak or a Cossack, Berber or Breton, French or English, English or Scot-
> tish, and one belonged to that parish, synagogue, or mosque, and that group,
> lineage, totem, island, or valley.[28]

For him, pre-modern identities were simple and mutually exclusive. Yet this
is highly romanticized, and clearly in service of underscoring the complexities of globalization's effect on identity formation. Evidence from antiquity shows that they were equally complex and that Nancy and others have
overlooked such complexity in order to treat it as a kind of Golden Age.
One need only glance at one of Paul's letters such as 1 Corinthians to understand this complexity. Paul imagined people in his audience who were male,
female, wealthy, of modest means, Christ-believers, pagan temple attend-
ees, educated, uneducated, and proficient in spiritual gifts, among many
other traits, which were not always mutually exclusive. To fix a label such
as "Corinthian Christian community" on such diversity homogenizes it too
much. From a modern vantage point, of course, one's interest in Jesus or
Christ in antiquity may *seem* like a person's defining feature. For some, it
no doubt was. But it is just as plausible that if we asked those people which
"community" they were from, a *whole host of other affiliations* would be
equally important. Even to answer that they were from a group with an
interest in Christ tells us little about what such people did, how they related
to one another, and what specific ideas they had in common. "Community"
is thus a sociologically ambiguous term.

   To complicate matters even more, seeking "early Christian communities"
embodies modern understandings of what religious affiliation is. Several
influential studies have called into question the notion that "religion" as an
autonomous and articulated sphere of life existed in the pre-modern period.
Without dwelling too long on these important studies, I will simply note some
highlights. Talal Asad has famously challenged universal, cross-cultural definitions of religion on the grounds that they privilege ideas over practice and
are based on modern Christian presumptions about what religion must be.[29]
Similarly, Tomoko Masuzawa has convincingly shown that homogenous
"world religions" categories appeared in western discourse relatively recently;[30] western thinkers imposed these categories on the peoples they encountered, because there was often no native category for what they had come to

---

   28.   Jean-Luc Nancy, *Identity: Fragments, Frankness* (trans. François Raffoul; New
York: Fordham University Press, 2015), 28–9.
   29.   See Talal Asad, *Genealogies of Religion: Discipline and Reasons of Power in
Christianity and Islam* (Baltimore, MD: Johns Hopkins University Press, 1993).
   30.   Cf. Tomoko Masuzawa, *The Invention of World Religions: Or, How European*

understand as a "religious system of belief and practice." So, religion emerged in modernity as an autonomous sphere of life and began to be applied to the ancient world, and as Brent Nongbri recently reminds us, the category has no counterpart in the Roman Empire.[31]

Furthermore, as Peter Harrison explores in his study on the concepts of "religion" and "science," what many people now assume is ancient Christian "religion" was actually understood quite differently in its antique context, at least by literate theologians. By analyzing thinkers such as Origen and Tertullian who had a great deal to say about what "true religion" was, Harrison notes that Christianity had most in common with philosophical practices to improve the self and achieve a properly ordered life. While Christians clearly had doctrines, these doctrines were also simultaneously "exercises" (practices) that were meant to inculcate a certain mental and spiritual habit in the person in their efforts to improve the self.[32] In fact, some of the Christian authors who tried to defend their ideas to others did so without reference to belief. *The Epistle to Diognetus*, for instance, uses the following substantive terms to describe Christianity: "godliness"; "worship"; "race"; and "way of life."[33] Harrison observes that "[n]one of these terms is suggestive of a commitment to a system of propositions."[34]

In other words, not only is it problematic to single out one dimension of a person's identity and to assume that a community could be sustained on the basis of a group elevating this dimension to primacy, but also the very strategy of using the category "religion" as this dimension in antiquity is questionable too. Ancient peoples would not have segmented off their private beliefs about deities and their cultic activities as a special feature of their being; they were intertwined with and animated their engagement with society, politics, and even economic activity.[35] Harrison points out that Christian

Universalism Was Preserved in the Language of Pluralism (Chicago, IL: University of Chicago Press, 2005).

31. See Brent Nongbri, *Before Religion: A History of a Modern Concept* (New Haven, CT: Yale University Press, 2013).

32. See Peter Harrison, *The Territories of Science and Religion* (Chicago, IL: University of Chicago Press, 2015), 45–6.

33. Harrison, *Science and Religion*, 34–5.

34. Harrison, *Science and Religion*, 36.

35. Furthermore, there remains an issue that I have not even touched upon: the anachronism of the term "Christian." In some ways, this takes us too far beyond the bounds of the present discussion, but it suffices to say that many others have shown persuasively that the term "Christian" and the associated identity enters ancient discourse much later that we had previously thought. Most of the struggles to define identity in Paul's letters and the gospels concern how to reconcile an interest with Jesus with a Jewish affiliation. Thus, to decode "Christian communities" behind this discourse makes little sense.

theologians/philosophers eventually "disembedded" Christianity from time and space, in order to claim that Christianity contained universal philosophical truths that had existed since the beginning of time and that Jewish, Greek, and Roman thinkers had simply not accessed its truest expression. This "disembedding," he then proposes, becomes the "precondition from the idea of a generic religion that will crystalize in the early modern period."[36]

The Concept of "Community" as a Modern Development

In addition to the sociological ambiguity of the concept, a particular intellectual heritage is responsible for its entrenchment in biblical studies, namely a combination of German nationalism (and Romanticism) and an earlier Protestant theology. Curiously, the way we now understand religious communities thus came about at the same time as religion started to be hived off as a special segment of life.

German Nationalism and Romanticism

Others have located the genesis of biblical scholarship in both German Romanticism and German nationalism (by this latter notion, I mean *only* the ideological efforts of forming the modern nation state of Germany, not anything to do with later National Socialist ideologies), so I will be brief here. In short, both of these movements encouraged scholars to see an animating *Volk* (people) preserved behind texts. Let me quote from Regina Schwartz, one proponent of such view:

> A key movement in the history of biblical interpretation occurred during the transition from the predominantly sacred to the largely secular worlds that spanned the seventeenth and eighteenth centuries ... Whether Hegelian, romantic, pietist, or none of the above, [biblical scholars] were imbued with nascent German nationalism. Could it really be a coincidence that biblical higher criticism and the ideology of radical modern nationalism were born in the same period in the same place? The Bible's preoccupation with collective identity was read though the lenses of German nationalism.[37]

Thus, she notes the evident "intersections of biblical identity formations and later secular beliefs about collective identity."[38] As I understand this, she is recognizing the way in which ordinary collective identification strategies in biblical texts are invested with a kind of prestige by modern interpreters and made to stand for discrete, coherent communities, akin to nationalist

36. Harrison, *Science and Religion*, 44.
37. Schwartz, *Curse of Cain*, 10–1.
38. Schwartz, *Curse of Cain*, 13.

entities emerging in the eighteenth century—the context in which these very modern interpreters were embedded. More recently, Stanley Stowers has observed that commentators as early as Johan Gottfried Herder (late eighteenth century) have supposed that "[t]he more authentic and Geist-filled literature [of the Bible] came not from the rational manufacture of authors, but grew organically from peoples, cultures and communities,"[39] which embodied ideologies of German Romanticism. Robyn Faith Walsh has similarly clarified the influence of Romanticism: "In treating ... the gospels more or less like folk literature, we have preserved an approach to these writings that focuses on using a given text to reconstruct (usually non-literate) 'implied audiences' or communities and their stories, teaching and other forms of oral exchange."[40] This approach, she goes on to note, portrays authors as "mere spokespersons for the oral speech of a vaguely defined community of people."[41] Thus, fueled by German nationalism and Romanticism, biblical studies emerged from this context primed to peer behind texts to imagine the communities which were made alive in them.

Early Protestant Theology

But perhaps this intellectual heritage can be found even earlier. I would like to propose that we *also* have familiar Protestant thinkers to thank for the all too ordinary text-community connection. Given the considerable shifts in thinking both about religion and about the individual as a social actor in this period, we can further flesh out the roots of what now seems the obvious conclusion about early Christian communities.

During and in the wake of the Protestant Reformation, there were fundamental shifts in thinking about the category "religion" that helped set the stage for envisioning communities associated with texts of different ideologies. Peter Harrison observes that Protestant reformers in this period started to become "insistent that religious faith be 'explicit'" and began to encourage Christians to "be able to articulate the doctrines they professed, and do so in propositional terms."[42] He explains:

> a largely unintended consequence of an insistence on explicit belief and creedal knowledge was thus the invention of the Christian religion, constituted by beliefs. Henceforth both Protestant and Catholic reform movements will emphasize the importance of doctrinal knowledge, with the consequence

39. Stowers, "Concept of 'Community'," 239.
40. Walsh, "Q and the 'Big Bang' Theory."
41. Walsh, "Q and the 'Big Bang' Theory."
42. Harrison, *Science and Religion*, 92.

that propositional beliefs become one of the central characteristics of the new "religion."[43]

Brent Nongbri takes these consequences even further in his history of the concept "religion." According to Nongbri, the Protestant fragmentation that resulted from the split with the Catholic Church invited, in addition to efforts to articulate propositions of belief, a new intellectual anxiety: which resulting denomination (that is, which set of propositions) was the true? Prior to the Reformation, different beliefs were wrong and heretical; now, they had become *different Christianities* and hence *different possible truths*. In response to this anxiety, different "sects" started producing literature ("tracts") that articulated their particular "propositions" for salvation.[44] Competing denominations, as one might expect, had competing propositions. Thus, we see in this historical moment how each social formation now came to have a particular set of intellectual propositions (doctrines) associated with it—a unique theology. And adherents were expected to be piously aware of them. Prior to this fracturing, competing theologies had existed in the form of heresies, but in this new setting, different theological propositions were tolerated without necessarily being considered heretical.

Martin Luther's own writings reflect the tendency to assume that competing theologies correspond to competing social groups. Consider his exasperated complaint:

> There are almost as many sects and beliefs as there are heads; this one will not admit baptism; that one rejects the Sacrament of the altar; another places another world between the present one and the day of judgment; some teach that Jesus Christ is not God. There is not an individual, however clownish he may be, who does not claim to be inspired by the Holy Ghost, and who does not put forth as prophecies his ravings and dreams.[45]

For Luther, each "sect" had a distinct version of beliefs that sustained their social formation: some had particular beliefs about baptism; some about the day of judgment; some about Jesus's divinity. Were one to identity the intellectual propositions to which a person adhered, one would be able to place them definitely in a "community." Steeped in a largely Protestant legacy, biblical scholars would be ready to work from the premise that texts and literature evincing distinct and particular "theologies" represented identifiable communities.

43. Harrison, *Science and Religion*, 93–4.
44. Nongbri, *Before Religion*, 91. So also, Harrison, *Science and Religion*, 63, 94.
45. Cited in Leslie Rumble, *Bible Quizzes to a Street Preacher* (Rockford, IL: TAN Books, 1976).

Is it necessarily correct that differing theologies and distinct intellectual propositions correspond to particular communities? On one hand, we are especially conditioned today to outline political ideologies of self-consciously formed groups, so people adhering to a list of articulated ideas seems natural. So-called "covenantal communities," which define themselves as a people following a distinct body of law, have been claimed to be "among our most enduring political formations."[46] Yet I maintain that scholars too easily forget that *the production of distinct intellectual propositions for a particular ideological position can be completely divorced from group formation.* The ideology may simply exist at the level of discourse and not in the lived experience of any identifiable people, practitioners, or adherents. We should thus be absolutely wary that a so-called "negative correlation" could exist between a text and a social group. That is to say, the text may not *reflect* or dictate anything constructive about the community, but rather reflects precisely what does not exist and what the author *wants* to exist. The fusion of articulated ideological propositions and group formation, especially when it comes to religious ideologies, is in part, to my mind, a Protestant legacy.

I close this section with some insightful, though somewhat long, comments by Giovanni Bazzana on the theoretically crude nature of sociological analyses that purport to find communities behind early Christian texts:

> [M]ost of the sociological analyses focused on early Christianity seem unable to avoid looking as mere rewritings of old theological accounts recast in a new—now sociologically flavored—jargon. This might be due in part to the fact that in several countries—notably in Germany and in a majority of North American academic institutions—New Testament scholars are trained primarily as theologians. Be this as it may, such a distinctive phenomenon is nowhere more evident than in the many inquiries of the social location of the "communities" that produced various New Testament books. Thus, if a given text deals with issues of Mosaic observance, then its "community" is deemed "Jewish." If a text contains some polemical pieces directed against the Pharisees, it must have been produced by a group that had been recently expelled from a Jewish synagogue. If a text refers to public rejection and opposition, it must have come from a persecuted group of Jesus believers. Methodologically, such historical and sociological results are highly questionable because they are derived from texts without considering the very likely possibility of rhetorical accommodation or even fictional invention as parts of their compositional processes.[47]

As we see in this perceptive passage, these streams of influence (both historical and theoretical) that I have outlined above contribute to a situation in which slippage between text and community easily becomes routine in

---

46. Schwartz, *Curse of Cain*, 26.

47. Giovanni B. Bazzana, *Kingdom of Bureaucracy, The Political Theology of the Village Scribes in the Sayings Gospel Q* (Leuven: Peeters, 2015), 7–8.

biblical studies. Furthermore, as Bazzana observes, theological interests to find certain religious beliefs and practices that can be readily understood by the modern reader fuel this slippage. But if I and others are correct, there can be no simple or even necessary relationship between a text and a so-called religious community lying behind it.

Excursis: Paul's Audiences as Communities

One major objection might follow from the points raised in this essay: in his letters Paul is clearly writing to groups of people who have some sort of self-identity *as a group*. These groups, the objection might further suppose, could be described as a community akin to modern religious groups. The chapter already noted above one problem with this line of thinking: Paul's groups could be described with numerous dimensions of identity, such that a homogenous community of people held together by a common belief about Christ was extremely unlikely—especially given the obvious misunderstanding that many of them seem to have about Paul's ideas about Christ and his significance. The problem is, however, even more complex than that.

For one, the imagined audience of a written document should not be equated with the real audience. Paul likely had certain idealizations about the people who received and read his letters (and how they reacted), but he simply could not control those who actually encountered them, that is, the real audience. This real audience, in turn, should not be conflated with any fixed community. We have little evidence for how the recipients received his letters—based on, for example, 2 Corinthians or Galatians, we might assume a rather negative reception. It is also unclear whether or not his recipients expressed his advice and proscriptions in a visible or meaningful way. That is, depending on whether his readership believed what he said and carried out his advice, they may or may not have expressed the "community" that he desired them to be.

For another, the most recent sociological models that have been used to help redescribe Paul's groups (in particular, household networks and voluntary associations[48]) resist an undertheorized model of community. For cultic groups that arise out of household structures and networks, we are often

---

48. On the phenomenon of voluntary associations, see John S. Kloppenborg and Stephen G. Wilson, eds., *Voluntary Associations in the Graeco-Roman World* (London: Routledge, 1996). For two detailed comparative studies between voluntary association and Paul's groups, see Richard Last, *The Pauline Church and the Corinthian Ekklēsia: Greco-Roman Associations in Comparative Context* (Cambridge: Cambridge University Press, 2015); Richard S. Ascough, *Paul's Macedonian Associations: The Social Context of Philippians and 1 Thessalonians* (Tübingen: Mohr Siebeck, 2003).

dealing with a group that emerges at the behest of the *pater familias*. Subordinate figures in the household, such as wives, children, and slaves, may have had little say in their affiliation with and participation in the group. This certainly resists a Protestant model of community, wherein such a phenomenon organically rises from those who share similar beliefs. Voluntary associations, whose group affiliations could be based on anything from a common deity to a neighborhood sociality to a similar trade or occupation, were exceptionally transient in terms of identity. People could belong to more than one association if their finances allowed. Many of the associative practices were periodic at best: monthly meetings, occasional banquets and honorific meals, and other festivities. More to the point, while such groups could have extremely elaborate rules and regulations for meetings, most of the regulations to distinguish the group only came into being during meetings. Outside of such encounters, the voluntary associations and their practices did not necessarily determine the identity of the members, and abstract, mutually exclusive "communities" do not seem to have resulted from associative activity.

It bears repeating: when it comes to Paul's letters, we encounter the "groupness" of his recipients only in the textual form and only from Paul's perspective. It is nearly impossible to know the extent to which the people he writes to see themselves as a coherent group in the manner that he does, or see themselves as a group at all. Evidence such as 1 Corinthians 1.11-7 suggests that many people in Paul's audiences were fundamentally confused about their group affiliation and allegiances. (Evidence throughout 1 Corinthians and other letters suggests that they were fundamentally confused on *many* points.) This extends Stowers's previously mentioned insight that Paul's letters are not a *reflection* of groups, but rather, the attempt to *create* them. This means that for scholars to project a coherent "Corinthian Christian community" behind such letters is likely wishful thinking.

Concluding Remarks

My argument has been that there are several interrelated problems with the category of "early Christian communities." First, it is sociologically ambiguous to the point that it lacks heuristic utility. Second, it results from a modern intellectual legacy that inherits early Protestant theology and later German nationalism and Romanticism. These ideologies make it possible to suppose that doctrinal differences observed in texts corresponded to—indeed expressed—the coherent ideas of a community lying just behind them. I end with a brief nod to an alternative way of discussing identity and group formation that is more promising than the concept of community. Instead of imagining a community that is embodied in a text, it is better to speak in terms of a *common discourse* about Jesus, with various people *participating* and *using* it as a resource (among many others) for understanding identity. When it comes to authors, we are not dealing with community leaders who write texts *for* coherent communities; the authors are intellectuals and custodians of these shared resources, who mediate them to audiences, whether imagined or real.

Biographical Note

Sarah E. Rollens is Assistant Professor of Religious Studies at Rhodes College, Memphis TN, USA. She is the author of *Framing Social Criticism in the Jesus Movement: The Ideological Project of the Sayings Gospel Q* (Mohr Siebeck, 2014) and has also published on the synoptic problem, violence in early Christianity, and Graeco-Roman associations. She is currently working on her second monograph discussing violence in early Christianity. She has taught courses on the study of religion and early Christianity at the University of Alabama, the University of Toronto, and the University of North Carolina at Wilmington.

Bibliography

Asad, Talal. *Genealogies of Religion: Discipline and Reasons of Power in Christianity and Islam*. Baltimore, MD: Johns Hopkins University Press, 1993.

Ascough, Richard S. *Paul's Macedonian Associations: The Social Context of Philippians and 1 Thessalonians*. Tübingen: Mohr Siebeck, 2003.

Baker, Coleman A. *Identity, Memory, and Narrative in Early Christianity: Peter, Paul, and Recategorization in the Book of Acts*. Eugene, OR: Pickwick Publications, 2011.

Bauckham, Richard. "For Whom Were the Gospels Written?" 9–48 in Bauckham, ed., *Gospels for All Christians*, 1998.

—"Introduction," 1–7 in Bauckham, ed., *Gospels for All Christians*, 1998. https://doi.org/10.1163/9789004267411_002

—ed. *The Gospels for All Christians: Rethinking the Gospel Audiences*. Grand Rapids, MI: Eerdmans, 1998.

Bazzana, Giovanni B. *Kingdom of Bureaucracy, The Political Theology of the Village Scribes in the Sayings Gospel Q*. Leuven: Peeters, 2015.

Botha, Pieter J. J. "Authorship in Historical Perspective and Its Bearing on New Testament and Early Christian Texts and Contexts," *Scriptura* 102 (2009): 495–510. https://doi.org/10.7833/102-0-610

Bultmann, Rudolf. "The New Approach to the Synoptic Problem," *Journal of Religion* 6.4 (1926): 337–62. https://doi.org/10.1086/480591

—*The History of the Synoptic Tradition*. Translated by John Marsh. New York: Harper & Row, 1963.

Cohen, Anthony. *The Symbolic Construction of Community*. London: Routledge, 1985. https://doi.org/10.4324/9780203323373

Crook, Zeba A. *Reconceptualising Conversion: Patronage, Loyalty, and Conversion in the Religions of the Ancient Mediterranean*. Berlin: Walter de Gruyter, 2004. https://doi.org/10.1515/9783110915600

—"Honor, Shame, and Social Status Revisited," *Journal of Biblical Literature* 128.3 (2009): 591–611. https://doi.org/10.2307/25610205

Dunn, James. "Jesus in Oral Memory: The Initial Stages of the Jesus Tradition," 287–326 in *SBL Seminar Papers* 39. Atlanta, GA: Society of Biblical Literature, 2000.

—"Social Memory in the Oral Jesus Tradition," 230–47 in *The Oral Gospel Tradition*. Edited by James Dunn. Grand Rapids, MI: Eerdmans, 2013.

Harrison, Peter. *The Territories of Science and Religion*. Chicago, IL: University of Chicago Press, 2015. https://doi.org/10.7208/chicago/9780226184517.001.0001

Hengel, Martin. *The Four Gospels and the One Gospel of Jesus Christ*. Harrisburg, PA: Trinity, 2000.

Klink III, Edward W. "The Gospel Community Debate: State of the Question," *Currents in Biblical Research* 3.1 (2004): 60–85. https://doi.org/10.1177/1476993X0400300104

Kloppenborg, John S., and Stephen G. Wilson, eds. *Voluntary Associations in the Graeco-Roman World*. London: Routledge, 1996.

Last, Richard. *The Pauline Church and the Corinthian* Ekklēsia: *Greco-Roman Associations in Comparative Context*. Cambridge: Cambridge University Press, 2015.

Masuzawa, Tomoko. *The Invention of World Religions: Or, How European. Universalism Was Preserved in the Language of Pluralism*. Chicago, IL: University of Chicago Press, 2005. https://doi.org/10.7208/chicago/9780226922621.001.0001

Nancy, Jean-Luc. *Identity: Fragments, Frankness*. Translated by François Raffoul. New York: Fordham University Press, 2015.

Nongbri, Brent. *Before Religion: A History of a Modern Concept*. New Haven, CT: Yale University Press, 2013. https://doi.org/10.12987/yale/9780300154160.001.0001

Pearson, Birger. "A Q Community in Galilee?" *New Testament Studies* 50 (2004): 476–94. https://doi.org/10.1017/S002868850400027X

Rohrbaugh, Richard L. *The New Testament in Cross-Cultural Perspective*. Eugene, OR: Cascade, 2007.

Rumble, Leslie. *Bible Quizzes to a Street Preacher*. Rockford, IL: TAN Books, 1976.

Schwartz, Regina M. *The Curse of Cain: The Violent Legacy of Monotheism*. Chicago, IL: University of Chicago Press, 1997.

Sen, Amartya. *Identity and Violence: The Illusion of Destiny*. New York: W. W. Norton, 2006.

Stegemann, Wolfgang, Bruce J. Malina, and Gerd Theissen, eds. *The Social Setting of Jesus and the Gospels*. Minneapolis, MN: Fortress Press, 2002.

Stowers, Stanley. "The Concept of 'Community' and the History of Early Christianity," *Method & Theory in the Study of Religion* 23 (2011): 238–56. https://doi.org/10.1163/157006811X608377

Streeter, B. H. *The Four Gospels, A Study of Origins, The Manuscript Tradition, Sources, Authorship, & Dates*. Oxford: MacMillan, 1924.

Triandis, Harry C. "Cross Cultural Studies in Individualism and Collectivism," 41–133 in *Nebraska Symposium on Motivation*. Edited by Richard A. Diensber and John J. Berman. Lincoln, NE: University of Nebraska Press, 1990.

Walsh, Robyn Faith. "Q and the 'Big Bang' Theory of Christian Origins," Paper presented at the Annual Meeting of the Society of Biblical Literature. Baltimore, MD, 2014.

PART V

TOPICS IN THE STUDY OF (ANCIENT) RELIGION

Chapter Sixteen

Cognitive Study of (Ancient) Religions

Leonardo Ambasciano

> Historical events involve acting subjects with cognitive systems. Knowledge of the constraints and mechanisms imposed by such systems can therefore help historians understand historical events.
>
> —Jesper Sørensen[1]

> Because cognitive functions are finally based upon and explainable by tractable biochemical and neurophysiological processes, they belong to the material causes of socio-historical formations and should be considered alongside physical influences, economic forces, the effects of political power, etc.
>
> —Luther H. Martin[2]

Historiography and the Longue Durée *of Cognition: An Introductory Note*

At the end of the *Origin of Species*, Charles Darwin famously wrote:

> There is grandeur in this view of life, with its several powers, having been originally breathed into a few forms or into one; and that, whilst this planet has gone cycling on according to the fixed law of gravity, from so simple a beginning endless forms most beautiful and most wonderful have been, and are being, evolved.[3]

Later, in *The Descent of Man*, Darwin set out to show that evolved psychological features critical for the elaboration of religious thought—like agency detection and related emotional responses—are present in different degrees in nonhuman animals.[4] Since the very beginning of modern scientific research,

---

1.   Jesper Sørensen, "Religion in Mind: A Review Article of the Cognitive Science of Religion," *Numen* 52.4 (2005): 487.

2.   Luther H. Martin, "Cognitive Science, Ritual and the Hellenistic Mystery Religions," in *Deep History, Secular Theory: Historical and Scientific Studies of Religion* (Berlin: Walter de Gruyter, 2014), 318.

3.   Charles R. Darwin, *On the Origin of Species by Means of Natural Selection, or the Preservation of Favoured Races in the Struggle for Life* (London: John Murray, 1859), 490.

4.   See Charles R. Darwin, *The Descent of Man, and Selection in Relation to Sex* (London: John Murray, 1871), 67; cf. Stewart E. Guthrie, "Animal Animism: Evolutionary

thus, cognition was strictly intertwined with evolution. Confronted with the "grandeur in this view of life," which entailed a breath-taking historicization of biology while advancing a secular and materialistic way to study the deep roots of religious behaviors and beliefs,[5] the mainstream historiographical and academic study of religion(s) reacted demonstrating either indifference, reticence, or a surprising inclination for distortion.[6]

As soon as the twentieth century began, it was clear that the fate of the evolutionary and cognitive study of religion was meant to be bleak. Modern evolutionary psychology rose and prematurely fell apart with the works of James M. Baldwin (1861–1934), which anticipated the modern formalization of the theory of mind (to which I will return below), as well as the evolutionary mechanisms which regulate the selection, retention, and transmission of ideas.[7] Likewise, precocious attempts at understanding "Religious studies as a life science,"[8] focusing in particular on behavioral patterns as the engine for group selection and on the evolutionary pressures behind cognitive mechanisms, were destined to be largely ignored.[9]

Roots of Religious Cognition," in *Current Approaches in the Cognitive Science of Religion* (ed. Ilkka Pyysiäinen and Veikko Anttonen; London: Continuum, 2002), 38–67; Matthew Day, "Godless Savages and Superstitious Dogs: Charles Darwin, Imperial Ethnography, and the Problem of Human Uniqueness," *Journal of the History of Ideas* 69.1 (2008): 59; Vittorio Girotto, Telmo Pievani, and Giorgio Vallortigara, "Supernatural Beliefs: Adaptations for Social Life or By-products of Cognitive Adaptations?" in *Evolved Morality: The Biology and Philosophy of Human Conscience* (ed. Frans B. M. de Waal et al.; Leiden: Brill, 2014), 249–66.

5.   See Salvador E. Luria, Stephen J. Gould, and Sam Singer, *A View of Life* (Menlo Park, CA: Benjamin/Cummings, 1981), 585; Luther H. Martin, "The Origins of Religion, Cognition and Culture: The Bowerbird Syndrome," in *Origins of Religion, Cognition and Culture* (ed. Armin W. Geertz; Routledge, 2013), 178–9.

6.   See Leonardo Ambasciano, "Mind the (Unbridgeable) Gaps: A Cautionary Tale about Pseudoscientific Distortions and Scientific Misconceptions in the Study of Religion," *Method & Theory in the Study of Religion* 28.2 (2016): 141–225; *An Unnatural History of Religions: Academia, Post-truth and the Quest for Scientific Knowledge* (London: Bloomsbury, 2018).

7.   See Henry Plotkin, *Evolutionary Thought in Psychology* (Oxford: Blackwell, 2004), 76–7.

8.   See Joseph Bulbulia and Edward Slingerland, "Religious Studies as a Life Science," *Numen* 59.5–6 (2012): 564–613.

9.   See Alexander Macalister, *Evolution in Church History* (Dublin: Hodges & Figgis, 1882) and Jane E. Harrison, "The Influence of Darwinism on the Study of Religions," in *Darwin and Modern Science: Essays in Commemoration of the Centenary of the Birth of Charles Darwin and the Fiftieth Anniversary of the Publication of the 'Origin of Species'* (ed. Albert Charles Seward; Cambridge: Cambridge University Press, 1909), 494–511, respectively. Cf. Luther H. Martin, "Evolution, Cognition and History," in *Deep History*, 163–5.

Justified by the specious idea that human behavior is far too complex to be put under the reductionistic lenses of science, the majority of past historians and scholars interested in the academic study of religion(s) neglected or discarded the importance of our biological heritage as a primate *taxon*.[10] This unfortunate state of affairs was promoted, and further supported, by a humanistic point of view which considered the gap between the civilized *taxon Homo sapiens* and the naturalistic ontology of the cosmos as basically unbridgeable.[11]

Suspicion arose among the humanities scholars whenever alternative attempts at uniting psychology and historiography on the basis of a naturalistic

---

10. However, a minority of noteworthy exceptions is attested. E.g., Benson Saler, "Culture in Phylogenetic Perspective: An Appreciation of the Contributions of A. I. Hallowell," in *Understanding Religion: Selected Essays* (Berlin: Walter de Gruyter, 2009), 82–91 on cultural anthropologist A. Irving Hallowell (1892–1974).

11. The following list provides some of the most influential ideas that prevented the correct adoption of a Darwinian framework: (a) theological biases (Luther H. Martin and Donald Wiebe, "Religious Studies as a Scientific Discipline: The Persistence of a Delusion," *Journal of the American Academy of Religion* 80.3 [2012]: 587–97); (b) anthropodenial and pithecophobia, i.e., the denial or neglect of the primate ascendance of *H. sapiens* (Frans B. M. De Waal, *The Bonobo and the Atheist: In Search of Humanism Among the Primates* [New York: W. W. Norton, 2013]; see Ambasciano, "Mind the (Unbridgeable) Gaps"); (c) the naïve idea that evolution equates quasi-eschatological progress towards increasing complexity, which is chauvinistically identified in a specific form of human culture/religion *tout court* (Stephen Jay Gould, *Wonderful Life: The Burgess Shale and the Nature of History* [New York: W. W. Norton, 1989]; Jonathan Z. Smith, "Classification," in *Guide to the Study of Religion* [ed. Willi Braun and Russell T. McCutcheon; London: Cassell, 2000], 35–44); (d) the adoption of Neo-Lamarckism and Spencerian progressionism to explain the historical development of culture(s) and religion(s) (cf. Ambasciano, "Mind the (Unbridgeable) Gaps"); (e) the toxic legacy of the anthropological prejudices of old which fallaciously equate "evolutionary studies" with "racism" (Mark Isaak, *The Counter-Creationism Handbook* [Berkeley, CA: University of California Press, 2007], 5; Day, "Godless Savages"; Robert J. Richards, "Myth 19: That Darwin and Haeckel Were Complicit in Nazi Biology," in *Galileo Goes to Jail and Other Myths about Science and Religion* [ed. Ronald L. Numbers; Cambridge, MA: Harvard University Press, 2009], 170–7; Adrian Desmond and James Moore, *Darwin's Sacred Cause: How a Hatred of Slavery Shaped Darwin's Views on Human Evolution* [Boston, MA: Harcourt, 2009]); (f) the blank slate paradigm once *en vogue* in the humanities, namely the idea that human beings are born with no binding innate biological constraints (Steven Pinker, *The Blank Slate: The Modern Denial of Human Nature* [New York: Viking, 2002]); (g) the postmodern stance according to which science is at best just another explanation among many other equal alternatives and, at worst, a coercive control device which we should get rid of (Alan Sokal and Jean Bricmont, *Intellectual Impostures: Postmodern Philosophers' Abuse of Science* [London: Profile Books, 1998]; Alan Sokal, *Beyond the Hoax: Science, Philosophy and Culture* [Oxford: Oxford University Press, 2010]).

foundation were advanced in a tautological loop. Their eventual downfall would seal the uselessness of such approaches. The failure of psychohistory, which was a largely psychoanalytic discipline methodologically based on the "underlying unity of motive of historical actors" in their socio-historical settings,[12] was basically due to the epistemological shortcomings of psychoanalysis itself,[13] yet the fundamental idea of reaching a better understanding of the psychology of historical agents was far from being useless. Indeed, one way or another, historians have always tried to penetrate and understand the minds behind social, political, and cultural products.[14]

Notwithstanding theoretical approaches that emphasized the virtues of a more cognitively oriented epistemology and methodology in the study of cultural and religious phenomena,[15] specific historico-religious attempts at scientific theorizing remained extremely rare. Among the few forerunners, one might recall Jonathan Z. Smith (1938–2017), who advocated the adoption of phylogenetic and quantitative methods to overhaul classical taxonomies of religions; indologist Frits Staal (1930–2012), who proposed the idea that ritual has no rational meaning *prima facie* but should be understood as part and parcel of biological and behavioral patterns; classicist Walter Burkert (1931–2015), who studied the similarities between rituals and ethological behaviors from a sociobiological perspective; historians of religions

12. See Fred Weinstein, "Psychohistory and the Crisis of the Social Sciences," *History and Theory* 34.4 (1995): 302.

13. E.g., Stephen Jay Gould, "Freud's Evolutionary Fantasy," in *I Have Landed: The End of a Beginning in Natural History* (New York: Harmony Books, 2002), 147–58; Frank Cioffi, "The Case of Freud's Sexual Etiology of the Neuroses," in *Philosophy of Pseudoscience: Reconsidering the Demarcation Problem* (ed. Massimo Pigliucci and Maarten Boudry; Chicago, IL: University of Chicago Press, 2013), 321–40; Maurilio Orbecchi, *Psicologia dell'anima* (Turin: Bollati Boringhieri, 2015).

14. See David G. Shaw, "The Return of Science," *History and Theory* 38.4 (1999): 8; Jeremy T. Burman, "Bringing the Brain into History: Behind Hunt's and Smail's Appeals to Neurohistory," in *Psychology and History: Interdisciplinary Explanations* (ed. Cristian Tileagă and Jovan Byford; Cambridge: Cambridge University Press, 2014), 67; and the following articles by Luther H. Martin: "The Promise of Cognitive Science for the Study of Early Christianity," in *Deep History*, 202; "Evolution, Cognition and History," 163; "The Future of the Past: The History of Religions and Cognitive Historiography," in *Deep History*, 347.

15. These studies were initially focused on a critical re-evaluation of semiotics, anthropomorphism, and Chomskyan universal grammar: see Dan Sperber, *Rethinking Symbolism* (trans. Alice L. Morton; Cambridge: Cambridge University Press, 1975); Stewart E. Guthrie, "A Cognitive Theory of Religion," *Current Anthropology* 21.2 (1980): 181–203 and *Faces in the Clouds: A New Theory of Religion* (Oxford: Oxford University Press, 1993); E. Thomas Lawson and Robert N. McCauley, *Rethinking Religion: Connecting Cognition and Culture* (Cambridge: Cambridge University Press, 1990), respectively.

William E. Paden, who sought to retrieve some of the classic notions of the academic history of religions (HoR) as part of the cultural niche construction and imaginary world-making of *H. sapiens*; and Luther H. Martin, who combined the explanatory devices of Foucaultian post-structuralism with a bottom-up evolutionary perspective focused on in-group fictive kinship.[16]

The interdisciplinary and scientific study of religion experienced a remarkable increase in both quantity and quality of research between the late 1990s and the early 2000s, which led to the official birth of the cognitive science of religion (CSR) in 2000.[17] Meanwhile, after a long hiatus,[18] the *Annales* school of historiography, with its penchant for quantitative models and interdisciplinarity, was revived and updated thanks to a growing interest in the identification of historical patterns constrained by intertwined evolutionary, cultural, and environmental factors.[19] Among these trends,

16. See, Jonathan Z. Smith's works: "Fences and Neighbours," in *Imagining Religion: From Babylon to Jonestown* (Chicago, IL: University of Chicago Press, 1982), 1–18; *Drudgery Divine: On the Comparison of Early Christianities and the Religions of Late Antiquity* (London: School of Oriental and African Studies, 1990), 47–8 and n. 15; "Classification"; and "When the Chips Are Down," in *Relating Religion: Essays in the Study of Religion* (Chicago, IL: University of Chicago Press, 2004), 22. Also: Frits Staal, "The Meaninglessness of Ritual," *Numen* 26.1 (1979): 2–22 and *Rules Without Meaning: Ritual, Mantras, and the Human Science* (Bern: Peter Lang, 1989); Walter Burkert, *Creation of the Sacred: Tracks of Biology in Early Religions* (Cambridge, MA: Harvard University Press, 1996); William E. Paden, "Elements of a New Comparativism," *Method & Theory in the Study of Religion* 8.1 (1996): 5–14 and "A New Comparativism: Reply to the Panelists," *Method & Theory in the Study of Religion* 8.1 (1996): 37–49; Luther H. Martin, "Biology, Sociology and the Study of Religions: Two Lectures," *Religio: revue pro religionistiku* 5.1 (1997): 21–35.

17. See Harvey Whitehouse, *Inside the Cult: Religious Innovation and Transmission in Papua New Guinea* (Oxford: Oxford University Press, 1995); Roy D'Andrade, *The Development of Cognitive Anthropology* (Cambridge: Cambridge University Press, 1995); Dan Sperber, *Explaining Culture: A Naturalistic Approach* (Oxford: Blackwell, 1996); Maurice Bloch, *How We Think They Think: Anthropological Approaches to Cognition, Memory and Literacy* (Boulder, CO: Westview Press, 1998); Justin L. Barrett, "Exploring the Natural Foundations of Religion," *Trends in Cognitive Sciences* 4.1 (2000): 29–34; E. Thomas Lawson, "Towards a Cognitive Science of Religion," *Numen* 47.3 (2000): 338–49; Pascal Boyer, *Religion Explained: The Evolutionary Origins of Religious Thought* (New York: Basic Books, 2001); Harvey Whitehouse, "Modes of Religiosity: Towards a Cognitive Explanation of the Sociopolitical Dynamics of Religion," *Method & Theory in the Study of Religion* 143.3–4 (2000): 293–315.

18. See Michael Shermer and Alex Grobman, *Denying History: Who Says the Holocaust Never Happened and Why Do They Say It?* (Berkeley, CA: University of California Press, 2009), 20–31.

19. For example, see Frank J. Sulloway, *Born to Rebel: Birth Order, Family Dynamics, and Creative Lives* (New York: Pantheon, 1996); Jared Diamond, *Guns, Germs, and Steel: The Fates of Human Societies* (New York: W. W. Norton, 1997); Jared Diamond

particularly fertile has been Fernand Braudel's (1902–1985) idea of the *longue durée* as the temporal frame within which the study of the *mentalité* should take place.[20] What has dramatically changed since Braudel's original proposal is the chronological extent: as the *longue durée* now coincides with the deep time of evolutionary history,[21] the analysis of the proximate and ultimate mechanisms by which the *mentalité* is expressed in historical times are currently rooted in the deep history of the human species.[22]

In the last decade, two among the main branches of CSR, that is, the more historiographical one (namely, cognitive historiography) and the cognitively-oriented evolutionary science of religion (ESR), have gradually assimilated this renewed concept of the *longue durée*. At the same time, a shift from general and theoretical approaches to more scientifically-informed or experimental analyses gained momentum.[23] From such perspectives, the two sub-fields are respectively producing in-depth qualitative re-analyses of

and James Robinson, eds., *Natural Experiments of History* (Cambridge, MA: The Belknap Press of Harvard University Press, 2010); Luther H. Martin and Jesper Sørensen, eds., *Past Minds: Studies in Cognitive Historiography* (London: Routledge, 2011); David Armitage, "What's the Big Idea? Intellectual History and the *Longue Durée*," *History of European Ideas* 38.4 (2012): 493–507; Jo Guldi and David Armitage, *The History Manifesto* (Cambridge: Cambridge University Press, 2014).

20. Cf. Fernand Braudel, "History and the Social Sciences: The Longue Durée," in *On History* (Chicago, IL: University of Chicago Press, 1980), 25–45; John Arnold, *History: A Very Short Introduction* (Oxford: Oxford University Press, 2000), 99; André Burguière, *The Annales School: An Intellectual History* (Trans. Jane Marie Todd; Ithaca, NY: Cornell University Press, 2009), 61; Immanuel Wallerstein, "Braudel on the Longue Durée: Problems of Conceptual Translation," *Review: Fernand Braudel Center* 32.2 (2009): 155–70; Jesper Sørensen, "Past Minds: Present Historiography and Cognitive Science," in Martin and Sørensen, eds., *Past Minds*, 179–96.

21. See Daniel Lord Smail, *On Deep History and the Brain* (Berkeley, CA: University of California Press, 2008); Andrew Shryock and Daniel Lord Smail, eds., *Deep History: The Architecture of Past and Present* (Berkeley, CA: University of California Press, 2011); David Christian, *Maps of Time: An Introduction to Big History* (Berkeley, CA: University of California Press, 2011); Edmund Russell, *Evolutionary History: Uniting History and Biology to Understand Life on Earth* (Cambridge: Cambridge University Press, 2011).

22. See Sørensen, "Past Minds"; cf. Mark Fedyk, "How (Not) to Bring Psychology and Biology Together," *Philosophical Studies* 172.4 (2015): 949–67. However, misunderstandings about the evolutionary and cognitive extent of such a renewed historiography, expressed by more traditional scholars, are still common. E.g., Guldi and Armitage, *History Manifesto*, 9, 87; David Armitage and Jo Guldi, "Le retour de la longue durée: une perspective anglo-américaine," *Annales. Histoire, Sciences sociales* 70.2 (2015): 315; Tim Whitmarsh, *Battling the Gods: Atheism in the Ancient World* (London: Faber & Faber, 2016), 5.

23. For the experimental branch devoted to anthropology and psychology, see Joseph Bulbulia, "The Arts Transform the Cognitive Science of Religion," *Journal for the Cognitive Science of Religion* 1.2 (2013): 141–60 and Dimitris Xygalatas, "Special

ancient religious beliefs and behaviors[24] and performing quantitative studies to test competing historiographical hypotheses against the backdrop of
H. sapiens' deep time.[25]

   In a sense, thanks to CSR and ESR, the historical study of religion(s) has
finally returned to Darwin's original intuition both in terms of methodology
and epistemology. In the following paragraphs, I will focus on the descriptive, qualitative aspect of cognitive historiography.

Building Blocks

The examination of the neurophysiological and mental mechanisms behind
religious cognition has contributed to deconstructing the concept of religion itself.[26] Just like an artificial group of animals taxonomically grouped
together on the intuitive basis of superficially similar characteristics, yet separated by a different evolutionary background reflected by peculiar internal

Issue on the Experimental Research of Religion," *Journal for the Cognitive Science of
Religion* 1.2 (2013): 137–9.

   24.   E.g., Harvey Whitehouse and Luther H. Martin, eds., *Theorizing Religions Past:
Archaeology, History, and Cognition* (Walnut Creek, CA: AltaMira Press, 2004); Panayotis Pachis and Donald Wiebe, eds., *Chasing Down Religion: In the Sights of History
and the Cognitive Sciences* (Sheffield, UK: Equinox, 2009); Martin and Sørensen, eds.,
Past Minds; Armin W. Geertz, "Whence Religion? How the Brain Constructs the World
and What This Might Tell Us About the Origins of Religion, Cognition and Culture,"
in *Origins of Religion*, 17–70; Panayotis Pachis, "Healing Gods, Heroes and Rituals
in the Graeco-Roman World," *Open Library of Humanities* (2016), online: https://olh.
openlibhums.org/collections/special/healing-gods-heroes-and-rituals-in-the-graeco-ro-
man-world/ and see also the *Journal of Cognitive Historiography*.

   25.   E.g., Nicolas Baumard et al., "Increased Affluence Explains the Emergence of
Ascetic Wisdoms and Moralizing Religions," *Current Biology* 25.1 (2015): 10–15; Peter
Turchin et al., "*Seshat*: The Global History Databank," *Cliodynamics: The Journal of
Quantitative History and Cultural Evolution* 6.1 (2015): 77–107, online: http://escholar-
ship.org/uc/item/9qx387; Joseph Watts et al., "Broad Supernatural Punishment but Not
Moralising High Gods Precede the Evolution of Political Complexity in Austronesia,"
Proceedings of the Royal Society B 282.1804 (2015): 1–7; Joseph Watts et al., "Pulotu:
Database of Austronesian Supernatural Beliefs and Practices," *PLoS ONE* 10.9 (2015):
1–17; Ara Norenzayan et al., "The Cultural Evolution of Prosocial Religions," *Behavioral
and Brain Sciences* 39 (2016); Hervey C. Peoples, Pavel Duda, and Frank W. Marlowe,
"Hunter-Gatherers and the Origins of Religion," *Human Nature* 27.3 (2016): 261–82; but
cf. Leonardo Ambasciano, "Exiting the *Motel of the Mysteries*? How Historiographical
Floccinaucinihilipilification Is Affecting CSR 2.0," in *Religion Explained? The Cognitive
Science of Religion After Twenty-Five Years* (ed. Luther H. Martin and Donald Wiebe;
London: Bloomsbury, 2017), 107–22.

   26.   For an overview, see Ambasciano, "Mind the (Unbridgeable) Gaps" and *An
Unnatural History of Religions*.

features and specific ancestors (e.g., crocodiles and lizards, the former being more closely related to birds than the latter), religion as a whole is an intuitively aggregated, componential system of many different things put together in distinctive ways in particular cultural and historical settings.[27] Therefore, there is no such thing as a religious mind, but only religious thoughts and behaviors. Given their non-exclusive cognitive nature, each one of these components may be obviously exploited for ordinary non-religious purposes, or even consciously disassembled for criticism.[28] This is because, basically, there is no neurophysiological distinction between non-religious and religious cognition, and no "God spot" in the brain.[29]

The most basic cognitive building blocks for religious thoughts are agency detection, teleological reasoning, and intuitive mind/body dualism.[30] Theory of Mind (ToM), or mind-reading, is the paramount ability to read the intentionality of other agents, in order to interact with them via the recognition of their specific mental states (desires, beliefs, etc.). Agents are important because they are intuitively considered the main force that will

27. E.g., Harvey Whitehouse, "Religion, Cohesion, and Hostility," in *Religion, Intolerance, and Conflict: A Scientific and Conceptual Investigation* (ed. Steve Clarke, Russell Powell, and Julian Savulescu; Oxford: Oxford University Press, 2013), 36; Juraj Franek, "Has the Cognitive Science of Religion (Re)defined 'Religion'?" *Religio: Revue pro religionistiku* 22.1 (2014): 3–27; Jonathan Jong, "On (Not) Defining (Non)religion," *Science, Religion and Culture* 2.3 (2015): 15–24. On the legitimacy and applicability of the modern category "religion" in classical antiquity, see Brent Nongbri, *Before Religion: A History of a Modern Concept* (New Haven, CT: Yale University Press, 2013).

28. E.g., Georges Minois, *Histoire de l'athéisme. Les incroyants dans le monde occidental des origines à nos jours* (Paris: Fayard, 1998); Armin W. Geertz and Guð-mundur Ingi Markússon, "Religion Is Natural, Atheism Is Not: On Why Everybody Is Both Right and Wrong," *Religion* 40.3 (2010): 152–65; Juraj Franek, "Presocratic Philosophy and the Origins of Religion," *Graeco-Latina Brunensia* 18.1 (2013): 57–74; Whitmarsh, *Battling the Gods*.

29. See Boyer, *Religion Explained*; Justin L. Barrett, *Why Would Anyone Believe in God?* (Lanham, MD: AltaMira Press, 2004); Armin W. Geertz, "When Cognitive Scientists Become Religious, Science Is in Trouble: On Neurotheology from a Philosophy of Science Perspective," *Religion* 39.4 (2009): 319–24. The following paragraphs provide a succint introduction to some of the fundamental tenets of CSR. They merely serve as an illustrative account and should not be considered exhaustive; those interested in delving deeper into the topic may wish to consult other specialized sources, such as: Sørensen, "Religion in Mind"; Jason D. Slone, ed., *Religion and Cognition: A Reader* (London: Equinox, 2006); Ilkka Pyysiäinen, "Cognitive Science of Religion: State-of-the-Art," *Journal for the Cognitive Science of Religion* 1.1 (2012): 5–28; Luther H. Martin, "Religion and Cognition," in *Deep History*, 182–201; Jeppe Sinding Jensen, *What Is Religion?* (London: Routledge, 2014). For the sake of brevity, ontogeny and neurodiverse or non-neurotypical cognitions and conditions are not taken into account in what follows.

30. E.g., Jensen, *What Is Religion?*

things to happen.[31] The intentionality of agents can be the result of beliefs which prompt them to do things and perform actions. Beliefs are here intended as "the state of a cognitive system holding information (not necessarily in propositional or explicit form) as true in the generation of further thought and behavior."[32] The resulting feedback loop between action and thinking involves also neuroendocrinological two-way interconnections.[33]

Evolutionary pressures, such as in-group interactions and predation-avoidance, have selected for a peculiar sensitivity to agency in natural environments. However, agency detection can misfire and signal non-agentive events in natural and non-natural environments as if they were the result of an agent's action.[34] Thus, ToM is not a perfect device, yet evolution is not meant to be perfect, as it is all about sufficiently good-enough solutions resulting from the continuous tinkering of already existing materials.[35] Therefore, although not selected against because of their value as quick heuristics, cognitive constraints may reveal evolutionary limitations. Causal cognition, for instance, is affected by teleological reasoning, an intuitive bias according to which natural things serve anthropomorphically imagined purposes.[36] Another common-sense stance which underpins the illusory perception of the mind as something detached from the body is Cartesian (or mind-body) dualism. A religious consequence of this fallacious

31. See Barber Elizabeth Wayland and Paul T. Barber, *When They Severed Earth from Sky: How the Human Mind Shapes Myth* (Princeton, NJ: Princeton University Press, 2004), 41.

32. Justin L. Barrett and Jonathan A. Lanman, "The Science of Religious Beliefs," *Religion* 38.2 (2008): 110.

33. For the role of emotions, see Robert M. Sapolsky, *Why Zebras Don't Get Ulcers?* (3rd ed.; New York: Henry Holt, 2004); Armin W. Geertz, "Brain, Body and Culture: A Biocultural Theory of Religion," *Method & Theory in the Study of Religion* 22.4 (2010): 304–21; Jan Panksepp and Lucy Biven, *The Archaeology of Mind: Neuroevolutionary Origins of Human Emotions* (New York: W. W. Norton, 2012).

34. See Guthrie, "Cognitive Theory" and *Faces in the Clouds*; Barrett, "Natural Foundations" and *Why Would Anyone Believe*; Anders Lisdorf, "What's HIDD'n in the HADD?" *Journal of Cognition and Culture* 7.3–4 (2007): 341–53; Peter Westh, "Anthropomorphism in God Concepts: The Role of Narrative," in *Origins of Religion*, 396–413.

35. See François Jacob, "Evolution and Tinkering," *Science* 196.4295 (1977): 1161–6.

36. See Robert N. McCauley, *Why Religion Is Natural and Science Is Not* (Oxford: Oxford University Press, 2011); Deborah Kelemen, "Functions, Goals and Intentions: Children's Teleological Reasoning about Objects," *Trends in Cognitive Sciences* 3.12 (1999): 461–8 and "Why Are Rocks Pointy? Children's Preference for Teleological Explanations of the Natural World," *Developmental Psychology* 35.6 (1999): 1440–52; Deborah Kelemen and Evelyn Rosset, "The Human Function Compunction: Teleological Explanation in Adults," *Cognition* 111.1 (2009): 138–43.

intuition is the survival of the mind (i.e., the "soul") as a continued source of immaterial agency after death.[37]

Cognitive processing of information is also constrained by a set of intuitive domain-specific mechanisms shaped by evolution to respond to environmental cues, infer adequate responses, and anticipate predictable outcomes—sometimes at the expense of precision.[38] Five ontological domains (person, animal, plant, natural object, artefact) and three basic categories of folk knowledge (physics, biology, psychology) provide the default combinatory procedures by which we access the world. Therefore, the resulting basic combinatory pattern consists of just fifteen slots, whose historical presence in human cultures is unequal: a systemic preference for the violations that affects human(-like) agency and ToM further restricts the available narrative pool (see Table 1).[39]

CATEGORY / DOMAIN	PERSON	ANIMAL	PLANT	NATURAL OBJECT	ARTEFACT
Physics	Altar with men in the sky	Disappearing dancing snakes	Laurel unconsumed by fire	Two suns seen in the sky	Statues falling from the skies
Biology	Child born with an elephant head	Gold-eating mice	Palmtree growing from an altar	River running with blood	Spears moving by themselves
Psychology	Newborn speaking	Bird moaning in a human-like way	/	Sun and moon fighting	Crying statue of a goddess

Table 1. Templates of intuitive violations from the Roman *prodigia* (ancient sources listed in Anders Lisdorf, "The Spread of Non-Natural Concepts: Evidence from the Roman Prodigy Lists," *Journal of Cognition and Culture* 4.1 [2004]: 169–71).

Even so, not all kinds of stories are compelling or attention-grabbing enough to account for religious schemata (i.e., cognitive templates), but only those

37. E.g., Guthrie, "Cognitive Theory"; Paul Bloom, "Religion Is Natural," *Developmental Science* 10.1 (2007): 147–51. For a historical perspective, cf. Minois, *Histoire de l'athéisme* and for critical reflections, see K. Mitch Hodge, "Descartes' Mistake: How Afterlife Beliefs Challenge the Assumption that Humans Are Intuitive Cartesian Substance Dualists," *Journal of Cognition and Culture* 8.3 (2008): 387–415.

38. See, for example, H. Clark Barrett and Robert Kurzban, "Modularity in Cognition: Framing the Debate," *Psychological Review* 113.3 (2006): 628–47.

39. See Pascal Boyer, "Functional Origins of Religious Concepts: Ontological and Strategic Selection in Evolved Minds," *Journal of the Royal Anthropological Institute* 6.2 (2000): 198–9.

that share an optimal and minimal number of violations of the ontological domains (usually one or two). A talking bush which burns unconsumed (e.g., psychological and physical violations), a talking animal (psychological violation), or a (super-)human being that transforms into a serpent (biological violation) are good enough, while a flying, invisible mountain that speaks telepathically with its sister every other Monday may be too off the mark: only minimally counterintuitive elements boost memorability and promote the diffusion of the religious content.[40]

Likewise, culturally relevant superhuman agents are only those that are the recipients of minimally counterintuitive storytelling as described above, that are believed to have full access to strategic information, that are able to generate further shared commitment through well-established traditions of so-called credibility-enhancing displays, and whose continuous transmission and teaching are guaranteed by vertical indoctrination or horizontal/oblique imitation.[41] Other intuitive heuristics and cognitive biases such as group conformity, prestige bias, contamination-avoidance, and even reasoning concur to shape the environmental habitat for religious thoughts and behaviors.[42]

40. See Pascal Boyer and Charles Ramble, "Cognitive Templates for Religious Concepts: Cross-Cultural Evidence for Recall of Counter-Intuitive Representations," *Cognitive Science* 25.4 (2001): 535–64; Boyer, *Religion Explained*. On the role of imagination, see Maurice Bloch, "Why Religion Is Nothing Special But Is Central," *Philosophical Transactions of the Royal Society B* 363.1499 (2008): 2055–61.

41. See Boyer, *Religion Explained*; Joseph Henrich, "The Evolution of Costly Displays, Cooperation and Religion: Credibility Enhancing Displays and Their Implications for Cultural Evolution," *Evolution and Human Behavior* 30.4 (2009): 244–60; Azim Shariff, Ara Norenzayan, and Joseph Henrich, "The Birth of High Gods: How the Cultural Evolution of Supernatural Policing Influenced the Emergence of Complex, Cooperative Human Societies, Paving the Way for Civilization," in *Evolution, Culture, and the Human Mind* (ed. Mark Schaller et al.; New York: Psychology Press-T&F, 2010), 119–36; Luigi Luca Cavalli-Sforza and Marcus Feldman, *Cultural Transmission and Evolution: A Quantitative Approach* (Princeton, NJ: Princeton University Press, 1981); cf. Daniel C. Dennett, *Breaking the Spell: Religion as a Natural Phenomenon* (New York: Viking, 2006), 326.

42. Nigel Warburton, *Thinking from A to Z* (3rd ed., London: Routledge, 2007). See also Dan Sperber, "The Guru Effect," *Review of Philosophy and Psychology* 1.4 (2005): 583–92; Daniel Kahneman, *Thinking Fast and Slow* (New York: Farrar, Straus and Giroux, 2011); McCauley, *Why Religion Is Natural*; Hugo Mercier and Dan Sperber, "Why Do Humans Reason? Arguments for an Argumentative Theory," *Behavioral and Brain Sciences* 34.2 (2011): 57–111; Yitzhaq Feder, "Contamination Appraisals, Pollution Beliefs, and the Role of Cultural Inheritance in Shaping Disease Avoidance Behavior," *Cognitive Science* 40.6 (2016): 1561–85. For biases in academic historiography, cf. David Hackett Fischer, *Historians' Fallacies: Toward a Logic of Historical Thought* (New York: Harper Perennial, 1970); for the incidence of biases and fallacies in mythmaking and the oral transmission of myths and folk tales, see Wayland Barber

Reverse Engineering: From Cognition to History and Back Again

As John Donne wrote in 1623, "[n]o man is an island, entire of itself; every man is a piece of the continent, a part of the main." In the same way, each individual brain-body system occupies a knot within the network of interacting brain-body systems where socio-cognitive chains of cultural representations are being selected and discarded, creating the constraining cultural preconditions for further interactions—and so on. In this sense, religious historiography offers the possibility to activate a reverse engineering of each combination of psychological building blocks and socio-cognitive interactions, chronologically collocated in specific geographical and political patterns.[43]

All else being equal, the transmission of ideas along these networks entails the imperfect copy of the content due to specific cognitive constraints and the shift towards certain intuitive and stabilizing attractors. However, when clusters of sufficiently homogeneous cultural representations (i.e., ideas and beliefs) are widely spread and shared in such a way that an "imagined community" is possible, a sort of unstable balance and temporary stasis is possible.[44] Jesper Sørensen calls this frame *meso-history*, which is a middle connector in a spectrum that conjoins the proximate environment in which mental representations are transmitted or retained via the cognitive mechanism recalled in the previous paragraph (*micro-history*, according to Sørensen) with the evolutionary processes and ultimate causes that are responsible for adaptation, co-evolution between culture and biology, and neurohistory. The latter frame is called *macro-history* (see Fig. 1).[45]

In particular, neurohistory, also known as Deep History, refers to the neuroendocrinological patterns of conscious and unconscious manipulation of "moods, emotions, and predispositions inherited from the ancestral past," experienced via behaviors and activities—such as rituals and beliefs,

and Barber, *When They Severed Earth From Sky*; for the overall incidence of cognitive biases in theological thinking, see Helen De Cruz and Johan De Smedt, *A Natural History of Natural Theology: The Cognitive Science of Theology and Philosophy of Religion* (Cambridge, MA: The MIT Press, 2015).

43. See Paul DiMaggio, "Culture and Cognition," *Annual Review of Sociology* 23 (1997): 263–87; Geertz, "Brain, Body and Culture"; Dan Sperber, "A Naturalistic Ontology for Mechanistic Explanations in the Social Sciences," in *Analytical Sociology and Social Mechanisms* (ed. Pierre Demeulenaere; Cambridge: Cambridge University Press, 2011), 64–77.

44. See Whitehouse, "Religion, Cohesion, and Hostility," 42; cf. Benedict Anderson, *Imagined Communities: Reflections on the Origin and Spread of Nationalism* (London: Verso, 1991) and Jesper Sørensen, "Religion, Evolution, and an Immunology of Cultural Systems," *Evolution and Cognition* 10.1 (2004): 61–73.

45. Sørensen, "Past Minds," 186–93.

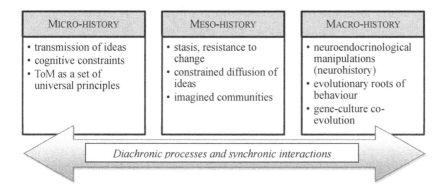

Figure 1. Meta-theoretical interactions between historical, psychological, and socio-cultural systems/timeframes (source: Sørensen, "Past Minds"). Legend: ToM: theory of mind.

gender norms, food consumption, and so on—and modulated/mediated by neurochemicals.[46] As such, neurohistory is a powerful and much needed instrument to study social change through time. From a neurophysiology-informed *longue-durée* perspective, particularly important are religious beliefs and behaviors exploited to exert control over subordinates.[47] Hence, androcentric agency and patriarchal authority are to be explored as social technologies apt to piggyback intra- and inter-sexual competition as well as to evoke favourable cognitive schemata, whether boosted by legitimized religious storytelling or ingrained via coercive social policy.[48]

Cognitive templates are important, yet constraints tell only one part of the story. Constraints, in the deep time of evolution, might be the source of countless variations of a theme.[49] While all the features previously listed restrain the realization of religious items along precise patterns,[50] their continuous interaction within the deep-historical continuum accounts for the

46. For antiquity, see Smail, *On Deep History*, 117.

47. E.g., Jason D. Slone and James A. Van Slyke, eds., *The Attraction of Religion: A New Evolutionary Psychology of Religion* (London: Bloomsbury, 2015).

48. See Jonathan Gottschall, *The Rape of Troy: Evolution, Violence, and the World of Homer* (Cambridge: Cambridge University Press, 2008); Jason D. Slone, "The Opium or the Aphrodisiac of the People? Darwinizing Marx on Religion," in *Mental Culture: Classical Social Theory and the Cognitive Science of Religion* (ed. Dimitris Xygalatas and William W. McCorkle; London: Routledge, 2013), 52–65; Hector Garcia, *Alpha God: The Psychology of Religious Violence and Oppression* (New York: Prometheus, 2015).

49. Cf. Stephen Jay Gould, "The Evolutionary Biology of Constraint," *Daedalus* 109.2 (1980): 39–52.

50. See Lawson, "Towards a Cognitive Science," 342.

mind-blowing, differential modulation of culture on the basis of cognitive proclivities and universal behaviors.[51] For instance, gathering, exchange, production, and storage of surpluses, goods, and foods are crucial variables for social organization which depend on constraining environmental factors—and yet they are an outstanding source of cultural variation. Moreover, they are key factors in predicting religious and social organizations.[52]

Thus, any scientific analysis of ancient cults should properly take into account the manifold "socioecological challenges that societies face" and that are encoded in the gods' own mental and emotional lives and social interactions as imagined by their devotees.[53] To do so is to acknowledge the socio-cognitive bridging role of rituals.

A Different View of Ritual

As human beings, we develop some maturationally cognitive inclinations that hinge upon the interplay between inborn features and environmental or developmental scaffolding.[54] Like the universal grammar posited by Noam Chomsky, which argues that the computational rules that underpin language are innate, ritual action is cognitively supported by some very basic tenets regarding the mental organization of ordinary sequences involving active agent, action, object, and passive patient. In both cases, cultural differentiation is the historical result of the selective accumulation of variation through time.

The *theory of religious ritual competence*, in particular, postulates that religious rituals are conceptually thought of and performed as a subset of ordinary actions where agents are supposed to participate as actors or patients, possibly by means of specific tools. The actual implementation of religious rituals hinges on the propositional slot occupied by "culturally postulated superhuman agents." The complementary *ritual form hypothesis* posits that high levels of sensory pageantry (being it emotionally euphoric or dysphoric) characterize the virtual presence—through surrogates and/

---

51. E.g., culture as a "distributed cognitive network" (Jensen, *What Is Religion?*, 36).

52. See Diamond, *Guns, Germs, and Steel*; Quentin D. Atkinson and Harvey White-house, "The Cultural Morphospace of Ritual Form: Examining Modes of Religiosity Cross-Culturally," *Evolution and Human Behavior* 32.1 (2011): 50–62; Peter Turchin et al., "A Historical Database of Sociocultural Evolution," *Cliodynamics: The Journal of Theoretical and Mathematical History* 3.2 (2013): 271–93.

53. See Benjamin G. Purzycki and Rita A. McNamara, "An Ecological Theory of Gods' Minds," in *Advances in Religion, Cognitive Science, and Experimental Philosophy* (ed. Helen De Cruz and Ryan Nichols; London: Bloomsbury, 2016), 143–67.

54. See, e.g., McCauley, *Why Religion Is Natural*.

or altered states of consciousness—of the superhuman agent in the cult. Given the cognitive expectations as to action, the effects of this kind of special agent ritual are mostly considered permanent (e.g., Christian baptism, Graeco-Roman initiatory rites).[55] Repetitiveness, instead, is the mark of the second and third type of ritual, in which the superhuman entity is represented in connection with a special patient (the recipient of the act) or a special instrument (e.g., Roman sacrifices). These rituals, which feature a much lower degree of experiential involvement, must be routinely repeated and their effects are temporary (see Table 2).

	SPECIAL AGENT RITUAL	SPECIAL PATIENT (OR INSTRUMENT) RITUAL
Accountable agents	CPSA	People
CPSA involvement	Direct/active (ASC/surrogate)	Indirect or passive (instrument)
Performance frequency	Low	High
Consequences	Lasting	Temporary
Repetition	Unnecessary	Necessary
Ritual substitutions	Rare	Common
Sensory pageantry	High	Low
Memory	Episodic	Semantic/procedural

Table 2. Ritual form hypothesis (adapted from Jennifer Larson, *Understanding Greek Religion* [London: Routledge, 2016], 196; see McCauley and Lawson, *Bringing Ritual to Mind*). Legend: CPSA: culturally postulated superhuman agents (gods, ancestors, spirits, etc.); ASC: altered states of consciousness.

Memory plays an important role in the definition, organization, and implementation of religious traditions often characterized by cognitively non-optimal and complex theological elaborations. Different kinds of memory are stimulated by different patterns and frequency of actions, with varying degrees of attention and shared motivation, thus affecting the social organization of religious behaviors and beliefs. The *theory of the modes of religiosity* takes into account these specific factors. Emotionally arousing rituals that take place occasionally (e.g., initiations) stimulate episodic memory, which in turn supports spontaneous exegetical reflections among the participants and strengthens in-group cohesion. This mode describes small groups with low levels of orthodoxy and without formalized leadership.

55. See Lawson and McCauley, *Rethinking Religion*; Robert McCauley and E. Thomas Lawson, *Bringing Ritual to Mind: Psychological Foundations of Cultural Forms* (Cambridge: Cambridge University Press, 2002).

Conversely, frequent rituals based on repetitive and standardized routiniza-
tion rely on semantic and procedural memory and are often typical of vast
communities in which participants might not know each other (e.g., Christian Sunday mass). These ritual procedures are usually supervised by hierarchical organizations on the basis of canonized written texts. These two
modes of religiosity are respectively known as *imagistic* and *doctrinal* (see
Table 3).[56]

	DOCTRINAL MODE	IMAGISTIC MODE
Psychological features		
Transmissive frequency	High	Low
Level of arousal	Low	High
Memory system	Semantic/implicit	Episodic/flashbulb memory
Ritual meaning	Learned/acquired	Internally generated
Techniques of revelation	Rhetoric, narrative, logical integration	Iconicity, multivocality, multivalence
Sociopolitical features		
Social cohesion	Diffused	Intense
Leadership	Dynamic	Passive/absent
Inclusivity/ Exclusivity	Inclusive	Exclusive
Diffusion	Rapid, efficient	Slow, inefficient
Scale	Large	Small
Degree of uniformity	High	Low
Structure	Centralized	Noncentralized

Table 3. Modes of religiosity (adapted from Whitehouse and Martin, *Theorizing Religions Past*, 11; Whitehouse "Modes of Religiosity," 74).

Nonetheless, theological incorrectness, that is, the difficult retention of
extremely counterintuitive theological elaborations (e.g., omnipotence,
omniscience, omnipresence, and so on; cf. the concept of Christian Trinity),
cannot be avoided since human brains naturally revert to a default agentive
mode (e.g., anthropomorphic understanding of agents' constrained interactions in time and space).[57]

56. See Whitehouse, "Modes of Religiosity" and *Modes of Religiosity: A Cognitive
Theory of Religious Transmission* (Walnut Creek, CA: AltaMira Press, 2004).
57. E.g., Justin L. Barrett and Frank C. Keil, "Conceptualizing a Nonnatural Entity:

All the patterns for religious organization advanced by the three theories recalled above are not supposed to be found in their "pure" form throughout history. Rather, they all represent a set of context-dependent attractors around which actual religious instantiations gravitate, more often than not in mixed and unexpected forms. In any case, the possible historical outcomes appear to be constrained by the hardwired understanding of action. As a result, the "predictable patterns" imposed by "cognitive constraints" present ancient historians with the possibility to "fill in the gaps of historical knowledge" in a scientific way never dreamt of before.[58] Historians have also the possibility and the duty to check, test, and revise these theories not just from present, and limited, psychological or anthropological perspectives but, rather, on a virtual cultural database consisting of the whole human history. Yet, not all historians might be willing to accept this methodological framework.

Stumbling Blocks: The Case of Roman Historiography

Given the sheer impossibility to account for every relevant and updated cognitive and evolutionary research in the blooming field of cognitive historiography, in the following paragraphs I will focus on a specific sub-discipline (Graeco-Roman historiography) and a particular setting (ancient Rome).[59]

The history of ancient cults usually comes with a long history of accumulated and dedicated historiography. In the case of Roman religion, and until very recently, academic scholarship was dominated by a specific perspective which somewhat tended to depreciate or, at least, to downplay belief *per se*. It is interesting to note that, right from the outset, academic research on Roman religion was ideologically committed to the *a priori* identification of degenerative ritualistic trends from late Republic onwards, variously interpreted as pragmatic, cynical, distant, risible, or cold.[60] As a result of the

Anthropomorphism in God Concepts," *Cognitive Psychology* 31.3 (1996): 219–47; Jason D. Slone, *Theological Incorrectness: Why Religious People Believe What They Shouldn't* (Oxford: Oxford University Press, 2004); Andrew Mahoney, "The Evolutionary Psychology of Theology," in Slone and Van Slyke, eds., *Attraction of Religion*, 189–210.

58.   Martin, "Religion and Cognition," 196.

59.   Jennifer Larson, *Understanding Greek Religion* (London: Routledge, 2016) and Jacob L. Mackey, *Belief and Cult: From Intuitions to Institutions in Roman Religion* (Princeton: Princeton University Press, forthcoming) are dedicated to Greek and Roman religions, respectively.

60.   E.g., Theodor Mommsen, *The History of Rome* (trans. William Purdie Dickson; London: R. Bentley & Son, 1862–1866), Vol. I, 222–3, 227; Vol. II, 433; Franz Cumont, *Les religions orientales dans le paganisme romaine* (Paris: Leroux, 1909), 36; Arthur

Protestant point of view embedded in most of those discourses, "faith" and "belief" were implicitly tied to an emic depreciation of certain characteristics identified as negative since the Reformation's anti-Catholic polemic, for example, against ritual *per se*.[61] Therefore, ritual was often, and more or less explicitly, disregarded as an unreflective custom.

In the second half of the twentieth century, the new critical attention to the translatability of the concept of "belief" in non-western, non-Christian, past and present social environments overcame the aforementioned judgmental perspective by relativizing the concept *tout court*: belief has a particular historical development; consequently, it can be present or absent.[62] In the Roman case, it was absent until the spread of Christianity. Thus, belief became an anachronistic and useless analytical tool to describe Roman religion(s). By positing a discontinuity between the components of Christian faith and ancient Roman practices, this in turn enforced a radical dichotomy between belief and action.[63] As Mary Beard recently synthesized, Roman religion "was a religion of doing, not believing."[64]

Does that really imply that "[religious] experiences, beliefs and disbeliefs had no particularly privileged role in defining an individual's action,

Darby Nock, "Religious Developments from the Close of the Republic to the Death of Nero," in *The Cambridge Ancient History.* Vol. X: *The Augustan Empire, 44 b.C.-a.D.70* (ed. S. A. Cook et al.; Cambridge: Cambridge University Press, 1934), 465. Bibliography and discussions are available in Jacob L. Mackey, "Rethinking Roman Religion: Action, Practice, and Belief," (PhD dissertation, Princeton University, 2009), 1–6.

61. See Jonathan Z. Smith, *To Take Place: Toward Theory in Ritual* (Chicago, IL: University of Chicago Press, 1987), 96–103. "Emic" is an anthropological term which defines the insiders' description/interpretation of their own worldviews. "Etic," instead, refers to the specialists' description/interpretation of the insiders' own description/interpretation (a meta-representation; see Purzycki and McNamara, "Ecological Theory," 155–6).

62. Cf. Rodney Needham, *Belief, Language, and Experience* (Oxford: Blackwell, 1972), 188.

63. See Andreas Bendlin, "Looking Beyond the Civic Compromise: Religious Pluralism in Late Republican Rome Religion," in *Archaic and Republican Rome and Italy: Evidence and Experience* (ed. Edward Bispham and Christopher Smith; Edinburgh, UK: Edinburgh University Press, 2000), 123.

64. Mary Beard, *SPQR: A History of Ancient Rome* (London: Profile, 2015), 103. Space limitations prevent me from delving deeper into the pivotal disciplinary concept of "demythicization," which defines the re-imagination, re-elaboration, or re-invention— sometimes in quasi-mythical terms—of fundamental events lost in the proto-historical, most prestigious time of Rome by the Romans themselves; e.g., Greg Woolf, "World Religion and World Empire in the Ancient Mediterranean," in *Die Religion des Imperium Romanum: Koine und Konfrontationen* (ed. Hubert Cancik and Jörg Rüpke; Tübingen: Mohr Siebeck, 2009), 33; cf. Emilio Gabba, *Dionysius and the History of Archaic Rome* (Berkeley, CA: University of California Press, 1991).

behavior or sense of identity"?[65] This explanation, which incidentally rescues and reinforces the much older paradigm, really seems like a forced conclusion in that it implicitly posits, and leaves unexplained, a different psychology for the *H. sapiens* members of the ancient Roman society.[66] The recent disciplinary shift towards individuals and everyday lived religion makes the coexistence of these paradigms quite problematic.[67] What to do, then? Enter cognitive historiography.

What Does a Cognitive Description of an Ancient Religion Look Like?

A cognitive redescription of Roman religion entails a most compelling example of the historical hybridization and mix between different modes of religiosity and ritual forms.

First of all, Roman devotees were not some cognitively anomalous "creatures from planet Zog,"[68] nor were they zombies deprived of conscious key features of meta-cognition (e.g., unable to represent themselves the representation of belief).[69] They were members of the genus *Homo*, species *sapiens*. As such, it is a safe bet to presume that they were agents with beliefs, desires, and intentions.[70] Therefore, their gods might be understood as the result of the imaginative thinking of *H. sapiens*' own anthropomorphic ToM: emic superhuman agentive thinking could not be engaged in a *do-ut-des* transaction, be it a petitionary prayer or a ritual, if the gods were not externally and properly informed in a visual or audible manner about the believer's state of mind.[71] The necessity to make the gods fully aware of the intentions of the believers explains the well-known ancient Roman

65. Mary Beard, John North, and Simon Price, *Religions of Rome*. Vol. I: *A History* (Cambridge: Cambridge University Press, 1998), 42.

66. See Bendlin, "Beyond the Civic Compromise," 122–3, 128.

67. E.g., Clifford Ando, "'Evidence and Orthopraxy': Review of J. Scheid: *Quand faire, c'est croire. Les rites sacrificiels des Romains*," *Journal of Roman Studies* 99 (2009): 177.

68. Rita Astuti and Maurice Bloch, "Anthropologists as Cognitive Scientists," *Topics in Cognitive Science* 4.3 (2012): 454.

69. For the "zombie argument" in philosophy of mind, see Robert Kirk, "Zombies," in *The Stanford Encyclopedia of Philosophy* (ed. Edward N. Zalta, 2015), online: http://plato.stanford.edu/archives/sum2015/entries/zombies/; cf. Massimo Pigliucci, "P-zombies Are Inconceivable: With Notes on the Idea of Metaphysical Possibility," *Scientia Salon* (4 August 2014), online: https://scientiasalon.wordpress.com/2014/08/04/p-zombies-are-inconceivable-with-notes-on-the-idea-of-metaphysical-possibility/.

70. See Mackey, *Cult and Cognition*.

71. Cf. Justin L. Barrett, "Smart Gods, Dumb Gods, and the Role of Social Cognition in Structuring Ritual Intuitions," *Journal of Cognition and Culture* 2.3 (2002): 183–93.

stress on the formal execution of ritual sequences of actions (i.e., ortho-praxy),[72] as well as prayers recited aloud.[73] No need to postulate any special pleading in order to justify a supposed Roman anomaly. Roman agents thought of and interacted with interested superhuman agents via their ordinary cognitive machinery.

The "practical understanding of generalized reciprocity" (i.e., intuitive fair relationship)[74] was important on every level of the social ladder: Roman deities were legislatively embedded in the patriarchal network of the community which created (or borrowed) them.[75] The collective management of these relationships was implemented via the *sacra publica*, that is, the official devotion scrupulously sanctioned by political institutions. These rites, which comprised "sacrifices … offerings, banquets, prayers, vows, games (either in the forms of theatrical shows or circus games) and supplications,"[76] were mostly adapted to serve as doctrinal mode (barring sacred books, usually exploited as a technological device for merely oracular and historiographical purposes; see Table 4). On a complementary and more exclusive level, every *pater familias* (i.e., the male head of each family or household) was in charge of the household's cults, based on the optimal stability of cognitive contents (i.e., no special mnemonic supports needed) and the everyday ritual actions between humans and superhuman agents such as ancestors and household deities.[77]

72. See John Scheid, *Quand faire, c'est croire. Les rites sacrificiels des Romains* (Paris: Aubier, 2005); for a reappraisal, see Ando, "'Evidence and Orthopraxy'."

73. See Aleš Chalupa, "Why Did Greeks and Romans Pray Aloud? Anthropomorphism, Dumb Gods and Human Cognition," in Pachis and Wiebe, eds., *Chasing Down Religion*, 81–95; on communication, see Deirdre Wilson and Dan Sperber, "Relevance Theory," in *The Handbook of Pragmatics* (ed. Laurence R. Hornand and Gregory Ward; Oxford: Blackwell, 2004), 607–32.

74. See Daniel Ullucci, "Towards a Typology of Religious Experts in the Ancient Mediterranean," in *The One Who Sows Bountifully: Essays in Honor of Stanley K. Stowers* (ed. Caroline Johnson Hodge et al.; Providence, RI: Brown Judaic Studies, 2013), 97; for an evolutionary background, cf. de Waal, *Bonobo and the Atheist*, 228–35.

75. See Anders Lisdorf, "Prisons of the *Longue Durée*: The Circulation and Acceptance of *Prodigia* in Roman Antiquity," in Martin and Sørensen, eds., *Past Minds*, 89–106.

76. Aleš Chalupa, "Religious Change in Roman Religion from the Perspective of Whitehouse's Theory of the Two Modes of Religiosity," in *Imagistic Traditions in the Graeco-Roman World: A Cognitive Modeling of History of Religious Research* (ed. Luther H. Martin and Panayotis Pachis; Thessaloniki: Vanias, 2009), 115.

77. See Ullucci, "Typology of Religious Experts," 97; Douglas L. Gragg, "Old and New in Roman Religion: A Cognitive Account," in Whitehouse and Martin, eds., *Theorizing Religions Past*, 69–86.

Standard Doctrinal Mode	Roman *sacra publica*	
	Chalupa (2009)	Griffith (2009)
	Psychological features	
High frequency	✓	✓
Low level of arousal	✓	✓
Semantic schemata and implicit scripts	✓	✓
Learned/acquired ritual meaning	✗	✗
Techniques of revelation[1]	✗	✗
	Sociopolitical features	
Diffused social cohesion	✓	✓
Dynamic leadership	✓	✓
Inclusivity	✓	✓
Rapid/efficient diffusion	✗	✗
Large scale	✓	✓
High degree of uniformity	✗	✓
Centralized structure	✗	✓

Table 4. Organization of the Roman republican religion (*sacra publica*) according to the modes of religiosity (sources: Chalupa, "Religious Change," 124; Griffith "Modes Theory," 164). Differences between interpretations and/or absence of standard doctrinal characteristics reflect the diachronic and synchronic mix of not-strictly doctrinal and imagistic features (see text for description). *Note*[1]: normative and logical explanations as compulsory doctrinal basis.

Both institutions and *patres familias* were basically engaged in a set of routinized, low-emotional special patient rituals, which formed the bedrock of standard Roman religion. Tedium effect due to dissatisfaction and repetitiveness, therefore, had to be tentatively avoided via an imagistic balance supported by highly emotional occasions that provided contextual relief, for example, *triumphi*, extraordinary *ludi* ("games"), and other specific collective celebrations.[78]

One of the most ancient imagistic devices exploited by institutions was the *prodigium*, that is, a report of an unusual event from the territories near Rome. *Prodigia* were fragments of intentional communication between human and superhuman agents that signaled an institutional break in their relationship. The most remarkable and contextually relevant to

78. On the *triumphi*, see Mary Beard, *The Roman Triumph* (Cambridge, MA: The Belknap Press of Harvard University Press, 2007); on the *ludi*, see Augusto Fraschetti, "Le feste, il circo, i calendari," in *Storia di Roma* (ed. Andrea Giardina and Aldo Schiavone; Turin: Einaudi, 1999), 805–24.

socio-political events were to be carefully decoded by Roman legislative bodies.[79] Usually, superhuman agency was identified in the disruption of normal expectations in the physical, psychological, and biological ontologies of the world (e.g., rains of stones, talking newborns, and so on), meeting thus the basic requirements of Boyer's minimal counterintuitive contents as well as Justin Barrett and Melanie Nihof's variant category of the "bizarre," that is, unexpected deviation from locally codified norms (e.g., temples struck by lightning, daytime owls, and so on; see Table 1).[80] Given the main cognitive underpinnings of the *prodigia* (i.e., ToM), a correct expiation (i.e., a repairing act to appease the superhuman agents) was therefore the basic precondition to re-establish a good balance between the two communities of agents.[81] This agentive *modus operandi* was intuitively drawn into play also for social and natural catastrophes such as epidemics.[82]

More specifically, certain imagistic cults were allowed to coexist inside the fabric of the *sacra publica* insofar as—being rigidly circumscribed "ritualized transgressions" and thanks to their neuroendocrinological effects[83]—they allowed devotees to better cope with and tolerate the overall socio-political control (e.g., the Republican December cult of Bona Dea for women).[84] Likewise, other mystery cults, with their emotionally arousing pageantry and

79. See Alison B. Griffith, "The 'Modes Theory' and Roman Religion: National Catastrophe and Religious Response in the Second Punic War," in Martin and Pachis, eds., *Imagistic Traditions*, 167.

80. See Lisdorf, "Prisons of the *Longue Durée*," 158. Cf. Justin L. Barrett and Melanie Nihof, "Spreading Non-natural Concepts: The Role of Intuitive Conceptual Structures in Memory and Transmission of Cultural Materials," *Journal of Cognition and Culture* 1.1 (2001): 69–100.

81. See Lisdorf, "Non-Natural Concepts: 151–73 and "Prisons of the *Longue Durée*."

82. See Leonardo Ambasciano, "The Fate of a Healing Goddess: Ocular Pathologies, the Antonine Plague, and the Ancient Roman cult of Bona Dea," *Open Library of Humanities* 2.1 (2016): 1–34. On the intuitive belief in immanent justice, cf. Nicolas Baumard and Coralie Chevallier, "What Goes Around Comes Around: The Evolutionary Roots of the Belief in Immanent Justice," *Journal of Cognition and Culture* 12.1–2 (2012): 67–80; also, Maarten Boudry and Johan De Smedt, "In Mysterious Ways: On Petitionary Prayer and Subtle Forms of Supernatural Causation," *Religion* 41.3 (2011): 449–69.

83. See Maurice Bloch and Dan Sperber, "Kinship and Evolved Psychological Dispositions: The Mother's Brother Controversy Reconsidered," *Current Anthropology* 43.5 (2002): 723–48.

84. See Hendrik H. J. Brouwer, *Bona Dea: The Sources and a Description of the Cult* (Leiden: Brill, 1989) and Leonardo Ambasciano, "The Gendered Deep History of the Bona Dea Cult," *Journal of Cognitive Historiography* 3.1–2 (2016): 134–56. On the suppression of the *Bacchanalia*, instead, see Douglas L. Gragg, "'Another People': Understanding the Roman Senate's Suppression of the *Bacchanalia*," in Martin and Pachis, eds., *Imagistic Traditions*, 137–52.

special-agent ritual initiations, were tolerated by the Roman socio-religious system as long as they were able to piggyback the pre-existing networks' mindscapes.[85]

Remarkably, each cult might also be potentially studied in itself as a modular network composed by multiple rituals and beliefs. The more cognitively balanced the cult, that is, able to integrate different modes and ritual actions in different settings, the more successful, namely, prone to be diffused and to co-evolve within its historical setting.[86]

As a matter of fact, much remains to be done to understand the complex history of competition and interbreeding between doctrinal, imagistic, and optimally cognitive cultural representations that shaped the cultural and religious dynamics of the ancient Mediterranean.[87]

Final Remarks

Any historical system, be it cultural or evolutionary, is composed by intertwined evident patterns and underlying processes. "Without patterns," as zoologist Ferdinando Boero has noted, "processes are ghosts, and without processes, patterns are corpses."[88] The pattern of apparently monolithic longevity of the overall Roman system was assured by constant adjustments between top-down and bottom-up tweaks and pressures, resulting in the continuous socio-political re-networking of beliefs and behaviors.[89] The

---

85. E.g., Luther H. Martin, "Why Christianity Was Accepted by Romans But Not by Rome," in *Deep History*, 298–387; also his "Roman Mithraism and Christianity," in *The Mind of Mithraism: Historical and Cognitive Studies in the Roman Cult of Mithras* (London: Bloomsbury, 2015), 9–20. On Hellenistic cults, cf. Martin, "Cognitive Science."

86. E.g., Mithraism: see Luther H. Martin, "Ritual Competence and Mithraic Ritual," in *Mind of Mithraism*, 41–56 and Aleš Chalupa, "What Might Cognitive Science Contribute to Our Understanding of the Roman Cult of Mithras?" in Martin and Sørensen, eds., *Past Minds*, 115 n. 29.

87. See, for example, Ullucci, "Typology of Religious Experts"; Greg Woolf, "Isis and the Evolution of Religion," in *Power, Politics and the Cults of Isis* (ed. Laurent Bricault and Miguel J. Versluys; Leiden: Brill, 2014), 62–92. For instances of religious change, cf. Aleš Chalupa, "How Did Roman Emperors Become Gods? Various Concepts of Imperial Apotheosis," *Anodos* 6–7 (2006–2007): 201–7 and "The Religio-Political Change in the Reign of Augustus: The Disappearance of Public Prodigies," *Graeco-Latina Brunensia* 17.2 (2012): 57–67; on competing initiations, see Douglas L. Gragg, "Do the Multiple Initiations of Lucius in Apuleius' *Metamorphoses* Falsify the Ritual Form Hypothesis?" in Martin and Sørensen, eds., *Past Minds*, 125–30.

88. Ferdinando Boero, "Evolution: Is Celebrating Darwin Still Worthwhile?" *Italian Journal of Zoology* 82.1 (2015): 1.

89. On the "technologies of the cult," see Ando, "'Evidence and Orthopraxy'," 180;

dynamics of the process, in turn, were directed by interrelated proximate and ultimate socio-cognitive and ethological-evolutionary causes. Obviously, this stress on the historical interconnectedness between cultural and cognitive factors also applies to any ancient religion.

Arnaldo Momigliano wrote in 1974 that

> [t]he historian understands men and institutions, ideas, beliefs, emotions, and the needs of individuals who no longer exist. He understands all this because the documents that lie before him, when correctly interpreted, offer themselves up as real situations.[90]

And yet, behind any ancient document whatsoever there is a mind that occupied a knot in a diffused cultural network of other minds. In order to understand ancient religious documents as the products of a specific biological species, and to avoid the proliferation of potentially fallacious interpretations,[91] it is time to bring back cognition and evolution to the study of historiography. Mind-blind aliens from planet Zog and unconscious zombies can wait.

Biographical Note

Leonardo Ambasciano earned his PhD in Historical Studies at the University of Turin, Italy, in 2014 with a cognitive and evolutionary analysis of the ancient Roman female cult of Bona Dea. In 2016, he was Visiting Lecturer of Religious Studies at Masaryk University, Brno, Czech Republic. He is the author of *An Unnatural History of Religions: Academia, Post-Truth, and the Quest for Scientific Knowledge* (London: Bloomsbury, 2018), and of various articles, book reviews, and chapters, the most recent of which is "Politics of Nostalgia, Logical Fallacies, and Cognitive Biases: The Importance of Epistemology in the Age of Cognitive Historiography," in *A New Synthesis for the Study of Religion: Cognition, Evolution, and History in the Study of Religion*, edited by Anders Klostergaard Petersen, Gilhus Ingvild Sælid, Luther H. Martin, Jeppe Sinding Jensen and Jesper Sørensen (Leiden: Brill, 2018). He is Managing Editor of the *Journal of Cognitive Historiography*.

Chalupa, "Religious Change," 127–8; cf. Griffith, "'Modes Theory'"; Greg Woolf, "Only Connect? Networks and Religious Change in the Ancient Mediterranean," CRASIS lecture (University of Groningen, 9 February 2012), online: http://www.rug.nl/research/centre-for-religious-studies/crasis/activities/annual-meeting/greg_woolf_crasis_lecture.pdf; Beard, *SPQR*, 530–2.

90. Arnaldo Momigliano, "The Rules of the Game in the Study of Ancient History," (trans. Kenneth W. Yu) *History and Theory* 55.1 (2016): 45.

91. Momigliano, "Rules of the Game," 42.

Bibliography

Ambasciano, Leonardo. "Mind the (Unbridgeable) Gaps: A Cautionary Tale about Pseudoscientific Distortions and Scientific Misconceptions in the Study of Religion," *Method & Theory in the Study of Religion* 28.2 (2016): 141–225. https://doi.org/10.1163/15700682-12341372

—"The Fate of a Healing Goddess: Ocular Pathologies, the Antonine Plague, and the Ancient Roman cult of Bona Dea," *Open Library of Humanities* 2.1 (2016): 1–34.

—"Exiting the *Motel of the Mysteries*? How Historiographical Floccinaucinihilipilification Is Affecting CSR 2.0," 107–22 in *Religion Explained? The Cognitive Science of Religion After Twenty-Five Years*. Edited by Luther H. Martin and Donald Wiebe. London: Bloomsbury, 2017.

—"The Gendered Deep History of the Bona Dea Cult," *Journal of Cognitive Historiography* 3.1–2 (2016): 134–56.

—*An Unnatural History of Religions: Academia, Post-truth and the Quest for Scientific Knowledge*. London: Bloomsbury, 2018.

Anderson, Benedict. *Imagined Communities: Reflections on the Origin and Spread of Nationalism*. London: Verso, 1991.

Ando, Clifford. "'Evidence and Orthopraxy': Review of J. Scheid: *Quand faire, c'est croire. Les rites sacrificiels des Romains*," *Journal of Roman Studies* 99 (2009): 171–81. https://doi.org/10.3815/007543509789744864

Armitage, David. "What's the Big Idea? Intellectual History and the *Longue Durée*," *History of European Ideas* 38.4 (2012): 493–507. https://doi.org/10.1080/01916599.2012.714635

Armitage, David, and Jo Guldi. "Le retour de la longue durée: une perspective anglo-américaine," *Annales. Histoire, Sciences sociales* 70.2 (2015): 289–318. https://doi.org/10.1353/ahs.2015.0033

Arnold, John. *History: A Very Short Introduction*. Oxford: Oxford University Press, 2000. https://doi.org/10.1093/actrade/9780192853523.001.0001

Astuti, Rita, and Maurice Bloch. "Anthropologists as Cognitive Scientists," *Topics in Cognitive Science* 4.3 (2012): 453–61. https://doi.org/10.1111/j.1756-8765.2012.01191.x

Atkinson, Quentin D., and Harvey Whitehouse. "The Cultural Morphospace of Ritual Form: Examining Modes of Religiosity Cross-Culturally," *Evolution and Human Behavior* 32.1 (2011): 50–62. https://doi.org/10.1016/j.evolhumbehav.2010.09.002

Barrett, H. Clark, and Robert Kurzban. "Modularity in Cognition: Framing the Debate," *Psychological Review* 113.3 (2006): 628–47. https://doi.org/10.1037/0033-295X.113.3.628

Barrett, Justin L. "Exploring the Natural Foundations of Religion," *Trends in Cognitive Sciences* 4.1 (2000): 29–34. https://doi.org/10.1016/S1364-6613(99)01419-9

—"Smart Gods, Dumb Gods, and the Role of Social Cognition in Structuring Ritual Intuitions," *Journal of Cognition and Culture* 2.3 (2002): 183–93. https://doi.org/10.1163/15685370260225080

—*Why Would Anyone Believe in God?* Lanham, MD: AltaMira Press, 2004.

Barrett, Justin L., and Frank C. Keil. "Conceptualizing a Nonnatural Entity: Anthropomorphism in God Concepts," *Cognitive Psychology* 31.3 (1996): 219–47. https://doi.org/10.1006/cogp.1996.0017

Barrett, Justin L., and Melanie Nihof. "Spreading Non-natural Concepts: The Role of Intuitive Conceptual Structures in Memory and Transmission of Cultural

Materials," *Journal of Cognition and Culture* 1.1 (2001): 69–100. https://doi.org/10.1163/156853701300063589

Barrett, Justin L., and Jonathan A. Lanman. "The Science of Religious Beliefs," *Religion* 38.2 (2008): 109–24. https://doi.org/10.1016/j.religion.2008.01.007

Baumard, Nicolas, A. Hyafil, I. Morris, and P. Boyer. "Increased Affluence Explains the Emergence of Ascetic Wisdoms and Moralizing Religions," *Current Biology* 25.1 (2015): 10–15. https://doi.org/10.1016/j.cub.2014.10.063

Baumard, Nicolas, and Coralie Chevallier. "What Goes Around Comes Around: The Evolutionary Roots of the Belief in Immanent Justice," *Journal of Cognition and Culture* 12.1–2 (2012): 67–80.

Beard, Mary. *The Roman Triumph.* Cambridge, MA: The Belknap Press of Harvard University Press, 2007. https://doi.org/10.4159/9780674020597

—*SPQR: A History of Ancient Rome.* London: Profile, 2015.

Beard, Mary, John North, and Simon Price. *Religions of Rome.* Vol. I: *A History.* Cambridge: Cambridge University Press, 1998.

Bendlin, Andreas. "Looking Beyond the Civic Compromise: Religious Pluralism in Late Republican Rome Religion," 115–35 in *Archaic and Republican Rome and Italy: Evidence and Experience.* Edited by Edward Bispham and Christopher Smith. Edinburgh, UK: Edinburgh University Press, 2000.

Bloch, Maurice. *How We Think They Think: Anthropological Approaches to Cognition, Memory and Literacy.* Boulder, CO: Westview Press, 1998.

—"Why Religion Is Nothing Special But Is Central," *Philosophical Transactions of the Royal Society B* 363.1499 (2008): 2055–61. https://doi.org/10.1098/rstb.2008.0007

Bloch, Maurice, and Dan Sperber. "Kinship and Evolved Psychological Dispositions: The Mother's Brother Controversy Reconsidered," *Current Anthropology* 43.5 (2002): 723–48. https://doi.org/10.1086/341654

Bloom, Paul. "Religion Is Natural," *Developmental Science* 10.1 (2007): 147–51. https://doi.org/10.1111/j.1467-7687.2007.00577.x

Boero, Ferdinando. "Evolution: Is Celebrating Darwin Still Worthwhile?" *Italian Journal of Zoology* 82.1 (2015): 1–2. https://doi.org/10.1080/11250003.2015.1023042

Boudry, Maarten, and Johan De Smedt. "In Mysterious Ways: On Petitionary Prayer and Subtle Forms of Supernatural Causation," *Religion* 41.3 (2011): 449–69. https://doi.org/10.1080/0048721X.2011.600464

Boyer, Pascal. "Functional Origins of Religious Concepts: Ontological and Strategic Selection in Evolved Minds," *Journal of the Royal Anthropological Institute* 6.2 (2000): 195–214. https://doi.org/10.1111/1467-9655.00012

—*Religion Explained: The Evolutionary Origins of Religious Thought.* New York: Basic Books, 2001.

Boyer, Pascal, and Charles Ramble. "Cognitive Templates for Religious Concepts: Cross-Cultural Evidence for Recall of Counter-Intuitive Representations," *Cognitive Science* 25.4 (2001): 535–64. https://doi.org/10.1207/s15516709cog2504_2

Braudel, Fernand. "History and the Social Sciences: The Longue Durée," 25–45 in *On History.* Chicago, IL: University of Chicago Press, 1980.

Brouwer, Hendrik H. J. *Bona Dea: The Sources and a Description of the Cult.* Leiden: Brill, 1989. https://doi.org/10.1163/9789004295773

Bulbulia, Joseph. "The Arts Transform the Cognitive Science of Religion," *Journal for the Cognitive Science of Religion* 1.2 (2013): 141–60. https://doi.org/10.1558/jcsr.v1i2.141

Bulbulia, Joseph, and Edward Slingerland. "Religious Studies as a Life Science," *Numen* 59.5–6 (2012): 564–613.

Burguière, André. *The Annales School: An Intellectual History*. Translated by Jane Marie Todd. Ithaca, NY: Cornell University Press, 2009.

Burkert, Walter. *Creation of the Sacred: Tracks of Biology in Early Religions*. Cambridge, MA: Harvard University Press, 1996.

Burman, Jeremy T. "Bringing the Brain into History: Behind Hunt's and Smail's Appeals to Neurohistory," 64–82 in *Psychology and History: Interdisciplinary Explanations*. Edited by Cristian Tileagă and Jovan Byford. Cambridge: Cambridge University Press, 2014. https://doi.org/10.1017/CBO9781139525404.006

Cavalli-Sforza, Luigi Luca, and Marcus Feldman. *Cultural Transmission and Evolution: A Quantitative Approach*. Princeton, NJ: Princeton University Press, 1981.

Chalupa, Aleš. "How Did Roman Emperors Become Gods? Various Concepts of Imperial Apotheosis," *Anodos* 6–7 (2006–2007): 201–7.

—"Religious Change in Roman Religion from the Perspective of Whitehouse's Theory of the Two Modes of Religiosity," 113–35 in Martin and Pachis, eds., *Imagistic Traditions*, 2009.

—"Why Did Greeks and Romans Pray Aloud? Anthropomorphism, Dumb Gods and Human Cognition," 81–95 in Pachis and Wiebe, eds., *Chasing Down Religion*, 2010.

—"What Might Cognitive Science Contribute to Our Understanding of the Roman Cult of Mithras?" 107–24 in Martin and Sørensen, eds., *Past Minds*, 2011.

—"The Religio-Political Change in the Reign of Augustus: The Disappearance of Public Prodigies," *Graeco-Latina Brunensia* 17.2 (2012): 57–67.

Christian, David. *Maps of Time: An Introduction to Big History*. Berkeley, CA: University of California Press, 2011.

Cioffi, Frank. "The Case of Freud's Sexual Etiology of the Neuroses," 321–40 in *Philosophy of Pseudoscience: Reconsidering the Demarcation Problem*. Edited by Massimo Pigliucci and Maarten Boudry. Chicago, IL: University of Chicago Press, 2013.

Cumont, Franz. *Les religions orientales dans le paganisme romaine*. Paris: Leroux, 1909.

D'Andrade, Roy. *The Development of Cognitive Anthropology*. Cambridge: Cambridge University Press, 1995. https://doi.org/10.1017/CBO9781139166645

Darwin, Charles R. *On the Origin of Species by Means of Natural Selection, or the Preservation of Favoured Races in the Struggle for Life*. London: John Murray, 1859.

—*The Descent of Man, and Selection in Relation to Sex*. London: John Murray, 1871.

Day, Matthew. "Godless Savages and Superstitious Dogs: Charles Darwin, Imperial Ethnography, and the Problem of Human Uniqueness," *Journal of the History of Ideas* 69.1 (2008): 49–70. https://doi.org/10.1353/jhi.2008.0006

De Cruz, Helen, and Johan De Smedt. *A Natural History of Natural Theology: The Cognitive Science of Theology and Philosophy of Religion*. Cambridge, MA: The MIT Press, 2015.

De Waal, Frans B. M. *The Bonobo and the Atheist: In Search of Humanism Among the Primates*. New York: W. W. Norton, 2013.

Dennett, Daniel C. *Breaking the Spell: Religion as a Natural Phenomenon*. New York: Viking, 2006.

Desmond, Adrian, and James Moore. *Darwin's Sacred Cause: How a Hatred of Slavery Shaped Darwin's Views on Human Evolution*. Boston, MA: Harcourt, 2009.

Diamond, Jared. *Guns, Germs, and Steel: The Fates of Human Societies*. New York: W. W. Norton, 1997.

Diamond, Jared, and James Robinson, eds. *Natural Experiments of History*. Cambridge, MA: The Belknap Press of Harvard University Press, 2010.

DiMaggio, Paul. "Culture and Cognition," *Annual Review of Sociology* 23 (1997): 263–87. https://doi.org/10.1146/annurev.soc.23.1.263

Feder, Yitzhaq. "Contamination Appraisals, Pollution Beliefs, and the Role of Cultural Inheritance in Shaping Disease Avoidance Behavior," *Cognitive Science* 40.6 (2016): 1561–85. https://doi.org/10.1111/cogs.12293

Fedyk, Mark. "How (Not) to Bring Psychology and Biology Together," *Philosophical Studies* 172.4 (2015): 949–67. https://doi.org/10.1007/s11098-014-0297-9

Fischer, David Hackett. *Historians' Fallacies: Toward a Logic of Historical Thought*. New York: Harper Perennial, 1970.

Franek, Juraj. "Presocratic Philosophy and the Origins of Religion," *Graeco-Latina Brunensia* 18.1 (2013): 57–74.

—"Has the Cognitive Science of Religion (Re)defined 'Religion'?" *Religio: Revue pro religionistiku* 22.1 (2014): 3–27.

Fraschetti, Augusto. "Le feste, il circo, i calendari," 805–24 in *Storia di Roma*. Edited by Andrea Giardina and Aldo Schiavone. Turin: Einaudi, 1999.

Gabba, Emilio. *Dionysius and the History of Archaic Rome*. Berkeley, CA: University of California Press, 1991.

Garcia, Hector. *Alpha God: The Psychology of Religious Violence and Oppression*. New York: Prometheus, 2015.

Geertz, Armin W. "When Cognitive Scientists Become Religious, Science Is in Trouble: On Neurotheology from a Philosophy of Science Perspective," *Religion* 39.4 (2009): 319–24. https://doi.org/10.1016/j.religion.2009.08.001

—"Brain, Body and Culture: A Biocultural Theory of Religion," *Method & Theory in the Study of Religion* 22.4 (2010): 304–21. https://doi.org/10.1163/157006810X531094

—"Whence Religion? How the Brain Constructs the World and What This Might Tell Us About the Origins of Religion, Cognition and Culture," 17–70 in Geertz, ed., *Origins of Religion*, 2013.

—ed. *Origins of Religion, Cognition and Culture*. London: Routledge, 2013.

Geertz, Armin W., and Guðmundur Ingi Markússon. "Religion Is Natural, Atheism Is Not: On Why Everybody Is Both Right and Wrong," *Religion* 40.3 (2010): 152–65. https://doi.org/10.1016/j.religion.2009.11.003

Girotto, Vittorio, Telmo Pievani, and Giorgio Vallortigara. "Supernatural Beliefs: Adaptations for Social Life or By-products of Cognitive Adaptations?" 249–66 in *Evolved Morality: The Biology and Philosophy of Human Conscience*. Edited by F. B. M. de Waal, P. S. Churchland, T. Pievani, and S. Parmigiani. Leiden: Brill, 2014. https://doi.org/10.1163/9789004263888_019

Gottschall, Jonathan. *The Rape of Troy: Evolution, Violence, and the World of Homer*. Cambridge: Cambridge University Press, 2008.

Gould, Stephen Jay. "The Evolutionary Biology of Constraint," *Daedalus* 109.2 (1980): 39–52.

—*Wonderful Life: The Burgess Shale and the Nature of History*. New York: W. W. Norton, 1989.

—"Freud's Evolutionary Fantasy," 147–58 in *I Have Landed: The End of a Beginning in Natural History*. New York: Harmony Books, 2002. https://doi.org/10.4159/harvard.9780674063419

Gragg, Douglas L. "Old and New in Roman Religion: A Cognitive Account," 69–86 in Whitehouse and Martin, eds. *Theorizing Religions Past*, 2004.

—"'Another People': Understanding the Roman Senate's Suppression of the *Bacchanalia*," 137–52 in Martin and Pachis, eds., *Imagistic Traditions*, 2009.

—"Do the Multiple Initiations of Lucius in Apuleius' *Metamorphoses* Falsify the Ritual Form Hypothesis?" 125–30 in Martin and Sørensen, eds., *Past Minds*, 2011.

Griffith, Alison B. "The 'Modes Theory' and Roman Religion: National Catastrophe and Religious Response in the Second Punic War," 153–78 in Martin and Pachis, eds., *Imagistic Traditions*, 2009.

Guldi, Jo, and David Armitage. *The History Manifesto*. Cambridge: Cambridge University Press, 2014. https://doi.org/10.1017/9781139923880

Guthrie, Stewart E. "A Cognitive Theory of Religion," *Current Anthropology* 21.2 (1980): 181–203. https://doi.org/10.1086/202429

—*Faces in the Clouds: A New Theory of Religion*. Oxford: Oxford University Press, 1993.

—"Animal Animism: Evolutionary Roots of Religious Cognition," 38–67 in *Current Approaches in the Cognitive Science of Religion*. Edited by Ilkka Pyysiäinen and Veikko Anttonen. London: Continuum, 2002.

Harrison, Jane E. "The Influence of Darwinism on the Study of Religions," 494–511 in *Darwin and Modern Science: Essays in Commemoration of the Centenary of the Birth of Charles Darwin and the Fiftieth Anniversary of the Publication of the "Origin of Species"*. Edited by Albert Charles Seward. Cambridge: Cambridge University Press, 1909.

Henrich, Joseph. "The Evolution of Costly Displays, Cooperation and Religion: Credibility Enhancing Displays and Their Implications for Cultural Evolution," *Evolution and Human Behavior* 30.4 (2009): 244–60. https://doi.org/10.1016/j.evolhumbehav.2009.03.005

Hodge, K. Mitch. "Descartes' Mistake: How Afterlife Beliefs Challenge the Assumption that Humans Are Intuitive Cartesian Substance Dualists," *Journal of Cognition and Culture* 8.3 (2008): 387–415.

Isaak, Mark. *The Counter-Creationism Handbook*. Berkeley, CA: University of California Press, 2007.

Jacob, François. "Evolution and Tinkering," *Science* 196.4295 (1977): 1161–6. https://doi.org/10.1126/science.860134

Jensen, Jeppe Sinding. *What Is Religion?* London: Routledge, 2014. https://doi.org/10.4324/9781315729466

Jong, Jonathan. "On (Not) Defining (Non)religion," *Science, Religion and Culture* 2.3 (2015): 15–24. https://doi.org/10.17582/journal.src/2015/2.3.15.24

Kahneman, Daniel. *Thinking Fast and Slow*. New York: Farrar, Straus & Giroux, 2011.

Kelemen, Deborah. "Functions, Goals and Intentions: Children's Teleological Reasoning about Objects," *Trends in Cognitive Sciences* 3.12 (1999): 461–8. https://doi.org/10.1016/S1364-6613(99)01402-3

—"Why Are Rocks Pointy? Children's Preference for Teleological Explanations of the Natural World," *Developmental Psychology* 35.6 (1999): 1440–52. https://doi.org/10.1037/0012-1649.35.6.1440

Kelemen, Deborah, and Evelyn Rosset. "The Human Function Compunction: Teleological Explanation in Adults," *Cognition* 111.1 (2009): 138–43. https://doi.org/10.1016/j.cognition.2009.01.001

Kirk, Robert. *s.v.* "Zombies," in *The Stanford Encyclopedia of Philosophy*. Edited by

Edward N. Zalta, 2015. Online: http://plato.stanford.edu/archives/sum2015/entries/zombies/ (accessed 5 August 2016).

Larson, Jennifer. *Understanding Greek Religion*. London: Routledge, 2016. https://doi.org/10.4324/9781315647012

Lawson, E. Thomas. "Towards a Cognitive Science of Religion," *Numen* 47.3 (2000): 338–49. https://doi.org/10.1163/156852700511586

Lawson, E. Thomas, and Robert N. McCauley. *Rethinking Religion: Connecting Cognition and Culture*. Cambridge: Cambridge University Press, 1990.

Lisdorf, Anders. "The Spread of Non-Natural Concepts: Evidence from the Roman Prodigy Lists," *Journal of Cognition and Culture* 4.1 (2004): 151–73. https://doi.org/10.1163/156853704323074796

—"What's HIDD'n in the HADD?" *Journal of Cognition and Culture* 7.3–4 (2007): 341–53.

—"Prisons of the *Longue Durée*: The Circulation and Acceptance of *Prodigia* in Roman Antiquity," 89–106 in Martin and Sørensen, eds., *Past Minds*, 2011.

Luria, Salvador E., Stephen J. Gould, and Sam Singer. *A View of Life*. Menlo Park, CA: Benjamin/Cummings, 1981.

Macalister, Alexander. *Evolution in Church History*. Dublin: Hodges & Figgis, 1882.

Mackey, Jacob L. "Rethinking Roman Religion: Action, Practice, and Belief," PhD thesis, Princeton University, 2009.

—*Belief and Cult: From Intuitions to Institutions in Roman Religion*. Princeton: Princeton University Press, forthcoming.

Mahoney, Andrew. "The Evolutionary Psychology of Theology," 189–210 in Slone and Van Slyke, eds., *Attraction of Religion*, 2015.

Martin, Luther H. "Biology, Sociology and the Study of Religions: Two Lectures," *Religio: revue pro religionistiku* 5.1 (1997): 21–35.

—"The Origins of Religion, Cognition and Culture: The Bowerbird Syndrome," 178–202 in Geertz, ed., *Origins of Religion*, 2013.

—*Deep History, Secular Theory: Historical and Scientific Studies of Religion*. Berlin: Walter de Gruyter, 2014. https://doi.org/10.1515/9781614515005

—"Cognitive Science, Ritual and the Hellenistic Mystery Religions," 298–307 in *Deep History*, 2014.

—"Evolution, Cognition and History," 163–74 in *Deep History*, 2014.

—"Religion and Cognition," 182–201 in *Deep History*, 2014.

—"The Future of the Past: The History of Religions and Cognitive Historiography," 343–57 in *Deep History*, 2014.

—"The Promise of Cognitive Science for the Study of Early Christianity," 202–20 in *Deep History*, 2014.

—"Why Christianity Was Accepted by Romans But Not by Rome," 308–22 in *Deep History*, 2014.

—*The Mind of Mithraism: Historical and Cognitive Studies in the Roman Cult of Mithras*. London: Bloomsbury, 2015.

—"Roman Mithraism and Christianity," 9–20 in *Mind of Mithraism*, 2015.

—"Ritual Competence and Mithraic Ritual," 41–56 in *Mind of Mithraism*, 2015.

Martin, Luther H., and Panayotis Pachis, eds. *Imagistic Traditions in the Graeco-Roman World: A Cognitive Modeling of History of Religious Research*. Thessaloniki: Vanias, 2009.

Martin, Luther H., and Jesper Sørensen, eds. *Past Minds: Studies in Cognitive Historiography*. London: Routledge, 2011.

Martin, Luther H., and Donald Wiebe. "Religious Studies as a Scientific Discipline: The Persistence of a Delusion," *Journal of the American Academy of Religion* 80.3 (2012): 587–97. https://doi.org/10.1093/jaarel/lfs030

McCauley, Robert N. *Why Religion Is Natural and Science Is Not*. Oxford: Oxford University Press, 2011.

McCauley, Robert N., and E. Thomas Lawson. *Bringing Ritual to Mind: Psychological Foundations of Cultural Forms*. Cambridge: Cambridge University Press, 2002. https://doi.org/10.1017/CBO9780511606410

Mercier, Hugo, and Dan Sperber. "Why Do Humans Reason? Arguments for an Argumentative Theory," *Behavioral and Brain Sciences* 34.2 (2011): 57–111. https://doi.org/10.1017/S0140525X10000968

Minois, Georges. *Histoire de l'athéisme. Les incroyants dans le monde occidental des origines à nos jours*. Paris: Fayard, 1998.

Momigliano, Arnaldo. "The Rules of the Game in the Study of Ancient History." Translated by Kenneth W. Yu. *History and Theory* 55.1 (2016): 39–45. https://doi.org/10.1111/hith.10786

Mommsen, Theodor. *The History of Rome*. Vols. 1–4. Translated by William Purdie Dickson. London: R. Bentley & Son, 1862–1866.

Needham, Rodney. *Belief, Language, and Experience*. Oxford: Blackwell, 1972.

Nock, Arthur Darby. "Religious Developments from the Close of the Republic to the Death of Nero," 465–511 in *The Cambridge Ancient History. Vol. X: The Augustan Empire, 44 b.C.-a.D.70*. Edited by S. A. Cook, F. E. Adcock, and M. P. Charlesworth. Cambridge: Cambridge University Press, 1934.

Nongbri, Brent. *Before Religion: A History of a Modern Concept*. New Haven, CT: Yale University Press, 2013. https://doi.org/10.12987/yale/9780300154160.001.0001

Norenzayan, Ara, A. F. Shariff, W. M. Gervais, A. K. Willard, R. A. McNamara, E. Slingerland, and J. Henrich. "The Cultural Evolution of Prosocial Religions," *Behavioral and Brain Sciences* 39 (2016). https://doi.org/10.1017/S0140525X14001356

Orbecchi, Maurilio. *Psicologia dell'anima*. Turin: Bollati Boringhieri, 2015.

Pachis, Panayotis. "Healing Gods, Heroes and Rituals in the Graeco-Roman World," *Open Library of Humanities* (2016). Online: https://olh.openlibhums.org/collections/special/healing-gods-heroes-and-rituals-in-the-graeco-roman-world/ (accessed 20 May 2016).

Pachis, Panayotis, and Donald Wiebe, eds. *Chasing Down Religion: In the Sights of History and the Cognitive Sciences*. Sheffield, UK: Equinox, 2009.

Paden, William E. "Elements of a New Comparativism," *Method & Theory in the Study of Religion* 8.1 (1996): 5–14. https://doi.org/10.1163/157006896X00026

—"A New Comparativism: Reply to the Panelists," *Method & Theory in the Study of Religion* 8.1 (1996): 37–49. https://doi.org/10.1163/157006896X00062

Panksepp, Jan, and Lucy Biven. *The Archaeology of Mind: Neuroevolutionary Origins of Human Emotions*. New York: W. W. Norton, 2012.

Peoples, Hervey C., Pavel Duda, and Frank W. Marlowe. "Hunter-Gatherers and the Origins of Religion." *Human Nature* 27.3 (2016): 261–82. https://doi.org/10.1007/s12110-016-9260-0

Pigliucci, Massimo. "P-zombies are Inconceivable: With Notes on the Idea of Metaphysical Possibility." *Scientia Salon*, 4 August 2014. Online: https://scientiasalon.wordpress.com/2014/08/04/p-zombies-are-inconceivable-with-notes-on-the-idea-of-metaphysical-possibility/ (accessed 20 August 2016).

Pinker, Steven. *The Blank Slate: The Modern Denial of Human Nature*. New York: Viking, 2002.

Plotkin, Henry. *Evolutionary Thought in Psychology*. Oxford: Blackwell, 2004. https://doi.org/10.1002/9780470773840

Purzycki, Benjamin G., and Rita A. McNamara. "An Ecological Theory of Gods' Minds," 143–67 in *Advances in Religion, Cognitive Science, and Experimental Philosophy*. Edited by Helen De Cruz and Ryan Nichols. London: Bloomsbury, 2016.

Pyysiäinen, Ilkka. "Cognitive Science of Religion: State-of-the-Art," *Journal for the Cognitive Science of Religion* 1.1 (2012): 5–28. https://doi.org/10.1558/jcsr.v1i1.5

Richards, Robert J. "Myth 19: That Darwin and Haeckel Were Complicit in Nazi Biology," 170–7 in *Galileo Goes to Jail and Other Myths about Science and Religion*. Edited by Ronald L. Numbers. Cambridge, MA: Harvard University Press, 2009.

Russell, Edmund. *Evolutionary History: Uniting History and Biology to Understand Life on Earth*. Cambridge: Cambridge University Press, 2011. https://doi.org/10.1017/CBO9780511974267

Saler, Benson. "Culture in Phylogenetic Perspective: An Appreciation of the Contributions of A. I. Hallowell," 82–91 in *Understanding Religion: Selected Essays*. Berlin: Walter de Gruyter, 2009.

Sapolsky, Robert M. *Why Zebras Don't Get Ulcers?* 3rd ed. New York: Henry Holt, 2004.

Scheid, John. *Quand faire, c'est croire. Les rites sacrificiels des Romains.* Paris: Aubier, 2005.

Shariff, Azim, Ara Norenzayan, and Joseph Henrich. "The Birth of High Gods: How the Cultural Evolution of Supernatural Policing Influenced the Emergence of Complex, Cooperative Human Societies, Paving the Way for Civilization," 119–36 in *Evolution, Culture, and the Human Mind*. Edited by M. Schaller, A. Norenzayan, S. J. Heine, T. Yamagishi, and T. Kameda. New York: Psychology Press-T&F, 2010.

Shaw, David G. "The Return of Science," *History and Theory* 38.4 (1999): 1–9. https://doi.org/10.1111/0018-2656.00101

Shermer, Michael, and Alex Grobman. *Denying History: Who Says the Holocaust Never Happened and Why Do They Say It?* Berkeley, CA: University of California Press, 2009.

Shryock, Andrew, and Daniel Lord Smail, eds. *Deep History: The Architecture of Past and Present*. Berkeley, CA: University of California Press, 2011.

Slone, Jason D., *Theological Incorrectness: Why Religious People Believe What They Shouldn't*. Oxford: Oxford University Press, 2004. https://doi.org/10.1093/0195169263.001.0001

—ed. *Religion and Cognition: A Reader*. London: Equinox, 2006.

—"The Opium or the Aphrodisiac of the People? Darwinizing Marx on Religion," 52–65 in *Mental Culture: Classical Social Theory and the Cognitive Science of Religion*. Edited by Dimitris Xygalatas and William W. McCorkle. London: Routledge, 2013.

Slone, Jason D., and James A. Van Slyke, eds. *The Attraction of Religion: A New Evolutionary Psychology of Religion*. London: Bloomsbury, 2015.

Smail, Daniel Lord. *On Deep History and the Brain*. Berkeley, CA: University of California Press, 2008.

Smith, Jonathan Z. "Fences and Neighbours," 1–18 in *Imagining Religion: From Babylon to Jonestown*. Chicago, IL: University of Chicago Press, 1982.

—*To Take Place: Toward Theory in Ritual*. Chicago, IL: University of Chicago Press, 1987.

—*Drudgery Divine: On the Comparison of Early Christianities and the Religions of Late Antiquity*. London: School of Oriental and African Studies, 1990.

—"Classification," 35–44 in *Guide to the Study of Religion*. Edited by Willi Braun and Russell T. McCutcheon. London: Cassell, 2000.

—"When the Chips Are Down," 1–60 in *Relating Religion: Essays in the Study of Religion*. Chicago, IL: University of Chicago Press, 2004.

Sokal, Alan. *Beyond the Hoax: Science, Philosophy and Culture*. Oxford: Oxford University Press, 2010.

Sokal, Alan, and Jean Bricmon. *Intellectual Impostures: Postmodern Philosophers' Abuse of Science*. London: Profile Books, 1998.

Sørensen, Jesper. "Religion, Evolution, and an Immunology of Cultural Systems," *Evolution and Cognition* 10.1 (2004): 61–73.

—"Religion in Mind: A Review Article of the Cognitive Science of Religion," *Numen* 52.4 (2005): 465–94. https://doi.org/10.1163/156852705775219974

—"Past Minds: Present Historiography and Cognitive Science," 179–96 in Martin and Sørensen, eds., *Past Minds*, 2011.

Sperber, Dan. *Rethinking Symbolism*. Translated by Alice L. Morton. Cambridge: Cambridge University Press, 1975.

—*Explaining Culture: A Naturalistic Approach*. Oxford: Blackwell, 1996.

—"The Guru Effect," *Review of Philosophy and Psychology* 1.4 (2005): 583–92. https://doi.org/10.1007/s13164-010-0025-0

—"A Naturalistic Ontology for Mechanistic Explanations in the Social Sciences," 64–77 in *Analytical Sociology and Social Mechanisms*. Edited by Pierre Demeulenaere. Cambridge: Cambridge University Press, 2011. https://doi.org/10.1017/CBO9780511921315.004

Staal, Frits. "The Meaninglessness of Ritual," *Numen* 26.1 (1979): 2–22. https://doi.org/10.1163/156852779X00244

—*Rules Without Meaning: Ritual, Mantras, and the Human Science*. Bern: Peter Lang, 1989.

Sulloway, Frank J. *Born to Rebel: Birth Order, Family Dynamics, and Creative Lives*. New York: Pantheon, 1996.

Turchin, Peter, H. Whitehouse, P. Francois, E. Slingerland, and M. Collard. "A Historical Database of Sociocultural Evolution," *Cliodynamics: The Journal of Theoretical and Mathematical History* 3.2 (2013): 271–93.

Turchin, Peter, R. Brennan, T. Currie, K. Feeney, P. Francois, D. Hoyer, J. Manning, A. Marciniak, D. Mullins, A. Palmisano, P. Peregrine, E. A. L. Tylor, and H. Whitehouse. "*Seshat*: The Global History Databank," *Cliodynamics: The Journal of Quantitative History and Cultural Evolution* 6.1 (2015): 77–107. Online: http://escholarship.org/uc/item/9qx387 (accessed 22 June 2016).

Ullucci, Daniel. "Towards a Typology of Religious Experts in the Ancient Mediterranean," 89–103 in *The One Who Sows Bountifully: Essays in Honor of Stanley K. Stowers*. Edited by C. J. Hodge, S. M. Olyan, D. Ullucci, and E. Wasserman. Providence, RI: Brown Judaic Studies, 2013.

Wallerstein, Immanuel. "Braudel on the Longue Durée: Problems of Conceptual Translation," *Review: Fernand Braudel Center* 32.2 (2009): 155–70.

Warburton, Nigel. *Thinking from A to Z*. 3rd ed. London: Routledge, 2007.

Watts, Joseph, S. J. Greenhill, Q. D. Atkinson, T. E. Currie, J. Bulbulia, and R. D. Gray. "Broad Supernatural Punishment but Not Moralising High Gods Precede the Evolution of Political Complexity in Austronesia," *Proceedings of the Royal Society B* 282.1804 (2015): 1–7.

Watts, Joseph, O. Sheehan, S. J. Greenhill, S. Gomez-Ng, Q. D. Atkinson, J. Bulbulia, and R. D. Gray. "Pulotu: Database of Austronesian Supernatural Beliefs and Practices." *PLoS ONE* 10.9 (2015): 1–17. https://doi.org/10.1371/journal. pone.0136783

Wayland, Barber Elizabeth, and Paul T. Barber. *When They Severed Earth from Sky: How the Human Mind Shapes Myth.* Princeton, NJ: Princeton University Press, 2006.

Weinstein, Fred. "Psychohistory and the Crisis of the Social Sciences," *History and Theory* 34.4 (1995): 299–319. https://doi.org/10.2307/2505404

Westh, Peter. "Anthropomorphism in God Concepts: The Role of Narrative," 396–413 in Geertz, ed., *Origins of Religion*, 2013.

Whitehouse, Harvey. *Inside the Cult: Religious Innovation and Transmission in Papua New Guinea.* Oxford: Oxford University Press, 1995.

—"Modes of Religiosity: Towards a Cognitive Explanation of the Sociopolitical Dynamics of Religion," *Method & Theory in the Study of Religion* 143.3–4 (2002): 293–315.

—*Modes of Religiosity: A Cognitive Theory of Religious Transmission.* Walnut Creek, CA: AltaMira Press, 2004.

—"Religion, Cohesion, and Hostility," 36–47 in *Religion, Intolerance, and Conflict: A Scientific and Conceptual Investigation.* Edited by S. Clarke, R. Powell, and J. Savulescu. Oxford: Oxford University Press, 2013. https://doi.org/10.1093/ac-prof:oso/9780199640911.003.0002

Whitehouse, Harvey, and Luther H. Martin, eds. *Theorizing Religions Past: Archaeology, History, and Cognition.* Walnut Creek, CA: AltaMira Press, 2004.

Whitmarsh, Tim. *Battling the Gods: Atheism in the Ancient World.* London: Faber & Faber, 2016.

Wilson, Deirdre, and Dan Sperber. "Relevance Theory," 607–32 in *The Handbook of Pragmatics.* Edited by Laurence R. Hornand and Gregory Ward. Oxford: Blackwell, 2004.

Woolf, Greg. "World Religion and World Empire in the Ancient Mediterranean," 19–35 in *Die Religion des Imperium Romanum: Koine und Konfrontationen.* Edited by Hubert Cancik and Jörg Rüpke. Tübingen: Mohr Siebeck, 2009.

—"Only Connect? Networks and Religious Change in the Ancient Mediterranean," CRASIS lecture (University of Groningen, 9 February 2012). Online: http://www. rug.nl/research/centre-for-religious-studies/crasis/activities/annual-meeting/greg_ woolf_crasis_lecture.pdf (20 May 2016).

—"Isis and the Evolution of Religion," 62–92 in *Power, Politics and the Cults of Isis.* Edited by Laurent Bricault and Miguel J. Versluys. Leiden: Brill, 2014.

Xygalatas, Dimitris. "Special Issue on the Experimental Research of Religion," *Journal for the Cognitive Science of Religion* 1.2 (2013): 137–9. https://doi.org/10.1558/ jcsr.v1i2.137

Chapter Seventeen

Cultural Geography

Justin K. H. Tse

Introduction:
The Strangeness of Pairing Cultural Geography with Ancient Religion

To have a chapter on cultural geography in a book on ancient religion presumes that cultural geographers have something to say about the topic. This
would probably be of more surprise to cultural geographers than to scholars of ancient religion. In the academic study of religion, the spatial turn
has generated a laundry list of buzzwords like "space," "place," "cartogra-
phy," and even "geography."[1] New conventions using geographical terminology seem to be constantly emerging in religious studies, with even sites
in antiquity theorized as "thirdspace" and "real-and-imagined spaces"[2] and
references aplenty to the likes of Henri Lefebvre, Yifu Tuan, Edward Soja,
and David Harvey.[3]

---

1. See Manuel A. Vásquez and Marie F. Marquardt, *Globalizing the Sacred:
Religion Across the Americas* (New Brunswick, NJ: Rutgers University Press, 2003);
Thomas Tweed, *Crossing and Dwelling: A Theory of Religion* (Cambridge, MA: Harvard University Press, 2008); Kim Knott, "Religion, Space, and Place: The Spatial Turn
in Research on Religion," *Religion and Society* 1 (2010): 29–43.
2. E.g., John L. Berquist and Claudia L. Camp, eds., *Constructions of Space I:
Theory, Geography, and Narrative* (London: Bloomsbury T&T Clark, 2008) and *Constructions of Space II: The Biblical City and Other Imagined Spaces* (London: Bloomsbury T&T Clark, 2008).
3. See: Henri Lefebvre, *The Production of Space* (trans. Donald Nicholson-Smith;
Oxford: Wiley-Blackwell, 1992 [1974]); Yifu Tuan, *Topophilia: A Study of Environmental Perceptions, Attitudes, and Values* (New York: Columbia University Press, 1990
[1974]) and *Space and Place: The Perspective of Experience* (Minneapolis, MN: University of Minnesota Press, 2001 [1977]); Edward Soja, *Thirdspace: Journeys to Los
Angeles and Other Real-and-Imagined Places* (Oxford: Wiley-Blackwell, 1996) and
Postmodern Geographies: The Reassertion of Space in Critical Social Theory (London:
Verso, 2011 [1989]); David Harvey, *The Condition of Postmodernity: An Enquiry into
the Origins of Cultural Change* (Oxford: Wiley-Blackwell, 1989), as well as *The Limits
to Capital* (2nd ed.; London: Verso, 2007), and *Social Justice and the City* (2nd ed.;
Athens, GA: University of Georgia Press, 2009).

All of this would come as a surprise to cultural geographers. For us, ancient religion can feel a little old for our trendy theories. Indeed, when the occasional presentation from antiquity is made at the annual Anglophone geography conferences, I have personally witnessed more than one eyebrow raised, often at a presenter from outside of the discipline trying to put old wine into new wineskins (which I suppose is technically fine but we do notice it). In other words, the impression that geography is hip and trendy probably comes from geographers ourselves. Our topics tend to encompass the more trend-setting items of today, with words like "critical geopolitics," "alternative economies," "post-Anthropocene," and "affective relations" circulating through our discourse.[4] We want to explore "new materialisms," theorize "relational geographies of encounter," engage in "creative co-production" with contemporary artists, and (above all) "fuck neoliberalism."[5] There is a dedicated subfield called the "geography of religion," but as one of our leading luminaries Lily Kong has encouraged us, religiosity must be put in conversation with the "global shifts" and "theoretical shifts" that are reshaping our planet right now: "rapid urbanization, environmental devastation, ageing populations, and human mobilities."[6] For geographers, the Hittites, Girgishites, Amorites, Canaanites, Perezites, Hivites, and Jebusites may as well be termites.

What on earth, then, does geography as a discipline have to do with ancient religion, and if it is a fad, is it destined to go the way of the Philistine? The simple case that I want to make in this chapter is that cultural

---

4.   On "critical geopolitics," see Gearóid Ó Tuathail, *Critical Geopolitics: The Politics of Writing Global Space* (Minneapolis, MN: University of Minnesota Press, 1996); on "alternative economies," see J. K. Gibson-Graham, *The End of Capitalism (As We Knew It): A Feminist Critique of Political Economy* (Oxford: Blackwell, 1996) and *A Postcapitalist Politics* (Minneapolis, MN: University of Minnesota Press, 2006); on "post-Anthropocene," see Elizabeth Johnson et al., "After the Anthropocene: Politics and Geographic Inquiry for a New Epoch," *Progress in Human Geography* 38.3 (2014): 439–56; on "affective relations," see Nigel Thrift, *Non-Representational Theory: Space, Politics, Affect* (London: Routledge, 2008). Cf., of course, Michel Foucault, *Discipline and Punish* (trans. Alan Sheridan; New York: Vintage, 1995 [1975]).

5.   See Sarah Whatmore, *Hybrid Geographies: Natures Cultures Spaces* (London: Sage, 2002) and Kay Anderson and Colin Perrin, "New Materialism and the Stuff of Humanism," *Australian Humanities Review* 58 (2015): 1–15; Gill Valentine, "Living with Difference: Reflections on Geographies of Encounter," *Progress in Human Geography* 32.3 (2008): 323–37; Harriet Hawkins, "Creative Geographies: Knowing, Representing, Intervening," *Cultural Geographies* 22.2 (2015): 247–68; Simon Springer, "Fuck Neoliberalism," *ACME: An International E-Journal for Critical Geographies* 15.2 (2016): 285–92, respectively.

6.   Lily Kong, "Global Shifts, Theoretical Shifts: Changing Geographies of Religion," *Progress in Human Geography* 34.6 (2010): 765.

geography is neither new nor emerging in the study of ancient religion because the two disciplines have in fact been intertwined for quite some time. In fact, my argument is that because cultural geography—the discipline seeking to theorize the practices that go into making a place—influenced historian of religion Mircea Eliade's understanding of the irruption of the sacred in specific sites, geographers and scholars of ancient religion share the most common ground when they seek to understand the ideologies (and perhaps also theologies) that are embedded in material space.[7] In other words, cultural geography is not trendy for scholarship on ancient religion; it is foundational.

My attempt to recover Eliade in the contemporary study of geography and religion is an expansion of a somewhat contested segment of an argument that I have previously lodged in one of geography's flagship journals, *Progress in Human Geography*. Geographers, I contended, are interested in "grounded theologies," which I described as "performative practices of placemaking informed by understandings of the transcendent."[8] More contentiously (I suspect) for religious studies scholars than geographers, I suggested further that "mapping grounded theologies entails a critical recovery of Eliade's spatial understanding of *homo religiosus*, that humanity retains a sense of transcendence despite the advent of modernity."[9] It is my aim in this chapter to fully flesh out this claim and its implications for contemporary scholarship on ancient religion.

I realize that bringing up Mircea Eliade is to risk becoming a laughing-stock among religious studies scholars, and although my return to Eliade is qualified by the word "critical," I am more than aware that Eliade is the furthest thing from hip and trendy for both geographers and ancient religion-ists alike. What is worse, to invoke Eliade may appear as if geographers like me are poaching from the ancient history of religious studies, which is not unlike how geographers might feel when they hear that works from the 1970s and 1980s by Lefebvre, Soja, Tuan, and Harvey are being paraded by religious studies scholars as "emerging." To that end, I want to first get a sense of the terrain of ancient religion from where I am standing as a geographer, operationalizing the field so that an encounter between the two disciplines can be realized. Second, I will revisit the contests in religious studies over Eliade and his understanding of "hierophany," the irruption of the divine into the earthly realm, in geographical terms. Realizing that these

---

7.   See Mircea Eliade, *The Sacred and the Profane: The Nature of Religion* (trans. Willard R. Trask. New York: Harcourt, 1999 [1959]).

8.   Justin K. H. Tse, "Grounded Theologies: 'Religion' and the 'Secular' in Human Geography," *Progress in Human Geography* 38.2 (2014): 202.

9.   Tse, "Grounded Theologies," 205.

not-so-current debates hearken back to the 1990s at best and the 1940s at worst (and are therefore not only untrendy and unhip, but also possibly unseemly for current discussion), I will end by sketching the contemporary implications of situating cultural geography as not so much hip and trendy, but foundational, for the study of the material order of ancient religion.

Operationalizing Ancient Religion for Geography: A Foundational Disciplinary Encounter

As a geographer, I have virtually no training in ancient religion; in this sense, I feel that I have quite a bit of common ground with scholars of ancient religion who have virtually no training in geography. Because of this, let me begin by proposing a common research agenda that our two disciplines might be able to share. At least as far as I understand it, the study of "ancient religion" encompasses a broad field of inquiry concerning how persons and societies approached "the one transcendent God, or ... Gods or spirits, or magic forces, or whatever" prior to the advent of a "modern" self-consciousness concerned with an individual quest for fullness developed in the late Middle Ages around the fifteenth to seventeenth centuries.[10] In this way, I understand studying "ancient" religion as taking seriously what Robinson Crusoe, the quintessential modern protagonist, meant as a farce when he discusses his father, "who was very ancient."[11] In this early modern English classic, "ancient" seems to be a pejorative for all of the old-fashioned attitudes that presumably came before the individualized, self-reflexive, "can do" attitude of modernity. Studies of ancient religions, as far as I know, critique this word "ancient" in the same way that critical scholars have critiqued the presumption that "orientals" and "mediaevals" are *a priori* relegated to a static past of inaction. I understand, then, that scholars in this field explore the agency of place-making actors who did not need the modern obsession with self-consciousness in order to act, but nonetheless worshiped, theologized, mythologized, and historicized in real places and performed such liturgical imaginations in their acts of everyday placemaking.[12]

As a sustained attempt to articulate how persons and other beings cultivate meaning in concrete sites, "cultural geography" is already latent in the foregoing description of the study of ancient religion. The "culture" is in

10. See Charles Taylor, *A Secular Age* (Cambridge, MA: The Belknap Press of Harvard University Press, 2007), 16.

11. Daniel Defoe, *Robinson Crusoe* (ed. Michael Shinagel; New York: W. W. Norton, 1993 [1719]), 4.

12. See Michel de Certeau, *The Practice of Everyday Life* (trans. Steven Rendall; Berkeley, CA: University of California Press, 1984).

the "cultivating," and the "geography" is in the concrete sites in which culture materializes. Usually, such concrete cultivation ends up being a political task leading to contestation because articulating what the material order
is and why it is significant often leads to disagreement, not consensus. This
point is made especially more acute in our current intellectual climate, as
"new materialist" rejections of the binary between "nature" (that which is
uncultivated by human consciousness and yet still has agency) and "culture"
(that which is cultivated by human minds) makes cultivation itself contested.[13] Still, what holds the discipline together, at least as I see it, is a focus on
what happens to *ideology* when it is put to work on the ground. In this sense,
ideology remains important to cultural geographers because the meanings of
concrete sites and the future of their development often involve the imagination. To discuss ideology is therefore to discuss geography because geography is what happens when ideology gets put to work in the material world.

A real intellectual encounter between cultural geographers invested in
these debates about concrete cultivations and scholars of ancient religion
would do both parties some good, I claim. It would remind geographers that
theorizing about ancient religion has always been central to what we do as
"cultural geographers" as we theorize the relationship between the affective
and the material, whether in the time frame demarcated by "modernity" or
not. By looking at how cultural geographers actually do our work, scholars
of ancient religion could also be given an opportunity to understand the theoretical concerns of our discipline, instead of being content with the buzzword
crumbs that fall from our table. Put in a more personal way, I am a geographer who wants to be disabused of my modern fundamentalism, and I am
not content with scholars of ancient religion and cultural geographers simply
poaching from each other's disciplines. A real engagement has to happen.

What that means, I think, is that our two disciplines—cultural geography
and ancient religion—do not really need to be *made* to interact, for we have
in fact been interacting for quite some time and have continued that interaction to the present day, although there is some denial on both sides that such
engagement actually happens. I claim, therefore, that the denial of our constant, longstanding, productive interaction must cease. Accordingly, I refuse
to prescribe ways that scholars of ancient religion can use cultural geography

13.   See Kay Anderson, *Race and the Crisis of Humanism* (London: Routledge, 2006);
Sarah Whatmore, "Materialist Returns: Practicing Cultural Geography in and for a More-
Than-Human World," *Cultural Geographies* 13.4 (2006): 600–9; Jane Bennett, *Vibrant
Matter: A Political Ecology of Things* (Durham, NC: Duke University Press, 2010); Divya
Tolia-Kelly, "The Geographies of Cultural Geography III: Material Geographies, Vibrant
Matters and Risking Surface Geographies," *Progress in Human Geography* 37.1 (2013):
153–60.

productively; rather, I seek to describe how conversations between our two disciplines have already been productive. Indeed, in what follows, I hope to show that Eliade's engagement with cultural geography for the study of ancient religion may be the unexpected way forward for our ongoing disciplinary encounter.

Revisiting the Eliade-Smith Debate: Hierophany and Geographical Exploitation

So as not to become a *complete* laughingstock (I am fine, however, with being partially one), let me situate my reflections on Eliade in the context of the later contest that Jonathan Z. Smith had with him over how to interpret ancient religion. That Eliade is a contested scholar in religious studies may come as a surprise to most geographers because, as Kim Knott points out, "it is with Eliade that most accounts of sacred space begin."[14] Unfortunately for those who think of geographers as current on all contemporary issues, this focus on Eliade also means that "relatively few geographers of religion are well versed in work on space, place, and geography by those in the field of religious studies per se,"[15] which means that many geographers will not be aware that Eliade is a bit of a *persona non grata* in the religionist guild. To press home her point, Knott chides Chris Park[16] for failing "in his major survey of geography and religion, *Sacred Worlds*" to "cite the work of either Jonathan Z. Smith or Paul Wheatley, though Mircea Eliade and Ninian Smart (whose name is not particularly associated with the study of sacred space) are mentioned in passing."[17] By complaining about Eliade, Knott thus inadvertently reveals that he remains very much a reference point for geographers understanding religious studies, especially ancient religions. Departing from Knott, I propose that we can simply be honest that while Eliade is very much dead in religious studies, he is very much alive in geography. Hopefully, my account of how Eliade remains useful for geographers will show in turn that Eliade might also be usefully recovered for the study of ancient religion, albeit in a critical way.

Conventions in religious studies usually make Smith's debate with Eliade out to be a contest over how to articulate the elusive meaning of "religion." In our religious studies classrooms, we typically pit Eliade's concept of

---

14. Knott, "Religion, Space, and Place," 95.
15. Knott, "Religion, Space, and Place," 104.
16. Chris C. Park, *Sacred Worlds: An Introduction to Geography and Religion* (London: Routledge, 1994).
17. Knott, "Religion, Space, and Place," 104.

hierophany ("*something sacred that shows itself to us*"[18]) against Smith's insistence that sacred places are *sacralized* in ways that are "relentlessly intentional and constructivist."[19] Committed as we are to probing the word "religion," we tell ourselves and our students that the fundamental difference between Eliade and Smith is that they do not agree on what "religion" is. Eliade, we say, relies on overly romantic conceptions of what Rudolf Otto calls the "numinous"[20]—a real sacred that is able to strike real terror—whereas Smith is the sane voice of secular reason who reminds us that religion is a social construct. Religion for Eliade (as Smith himself claims) is really "cosmological"; religion for Smith is mundanely political.[21] Smith thus criticizes Eliade for taking an all-too-uncritical view of ancient religion; after all, Eliade actually believes that there is a *there* there when it comes to the sacred. By contrast, Smith sees himself as engaging in a truly critical exegesis of the ancient texts in order to excavate the politics being covered up by what looks numinous but is really just ideology. There is a real transcendent for Eliade, but transcendence is all ideological smoke-and-mirrors for Smith.

Interesting as the probing of the word "religion" may be, the gap between Eliade and Smith is in fact not so wide when framed within the disciplinary rubrics of cultural geography. In fact, I claim that cultural geography, not the dispute over the definition of religion, is what is primarily at stake in this exchange—an interaction that, upon a closer reading, is not altogether oppositional. Not only do both Eliade and Smith get down and dirty in the doing of geography, but they have also both been influenced by and then exert their influence on geographers. They do disagree with each other—significantly even—but the "politics of religion," as Lily Kong puts it, do not negate the "poetics of religion" in the making and contesting of places.[22] Eliade and Smith form a dialectic, not a divorce.

Indeed, there is profound agreement between Eliade and Smith on Émile Durkheim's premise that the study of religion is interesting not only because it provides insight into the institutional organization of societies, but also because social organizations occupy actual space. Put another way, sociologists seek to understand society because they want to say something

18.   Eliade, *Sacred and the Profane*, 11 (emphasis in the original).

19.   Jonathan Z. Smith, *To Take Place: Toward Theory in Ritual* (Chicago, IL: University of Chicago Press, 1987), 18.

20.   See Rudolf Otto, *The Idea of the Holy: An Inquiry Into the Non-Rational Factor in the Idea of the Divine and Its Relation to the Rational* (trans. John W. Harvey; Oxford: Oxford University Press, 1923).

21.   See Smith, *To Take Place*, 17.

22.   See Kong, "Global Shifts."

about spatial ontology. As Durkheim puts it, "the social organization has been the model for the spatial organization and a reproduction of it."[23] The organization of societies is important for Durkheim because one can only speak of societies if space is organized unevenly with different hierarchies of experience:

> Spatial representation consists essentially in a primary co-ordination of the data of sensuous experience. But this co-ordination would be impossible if the parts of space were qualitatively equivalent and if they were really interchangeable.[24]

For Durkheim, this spatial unevenness can be understood through the "elementary forms of religion"—that is, *ancient religion*, with reference to the sacralized hierarchies (the "totem"), beliefs in numinous power (the "mana"), and practical "taboos" of Australian indigenous tribes. Theorizing about ancient religion thus underlies Durkheim's entire sociological system, as he argues that the organization of societies in actual spaces have religious origins and still may carry this religiosity into the making of modern geographies. Admittedly, the ancient religion in question here (and in Eliade and Smith) is more properly *indigenous religion*, and a settler colonial reading at that; as much as I want to blast this sensibility into oblivion, my aims here are more modest, as I am simply trying to show that ancient religion lies at the heart of Durkheimian sociology, but sociology (at least a Durkheimian one) serves the primary task of doing geography, that is, theorizing space.

With ancient (indigenous) religion as the common topic of discussion, Eliade and Smith agree that what Durkheim is up to is not just "sociology" (and definitely *not* just trying to define what "religion" is for its own sake), but *geography*. Readers in religious studies will no doubt be familiar with the first chapter of Eliade's *Sacred and the Profane* (1959), if not from reading Eliade himself, then from Smith's parody opening in *To Take Place* (1987). Titled "Sacred Space and Making the World Sacred," Eliade sets himself to the task of theorizing what space is—invoking Durkheim's insistence on the unevenness of spatial experience, no less: "For religious man, space is not homogeneous; he [*sic*] experiences interruptions, breaks in it; some parts of space are qualitatively different from others."[25] That Eliade focuses on religion is a bit of a red herring; by the end of the book, we learn that Eliade thinks that *homo religiosus* is basically everyone. "Modern religious man," he admits, "assumes a new existential situation; he regards himself solely as

23. Émile Durkheim, *The Elementary Forms of the Religious Life* (trans. Joseph Ward Swain; New York: Free Press, 1915), 25.
24. Durkheim, *Elementary Forms*, 23.
25. Eliade, *Sacred and the Profane*, 20.

the subject and agent of history, and he refuses all appeal to transcendence." Then he adds: "But this nonreligious man descends from *homo religiosus* and, whether he likes it or not, he is also the work of religious man; his formation begins with the situations assumed by his ancestors. In short, he is the result of a process of desacralization."[26] Contrary to those who might hail such a decline of religion as a triumph, Eliade turns what seems to be his defeat into a victory, claiming that the "majority of the 'irreligious' still behave religiously, even though they are not aware of the fact" of their "large stock of camouflaged myths and degenerated rituals":

> But this means that nonreligious man has been formed by opposing his predecessor, by attempting to "empty" himself of all religion and all trans-human meaning. He recognizes himself in proportion as he "frees" and "purifies" himself from the "superstitions" of his ancestors. In other words, profane man cannot help preserving some vestiges of the behavior of religious man, though they are emptied of religious meaning. Do what he will, he is an inheritor. He cannot utterly abolish his past, since he is himself the product of his past. He forms himself by a series of denials and refusals, but he continues to be haunted by the realities that he has refused and denied. To acquire a world of his own, he has desacralized the world in which his ancestors lived; but to do so he has been obliged to adopt the opposite of an earlier type of behavior, and that behavior is still emotionally present to him, in one form or another, ready to be reactualized in his deepest being.[27]

In other words, Eliade's exploration of religious space is not limited to "the religious"; he is simply doing geography, period, because all geographies in relation to the human person are foundationally religious, as the human person is essentially *homo religiosus*.

The dispute between Eliade and Smith is over how these geographies are constituted, and the passage under debate focuses (like Durkheim) on an Australian tribe, the Tjilpa ("Achilpa" in Eliade). This case study is important, Smith notes, because Eliade uses it to set the stage for comparison to other ancient religions, such as "two sacred centers in Jerusalem that provided rich clusters of symbolic meanings: the Temple and the Church of the Holy Sepulcher."[28] In other words, it is perfectly legitimate, according to both Eliade and Smith, to extrapolate theoretically from their row over indigenous religion to claims about ancient religion more generally. As Smith quotes at length from Eliade:

> According to the traditions of an Arunta tribe, the Achilpa, in mythical times the divine being Numbakula cosmicized their future territory, created their

26. Eliade, *Sacred and the Profane*, 203.
27. Eliade, *Sacred and the Profane*, 204–5.
28. Smith, *To Take Place*, 3–4.

Ancestor, and established their institutions. From the trunk of a gum tree Numbakula fashioned the sacred pole (*kauwa-auwa*), and, after anointing it with blood, climbed it and disappeared into the sky. This pole represents a cosmic axis, for it is around the sacred pole that territory becomes habitable, hence is transformed into a world. The sacred pole consequently plays an important role ritually. During their wanderings the Achilpa always carry it with them and choose the direction they are to take by the direction toward which it bends. This allows them, while being continually on the move, to be always in "their world" and, at the same time, in communication with the sky into which Numbakula vanished.

For the pole to be broken denotes catastrophe; it is like "the end of the world," reversion to chaos. Spencer and Gillen report that once, when the pole was broken, the entire clan were in consternation; they wandered about aimlessly for a time, and finally lay down on the ground together and waited for death to overtake them.[29]

For Smith, everything about Eliade's analysis of the Tjilpa is wrong. Where Eliade posits that the pole is the center of the world, Smith points out that there is no center because the pole keeps moving. Where Eliade thinks that Numbakula communicates cosmically with the Tjilpa, Smith suggests that this cosmological association is an act of political ideology. Where Eliade reads the brokenness of the cosmic pole to have led to the disorientation and death-desire of the Tjilpa, Smith retrieves the original sources and finds that the only reason the Tjilpa wanted to die is because of exhaustion.

But if we are reading Eliade's account as geography, is Smith's critique really so devastating? A closer examination of Eliade's bibliography for this first chapter suggests that it is not. Indeed, while there are no endnotes in *The Sacred and the Profane*, the references are divided among each of the chapters, showing the influences on each part of Eliade's thinking. In this first chapter, there is a curious reference to Pierre Deffontaines's *Géographie et religions* (1948),[30] considered a classic of French cultural geography that operated primarily in the 1940s and 1950s by describing different kinds of spaces and categorizing them. I find Park's description of the book— from the very text that Kim Knott despises because Park seems to be ignorant of the spatial turn in religious studies—especially prescient, even though it wildly understates Deffontaines's contribution to religious studies as a geographer:

> The most influential French geographer of the genre was Pierre Deffontaines … whose *Géographie et religions* (1948) offered a wide-ranging though entirely descriptive treatment of relevant themes … Although Eliade (1959) was not a geographer, he has had a lasting impact on the development of

---

29. Smith, *To Take Place*, 1–2 citing Eliade, *Sacred and the Profane*, 32–3.
30. Pierre Deffontaines, *Géographie et religions* (Paris: Gallimard, 1948).

geographical studies of religion, particularly in distinguishing the sacred
from the profane (secular).[31]

It would be all too easy for scholars of ancient religion to mock these two
sentences; for example, we all know that the point of *The Sacred and the
Profane* is quite the opposite of Park's assessment—for Eliade, the profane and the sacred are almost indistinguishable geographically! But what
is useful about this flawed passage is that Park recognizes implicitly that
there is a connection between Deffontaines's French geography and Eliade's work, suggesting that Eliade is more properly read not within the
canon of religious studies, but as part of the guild of geographers citing a
colleague in a shared effort to theorize space.

More explicitly, then, it becomes clear on a re-reading of Eliade's first
chapter that Deffontaines is everywhere to be found in his account of the
axis mundi, the sacred place as the center of the world. Deffontaines's geography of religion is divided into five parts: (1) the influence of religion on
geographies of dwelling, whether of the living, the dead, or the gods; (2) the
impact of religion on human settlement; (3) the relationship between religion and the exploitation of the earth in geographies of agriculture, industry, and consumption; (4) religious migrations of the living (e.g., business
and pilgrimage) and the dead; and (5) the geographies of lifestyle, including religious ones.[32] In other words, the key to Deffontaines's descriptive
geography of religion is the centrality of the dwelling for human geography,
for it is from the home that the everyday life of the human population radi-
ates. This domesticity is recapitulated in Eliade's account of the *axis mundi*
as he moves beyond Deffontaines's descriptive *modus operandi* to theorize space. The details of dwelling, settlement, farming, industrialization,
migration, and lifestyle are all secondary for Eliade. What is instead important is Eliade's central argument: "To us, it seems an inescapable conclusion that *the religious man sought to live as near as possible to the Center
of the World.*"[33] This dwelling, Eliade continues, did not only refer to *homo
religiosus*'s country, city, temple, or palace, but "he also wanted to his own
house to be at the Center and to be an *imago mundi*," so much so that homes
were built "on the microcosmic scale, to reproduce the universe."[34] In other
words, Eliade brings out explicitly what Deffontaines leaves implicit in his
descriptive geography: if the geographical task is to describe the dwelling
place of the living and the dead and has some relationship with religion,

31. Park, *Sacred Worlds*, 17.
32. Deffontaines, *Géographie et religions*.
33. Eliade, *Sacred and the Profane*, 43 (emphasis in the original).
34. Eliade, *Sacred and the Profane*, 43.

then ancient geographies reveal the centrality of religion in the practices of making a home the center of the world. If everyone has to live somewhere, the sacred and the profane really are not so far apart.

Does it really matter, then, whether this dwelling is either cosmological or ideological? Is it really consequential for understanding a place whether it is the cosmic divine or the political fantasy of the powerful for centering one's home in the world? Does the opposition between Eliade and Smith really have to be a zero-sum game? In cultural geography, the answer to these questions seem to be no. Lily Kong's magisterial argument for the coherence of geographies of religion as a field gives equal weight to both ways of conceptualizing sacred space. She achieves this balancing act through a sideways reading of David Chidester and Edward Linenthal's understanding of "sacralization,"[35] one that is close to Smith's:

> Chidester and Linenthal (1995: 5) draw parallels between the politics and poetics of the sacred with the situational and substantial sacred. Citing Durkheim, they argue that the sacred is situational because it is "at the nexus of human practices and social projects." Hence, "nothing is inherently sacred" (Chidester and Linenthal, 1995: 6). Similarly, Levi-Strauss has emphasized that the sacred is "a value of indeterminate signification, in itself empty of meaning and therefore susceptible to the reception of any meaning whatsoever" (Chidester and Linenthal, 1995: 6). The sacred is thus tied up with, and draws meaning from, social and political relationships. In contrast, the "substantial" sacred parallels the poetics of the sacred. Hence, the "sacred" is thought to have an essential character (Chidester and Linenthal, 1995: 5).[36]

As Kong herself notes, Chidester and Linenthal are far from friendly to the sort of sacred essentialism by which "Eliade's (1959) work immediately comes to mind."[37] However, she does not share their skepticism; instead, she posits the substantial sacred as a parallel, not an opposition, to the situational. Of course, it is imaginable that religious studies scholars may scoff at Kong's parallelism between the "situational and substantial sacred." But to do so would be to miss Kong's point. What she is really saying is that where there is no real conflict for theorizing a place, no schism need exist. What Smith's approach would achieve is an account of the political, but one that denies the poetry of the sacred; what Eliade gives us is pure poetry with political naïveté. Both, Kong suggests, are needed for a comprehensive

---

35. David Chidester and Edward T. Linenthal, "Introduction," in *American Sacred Space* (ed. David Chidester and Edward T. Linenthal; Bloomington, IN: Indiana University Press, 1995), 1–42.

36. Lily Kong, "Mapping 'New' Geographies of Religion: Politics and Poetics in Modernity," *Progress in Human Geography* 25.2 (2001): 212–3.

37. Kong, "Mapping 'New' Geographies," 218.

geography of religion; there is not only room for both, but both ends of the dialectic must be maintained. Or as the religious philosopher Simone Weil (who would have been no friend to Smith, Chidester, and Linenthal) says: "Foolish as the theory of Durkheim may be in confusing what is religious with what is social, it yet contains an element of truth; that is to say that the social feeling is so much like the religious as to be mistaken for it."[38]

To put it starkly, to describe a place is to theorize it, and to theorize space is the task of cultural geography. This task, I have argued, lies at the heart of studying ancient religion, not least because geographers like Deffontaines and Eliade were foundational to the study of ancient religions, deny it as scholars in this field might. In other words, there is nothing hip and trendy about geography in the study of ancient religion; it is rather quite old and boring because geographers have been woven into the enterprise from the beginning, from Smith back to Eliade, and Eliade back to Deffontaines, and all of them back to Durkheim, who himself claims that the task of sociology is ultimately geographical. There is nothing flashy about theorizing the spaces of ancient religion; if anything, they are just deep reflections on thick description. Indeed, for Kong, this means that all placemaking may have something to do with religion, leading to her call for geographers to map religious territoriality "beyond the officially sacred."[39] Geographers thus shamelessly continue to use Eliade, discredited though he may be in religious studies, for Eliade's theorization of Deffontaines's descriptiveness highlights the transcendent dimension in the making of everyday places that may not even be considered sites of official religious worship, especially homes. Perhaps the task, as I have suggested, is a critical recovery of Eliade, much like Kong, appreciating his poetics of religious space, but recognizing the social and political dimensions of its construction. Indeed, such usages of Eliade have been undertaken for quite some time in geography. It is to them finally that we now turn.

Political Phenomenology:
The Ubiquity of Eliade and Ancient Religion in Geography

Cultural geography is not a new trend in the study of ancient religion(s) because it is foundational to the discipline, especially because it is the basis by which religious studies scholars interpret the material order, the ideologies embedded in it, and the possible theological readings of it. The divergence of our two disciplines, however, has caused some misunderstanding,

---

38.   Simone Weil, *Waiting on God* (Abingdon, UK: Routledge, 2010 [1951]), 4.
39.   Kong, "Mapping 'New' Geographies," 226.

perhaps generating possible disdain between scholars in both fields because we are not aware of each other's debates. This rift can most likely be attributed to Erich Isaac, who differentiated *religious geography*, an apologetic geography seeking to describe a religious way of being from within, from the *geography of religion*, the description of how religions affect material processes on the earth.[40] For Isaac, only geography of religion was appropriate for geographers to conduct; religious geographies, he thought, were best left up to theologians and religious studies scholars. Not only was this a conflation of theology and religious studies in geography, but it inculcated geographers with the notion that the legitimacy of even engaging with religious studies was an open question in the discipline,[41] a form of disciplinary policing that Kong decisively rejected when she called on geographers to give some attention "to how we can collectively make an impact beyond geography" by actively publishing and presenting in interdisciplinary religious studies contexts.[42] Given the nearly forty-year absence of geography from religious studies, though, it is perhaps of little surprise that geographers may have missed the memorandum that Eliade had died and that his thought has been replaced by Smith and his disciples.

However, I claim that the failure of geographers to appreciate Eliade's demise in religious studies has been productive in cultural geography. Despite the turn in religious studies to a critical appraisal of placemaking—so much so that Eliade has been discarded—it turns out that the turn within geography to critically assess the politics of placemaking has relied heavily on Eliade when discussion turns to ancient religion. This preference for Eliade may well be attributed to an implicit radical shift that occurred in geography in the 1970s that has set the stage for the acceptance of a transcendent plane of existence, likely due to ongoing interest in phenomenology—the study of personal consciousness in a world of material phenomena—as a mode of geographical analysis. Yi-fu Tuan's *Topophilia* (1990) is the classic, if not foundational, work in this vein, one that even deals explicitly with ancient religion. Tuan's inquiry revolves around how human persons consciously come to love certain sites, invoking especially the spectacular ancient landscapes of gardens, palaces, and temples as monuments attempting to capture the mystery of the cosmos. Eliade is one helpful theorist of space that Tuan engages because "if Mircea Eliade is right, an early and fundamental idea in the sacredness of place is that it represents the center, the axis, or the navel

40. Erich Isaac, "Religious Geography and the Geography of Religions," in *Man and the Earth* (Boulder, CO: University of Colorado Press, 1965), 1–14.
41. See Lily Kong, "Geography and Religion: Trends and Prospects," *Progress in Human Geography* 14.3 (1990): 360–1.
42. Kong, "Mapping 'New' Geographies," 770.

of the world," which means that "every effort to define space is an attempt to create order out of disorder," sharing "some of the significance of the primordial act of creation and hence the sacred character of that act" not only in "the building of a sanctuary, but the building of a house and of a town traditionally called for the ritual transformation of profane space."[43] As Paul Wheatley also notes in his study of ancient Chinese cities, urban economic centers in imperial China only became so because they were first known as ritual sites, leading to the conclusion that "for the ancients the 'real' world transcended the pragmatic realm of textures and geometrical space, and was perceived schematically in terms of an extra-mundane, sacred experience," meaning that "only the sacred was 'real,' and the purely secular—if it could be said to exist at all—could never be more than trivial."[44] Tuan thus claims that part of the phenomenological draw to certain places is their sacred character, and it is Eliade—not his critics—who are helpful for talking about the numinous quality of that affective relation. *Topophilia* can thus be read as an implicit rejection of Isaac's strict dichotomization of religious geography and geography of religion because, for Tuan, geographers describe the emotional relations between conscious persons and material places, even if these feelings originate from religion, even ancient ones.

This phenomenological approach to geography took on a political ring because geographers found that most places are constituted by contests among various ideological and even theological imaginations. While Tuan's readers outside of geography seem to understand him as offering a typology of geographies (the most popular being the contrast between meaningless space and meaningful place),[45] this move toward the politics of placemaking can also be seen as a development of Tuan's phenomenology. As the renowned cultural geographer Denis Cosgrove put it, "[i]n the construction of human landscapes the anthropomorphism of environmental symbolism and of sacred geometry has been recognized and its cross-cultural replication noted by writers like Mircea Eliade (1959), Paul Wheatley (1971), and Yi-Fu Tuan (1974)."[46] Here, again, Eliade is included with Wheatley and Tuan, as Eliade offers geographers a way of describing sacred phenomenologies from within, especially as they deal with ancient religions. James Duncan's masterpiece *The City as Text* (1990) is one such example as a study of how the urban

43. Tuan, *Topophilia*, 146.

44. Paul Wheatley, *The Pivot of the Four Quarters: A Preliminary Enquiry into the Origins of the Ancient Chinese City* (Edinburgh, UK: Edinburgh University Press, 1971), 304.

45. See Tuan, *Space and Place*.

46. Denis E. Cosgrove, *Social Formation and Symbolic Landscape* (Madison, WI: University of Wisconsin Press, 1994), 57.

landscape of the ancient city of Kandy was infused with the clash between an "Asokan" understanding of kingship as benevolence derived from Buddhist sources and "Sakran" ideologies of sovereignty emphasizing kingly pomp by making Buddhist practice revolve around the king. While Duncan is aware of Smith's complaint that Eliade misinterprets his sources and overly generalizes them,[47] he actively uses Eliade throughout his study of Kandy because it is Eliade, not Smith, who shows the connection between ritual landscapes and cosmic realities. Duncan's specific invocations of Eliade include: the Sakran king's pomp as the representation of "energy and fertility"; Kandy's "Ocean of Milk" as part of a "philosophical system with water seen as the source of all existence, as that which contained the potentiality of existence in unbroken unity"; Mount Meru as the cosmic "realm of gods" in the Sakran discourse; the *mandala* as a parallel to cosmic reality; and Raja Sinha II's burial of treasure under the water during the seventeenth-century Portuguese invasion of Kandy as "acting like Kuvera, the god of wealth, who buried his treasure at the bottom of the ocean."[48]

In each of these cases, Duncan is concerned about the phenomenological implications of ritual actions on the landscape, pragmatically using Eliade to analyze the political dimensions of these ideological invocations of cosmology. Similarly, Brenda Yeoh calls on Eliade to interpret ancient Chinese burial practices in the contests between the colonized Chinese population and the British colonial regime in late nineteenth- and early twentieth-century Singapore: "According to Mircea Eliade, the act of settlement itself is perceived as a re-enactment of the mythical creation of the world,"[49] which meant that British attempts to displace Chinese settlements, especially in burial plots, could be read as acts of desecration, thus involving the cosmic dimension in political negotiation. The phenomenology of ancient religion, caught as it often is in a colonial matrix, is political stuff indeed, and the theorist that geographers have preferred in these postcolonial phenomenological endeavors has been Eliade. Indeed, the real complaint within geography about Eliade has come from Julian Holloway, who complains that Eliade still "takes the sequestration of the sacred too far" by assuming that spaces are profane until the sacred irrupts in them.[50] In other words, Holloway is lodging quite the opposite disagreement from Smith: instead of Eliade being too obsessed with

47. See James S. Duncan, *The City as Text: The Politics of Landscape Interpretation in the Kandyan Kingdom* (Cambridge, UK: Cambridge University Press, 1990), 198 n. 20.

48. Duncan, *City as Text*, 39, 44, 47, 49, 68, respectively.

49. Brenda Yeoh, *Contesting Space in Colonial Singapore: Power Relations and the Urban Built Environment* (Singapore: Singapore University Press, 2003), 281.

50. Julian Holloway, "Make-Believe: Spiritual Practice, Embodiment, and Sacred Space," *Environment and Planning A* 35.11 (2003): 1962.

the essential character of the sacred, Holloway finds that Eliade is not nearly sacred enough to be used as a theorist to understand spiritual geographies.

While Smith has led religious studies in a secularizing direction, then, the politicization of geography has gone in quite the opposite direction, prioritizing a phenomenology of the transcendent as a mode of postcolonial scholarship. Such phenomenologies, as I have shown, depend on understandings of ancient religion as the basis for understanding the emotional pull of certain places, emotions that often turn out to be political when multiple landscape ideologies vie for dominance in a specific site. What this means, then, is that just as cultural geography has been foundational to the study of ancient religion, ancient religions provide the foundations for geographical thought about space, place, and emotion. It is probably fair to say, then, that if geographers were to be given the memorandum that Eliade has been discredited for playing fast and loose with the details, we probably could not care less. After all, interrogating these phenomenologies means that we have fallen far indeed from Isaac's insistence on a distinction between religious geography and geography of religion. We are all doing religious geography now, and it does not matter whether it is fact or fiction, for geographers are interested in the operational power of fictions on the material landscape.

Conclusion

Etymologically, "geography" is simply the "writing of the earth." I hope to have shown that far from being hip and trendy, geography is foundational to the study of ancient religion. Indeed, I have attempted to show that geography and ancient religious studies are co-constitutive disciplines, even though they have not been in direct dialogue for quite some time. Although this perhaps means that geographers have been ignorant of developments within religious studies writ large, this may well be a blessing in disguise, as we are able to offer Eliade back to the study of ancient religion in a critical way.

As cultural geographers and scholars of ancient religion move forward together, perhaps the foregoing review of the *longue durée* of our disciplines may reveal a shared research agenda. If indeed geographers are interested in the materialization of operating fictions and scholars of ancient religion want to theorize the places that they study, what scholars of ancient religion could perhaps offer geographically is an account of how the materializing of ancient religious practices led to the creation of fictions that are at work even today. But what is foundational for this shared research must be the rejection of the spatial turn as a fad. As far as I am concerned, there has been no turn. We have always been working on theorizing space, from Durkheim to Eliade to Smith. Because of this, we can dare to hope that there will be no turn away from geography in the future of theorizing about ancient religion. Let us happily write our fictions together forever!

Biographical Note

Justin K. H. Tse is Visiting Assistant Professor of Asian American Studies at Northwestern University, Evanston IL, USA. Previously, he taught at the University of Washington's Henry M. Jackson School of International Studies in Seattle, WA, USA and human geography at Simon Fraser University in Burnaby, BC, Canada. His research interests revolve around geographies of religion in the Pacific region. He is the editor (with Jonathan Y. Tan) of *Theological Reflections on the Hong Kong Umbrella Movement* (Palgrave, 2016) and his work has appeared in *Progress in Human Geography*, *Global Networks*, and *Population, Space, Place: A Journal of Population Geography*.

Bibliography

Anderson, Kay. *Race and the Crisis of Humanism*. London: Routledge, 2006.

Anderson, Kay, and Colin Perrin. "New Materialism and the Stuff of Humanism," *Australian Humanities Review* 58 (2015): 1–15.

Berquist, John L., and Claudia L. Camp, eds. *Constructions of Space I: Theory, Geography, and Narrative*. London: Bloomsbury T&T Clark, 2008.

—eds. *Constructions of Space II: The Biblical City and Other Imagined Spaces*. London: Bloomsbury T&T Clark, 2008.

Bennett, Jane. *Vibrant Matter: A Political Ecology of Things*. Durham, NC: Duke University Press, 2010.

de Certeau, Michel. *The Practice of Everyday Life*. Translated by Steven Rendall. Berkeley, CA: University of California Press, 1984.

Chidester, David, and Edward T. Linenthal. "Introduction," 1–42 in *American Sacred Space*. Edited by David Chidester and Edward T. Linenthal. Bloomington, IN: Indiana University Press, 1995.

Cosgrove, Denis E. *Social Formation and Symbolic Landscape*. Madison, WI: University of Wisconsin Press, 1994.

Deffontaines, Pierre. *Géographie et religions*. Paris: Gallimard, 1948.

Defoe, Daniel. *Robinson Crusoe*. Edited by Michael Shinagel. New York: W. W. Norton, 1993 [1719].

Duncan, James S. *The City as Text: The Politics of Landscape Interpretation in the Kandyan Kingdom*. Cambridge, UK: Cambridge University Press, 1990.

Durkheim, Émile. *The Elementary Forms of the Religious Life*. Translated by Joseph Ward Swain. New York: Free Press, 1915.

Eliade, Mircea. *The Sacred and the Profane: The Nature of Religion*. Translated by Willard R. Trask. New York: Harcourt, 1999 [1959].

Foucault, Michel. *Discipline and Punish*. Translated by Alan Sheridan. New York: Vintage, 1995 [1975].

Gibson-Graham, J. K. *The End of Capitalism (As We Knew It): A Feminist Critique of Political Economy*. Oxford: Blackwell, 1996.

—*A Postcapitalist Politics*. Minneapolis, MN: University of Minnesota Press, 2006.

Harvey, David. *The Condition of Postmodernity: An Enquiry into the Origins of Cultural Change*. Oxford: Wiley-Blackwell, 1989.

—*The Limits to Capital*. 2nd ed. London: Verso, 2007.

—*Social Justice and the City*. 2nd ed. Athens, GA: University of Georgia Press, 2009.

Hawkins, Harriet. "Creative Geographies: Knowing, Representing, Intervening," *Cultural Geographies* 22.2 (2015): 247–68. https://doi.org/10.1177/1474474015569995

Holloway, Julian. "Make-Believe: Spiritual Practice, Embodiment, and Sacred Space," *Environment and Planning A* 35.11 (2003): 1961–74. https://doi.org/10.1068/a3586

Isaac, Erich. "Religious Geography and the Geography of Religions," 1–14 in *Man and the Earth*. Boulder, CO: University of Colorado Press, 1965.

Johnson, Elizabeth, H. Morehouse, S. Dalby, J. Lehman, S. Nelson, R. Rowan, S. Wakefield, and K. Yusoff. "After the Anthropocene: Politics and Geographic Inquiry for a New Epoch," *Progress in Human Geography* 38.3 (2014): 439–56.

Knott, Kim. "Religion, Space, and Place: The Spatial Turn in Research on Religion," *Religion and Society* 1 (2010): 29–43.

Kong, Lily. "Geography and Religion: Trends and Prospects," *Progress in Human Geography* 14.3 (1990): 355–71.

—"Mapping 'New' Geographies of Religion: Politics and Poetics in Modernity," *Progress in Human Geography* 25.2 (2001): 211–33.

—"Global Shifts, Theoretical Shifts: Changing Geographies of Religion," *Progress in Human Geography* 34.6 (2010): 755–76. https://doi.org/10.1177/0309132510362602

Ó Tuathail, Gearóid. *Critical Geopolitics: The Politics of Writing Global Space*. Minneapolis, MN: University of Minnesota Press, 1996.

Otto, Rudolf. *The Idea of the Holy: An Inquiry into the Non-Rational Factor in the Idea of the Divine and Its Relation to the Rational*. Translated by John W. Harvey. Oxford: Oxford University Press, 1923.

Park, Chris C. *Sacred Worlds: An Introduction to Geography and Religion*. London: Routledge, 1994.

Smith, Jonathan Z. *To Take Place: Toward Theory in Ritual*. Chicago, IL: University of Chicago Press, 1987.

Soja, Edward. *Thirdspace: Journeys to Los Angeles and Other Real-and-Imagined Places*. Oxford: Wiley-Blackwell, 1996.

—*Postmodern Geographies: The Reassertion of Space in Critical Social Theory*. London: Verso, 2011 [1989].

Springer, Simon. "Fuck Neoliberalism," *ACME: An International E-Journal for Critical Geographies* 15.2 (2016): 285–92.

Taylor, Charles. *A Secular Age*. Cambridge, MA: The Belknap Press of Harvard University Press, 2007.

Thrift, Nigel. *Non-Representational Theory: Space, Politics, Affect*. London: Routledge, 2008.

Tolia-Kelly, Divya. "The Geographies of Cultural Geography III: Material Geographies, Vibrant Matters and Risking Surface Geographies," *Progress in Human Geography* 37.1 (2013): 153–60. https://doi.org/10.1177/0309132512439154

Tse, Justin K. H. "Grounded Theologies: 'Religion' and the 'Secular' in Human Geography," *Progress in Human Geography* 38.2 (2014): 201–20. https://doi.org/10.1177/0309132512475105

Tuan, Yi-Fu. *Topophilia: A Study of Environmental Perceptions, Attitudes, and Values.* New York: Columbia University Press, 1990 [1974].

—*Space and Place: The Perspective of Experience.* Minneapolis, MN: University of Minnesota Press, 2001 [1977].

Tweed, Thomas. *Crossing and Dwelling: A Theory of Religion.* Cambridge, MA: Harvard University Press, 2008.

Valentine, Gill. "Living with Difference: Reflections on Geographies of Encounter," *Progress in Human Geography* 32.3 (2008): 323–37. https://doi.org/10.1177/0309133308089372

Vásquez, Manuel A., and Marie F. Marquardt. *Globalizing the Sacred: Religion Across the Americas.* New Brunswick, NJ: Rutgers University Press, 2003.

Weil, Simone. *Waiting on God.* Abingdon, UK: Routledge, 2010 [1951].

Whatmore, Sarah. *Hybrid Geographies: Natures Cultures Spaces.* London: Sage, 2002.

—"Materialist Returns: Practicing Cultural Geography in and for a More-Than-Human World," *Cultural Geographies* 13.4 (2006): 600–9. https://doi.org/10.1191/1474474006cgj377oa

Wheatley, Paul. *The Pivot of the Four Quarters: A Preliminary Enquiry into the Origins of the Ancient Chinese City.* Edinburgh, UK: Edinburgh University Press, 1971.

Yeoh, Brenda. *Contesting Space in Colonial Singapore: Power Relations and the Urban Built Environment.* Singapore: Singapore University Press, 2003. https://doi.org/10.2307/j.ctv1ntj2v

Chapter Eighteen

Texts

James Crossley

Introduction:
Unstable Texts with Stable Meanings

The field of biblical studies, including its subfields (e.g., "Hebrew Bible studies," "Old Testament studies," "New Testament studies"), works with an intellectual (and somewhat Protestant) history of something assumed to be a "text" (or, in earlier parlance, a "document") or a collection of "texts." These assumptions are, on the surface, relatively straightforward. We know that we have individual texts such as Deuteronomy, the Book of Esther, the Gospel of Matthew, the Letter to the Romans and so on, often, in the hands of biblical scholars, incorporating hypothetical source texts like the Priestly Source or "Q." Collectively they make up an overarching text, whether the Hebrew Bible, the Old Testament, the New Testament, or the Bible itself, which might include sub-classifications such as the Pentateuch, Minor Prophets, Apocrypha, Gospels, and the Pauline Letters. Zooming in more closely, we might think of smaller units of texts, such as a given biblical passage, creation stories, prophetic laments, prayers, miracle stories, parables, which make up the bigger text. For those who contextualize such texts in the ancient world, there is also the implicit or explicit notion of "background texts," themselves classified and subclassified, notably including ethnic and geographical labels. So, for instance, people might use the Mesopotamian Epic of Gilgamesh to understand the Eden or flood stories of Genesis, Egyptian or Hellenistic texts to understand Wisdom genres, Jewish or Graeco-Roman texts to understand the New Testament, or Graeco-Roman biographies to understand the Gospels. And once again, subcategories exist. Dead Sea Scrolls, Apocrypha, Pseudepigrapha, rabbinic literature, and Hellenistic, are among the more common classifications of Jewish literature.

The standard and obvious assumption of the definition of a text is that it is a discreet unit in its own right, fairly coherent or can be made to be coherent once problematic elements are resolved, and that it fits with like-minded texts. If it is not coherent then more coherent earlier versions can be reconstructed in the hands of the scholar, as Rudolf Bultmann did when faced with perceived inconsistencies or perceived problematic themes (e.g., eschatology) in John's Gospel[1] or as countless biblical scholars have done when faced with smaller passages they deem incoherent and are thus sub-categorized in to smaller sources and editorial accretions. But whatever these "texts" may be, what ancient historians know about them already makes them unstable, or ought to. The Bible as the object of study for biblical studies is already problematized by the question of "which Bible"? Protestant? Catholic? Ethiopic? Jewish? Indeed, these labels already suggest, of course, that we are not dealing with classifications that are purely ancient. The canonizing process of the Bible, the Hebrew Bible, the Old Testament, and/or the New Testament took centuries, and unsurprisingly decisions about what is in and what is out reflect the interests and contexts of those involved in the canonization process. The various subcategories are likewise problematized by the question of "which text"? What goes by the name of "Jeremiah" looks very different in Hebrew and Greek versions which suggests that *the* text of Jeremiah may to some extent be a scholarly construct. Throughout the books of the Bible, textual variants have been the focus of scholarly reconstruction and so, at the very least, the notion of a pristine "text" is problematic before we start explaining its meaning. Other classifications or subclassifications likewise resist the idea of a stable "text." Among the Dead Sea Scrolls are different versions of the same text, while texts included in the Pseudepigrapha are effectively defined as a range of Jewish texts which did not make it into the Old Testament canon and, in some cases, have no obvious connection with one another other than not being written by who they might claim they are written by and being assumed to be Jewish. And even the Jewish assumption is problematic as it is typically stressed that there is a Christianizing tendency in various books, and that is still to assume that redactors themselves worked with a strict Jewish-Christian binary.

Assumptions about ancient texts are further problematized by notions of interpretation. Even if we could assume a fairly precise location for the writing of a given text, we are still left with problems of audience or, rather, audiences. Presumably not every audience member would pick up the subtle allusions noted by the learned scholarly exegete, while some might see certain allusions that even the author or authors never intended.[2] Indeed,

1.   See Rudolf Bultmann, *The Gospel of John: A Commentary* (Louisville, KY: WJK, 1971).

2.   Cf. Christopher D. Stanley, *Arguing with Scripture: The Rhetoric of Quotations in the Letters of Paul* (London: T&T Clark, 2004); Brian J. Abasciano, "Diamonds in the Rough: A Reply to Christopher Stanley Concerning the Reader Competency of Paul's Original Audiences," *Novum Testamentum* 49 (2007): 153–83.

even if we were to concede some notion, no matter how hazy, of authorial intention (or the author's own interpretation of their own work), we are
rarely in a position to be able to say much about the author, if anything at
all. In probably most cases we do not even know if we have one or many
authors in many of the texts subsumed under the classifications mentioned
above. Some were written over a long period of time (centuries, even),
some given pseudepigraphical authorship, some texts (e.g., Hebrews) were
written anonymously. Even the date and location of writing of texts are regularly disputed. So, authorial or community intention, as well as authorship and context, is something that has, to a large degree, to be gleaned
from the text itself ... before being applied to the interpretation of the same
text. Where there is a little more precision about authorship and provenance
available (e.g., Paul's letters) the details about the author remain scant. In
the case of Paul, we are effectively reliant on his letters to specific communities and the Acts of the Apostles. Certainly, a skeletal outline of Paul's life
can be worked out but is this enough for establishing some degree of authorial intention? By way of comparison, I also work on contemporary English
political figures and writers. We have voluminous amounts of data for the
activities of, say, George Orwell or Margaret Thatcher. I can find out what
year, month, day, and even time such speeches were presented or articles
submitted and still questions of authorial intention are problematic. How
much more of a problem is this for the interpreter of ancient texts, certainly
those categorized in the field of biblical studies!

None of this should be news to biblical scholars. However, it remains
that broad assumptions about the text and what it means remain an integral part of the history of biblical studies, whether the ways in which teaching is structured or research is carried out. Arguments remain heated and
levels of confidence remain surprisingly high about the location, interpretation, and the meanings of these texts. Understandings of texts are as
much about mythmaking as the category "religion" or reverence (or otherwise) of "great" individuals. Indeed, it is the mythmaking that orders the
chaos of the unstable texts and renders them meaningful. This is not to say
that scholarly arguments cannot be correct or that all understanding of the
ancient world is futile or that contemporary figures are immune to mythmaking (it was not without reason that I mentioned Orwell and Thatcher).
Nevertheless, the relatively fixed notion of a "text" from which meaning is
still extracted by some methodology or other[3] is broadly assumed in biblical
studies despite the enormous gaps in data. That the enormous gaps in data

---

3.   Cf. Terry Eagleton, *Literary Theory: An Introduction* (Minneapolis, MN: University of Minnesota Press, 2008), 77.

can be filled should already indicate that we are dealing with a field that carries much investment for the biblical scholars who write so much and pack out annual conferences in their thousands.

As we all know, classification is a political act and in the rest of this chapter I want to reveal some (and only some) of the politicized mythmaking which often unintentionally accompanies such processes. We will see that the Bible continues to function as a source of cultural and political authority in areas where academic biblical studies is most dominant (North America and Europe). In particular, I want to look at some repetitive (and usually unintentional) versions of the Bible and politicized assumptions of biblical texts: the Enlightenment Bible; the Strange Bible; the Liberal Bible; and the Radical Bible. Much of what I say could be reapplied to the study of any number of categorized areas in the study of the ancient world (e.g., "Classics," "Ancient Near East," "Philosophy," "Patristic Literature") but constraints of space and limits of expertise mean that I will focus on this one classification of literature from the ancient world. Constrained as I am by the classifications noted above, my focus will often be narrower still by largely looking at how New Testament texts function ideologically.

Enlightenment Bible

In his detailed study of the development of biblical scholarship, Jonathan Sheehan provides the label, among others, of the Enlightenment Bible or the Cultural Bible.[4] For Sheehan, the Enlightenment gave us the construct of the Bible understood (and sometimes contradictorily) as a philological and pedagogical resource, a literary classic, a moral guidebook, and a historical archive, all in their own ways interacting with developing ideas of secularization. Sheehan's work and the legacy of the Enlightenment Bible has been worked into genealogies of biblical scholarship by Stephen Moore and Yvonne Sherwood.[5] In other words, the Enlightenment Bible in one form or another is the assumed text of biblical scholarship. We might think, for instance, about dictionaries of ancient words grounded in some construction of the Bible, the idea of the Bible and biblical texts as works of literary geniuses, studies of the ethics of the Bible or subclassifications of the Bible, or the reconstruction of earlier texts, effectively mini-historical archives in and of themselves. While it is difficult to dispute the general

---

4.   See Jonathan Sheehan, *The Enlightenment Bible: Translation, Scholarship, Culture* (Princeton, NJ: Princeton University Press, 2007).

5.   See Stephen D. Moore and Yvonne Sherwood, *The Invention of the Biblical Scholar: A Critical Manifesto* (Minneapolis, MN: Fortress Press, 2011).

case made by Sheehan and Moore and Sherwood, it is worth adding one important qualification made by Deane Galbraith: theology has likewise been integral to the story of biblical studies.[6] We might think, for instance, about the close connections between scholarship and theological institutions, the genre of "The Theology of" a given book, or the focus of some of the most prominent questions which continue to dominate (should we read the creation stories "symbolically"? Is the Bible pro- or anti-Empire? Was Jesus mistaken? What did Paul mean by "justification"?). This qualification runs throughout some of the major constructions about the meaning of the text(s) of the Bible that I present here.

The Bible: Ancient and Strange … But Not That Strange

A further emphasis should also be added: the ways in which these understandings of the Bible engaged with political movements which gained momentum from the Enlightenment onwards. The Enlightenment Bible developed amidst emerging nationalism and Orientalism and these too continue to leave their mark on assumptions of textual meaning,[7] including the subcategorization of "background texts" that has played the role of elevating the biblical text or texts. The development of the critical study of the Bible in the nineteenth century would in its own way deal with "the Jewish Question" simultaneously in relation to biblical texts and contemporary nationalism which would reach its most notorious point in twentieth-century Nazi scholarship, where biblical texts were purged of elements deemed too Jewish.[8] The standard *Theological Dictionary of the New Testament* would produce a series of "background texts" with which New Testament texts could be compared and, of course, contrasted. A startling example is the article on words concerning "Jew" and "Hebrew," where sources which contained the relevant words but did not fit the agenda of the author—the Nazi party member, K. G. Kuhn—were not discussed.[9] Smaller units of pre-Gospel texts were at the heart of the form-critical enterprise

---

6.   See Deane Galbraith, "Review of S. D. Moore and Y. Sherwood: *The Invention of the Biblical Scholar: A Critical Manifesto*," *Relegere* 3 (2013): 413–4.

7.   Cf. Halvor Moxnes, *Jesus and the Rise of Nationalism: A New Quest for the Nineteenth Century Historical Jesus* (London: I. B. Tauris, 2011).

8.   See Maurice Casey, "Some Anti-Semitic Assumptions in *The Theological Dictionary of the New Testament*," *Novum Testamentum* 41 (1999): 280–91; Peter Head, "The Nazi Quest for an Ayrian Jesus," *Journal for the Study of the Historical Jesus* 2 (2004): 55–89; Susannah Heschel, *The Aryan Jesus: Christian Theologians and the Bible in Nazi Germany* (Princeton, NJ: Princeton University Press, 2008).

9.   See Casey, "Some Anti-Semitic Assumptions."

which also served the function of avoiding anything deemed too Jewish. These smaller units supposedly had a "setting in life" but the focus shifted to a "setting in faith" as Jewish social contexts were typically either ignored or used as a foil for superiority, while form criticism's focus on church life avoided the problems of a Jewish man emerging from behind the traditions.[10] Form criticism's main proponents may not have been supporters of the Nazi Party but form criticism was part of the dominant anti-Jewish traits in German cultural discourses after World War I.

But even after the Holocaust, biblical New Testament scholarship dominated by Rudolf Bultmann and Ernst Käsemann would continue to present its texts over against their "background." In New Testament studies, this meant the background of Jewish texts—not uncommonly taken from the summarizing presentations by Hermann Leberecht Strack and Paul Billerbeck. In the hands of biblical scholars, such background texts now infamously showed that Paul's letters promote grace and love in contrast to Jewish texts, which were more about cold, harsh legalism and works-righteousness. The most successful challenge to this view was E. P. Sanders's *Paul and Palestinian Judaism* (1977), which had the telling subtitle, *A Comparison of Patterns of Religion*.[11] Here the comparative Jewish texts were categorized in familiar ways we have seen (e.g., "Tannaitic Literature," "The Dead Sea Scrolls," "Apocrypha and Pseudepigrapha") in order to show a common pattern of "covenantal nomism" whereby Jews were deemed to be elected by God and sought to stay in the covenant through observance of the Law. For Sanders, this provided a point of similarity with Paul and the difference maker was effectively Christ.

Sanders's work ushered in what soon became labelled the "New Perspective" on Paul,[12] a catch-all term for different scholarly views which broadly accepted Sanders's reading of Jewish texts. But the assumed construction of the "background texts" still functioned as a difference maker from the texts assumed to be "ours," as well as being part of changing cultural and political histories. New Perspective writers on Paul's letters have presented

10. See Maurice Casey, "Who's Afraid of Jesus Christ? Some Comments on Attempts to Write a Life of Jesus," in *Writing History, Constructing Religion* (ed. James G. Crossley and Christian Karner; Aldershot, UK: Ashgate, 2005), 133; James G. Crossley, *Why Christianity Happened: A Sociohistorical Account of Christian Origins 26–50CE* (Louisville, KY: WJK, 2006), 4–5.

11. E. P. Sanders, *Paul and Palestinian Judaism: A Comparison of Patterns of Religion* (London: SCM, 1977).

12. Cf., N. T. Wright, "The Paul of History and the Apostle of Faith," *Tyndale Bulletin* 29 (1978): 61–88; James D. G. Dunn, "The New Perspective on Paul," *Bulletin of the John Rylands Library* 65 (1983): 95–122.

difference from Judaism without bringing in the triumphalism and negativity associated with the Old Perspective on Paul. Instead of the overt rhetoric of Christian superiority, such New Perspective approaches[13] have used the language of Jewish "boundary markers" and Jewish nationalism to show how Paul's letters reject these categories when they impact upon the early church. But the typically unmentioned implications of this for the construction of Judaism is that things like circumcision, Sabbath, or whatever else is deemed a "boundary marker" in early Jewish texts, are sufficiently alien to the exegete to be dropped.[14]

This sort of "Jewish but not that Jewish" pattern, it should be added, has been typical of New Testament scholarship more generally.[15] In terms of historical Jesus scholarship, for instance, a "very Jewish Jesus" could be reconstructed from the texts (usually the Synoptic Gospels, although sometimes also the tellingly italicized "noncanonical" texts like Thomas) where he too emerged "Jewish ... but not that Jewish" after extensive textual analysis, whether John Meier's "marginal Jew"[16] or N. T. Wright's claim about "a very Jewish Jesus who was nevertheless opposed to some high-profile features of first-century Judaism."[17] To take the example of Wright, he argued that the saying "let the dead bury their own dead" (Matthew 8.21-2; Luke 9.59-60) "is, quite frankly, outrageous. Many scholars have pointed out that Jesus is here advocating behavior that his contemporaries, both Jewish and non-Jewish, would have regarded as scandalous."[18] The "background" ancient texts Wright used to highlight how this Jesus saying would have been shocking are a brief summary of "Tannaitic literature" and passing reference to a handful of chapters and verses from the Hebrew Bible/

---

13. E.g., N. T. Wright, *The Climax of the Covenant: Christ and the Law in Pauline Theology* (London: T&T Clark, 1991) and *Paul and the Faithfulness of God* (London: SPCK, 2013); James D. G. Dunn, *The Theology of Paul the Apostle* (Grand Rapids, MI: Eerdmans, 1998) and *The New Perspective on Paul: Collected Essays* (Tübingen: Mohr Siebeck, 2005).

14. See James G. Crossley and Katie Edwards, "Paul and the Faithfulness of God as Postmodern Scholarship," in *God and the Faithfulness of Paul: A Critical Examination of the Pauline Theology of N.T. Wright* (ed. Christoph Heilig, J. Thomas Hewitt, and Michael F. Bird; Tübingen: Mohr Siebeck, 2016), 603–21.

15. Cf. James G. Crossley, *Jesus in an Age of Terror: Scholarly Projects for a New American Century* (London: Equinox, 2008), as well as *Jesus in an Age of Neoliberalism: Quests, Scholarship and Ideology* (London: Equinox, 2012) and "A 'Very Jewish' Jesus: Perpetuating the Myth of Superiority," *Journal for the Study of the Historical Jesus* 11 (2013): 109–29.

16. See John P. Meier, *A Marginal Jew: Rethinking the Historical Jesus.* Vol. 1: *The Roots of the Problem and the Person* (New York: Doubleday, 1991).

17. N. T. Wright, *Jesus and the Victory of God* (London: SPCK, 1996), 93.

18. Wright, *Jesus and the Victory of God*, 401.

Old Testament. There are numerous problems with Wright's argument but what is notable about the use of such texts is the power they are given to control who-knows-what complexity and contradiction of opinion there was in early Judaism, not to mention texts which may not quite support his view.[19] The Protestant notion of authoritative "texts" remains powerful in such scholarship.

Such constructions of the New Testament text(s) in relation to Judaism and Jewish texts are part of ideological shifts from the late 1960s onwards. While a Christian tradition of superiority over Judaism obviously has an ongoing influence, such developments are part of liberal multicultural-ism developing since the 1960s, where the palatable bits of the Other are embraced and where problematic otherness is pushed away.[20] In terms of the representation of New Testament texts over the past forty years, we might think of the ongoing rhetoric of how "thoroughly Jewish" such texts are and yet remove problematic bits that are constructed (by scholars) as core aspects of Jewish identity (e.g., circumcision, much of the Law). William Arnal has also identified how a scholarly form of essentialized Judaism with a (super-ficial) philo-Semitism emerged during this period. Arnal showed how this was a reaction against globalization and fractured postmodern identities, the dominance of pre-1970s German scholarship, and a desire for Christian scholars to show that Christianity is not anti-Semitic at its core in order to distance Christianity from complicity in the Holocaust.[21] To this we might add that the rhetoric of Jesus' "Jewishness" was part of a post-1967 cultural shift including the first widespread interest in the Holocaust and a favorable attitude towards Israel in Anglo-American political, educational, and popu-lar culture after the Six Day War. Yet this philo-Semitism nevertheless per-petuated attitudes of cultural and religious superiority in relation to Jews, Judaism, and Israel, and all as part of a general shift of the center of biblical scholarship from Germany to North America.[22]

---

19. See Markus Bockmuehl, *Jewish Law in Gentile Churches: Halakhah and the Beginning of Christian Public Ethics* (Edinburgh, UK: T&T Clark, 2000), 23–48; Cross-ley, "A 'Very Jewish' Jesus."

20. See Slavoj Žižek, "Multiculturalism, or, the Cultural Logic of Multinational Capital-ism," *New Left Review* 225 (1997): 28–51 and "Liberal Multiculturalism Masks an Old Bar-barism with a Human Face," *Guardian* (3 October 2010), online: http://www.theguardian.com/commentisfree/2010/oct/03/immigration-policy-roma-rightwing-europe. Cf. David Theo Goldberg, *The Threat of Race: Reflections on Racial Neoliberalism* (Oxford: Wiley-Blackwell, 2009); Alana Lentin and Gavan Titley, *The Crises of Multiculturalism: Racism in a Neoliberal Age* (London: Zed Books, 2011).

21. See William Arnal, *The Symbolic Jesus: Historical Scholarship, Judaism and the Construction of Contemporary Identity* (London: Equinox, 2005), 39–72.

22. See Crossley, *Jesus in an Age of Terror*, 143–94.

Such concern with what constitutes "Jewish texts" is, then, part of a long Orientalist discourse in New Testament studies, although also with its own particular developments in "Old Testament" or "Hebrew Bible" studies.[23] There is also another, lesser-known, Orientalist history intertwined with biblical studies—the construction of "the Mediterranean"—often implicit code for "the Arab world" or "the Muslim world."[24] For example, the Bruce Malina-inspired social scientific approaches to the Bible have dominated contemporary approaches to social sciences and the New Testament—particularly over the past thirty years—and brought a number of now well-known issues to the fore (e.g., honor and shame, limited good, dyadic personality, etc.). Following a virtual absence of social scientific approaches in New Testament studies between (approximately) the 1930s and the 1970s (partly because of the not wholly unjustified association of social sciences with atheistic Marxism and, by implication, Soviet Communism), they came back powerfully. One key reason among a myriad of reasons was the heavy (re-)emphasis in Anglo-American culture from the 1970s onwards on the "Arab world," "the Arab mind," "the Middle East," and a number of Orientalist and ideologically convenient stereotypes which fed into the world of the influential Malina, as well as his key colleagues such as Richard Rohrbaugh and John Pilch, and their use of the static construction of "the Mediterranean."

In such constructions, the equation of "the Mediterranean" and "the Arab world" is explicit, particularly in the work of Malina. The following example (from his book on the Gospels, lest we forget) apparently holds for "village Mediterraneans" in general and comes by way of Raphael Patai, *The Arab Mind*:

> [P]ersonalization of problems goes so far in the Arab countries that even material, technical difficulties accompanying the adoption of elements of western civilization are considered as resulting from human malevolence and felt to be a *humiliation* ... Where the Arab encounters an obstacle he imagines that an enemy is hidden. Proud peoples with a weak "ego structure" tend to interpret difficulties on their life path as personal humiliations and get entangled in *endless lawsuits* or throw themselves into the arms of *extremist political movements. A defeat in elections*, a risk that every politician must face in a democracy, appears to be such a humiliation that an Arab can thereby be induced without further ceremony to take up arms against the victor and the legal government.[25]

---

23. Cf. Yvonne Sherwood, *A Biblical Text and Its Afterlives: The Survival of Jonah in Western Culture* (Cambridge: Cambridge University Press, 2000).

24. See Crossley, *Jesus in an Age of Terror*, 112–6.

25. Bruce J. Malina, *The Social World of Jesus and the Gospels* (London: Routledge,

Intentionally or not (most likely not), this argument obviously complements the neo-Orientalism of the contemporary clash-of-civilizations rhetoric and ideas of how Iraq and the Middle East are not inherently "suited" to democracy, or at least not without "our" help. Likewise, the idea of Arab or Muslim "humiliation" is a common category with which the problems of "the Arab" and "the Muslim" in Iraq and Palestine are conveniently explained. Furthermore, Patai's work on "the Arab mind" has been used in governmental and military circles as a means to understand Iraq and was partly the thinking behind the acts carried out by the US military in Abu Ghraib.[26]

What is also significant is that Malina's work on this "background" to the New Testament is often simply assumed in scholarship as another way to extract meaning from the text. For instance, mainstream New Testament scholars not known for their interest in anthropology[27] simply refer the reader to Malina or Malina-inspired work in order to further appreciate "the context" and its relevance for the act of interpretation. In addition to a reference to a handful of texts on family, Wright further adds a reference to Malina and Rohrbaugh to show how the theme of family in the Gospel tradition would have been "socially deviant."[28] But one of the most high-profile users of such scholarship has been John Dominic Crossan who does something strikingly similar to the construction of "the Jewish background" in New Testament scholarship. Against this anthropological background systematically applied, Crossan provides an elaborate trajectory of texts, from small passages through hypothetical source texts to gospels, in order to construct a historical Jesus who becomes arguably the most famous liberalized (in a widely recognized popular sense) Jesus of recent times. For all the anti-imperial rhetoric of Crossan it is noticeable that Crossan's Jesus stands over against the alien Mediterranean world. The world of honor and shame which supposedly characterizes "the Mediterranean" is, so the argument goes, profoundly challenged. And against this fixed Mediterranean world is a Jesus with common table fellowship and a brokerless kingdom, subverting the system, playing around with gender categories, and so on.[29] Crossan's Jesus is, in many ways, and almost

1996), 63, quoting Raphael Patai, *The Arab Mind* (New York: Scribner, 1983) (emphasis in the original).

26. See Seymour Hersh, "Annals of National Security: The Gray Zone – How a Secret Pentagon Program Came to Abu Ghraib," *The New Yorker* (15 May 2004).

27. E.g., Wright, *Jesus and the Victory of God*, 52–3, 430; Meier, *Marginal Jew*, 10–1; John P. Meier, *A Marginal Jew: Rethinking the Historical Jesus.* Vol. 3: *Companions and Competitors* (New York: Doubleday, 2001), 67.

28. See Wright, *Jesus and the Victory of God*, 403.

29. Cf. John H. Elliott, "Jesus Was Not an Egalitarian: A Critique of an Anachronistic and Idealist Theory," *Biblical Theology Bulletin* 32 (2002): 75–91.

certainly unintentionally, representative of liberal America, or perhaps the liberal West, overcoming the brutal, backwards East.

The Liberal Bible and the Radical Bible

Reconstructions such as Crossan's implicitly fit into what Yvonne Sherwood labelled the "Liberal Bible."[30] Sherwood has shown how this Liberal Bible is an understanding of the Bible as supportive of freedom of conscience, rights, law, government, and consensus, and which is a development from early modern Europe. The Liberal Bible has also produced the (mistaken) assumption that the Bible is the foundation, and consonant with the principles, of western democracies, and is constructed against its opposites: tyranny, terror, and a lack of democratic values. Unsurprisingly, it can follow from this anachronistic perspective that the Bible can be believed to be more representative of democracy than the Qur'an. While politicians may typically be more explicit than biblical scholars in foregrounding the alleged liberalness of the biblical text, there remain striking similarities. Crossan is one example among many. An example from the study of the Hebrew Bible is Joel Baden who goes through the contradictions in the Hebrew Bible (especially the two creation stories) and accepts the importance of contradiction because it shows that the Bible does not have a singular meaning. Instead, he argues, the Bible accepts a combination of voices and many truths. For Baden, the Bible is like contemporary religious pluralism founded on dialogue and inclusion and the authority and power of the Bible can still, then, have relevance if harnessed "correctly," that is, in a liberal, tolerant, democratic way.[31] What is notable about Baden's view is that, while dismissing a singular meaning of overall text, he simultaneously gives the multiple texts and contradictions an overarching liberal meaning. This allows the contradictions to coexist, the text to take on a different kind of (ideological) coherence, and allows the Bible to be the text of American society in a way that "rescues" it from the assumed extremes of the Christian Right.

But there is another angle on the assumption of liberal values: the Bible and biblical texts as a host for *illiberal* values which much be resisted. In a series of books, Burton Mack has challenged the moral vision of the "myth

---

30. E.g., see Yvonne Sherwood, "Bush's Bible as a Liberal Bible (Strange Though That Might Seem)," *Postscripts* 2 (2006): 47–58 and "On the Genesis Between the Bible and Rights," in *Bible and Justice: Ancient Texts, Modern Challenges* (ed. M. J. M. Coomber; London: Equinox, 2011), 13–42.

31. See Joel Baden, "The Bible Doesn't Say What You Think It Does," *The Nantucket Project* (2014), online: https://www.nantucketproject.com/joel-baden-what-use-is-the-bible.

of innocence," most influentially found in Mark's Gospel, arguing for its profound and typically malevolent influence.[32] Such influence reinforces the notion of a strong, influential "text" because material factors do not play a major role in Mack's approach. Often lacking Mack's historical scope, the emergence of New Atheism and the online popularity of Mythicism (effectively the idea of the nonexistence of Jesus) where the biblical text is fundamentally unreliable, both historically and morally. The texts themselves are so morally problematic that they do not match up to contemporary ethical (and liberal capitalist) assumptions, not even the much vaunted sayings of Jesus.[33] The lateness of manuscripts or the dates and contexts of the sources themselves in relation to the historical figure, like David or Jesus, are deemed to make the underlying historical figure even more distant and unknowable, even if they were to exist.[34] Indeed, even Bart Ehrman, one of the most high-profile opponents of Mythicism, has had his books carefully marketed to a related audience, most notably one with the title *Misquoting Jesus: The Story Behind Who Changed the Bible and Why*, a title which helped manufacture its own controversy. The arguments made in the book might not be especially radical in terms of biblical scholarship but the marketing plays into a known understanding of what the biblical texts *really* mean.[35] Once again, we see a privileging of the power of the text and its interpretation, at the expense of material changes and conditions, in order to explain the world.

Another flipside to the liberal understandings of the Bible is the idea of a text of hypothetical texts as politically radical, an understanding of the texts which has resisted the dominant political norms of the day. This Radical Bible—probably best known in the form of Liberation Theology—typically involves a kind of proto-Socialism or even revolutionary transformation, including the idea of a transformation of the social, economic, and political order.[36] Indeed, the development of early critical biblical scholarship has

---

32. See Burton Mack, *A Myth of Innocence: Mark and Christian Origins* (Philadelphia, PA: Fortress Press, 1988), as well as *Myth and the Christian Nation: A Social Theory of Religion* (London: Equinox, 2008) and *Christian Mentality: The Entanglements of Power, Violence and Fear* (London: Equinox, 2011).

33. I owe this point to Robert Myles.

34. For academic representatives of such views, see, e.g., Hector Avalos, *The End of Biblical Studies* (Amherst, NY: Prometheus, 2007) and *The Bad Jesus: The Ethics of New Testament Ethics* (Sheffield, UK: Sheffield Academic Press, 2015); Richard Carrier, *On the Historicity of Jesus: Why We Might Have Reasons for Doubt* (Sheffield, UK: Sheffield Academic Press, 2014).

35. See Bart D. Ehrman, *Misquoting Jesus: The Story Behind Who Changed the Bible and Why* (New York: HarperCollins, 2005).

36. See James G. Crossley, *Harnessing Chaos: The Bible in English Political Discourse since 1968* (London: Bloomsbury T&T Clark, 2016), 18–32.

given texts, or hypothetical texts which were later distorted, a revolutionary reading, from Reimarus, Proudhon, Engels, and Karl Kautsky through Gottwald, Schüssler Fiorenza, Schottroff, and Horsley. However, the rhetoric of radical and subversive texts (e.g., in the work of Crossan, Wright, and Marcus Borg) and the prominent notion of an "anti-imperial" Bible or biblical texts has been co-opted in liberal capitalism.[37] The neoliberal context of the past forty years also absorbs such seemingly radical critique in that anti-capitalist rhetoric has simultaneously become widespread.[38] As Slavoj Žižek put it:

> Today, when everyone is "anticapitalist," up to the Hollywood "socio-critical" conspiracy movies (from *The Enemy of the State* to *The Insider*) in which the enemy are the big corporations with their ruthless pursuit of profit, the signifier "anticapitalism" has lost its subversive sting. What one should problematize is rather the self-evident opposite of this "anticapitalism": the trust in the democratic substance of the honest Americans to break up the conspiracy.[39]

One example of this in practice can be found in Žižek's review of the film *Avatar* for the *New Statesman*.[40] Žižek pointed out that, at the same time as *Avatar* was generating one billion dollars in under three weeks, there was in fact something resembling its plot happening in the Indian state of Orissa. Here, land was sold to mining companies which provoked an armed rebellion. Consequently, there were propaganda and military attacks from the Indian state and a vicious conflict ensued. Žižek added:

> So where is Cameron's film here? Nowhere: in Orissa, there are no noble princesses waiting for white heroes to seduce them and help their people, just the Maoists organising the starving farmers. The film enables us to practise a typical ideological division: sympathising with the idealised aborigines while rejecting their actual struggle. The same people who enjoy the film and admire its aboriginal rebels would in all probability turn away in horror from the Naxalites, dismissing them as murderous terrorists. The true avatar is thus *Avatar* itself—the film substituting for reality.[41]

---

37. See James G. Crossley, *Jesus and the Chaos of History: Redirecting the Life of the Historical Jesus* (Oxford: Oxford University Press, 2015), 5–9; Robert Myles, "The Fetish for a Subversive Jesus," *Journal for the Study of the Historical Jesus* 14.1 (2016): 52–70.

38. See Mark Fisher, *Capitalist Realism: Is There No Alternative?* (Winchester, UK: Zero Books, 2009); Colin Cremin, *Capitalism's New Clothes: Enterprise, Ethics and Enjoyment in Times of Crisis* (London: Pluto Press, 2011).

39. Slavoj Žižek, "Do We Still Live in a World?" (n.d.), online: http://www.lacan.com/zizrattlesnakeshake.html.

40. See Slavoj Žižek, "Return of the Natives," *New Statesman* (4 March 2010), online: http://www.newstatesman.com/film/2010/03/avatar-reality-love-couple-sex.

41. Žižek, "Return of the Natives."

Putting the motivations, beliefs, and practices of individual scholars to one side, it is difficult to see how the Bible in the hands of biblical scholars is having any significant oppositional political impact. But did we ever expect scholars' presentations of their texts to have such an impact? Arguably the most significant ideological function of the voluminous anti-imperial texts produced is to sell books to liberal audiences on a large scale.[42] Strands of Liberation Theology provide an important point of comparison, because here we have an influential movement dedicated to socio-economic liberation in contexts which have faced serious peasant exploitation and the brutal effects of imperialism of the sort that might form the backdrop for certain scholarly works on the anti-imperial Bible or biblical texts. And Liberation Theology *has* had an impact, hence the reason various figures came under fatal attack.[43] However, this is not the fate of the humble biblical scholar. To paraphrase Mark Fisher's analysis of *Wall-E*,[44] the scholarly construction of radical texts performs our anti-capitalism and radicalism for us, allowing us to consume anti-imperial books with impunity.

Concluding Remarks

Postmodernity may have provided serious challenges to the notion of a fixed text, and, perhaps contrary to my presentation, some such critiques have indeed come through in biblical studies (most famously in the work of Stephen Moore), and appear to be coming through further in recent and widespread study of memory in the field. Nevertheless, a relatively fixed notion of text (whether the Bible, a biblical book, or smaller units) continues to be the working model of much of biblical studies where meaning is regularly ascribed to them. In the hands of the biblical scholars, ancient texts such as the Bible and biblical texts—for all the uncertainty, instability, and basic problems of authorship, provenance, audience, and early editions—function implicitly or explicitly as a higher source of authority and a carrier of contemporary political ideals. In his most significant academic publication, *Nationalism and Culture* (1937), Rudolf Rocker argued that throughout its history "religion" has made humanity dependent upon a higher power which has been taken over, or intertwined with, political power and authority. For Rocker, "all politics is in the last instance religion," "all power has its

---

42. Cf. Rebekka King, "The Author, the Atheist, and the Academic Study of Religion: Bourdieu and the Reception of Biblical Criticism by Progressive Christians," *Bulletin for the Study of Religion* 41 (2012): 14–20.

43. See Noam Chomsky, *Understanding Power* (New York: New Press, 2002), 154.

44. See Fisher, *Capitalist Realism*, 12.

roots in God," and "all rulership is in its inmost essence divine."[45] We might update this thinking in a number of ways but one might be to suggest that, in the hands of the biblical scholar, all power now has its roots in the text.

Biographical Note

James Crossley is Professor of Bible, Society, and Politics at the St Mary's University, London, UK. He is the author of numerous articles in various academic journals, author of seven books, most recently *Cults, Martyrs and Good Samaritans: Religion in Contemporary English Political Discourse* (Pluto, 2018), *Jesus and the Chaos of History: Redirecting the Life of the Historical Jesus* (Oxford University Press, 2015), *Jesus in an Age of Neoliberalism: Quests, Scholarship, and Ideology* (Routledge, 2012), and *The New Testament and Jewish Law: A Guide for the Perplexed* (T&T Clark, 2010), and he has edited and co-edited three books, most recently *Judaism, Jewish Identities and the Gospel Tradition: Essays in Honour of Maurice Casey* (Routledge, 2014).

Bibliography

Abasciano Brian J. "Diamonds in the Rough: A Reply to Christopher Stanley concerning the Reader Competency of Paul's Original Audiences," *Novum Testamentum* 49 (2007): 153–83. https://doi.org/10.1163/156853607X185366

Arnal, William. *The Symbolic Jesus: Historical Scholarship, Judaism and the Construction of Contemporary Identity*. London: Equinox, 2005.

Avalos, Hector. *The End of Biblical Studies*. Amherst, NY: Prometheus, 2007.

—*The Bad Jesus: The Ethics of New Testament Ethics*. Sheffield, UK: Sheffield Academic Press, 2015.

Baden, Joel. "The Bible Doesn't Say What You Think It Does," *The Nantucket Project* (2014). Online: https://www.nantucketproject.com/joel-baden-what-use-is-the-bible (accessed 8 May 2016).

Bockmuehl, Markus. *Jewish Law in Gentile Churches: Halakhah and the Beginning of Christian Public Ethics*. Edinburgh, UK: T&T Clark, 2000.

Bultmann, Rudolf. *The Gospel of John: A Commentary*. Louisville, KY: WJK, 1971.

Carrier, Richard. *On the Historicity of Jesus: Why We Might Have Reasons for Doubt*. Sheffield, UK: Sheffield Academic Press, 2014.

Casey, Maurice. "Some Anti-Semitic Assumptions in *The Theological Dictionary of the New Testament*," *Novum Testamentum* 41 (1999): 280–91. https://doi.org/10.1163/156853699323281306

—"Who's Afraid of Jesus Christ? Some Comments on Attempts to Write a Life of Jesus," 129–46 in *Writing History, Constructing Religion*. Edited by James G. Crossley and Christian Karner. Aldershot, UK: Ashgate, 2005.

45. Rudolf Rocker, *Nationalism and Culture* (Los Angeles, CA: Rocker Publications Committee, 1937), 46, 48.

Chomsky, Noam. *Understanding Power*. New York: New Press, 2002.

Cremin, Colin. *Capitalism's New Clothes: Enterprise, Ethics and Enjoyment in Times of Crisis*. London: Pluto Press, 2011.

Crossley, James G. *Why Christianity Happened: A Sociohistorical Account of Christian Origins 26–50CE*. Louisville, KY: WJK, 2006.

—*Jesus in an Age of Terror: Scholarly Projects for a New American Century*. London: Equinox, 2008.

—*Jesus in an Age of Neoliberalism: Quests, Scholarship and Ideology*. London: Equinox, 2012.

—"A 'Very Jewish' Jesus: Perpetuating the Myth of Superiority," *Journal for the Study of the Historical Jesus* 11 (2013): 109–29. https://doi.org/10.1163/17455197-01102002

—*Jesus and the Chaos of History: Redirecting the Life of the Historical Jesus*. Oxford: Oxford University Press, 2015. https://doi.org/10.1093/acprof:oso/9780199570577.001.0001

—*Harnessing Chaos: The Bible in English Political Discourse since 1968*. London: Bloomsbury T&T Clark, 2016.

Crossley James G., and Katie Edwards. "Paul and the Faithfulness of God as Postmodern Scholarship," 603–21 in *God and the Faithfulness of Paul: A Critical Examination of the Pauline Theology of N.T. Wright*. Edited by Christoph Heilig, J. Thomas Hewitt, and Michael F. Bird. Tübingen: Mohr Siebeck, 2016.

Dunn, James D. G. "The New Perspective on Paul," *Bulletin of the John Rylands Library* 65 (1983): 95–122. https://doi.org/10.7227/BJRL.65.2.6

—*The Theology of Paul the Apostle*. Grand Rapids, MI: Eerdmans, 1998.

—*The New Perspective on Paul: Collected Essays*. Tübingen: Mohr Siebeck, 2005.

Eagleton, Terry. *Literary Theory: An Introduction*. Minneapolis, MN: University of Minnesota Press, 2008.

Ehrman, Bart D. *Misquoting Jesus: The Story Behind Who Changed the Bible and Why*. New York: HarperCollins, 2005.

Elliott, John H. "Jesus Was Not an Egalitarian: A Critique of an Anachronistic and Idealist Theory," *Biblical Theology Bulletin* 32 (2002): 75–91. https://doi.org/10.1177/014610790203200206

Fisher, Mark. *Capitalist Realism: Is There No Alternative?* Winchester, UK: Zero Books, 2009.

Galbraith, Deane. "Review of S. D. Moore and Y. Sherwood: *The Invention of the Biblical Scholar: A Critical Manifesto*," *Relegere* 3 (2013): 409–14. https://doi.org/10.11157/rsrr3-2-612

Goldberg, David Theo. *The Threat of Race: Reflections on Racial Neoliberalism*. Oxford: Wiley-Blackwell, 2009.

Head, Peter. "The Nazi Quest for an Ayrian Jesus," *Journal for the Study of the Historical Jesus* 2 (2004): 55–89. https://doi.org/10.1177/147686900400200103

Hersh, Seymour. "Annals of National Security: The Gray Zone – How a Secret Pentagon Program Came to Abu Ghraib," *The New Yorker* (15 May 2004).

Heschel, Susannah. *The Aryan Jesus: Christian Theologians and the Bible in Nazi Germany*. Princeton, NJ: Princeton University Press, 2008.

King, Rebekka. "The Author, the Atheist, and the Academic Study of Religion: Bourdieu and the Reception of Biblical Criticism by Progressive Christians," *Bulletin for the Study of Religion* 41 (2015): 14–20.

Lentin, Alana, and Gavan Titley. *The Crises of Multiculturalism: Racism in a Neoliberal Age*. London: Zed Books, 2011.

Mack, Burton. *A Myth of Innocence: Mark and Christian Origins*. Philadelphia, PA: Fortress Press, 1988.

—*Myth and the Christian Nation: A Social Theory of Religion*. London: Equinox, 2008.

—*Christian Mentality: The Entanglements of Power, Violence and Fear*. London: Equinox, 2011.

Malina, Bruce J. *The Social World of Jesus and the Gospels*. London: Routledge, 1996.

Meier, John P. *A Marginal Jew: Rethinking the Historical Jesus.* Vol. 1: *The Roots of the Problem and the Person*. New York: Doubleday, 1991.

—*A Marginal Jew: Rethinking the Historical Jesus.* Vol. 3: *Companions and Competitors*. New York: Doubleday, 2001.

Moore, Stephen D., and Yvonne Sherwood. *The Invention of the Biblical Scholar: A Critical Manifesto*. Minneapolis, MN: Fortress Press, 2011.

Moxnes, Halvor. *Jesus and the Rise of Nationalism: A New Quest for the Nineteenth Century Historical Jesus*. London: I. B. Tauris, 2011.

Myles, Robert. "The Fetish for a Subversive Jesus," *Journal for the Study of the Historical Jesus* 14.1 (2016): 52–70. https://doi.org/10.1163/17455197-01401005

Patai, Raphael. *The Arab Mind*. New York: Scribner, 1983.

Rocker, Rudolf. *Nationalism and Culture*. Los Angeles, CA: Rocker Publications Committee, 1937.

Sanders, E. P. *Paul and Palestinian Judaism: A Comparison of Patterns of Religion*. London: SCM, 1977.

Sheehan, Jonathan. *The Enlightenment Bible: Translation, Scholarship, Culture*. Princeton, NJ: Princeton University Press, 2007.

Sherwood, Yvonne. *A Biblical Text and Its Afterlives: The Survival of Jonah in Western Culture*. Cambridge: Cambridge University Press, 2000.

—"Bush's Bible as a Liberal Bible (Strange Though That Might Seem)," *Postscripts* 2 (2006): 47–58.

—"On the Genesis Between the Bible and Rights," 13–42 in *Bible and Justice: Ancient Texts, Modern Challenges*. Edited by M. J. M. Coomber. London: Equinox, 2011.

Stanley, Christopher D. *Arguing with Scripture: The Rhetoric of Quotations in the Letters of Paul*. London: T&T Clark, 2004.

Wright, N. T. "The Paul of History and the Apostle of Faith," *Tyndale Bulletin* 29 (1978): 61–88.

—*The Climax of the Covenant: Christ and the Law in Pauline Theology*. London: T&T Clark, 1991.

—*Jesus and the Victory of God*. London: SPCK, 1996.

—*Paul and the Faithfulness of God*. London: SPCK, 2013.

Žižek, Slavoj. "Multiculturalism, or, the Cultural Logic of Multinational Capitalism," *New Left Review* 225 (1997): 28–51.

—"Liberal Multiculturalism Masks an Old Barbarism with a Human Face," *Guardian* (3 October 2010). Online: http://www.theguardian.com/commentisfree/2010/oct/03/immigration-policy-roma-rightwing-europe (accessed 16 June 2016).

—"Return of the Natives," *New Statesman* (4 March 2010). Online: http://www.newstatesman.com/film/2010/03/avatar-reality-love-couple-sex (accessed 22 June 2016).

—"Do We Still Live in a World?" (n.d.). Online: http://www.lacan.com/zizrattlesnakeshake.html (accessed 2 July 2016).

Chapter Nineteen

Gender

Irene Salvo

How gender and sexualities are interconnected with religion, and how religion influences individuals' sexual life, is a topic that has been explored from a variety of theoretical approaches. Each term of this conceptual triad has been an object of debate, since each theory and discipline—from the history of religion to feminism—can define them differently. Without daring to condense the historiography of theories on gender and religion in a short chapter, this overview will focus on whether using transcultural theoretical paradigms for illuminating a given historical context, that is an ancient Mediterranean culture, is a valid intellectual enterprise.[1] It will try to recall some questions that are cross-culturally relevant as well as to highlight a selection of themes and data specific to the context of ancient societies, with a major attention to the Greek-speaking world from the Classical to the Imperial period. A key question will be whether and in what ways issues of gender were relevant to ancient religious experiences. Are contemporary theories on gender useful for decoding ancient religions and cults? Did agents of different genders practice religion in the same way? Were officers and roles assigned on the basis of gender? The first part will be devoted to putting into focus some of the major theoretical knots, while the second part will illustrate with four case studies how theories and data can interplay.

From a theoretical perspective, two main challenges need to be addressed: (1) the definition of the category of "gender" itself, and (2) its use in religious studies. Of the possibly never-ending debate on what gender means, only a few essential lines can be sketched here. From philosophy to history and from psychology to anthropology, the relationship of gender and sexual difference to the texture and structure of historical societies has been analyzed in multifarious ways. In the field of history, Joan Scott instructed the discussion

1.   This research has been supported by the Deutsche Forschungsgemeinschaft (DFG) at the University of Goettingen, Collaborative Research Centre 1136 *Bildung und Religion*, sub-project C01 *Aufgeklärte Männer - abergläubische Frauen? Religion, Bildung und Geschlechterstereotypen im klassischen Athen.*

on gender as historical process in a seminal article.[2] In her definition, "gender is a constitutive element of social relationships based on perceived differences between the sexes, and gender is a primary way of signifying relationships of power."[3] Being the product of conflict and interpretation of cultural symbols, gender is to be historically investigated beyond a fixed, permanent, and binary representation of the male/female opposition. However, as Jeanne Boydston has noted, Scott's definition of gender risks reaffirming the binary merely deflecting the biological opposition "from the *naturalized* body to the *perceived* body."[4] Boydston underlines that gender as represented in western culture is not universal, and inspiringly quotes the African historian Oyèrónké Oyewùmí, who writes: "gender, being a social construction, is also a historical and cultural phenomenon ... [I]t is logical to assume that in some societies, gender construction need not have existed at all."[5] This is extremely relevant to our discussion on the applicability of gender categories to ancient religions, and we will try to further explore non-western theoretical formulations. For example, among a West African ethnic group, the Yoruba, age and seniority influence power and social hierarchy, and their language is gender-neutral.[6] Spatial and chronological distance in the articulation of thought categories should make scholars more attentive to the methodological difficulties in using gender in non-Anglophone contexts. The relevance of gender cannot be assumed *a priori*, and English terminology might be problematic to translate in other languages. This can also be observed in the non-universality of the concepts of agency and performative agency, although its definition by Judith Butler has transformed the field of gender studies. As is well known, Butler has theorized the definition of gender identity as an act to be performed: sex and gender are expressed in doing constitutive acts rather than in being inscribed in the body. In Butler's own words, "gender proves to be performance—that is, constituting the identity it is purported to be. In this sense, gender is always a doing, though not a doing by a subject who might be said to pre-exist the deed."[7] Butler displaces binary norms of

2.   See Joan Scott, "Gender: A Useful Category of Historical Analysis," *American Historical Review* 91 (1986): 1053–75.

3.   Scott, "Gender," 1067.

4.   Jeanne Boydston, "Gender as a Question of Historical Analysis," *Gender & History* 20 (2008): 563 (emphasis in the original).

5.   Boydston, "Historical Analysis," 564ff.; Oyèrónké Oyewùmí, "Visualizing the Body: Western Theories and African Subjects," in *African Gender Studies: A Reader* (ed. Oyèrónké Oyewùmí; New York: Palgrave Macmillan, 2005), 11.

6.   Oyèrónké Oyewùmí, *The Invention of Women: Making an African Sense of Western Gender Discourses* (Minneapolis, MN: University of Minnesota Press, 1997).

7.   Judith Butler, *Gender Trouble: Feminism and the Subversion of Identity* (London: Routledge, 1990), 25.

gender and sexuality, opening the discourse of queerness and confronting the opposition between heteronormativity and homosexuality.[8] The conceptualization of gender as a spectrum and the fluidity of transgenderism can be particularly beneficial to the understanding of ancient religious practices, as we will further explore later.

Categorizations based on sexual differences cannot in any case be considered independently from other factors, such as race, ethnicity, kinship, age, social class, literacy, confessional identity, and political rights.[9] An individual identity is a multidimensional socio-historical product. Intersectionality influences the study of religion in particular in the choice of who can be elected to hold ordinary and high rank offices.

Now that we have at least a glimpse of feminist and queer theories on the conceptual definition of gender, we can consider how gender can be theorized in relation to ancient religions. Especially in the last twenty years, "religion" has attracted the attention of scholars who intended to write women's histories, since festival and rituals were considered one of the few occasions in which women could freely move within ancient cities. Politics and public affairs had primarily a male dimension, while "femaleness" was confined to the private space and the religious sphere. However, in antiquity the spheres of religion and politics, private and public, were strictly interconnected. Considering that in most of ancient societies the realms of politics and religion cannot be straightforwardly distinguished, power balance between men and women is a crucial theoretical point that has to be clarified by the evidence. As Scott writes, "gender is one of the recurrent references by which political power has been conceived, legitimated, and criticized."[10] In Greece, although women could not vote in the assembly or be members of a jury court, they were acting politically in guaranteeing a good relationship between the city and its gods. The current scholarly debate is rightly challenging, then, a rigid opposition between women's "religion inclusion" and their civic exclusion.[11] A more dynamic interpretation of gender, religion,

8.   See Judith Butler, *Bodies That Matter: On the Discursive Limits of "Sex"* (London: Routledge, 1993).

9.   See Boydston, "Historical Analysis," 577: "Gender is one set of historical relationships nested within a larger historical cluster of relationships from which it cannot, finally, be meaningfully disentangled." On the "politics of identity," cf. Virginia Burrus, "Mapping as Metamorphosis: Initial Reflections on Gender and Ancient Religious Discourse," in *Mapping Gender in Ancient Religious Discourse* (ed. Todd Penner and Caroline Vander Stichele; Leiden: Brill, 2006), 3.

10.   Scott, "Gender," 1073.

11.   See Angeliki Tzanetou, "Ritual and Gender: Critical Perspectives," in *Finding Persephone: Women's Rituals in the Ancient Mediterranean* (ed. Angeliki Tzanetou and Maryline Parca; Bloomington, IN: Indiana University Press, 2007), 3–26, and Tanja S.

and politics gives the opportunity to reveal an image of women as active social participants. Whether women could have social agency due to their religious roles and their participation in cults is one of the most promising research paths in the field.[12] What matters is how a gendered civic identity was shaped and invested with social power.

At different levels of analysis, the use of the category of gender in the study of ancient religions has produced multifarious results. A brief, and not exhaustive, overview will help in identifying how ancient religious practices can be understood through the lens of gender. Starting from ontological issues, the concept of gender has been applied to the analysis of the nature of ancient divine entities and their anthropomorphic representation in gods and goddesses.[13] However, more than one figure, as for example Athena or Dionysos, does not conform to a rigid separation between male and female characteristics.[14] The fluidity of gender boundaries and queer identities seems to be older than contemporary theorists.

From the perspective of human worshipers, it has been explored whether and in what ways sexual difference determined the choice of cultic officers and the possibility of performing sacral and cultic actions.[15] Furthermore, some cult practices and forms of devotion have emerged as gender-specific, such as the thesmophoric women-only festival or the male exclusivity of Mithraic initiations.[16] Fertility rituals have been linked mainly

Scheer, *Griechische Geschlechtergeschichte* (München: Oldenbourg Verlag, 2011), 111, with further bibliography.

12. The following quote is indicative of the debate and its complexity, see Barbara Goff, *Citizen Bacchae: Women's Ritual Practice in Ancient Greece* (Berkeley, CA: University of California Press, 2004), 12f.: "[I]n performing rituals women of ancient Greece exercise unusual agency and cultural presence and are constituted as active subjects of the ritual process. Yet at the same time and in the same gesture, if the ritual reproduces symbols or narratives that confirm the culture's account of women's inferiority, women may be reproducing the ideological constraints that govern their lives." See also Amy Richlin, "Carrying Water in a Sieve: Class and the Body in Roman Women's Religion," in *Women and Goddess Traditions: In Antiquity and Today* (ed. Karen L. King; London: Bloomsbury, 1998), 330–74.

13. See Nicole Loraux, "What Is a Goddess?" in *A History of Women: From Ancient Goddesses to Christian Saints* (ed. Pauline Schmitt Pantel and Georges Duby; Cambridge, MA: The Belknap Press of Harvard University Press, 1992), 11–44.

14. For a synthesis on these two much studied divine entities, see Susan Deacey, *Athena* (London: Routledge, 2008), and Richard Seaford, *Dionysos* (London: Routledge, 2006).

15. See, *ex plurimis*, Ross Shepard Kraemer, "Gender," in *The Cambridge Companion to Ancient Mediterranean Religions* (ed. Barbette Stanley Spaeth; Cambridge: Cambridge University Press, 2013), 281–308.

16. On the *Thesmophoria*, see Eva Stehle, "*Thesmophoria* and Eleusinian Mysteries:

only to women, since it is hard to abandon the association between women and motherhood.[17] The myth of matriarchy, and its overcoming by patriarchy, is another theory that has dominated the discussion, especially in the 1970s.[18] Similarly extremely influential, Foucault's construction of the discourse of power and knowledge has shaped classicists' research on sexuality in ancient societies and religions.[19] Finally, the debate on the relationship between "magic" and "religion" has included the gender factor, considering how magic is represented in literary sources as the domain of women, in opposition to the more "rational" and "pious" men, while the epigraphic evidence, as in the case of erotic curse tablets, attests several men as author of spells.[20] The relationship between gender and religion, in antiquity as in other historical periods, has been mainly explored so far in terms of participation—or rather lack of participation—of the female sex. A treatment of masculinity and religious practice still needs more scholarly efforts.[21]

In order to better elucidate the theoretical challenges of using gender in the study of ancient religions, it is essential to turn to the data. A glimpse into four examples from Greek religion can best contribute to clarifying the questions and issues at stake. Priesthood, the performance of sacrifice, access to the sacred space, and ritual transsexualism are the case studies that, in what follows, will try to illustrate in what ways theories and sources can interplay.

The Fascination of Women's Secret Ritual," in *Finding Persephone*, 165–85; on Mithraism, see John North, "Gender and Cult in the Roman West: Mithras, Isis, Attis," in *Women and the Roman City in the Latin West* (ed. Emily A. Hemelrijk and Greg Woolf; Leiden: Brill, 2013), 109–28. See also Ross Shepard Kraemer, *Unreliable Witnesses: Religion, Gender, and History in the Greco-Roman Mediterranean* (Oxford: Oxford University Press, 2011), 246: "in the ancient Mediterranean, much religion was gender specific."

17. See Scheer, *Griechische Geschlechtergeschichte*, 127, with further bibliography.

18. On matriarchy, see Stella Georgoudi, "Creating a Myth of Matriarchy," in Pantel and Duby, eds., *History of Women*, 449–63.

19. See Michel Foucault, *The History of Sexuality.* Vol. 1: *An Introduction* (New York: Vintage Books, 1980), *The History of Sexuality.* Vol. 2: *The Use of Pleasure* (New York: Vintage Books, 1985), and *The History of Sexuality.* Vol. 3: *The Care of the Self* (New York: Vintage Books, 1988). On Foucault and the Classics, see Wolfgang Detel, *Foucault and Classical Antiquity: Power, Ethics and Knowledge* (Cambridge: Cambridge University Press, 2005).

20. On magic and gender, see, e.g., Kimberly B. Stratton and Dayna S. Kalleres, *Daughters of Hecate: Women and Magic in the Ancient World* (Oxford: Oxford University Press, 2014).

21. See Robin Osborne, "Male/Female in the Greek World," in *ThesCRA VIII 5 Polarities in Religious Life: 5a Male/Female* (Los Angeles, CA: J. Paul Getty, 2012), 248: "The religious aspects of what happened to boys and men has been much less discussed, and cults limited to men and the myths by which men's lives are shaped have received little specific attention."

In ancient Greek societies, one of the more balanced relationships between men and women was achieved in the ministry of priesthood. Generally, but not always, a male divinity was a served by a male priest and a female divinity by a female priestess. However, responsibilities, privileges, and importance of the public office of a priest and a priestess were not differentiated on the basis of sex. Priestesses could manage funds and money; they maintained the relations with the popular assembly or civic magistrates; and they could gain public honors and achieve high social recognition. The identity of a priestess was profoundly determined by her kinship ties and by her "ethnicity," as it is evident from an inscription from Halikarnassos (Asia Minor), dated to the third century BCE, showing that the priesthood of Artemis Pergaia was held by a woman living in the city, whose parents were both citizens going back three generations.[22] The adjective *astos*, in the fifth line of this text, designates a person with civil—but not political—rights, in opposition to citizens with full rights, the *polites*. As the same inscription demonstrates, especially in Hellenistic Asia Minor, the economic factor was determinant, since priesthoods were usually expensive to buy. An exception seems to be the case of the priesthood of Athena Nikē in Athens: the priestess was appointed by lot from all the Athenian women, as an attic tombstone testifies.[23] Among the various theoretical approaches possible for the

---

22. *Lois sacrées de l'Asie Mineure* 73.4-14:

> ὁ πριάμε[νο]ς [τ]ὴν ἱερητείαν τῆς Ἀρτέμιδος τῆς Περγαίας πα[ρέξ]εται ἱέρειαν ἀστὴν ἐξ ἀστῶν ἀμφοτέρων ἐπὶ [τρε]ῖς γενεὰς γεγενημένην καὶ πρὸς πατρὸς καὶ πρὸς [μη]τρός, ἡ δὲ πριαμένη ἱεράσεται ἐπὶ <ζ>ωῆς τῆς αὐτῆς καὶ θύσει τὰ ἱερὰ τὰ δημό[σ]ια καὶ τὰ ἰδιωτικὰ καὶ λήψεται τῶν θυομένων δημοσίαι ἀφ᾽ ἑκάστου ἱερείου κωλῆν καὶ τὰ ἐπὶ κω<λ>ῆι νεμόμενα καὶ τεταρτημορίδα σπλάγχνων καὶ τὰ δέρματα, τῶν δὲ ἰδιωτικῶν λήψεται κωλῆν καὶ τὰ ἐπὶ κωλῆ νεμόμενα καὶ τεταρτημορίδα σπλάγχνων.

> The man who purchases the priesthood of Artemis *Pergaia* will present a priestess who is a townswoman, descended from citizens on both sides, on the mother's side and the father's side, over three generations. The woman who will buy the priesthood will be priestess for her lifetime, and she will perform the public and private sacrificial rites. From each of the victims sacrificed publicly, she will take the thigh, the joints around the thigh, and a fourth part of the viscera, and the skins; and she will take the thigh, the joints around the thigh, and a fourth part of the viscera of privately sacrificed victims.

Translation taken from Robin Osborne, "Women and Sacrifice in Classical Greece," in *Oxford Readings in Greek Religion* (ed. Richard Buxton; Oxford: Oxford University Press, 2000), 304 n. 33, slightly modified.

23. *Inscriptiones Graecae* I³1330.11-6, Athens, c. 430–400 BCE: πρώτε Ἀθηναίας Νίκες ἕδος ἀμφεπόλευσεν ἐκ πάντων κλήρωι, Μυρρίνη εὐτυχίαι [As the first there she served the shrine of Athena Nike Myrrhina, chosen by lot from all, with good fortune]. Translation taken from Simon Price, *Religions of the Ancient Greeks* (Cambridge: Cambridge University Press, 1999), 176.

interpretation of these data, it can be useful to resort to Pierre Bourdieu and his sociology of religion. After refocusing his mainly Franco-catholic perspective,[24] Bourdieu's sociology can be used in different cultural contexts. As Marta Trzebiatowska writes, his concept of *habitus*

> can be understood as transcending the individual/structure dualism but only in the sense that individuals are active in the world where structure refers to nothing more than the historically positioned interactions between groups of individuals in possession of various amounts of capital, competing in fields of social life where symbolic violence is exercised but also resisted and challenged. The task of researching the intersection of gender, sexuality and religion poses a number of difficulties because all elements continuously shift internally and in relation to one another in a manner of images in a kaleidoscope. In order to produce a most complete and balanced account of such shifts, we must pay attention to the sum of historical interaction between the parts, instead of assuming a reified structure that rules over and determines all of them.[25]

Applying this to our case, it is worth noting that both Greek male and female priestly officers were possessing a similar amount of cultural capital. Moreover, symbolic violence against women, and in favor of misogyny, was resisted and challenged in the institution of priesthood, that gave power and social respect to both sexes. The situation is further articulated in other ancient religions, as for example in Roman religion. Roman women could not be nominated as magistrates or members of the most prestigious priestly colleges: only the wives of magistrates could have a role, as the *regina sacrorum* or the *flaminica Dialis*. Their religious role—and consequently their social authority—is more evident when they acted as priestesses, benefactors, and dedicators. The role of gender in the structure of Roman religious life, however, should not be subject to generalization. Each single cult regulated the admission to its practices as well as the roles played by the ritual personnel and the worshipers. In any case, it should be remembered that the privilege of overseeing the communication with the gods was primarily influenced by: "ethnicity"—to be Roman; by wealth—to be a member of an elite family; and by personal reputation and model behavior, although the standard for female priestesses was much more strict and demanding than that of male priests.[26]

---

24. See Andrew McKinnon, Marta Trzebiatowska, and Christopher C. Brittain, "Bourdieu, Capital and Conflict in a Religious Field: The Case of the Anglican Communion," *Journal of Contemporary Religion* 26 (2011): 355–70.

25. Marta Trzebiatowska, "Beyond Habitus: Researching Gender and Religion Through the Ontology of Social Relations," in *Sociological Theory and the Question of Religion* (ed. Andrew McKinnon and Marta Trzebiatowska; Farnham, UK: Ashgate, 2014), 256.

26. On women in Roman religion, see Celia E. Schultz, *Women's Religious Activity*

The significance of gender can be further tested exploring the degree of gendered participation in Greek cult, in particular analyzing the central act of ancient worship: animal sacrifice. Because of space constraints, it is impossible to offer an in-depth treatment of Greek women and their role in the actual performance of animal sacrifice, but it is important to mention a few key points. In the 1970s, the structuralist view of Marcel Detienne was dominant. The Belgian scholar marked a sharp division between the feminine and the masculine in Greek sacrificial practices. According to his view, priestesses consecrated the victim with lustral water before the killing, but they could not hold the sacrificial knife, they did not actually slaughter the animal, and they did not partake in the sharing of the meat.[27] On this path, in her cross-cultural analysis of gender and sacrifice, Nancy Jay has argued that animal sacrifice socially constructed the male lines of descent, expelling femaleness from a patrilineal and patriarchal generative system.[28] Furthermore, an analogy between the menstrual and lochial blood and the blood of the animal victim in the Greek medical writings has been highlighted: while women were fertile and bleeding they could not shed blood in sacrifice.[29] However, many scholars working on Greek and Roman religions have criticized this picture. Robin Osborne has firstly showed that in Greek inscriptions a clause explicitly excluding women from sacrifice is more frequent than clauses about their inclusion. The epigraphic evidence seems to suggest that women were not regularly excluded from the sharing of sacrificial meat, and eventual prohibitions to their participation varied from cult to cult and from city to city.[30] An inscription from the island of Chios proves that women could have been responsible for the sacrifice and could have eaten the sacrificial meat:

> If a private person performs (a sacrifice), a portion (of meat) shall be given
> from the victim, so as to be placed in the basket, and the priestly prerogative,

in the Roman Republic (Chapel Hill, NC: University of North Carolina Press, 2006); Emily A. Hemelrijk, *Hidden Lives, Public Personae: Women and Civic Life in the Roman West* (Oxford: Oxford University Press, 2015).

27. See Marcel Detienne, "Violentes Eugenies: En pleines Thesmophories des femmes couvertes de sang," in *La cuisine du sacrifice en pays grec* (ed. Marcel Detienne and Jean-Pierre Vernant; Paris: Gallimard, 1979), 183–214.

28. Cf. Nancy Jay, *Throughout Your Generations Forever: Sacrifice, Religion, and Paternity* (Chicago, IL: University of Chicago Press, 1992).

29. See Helen King, *Hippocrates' Woman: Reading the Female Body in Ancient Greece* (London and New York: Routledge, 1998), 88–98.

30. See Osborne, "Women and Sacrifice." On Roman religion, with previous bibliography, see James Rives, "Women and Animal Sacrifice in Public Life," in Hemelrijk and Woolf, eds., *Women and the Roman City*, 129–46.

and the tongue. These shall be consumed on the spot with the women who performed the sacrifice.[31]

The cult in question is that of Eileithuia, the Greek goddess of birth, and the women mentioned are probably members of the cult personnel involved in the performance of the rites together with the priestess. From a theoretical point of view, the supposed sacrificial incapability of women is indeed problematic, since it asserts a perpetuation of patriarchal domination, using a framework that has now been superseded.

Another good example for illustrating ways of thinking gender and religion in antiquity—and for assessing whether ancient religious practices privileged men and male power—concerns the access to the sacred space. Greek religion manipulated the relationship between gender identity and the sacred regulating symbolic markers such as the style of clothing, jewelry, make-up, and hairstyle.[32] In order to preserve the ritual purity of the sacred space, many sanctuaries regulated the access to the site, forbidding entrance to men and women wearing inappropriate clothes, or bringing with them forbidden items such as sandals of goat skin, belts, arms, or metal objects.[33] We have laws on clothing in the sacred space concerning men and women alike, or laws specifically for women—especially in the case of women-only festivals. A law can distinguish regulations for men and women depending on their hairstyles, as in the following text:

> It is not permitted to enter the temple of the Lady Goddess with any object of gold on one's person, unless it is intended for an offering, or to wear a purple or brightly-colored or black garment, or shoes, or a finger-ring. But if one enters wearing any forbidden object, it must be dedicated to the temple. Women are not to have their hair bound up, and men must enter with bared head.[34]

---

31. See, e.g., *Supplementum Epigraphicum Graecum* XXXV 923A.4-10, Chios (Aegean islands), c. 400 BCE: ἢν δὲ ἰδιώτης ποι[ῇ], δίδοσθαι ἀπὸ τõ ἱερ[õ], ὥστε ἐς [τὸ] λ[ί]κνον ἐνθεῖ[ν]αι [μ]οῖ ραν καὶ γέρας καὶ γλῶσσαν [καὶ] τάδε ἀναλ[ί]σκεσθαι αὐτõ μ[ε]τὰ τῶν γυναικῶν τῶν π[ο]ι[η]σασέ[ων] τὰ ἱρά. Translation taken from Eran Lupu, *Greek Sacred Law: A Collection of New Documents* (Leiden: Brill, 2005), 304.

32. On regulating the attire of worshipers in sanctuaries, see most recently Mireille M. Lee, *Body, Dress, and Identity in Ancient Greece* (Cambridge: Cambridge University Press, 2015), 215ff.

33. *Lois sacrées des cités grecques: Supplément* 56, Delos (Aegean islands), second century BCE: γυναῖκα μὴ προσάγειν μηδὲ ἐν ἐρεοῖς ἄνδρα· κατὰ πρόσταγμα [In accordance with the ordinance, women should not participate, men are not to wear wool].

34 *Lois sacrées des cités grecques* 68.2-11, Lykosoura (Arkadia, Greece), third century BCE: μὴ ἐξέστω παρέρπην ἔχοντας ἐν τὸ ἱερὸν τᾶς Δεσποίνας μὴ χρ[υ]σία ὅσα <μ>ὴ ἰν ἀνάθεμα μηδὲ πορφύρεον εἱματισμὸν μηδὲ ἀνθινὸν μηδὲ [μέλ]ανα μηδὲ ὑποδήματα μηδὲ δακτύλιον· εἰ δ' ἄν τις παρένθη ἔχων τι τῶν ἁ στάλα [κ]ωλύει, ἀναθέτω ἐν τὸ ἱερόν. μηδὲ τὰς τ[ρί]χας ἀμπεπλεγμένας μηδὲ κεκαλυμμένος. Translation taken

In order to make sense of these data, ancient historians could profit from cognitive theories about how the extended mind can influence a cultic experience. Cognitive scientists suggest that the human mind functions not only within the cranial box, but needs a variety of external objects in order to think and act. Our thinking is embodied, incorporated in our movements, gestures, and language, and also extended into the environment. The extended mind thesis, supported by a continuously growing literature, is now being applied to religion and personal identity. As Joel Krueger notes, material culture and objects shape religious thought and are anchors that help us to think about the divine.[35] Applying cognitive concepts into our field, rituals can be interpreted as whole-body experiences in which external inputs contribute to the scaffolding of emotions in actors, participants, and viewers. In other words, objects and prompts provide a framework that supports the worshipers in developing a contact with the sacred. In Greek religion, impure and pure elements like fabric, materials, and colors of clothes, to mention just a few, helped to create an emotional and psychological state of awe and concentration. This process could have had a gendered connotation, for example when women had to bind up their hair, while men should have bared heads. However, norms on dress code and the attire were also gender-neutral, when for example knots or iron were prohibited in the sanctuary. To conclude on this point, cognitive studies can help us to understand better the shaping of personal identity and emotions during a religious experience, and in this way it can also usefully highlight whether and when gender was a relevant discrimen.[36]

Indeed, an exact definition and differentiation between male and female sex was sometimes unnecessary, as our fourth topic—ritual transexualism—will indicate. On the level of ritual and cult, sexual ambivalence was accepted and performed. A well-known example is that of the *Galloi*, Cybele's emasculated priests in Anatolian temples. While Christian writers abhorred this gender transgression, Sextus Empiricus notes that "the Mother of the Gods also admits effeminates, and the Goddess would not judge so, if by nature unmanliness were a trivial thing"[37] Transvestism was customary in Bacchic dances and in some Athenian religious festivals such as the *Oschophoria* and

from Harrianne Mills, "Greek Clothing Regulations: Sacred and Profane?" *Zeitschrift für Papyrologie und Epigraphik* 55 (1984): 255–65.

35. See Joel Krueger, "Extended Mind and Religious Cognition," in *Religion: Mental Religion* (ed. Niki Kasumi Clements; Farmington Hills, MI: Gale Cengage Learning, 2016), 237–54.

36. For more on the cognitive study of religion and antiquity, see Chapter Sixteen, this volume.

37. Sextus Empiricus, *Outline of Pyrrhonism* 217-8.

perhaps also in the *Scirophories*. During wedding rites at Sparta, the bride was bald and in male clothes, in Argos she wore a false beard, and in Kos the husband wore a female dress. As Marie Delcourt wrote, "[transvestism] certainly had a positive value; it had power to promote health, youth, strength, longevity, perhaps even to confer a kind of immortality."[38] Gender identities could be fluidly negotiated, and this fluidity was socially accepted, at least in certain ritual contexts. Socio-constructionist and non-binary understandings of sex and gender seem to be anticipated by these rituals. Gender identity was expressed in a way reminiscent of the Butlerian definition of the performativity of gender.

The rise of Christianity dismantled the links between cult practice, space, and ethnicity, since the new religion aimed at a universal trans-cultural faith. And, at least in the early Christian communities of the first four centuries of our era, gender seems not to have played a significant role in the appointment of priestly officers. Inscriptions attest the title of presbytera. However, Christian writers of the third and fourth centuries condemn women who bless the Eucharist and baptize: it was considered a heresy that women functioned as priests, since—among other reasons—the twelve apostles were male and the bishops have succeeded them.[39] John Chrysostom wrote:

> The divine law indeed has excluded women from the ministry, but they try to thrust themselves into it; and since they can effect nothing of themselves, they do all through the agency of others; and they have become invested with so much power that they can appoint or remove priests at their will.[40]

It is enlightening to compare Chrysostom's passage with an excerpt from an encyclical letter by Pope Francis:

> The reservation of the priesthood to males, as a sign of Christ the Spouse who gives himself in the Eucharist, is not a question open to discussion, but it can prove especially divisive if sacramental power is too closely identified with power in general. It must be remembered that when we speak of sacramental power "we are in the realm of function, not that of dignity or holiness."[41]

The last sentence, within quotation marks, is of Pope John Paul II. Both Chrysostom and Pope Francis put an emphasis on power. In order to justify the exclusion of women from priesthood, Pope Francis needs to separate the

---

38. Marie Delcourt, *Hermaphrodite: Myths and Rites of the Bisexual Figure in Classical Antiquity* (London: Studio Books, 1961), 22.

39. Ross Shepard Kraemer, *Her Share of the Blessings: Women's Religions Among Pagans, Jews and Christians in the Greco-Roman World* (Oxford: Oxford University Press, 1992) and Kraemer, *Unreliable Witnesses*.

40. John Chrysostom, *On the Priesthood* 3.9.

41. Pope Francis, *The Joy of the Gospel* (24 XI 2013), ch. 2 §104.

sacramental function from dignity and power. Women are not less power-ful, authoritative, or respectable than men even if they cannot have priestly duties. In response to Pope Francis, one might remember the Foucauldian theorization on the fact that the discourse of power/knowledge *does* define social identities. Power, authority, and social identity are the key issues here. The more hierarchical is the religious system, the more unequal and unbal-anced are the gender roles. Feminist scholars have explained the exclusion of women from the hierarchies of religions underlining that men fear wom-en's authority over men. The main three monotheistic religions—Islam, Judaism, and Christianity—have represented God as male, and therefore the officers must be men. Or, using Mary Douglas's terminology, the egali-tarianism of Jesus was soon wiped out by a high grid society.[42] Furthermore, excluding women, the number of individuals competing for leadership roles decreases almost by half, and there are less people involved in the deci-sion-making process. Gender and religion, ultimately, have a relationship based on the balance of social and cultural power.

This brief overview has tried to show how from Bourdieu to Butler, from challenging patriarchy to cognitive sciences, a variety of theoreti-cal approaches can illuminate gender and religion in antiquity. A commit-ment to a single analytical framework lies in the choice of the researcher. Each document or phenomenon can be better understood thanks to a partic-ular theory. This advocates for a flexible relationship between theories and historical contexts. Before starting any analytical enterprise on this topic, scholars should examine first whether the discourse on gender in the reli-gious field actually preoccupied ancient societies. As Carlo Ginzburg indi-cates, historians ask anachronistic questions, but they should try to gain from their texts answers "that are articulated in the actors' language, and related to categories peculiar to their society ... One starts from *etic* ques-tions aiming to get *emic* answers."[43] In ancient religions, sexual difference was an important factor in regulating the approach to the divine as well as in structuring funerary rites, processions, festivals, and mantic proce-dures. However, additional factors such as age, personal reputation, eth-nicity, and social status determined who was chosen to function as a ritual actor. The application of our category of "gender " is certainly productive in the study of ancient religious experience, since it allows us to identify the profiles of those who participated in cults and who were responsible for

42. See Mary Douglas, *Natural Symbols: Exploration in Cosmology* (London: Barrie and Rockliff, 1970).

43. Carlo Ginzburg, "Our Words, and Theirs: A Reflection on the Historian's Craft, Today," in *Historical Knowledge* (ed. Susanna Fellman and Marjatta Rahikainen; New-castle, UK: Cambridge Scholars Publishing, 2012), 108 (emphasis in the original).

the transmission of beliefs and theological concepts. However, an uncritical transposition of definitions of sex and gender might generate a misinterpretation of the sources, or, better, their overreading, intending by this term that process defined by literary theorists when "we find in narratives qualities, motives, moods, ideas, judgments, even events for which there is no direct evidence in the discourse."[44] How can we build our investigation on an idea that cannot even find a correspondent translation in the language of the society under study? Nevertheless, denying historiographical status to a phenomenon only because of its untranslatability is not a satisfactory argument. Following this line of thought, one should avoid studying "religion" altogether, considering that in the ancient Greek language the term, as we understand it, does not exist. Alternatively, one may advocate abandoning the category of "gender" and the writing of gender history to return to women's history, as it has been discussed recently.[45] However, this would exclude from the analysis manifestations of masculinity in the religious space, non-binary representation of sex, and transsexualism.

Historians can hardly avoid using their contemporary analytical categories in the study of ancient religions, and gender does not escape this methodological rule. Notwithstanding the anachronism and the challenges of its multifaceted definition, gender still offers a beneficial perspective from which to analyze the evidence on ancient cults and beliefs. What it is crucial, though, is to approach the sources without any pre-established ideas about the results of the inquiry. The partition of symbolic and religious power did not necessarily always favor men. Religion shaped gender through the allocation of power and authority, balancing social hierarchies and leadership roles between men and women. Differentiations in the performance of cults and ritual norms were not established following exclusively criteria based on the gender of priestly officers and worshipers. Divine entities and ritual participants did not align only to two sexes, but the boundaries between male and female identities were infringed and fluid characterizations of sex were explored.

Biographical Note

Irene Salvo is Postdoctoral Researcher at the Georg-August University Göttingen, Collaborative Research Centre 1136 *Bildung und Religion*

44. H. Porter Abbot, *The Cambridge Introduction to Narrative* (Cambridge: Cambridge University Press, 2002), 82.

45. On this debate see, *ex plurimis*, Scheer, *Griechische Geschlechtergeschichte*, 56ff; Violaine Sebillotte-Cuchet, "Touchée par le féminisme: L'Antiquité et le genre," in *Anthropologie de l'Antiquité: Anciens objets, nouvelles approches* (ed. Pascal Payen and Evelyne Scheid-Tissinier; Turnhout: Brepols Publishers, 2012), 143–72.

(Germany). After having earned her doctorate at the Scuola Normale Superiore (Pisa, Italy), from 2013 to 2015 she was Gerda Henkel Scholar in Ancient History at the Royal Holloway, University of London (UK). One of her main research interests is to explore the relationship between gender and religion from the evidence of Greek inscriptions of religious interest. She has published various articles on Greek social and cultural history, in particular on Greek epigraphy, education and history of knowledge, pollution and purification, and emotions.

Bibliography

Abbott, H. Porter. *The Cambridge Introduction to Narrative*. Cambridge: Cambridge University Press, 2002.

Boydston, Jeanne. "Gender as a Question of Historical Analysis," *Gender & History* 20 (2008): 558–83. https://doi.org/10.1111/j.1468-0424.2008.00537.x

Burrus, Virginia. "Mapping as Metamorphosis: Initial Reflections on Gender and Ancient Religious Discourse," 1–10 in *Mapping Gender in Ancient Religious Discourse*. Edited by Todd Penner and Caroline Vander Stichele. Leiden: Brill, 2006. https://doi.org/10.1163/ej.9789004154476.i-582.6

Butler, Judith. *Gender Trouble: Feminism and the Subversion of Identity*. London: Routledge, 1990.

—*Bodies That Matter: On the Discursive Limits of "Sex"*. London: Routledge, 1993.

Deacey, Susan. *Athena*. London: Routledge, 2008. https://doi.org/10.4324/9780203932148

Delcourt, Marie. *Hermaphrodite: Myths and Rites of the Bisexual Figure in Classical Antiquity*. London: Studio Books, 1961.

Detel, Wolfgang. *Foucault and Classical Antiquity: Power, Ethics and Knowledge*. Cambridge: Cambridge University Press, 2005. https://doi.org/10.1017/CBO9780511487156

Detienne, Marcel. "Violentes Eugenies: En pleines Thesmophories des femmes couvertes de sang," 183–214 in *La cuisine du sacrifice en pays grec*. Edited by Marcel Detienne and Jean-Pierre Vernant. Paris: Gallimard, 1979.

Douglas, Mary. *Natural Symbols: Exploration in Cosmology*. London: Barrie and Rockliff, 1970.

Foucault, Michael. *The History of Sexuality*. Vol. 1: *An Introduction*. New York: Vintage Books, 1980.

—*The History of Sexuality*. Vol. 2: *The Use of Pleasure*. New York: Vintage Books, 1985.

—*The History of Sexuality*. Vol. 3: *The Care of the Self*. New York: Vintage Books, 1988.

Georgoudi, Stella. "Creating a Myth of Matriarchy," 449–63 in Pantel and Duby, eds., *History of Women*, 1992.

Ginzburg, Carlo. "Our Words, and Theirs: A Reflection on the Historian's Craft, Today," 97–119 in *Historical Knowledge*. Edited by Susanna Fellman and Marjatta Rahikainen. Newcastle, UK: Cambridge Scholars Publishing, 2012.

Goff, Barbara. *Citizen Bacchae: Women's Ritual Practice in Ancient Greece*. Berkeley, CA: University of California Press, 2004.

Hemelrijk, Emily A. *Hidden Lives, Public Personae: Women and Civic Life in the Roman West*. Oxford: Oxford University Press, 2015. https://doi.org/10.1093/acprof:oso/9780190251888.001.0001

Hemelrijk, Emily A., and Greg Woolf, eds. *Women and the Roman City in the Latin West*. Leiden: Brill, 2013. https://doi.org/10.1163/9789004255951

Jay, Nancy. *Throughout Your Generations Forever: Sacrifice, Religion, and Paternity*. Chicago, IL: University of Chicago Press, 1992.

King, Helen. *Hippocrates' Woman: Reading the Female Body in Ancient Greece*. London: Routledge, 1998.

Kraemer, Ross Shepard. *Her Share of the Blessings: Women's Religions Among Pagans, Jews and Christians in the Greco-Roman World*. Oxford: Oxford University Press, 1992.

—*Unreliable Witnesses: Religion, Gender, and History in the Greco-Roman Mediterranean*. Oxford: Oxford University Press, 2011.

—"Gender," 281–308 in *The Cambridge Companion to Ancient Mediterranean Religions*. Edited by Barbette Stanley Spaeth. Cambridge: Cambridge University Press, 2013. https://doi.org/10.1017/CCO9781139047784.017

Krueger, Joel. "Extended Mind and Religious Cognition," 237–54 in *Religion: Mental Religion*. Edited by Niki Kasumi Clements. Farmington Hills, MI: Gale Cengage Learning, 2016.

Lee, Mireille M. *Body, Dress, and Identity in Ancient Greece*. Cambridge: Cambridge University Press, 2015. https://doi.org/10.1017/CBO9781107295261

Loraux, Nicole. "What Is a Goddess?" 11–44 in Pantel and Duby, eds., *History of Women*, 1992.

Lupu, Eran. *Greek Sacred Law: A Collection of New Documents*. Leiden: Brill, 2005.

McKinnon, Andrew, Marta Trzebiatowska, and Christopher C. Brittain. "Bourdieu, Capital and Conflict in a Religious Field: The Case of the Anglican Communion," *Journal of Contemporary Religion* 26 (2011): 355–70. https://doi.org/10.1080/13537903.2011.616033

Mills, Harrianne. "Greek Clothing Regulations: Sacred and Profane?" *Zeitschrift für Papyrologie und Epigraphik* 55 (1984): 255–65.

North, John. "Gender and Cult in the Roman West: Mithras, Isis, Attis," 109–28 in Hemelrijk and Woolf, eds., *Women and the Roman City*, 2013. https://doi.org/10.1163/9789004255951_008

Osborne, Robin. "Women and Sacrifice in Classical Greece," 294–313 in *Oxford Readings in Greek Religion*. Edited by Richard Buxton. Oxford: Oxford University Press, 2000.

—"Male/Female in the Greek World," 247–61 in *ThesCRA VIII 5 Polarities in Religious Life: 5a Male/Female*. Los Angeles, CA: J. Paul Getty, 2012.

Oyewùmí, Oyèrónké. *The Invention of Women: Making an African Sense of Western Gender Discourses*. Minneapolis, MN: University of Minnesota Press, 1997.

—"Visualizing the Body: Western Theories and African Subjects," 3–21 in *African Gender Studies: A Reader*. Edited by Oyèrónké Oyewùmi. New York: Palgrave Macmillan, 2005. https://doi.org/10.1007/978-1-137-09009-6_1

Pantel, Pauline Schmitt, and Georges Duby, eds. *A History of Women: From Ancient Goddesses to Christian Saints*. Cambridge, MA: The Belknap Press of Harvard University Press, 1992.

Price, Simon. *Religions of the Ancient Greeks*. Cambridge: Cambridge University Press, 1999. https://doi.org/10.1017/CBO9780511814488

Richlin, Amy. "Carrying Water in a Sieve: Class and the Body in Roman Women's Religion," 330–74 in *Women and Goddess Traditions: In Antiquity and Today*. Edited by Karen L. King. London: Bloomsbury, 1998.

Rives, James. "Women and Animal Sacrifice in Public Life," 129–46 in Hemelrijk and Woolf, eds., *Women and the Roman City*, 2013. https://doi.org/10.1163/9789004255951_009

Seaford, Richard. *Dionysos*. London: Routledge, 2006. https://doi.org/10.4324/9780203358016

Sebillotte-Cuchet, Violaine. "Touchée par le féminisme. L'Antiquité et le genre," 143–72 in *Anthropologie de l'Antiquité: Anciens objets, nouvelles approaches*. Edited by Pascal Payen and Evelyne Scheid-Tissinier. Turnhout: Brepols Publishers, 2012.

Scheer, Tanja S. *Griechische Geschlechtergeschichte*. München: Oldenbourg Verlag, 2011. https://doi.org/10.1524/9783486713879

Schultz, Celia E. *Women's Religious Activity in the Roman Republic*. Chapel Hill, NC: University of North Carolina Press, 2006.

Scott, Joan. "Gender: A Useful Category of Historical Analysis," *American Historical Review* 91 (1986): 1053–75. https://doi.org/10.2307/1864376

Stehle, Eva. "*Thesmophoria* and Eleusinian Mysteries: The Fascination of Women's Secret Ritual," 165–85 in Tzanetou and Parca, eds., *Finding Persephone*, 2007.

Stratton, Kimberly B., and Dayna S. Kalleres. *Daughters of Hecate: Women and Magic in the Ancient World*. Oxford: Oxford University Press, 2014. https://doi.org/10.1093/acprof:oso/9780195342703.001.0001

Trzebiatowska, Marta. "Beyond Habitus: Researching Gender and Religion Through the Ontology of Social Relations," 243–60 in *Sociological Theory and the Question of Religion*. Edited by Andrew McKinnon and Marta Trzebiatowska. Farnham, UK: Ashgate, 2014.

Tzanetou, Angeliki. "Ritual and Gender: Critical Perspectives," 3–26 in Tzanetou and Parca, eds., *Finding Persephone*, 2007.

Tzanetou, Angeliki, and Maryline Parca, eds., *Finding Persephone: Women's Rituals in the Ancient Mediterranean*. Bloomington, IN: Indiana University Press, 2007.

Chapter Twenty

Epilogue
The Jabberwocky Dilemma: Take Religion for Example

Luther H. Martin

The past is a foreign country:
they do things differently there.

— Leslie P. Hartley[1]

Introduction

As Leslie Hartley notably reminds us in the opening line of his novel, *The Go-Between*, historiography is inseparable from comparative research. As such, an edited volume with the theme *Theorizing "Religion" in Antiquity* initially and inevitably raises issues of its temporal and geographical frame, that is, what exactly is the historical period and geographical frame designated by antiquity that is stipulated (presumed?) by contributors to this volume?

As with any historical periodization, antiquity is a fungible category that is defined by the interests of various historians and by those of the historical age in which they work.[2] Most generally, antiquity is used by contributors to the present volume as a western, in contrast to an Asian or American, geographical designation. Consequently, the history of these latter regions in antiquity is often ignored, for example, that of the Asian Denisovians to the early dynasties of China, that of the Samhitic traditions of the Indian subcontinent, or that of the much later (ancient) history of the Anaszi to that of the Incas in the Americas. European historians conventionally refer to the time prior to the fall of Rome and its inauguration of a European Middle Ages at the end of the fourth and the beginning of the fifth centuries CE as antiquity. For contributors to this volume, considerations of ancient religions during this indiscriminately lengthy period range capriciously from second-millennium BCE Egypt to the Christianities and post-biblical Judaisms of the late Roman Empire.

---

1. Leslie P. Hartley, *The Go-Between* (Harmondsworth, UK: Penguin, 1997 [1953]), 1.
2. Luther H. Martin, *Hellenistic Religions: An Introduction* (Oxford: Oxford University Press, 1987), 4–6.

And, it is unclear what contributors to the present volume mean by modernity, as when they criticize the use of the category religion for historical research as modern.[3] For the European historians, modernity refers to the temporal period since the end of the Middle Ages and the beginning of the Enlightenment.[4] For social and cultural analysists, however, modernity refers to an "experience of space and time, of the self and others, of life's possibilities and perils,"[5] which includes perhaps even postmodernism? Do contributors to the volume mean by modernity the one or the other? (Or both indiscriminately.)

And what of the religious things done differently there? Since the founding of religious studies as an academic field in the late nineteenth century, a definition of religion as an object of study has confounded researchers in the field. Some contributors to the present volume even question whether there is anything that might be defined as religion at all during the wide-ranging time period of antiquity—including, apparently, the Christianities and the post-biblical Judaisms of the first four centuries of the common era. But, if the early Christianities and Judaisms of western antiquity are excluded from the category of religion, what then might be the object of any history of religions study?

Religion as an Object of Historiographical Study

Beware the Jabberwock, my son!
The jaws that bite, the claws that catch!
Beware the Jubjub bird, and shun
The frumious Bandersnatch!

— Lewis Carroll[6]

Historians must perforce stipulate from their generally incomplete and fragmented data an object for their study. The question that preoccupies a number of the contributors to the current volume is whether "religion" is an

3.   E.g., Brent Nongbri, *Before Religion: A History of a Modern Concept* (New Haven, CT: Yale University Press, 2013), 2.
4.   Other periodizations of modernity differ between disciplines. Western literary historians, for example, mark the turn to modernity with the late eighteenth-century novels of Jane Austen, while art historians refer to modernism as the changes and developments in art from the late nineteenth century, and modernism in music and architecture is associated with those challenges to older form from the beginning of the twentieth century, etc.
5.   Marshall Berman, *All That Is Solid, Melts into the Air: The Experience of Modernity* (New York: Penguin, 1988), 15.
6.   Lewis Carroll, *Through the Looking Glass and What Alice Found There* (London: Macmillan, 1871), 33; ed. cited: PDFreeBooks.org (2010): https://archive.org/details/ThroughTheLookingGlassAndWhatAliceFoundThere.

appropriate category for delineating from their evidence a coherent object of study in antiquity. These contributors largely base their apprehensions on the genealogical study of this category by Brent Nongbri in his *Before Religion: A History of a Modern Concept* (2013).

Nongbri, who also wrote the Introduction for this volume, argues that religion is a modern (Christian) concept and, consequently, that its employment for identifying a conceptual area for the historical study of religions in antiquity is problematic (at best). In fact, he concludes that since "no ancient language has a term that really corresponds to what modern people mean when they say 'religion',"[7] there simply is no "such a thing as 'ancient religion'."[8] Steven Mason, in his initial contribution to the current volume on "Religious Categories" (Chapter 2),[9] is among those who most strongly agrees with Nongbri's conclusion (29), as is Jason Davies who argues a similar case for the related "religious" category of belief (Chapter 4).

Nongbri's view of language is one of jabberwockian randomness, in which words or categories simply have no shared or public meaning—or no meaning at all—from one historical setting or comparative context to another. Although he is correct that linguistic referents accumulate cultural baggage over time, the cognitive stability of the species *Homo sapiens* over evolutionary time nevertheless argues for some familiarity with linguistic referents, especially over the circumscribed period of historical time. For example, does it mean that no one in antiquity saw the color blue simply because many civilizations of antiquity had no proper word for it?[10] Homer, for example, spoke of the blue Aegean Sea as "wine dark" (*Odyssey* 1.178). Although the color blue was significant for ancient art, architecture, and symbolism, the word for it, like that of religion, is a modern word, derived from (among several other mediaeval languages) the middle English *bleu* or *blewe*. Significantly, however, the wavelength of light on the visible optical spectrum of between four hundred and fifty and four hundred and ninety-five nanometers corresponds to the color the modern term refers to and it is highly unlikely that the neurophysiological response of the human eye has changed in this regard over the past four or five millennia—whether or not there is a specific word in antiquity naming that visual response.

7.   Nongbri, *Before Religion*, 2.
8.   Nongbri, *Before Religion*, 8.
9.   Unless otherwise noted, all chapter and page references are to this volume.
10.   Guy Deutscher, *Through the Language Glass: Why the World Looks Different in Other Languages* (New York: Metropolitan Books/Henry Holt, 2010), 43–4, 60–1. The Egyptians, who developed the technology of blue dyes and pigments, *may* have had a word for blue (56).

Or, can it be argued that no one in antiquity ever died from malaria since, in antiquity, there was no word for this disease? Although the historical record attests to the devastation apparently exacted on ancient civilizations, particularly the Roman Empire, by what in the Hippocratic era was known simply as πυρετός, "the fever," the modern category of malaria is derived from the medieval Italian *mala aria*, meaning "bad air," presumably a cause of the fever. However, in December 2016, a group of anthropological and biomedical researchers reported in the journal of *Current Biology* that DNA evidence extracted from the molars of two individuals recovered from two cemeteries in Southern Italy, one in Velia and the other in Vagnari, dating to the first–second century CE, now confirms the presence of the malaria parasite *Plasmodium falciparum* as the cause of their death.[11]

Now, no one expects there to be any objective referent for the category religion, as there is for the wavelength on the optical spectrum that corresponds to the color blue, or for a certain protozoan parasite multiplying in the red blood cells of its hosts; religion is not a natural reality. However, like identifying ancient uses of hues in art and architecture with modern categories of wavelength refraction, or the symptoms of disease with a modern pathological category, shades and symptoms of that human behavior commonly associated with religion may be identified in the cultures of antiquity. As Alan Lenzi notes in his contribution to this volume on "Ancient Mesopotamian Scholars" (Chapter 8): "[w]hile there is no Akkadian word for 'religion,' there is also no general word for 'ethics,' 'law,' 'music,' 'art,' 'science,' 'economy,' 'technology,' 'government,' 'media,' or 'culture' (154). And Nickolas Roubekas, in his contribution on Herodotus (Chapter 7), cites classicist Robert L. Fowler, who similarly notes that the Greeks "had no categories for 'economy,' 'society,' or 'psychology' either, but we can study them nonetheless" (131).[12] As Irene Salvo concludes in her contribution on gender (Chapter 19), "denying historiographical status to a phenomenon only because of its untranslatability is not a satisfactory argument" (410).

In other words, the problem of studying religion in antiquity is not one of translational equivalence but simply the historical problem of stipulating the object of study in a way that is devoid of presentist biases. This would seem to be an issue which anyone with even a cursory knowledge of another language would recognize, or with which any historian persistently

11. See Stephanie Marciniak et al., "*Plasmodium falciparum* Malaria in 1st–2nd century CE Southern Italy," *Current Biology* 26.33 (2016): R1220–22; Kevin Schilbrack, in his contribution to this volume (Chapter 4) makes a comparable argument about the modern category of tuberculosis; 67.

12. Robert L. Fowler, "Thoughts on Myth and Religion in Early Greek Historiography," *Minerva* 22 (2009): 22–3.

grapples, or even which anyone critically reading literature in translation is aware.

"In the academic field of religious studies," Nongbri confirms, "the claim that religion is a modern invention is not really news"[13]—nor should it be. Nongbri cites, for example, his reading of Wilfred Cantwell Smith's "major (and still highly influential) study," *The Meaning and End of Religion: A New Approach to the Religious Traditions of Mankind* (1963), as awakening his "initial curiosity about the history of the concept of religion."[14] Indeed, the recognition that religion is a culturally contingent category goes back at least to Max Müller, the comparative philologist considered to be one of the founders of the modern academic study of religion. Already in 1878, Müller wrote in his *Lectures on the Origin and Growth of Religion* that:

> It may be said that, when Herakleitos pondered on ὅίησις, or belief, he meant something very different from what we mean by religion ... [F]or if there is a word that has changed from century to century, and has a different aspect in every country in which it is used ... it is religion.[15]

So, for example, if

> in translating the hymns of the Vedas we always translate *deva* by *deus*, or by god, we should sometimes commit a mental anachronism of a thousand years.[16]

13. Nongbri, *Before Religion*, 3.

14. Nongbri, *Before Religion*, 4. Cf. Wilfred Cantwell Smith, *The Meaning and End of Religion: A New Approach to the Religious Traditions of Mankind* (New York: Macmillan, 1963).

15. F. Max Müller, *Lectures on the Origin and Growth of Religion* (London: Longmans, Green, 1878), 8.

16. Müller, *Origin and Growth of Religion*, 190. In his history and assessment of Müller's monumental editorial project, *Sacred Books of the East*, Dutch historian of religions Arie L. Molendijk has written that "[c]rucial to the whole programme of the *Sacred Books of the East* is the idea of translation. Therefore, it is no coincidence that Müller devoted a large part of the preface to the series as a whole to the character of the original texts and to the question how to translate these in a proper way. [In the initial volume of *SBE*, the *The Upanishads*, Müller] formulated three 'cautions', the first concerning the character of the translated texts, the second with regard to the 'difficulties making a proper use of translations', and the third about the possibilities and impossibilities of rendering 'ancient thought into modern speech'" (*Friedrich Max Müller and the Sacred Books of the East* [Oxford: Oxford University Press, 2016], 96, with reference to F. Max Müller, "Preface," in *Sacred Books of the East.* Vol. 1: *The Upanishads*, Part 1 [Oxford: Clarendon Press, 1879]), ix, the same year in which Müller's *Lectures on the Origin and Growth of Religion* was published). I am indebted to Nickolas Roubekas for calling my attention to this reference. Other recent scholars who have called attention to the inadequacy of imposing familiar "discursive formations" on the cultures of others, include Michel Foucault, *The Archaeology of Knowledge* (trans. A. M. Sheridan; New York: Pantheon, 1972), 22 and Louis Dumont, "Religion, Politics, and Society in the Individualistic Universe,"

And, this recognition of religion as a non-natural, socio-historically contingent category has more recently been adroitly re-emphasized by the historian of religion Jonathan Z. Smith in the oft-cited "Introduction" to his monograph *Imagining Religion*.[17]

The problem, in other words, is not with genealogical studies of academic categories like "religion," such as those by Müller, W. C. Smith, Nongbri, and so on; such studies make valuable contributions to the history of ideas and/or to cultural history. The problem, however, given the long history acknowledging the concept of religion as both modern and contingent, is why this recognition continues to preoccupy the attention of so many modern historians of religion. Perhaps it is the result of a contemporary de-emphasis on learning other languages by graduate programs in the study of religion? Or, perhaps it is a general deficit in this education about the theoretical and methodological history of the field in which students of religion work? Or, perhaps, it is a presentist bias in historical research itself, an ahistorical narcissism by which many have characterized American culture?[18] Or, perhaps it is, among a number of religious studies scholars, a recognition of and reaction against a lingering theological bias of liberal Protestantism from which context the modern academic study of religion was spawned? Or, perhaps it is an over-reach of a post-modernist emphasis on cultural relativity? Or, perhaps, it is the one hundred and fifty-year failure of scholars of religion to agree on any definition for their object of study? However, if there is to be an academic field of history of religions, the object of its study, religion, can be—must be—simply stipulated by the author(s) of that study.

Kevin Schilbrack, for example, agrees with Mason and Davies in questioning how the connotation of modern terms like religion and belief can "accurately capture a social reality that operated long before the concept emerged?" (59). However, the issue for Schilbrack is to differentiate between the ontology of the natural world and that of the social world, as well as being cognizant of how present theorizing influences our understanding of the past (59). The problem with the approach of a number of contemporary historians is that they deal with religion as a social reality from the perspective of social construction—an exercise in redescription rather than a theoretical explanation. Schilbrack's thesis, on the other hand,

Proceedings of the Royal Anthropological Institute of Great Britain and Ireland for 1970: 31–41 and *Homo Hierarchicus: The Caste System and Its Implications* (trans. M. Sainsbury; rev. ed.; Chicago, IL: University of Chicago Press, 1980), 1–20.

17.   Jonathan Z. Smith, *Imagining Religion: From Babylon to Jonestown* (Chicago, IL: University of Chicago Press, 1982), xi; also influential for Nongbri, *Before Religion*, 13.

18.   E.g., Christopher Lasch, *The Culture of Narcissism: American Life in an Age of Diminishing Expectations* (New York: W. W. Norton, 1978).

is "that when historians recognize that 'religion' is a modern invention, they are not forced to treat the use of the term for premodern history as illegitimately anachronistic." Rather, they can choose an approach of "critical realism" that "says that something like what modern people call religion did, in fact, exist in antiquity" (60; also Roubekas, 131). Schilbrack suggests that a primary symptom of religions in antiquity might be those "forms of life predicated on the existence of superempirical realities" (73).

Similar to Schilbrack's proposal, a number of contemporary scholars of religion are now stipulating that religions—ancient and modern alike—are (something like) those groups and social institutions, and their related practices, that "Claim Legitimation from the Authority of Superhuman Agents" (CLASA).[19] Such claims may, of course, be explicit or implicit, that is, formally professed or inferred from practices and behaviors (as, e.g., in the ritual speech outlined by Lenzi, 153–5, see below, p. 429).

Religions as social and institutionalized formations *per se* (or cognitively, as discrete objects of thought) can be traced from the hierarchical divisions of labor—between political rulers, religious specialists, tradesmen and craftsmen, laborers, farmers and peasants, and slaves—that developed historically from the period of the Holocene some 11,700 years ago. From this time to the present any social institution, of course, could, and did, make CLASA a basis for its authority, for example, claims to rule by divine right made by political authorities. In support of their rhetorical claims to divine right, however, political authorities also typically controlled a formidable military and daunting police force in actual support of their claims to legitimacy and in concrete enforcement of their authority; the authority of religions, however, rely *solely* on such claims.

The characterization of religions as those social institutions and their related behaviors that are legitimated by CLASA does not, of course, presume any necessary institutional relationship (or differentiation) between a sacred and a secular realm or between a religious and a non-religious reality, nor does it problematize religion as necessarily separate from the political, the economic, the social, the military, and so on (Mason, 19–20). Already in 1941, Michael Rostovtzeff opened his monumental study of *The Social and Economic History of the Hellenistic World* by observing the general interconnection between social, economic, and political developments following the death of Alexander the Great.[20] Much of the evidence for Rostovtzeff's

---

19. E.g., Nongbri, *Before Religion*, 157; also, in this volume, Pachis, 198; Tse, 363 and, especially, Ambasciano, Chapter 16.

20. Michael I. Rostovtzeff *The Social and Economic History of the Hellenistic World* (Oxford: Clarendon Press, 1941), 1.

discussion relies on documentary evidence from contemporaneous excavations of Greek, Roman, and Egyptian religious sites.[21] These relationships are exemplified by various overlapping *raisons d'être*—social, political, economic, religious—of the voluntary associations and special interest clubs that proliferated during the Hellenistic period.[22] Subsequently, it became something of a truism that what modern scholars study as Graeco-Roman religions are beliefs and practices that are embedded in social, economic, and political institutions and their practices generally.[23] CLASA does, however, differentiate, from a theoretical position, religion as a particular aspect of the broader cultural environment, whatever status and relationship of that object of study might be to that wider environment, and it poses, thereby, the historiographical challenge of untangling and explaining the specific reasons behind their entanglement (Pachis, 197–8).[24]

While a characterization of religion as CLASA may be a necessary marker for an initial identification of religion, it remains insufficient for any complete definition. In addition to CLASA, for example, Leonardo Ambasciano, suggests that "religion … is an aggregated, componential system of many different … [cognitive biases documented from the evolutionary history of *H. sapiens* that are] put together in distinctive ways in particular cultural and historical settings," for example, agency detection and intentionality, teleological reasoning, mind/body dualism (334), group conformity, prestige bias, contamination-avoidance, and so on (337). Other pan-human behaviors generally recruited by religions (but not exclusively) include, the pursuit of altered states of consciousness,[25] social bonding through ritualized synchronizing behaviors such as chorusing and dancing (documented also from other species), or story-telling (about fictive agents, for example),[26] and so on.

21. Rostovtzeff, *Social and Economic History*, 1313 n. 1.
22. Philip A. Harland, *Associations, Synagogues, and Congregations: Claiming a Place in Ancient Mediterranean Society* (Minneapolis, MN: Fortress Press, 2003); John S. Kloppenborg and Stephen G. Wilson, eds., *Voluntary Associations in the Graeco-Roman World* (London: Routledge, 1996).
23. E.g., Bruce J. Malina, *Christian Origins and Cultural Anthropology* (Atlanta, GA: John Knox Press, 1986), ch. 2 and *The New Testament World: Insights from Cultural Anthropology* (Atlanta, GA: John Knox Press, 1986), 85–6.
24. Pachis offers some direction for such an analysis (204–5), following the suggestions of Bruce Lincoln, *Discourse and the Construction of Society: Comparative Studies of Myth, Ritual, and Classification* (Oxford: Oxford University Press, 1989), 8–9.
25. Daniel Lord Smail, *On Deep History and the Brain* (Berkeley, CA: University of California Press, 2008).
26. Robin Dunbar, *Human Evolution: Our Brains and Behavior* (Oxford: Oxford University Press, 2016), chs. 6, 7, and 8 (esp. 277–80).

In other words, religions in antiquity might, like strains of disease, be identified by their symptoms. Of course, each of these aggregate symptoms have their own evolutionary and cultural history, exhibit various behavioral forms across groups, and are exploited by all social institutions (as Davies notes, 42–43). Nevertheless, it may be useful to retain CLASA as a preliminary marker for those aggregated social behaviors and their institutionalizations that might be identified as religious, past or present; to do so certainly should give no rise to categorical misapprehensions.[27] However, it needs to be asked how and why the components of the aggregates became assembled around the CLASAs in just the way they were to form a given religious system—and that is the work of historiographical theorizing (Schilbrack, 65–66).

Theorizing Ancient Religions

And you thought you'd give me some more material?
Alas, I've got too much already ... I don't need any more data.
What I need is a theory to explain it all.

— Morris Zapp[28]

What does the theme of this volume, "theorizing ancient religions," refer to? To a discernment of (implicit) views about religion held by ancient authors? Or might this theme refer to establishing an *object* for study (i.e., ancient religions) from an explicit theoretical position? Or might it refer to stipulating an appropriate or a productive modern theoretical approach to ancient religions? Or, might it even refer to theorizing about ancient theorizings about religion? In any case, what is meant by theory needs to be determined.

Mason opens his contribution to this volume with the observation that "[m]ost of our surviving evidence for the Graeco-Roman world ... involves language," whether "literary, inscriptional, or numismatic" (11). This, of course, is more of a philological observation than a theoretical insight. And, in his contribution on "Texts" (Chapter 18), James Crossley emphasizes that any notion of a pristine or fixed text, which might clearly convey any empirical evidence is problematic, as is determining the audience of a text

---

27. CLASA as the cultural marker for identifying religion and religious institutions excludes, of course, the so-called "atheistic religions" of Confucianism, some forms of Buddhism (or even some theological expressions of Christianity e.g., Paul Tillich's identification of religion in individualistic terms of "ultimate concern"). However, these occasional *philosophical* formulations are belied by visits to any Confucian or Buddhist temple with their broad representations of resident superhuman agents.

28. David Lodge, *Small World: An Academic Romance* (New York: Penguin, 1984), 28.

or its authorial intention (381–2). This is, of course, a familiar observation for those who work with ancient texts, especially biblical scholars and classicists (as Crossley points out, 383). Further, the surviving evidence for some ancient religions is almost entirely non-linguistic—for example, that of the agrarian culture of the Incan Empire, which never developed a system of writing, or that of the Roman cult of Mithras, which is documented solely by archaeological evidence. In fact, material cultural remains from western antiquity are increasingly adding to—and in some cases, challenging—those of linguistic accounts.[29] Given the steady accumulation of data, of more kinds of data, and even of contradictory data, the historian of religion, like Morris Zapp, the fabled if fictive scholar of David Lodge's satiric novels of academic life,[30] craves a theory that might be able to explain it all.

When historians categorize their data in order to make sense of them, they are theorizing. Some explicitly employ some type of formal theorizing, others do so implicitly and informally. The latter may fall prey, for example, to their commonsense assessments, an approach that been defined by Giambattista Vico as "judgment without reflection" that is shared by a particular social group.[31] Or they may do so in terms of implicit folk categories that are characteristic of the unreflective cognition of *H. sapiens* (as noted by Davies with respect to belief, 33). What is required in order for historians to guard against such reflexive common sense or of folk categorizations in their research is, of course, a reflective or explicit theoretical approach to their evidence.

Most broadly, theorizing can be described as formulating generalizations, hypotheses, or models that might predictively—or, in the case of historiography, retrodictively—explain some stipulated set of data in terms of the fewest number of principles, and that these generalizations can somehow be inter-subjectively testable/assessable with empirical data (experimental, historical, or ethnographic) and, thus, be judged to be provisionally valid (i.e., as subject to future modification or falsification).[32] By this

29. The third- and fourth-century material evidence for early Christian practices, for example, diverges from those documented from the literary record of the orthodox gospels. See Graydon F. Snyder, *Archaeological Evidence of Church Life Before Constantine* (2nd ed.; Macon, GA: Mercer University Press, 2003).

30. David Lodge, *Changing Places: A Tale of Two Campuses* (New York: Penguin, 1975) and *Small World*.

31. Giambattista Vico, *The New Science* (translated, revised, and abridged by T. G. Bergin and M. H. Fisch; Ithaca, NY: Cornell University Press, 1948 [1744]), 142.

32. Luther H. Martin, "Secular Theory and the Academic Study of Religion," in *Secular Theories on Religion: A Selection of Recent Academic Perspectives* (ed. Tim Jensen and Mikael Rothstein; Copenhagen: Museum Tusculanum Press, 2000), 137–48; Max Weber, "Science as a Vocation," in *From Max Weber: Essays in Sociology* (translated,

disenchanting view of enquiry, surprisingly few researchers in the field of religious studies forthrightly address issues of theory (Lenzi, 158; Ambasciano, 368).

Schilbrack asserts that theorizing has to do with questions of power (65), while Roubekas writes that theorizing has to do with questions of origins (130, 141). Justin Tse contributes more substantively to a discussion of theory in his contribution on "Cultural Geography" (Chapter 17) where he observes that "theorizing about ancient religion [in terms of space] has always been central to what 'cultural geographers'" do (365, see Tse below pp. 426). Spencer Cole also presents a useful overview of how ancient authors theorized religions (227–37),

Mason implies an interesting theoretical direction when he proposes that the "ancient evidence will require us to enter into the mentality and discourse of those who wrote and understood it" (15). The most appropriate way for doing so, he argues, is by recognizing the authors of ancient works as "fellow human beings" (18). Mason opts for social discourse analysis to access the mentality of those who produced ancient evidence (18),[33] (as do a number of other contributors to the volume, for example, Schilbrack, Satlow, Rollens, and Salvo). However, isn't the category of discourse itself as modern as those of religion, belief, and ritual?

As Ambasciano points out, however, there is behind all ancient evidence "a mind that occupied a knot in a diffused cultural network of other minds" (338, 350). Investigation of minds, in other words, would seem to underlie and logically precede discourse analysis. Consequently, Mason's recognition of the fellow mentality of *H. sapiens* (15) would seem rather to suggest some form of psychological theorizing that explores a mentality shared by all humans. The most robust form of such a psychological theory is that of contemporary cognitive science. The relatively new approach of a cognitive science of religion would seem to offer a theoretical approach to the study of ancient as well as of modern religions, as is indeed suggested by several of the contributors to this volume (e.g., Lenzi [163], Cole [Chapter 11] and Ambasciano [Chapter 16]). Although Lenzi refers to cognitive studies of religion in support of his discussion of ancient Mesopotamian religions (163), he does not elaborate on its theoretical potential. And, although Davies is somewhat wary of this approach, he does concede that the cognitive science of religion does "permit us … to be sure that some things [i.e.,

---

edited, with an Introduction by H. H. Gerth and C. Wright Mills; New York: Oxford University Press, 1946 [1922]), 138–9.

33. In her short article, "A Jabberwockian Approach to Discourse Analysis," (*TESL Reporter* 1.1 [1969]: 3–4), Nancy A. Arapoff argues that words acquire meaning from their grammatical context.

historiographical interpretations?] are *less* problematic than they appear"
(45).[34] In his chapter devoted solely to the "Cognitive Study of (Ancient)
Religion" (Chapter 16), Ambasciano offers the most comprehensive discussion of that approach in this volume.

Analyses by cognitive scientists of the neurophysiological and mental
mechanisms underlying religious minds (and behaviors) have, according
to Ambasciano, contributed to a deconstruction of the concept of religion
(332–3, 338). Of course, a deconstruction of religion has been characteristic of the comparative study of religion since its nineteenth-century origins;
rather than a deconstruction of *religion* into its cognitive components, however, comparativists deconstructed *religions* into cross-cultural social types,
for example, into varieties of ritual actions (e.g., sacrifice, prayer), types
of beliefs (e.g., animistic, polytheistic, henotheistic, etc.), forms of social
organization (e.g., hierarchical or individualistic), categories of authority
(personal, traditional, textual), and so on.[35]

While comparative religionists have often employed a monothetic
approach for classifying religious types, Ambasciano begins his discussion
by identifying his approach as polythetic, as does Michael Satlow (Chapter 12).[36] This approach has been most forthrightly addressed for religious
studies a quarter of a century ago by anthropologist Benson Saler as one of
family resemblance. The problem with a family resemblance approach, of
course, is that it still presumes an *a priori* concept of religion that identifies
the family to be deconstructed.[37]

Rather than a reverse engineering of religion(s) from some presumed *a
priori* notion, the cognitive sciences recognize that the same neurophysiological and mental mechanisms underlying expressions or behaviors
that may be termed religious—ancient or modern—are available to—and
have, in fact, been historically exploited by—all socially successful institutions. This recognition of cognitive mechanisms available to and commonly
shared by all social institutions has rendered the category of religion largely
moot—apart, of course, from the stipulated exception, noted earlier, of the
CLASAs that are made uniquely by religions. Consequently, Ambasciano
concludes that, while much "remains to be done to understand the complex

34. A point I have frequently emphasized, e.g., Luther H. Martin, "The Promise of
Cognitive Science for the Study of Early Christianity," in *Deep History, Secular Theory:
Historical and Scientific Studies of Religion* (Berlin: Walter de Gruyter, 2014 [2007]),
202–3.

35. Benson Saler, *Conceptualizing Religion: Immanent Anthropologists, Transcendent Natives, and Unbounded Categories* (Leiden: Brill, 1993), 82.

36. Both follow the suggestions of Smith, *Imagining Religion*, 1–18.

37. As Saler, *Conceptualizing Religion*, 261, concedes.

history of competition and interbreeding between doctrinal, imagistic, and optimally cognitive actors that shaped the cultural and religious dynamics of the ancient Mediterranean" (349), the "predictable patterns" identified by cognitive scientists and imposed by the "cognitive constraints" upon human minds present ancient historians with the possibility of filling in "the gaps of historical knowledge" (343).

Cole follows the cognitive approach advocated by George Lakoff and Mark Johnson that explores the metaphorical and the cultural processing of religions.[38] He illustrates this approach with his example of concepts of death and divinity in the late Roman Republic. Cole recognizes that metaphors are simply the ways by which ancient authors conceptualized one mental domain in terms of another (222). This approach of cross-domain mapping and cognitive realignments (222), while drawing upon cognitive theorizing, is somewhat alternative to the identification of neurophysiological and mental mechanisms underlying religious cognition described by Ambasciano and more complementary to the discourse analyses proposed by other of the contributors to this volume.

Tse and Salvo also contribute to a discussion of formal theoretical approaches to the study of ancient religions. Tse proposes that a cultural geography is foundational for any theorizing of ancient religions (362–3, 373, 377). Agreeing with those who emphasize ritual over belief, he describes cultural geography as the discipline that seeks to theorize placemaking practices—for religious studies, those "performative practices of placemaking informed by understandings of the transcendent" (363–4, 373, 377; see above p. 424). Interestingly, Tse traces the genealogy of this theologizing task from Émile Durkheim to the classic study of Pierre Deffontaines on *Géographie et religions* (1948)[39] to Mircea Eliade and Jonathan Z. Smith (366–73, 377).

In her contribution on "Gender," Salvo questions "whether and in what ways issues of gender were relevant to the ancient religious reality" (398). She questions thereby the categories of gender that are often simply commonsensically presumed or that remain a matter of historiographical description (or redescription) but that are less often theoretically argued. Foremost, she argues, the category of gender must first be defined and then its theoretical employment in religious studies explored (398). With regard to definition, Salvo writes that the "conceptualization of gender as a spectrum and the fluidity of transgenderism can be particularly beneficial to the

38.   George Lakoff and Mark Johnson, *Metaphors We Live By* (Chicago, IL: University of Chicago Press, 2003).
39.   Pierre Deffontaines, *Géographie et religions* (Paris: Gallimard, 1948).

understanding of ancient religious practices" (400). In this regard, she cites the "well-known example … of the *Galloi*, Cybele's emasculated priests in Anatolian temples" (407). Ultimately, Salvo concludes, "[g]ender and religion have a relationship based on the balance of social and cultural power" (409). Consequently, she argues that, generally, "a male divinity was served by a male priest and a female divinity by a female priestess" (403). While this was the case, for example, with the Roman cult of Mithras, which was presided over by Fathers, it was not the case with the Roman cult of the goddess Isis, which was presided over by male priests. And, it might be asked, to what extent is an understanding of gender as a category with fluid boundaries a modern one that might be questionable for understanding ancient religions practices, for which binary categorizations of gender may have been presumed, however variably such cultures may have expressed those binary relationships?

Case Studies

Case studies [illustrate] how theories and data can interplay.
— Irene Salvo (398)

While overlapping with their theoretical reflections, a number of convergent contributions to the current volume also present specific historiographical studies that belie the concerns of some contributors concerning the propriety of studying religions in antiquity. These case studies can be grouped as studies making a contribution to the theme of the volume on the Greek presocratic philosophers, on ritual studies, and on questions of identity.

The Presocratics

One of the more interesting discussions in this volume is that of the contributions of the sixth century BCE presocratic philosophers to its theme. In the first of the case studies, Donald Wiebe's "Philosophical Reflections on the Presocratics" (Chapter 5), Wiebe challenges many of the culturally-relative linguistic and theoretical concerns expressed by a number of contributors to this volume. Implicit in the thought of the presocratic cosmologists, Wiebe argues, is a new kind of knowledge about the world and about states of affairs in the world that amounts to an espousal of an objectively existing reality that has rational and evidential support (81). This new knowledge provided the foundation for a genuinely scientific study not only of the natural world but of the social world as well (83). In fact, Wiebe points out that, from an evolutionary perspective, even our archaic forebears would have been unable to survive had they not been able to have some knowledge of the external world for what it is (92). While this archaic knowledge of the natural world was embedded in pragmatic social interests, the presocratics, Wiebe contends, moved that archaic knowledge necessary for survival towards a more focused and neutral interest in knowledge of the natural world for its own sake (92–93). They influenced, thereby, the rise of a proto-scientific historiography that was "capable of standing on its own and with a character and premises special to it" (99) and, consequently, Wiebe concludes, they portended a proto-scientific history of religions (100).

On the other hand, Emese Mogyoródi cautions, in her reflections on the "Rationalization of Religion in Classical Greece" (Chapter 6), that, while Wiebe's view represents the conventional interpretation of the presocratics (104), it is misleading to emphasize their empiricism, naturalism, or materialism too strongly (105). Rather, she concludes, with particular reference to Anaximander and Heraclitus, that "no Presocratic natural philosophical or theological (skeptical or critical) development directly resulted in the elimination of gods" (125). Similarly, Roubekas emphasizes, in his study of Herodotus's (later fifth-century BCE) *Histories* (Chapter 7), that claims about Herodotus's disbelief, atheism, or refusal of the existence of the gods are the result of misreading or misinterpreting the *Histories* since Herodotus continued to allow for divinity to function outside the direct empirical realm (through intermediaries, e.g., mediums and oracles, 132–3).

Still, Mogyoródi agrees with Wiebe's general view that the presocratic philosophers initiated a "novel way of thinking about the world" (104) by contributing to the advancement of the mathematical and physical sciences and, consequently, to an anti-religious trend. In this regard, she cites especially the cases of Protagoras, Prodicus, and Critias (or Euripides) in the *Sisyphus* who rationalized religion by making religious conceptions compatible with the changing social realities of the time—including with the new framework of explanation provided by history (106). In this way, she essentially agrees with Wiebe's conclusion that the presocratics contributed to a more secular view of nature and, thereby, implicitly to a proto-scientific history of religions (125–6).

The problem with any interpretation of the presocratics is, of course, that the surviving evidence for their philosophical thought is even more fragmentary than is that for many ancient religions. Perhaps, attributing to the presocratics fragments the conventional view that they collectively represent a new secular, proto-scientific kind of knowledge requires a more nuanced historical assessment? As Mogyoródi concludes, "[i]t can no longer [simply] be taken for granted that the philosophical efforts of the early Greek philosophers from Thales through Parmenides to Anaxagoras were all aiming at a single *telos* culminating in atomism, a system of thought that finally got rid of all super-natural agency or causation at work in nature" (105).

Ritual

There is, as we have seen, a consensus among many contributors to this volume, as among many historians of religion generally, that ritual is a more appropriate object of study for ancient religions than is belief. In two case studies of ancient religions that are antecedent to those of the Graeco-Roman focus of most contributors to this volume, Lenzi and Rita Lucarelli, rather than begging the jabberwockian dilemma, argue persuasively the priority of ritual for their cases. Lenzi focuses on "Mesopotamian Scholars" (Chapter 8) while Lucarelli discusses Pharaonic (as well as Graeco-Roman) Egyptian "Magic and Religion" (Chapter 9).

Lenzi argues that Mesopotamian scholars of the first millennium BCE dealt with divine-human relations through what he calls ritual speech (153). He defines ritual speech as "any human linguistic communication that was not used to communicate between humans but that sought by performative means to elicit or effect change in some situation for which the communication was invoked." It is that ritual speech which is directed at superhuman entities that marks it as religious (155).

Lucarelli identifies magical practices in ancient Egypt with ritual performance. Similar to the conclusions by Mogyoródi and Roubekas that the presocratics and Herodotus allowed for divinity to function outside the direct empirical realm, Lucarelli maintains that magical practices in ancient Egypt assumed an "impersonal and abstract force of creation provided by the gods for humankind" (177). As such, "magic was a necessary element of any kind of ritual and cultic performance" (176). She concludes with the suggestion that a comparative study of magic traditions in the ancient world "could lead scholars to think at a broader level and to propose new, more fluent, and less limited definitions of phenomena such as demons and demonology, which are an integral part of magic" (192)—as well as, it might be added, of (ancient) religions generally.

In contrast to Lenzi's and Lucarelli's (and others') focus on ritual as the object of study for ancient religion, Roubekas concludes—at least in regards to Greek culture—that it was a "belief in gods [that] constituted the crux of ancient … religion for many ancient thinkers, no matter how eagerly some scholars still prefer and promote the dichotomy between religious belief and religious practice within ancient … culture[s] by prioritizing the latter and depreciating or even rejecting the former" (131).

Surely ritual agents in antiquity were not devoid of cognitive commitments to expected outcomes of their performative activity. Didn't those Mesopotamians, who engaged in ritual speech or those Egyptians, who engaged in magical incantations, not have some prior belief regarding the anticipated outcome of their ritual activities? While such cognitive commitments were, of course, not necessarily a systematically defining characteristic of a given religious system (as is the case for Protestant theology), those who emphasize ritual performance as the appropriate object for the study of ancient religions might risk going too far by claiming that ancient religions are defined predominantly by ritual practices. Anthropologists have, for example, identified two types of religion, an imagistic type that is predominantly defined by ritual practices and a doctrinal type that is predominantly defined by belief systems. Both of these types of religions are, however, characterized by ritual transmission, the former by their infrequent performance but their high sensory pageantry while the latter are characterized by their frequent, even routinized, performances that are associated with the widespread affirmation and transmission of a commonly held set of beliefs. And while the imagistic type may antedate the doctrinal, the doctrinal type is not confined to modernity.[40]

And, isn't ritual as modern a category that has as long and as contested a history, with various interpretations and biases, as do religion and belief?[41] What the foregoing discussion does do is to suggest the formal possibility of theoretically uncoupling belief and ritual in order to analyze the effects of both before attempting to resolve the question of the place and role of ritual in ancient religions generally, and of the relationship of the one to the other.

Questions of Identity

Related to concerns raised about the use of modern categories, such as religion and belief, in historical research, Michael Satlow, Sarah Imhoff, Nickolas Roubekas, Sarah Rollens, and Panayotis Pachis present convergent challenges to modern notions of religious identity in the Hellenistic world—Satlow and Imhoff to that of Jewish identity (Chapters 12 and 13),

---

40. Harvey Whitehouse and Jonathan A. Lanman, "The Ties That Bind Us: Ritual, Fusion, and Identification," *Current Anthropology* 55.6 (2014): 674–95.

41. E.g., Jonathan Z. Smith, *To Take Place: Toward Theory in Ritual* (Chicago, IL: University of Chicago Press, 1987); Caroline Humphrey and James Laidlaw, *The Archetypal Actions of Ritual: A Theory of Ritual Illustrated by the Jain Rite of Worship* (Oxford: Oxford University Press, 1994).

Roubekas and Rollens to that of early Christians (Chapters 15 and 14) while Pachis reflects on socio-cultural processes of definitions and redefinitions of religious identities in the ancient world generally (Chapter 10).

In his contribution on "Defining Judaism," Satlow argues that first-order definitions of religions do not seek to describe a religious phenomenon but rather to create "authentic community by drawing lines between 'orthodox' and 'heterodox' manifestations." And, while such first-order self-definitions "are useful as data ... they are, far less useful as analytical or explanatory categories." Rather, Satlow argues, the study of religion must begin "with the development of second-order concepts and definitions" (251). Satlow illustrates historically shifting definitions with a concise genealogy of the designation of Judaism from the first use of the term in 2 Maccabees to Napoleon, and he suggests three "maps" onto which various Jewish identities might be plotted: a group's self-identity as Israel, its relationship to a claimed authority ascribed to the Hebrew Bible and the rabbinic textual tradition, and its transmitted ritual practices (254). He illustrates this mapping with Philo as a case study, concluding that Philo's approach to what we might call religion is "messy and incomplete." However, he concludes that his polythetic approach to all religions of the ancient Mediterranean might provide a rigorous paradigm for comparison between and among the different religions of this area (261–2).

Imhoff, in her contribution on the "Impossibility of Jewish Identity," agrees with Satlow that modern scholars should analyze the past using etic (second-order) categories but she also argues for analyzing religious identities as best as possible under the emic terms available from antiquity (266). With examples from Philo and Josephus, the *Third Sibylline Oracle*, the Essenes, and the rabbinic texts, Imhoff argues that groups claiming Jewish identity nevertheless shared a culture with their non-Jewish neighbors without any necessity of deciding to which category they belonged (e.g., religion, ethnicity, national group) (266–7). Still, the category of Jew, she argues, can help historians to "think about a long trajectory of ... history... [and this category, like that of religion generally] can help illuminate the intersections of ritual, material objects, and philosophies. 'Judean' and its related categories of 'ethnicity' and 'nation'," she concludes, can "train the eye on geographic, military, and political aspects of Jewishness [and of religions generally] in antiquity" (284).

In her contribution on "The Anachronism of 'Early Christian Communities'," Rollens maintains that "scholars too easily forget that the production of distinct intellectual propositions for a particular ideological position can be completely divorced from group formation" (320). Consequently, she argues that "there can be no simple or even necessary relationship between a text and a so-called religious community" (321).[42] Rather, Rollens argues that "ideology may simply exist at the level of discourse and not in the lived experience of any identifiable people, practitioners, or adherents." In other words, "the text may [simply reflect] what the author wants to exist" (320). For example, '[i]nstead of imagining a Christian community that is embodied in a text," Rollens argues that "it is better to speak in terms of a common discourse about Jesus, with various people participating and using it as a resource (among many others) for understanding identity" (323). Rollens' point about the varying views among the early Christians is well-illustrated from the "heterodox" writings of early Christians and by the evidence of their material culture collected by Graydon Snyder,[43] much of which contradicts the views preserved in the "orthodox" Christian texts.

Similar to Tse's advocacy of a cultural geography, Roubekas, in his chapter on "Christian Identity Formation" (Chapter 14), argues that "theorizing about the relationship between space and religion creates, enforces, and maintains new religious identities and … [that] classification, as a set of human relations and ideas, transforms places from ordinary and neutral into ideologically and 'religiously' charged spaces" (290). With his example of Tertullian's *De Spectaculis*, Roubekas shows that this early Christian theologian already sought to establish a specifically Christian identity by arguing against particular practices in distinct places, as was the case with Roman spectacles. By concentrating on space and spatializing practices, Roubekas sees Tertullian as an early exponent of a basic principle that scholars of religion have discussed in the last hundreds of years or so that has been succinctly summarized by religion scholar Craig Martin as "[t]he way we classify or divide up the world is fundamental to understand how religious traditions function to reinforce social order" (Roubekas, 291).[44] Thus, Roubekas concludes that the spatializing categories of Tertullian's *De Spectaculis* helped initiate a clear discourse on what it meant to be Christian in North Africa at the turn of the third century CE (Roubekas, 304).

In his chapter on "Manipulating 'Religion'" (Chapter 10), Pachis shows that Diodorus Siculus adopted but adjusted the ideas of Euhemerus, for example, in order "to justify the religio-political *status quo* of his time" (198; see also 125). Consequently, Pachis claims that Diodorus, "in contrast to Herodotus who dealt with the Egyptian tradition as a Greek of the classic period"

42. See also Pachis, 215 and Crossley, Chapter 18.
43. Snyder, *Archaeological Evidence*.
44. Citing Craig Martin, *A Critical Introduction to the Study of Religion* (London: Routledge, 2012), 20, referring also to Jonathan Z. Smith, "Classification," in *Guide to the Study of Religion* (ed. Willi Braun and Russell T. McCutcheon; London: Cassell, 2000), 35–44.

was "an exponent of the cosmopolitan spirit of the Hellenistic era" (212; see also Roubekas, 134, 146). In other words, Pachis, in agreement with Satlow, Imhoff, Roubekas, and Rollens, concludes that ancient religious identities were never static but were historically fluid, always formulated, and re-formulated to reflect contemporaneous socio-political contexts.

Conclusion

> "The question is," said Alice, "whether you can make words mean so many different things."
> "The question is," said Humpty Dumpty, "which is to be master—that's all."
> — Lewis Carroll[45]

Many, if not most, of the contributors to the present volume voice apprehension about employing modern categories in historical research, a topic that was most forthrightly addressed a quarter of a century ago by Benson Saler in his study of *Conceptualizing Religion*. This is a study (mentioned only by Davies, 35–36) that should be attentively revisited by any of those who continue to be exercised by this particular issue. Rather than the modern category of religion (or its related category of belief) as an object of historical research for ancient religions, a number of contributors to the volume identify "shared discourse" as an appropriate object of study (e.g., Mason, Schilbrack, Satlow, Rollens, Salvo); others suggest ritual as the appropriate object of historical research on ancient religions (e.g., Lenzi, Lucarelli, Tse). However, aren't the categories of discourse and ritual themselves as modern as those of religion and belief? In fact, isn't the use of any term or category that is contemporaneous with a historian, well … "modern"?

The problem with employing modern categories is less their modernity *per se* than their essentialization. Essentialism is basically a cognitive default whereby class inclusion is defined by some (presumed) necessary and timeless internal property or characteristic.[46] It is such essentializations that historians must explicitly guard against in their research. But they must also be wary of imposing modern de-essentialized categories on the historical evidence, for ancient categories may, in fact, be essentialized in the minds of their historical actors and, consequently, have informed their thoughts and behaviors (e.g., those of religio-political entanglement or gender).

Take the category of religion, for example. No stipulation by historians of religion about the meaning of this category has, during the past century

---

45. Carroll, *Through the Looking Glass*, 46.
46. Pascal Boyer, *The Naturalness of Religious Ideas: A Cognitive Theory of Religion* (Cambridge: Cambridge University Press, 1994), 171–3; Saler, *Conceptualizing Religion*, 10–1.

and a half, proven to be epistemologically robust. Perhaps it is time for such scholars to abandon their insulated, subjective, and relativistic humanistic musings and participate in—as well as contribute to—interdisciplinary studies of religion that incorporate approaches and theories from the sciences. For example, Kent State University classicist Jennifer Larson has published a consequential study of ancient Greek religion that not only exemplifies the significance of a (cognitive) scientific approach for theorizing ancient religions generally but, also belies apprehensions about the propriety of research on those "religions" with her respect for and careful but innovative interpretations of the particulars of the historical data.[47]

Many cognitive scientists of religion, as noted above, stipulate that religion (or whatever category historians might find congenial) can be identified as those institutions or groups that legitimate their beliefs and practices by claims to the authority of superhuman agents (CLASA). This stipulation is, of course, a neo-Tylorian "minimal" characterization of religion;[48] it is "neo-" because, in addition to Tylor's ethnographic data, this characterization is now supported by empirical research from the cognitive sciences.[49]

Of course, the nature of claims to the authority of superhuman authority must be culturally parsed. For example, whereas all supernatural agents are imagined as superhuman, not all superhuman agents are imagined as supernatural. For the religions of antiquity, super*human* must be differentiated from super*natural*, terms that are often used synonymously (Schilbrack prefers an inclusive category of superempirical, 73 and n. 44). Whereas the pantheon of the fourteenth-century Incan Empire (as of many ancient religions), for example, was natural, simply personified aspects of nature that were relevant to and important for their agrarian economy (e.g., sun, moon, earth, thunder, rain, rivers, etc.), the Mesopotamian and Graeco-Roman deities were imagined as superhuman, that is, as wielding power or knowledge greater than humans but dwelling together *with* humans *within* the bounds of the natural (cosmic) realm. Only the early Christian God was widely re-imagined in antiquity as super*natural*, that is, as transcendentally situated in a realm beyond the natural cosmos—a characteristic rooted initially

---

47. Jennifer Larson, *Understanding Greek Religion* (London and New York: Routledge, 2016).

48. Edward Burnett Tylor, *Primitive Culture: Researches into the Development of Mythology, Philosophy, Religion, Art, and Custom* (New York: Harper Torchbook, 1958 [1871]), Vol. II, 10.

49. E.g., Pascal Boyer, *Religion Explained: The Evolutionary Origins of Religious Thoughts* (New York: Basic Books, 2001), 137–67; E. Thomas Lawson and Robert N. McCauley, *Rethinking Religion: Connecting Cognition and Culture* (Cambridge: Cambridge University Press, 1990), 61, 89, 92–3, 123–4.

in the expanse of Ptolemaic cosmology, geographically in that of empire, and metaphysically in neo-Platonic philosophy. Supernatural deities are those now generally associated with the modern concepts of religion.

The particular spatial domain upon which deities are mapped—natural, this-worldly, other-worldly, whether that domain is mythologically, geographically, politically, or cosmologically inscribed—determines, of course, the ways in which divine-human relationships and rituals are imagined. These relationships, in turn, determine the shape of rituals. Compare, for example, the simple but ancient ritualized expressions of gratitude for the bounty of Mother Earth (or magical incantations to secure such bounty) among many agrarian cultures, with the joyous celebrations of fertility together with the deity in the early Dionysian bacchanalia, or with the solemn transcendental remembrances of the soteriological sacrifice in a Roman Catholic high mass. The numerous deities inhabiting cultural parsings are, of course, named from within their various mythological and historical discourses—and that is where historians of religion come in, faced, of course, with their abundant, if fragmentary, corpus of data that has survived from the past.

"The question is," to paraphrase Alice, *"how the abundance of historical data can seem to mean so many different things." "The question is,"* said Humpty Dumpty in response, *"which is to be master—that's all."* The mastering of so much different data is, as Morris Zapp reminds his fictive—as well as his actual modern—colleagues, the work of theory. And a theoretical reduction of claimed superhuman agents to their discursive expressions and cultural patterns, and, further, to their pan-human cognitive underpinnings, can provide meaningful empirical markers for ancient religions that do not presume any particular modern bias.

Despite my questions and some criticisms of the various and varying contributions, this volume is welcome and important. First of all, the contributors should be commended for their participation in a collegial and collaborative exercise that is all too often absent from the individualist pursuits characteristic of the humanistic research (itself a characteristic of modernity); and the editor should be congratulated for envisioning such a project and for overseeing its successful completion. Secondly, contributors to this volume call timely and discerning attention to an array of theoretical concerns focused on a particular theme, the study of ancient religions—some reminding us of issues long acknowledged, others challenging us with recent historical and theoretical concerns. Hopefully, this important volume will revive among historians of religion a renewed interest in neglected issues of historiographical theory and method, not only in the study of ancient religions but in the academic study of religion generally, issues that have too long been suppressed by the trendy embrace of post-modern jab-berwockianism in the modern research university.[50]

> *And hast thou slain the Jabberwock?*
> *Come to my arms, my beamish boy!*
> *O frabjous day! Callooh! Callay!*

Biographical Note

Luther H. Martin is Professor Emeritus of Religion at the University of Vermont, USA. He is the author of *Hellenistic Religion: An Introduction* (Oxford University Press, 1987), *The Mind of Mithraists: Historical and Cognitive Studies in the Roman Cult of Mithras* (Bloomsbury, 2015) and of numerous articles in this field of his historical specialization, many now collected in *Studies in Hellenistic Religions* (edited by Panayotis Pachis; Cascade Books, 2018). He has also published widely in the field of theory and method in the study of religion, especially in the area of cognitive theory and historiographical method, now collected in *Deep History, Secular Theory* (Walter de Gruyter, 2014), and he has co-edited several volumes in this area, including *Past Minds: Studies in Cognitive Historiography* (with Jesper Sørensen; Routledge, 2011). A founder of the North American Association for the Study of Religion, he is now a member of the Honorary Board of its journal, *Method & Theory in the Study of Religion.* He is also a founding member of the International Association for the Cognitive Science of Religion and co-editor of its *Journal of the Cognitive Science of Religion,* as well as a founding editor of the *Journal of Cognitive Historiography.*

Bibliography

Arapoff, Nancy A. "A Jabberwockian Approach to Discourse Analysis," *TESL Reporter* 1.1 (1969): 3–4.

Berman, Marshall. *All That is Solid, Melts into the Air: The Experience of Modernity.* New York: Penguin, 1988.

Boyer, Pascal. *The Naturalness of Religious Ideas: A Cognitive Theory of Religion.* Cambridge: Cambridge University Press, 1994.

---

50. Cf. Jürgen Habermas, *The Philosophical Discourse of Modernity* (Cambridge, MA: The MIT Press, 1987). On the significant contribution of postmodernism to the Trump era culture of "alternative facts," see Michiko Kakutani, *On the Death of Truth: Notes on Falsehood in the Age of Trump* (New York: Tim Duggan Books, 2018). On the relationship between postmodernist philosophy and pseudoscience, see Massimo Pigliucci and Maarten Boudry, eds., *Philosophy of Pseudoscience: Reconsidering the Demarcation Problem* (Chicago, IL: University of Chicago Press, 2013), esp. 4–5, 93, 102.

—*Religion Explained: The Evolutionary Origins of Religious Thoughts*. New York: Basic Books, 2001.

Carroll, Lewis. *Through the Looking Glass and What Alice Found There*. London: Macmillan, 1871. Online: PDFreeBooks.org (2010): https://archive.org/details/ThroughTheLookingGlassAndWhatAliceFoundThere.

Deffontaines, Pierre. *Géographie et religions*. Paris: Gallimard, 1948.

Deutscher, Guy. *Through the Language Glass: Why the World Looks Different in Other Languages*. New York: Metropolitan Books/Henry Holt, 2010.

Dumont, Louis. "Religion, Politics, and Society in the Individualistic Universe," *Proceedings of the Royal Anthropological Institute of Great Britain and Ireland for 1970* (1970): 31–41. https://doi.org/10.2307/3031738

—*Homo Hierarchicus: The Caste System and Its Implications*. Translated by M. Sainsbury. Rev. ed. Chicago, IL: University of Chicago Press, 1980.

Dunbar, Robin. *Human Evolution: Our Brains and Behavior*. Oxford: Oxford University Press, 2016.

Foucault, Michel. *The Archaeology of Knowledge*. Translated by A. M. Sheridan. New York: Pantheon, 1972.

Fowler, Robert L. "Thoughts on Myth and Religion in Early Greek Historiography," *Minerva* 22 (2009): 21–39.

Habermas, Jürgen. *The Philosophical Discourse of Modernity*. Cambridge, MA: The MIT Press, 1987.

Harland, Philip A. *Associations, Synagogues, and Congregations: Claiming a Place in Ancient Mediterranean Society*. Minneapolis, MN: Fortress Press, 2003.

Hartley, Leslie P. *The Go-Between*. Harmondsworth, UK: Penguin, 1997 [1953].

Humphrey, Caroline, and James Laidlaw. *The Archetypal Actions of Ritual: A Theory of Ritual Illustrated by the Jain Rite of Worship*. Oxford: Oxford University Press, 1994.

Kakutan, Michiko. *On the Death of Truth: Notes on Falsehood in the Age of Trump*. New York: Tim Duggan Books, 2018.

Kloppenborg, John S., and Stephen G. Wilson, eds. *Voluntary Associations in the Graeco-Roman World*. London: Routledge, 1996.

Lakoff, George, and Mark Johnson. *Metaphors We Live By*. Chicago, IL: University of Chicago Press, 2003. https://doi.org/10.7208/chicago/9780226470993.001.0001

Larson, Jennifer. *Understanding Greek Religion*. London: Routledge, 2016. https://doi.org/10.4324/9781315647012

Lasch, Christopher. *The Culture of Narcissism: American Life in an Age of Diminishing Expectations*. New York: W. W. Norton, 1978.

Lawson, E. Thomas, and Robert N. McCauley. *Rethinking Religion: Connecting Cognition and Culture*. Cambridge: Cambridge University Press, 1990.

Lincoln, Bruce. *Discourse and the Construction of Society: Comparative Studies of Myth, Ritual, and Classification*. Oxford: Oxford University Press, 1989.

Lodge, David. *Changing Places: A Tale of Two Campuses*. New York: Penguin, 1975.

—*Small World: An Academic Romance*. New York: Penguin, 1984.

Malina, Bruce J. *The New Testament World: Insights from Cultural Anthropology*. Atlanta, GA: John Knox Press, 1981.

—*Christian Origins and Cultural Anthropology*. Atlanta, GA: John Knox Press, 1986.

Marciniak, Stephanie, T. L. Prowse, D. A. Herring, J. Klunk, M. Kuch, A. T. Duggan, L. Bondioli, E. C. Holmes, and H. N. Poinar. "*Plasmodium falciparum* Malaria in 1st–2nd century CE Southern Italy," *Current Biology* 26.23 (2016): R1220–22. https://doi.org/10.1016/j.cub.2016.10.016

Martin, Craig. *A Critical Introduction to the Study of Religion*. London: Routledge, 2012.

Martin, Luther H. *Hellenistic Religions: An Introduction*. Oxford: Oxford University Press, 1987.

—"Secular Theory and the Academic Study of Religion," 137–48 in *Secular Theories on Religion: A Selection of Recent Academic Perspectives*. Edited by Tim Jensen and Mikael Rothstein. Copenhagen: Museum Tusculanum Press, 2000.

—"The Promise of Cognitive Science for the Study of Early Christianity," 202–20 in *Deep History, Secular Theory: Historical and Scientific Studies of Religion*. Berlin: Walter de Gruyter, 2014 [2007].

Molendijk, Arie L. *Friedrich Max Müller and the Sacred Books of the East*. Oxford: Oxford University Press, 2016. https://doi.org/10.1093/acprof:oso/9780198784234.001.0001

Müller, F. Max. *Lectures on the Origin and Growth of Religion*. London: Longmans, Green, 1878.

—"Preface," ix–xxxviii in *Sacred Books of the East*. Vol. 1: *The Upanishads*, Part 1. Oxford: Clarendon Press, 1879.

Nongbri, Brent. *Before Religion: A History of a Modern Concept*. New Haven, CT: Yale University Press, 2013. https://doi.org/10.12987/yale/9780300154160.001.0001

Pigliucci, Massimo, and Maarten Boudry, eds. *Philosophy of Pseudoscience: Reconsidering the Demarcation Problem*. Chicago, IL: University of Chicago Press, 2013. https://doi.org/10.7208/chicago/9780226051826.001.0001

Rostovtzeff, Michael I. *The Social and Economic History of the Hellenistic World*. Oxford: Clarendon Press, 1941.

Saler, Benson. *Conceptualizing Religion: Immanent Anthropologists, Transcendent Natives, and Unbounded Categories*. Leiden: Brill, 1993. https://doi.org/10.1163/9789004378797

Smail, Daniel Lord. *On Deep History and the Brain*. Berkeley, CA: University of California Press, 2008.

Smith, Jonathan Z. *Imagining Religion: From Babylon to Jonestown*. Chicago, IL: University of Chicago Press, 1982.

—*To Take Place: Toward Theory in Ritual*. Chicago, IL: University of Chicago Press, 1987.

—"Classification," 35–44 in *Guide to the Study of Religion*. Edited by Willi Braun and Russell T. McCutcheon. London: Cassell, 2000.

Smith, Wilfred Cantwell. *The Meaning and End of Religion: A New Approach to the Religious Traditions of Mankind*. New York: Macmillan, 1963.

Snyder, Graydon F. *Archaeological Evidence of Church Life Before Constantine*. 2nd ed. Macon, GA: Mercer University Press, 2003.

Tylor, Edward Burnett. *Primitive Culture: Researches into the Development of Mythology, Philosophy, Religion, Art, and Custom*. New York: Harper Torchbook, 1958 [1871].

Weber, Max. "Science as a Vocation," 129–56 in *From Max Weber: Essays in Sociology*. Translated, edited, and with an Introduction by H. H. Gerth and C. Wright Mills. New York: Oxford University Press, 1946 [1922].

Vico, Giambattista. *The New Science*. Translated, revised, and abridged by T. G. Bergin and M. H. Fisch. Ithaca, NY: Cornell University Press, 1948 [1744].

Whitehouse, Harvey, and Jonathan A. Lanman. "The Ties That Bind Us: Ritual, Fusion, and Identification," *Current Anthropology* 55,6 (2014): 674–95. https://doi.org/10.1086/678698

Index

CPSIA information can be obtained
at www.ICGtesting.com
Printed in the USA
JSHW020544160520
5718JS00002B/28